THE HISTORY OF THE INDIES OF NEW SPAIN

By Fray Diego Durán

Translated, Annotated,
and with an Introduction
by Doris Heyden

University of Oklahoma Press : Norman

Portions of this translation are reprinted from *The Aztecs* by Fray Diego Durán, translated by Doris Heyden and Fernando Horcasitas, Copyright © The Orion Press, Inc., 1964, by permission of Viking Penguin, a division of Penguin Books USA Inc. The appendix, "Durán's *Historia* and the *Crónica X*," by Ignacio Bernal, is reprinted from the introduction to *The Aztecs*, by Fray Diego Durán, translated by Doris Heyden and Fernando Horcasitas, The Orion Press, 1964. It is used here with the permission of Ignacio Bernal.

The frontispiece and illustrations 1 to 62 of *The History of the Indies of New Spain* by Fray Diego Durán are reproduced courtesy of the Biblioteca Nacional, Madrid. Copies were made in the photo laboratory of the Biblioteca Nacional.

This book is published with the generous assistance of the McCasland Foundation, Duncan, Oklahoma.

Durán, Diego, d. 1588?
  [Historia de las Indias de Nueva-España y Islas de Terra Firme. English]
  The history of the Indies of New Spain / by Diego Durán ; translated, annotated, and with an introduction by Doris Heyden.
      p.   cm.— (Civilization of the American Indian series ; v. 210)
  Translation of: Historia de las Indias de Nueva-España y Isla de Terra Firme.
  Includes bibliographical references (p.   ) and index.
  ISBN 978-0-8061-4107-7
  1. Aztecs—History. 2. Aztecs—Social life and customs. 3. Mexico—History—To 1519. 4. Mexico—History—Conquest, 1519-1540. I. Heyden, Doris. II Title. III. Series.
F1219.73.D8713   1994
972'.018—dc20   93-48624
                                                                        CIP

The History of the Indies of New Spain is Volume 210 in The Civilization of the American Indian Series.

The paper in this book meets the guidelines for permanence and durability of the Committee on Production Guidelines for Book Longevity of the Council on Library Resources, Inc. ∞

Copyright © 1994 by the University of Oklahoma Press, Norman, Publishing Division of the University. Manufactured in the U.S.A. Paperback published 2009.

All rights reserved. No part of this publication may be reproduced, stored in a retrieval system, or transmitted, in any form or by any means, electronic, mechanical, photocopying, recording, or otherwise—except as permitted under Section 107 or 108 of the United States Copyright Act—without the prior written permission of the University of Oklahoma Press.

Dedicated to
FERNANDO HORCASITAS
In Memoriam

CONTENTS

Acknowledgments		VIII
Preface		XV
Translator's Introduction		XIX
The History of the Indies of New Spain		
Chapter I.	The possible place of origin of the Indians of New Spain	3
Chapter II.	How the Indians left their Seven Caves	12
Chapter III.	The arrival of the Aztecs in Mexico	20
Chapter IV.	What befell the Aztecs after their arrival at Chapultepec	31
Chapter V.	How the Aztecs went to seek the prickly pear cactus and the eagle, and how they found them	42
Chapter VI.	The first king os Mexico, Acamapichtli	51
Chapter VII.	The second king of Mexico, Huitzilihuitl	58
Chapter VIII.	The third king of Mexico, Chimalpopoca	66
Chapter IX.	The election of King Itzcoatl, and how he liberated the city of Mexico	73
Chapter X.	How the Tepanecs of Coyoacan waged war on the Aztecs, and how they were vanquished	84
Chapter XI.	How the lords of Mexico requested of King Itzcoatl that he give them titles	96
Chapter XII.	The great discord between the people of Xochimilco and the Aztecs, and how Xochimilco was vanquished	104

Contents

Chapter XIII.	How King Itzcoatl of Mexico ordered the distribution of the lands of Xochimilco	112
Chapter XIV.	How the people of Cuitlahuac rebelled against the Aztecs during the reign of King Itzcoatl, and how they were vanquished	116
Chapter XV.	The election of the fifth king of Mexico, Huehue Motecuhzoma, the first of this name	123
Chapter XVI.	How Motecuhzoma the First began to build the temple, and how Chalco waged war against Mexico and was defeated by the Aztecs	130
Chapter XVII.	The cruel attack made by the Chalcas upon the Aztecs between Amequemecan and Tepepulla, and how the Chalcas finally were defeated	141
Chapter XVIII.	How the people of Tepeaca waged war against the Aztecs, and how the former were defeated, harshly treated, and brought to Mexico-Tenochtitlan to be sacrificed	149
Chapter XIX.	The great discord between the Aztecs and the Huaxtecs of Tamapachco, Tochpan, and Tzincoac, and how the Huaxtecs were vanquished	160
Chapter XX.	The cruel sacrifice of the Huaxtecs at the hands of the Aztecs	169
Chapter XXI.	The war with Ahuilizapan, and how those people were defeated	175
Chapter XXII.	How King Motecuhzoma warred with Coaixtlahuaca, and how that city was destroyed	182
Chapter XXIII.	The sacrificial ceremony performed in honor of the stone called the *cuauhxicalli*, image of the sun	188
Chapter XXIV.	How the Province of Cuetlaxtlan rebelled again, and how they were vanquished a second time	194
Chapter XXV.	The great tribute and wealth received by the Aztecs	202

Chapter XXVI.	The laws, ordinances, statutes, and other conditions decreed by King Motecuhzoma, the first of this name	208
Chapter XXVII.	How King Motecuhzoma the First sought the Seven Caves	212
Chapter XXVIII.	How the people of Guaxaca killed the royal envoys, and how the Aztecs destroyed them and settled the city with Aztecs, Tezcocans, and Xochimilcas	223
Chapter XXIX.	How the king and nobility decided to wage perpetual war on Tlaxcala, Huexotzinco, Cholula, Atlixco, Tecoac, and Tliliuhquitepec	233
Chapter XXX.	The great famine that devastated this land for three years during the reign of Motecuhzoma the First, and how this ruler came to the aid of the people of Mexico-Tenochtitlan	238
Chapter XXXI.	How King Motecuhzoma had his likeness carved upon a rock on the Hill of Chapultepec, and a description of his last days and death	242
Chapter XXXII.	The election of King Axayacatzin and the events that occurred in his time	247
Chapter XXXIII.	A fierce battle between the Aztecs of Tlatelolco and those of Tenochtitlan	251
Chapter XXXIV.	The second battle between the Aztecs of Tenochtitlan and Tlatelolcas and how the latter were defeated	258
Chapter XXXV.	How the people of Tenantzinco asked the Aztecs for aid against Toluca and Matlatzinco, and how this help was sent and those cities were destroyed	263
Chapter XXXVI.	How the two carved stones were set in their places and how the Matlatzincas were sacrificed upon them	272
Chapter XXXVII.	How war was waged against Mechoacan, and how the Aztec army was defeated	278

Contents

Chapter XXXVIII.	The long funeral rites with which the Aztecs honored those who had died in war	283
Chapter XXXIX.	The gifts that the lords brought to the deceased King Axayacatl, the speeches that were made, and the election of the seventh king, Tizocicatzin	291
Chapter XL.	How the Aztecs waged war on Metztitlan	299
Chapter XLI.	How, after the funeral of King Tizoc, a younger brother of his was elected	309
Chapter XLII.	The festival that was held for the coronation of King Ahuitzotl	319
Chapter XLIII.	How King Ahuitzotl finished the construction of the Great Temple, and the solemn feast made for its inauguration	328
Chapter XLIV.	How the solemn ceremony and sacrifice began	337
Chapter XLV.	How Aztec and Otomi colonists were sent to repopulate Alauiztlan and Oztoman	344
Chapter XLVI.	How the Aztecs waged war upon Tecuantepec, Izhuatlan, Miauatlan, and Amaxtlan	349
Chapter XLVII.	How King Ahuitzotl visited all the temples when he returned from war	355
Chapter XLVIII.	The death of Tlacaelel, how King Ahuitzotl asked the ruler of Coyoacan for water from Acuecuexco, the excuse that was given to him, and how Ahuitzotl had this ruler killed	361
Chapter XLIX.	How the waters entered Tenochtitlan, how they were welcomed, and how the city was flooded and the inhabitants were forced to flee	367
Chapter L.	How Mexico learned that Xoconochco, Xolotla, and the province of the Mazatecs had mistreated the people of Tecuantepec, with a description of the war the Aztecs waged on them	374

Chapter LI.	The death of King Ahuitzotl, and the funeral rites in his honor	382
Chapter LII.	The solemn council that was formed to elect the new king of Mexico-Tenochtitlan, and how Motecuhzoma the Second was chosen	387
Chapter LIII.	The order and harmony decreed by King Motecuhzoma for his personal service and that of his household and other things commanded by him	394
Chapter LIV.	The solemn festivities that were held at the coronation	402
Chapter LV.	How Motecuhzoma conquered the provinces of Cuatzontlan and Xaltepec	409
Chapter LVI.	The reasons Motecuhzoma had for warring against Quetzaltepec and Tototepec, the strong resistance he met, and how he conquered them	417
Chapter LVII.	The cruel battle waged between the Aztecs and the men of Huexotzinco, and how Tenochtitlan and Tezcoco perished and the Huexotzincas triumphed	425
Chapter LVIII.	How Motecuhzoma had the Temple of Coatlan built within that of Huitzilopochtli, and the solemn festival that was held	431
Chapter LIX.	How Cholula defied the Aztecs on the road to Atlixco, with a description of the battle that took place	438
Chapter LX.	The enmity and war between Tlaxcala and Huexotzinco, how the Huexotzincas asked the king of Tenochtitlan for help, and how this plea was granted	445
Chapter LXI.	How Nezahualpiltzintli, king of Tezcoco, informed Motecuhzoma that the Spaniards would soon arrive and the Aztecs would have few victories over their enemies	452

Contents

Chapter LXII.	The cruel sacrifice of the Tlaxcalan victims on the feast of the goddess Toci, and how the Huexotzincas were angered by this and burned her temple at night	456
Chapter LXIII.	How a comet appeared in the sky, how it troubled Motecuhzoma, and how he consulted the king of Tezcoco to discover its meaning	460
Chapter LXIV.	The death of Nezahualpilli, king of Tezcoco, and the election of a new ruler called Quetzalacxoyatl	465
Chapter LXV.	How the people of Coaixtlahuaca were bringing their tribute to Mexico-Tenochtitlan, and how the men of Tlachquiauhco attacked them on the road and robbed them, with an account of the war Motecuhzoma waged against the latter	470
Chapter LXVI.	How Motecuhzoma ordered that the largest stone that could be found be brought for the sacrifice of the Flaying of Men	477
Chapter LXVII.	How Motecuhzoma decided to abandon the city and hide himself where he could not be found	483
Chapter LXVIII.	How Motecuhzoma ordered the authorities of the city to investigate the dreams of the old people regarding the coming of some phenomenon that they might have anticipated, and how he had many killed because they revealed dreams contrary to his desires	490
Chapter LXIX.	How a ship from Cuba arrived in this land and how Motecuhzoma sent emissaries, and a description of the events that followed	495
Chapter LXX.	How Motecuhzoma ordered an artist to paint pictures of the Spaniards according to the description given by Tlillancalqui Teuctlamacazqui	503
Chapter LXXI.	How Don Hernán Cortés disembarked at the port of Chalchiuhcueyecan, and how Mote-	508

	cuhzoma ordered provisions to be sent to Cortés	
Chapter LXXII.	How Motecuhzoma sent a chieftain to bring Cortés, how he guided the Spaniards along a difficult path to a cliff, how two horses fell and two Spaniards were killed, and how the chieftain fled and later was executed by Motecuhzoma	515
Chapter LXXIII.	How the Tlaxcalans held a meeting and decided to receive Cortés in peace and deliver the city to him	522
Chapter LXXIV.	How Hernán Cortés was welcomed in Mexico-Tenochtitlan by Motecuhzoma and his dignitaries, how he was lodged in a palace in the city and was well served there, and how King Motecuhzoma was taken prisoner	528
Chapter LXXV.	How Pánfilo de Narváez arrived at Veracruz, how Cortés captured him and sent him away, how Cortés returned to Tenochtitlan with his men, and how a rebellion broke out among the natives against the Spaniards	534
Chapter LXXVI.	How Don Hernán Cortés fled from his quarters, how the Indians were aware of his departure, and how many Spaniards and Indians were killed in that flight	542
Chapter LXXVII.	How Cortés came from Tlaxcala to Tezcoco, built brigantines there, and went on to Tenochtitlan, and how King Cuauhtemoc defended himself with great valor	549
Chapter LXXVIII.	How Don Hernán Cortés, after having conquered Mexico, left that city in good order, and how he set out to conquer other provinces, with a description of the death of Cuauhtemoctzin	558

Appendix: Durán's *Historia* and the *Crónica X*, by Ignacio Bernal   565

Chronology of Aztec Kings   579

Contents

Glossary 581

Bibliography 595

Index 609

ACKNOWLEDGMENTS

This book was made possible by a National Endowment for the Humanities grant. Thanks to this generous support I was able to do extensive work on two separate occasions in archives and libraries in Spain. Further research has been supported by a grant from the American Philosophical Society and a fellowship from the John Simon Guggenheim Memorial Foundation.

My deepest thanks to the personnel of the Biblioteca Nacional de Madrid, where the original Durán manuscript is housed, especially to Manuel Sánchez Mariana, keeper of rare documents.

I am grateful for the continuous encouragement given me by my colleagues and the authorities at Mexico's National Institute of Anthropology and History, where I am a researcher in ancient religions and history, as well as an archaeologist. I also extend my gratitude for recent support from Mexico's Sistema Nacional de Investigadores.

The study of the *Crónica X*, published in our 1964 edition, is included in the present volume through the generosity of its author, the late Ignacio Bernal. The present edition is based partly on the 1964 translation by Doris Heyden and Fernando Horcasitas.

For encouragement and advice during the long process of translation and annotation, I thank Miguel León-Portilla, Karen Dakin, Elizabeth H. Boone, N. C. Christopher Couch, H. B. Nicholson, Debra Nagao, Dana Leibsohn, and Scott O'Mack. I especially thank Benjamin Keen, Louise Burkhart, and James Lockhart for reading the finished manuscript and offering constructive suggestions.

PREFACE

This new English translation of the *History* by Fray Diego Durán presents a work written by one of the great missionary-ethnographers of sixteenth-century Mexico. Modern research is indebted to chroniclers such as Durán for much of its knowledge of Aztec civilization in particular and Mesoamerican culture in general. In the wake of the Spanish conquest, which violently truncated the development of civilizations in the New World, a handful of enlightened men salvaged enough information about the conquered culture to allow a detailed ethnographic and historical reconstruction of this ancient empire. Since all but a few of the indigenous historical and ritual manuscripts were destroyed during or soon after the conquest, we have little besides these colonial chronicles to supplement the information recoverable by archaeological techniques. These documents were requested by the religious Orders and by royal and civil authorities in order to document the life and customs of the people of New Spain for purposes of extirpating idolatry and organizing the natural and human resources of the colony. They constitute a key to the understanding of ancient Mexican civilization and, through this, of present-day Latin America. Each chronicle contains precious information not found elsewhere. The dissemination of these works is thus essential to Latin American studies.

Fray Diego Durán's works are exceptional for their accuracy and thoroughness, and many of his descriptions of Aztec history and culture are not to be found in other sources. Durán was one of the few early chroniclers to have contact with native informants old enough to have experienced the preconquest world. He was a perceptive and sympathetic investigator who had access to many informants and sources of information not available to other writers of his time. Because of his command of the native language—Nahuatl—Fray Diego was able to gain the confidence of native informants who told him the stories, histories, myths, and anecdotes of their ancestors. His other informants included Spanish eyewitnesses to the conquest. He also consulted prehispanic pictorial codices and accounts written in the sixteenth century by other friars. His accounts of the dynastic history and ceremonial activities of the Aztec kings have been particularly valuable in recent years in interpreting archaeological discoveries in Mexico, such as the important Templo Mayor or Great Temple, heart of Tenochtitlan, ancient capital of the Aztecs, now Mexico City.

Inasmuch as Durán grew up in Tezcoco, even his contemporaries considered him "a son of Mexico." In a way he was, since he left Spain

Preface

with his family at a very early age. He was a son of Mexico only by adoption, however, although this was the country nearest to his heart. In a document related to the Inquisition that Fernández del Castillo discovered in 1925 in the Archivo General de la Nación in Mexico (Rama de la Inquisición, vol. 232, fols. 227–51), Durán clearly stated that he was a native of Seville.[1] Garibay, citing Fernández del Castillo, mentions that Diego came to Mexico "almost in the arms of his father" (Durán 1967:xii). The "almost" in this citation makes us wonder if Diego was barely walking or if he was a child of four or five. The present translation aims to correct some misconceptions regarding Durán and his times.

Mentions of Durán appeared now and then, like lights that flash on and then disappear. In 1639 the bibliographer León Pinelo called Durán's treatises "remarkable books." In 1755 Juan José Eguiara y Eguren mentioned Durán, and in 1816–20 José Mariano Baristáin y Souza praised the Dominican's writings, though neither he nor Eguiara y Eguren was acquainted with the manuscript.[2]

It was not until the 1850s that the Mexican scholar José Fernando Ramírez discovered the forgotten Durán manuscript in the Biblioteca Nacional de Madrid. By that time it had suffered mutilations: the title page had been lost and in the nineteenth century—perhaps after Ramírez's discovery—the manuscript had been bound in a way that cut off parts of some of the illustrations and eliminated some letters in the text. Nevertheless, Ramírez, with the help of Francisco González de Vera, librarian of the Ministry of War in Madrid, had a scribe copy the manuscript and an artist copy the illustrations. This copy was completed on April 1, 1854, and was sent to Mexico, where it now is preserved in the Historical Archive of the National Library of Anthropology and History.[3] Although Ramírez had decided to publish this valuable historical work, political unrest in Mexico made the entire project impossible. Sixty-eight chapters of the *Historia* (called vol. I by Ramírez) were actually published in 1867, but at that time Emperor Maximilian of Mexico was overthrown and Ramírez, one of his supporters, went into exile. The publication of Durán's works did not continue. After the fall of the Second Empire, the Durán copy and the illustration plates were preserved in the School of Mines in Mexico City (before they went to the National Library). In 1873 Eduardo Gallo published *Hombres ilustres mexicanos* with eight illustrations from the Ramírez copy of Durán. We do not know how these were obtained. In

[1] Fernández del Castillo 1925:228. See also Colston 1973:6, 34.
[2] See Miguel León-Portilla, in Durán's *Book of the Gods and Rites* (1971; 2nd. ed. 1977:v–vi). This volume is hereafter cited as Durán 1977.
[3] AHINAH = Archivo Histórico, Instituto Nacional de Antropología e Historia.

1880 the director of the National Museum of Mexico, Gumesindo Mendoza, managed to have the second volume of the Ramírez edition and the *Atlas* (illustrations) published, together with the first volume. In all they contained what we now know as the last part of the *History*, the *Book of the Gods and Rites*, *The Ancient Calendar*, and the *Atlas*. The work also contained a study by Alfredo Chavero. A facsimile edition of this 1867–80 publication was printed in 1951. Unfortunately, this is plagued with errors and continues to be used, although the 1967 two-volume Garibay edition is superior to it.[4]

An important study on the style of the illustrations for Durán's work by Donald Robertson can be found in the 1977 edition of Durán's *Book of the Gods and Rites* (pp. xvi–xviii).

As I have stated in the introduction to this book, Fernando Horcasitas and I made a translation into English of Durán's *History*, which was published by Orion Press in 1964. Up to that time and despite the importance of Durán's accounts, there had been no complete English translation of his works. Since this edition was directed toward a public audience there were some unfortunate deletions and all the illustrations were not published. The present translation has been made directly from the sixteenth-century document in Madrid with only occasional references to the 1964 edition.

The Durán manuscript presents several problems to the translator. The original manuscript has very little punctuation; therefore, any translation involves a considerable amount of editing. Although a disciplined and meticulous investigator, Durán as a writer was repetitious, sometimes using several synonyms to describe a single act or object. Such redundancy does not read with fluidity in translation and I have attempted to reduce repetition here, without losing any of the meaning. As a product of the sixteenth century, the language of Durán's manuscript reflects the style of that period; thus, a knowledge of this Spanish is necessary in order to find the exact equivalent meaning. Furthermore, a knowledge of Nahuatl, I found, is useful, for native terms are scattered throughout the manuscript.

These are but a few aspects of the translation of Diego Durán's work, so valuable to both scholars and the general reader. Since this sixteenth-century Dominican friar has been called one of the earliest and most knowledgeable of ethnographers, it is with pleasure that I here present my grain of sand as part of the extensive field that covers Mexican culture and history. It is my hope that the illustrations to Durán's *History* will be reproduced elsewhere in color at a future date.

[4]For a more complete description of the adventures that befell Durán's writings, see "Bibliographical Note" in Durán 1977:xii–xviii.

TRANSLATOR'S INTRODUCTION

On August 13, 1521, the last Aztec *tlatoani*, or ruler, of Tenochtitlan, Cuauhtemoc, surrendered to the Spanish conqueror Hernán Cortés at Tlatelolco in the northern part of the Aztec capital. A modern plaque installed at the site reads, "This was neither a triumph nor a defeat but was the painful birth of the mestizo people who are the Mexico of today."

This painful birth and events before and after it are recorded in the works of friars who initially crossed the Atlantic Ocean by order of the king of Spain, Charles V, to take the Christian doctrine to the natives of the New World. Three mendicant Orders sent missions soon after the conquest, the Franciscans arriving in 1524, the Dominicans in 1526, and the Augustinians in 1533. Diego Durán, author of the present *History*, did not, however, come with the first group of twelve Dominicans.[1] He arrived a little later as a small child with his family, having been born in Seville (Fernández del Castillo [1925:223–29] cites a document in the Archivo General de la Nación in Mexico written by Durán, stating this). Durán's family was not among the *encomenderos*, or Spaniards granted rights to Indian land and labor; perhaps his father held a position in the Spanish colonial government. That they were not of humble station is seen by Durán's own comment that he saw slaves marked by branding in the homes of his relatives (chapter LXXVIII of the *History*). Diego says that "although I did not acquire my milk teeth in [Tezcoco], I got my second ones there" (chapter II), indicating that his birth date was around 1537. It was in Tezcoco that he learned Nahuatl, the language of the Aztecs.

When Diego was still young his family moved to nearby Mexico City, where the boy attended school (we don't know which). He witnessed the consolidation of the new capital, was enchanted by agile Indian gymnasts and dancers, saw games and even fights among the blacks whose families had been brought from Africa as slaves, and at times was confused by the mixture of peoples and races, to the extent

---

[1]A discussion of Diego Durán's works and a biography of this Dominican friar by Fernando Horcasitas and Doris Heyden, as well as a foreword by Miguel León-Portilla, are found in the first volume of Durán's writings published by the University of Oklahoma Press in 1971 (2nd ed. 1977:v–vi, xii–xviii, 12–47). In my introduction here I have made a summary of the 1977 biography and bibliographical note and have added a new study on changes in the sixteenth century that affected writings by the clerics.

that he later wrote, "one can barely tell who is the knight, who the muleteer, who the squire, who the sailor" (1977:180–81, 195).

Diego matured as a member of this changing society and in 1556, in his late teens, entered the Dominican Order as a novice, later to be deacon in the convent there (Colston 1973:9). In 1529 the Dominicans had acquired a site in the center of Mexico City and soon had built their first residence (called *convento* in Mexico, rather than monastery) and the church of Santo Domingo, a handsome structure still standing. The Dominicans had been authorized by a *cédula* or decree issued by Charles V on September 14, 1526, to preach in rural villages. Therefore, Fray Domingo de Betanzos, first Dominican Provincial, named in 1535, had established residences among the Indians in their towns. The first three *conventos* founded outside Mexico City in the early 1530s were in Oaxtepec, Chimalhuacan-Chalco, and Coyoacan. Also in the 1530s, it was decided to establish a *convento* in Antequera, now the city of Oaxaca. It had been decreed in Rome in 1532 that this new Province of Santiago, centered at Oaxaca, also included the Dioceses of Tlaxcala, Michoacan, Yucatan, Chiapa, and others. The ceremony officially accepting the papal bull establishing the province took place in Mexico City on July 24, 1534 (Mullen 1975:22, 23).

Durán is said to have been sent to the Dominican convent in Oaxaca in 1561 (Sandoval 1945:8; Garibay in Durán 1967:I:xii; Colston 1973:9). But as Bernal notes in the study published in the present volume, Durán is never mentioned among the Dominicans who labored in Oaxaca and once even asked a Spaniard who had been there what the region was like (Durán 1977:63). Fray Diego speaks lovingly of the Marquesado, now the state of Morelos, "one of the most beautiful lands in the world." He resided for a time in the *convento* at Oaxtepec (which he spells Huaxtepec), where he was influenced by "a most honest priest, a man who was jealous of the glory of God and of His doctrines," who, we believe, was Fray Francisco de Aguilar (Durán 1977:15, 31). Aguilar had been a soldier under Cortés before entering the Dominican Order and had much to tell Durán about the conquest. Fray Diego cites him frequently in the *History*. Durán also was vicar in Hueyapan, a town high on the southern slopes of the volcano Popocatepetl, the Dominican *convento* there dating from 1563. In that Nahuatl-speaking region Durán found many informants for his *History*. One of the important characteristics of his research is that he ventured into rural areas, questioning the old and the young in their own language, observing their customs, and always searching for ancient documents, which he thought might include lost Holy Scripture written in Hebrew. He suspected, as did many in his day, that the people of Mexico were one of the lost tribes of Israel and that

Topiltzin-Quetzalcoatl, the hero-god of native history, was the apostle Saint Thomas (1977:23–31). In his search for evidence in support of this idea and in concert with his missionary work among the native people, he discovered pictorial manuscripts that he incorporated into his *History*, which unfortunately have not been preserved (1977:67).

By speaking the language of the people and by participating actively in the same colonial milieu, Durán had access to many customs and beliefs that might otherwise have escaped him, and much of this information found its way into his writings. As Garibay (Durán 1967:I:xvi) puts it, it would be difficult to find a Spanish author of the sixteenth century whose writings about Mexico were more important than those of Durán, for even the great Franciscan Fray Bernardino de Sahagún, whose encyclopedic account of Aztec culture is without compare, was not nearly so Mexican, even if Durán was so by assimilation and not by birth.

Durán's close association with the Mexicans and his understanding of their ways brought him to criticize the clerics and conquerors who did not bother to learn the native language. He writes that "they should know the language well and understand [the people] if they have any pretense of obtaining fruit. . . . And [the ministers] should not acquiesce by saying that they know a little bit of the tongue in order to hear confession and that is enough." He adds that some religious men are satisfied with knowing the first words learned by the conquerors, *tleitoca*, "what do you call this?" and *huallaz*, "it will come." Other Nahuatl words learned by the Spanish soldiers were so "crude and rough" that the Indians laughed and scorned them, and Durán refrains from giving these (1977:23, 170, 171).

Although Durán's love for Mexico and the Mexicans is evident in his writings, he really was a child of two worlds. He was pulled between his admiration for the *pulicía* or good organization of the ancient Aztec world and the horror he felt at some of its practices, particularly human sacrifice. His Spanish background made him repudiate many of these practices for, after all, his mission was to evangelize the natives and he had been commissioned by his Order to carry out this task. The Dominican Order also requested that Fray Diego produce, as did other men dedicated to missionary work, a study of the ideas and ways of the Indians, especially their religion, as a guide to the ministers who were "workers in this divine task of the conversion of the natives." Durán writes that in order to administer the sacraments, "one needs more knowledge of the language, customs, and weaknesses of these people than most think" (1977:386). He was obliged to undertake this work by superiors in his Order, to write not only the present *History* but "another treatise on past events from the time of the plague to the unhappy present" (chap. LXXVIII, this volume).²

Although Durán's aims were to present a picture of "heathen practices" as a kind of manual for other missionaries who would Christianize the natives, he also felt his work would be "pleasant and gratifying," that it would please readers and provide useful information (1977:140, 154). This "useful information" can properly be called the collection of ethnographic research. Although centuries ago no one called the friars "ethnographers," indeed they were, as they went about questioning people, writing down their observations, and consulting the few ancient documents that had not been destroyed. Durán's style is not polished but some of the good breeding, courtesy, and fine manners of speaking so typical of the Tezcoco of his day did rub off and find their way into his writings.

Durán produced three works: the *Book of the Gods and Rites*, written between 1574 and 1576 (possibly begun earlier,³ when he had taken up his duties near Tezcoco, perhaps in Chimalhuacan-Atenco); the *Ancient Calendar*, finished in 1579;⁴ and the present *History*, written while Durán was *vicario* in Hueyapan. In his writings he often refers to another treatise he was obliged to write, but about which we have no information. If this does exist in some archive, we hope that an enterprising student of the Dominicans will one day discover it. All through his writings Fray Diego refers to another treatise he wrote: in chapter LXII of the *Gods and Rites* on the goddess Toci he twice refers to a description of ceremonies written "in the second part of this book," meaning, we presume, the *Ancient Calendar*. References to a "second part of this book" are also frequent in the *History*. In this chronological confusion it would seem that the first and second parts, published together in all printed editions, were written at the same time and in the same place, but, as already noted, the first was produced in 1574–76, the *Calendar* in 1579, the *History* in 1581. Since Durán refers to a second part in the historical book, however, this

---

²For a brief account of the Dominican Order in Mexico and a discussion of Durán's life and writings, see Durán (1977:xii–xviii, 3–47) and also Garibay (Durán 1967:I:xi–xlvii).

³Although Garibay dates the *Book of the Gods and Rites* to 1570 (Durán 1967:I:xvii), Durán himself states in chapter V of the book: "We [the Spaniards] have been here fifty-five years." If Fray Diego is referring to the arrival of Cortés (1519), the date of the writing of the book would be 1574. If he is referring to the consummation of the conquest of Mexico (1521), the date would be 1576. He cannot be referring to the arrival of the Dominicans in Mexico (1526), for the date would then be 1581, and we know that the second book, the *Ancient Calendar*, was finished in 1579. We believe that the *Book of the Gods and Rites* is no earlier than 1574–76 (Durán 1977:4n. 95).

⁴Published in Durán 1977.

suggests that while writing this he came upon information relating to the ceremonies and then added them to his first draft. Or perhaps he had written still another work that is also lost. The *History* evidently was written after he and other investigators had discovered what Barlow later called the *Crónica X*,[5] a document written in Nahuatl and translated by Fray Diego. Durán enriched this official Aztec history with material collected from informants and from manuscripts he consulted in the villages.

In 1585 Diego Durán was back in Mexico City in the Santo Domingo *convento*. He was in poor health but still found time to carry out his duties as translator from Nahuatl to Spanish for the Inquisition. His death came in 1588 (Durán 1977:45).

Durán's works were known by some of his contemporaries. Copyright laws did not exist in sixteenth-century New Spain and writings by both clerics and laymen were read in manuscript form and edited by one another. H. F. Cline has commented on the "Franciscan doctrine of anonymity and borrowing" (Dibble 1982:10), which evidently was common practice. In 1576 the Jesuit Juan de Tovar studied both written and pictorial manuscripts in Mexico by order of Viceroy Martín Enríquez. With the material he so gathered, Tovar wrote his *Primera relación*, which was sent to Spain. This manuscript is now lost. After Durán had finished his works, these were read by Tovar, who then wrote a *Segunda relación* (1583), basing much of his material on Durán's work. Although Tovar did not mention Durán by name, he stated in a letter to Joseph de Acosta, a fellow Jesuit, that in order to write this second *Relación* he had read a book written by a Dominican friar, a relative of his (perhaps a reference to Durán based on similarities in the text and illustrations shared by these manuscripts). In 1590 Acosta published his *Historia natural y moral de las Indias*, in which he stated that his principal source for works on Mexico was Juan de Tovar. Six years later Fray Agustín Dávila Padilla published the *Historia de la fundación y discurso de la Provincia de Santiago de México*, in which he mentions writings by his fellow Dominican, Fray Diego Durán. Durán's works on Mexican history were as yet unpublished, Dávila Padilla said, but could be consulted in part in Acosta's *Historia* because Tovar had passed his information on to him. This copying of data back and forth is cited by other authors of the period, including Antonio de Pinelo and Torquemada, but not in a critical sense or as an accusation of plagiarism. An interesting discussion of this and the above information is found in the prologue and second appendix of Acosta's *Historia* edited by Edmundo O'Gorman

---

[5] See essay by Bernal in this volume.

(1962:xi–xiii, lxxviii).

Durán worked hard at writing his chronicles. Aside from the three books that have come down to us, he talks of a first draft no longer extant. In this draft, in spite of his pro-Indian sentiments, he eliminated "Indian wordiness in telling fables . . . (when anyone is willing to listen to them they go on forever) . . . and irrelevant matters" (1977:70–71). With this wealth of material on Aztec Mexico, why did his works lie dormant until the nineteenth century, when José Fernando Ramírez discovered the manuscript in the National Library of Madrid? One clue can be found in the *Ancient Calendar*, where Durán wrote, "Some persons (and they are not few) say that my work will revive the ancient customs and rites among the Indians," to which he replied that "those who speak as outsiders . . . understand little about these things. Thus I swear that my intention is not to instruct the Indians regarding these [pagan] things, because they are already well informed. They are so careful in hiding their papers and ancient traditions, so secretive and so deceitful that they do not need an instructor!" (1977:411).

In spite of this last comment, Fray Diego admired the people of the country in which he grew up and often said so. His fluency in Nahuatl allowed him to penetrate many of the customs and beliefs of the people and to be accepted by them. But as Louise Burkhart has said, "Learning native languages enabled the friars to gain the Indians' acceptance, but it was also a factor in the friars' downfall: having bound themselves so closely to the Indians, they raised the suspicions of colonial authorities and the leaders of the secular Church hierarchy" (1989:11).[6] Burkhart also points out that the soul-saving mission during the first half of the sixteenth century was urgent and the friars learned the native tongues in order to accelerate this project; the alternative of first teaching Spanish to the Indians would have been considerably slower.

A CHANGING WORLD

In Durán's time, the Spanish colonial world as initially established was quickly changing. The seventeenth century, that great period of consolidation, was drawing near. New Spain appeared to be under control: disease had decimated the native population, work in the mines had destroyed still more native lives, while others had accepted the new faith and had adapted to the new order. Not only was the

---

[6]Reprinted from *The Slippery Earth: Nahua-Christian Moral Dialogue in Sixteenth Century Mexico*, by Louise M. Burkhart, by permission of the University of Arizona Press, copyright 1989 Arizona Board of Regents.

paternal attitude toward the Indians no longer welcome, but different men were in power and different laws prevailed, both in Spain and in New Spain.

Numerous recent studies have reevaluated the writings of chroniclers in view of the changes taking place in the course of the sixteenth century, particularly with respect to Sahagún.[7] Although little work has been done regarding what happened to Durán and the Dominicans, they obviously shared much the same fate as the Franciscans. The following is a brief reconstruction of events that forced the expropriation and sometimes loss of ethnographic material in the sixteenth century. I rely mainly on recent work concerning the Franciscans (especially those mentioned in note 7).

While Durán was carrying out his missionary work in Hueyapan and in Chimalhuacan-Atenco, at the same time interviewing native informants for material with which to finish his first two books, the spiritual climate in Mexico had been changing. The Inquisition had been installed in New Spain (actually, Durán took part in this as a translator), the mendicant Orders were being replaced by the secular clergy, and as early as 1570 financial support for scribes was withdrawn throughout Mexico (Dibble 1982:14).

From the very beginning, the intention of the mendicant friars had been to understand the native cultures, especially their religion, in order to carry out the evangelization. Sahagún himself said that a physician could not cure an ailment without understanding the cause of that illness (Cline 1989:1). Cortés had requested that missionaries be sent from Spain for this purpose and invited both the Franciscans and the Dominicans (Cortés 1971:334), but the Franciscans arrived two years earlier than the Dominicans, nine years before the Augustinians. Durán was eventually ordered to write both a history of the native people and a treatise on their customs, and the result is his three-book work.

The early friars, especially the Franciscans Fray Toribio de Benavente, or Motolonía, and Fray Gerónimo de Mendieta, had millenarian ideas, which eventually led the crown to fear a separatist movement and possible loss of the colony. The crown had reason to be wary: there were Indian revolts between 1541 and 1576 (the Mixton War of 1541–42 being a major one); Martín Cortés, son of the conqueror, headed an unsuccessful conspiracy (1565–66) for the establishment of an independent Mexico; a descendant of Motecuhzoma Xocoyotzin,

---

[7]See Jiménez Moreno 1938; Ricard 1966; Phelan 1970; Baudot 1974, 1983, 1988; Edmondson 1974; Anderson 1982; Dibble 1982; Todorov 1985; Klor de Alva et al. 1988; Burkhart 1989; S. L. Cline 1989.

Diego Luis de Motecuhzoma, had political pretensions (1576) unfavorable to Philip II of Spain. After the death of the president of the Council of the Indies, Juan de Ovando, who had been sympathetic to Sahagún and the mendicants, in 1575, the council adopted restrictive policies and condemned works written in native languages that were considered to be subversive.

A *cédula* of April 22, 1577, sent by Philip II to Viceroy Martín Enríquez, prohibited all writings referring to "superstitions and the way of life of the Indians" in any language and specifically ordered the confiscation of the extensive works of Sahagún, as well as of other writings of similar character (Baudot 1983:471–500). Many major chronicles were effectively repressed, some of them unknown until their rediscovery in the nineteenth century. Among the works hidden, lost, or mutilated are those written by Olmos, Motolinía, Sahagún, Las Navas, Martín de la Corona, Francisco Hernández, Mendieta, and López de Gómara, as well as the *Relación de Michoacán* and even the letters of Cortés. The writings of the Dominicans were of course included.

Rodrigo de Sequera, commissary general of the Franciscan Order, together with the heads of the Dominican and Augustinian Orders, argued that these works were to be used exclusively by the religious and thus would not foment idolatry. Thus, in 1581, the Inquisition finally relented, allowing the use of works in native languages (Cline 1989:14). Baudot points out that Torquemada's *Monarquía indiana* appeared in 1615, but, although he relied heavily on works by Olmos, Mendieta, and Motolonía, he was not obviously a millenarian. In addition, by the seventeenth century the native people of New Spain represented less of a threat than they had earlier, in part because they had suffered severe demographic losses (1983:501). Baudot also mentions that prohibitions of writings by the crown continued right up to the nineteenth century, just before Mexican Independence. In January 1820 the Inquisition ordered the seizure of a book on Indian "superstitions" written by Josef Meneses, but that book proved to be nonexistent (1983:488–89).

One result of the initial repression was the revision by Sahagún of book 12 of his magnum opus, the volume on the conquest of Mexico. Working from notes in 1585, shortly before his death, Sahagún claimed that his revision was undertaken for linguistic reasons, to provide a clearer translation of the native text, yet the changes he made were clearly the "product of a climate increasingly hostile to the early evangelical Franciscans" (Cline 1989:14). S. L. Cline has made a detailed study of statements in the 1585 version (book 12 of the *Florentine Codex*) and compared them with their counterparts in the 1579 version.

The 1585 version greatly favors Cortés and, in a new chapter, relates the conquest from the Spaniards' point of view, as well as using data from Tlaxcala informants, enemies of the Aztecs. For example, in 1585 Sahagún justified the looting of Motecuhzoma's treasure, claiming that by allowing his soldiers to sack the royal houses he kept their goodwill (Cline 1989:7). (This reminds us of occasions related by Durán when the Aztec soldiers were permitted in prehispanic times to plunder conquered towns as payment.) Sahagún justified Alvarado's massacre of the Aztec nobles as a means of forestalling a plot against the Spaniards. Sahagún later put words in the mouth of Cortés, justifying the entire conquest. The Spanish captain is seen as an instrument of God's will (Cline 1989:8, 9). Clearly, while the mendicants were given free reign under Charles V (1516–56), under Philip II (1556–98) they were significantly restricted in their actions, while the secular clergy was favored. The vicissitudes of the sixteenth century were reflected in the fate of the friars and their written works.

In the specific case of Durán's manuscript, entitled *Historia de las Yndias de Nueva España y Yslas de la Tierra Firme*, it eventually was deposited in the Biblioteca Nacional de Madrid in the Sección de Manuscritos, catalogued as Vit. 24-11. It is composed of 344 leaves, folio-size, which measure 32 cm high by 22 cm wide. The manuscript contains three separate treatises: the *Gods and Rites*, the *Ancient Calendar*, and the *History of the Aztec-Mexica*. Here it remained forgotten until the 1850s, when the renowned Mexican scholar José Fernando Ramírez discovered it and had it copied by a scribe. This copy is preserved in the Archivo Histórico of the Biblioteca Nacional de Antropología e Historia in Mexico (No. 556 [15585]). An incomplete edition came out in 1867 and the rest of it was published in 1880. The original remains in Madrid.[8]

The Madrid manuscript appears to have been written in different hands. Perhaps Durán wrote part in his own hand, then at times dictated to a scribe or scribes. On this original manuscript, chapters LXXIII to LXXVIII are full of corrections. In many places words have been repeated, then crossed out, which leads one to believe that Durán's manuscript (perhaps first written entirely by him) was rewritten by a scribe, who made these errors in the process of recording dictation or copying the manuscript. For example, on fol. 210v the word *estatua* was written twice, inked out once; on fol. 211r *de todo* was written twice, inked out once. Corrections in these chapters are in a different hand and may have been contributed by an editor or a

---

[8]See bibliographical note, Durán (1977:xii–xviii) and Garibay (Durán 1967:I:xv–xxvii).

censor. While some of these corrections were probably due to spelling or style, other changes affect the meaning. It would seem that there was a good deal of revision. Early in the document, words or parts of phrases are blocked out with thick horizontal lines. Later, another hand deleted some words with a series of curled circles. In chapter LXXVIII (fol. 221r in the manuscript), when Durán describes Cuauhtemoc's last days on the trip to Higueras, where the Aztec leader was killed, two lines are inked out precisely where Cuauhtemoc's end is being discussed. When deletions in the manuscript are considered to be important, these are indicated in the chapter notes.

THE PRESENT EDITION

With the decision of the University of Oklahoma Press to publish the historical part (volume III) of Diego Durán's *Historia de las Indias de Nueva España* in English as a companion volume to the ritual section (*Book of the Gods and Rites and the Ancient Calender*, 1977) based on the Heyden-Horcasitas book published in 1964 (see bibliography), I decided to do a completely new translation and annotation of this document directly from the sixteenth-century manuscript. My decision was determined by the twenty-five years that had passed since our first effort. Since that time I have spent many hours in archives and libraries in Mexico and other countries and have profited by this research. I have also benefited from suggestions and friendly criticism from colleagues such as Charles Gibson, H. B. Nicholson, and Miguel León-Portilla. By 1985, when I started the new translation, Fernando Horcasitas had died, so I carried on alone. My plan consisted of working with the original manuscript in Madrid, then checking my paleography with Garibay's 1967 edition of Durán, and finally comparing my translation with the 1964 Heyden-Horcasitas work. A few sections were left almost as they had been translated by us, but even in those cases I have made minor changes. It was also necessary to add numerous passages that had been deleted by the publisher in the earlier, abridged edition.

I have used modern English in translating the chronicle to facilitate the reading of the history and because Durán's writing is not poetic, as are, for example, many passages in Sahagún's work. Although Durán grew up in Tezcoco, the center of *pulicía* or good breeding in his time, he did not have the advantage of being educated at Salamanca, as did Sahagún. Durán's style is often redundant, at times tedious, though rich in historical and ethnographic material. I have translated the manuscript in a fairly literal style and have included an occasional redundancy in order to preserve some of the flavor of Durán's writing.

I have left proper names (people, places) as Durán recorded them, with a few exceptions. For example, Tehuantepec, as it is today, is spelled Tecuantepec by Durán; Soconusco was originally Xoconochco. Then I was confronted by Durán's referring to the ruler of the Aztecs as "king," although kings in the European sense did not exist in ancient Mexico. The *tlatoani*—"he who speaks, the speaker"—was the ruler, the *huey tlatoani* was the supreme leader, above the other *tlatoanime* and *tlatoque*; this *huey tlatoani* would have been the Aztec "king" according to Durán's informative document. Nevertheless, in respect for Durán's usage, I have used "king," although I sometimes substitute "ruler."

One of the problems facing me while doing the present translation was the use of the term "Aztec." I discussed this with Miguel León-Portilla, perhaps the major authority in this field. His suggestion was that it is now time to start calling the inhabitants of parts of prehispanic central Mexico "Mexica" (in Nahuatl *x* is pronounced *sh*), inasmuch as "Aztec" covers many Yuto-Aztecan groups in Mesoamerica. The people living in Tenochtitlan or Tlatelolco in ancient times were the Mexitin, also called the Mexica, the Mexicas, or the Aztecs. They were a subgroup of the Aztecs who originally lived in Aztlan (Aztec means "inhabitant of Aztlan"; for the etymology of Mexica, see the glossary). The people in the Aztec-Mexica capital in the Valley of Mexico, Tenochtitlan, were the Tenochca. Faced with all these possibilities, however, it was decided to continue to refer to the people about whom Durán wrote as the Aztecs or Mexicans, to establish consistency between this volume and the *Book of the Gods and Rites*, which uses the name Aztec.

Since I first started studying the works of Durán and other sixteenth- and seventeenth-century chroniclers almost thirty years ago, many scholars have discussed different aspects of Durán's works. Among these are Elizabeth H. Boone, Stephen Colston, Christopher Couch, and Donald Robertson. Their studies have greatly enriched our understanding of this Dominican's work and are included in the bibliography.

During my work on the Durán project I made numerous trips to places in the state of Morelos, where Fray Diego resided for a time in the Dominican monastery at Oaxtepec and in Hueyapan, one of the other Dominican establishments at the foot of the Popocatepetl volcano. I was enchanted with Hueyapan and found that there are still families in that town named Estrada and Partidor, possibly related to María Estrada, the woman who conquered this region under Cortés, as described in the last chapter of Durán's *History*. In nearby Zacualpan I studied church archives to see if I could discover records of Durán's activities in the region, but found that documents from the sixteenth and early seventeenth centuries relating to Hueyapan no longer existed. This was also the sad case in neighboring Tetela del Volcán.

No matter where Fray Diego resided or traveled, he invariably sought out informants and old documents (pictorial or written) in his constant search for information about the people of Mexico—information about their history, their customs, their religion, and their social and political organization. The result of his investigations is a rich account of a culture, partly destroyed and partly fused with a vastly different one. And in this fusion a new society and a new country—Mexico—were just beginning to be born.

DORIS HEYDEN

Mexico City

The History of the Indies of New Spain

The Basin of Mexico in Aztec times. Map by Aarón Flores Crispin, after Van Zantwijk, 1985.

CHAPTER I

Which treats of the possible place of origin of the Indians of these Indies, the Islands, and Mainland of this New Spain.

I n order to provide a truthful and reliable account of the origin of these Indian nations, an origin so doubtful and obscure, we would need some divine revelation or assistance to reveal this origin to us and help us understand it. However, lacking that revelation we can only speculate and conjecture about these beginnings, basing ourselves on the evidence provided by these people, whose strange ways, conduct, and lowly actions are so like those of the Hebrews. Thus we can almost positively affirm that they are Jews and Hebrews, and I would not commit a great error if I were to state this as fact, considering their way of life, their ceremonies, their rites and superstitions, their omens and hypocrisies, so akin to and characteristic of those of the Jews; in no way do they seem to differ. The Holy Scriptures bear witness to this, and from them we draw proofs and reasons for holding this opinion to be true.

As proof thereof, we know that this newly arrived nation, latecomers from strange and remote regions, made a long and tedious journey, searching and finally taking possession of this land. They spent many months and years in coming to this place. The truth of this matter can be found by drawing on their traditions and paintings and by talking to their elders, some of whom are very old.[1]

---

[1] Durán's ideas on the Hebrew origins of the natives of the Americas and the probable migration of people from the Near East to the New World constituted a favorite subject among the early colonial chroniclers. Columbus and Amerigo Vespucci were in agreement with the theory that Noah, after the great flood, had sent his children to all corners of the world. Joseph de Acosta, in his *Historia natural y moral de las Indias* (1962:45, 54), said in 1590 that he had little doubt that the settlers of the New World came, together with their animals, from Asia, from Europe, or from Africa, "although we would like to know how and why they came," he added (1962:45). The *Origen de los indios del Nuevo Mundo e Indias Occidentales* (1607), by Fray Gregorio García, and Fray Juan de Torquemada's *Monarquía indiana* (1615) both discuss the settling of the Americas by survivors of the flood, although García was ahead of his time in believing that the settlers in reality came from different parts of the Old World at different times. This chronicler and others also wrote of native ideas regarding their origins, such as the Mixtec belief that they came from a great tree and the Aztec claim that they came from Seven Caves. Belief in the ten lost tribes of Israel, based on vague texts in Genesis, persisted, however, until the nineteenth century and even later. One of

There are some people who tell fables about this subject. To wit, some say that the Indians were born of pools and springs; others that they were born of caves; still others, that they descended from the gods. All of this is clearly fabulous and shows that the natives themselves are ignorant of their origin and beginnings, inasmuch as they always profess to have come from strange lands. And I have found these things depicted in their painted manuscripts, where they portray great periods of hunger, thirst, and nakedness, with innumerable other afflictions that they suffered until they reached this land and settled it.[2]

All of these things confirm my suspicions that these natives are part of the ten tribes of Israel that Shalmaneser, king of the Assyrians, captured and took to Assyria in the time of Hoshea, king of Israel, and in the time of Ezekias, king of Jerusalem, as can be read in the fourth Book of Kings, chapter XVII. Here it is stated that Israel was taken

its exponents was the famous Lord Kingsborough, who in 1831 published his monumental work *Antiquities of Mexico*, consisting of numerous pictorial codices and other documents collected by the viscount, an enterprise which put him in debtors' prison, where he died.

[2] Mesoamerica, comprised mainly of Mexico and Guatemala and parts of Honduras, Nicaragua, and Salvador, was an area of high culture in prehispanic times and was a land of written books. These ancient codices or painted manuscripts were made of deerskin or bark paper in screenfold form, with pictographic writing painted in mineral colors combined with organic matter. There were also *lienzos*, sheets of cloth (although only colonial examples exist, since no *lienzos* have survived from the prehispanic period) and rolls, which are pictorial manuscripts rolled up rather than folded into screens. Themes included calendars, religious and divinatory material, genealogies, histories, and land claims. Few prehispanic pictorial codices survive since most were destroyed at the time of the conquest. Some were even destroyed or mutilated prior to this, in order to eliminate personages or events that rival factions wished to erase from the historical records.

Among the pictorial manuscripts believed to antedate the conquest are the five ritual-calendrical codices of the Borgia group from the Puebla–Tlaxcala–Western Oaxaca region (Borgia, Cospi, Fejérváry-Mayer, Laud, Vaticanus B); Mixtec manuscripts from Oaxaca; the Nuttall group (Becker I, Bodley, Colombino, Nuttall, Vienna), which are mainly historical-genealogical; and three ritual-calendrical screenfolds from the Maya area (Dresden, Paris, and Madrid) (Glass 1975:11-13).

There are perhaps no more than sixteen extant prehispanic pictorial manuscripts of the type mentioned here, although Durán must have been acquainted with many that portrayed the Aztec migration, in view of his comments. These undoubtedly were lost or destroyed, but may have been similar to the *Codex Boturini/Tira de la Peregrinación*, which is an early sixteenth century copy of an older document (or possibly the *Tira* is prehispanic). It is conserved in the National Museum of Anthropology in Mexico City. Or Durán may have seen manuscripts similar to the *Mapa de Sigüenza*, today in the Museum of Anthropology in Mexico, or the sixteenth-century *Azcatitlan Codex*, now in the Bibliothèque Nationale de Paris. The *Codex Borbonicus* is an important religious-ritual manuscript from central Mexico, probably an early copy of a prehispanic one, but does not include the migration.

from its own land to Assyria. And Ezra, in book four, chapter XIII, says about these people that they went to live in a remote and distant country that had never before been inhabited. There was a long and wearisome journey of a year and a half to reach the region of the Islands and the Mainland, to the west and beyond the seas, where today these people are found.

Other evidence found in the Holy Writ that can be cited to prove this idea is that God, in Hoshea, chapters I and II, and II up to XII, is said to have promised to multiply ten tribes of Israel, making them as numerous as sands of the sea. And the fact that they have taken possession of a large part of the world clearly and manifestly shows how great was this increase. But leaving [the biblical text] and coming to what the Spaniards saw in this country, one thing that amazed them was the large number of people they found here. This was remarked by [the Spaniards] who came early to this country, before the great plague of thirty-three years ago, when so many people died that not even a third of the Indians who lived here before the plague survived. And this does not include the innumerable men, women, and children killed by the Spaniards during the conquest a few years earlier.

The curious reader can find many other proofs in the Scriptures: in Deuteronomy, chapters IV and XXVIII and XXXII; in Isaiah, chapters XX, XXVIII, XLII; Jeremiah, Ezekiel, Micah, and Zephaniah, which tell of the rigorous punishment that God predicted would befall these ten tribes because of their wickedness and evil doings and infamous idolatries, which made them stray from belief in the true God, from whom they had received so many benefits. In the places I have mentioned it is told that, in return for such ingratitude, God promised a scourge and severe punishment. And it must be noted that it was prophesied that these people would lose their lands, homes, and treasures, their jewels and precious stones, their wives and children; and they would be taken to foreign lands and be sold there, while others were to take possession of their estate.

It seems to me that even without other explanation we have here sufficient proof that these Indians descend from the Hebrews. On their migration, during the long years of their journey, they were few in number, yet we have seen that they have multiplied like the sands of the sea.

And after they had populated this vast world, God tired of tolerating their abominations and evil doings and idolatries, so He brought alien people. Like an eagle that comes from the end of the earth, and with no respect for the old or the young, for the children or the women, without mercy He destroyed them. They were kept in hunger, in thirst, in nudity, and in perpetual exhaustion, until they were humbled, cowed, defeated.

Among the other misfortunes God foretold for these people was that they would have cowardly, pusillanimous, and fearful hearts, so that they, who were many, nevertheless would flee from few. This was true and proved when the Marqués del Valle [Hernán Cortés] disembarked on these shores with only three hundred men, half of whom were seafarers accustomed to work on ships, not trained in the art of war, yet they dared attack millions of Indians in this country. In this way they were guided by the hand of the Supreme Lord. It was His divine will that that the augury of the Sacred Scriptures be fulfilled and that three hundred men overcome so many people and that all those millions be possessed of such cowardly and frightened hearts that they would flee from the three hundred.[3]

Even today the natives are so weak and fearful in spirit that they dare not trust us in any way or give credence to us even in what concerns our Holy Catholic Faith and their salvation. But, Our Lord and God, we are witnesses to the fact that these miserable nations are now being subjected to all the labors and misery and punishments caused by their evil ways and abominations and idolatries. Let us see, o Lord, Your divine mercy and their true conversion to the Catholic Faith, which the same Scriptures promise, with renown and praise, to all people who of their own free will accepted the Holy Catholic Faith.

Having resolved the question whether these people are Hebrews and from the Jewish nation with the aid of authorities who have come to this country, I wish to prove the same idea with other reasons, such as those based on the authority of the Sacred Scriptures.

---

[3] Actually, there were not millions of inhabitants in Mexico who "would flee from the three hundred" Spaniards. In the city of Tenochtitlan, the Aztec capital, it is calculated that the population density was about 300,000 to 400,000 at the time of the conquest (van Zantwijk 1985:284–85). In other parts of the country not everyone fled from the Spaniards. Many joined them in the hope of freeing themselves from Aztec domination and the payment of tribute to the Aztec treasury and because the Spaniards appeared to be liberators from these overlords. It is well known that the Tlaxcalans and the Aztecs were rivals of long standing, as were the people of Michoacan and the Aztecs. Chapter XLIV of this volume clearly illustrates the extremes to which the Aztecs could go when a town refused to surrender. It is no wonder that this great power was both feared and hated. Bernal Díaz del Castillo (1939:94–97) describes the friendly welcome given Cortés and his men by the Totonacs of Cempoala in Veracruz, whose ruler Díaz calls the Fat Chief because of his girth. After feeding the Spaniards well and giving them gifts, the Fat Chief complained to Cortés of the treatment given the Totonacs by Motecuhzoma, "saying that having lately been compelled to submit to the yoke of that monarch, he had seized all his gold, and now held him completely enslaved." Other chieftains, in nearby Quiahuiztlan, joined "in bitter complaint of the tyranny of Montezuma," saying that the Aztecs took their children in slavery or for sacrifice. Obviously, under these conditions, many groups willingly allied themselves with the Europeans against the Aztecs.

Among the narrations of these people that tell of their coming to possess and inhabit this territory, I often find great differences among the old people who tell these tales regarding the events, toils, and afflictions that took place during their journey. Yet, when they narrate this story, some one way and some another, their different accounts seem to describe that long, tedious road traveled by the children of Israel who went from Egypt to the promised land, told so vividly that I could cite passages from Exodus or Leviticus to show the resemblance — but I do not want to be prolix. I do not intend to follow the order of these narrations. I only wish, in order to make my point, to relate some of the difficulties and misfortunes, famines and pestilences, that they claim they suffered during their migration. We shall see that in fact this is nothing other than the story told in the Sacred Scriptures, handed down by their ancestors.

These people have traditions regarding a great man. They told me that after he had suffered many afflictions and persecutions from his countrymen he gathered the multitude of his followers and persuaded them to flee from that persecution to a land where they could live in peace. Having made himself leader of those people, he went to the seashore and moved the waters with a rod that he carried in his hand. Then the sea opened up and he and his followers went through. And his enemies, seeing this opening made, pursued him, but the waters returned to their place and the pursuers were never heard of again.[4]

What clearer proof do we need that these people were Jews than their own reference to the flight from Egypt, wherein Moses moved the waters with his rod, the sea opened up, a path appeared, and after Pharaoh followed with his army God caused the sea to return to its place, with the result that all their enemies drowned in the deep? And if this account is not convincing enough, I should like to tell about another event that the Aztecs claim happened on their long migration.

While they were camped by some high hills, a great, frightful earthquake occurred. The earth opened up and swallowed certain evil men who were among them, an occurrence that filled the other people with dread. Having seen the painting of this event, I was reminded of the Book of Numbers, chapter XVI, where it is told how the earth opened up and swallowed Korah and Dathan and Abiram.

---

[4]Durán's leaning toward biblical interpretations is seen in his claim that Quetzalcoatl opened a path in the sea with his rod, the waters returning to their place and drowning the pursuers after the followers of the divine personage had fled to safety. Quetzalcoatl, whose name means "Feathered Serpent," was also called Ce Acatl, "One Reed," his birth date, and Topiltzin, "Our Lord." Durán in the present volume describes Motecuhzoma's belief that the Spanish conquerors arriving from the east represented Quetzalcoatl returning, or at least Cortés was thus identified.

The History of the Indies of New Spain

To provide another strong and clear proof of what I have been saying, I wish to relate that the same painting showed how sand or very fine hail rained on the people. When I inquired what this meant, I was told that sand from the sky rained on their forefathers continually during the journey they made to reach this land. If I am not deceived, this must be the same manna with which God sustained the Jews in the desert, as chapter XVI of Exodus relates.

That I may leave nothing untold, I wish to cite the Holy Writ in defense of my opinion. I take my theme from the first chapter of Genesis, which states: "In the beginning God created the heaven and the earth." Just so an aged man from Cholula, about one hundred years old, began to describe their origins to me. This man, who because of his great age walked bent over toward the earth, was quite learned in their ancient traditions. When I begged him to enlighten me about some details I wished to put into this history, he asked me what I wanted him to tell. I realized I had found an old and learned person, so I answered, all that he knew about the history of his Indian nation from the beginning of the world. He responded: "Take pen and paper, because you will not be able to remember all that I shall tell you." And began thus:

In the beginning, before light or sun had been created, this world lay in darkness and shadows and was void of every living thing. It was all flat, without a hill or ravine, surrounded on all sides by water, without even a tree or any other created thing. And then, when the light and sun were born in the east, men of monstrous stature appeared and took possession of this country. These giants, desirous of seeing the birth of the sun and its setting, decided to go seek [dawn and dusk], and they separated into two groups. One band walked toward the west and the other toward the east. The latter walked until the sea cut off their route; from here they decided to return to the place from which they had set out, called Iztac Zolin Inemian.[5]

Not having found a way to reach the sun but enamored of its light and beauty, they decided to build a tower so high that its summit would reach unto heaven. And gathering materials for this building, the giants found clay for bricks and an excellent mortar with which they began to build the tower very swiftly. When they had raised it as high as they could—and it seemed to reach to heaven—the Lord of the Heights became angry and said to the inhabitants of the heavens, "Have you seen that the men of the earth have built a proud and lofty tower in order to come up here, enamored as they are of the light of the

[5] According to Angel María Garibay's edition of Durán's *Historia* (1967:II:586), Iztac Zolin Inemian means "Where White Quails Dwell" and is an epithet of the site chosen by Huitzilopochtli.

sun and of its beauty? Come, let us confound them, for it is not right that these earthlings, made of flesh, mingle with us." Then swift as lightning those who dwell in the heavens came out from the four regions of the world and tore down the tower that had been constructed. And the giants, bewildered and filled with terror, separated and fled in all directions.[6]

That is how an Indian relates the creation of the world, and I do not believe it necessary to call attention to the resemblance of this account to chapters I and II of Genesis. [The sixth and eleventh chapters] of that book deal with giants and the tower of Babel and how men, ambitious to reach heaven, moved only by the desire to praise their own name, built the tower and because of this were confounded by God. Therefore I am convinced and wish to convince others that those who tell this account heard it from their ancestors; and these natives belong, in my opinion, to the lineage of the chosen people of God for whom He worked great marvels. And so the knowledge of the paintings of the things told in the Bible and its mysteries have passed from hand to hand, from father to son. The people assign those events to this land, believing that they took place here, for they are ignorant of their own origins.

It cannot be denied, nor do I deny, that there have been giants in this country. I can affirm this because I have seen them, I have met men of monstrous stature here. I believe there are some in the city of Mexico who will remember, as I do, a gigantic Indian who appeared in a procession of the feast of Corpus Christi. He was dressed in yellow silk with a halberd at his shoulder and a helmet on his head. And he was all of a *vara* taller than the others.[7]

I also believe that during such a long and tedious journey as that which these people pursued to come to this land they experienced great hardships. They tell of famines, plagues, thirst, tempests, wars, locusts that tormented them; of hailstorms that destroyed the fields they had sown along the way; and a thousand other obstacles and troubles that I find described in their chronicles. They undoubtedly brought chieftains and priests to guide them and instruct them in their ceremonies, although I doubt that these things were taken from the biblical account. Seeing that their stories are so like those found in

---

[6]Undoubtedly Durán was influenced by the Tower of Babel recorded in Genesis 11:7–9 (King James Version): "Go to, let us go down, and there confound their language, that they may not understand one another's speech.... Therefore is the name of it called Babel, because the Lord did there confound the language of all the earth; and from thence did the Lord scatter them abroad upon the face of all the earth."

[7]Durán evidently refers to men on stilts, not uncommon in Mexican festivities.

the Holy Scriptures I cannot help but believe that [these Indians are the children of Israel].

As proof of this, in order to make it clear, I wish to mention the rites, idolatries, and superstitions these people had. They made sacrifices in the mountains, and under trees, in dark and gloomy caves, and in the caverns of the earth. They burned incense, killed their sons and daughters, sacrificed them, and offered them as victims to their gods. They sacrificed children, ate human flesh, killed prisoners and captives of war. All of these were also Hebrew rites practiced by those ten tribes of Israel, and all were carried out with the greatest ceremony and superstitions one can imagine.

What most forces me to believe that these Indians are of Hebrew descent is their strange insistence in clinging to their idolatries and superstitions, for they pay them much heed, just as their ancestors did. As David states, in Psalm 106, when the people were afflicted by God, they pleaded that He forgive them in His mercy; but then they forgot and returned to idolatry:

> And they served their idols; which were a snare unto them. Yea, they sacrificed their sons and daughters unto devils. And shed innocent blood, even the blood of their sons and of their daughters, whom they sacrificed unto the idols of Canaan: and the land was polluted with blood.[8]

The only knowledge I have of the origins of these people, and the Indians know more than they relate, tells of the Seven Caves where their ancesters dwelt for such a long time, and which they abandoned in order to seek this land, some coming first and others later, until those caves were deserted. The caves are in Teocolhuacan, also called Aztlan, which we are told is found toward the north and near the region of La Florida.[9]

---

[8]This quotation is taken from Psalm 106:36–38 (King James Version).

[9]During early Spanish colonial times, La Florida referred not only to what is now the peninsula of this name in the United States but to the region north of Tamaulipas, which would include northeastern Mexico and southeastern Texas. Aztlan is considered the original home of the Aztecs and gave them their name, which means "People of Aztlan." Garibay (Durán 1967:II:584), however, claims that Aztatlan and not Aztlan is correct, for *aztatl* is "whiteness." There are many theories about the location of Aztlan. Jiménez Moreno (personal communication) suggests that it may be the Aztatlan discovered by Nuño de Guzmán in 1530, situated on an island in the Mezcatitlan Lagoon in Nayarit.

During colonial times these sites were confused with each other and the Seven Caves with the Seven Cities of Silver or Cíbola, sought by Coronado, who set out with three hundred Spaniards, one thousand Indians, and one thousand horses on a great expedition in search of wealth, like Ponce de León's search for the Fountain of Youth in Florida or Belcázar's hunt for El Dorado in Colombia.

At this first mention of sedentary life by Durán, some of the plants cultivated in ancient Mesoamerica can be mentioned. The four most important were maize or

Possible place of origin

Therefore, I shall now give the true account of these nations and their migration from the place of the caverns [according to the native accounts], although my own opinion of their origin seems more correct. But in everything I submit myself to the correction of the Holy Catholic Church. Thus, seven tribes of people went out from those seven caves called Chicomoztoc, where they lived, in search of this land. As they have no information relating to previous times and since they do not know their true origin, they claim that their ancestors were born of these caves. In the following chapter I shall treat of this departure.

Indian corn, beans, chile peppers, and squash. Others were the maguey or century plant, tomato, the tiny *chian* seed (a type of sage), gourds, *jícama* (a turnip-like fruit), the *texocotl* (similar to the crab apple), *nopal* or prickly pear cactus (whose fruit, the *tuna*, and tender leaves were important in the diet), cacao or chocolate, vanilla, avocado, manioc, and other plants and berries. Amaranth or *huauhtli* (*Amaranthus hypochondriacus* and *Amaranthus cruentus*), native to Mexico and one of the basic cereals, was and still is a popular food, rich in protein, adaptable to most climates and altitudes. It is presently being hailed as an answer to hunger in underdeveloped countries, along with *Spirulina* (protein-rich algae), which was also part of the prehispanic diet in Mexico (see chap. XXXI, note 3). It was not until the arrival of the Spaniards that cereals such as wheat, barley, and rice, fruits such as apples, pears, and oranges, and vegetables such as lettuce, carrots, and peas were added to the Indian diet of Mexico, while native American plants found their way to Europe.

CHAPTER II

Which treats of how these Indians left their Seven Caves in order to come to this land.

The Indian nations emerged from those Seven Caves, where they had lived a long time, in the year of Our Lord 820. It took them more than eighty years to reach this country because of the many delays that took place during the migration.[1] Along the way they built towns and settled in places that they saw were peaceful and pleasant and that they favored. But as they explored the country they found better, more advantageous sites, so they abandoned the other places and went on. The old people, the sick, and those who were exhausted were left behind; in this way those regions were populated.

The people erected great and curious buildings in each settlement along the way, so that today remains of these edifices are found in many places where they stayed. For this reason they tarried in coming here, although the distance [from Aztlan] is so short that it can be covered in a month. The cause of this was their stopping to sow and harvest, and their lingering to rest and build towns, all this being consistent with their natural temperament, which is deliberate and slow. In that way they reached this part of New Spain in the year 902.[2]

---

[1]Durán indicates that the people left Aztlan in A.D. 820, arriving in the Valley of Mexico about 900. The date usually accepted for the founding of Tenochtitlan is A.D. 1325, but the Aztecs must have been in the area before this, though perhaps not since 900. Although the Aztecs gave as their reason for leaving Aztlan-Chicomoztoc the offer of a promised land by their god Huitzilopochtli, the chronicler Cristóbal del Castillo (1908:55) relates that these people had been vassals of other Aztecs, humiliated and subjugated, forced to turn over to their overlords most of the lake products they collected daily. Thus, living in a rich aquatic environment did not free them from hunger or excessive work. The alternative was to migrate, as did other groups who may also have been subject to the rulers of Aztlan.

[2]That the Aztecs founded settlements and planted and harvested while on their migration indicates that they were a truly Mesoamerican people at that time and not nomadic barbarians, as has sometimes been suggested. The Aztecs did call themselves Chichimec at the beginning of their long journey and this term means "hunter," "seminomad," or "people who migrate." These are free definitions because the etymology of *chichimecatl* (pl. *chichimeca*) according to Simeón (1988:96) is "he who nurses." There is also a tradition which states that the Chichimecs descend from the union of a man and a dog, making the name mean "dog lineage" from *chichi*, "dog," and *mecatl*, "line, rope, or lineage."

The people who left the caves first were the following six tribes: the Xochimilcas, the Chalcas, the Tepanecs, the Colhuas, the Tlalhuicas, and the Tlaxcalans. It should be noted, however, that not all left together or in the same year, but some first and others later. In this way they abandoned the region of the caves, one tribe doing what it saw another do. These people are fond of imitating others, like monkeys or sheep: if one jumps they all jump after him.

So it was that first the Xochimilca left, followed by the Chalcas, then the Tepanecs, the Colhuas, and after them the Tlalhuicas and the Tlaxcalans. The Aztecs[3] remained behind, due to a divine command that will be spoken of later. These people affirm that God had promised them this land, for they are the people He held dearest, like the tribe of Judah among the Jews. Thus, they were loath to leave and did not abandon the place of the caves for three hundred and two years. It is evident from the count of the years that the other tribes came first and took possession of the land. The Aztecs, then, lived here three hundred and one years and the others, six hundred and two.

The Xochimilcas were the first to arrive and they made a circuit of the great lake. They saw that the place they occupy today had a good location, a pleasant one, so they settled there, finding everything they needed, without meeting opposition or causing injury to anyone. The leading men of that tribe took possession of the mountain ridge that today belongs to the Xochimilca nation and that stretches as far as a town called Tuchimilco or Ocopetlayuca, by another name. Other towns that form part of this nation and are still called by the same name include Ocuituco, Tetela, Hueyapan, Tlamimilolpan, Xumiltepec, Tlacotepec, Zacualpa and Temoac, Tlayacapa and Totolapan and Tepoztlan, Chimalhuacan, Ecatzinco, and Tepetlixpan, with all the other towns subject to Chimalhuacan. All these are part of the Xochimilca nation, and that is what all the territory of the Xochimilca people is called, including Cuitlahuac, Mezquic, and Culhuacan.[4]

Soon after the Xochimilca, the second group arrived. These were the Chalca lineage, who on their arrival joined the Xochimilca and

---

[3] When the Aztecs left Aztlan, they were called Aztecs and formed part of a larger group with this name, the "people of Aztlan." As noted in other parts of this book, the migrating Aztecs changed their name to Mexicans or Mexicas at Coatlicamac. Here a great tree split, which was seen as a sign that the group should separate from the others and change its name.

[4] Those towns under Xochimilca control include many that today are in the state of Morelos (for example, Ocuituco, Tetela, and Hueyapan on the slopes of the Popocatepetl volcano) and some in the present-day state of Mexico (such as Tlamimilolpan near Teotihuacan and Chimalhuacan). Xochimilco itself is now part of Mexico City, as are Chalco and the Tepanec centers. The Tezcocan cities are in the eastern part of the state of Mexico.

adjusted their common boundaries pacifically. They designated as their capital the town of Tlalmanalco. The leading men and chieftains of that lineage went out from here to live in those places, in the important towns that were in this province: Amequemecan, Tenango, and all those of Cuaxopas, Ayotzinco, Chalco, Atenco, San Martín, and all the villages, towns, and cities now found in the Chalco region. This is a much smaller area than that occupied by the Xochimilcas, because there were many more people among the Xochimilcas than among the Chalcas.

The Tepanecs came after the Chalcas and, just like the others, founded their main center. This was Tlacopan [Tacuba], although the court and principal people resided in Azcapotzalco. After some time had passed, the lords and principals spread out and occupied the towns of Tacubaya, Coyoacan, Azcapotzalco, Tlalnepantla, Tenayuca, and the entire range that runs to the border where the Otomi people live.

The fourth to arrive was the Tezcocan tribe, a group as numerous as that of Xochimilco. They were accompanied by many illustrious and courageous men. This fact is proved by the order and fine planning with which their city was built and the beauty with which they adorned and maintained it all the time they could. They made their capital that place which is now the city of Tezcoco, and from here they dispersed in order to build towns such as the other people had done. Some went to Huexutla and others to Coatlinchan, where the court of that nation resided long before they moved to Tezcoco. Still others built in Tepetlaoztoc, Acolman, Chiauhtla, Tecciztlan, Tepechpan, Otompan, and many other villages, towns, cities, and capitals, which I shall not mention so as not to waste time and paper. It is enough to state that [the Tezcocan nation] occupied as much land as that of Xochimilco; among these places were Coatepec and Chimalhuacan del Río, called thus in their language, and Chicualoapa, and all those along that part of the lake shore.

In this region there are beautiful towns and the inhabitants are in every way educated and courteous, clever, sagacious, of fine speech, elegant, and polished. Their refined style in speaking is so outstanding that it reminds one of the Castilian of Toledo in Spain. In comparison with these people, the others seem coarse and rough.[5] Some will

[5] The Nahuatl language, a branch of the Yuto-Aztecan linguistic family, was spoken all the way from Jalisco to Central America. It was also known as Mexica or Mexicano and was divided into a number of dialects. Several of the Spanish chroniclers comment on the superior attitude of the people of Tezcoco regarding their particular form of speaking this tongue, apparently considering their accent finer than that of Mexico City. The *o* was often written as *u* in the chronicles.

think that I am partial in speaking so well of Tezcoco; although I did not acquire my milk teeth in that city, I got my second ones there. Since the remarkable things of Tezcoco have been extolled by others, everything I say is already well known.

When the lake was completely encircled by these four tribes who occupied its shores and shared the land among themselves, the Tlalhuicas came, a very rough people in every way and of coarse speech. As the newcomers found everything occupied, they settled in the place that they inhabit today, making Cuauhnahuac the main center and capital of their province. From here the men of that group went out, like the others, to settle in other towns, some to Yauhtepec, others to Huaxtepec, to Acapichtlan, or to Tlaquiltenango, and to all the other towns and villages in this region, now called the Marquesado because it belonged to the most fortunate Marqués del Valle [Hernán Cortés]. This is certainly one of the most beautiful and pleasant lands in the world, and if it were not for the great heat here it would be another Garden of Eden. There are delightful springs, abundant rivers full of fish, the freshest of woods, and orchards of many kinds of fruit, many of them native to Mexico and others to Spain, which supply all the neighboring cities with this fruit. [The Marquesado] is full of a thousand different fragrant flowers and is very rich in cotton. The commerce in this product is carried on here by people from all over the country.[6]

After these five tribes had settled, the people of Tlaxcala, originally called Texcallan, arrived and, seeing that there was now no place where they could establish themselves on this side of the mountains, went behind the Sierra Nevada [the snow-capped ridges] to live, where they now have their home. They chose Tlaxcala as capital of their dominion, but as they were very numerous the lords dispersed toward

---

[6]The Marquesado del Valle de Oaxaca constituted the enormous extension of lands given to Hernán Cortés in a Royal Grant of June 6, 1529, at the same time that Cortés was given the title of Marqués (or Marquis). These properties included lands north of Mexico City near the Chichimec frontier down to the Valley of Oaxaca and the Isthmus of Tehuantepec. The entire territory was not assigned to Cortés as an *encomienda* but did include large areas controlled by the Marqués that paid tribute to him. In 1570 about half of Cortés's income was derived from tribute. The present state of Morelos, the region mainly described by Durán in his *History*, seems to have been a favorite of Cortés and the place where he established a sugar plantation (Barret 1977:21–27). Property controlled by Cortés in the present state of Morelos covered 4,100 square kilometers and included Cuernavaca and Cuautla—in all, some eighty towns and villages, eight *haciendas*, and two sugar plantations. His holdings in Oaxaca, Veracruz, and what is now the state of Mexico were also vast. In all the total extent of the Marquesado was 11,550 square kilometers. Cortés himself resided in Coyoacan (then not part of the capital but now a section of Mexico City) and in Cuernavaca (*Enciclopedia de México* 1977:VIII:575).

Huexotzinco, Calpan, and Cholula. If I were to mention all the lands occupied by the Tlaxcalans it would tire the reader without purpose, as the innumerable towns, villages, and dwelling places are well known. The king our lord has seen fit to exempt them from all tribute, since they were loyal and faithful subjects in the conquest of this country.

When these six tribes and different peoples had settled, they recorded [in their painted books] the type of land and kind of people found here. Among these there are two paintings that show two types of people, one from the west of the snow-covered mountains toward Mexico [City], and the other to the east, where Puebla and Cholula are found. The people from the first region were Chichimecs and those from the east were "giants," the Quiname, which means "men of great stature."

The few Chichimecs on the side of the Valley of Mexico were brutal, savage men; their name Chichimec means "hunters, those who live by the hunt." They were wild and rustic. And they were called thus because they lived among the peaks and in the harshest places of the mountain, where they led a bestial existence, with no propriety or human organization. They hunted food like beasts of the same mountain and went naked without any covering on their private parts. They hunted all day for rabbits, deer, hares, weasels, moles, wildcats, birds, snakes, lizards, mice, and they also collected locusts, worms, herbs, and roots, on which they lived. Their whole life was reduced to this, hunting for these things. They were skillful in this occupation: in order to kill a snake they spent an entire day crouching behind a bush, on their haunches, watching the snake at its lair as a cat, when it smells a mouse, will stalk it next to its hole.

These people slept in the hills, inside caves or under bushes, without any heed for sowing, cultivating, or gathering. They did not worry about the morrow but ate what they had hunted each day. Thus men and women went into the hills to search for food, just as a dog goes to a rubbish heap seeking something on which to gnaw. As the women accompanied their husbands, they left their little children well glutted with milk, hanging in small rush baskets from branches of trees, until they returned from the hunt. These few Chichimecs were so spread out that they had no contact with each other. They adored no gods and had no kind of ritual, nor did they recognize any ruler. They lived a carefree life according to natural law.

When the new nations came, these savage people did not resist them, nor did they show anger, but rather awe and fear. They fled toward the hills, hiding themselves there. They hid in the way they flee from us today, because it is true that we have not shown ourselves to be so kind and loving as to induce them to do otherwise. The newly arrived people seeing, then, that the land was left unoccupied and free, chose at will the finest and most peaceful places.

The other people who were found in Tlaxcala and Cholula and Huexotzinco are said to have been giants.[7] They were enraged and aggrieved by the coming of the invaders and tried to defend their land. I do not have a very reliable account of this; therefore, I shall not insist upon telling the story, the relation that I was told, even though it was long and worth hearing, of the battles the Cholultecs fought with the giants until they killed them or drove them from the country.

These giants lived no less bestially than [the Chichimecs], as they had abominable customs and ate the meat from the hunt raw. In some places of that region enormous bones of the giants have been found, which I myself have seen dug up in rugged places many times. These giants, while fleeing from the Cholultecs, flung themselves from the precipices and were killed, in order to avoid falling into the hands of the others. The Cholultecs had been extremely cruel to them, harassing them, not leaving them in peace, pursuing them from hill to hill, from valley to valley, molesting them, hounding them, until they were destroyed.

Even if we detain the reader a little, I should like to tell of the manner in which the people of Cholula and Tlaxcala annihilated that evil nation. This was done by treason and deceit. They pretended to want peace with the giants and after having assured them of their goodwill they invited them to dine and made a great banquet. An ambush was then prepared. Some men slyly robbed the guests of their

---

[7] The legend of giants is a favorite one in many parts of Mexico, as gigantic bones of Pleistocene animals such as the mammoth, *Bison antiquuus*, and a type of elephant have been found from prehistoric times and were formerly mistaken for human remains. Sahagún mentions that "giants" or Quinametin built Teotihuacan as well as Cholula (1969:III:111). So many of these immense bones have been disinterred in the Valley of Teotihuacan that before the conquest people named a site near the pyramids Acolman (from *acolli*, "tall" or "broad-shouldered," and *mani*, "where they are"; by extension, "where there are giants"). Furthermore, who but men-greater-than-men, giants or gods, could have constructed the pyramids of such extraordinary proportions at Teotihuacan, "Place of Gods"? This legend applies to Cholula not only because remains of the same type have been found there but because there was a strong relationship between Teotihuacan and that city. Mammoth bones were a curiosity to the Spaniards as well as to the Indians. Fossilized bones were sent to Spain during the sixteenth century, perhaps among the first "Mexican curios." Dr. Francisco Hernández, commissioned by the Spanish monarch to investigate many natural phenomena of New Spain, judged the "giants" to be more than five meters tall, based on the size of the mammoth bones. The Museum of Prehistory at Tepexpan in the Teotihuacan Valley has a comprehensive exhibit of gigantic bones, together with lithic instruments discovered here.

shields, clubs, swords, and many other kinds of weapons they used. Then, having feigned peace, having fed the guests, and having stolen their weapons while the others were off guard, some of the Cholultecs suddenly came out of hiding and attacked, killing all. The giants tried to defend themselves and, as they could not find their weapons, it is said that they tore branches from the trees with the same ease that one cuts a turnip, and in this way they defended themselves valiantly. But finally all were killed.

Once the giants were annihilated, the others built their towns and cities as they wished, without any opposition or difficulties. Thus, peacefully, they settled the boundaries among themselves in order to define their lands and possessions clearly. They communicated with one another, they intermarried, they lived in peace without problems or disputes, cultivating their lands and building their dwellings, their houses and their huts. They had no ceremonies and had no idols but adored only the sun, which they worshiped as God, the creator and cause of all things. They sacrificed to him the following way: when any game was killed they removed the blood-stained arrow and offered it, as a symbol of sacrifice, to the sun, recognizing him as a deity.

From this time on the Chichimec barbarians acquired a little culture and lived like rational people and covered themselves with clothing, because things that had seemed natural to them before now were regarded as shameful. They also made huts in which to live. They began to have relations with the other people and to trade and bargain with them, losing the fear they used to have of these neighbors, becoming related to them by marriage, beginning to have lords, recognizing the authority of some men over others. They congregated in different places; they opened their eyes to distinguish good from evil; they abandoned their savage life. But these Chichimecs always stayed in the hills and retired to the mountains, separated from the others.

Three hundred and two years after the six bands of people had left the caves where they had lived, in the region of Aztlan and Teocolhuacan, the seventh tribe, the Mexican nation, came to this land,[8] which they believed had been promised to them by their gods because they were the people closest to them. All were idolatrous and felt favored by their deities. Aside from this they were bellicose, courageous,

---

[8]At the beginning of this chapter Durán states that "the Indian nations" took more than eighty years to reach the Valley of Mexico, yet here he contradicts himself by saying that 302 years after the first six groups left the caves the Aztecs came to the central region. This question of Durán's dating is confusing. Nigel Davies has made a careful study of dates and events in the prehispanic Valley of Mexico: see *The Aztecs: A History* (1973:37); and *The Toltec Resurgence* (1986).

undertook great feats and exploits fearlessly, but also could be courteous and show some breeding.

As they tarried much on their journey, stopping at times for long periods, and as it is my intention to relate their history, it is necessary to write a special chapter regarding the events that took place during their migration. They suffered great trials in the hope that the country that was promised them by their prophets and chieftains would really be the promised land, fertile and full of plenty, with great riches and with everything that could be imagined or wished for. Anyone who knows this place and whose eyes are free of prejudice knows that the above description is true of this country, for, among all the lands in the world, this one can compare with the finest.

The Aztecs brought with them an idol called Huitzilopochtli,[9] who had four custodians to serve him. He prophesied to them in secret all the events that would take place on their journey. The people held this idol in such reverence and awe that no one but his keepers dared approach or touch him. He came concealed in a coffer of rushes, so that not one of the natives had ever seen the form of their idol. The priests made the people adore the idol as a god, preaching to them the conduct they were to follow, and the ceremonies and rites to be observed in honor of their divinity. This they did in all the places where they set up camp, just as the children of Israel did when they wandered in the wilderness.

---

[9]Huitzilopochtli, the god-hero of Durán's works, is presented at the beginning of the text as an idol or as a human being, a chieftain who led the Aztecs during their migration to find the promised land. Later in the chronicle he appears as a deity represented by an idol in the main temple in the city of Mexico-Tenochtitlan. The *Codex Boturini* or *Tira de la Peregrinación* represents Huitzilopochtli as a sacred bundle carried by the *teomamaque* or god-bearers. Since the deity's commands were interpreted through his priests he also can be considered an oracle. Durán's *Book of the Gods and Rites and the Ancient Calendar* (1977), companion to the present volume, describes Huitzilopochtli fully.

CHAPTER III

Which treats of the arrival of the Aztecs in this land of Mexico and of the events that took place before they reached it.

So great were the feats and exploits of the Aztecs, so full of adventure, that those who are not acquainted with these exploits and with these people will enjoy hearing of their ancient customs and of their origins and descendants, and of many other events regarding them that are worthy of remembrance. I am aware of the great difficulties in relating these ancient histories, especially since they begin so far back in the past. Moreover, some early friars burned ancient books and writings and thus they were lost. Then, too, the old people who could write these books are no longer alive to tell of the settling of this country, and it was they whom I would have consulted for my chronicle.

It also seems to me that it will be impossible to tell everything that has occurred in this New Spain, as it is such a large country. There are so many kingdoms, provinces, cities, and villages here, so many large towns where innumerable people lived, divided into many nations, languages, and ways of life, as well as dress and customs. The good and bad fortunes that befell a single one of these nations would be enough for one painstaking historian. He would still have enough to do in writing the exploits of only one people, even though he abbreviated the history, which is what I have attempted here.

However, this brief history will have a special purpose: that nothing regarding the Aztec nation be left unsaid, because although the feats of all the people were to be scattered over most of this New Spain during many epochs, and were achieved by courageous men, the real origin for all these valorous deeds was, after all, Mexico-Tenochtitlan. For it was here that information about all that passed in the other provinces and kingdoms was reported, because it was the head and center of them all. So great was the power and importance of this center that it has been my desire to revive it and bring it to life again after so long a time.

This happy land has produced sons of fine and subtle intellect, sons who could have revived its ancient glories and given it new life with their outstanding skills. Thus the ancient splendor would have lived forever in the memory of men and they would have been adorned with the beauty of their own qualities, so that newly arrived foreign peoples of different nations and from different regions, like those who come to this land, attracted by its fertility and richness, would have been pleased to observe these things. Thus they would lose the bad and false opinion that these Aztec people were barbarian and uncivilized, as they have been called. Because, although they showed blindness and diabolic self-deception in their rites and idolatries, in matters of government and good order, submission and reverence, majesty and authority, courage and fortitude, I have found no one to surpass them. And I want to point out all these things so the memory of these people will last forever.

With this in mind, and although I do not claim any greater power of intellect than anyone else possesses, the hope that I can realize this objective — and hope of success often overcomes greater difficulties — has helped me in this task of writing an account of those things of the country that interest me. And although I am ill equipped and prepared for this task, I venture to embark upon it and set out to bring to light this obscure and forgotten history. I shall refer to the most obvious and well-known facts, for some vestiges of the past can lead us to an understanding of former events. Even if we had no more record than the stones carved with the likenesses of the ancient kings in the enclosure at Chapultepec, where the rulers had their portraits carved at the end of their days, and many other images and sculptures one comes upon at every turn, these alone would suffice to tell of the grandeur, great deeds, origin, and descendants of these people. Although these images do not tell the whole story, at least they are an indication of the greatest achievements of these nations.

In the year one thousand one hundred and ninety-three after the birth of Our Redeemer, Jesus Christ, the Aztec nation reached this land. These people, like the others who populated the country, departed from the Seven Caves in a land where they had lived, called Aztlan. This name means "Whiteness" or "Place of the Herons." Because of this the people originally were called Aztec, which means "People of Whiteness." They were also called Mecitin or Mexicans, in honor of the priest and lord who guided them on their migration, whose name was Meci. The entire tribe took this name, just as the Romans took theirs from Romulus, the founder of Rome.

The Aztecs now have another name, which they acquired after they took possession of this land: Tenochca, from the *tenochtli* or prickly pear cactus that sprang from the rock in the place where they built their city. In this sense Tenochca means "the owners of the prickly pear cactus."

The Aztecs left the Seven Caves and embarked upon their journey in order to seek the land promised them by their gods, according to traditions left by their priests. I find in their painted manuscripts and

The History of the Indies of New Spain

in their oral traditions that the people made long stops on the migration and lived for years at a time in peaceful, fertile places abounding in water and forests. In some places they stayed twenty years, in others fifteen, and in others ten, more or less. In a painting that I was shown in Santiago Tlatelolco, I saw depicted many towns founded during this migration, some of them still inhabited and others now abandoned because the people there have died off. Only vestiges remain of the buildings and temples erected to their god; the first thing the people did in each place was to construct a temple.

The second thing the people did, when the temple was finished and ready to receive the coffer in which their god was carried, was to plant maize, chiles, which are a kind of pepper they eat, and all the other crops they depend upon, watered either by rains or by irrigation. And that done, they either had or did not have good crops, for if their god decreed a good harvest, then they reaped; if he determined otherwise, they abandoned the fields, except when the maize was ripe. Frequently these fields were left to old men and women and the sick who could not go on. In this way some places were settled and were left with the seeds of those crops that had been planted. This was the purpose of the Aztecs, to populate those places with their people and become rulers of the land and of its fruits.

We have mentioned how the people of this nation brought their principal god, without whom they dared not move. They also revered seven other gods who represented the Seven Caves out of which the seven tribes or groups had emerged. These seven gods were greatly esteemed and had their names and titles to indicate divine superiority, as today titles denote noblemen who possess them. These titles of honor and greatness confer solemn authority in name of those deities.

The god of the first barrio was called Yopican Tecutli, Lord of Yopican (Place of the Tlapanecs),

the second, Tlacochcalcatl Tecutli, Lord of the House of Darts,
the third, Huitznahuatl Tecutli, Lord of the South,
the fourth, Cuatecpan Tecutli, Lord of the Eagle Place,
the fifth, Chalmecatl, He of the Jade Lineage,
the sixth, Tlacatecpanecatl, He of the People's Palace,
the seventh, Izquitecatl, He of the Place of Toasted Maize.[1] The

---

[1] Although *teuctli* or *tecutli* can be translated as deity, as Durán says, it is possible that the names given here refer to *calpulli* chiefs, since *teuctli* or *tecuhtli* (pl. *tetecuhtin*) also means holder of titles and offices, dignitary. A *teuctli* was the head of a chiefly house (the *teucalli*), often acted as judge, was called upon to consult with the ruler, or could be the ruler himself, inasmuch as the *tlatoani*'s title included the word *teuctli*. Pedro Carrasco (1971:352) gives as an example Chichimecateuctli (Lord of the Chichimec) as the title of the ruler of Tezcoco. A *teuctli* held his position for life and his

Aztecs passed through the land of the Chichimecs, seeing this new country and the plains of Cíbola but nothing in that land pleased them, and finally they came to rest in the province that is now called Mechoacan, "Land of Those Who Have Fish," in a place called Patzcuaro. And before we continue, I wish to tell how that town and the rest of the province were founded, according to their account.

It should be noted that the Aztecs and those who are now called the Tarascans of Mechoacan, and those of the province of Malinalco, were of the same group or faction; they were related and all spoke the same language. When they had reached Patzcuaro and saw that it was so peaceful and pleasant, the priests consulted their god. They begged him, if this were not the land that had been promised them, that at least he allow them to leave part of their group there.[2]

The god Huitzilopochtli answered the priests in dreams, telling them he was happy to do what they asked of him, and it would be done in the following way: when certain men and women went to bathe in the great lake, as was their custom, after they had gone into the water, those who remained on shore should steal their clothing, the garments of the men and of the women. Then they should gather up their things and steal away, leaving the others naked.

While those in the lake were still enjoying the water, the Aztecs, obeying the order of their god, broke camp hastily and left the place and followed the route indicated by their god.

After the people in the lake had bathed with much contentment, they came out and looked for their clothing with which to cover themselves, but could not find the garments. Realizing that they had been tricked, they went to the camp where the other people had been and found it abandoned, with no one there to tell them what route the Aztecs had taken. Naked and forsaken and not knowing where to go, they decided to stay there and settle the land. Those who tell this story say that they remained dressed only in their own skin, men as well as

---

successor was appointed by the supreme lord or ruler, the *tlatoani*. Although the position of *teuctli* was not hereditary, a son of a deceased lord of this high position might be appointed to succeed his father.

Carrasco (1971:352–53, 363) lists the seven *calpultin* of Tenochtitlan as Yopica, Tlacochcalca, Huitznahuac, Tlacatecpaneca, Chalmeca, Yzquiteca, and Cihuatecpaneca (Palace of Women) instead of Cuatecpan.

[2]Actually, it is doubtful that the Aztecs passed by Patzcuaro on their migration, though the Toltecs of Nahuatl speech left remains in this region at an earlier date. The *chacmool*, a half-reclining, supine figure that forms an altar, typically Toltec in style, testifies to their presence in the area. The legend of the Tarascans' ire, which made them "change their language" out of spite, is probably due to later rivalry between these people and the Aztecs of Tenochtitlan, both strong political forces in historical times. The Aztecs tried but failed to conquer these people.

women, and as they were there a long time they came to lose shame and leave their private parts uncovered. These people used neither loincloths nor mantles, but eventually wore long tunics that reached the floor, like the robes of the Jews. I saw these robes some time ago, and I understand they are still used among the countrymen of that province.

The god of the Aztecs had a sister who was called Malinalxochitl [Wild Grass Flower], who had accompanied the group on its migration. She was beautiful and of spirited disposition and was so clever and cunning that she became skillful in the use of magic and sorcery. Her craftiness was so great that she caused much harm among the people and made herself feared in order to be adored later as a goddess. The people had endured her because she was the sister of Huitzilopochtli, but finally they asked the god to get rid of her. Huitzilopochtli advised the priest through dreams, as was his custom, to abandon her in the place he would indicate, together with her attendants and certain elders of her group.

In order to please the people, the priest told everyone of this revelation. He said:

"Your god, who beholds your sufferings, says that his sister, with her cunning and evil dealings, is dangerous to you. He is very offended by this and filled with wrath toward her because he sees the power she has acquired by illicit means over fierce and harmful creatures. With magic spells, she slays those who anger her by sending snakes and scorpions, centipedes, or deadly spiders to bite them.

"Therefore, in order to free you from this affliction, and because of the love he has for all of you, it is his will that this night when she is in her first slumber, when she is sleeping, together with her attendants and followers while we remain awake, we shall depart and abandon her. Not one of us will remain to show her the way, because your god says he did not come here to bewitch the people, or cast spells upon them or control them by these means.

"He wishes to aid them by the courage of their hearts and by the strength of their arms. He wishes to extol his own name and raise the Aztec nation to the heavens. He will make us lords of gold and silver and of all metals, of splendid feathers of many colors, and of precious stones of great value. Your people [the Aztecs] will build houses and temples of emeralds and rubies in his name, as he is the lord of precious stones on this earth, and lord of cacao and of richly worked mantles that he will wear.[3] These are the reasons for his blessed

---

[3]For "emerald," sometimes read "jade." For an explanation of jade in Mesoamerica, see Durán's *Book of the Gods and Rites* (1977:263–64n.), and Foshag (1959:51–60): "The

coming: he has troubled himself to guide us to these lands, to give us repose, and to bestow upon us rewards for the trials that we have undergone and those we are still to endure.

"Therefore he commands that his sister be abandoned in this place, with her evil sorcery."

After the priest had spoken and revealed these things, all those who were not followers of Malinalxochitl went away during the night. They abandoned her and her attendants who were asleep. They followed the road toward Tula, their deity leading them, and finally reached the summit of the hill called Coatepec.[4]

When morning came Malinalxochitl found herself alone with her followers. She wept sorrowfully and bemoaned the departure of her brother who had thus mocked her. As she did not know the way, she asked advice of her aides and of the people who had remained. They led her to a place now called Malinalco, where she and her partisans settled, naming the town for her, for the woman called Malinalxochitl, as I have said. That is why the town is called Malinalco. It is the custom of these people to name a town for its founder, which is also a Hebrew practice. The people of Malinalco to this day have the reputation of being wizards and sorcerers and it is said they inherited this custom from the woman who founded the city.

The Aztec nation was now divided into three parts. One had stayed in Mechoacan and settled that region, where they invented a special language so as not to be mistaken for Aztecs, since they were offended by the humiliation they had suffered. Another part of the nation remained in Malinalco. Very few people reached Coatepec, but those who did [the Mexica-Aztecs] were strong and courageous. Along the way, in two places called Ocopilla and Acahualtzinco, where they had spent some time replenishing their provisions, they left some aged and sick persons, and this diminished their number.

As the Aztecs went into the land of Tula, the Chichimecs and mountaineers of those regions became uneasy and showed their

---

word jade was derived from the Spanish term *piedra de ijada*, or 'stone of the loin,' in allusion to the virtue imputed to it of relieving pains of the side or of the kidneys. From the word jade was derived the specific name jadeite, applied to the pyroxenic mineral that constitutes one form of jade." Among the Aztecs, jadeite was known as *chalchihuitl*.

[4]The Aztecs reached Tula toward the end of the twelfth century, at the time of the collapse of the Toltec state. It is probable that the new arrivals contributed to this collapse; according to the *Anales de Cuauhtitlan*, they were in the area at that time, and Sahagún (*Florentine Codex* 1961:X:175) describes the Toltecs fighting people of the region who, according to Cuauhtitlan, would have been the Aztecs.

displeasure and anger. The Otomi people[5] were especially annoyed, complaining, "What people are these? They are daring and impudent, for they dare to occupy our lands without our permission! It is not possible that these are good people!"

The Aztecs, not heeding these complaints, almost immediately erected, as was their custom on settling a territory, the temple of their divinity, with the sacrifice stone that they used as an altar, around which were placed the other gods whom I have described. When they had settled down in their shelters around the temple, in the order that their god and their priest decreed, some to the east and others to the west, some to the south and others to the north, then in dreams the god commanded the priests to dam up the water of a river that passed close by. The water was to flow through the plain and form a lake around the hill where they had settled because the god wished to make a likeness of the land he had promised them.

When the dam was made, the river flowed over and covered the entire plain, forming a great lagoon. The people planted willows, cypresses, and poplars. They covered the shores with reeds and rushes, and the lake began to swell with all kinds of fish that are found in this land. Waterfowl appeared. Ducks, wild geese, herons, and coots covered the lagoon, and many other kinds of birds that are found and breed today by the lake in Mexico-Tenochtitlan.

The place became filled with aquatic flowers and cattails that attracted different types of thrushes and magpies, some red, some yellow. Their singing and chattering created great harmony and gladdened the entire place, which became pleasant and enjoyable. The Aztecs were so contented here, although it was no more than a model, no more than a pattern, of the promised land, that they did not want to leave it in order to search for an even more satisfactory place.

For this reason they began to sing and dance with songs inspired by the luxuriant verdure and beauty of the place. And, as many of the group (whose principal troublemaker was Huitznahua, together with a woman called Coyolxuah) did not want to go on farther because they had become fond of that place, they exclaimed to their god:

---

[5]Sahagún refers to the Otomi as being "untrained . . . miserable . . . blockhead . . . uncouth . . . covetous" but at the same time describes their society as being advanced, having "a civilized way of life" with social stratification, well-developed agriculture, religion, arts such as fine textiles, and other characteristics of high civilizations (*Florentine Codex* 1961:X:176–81). The Otomi were excellent warriors. Among the Aztecs there was a group of outstanding warriors called the Otomi, perhaps because of the fame of Otomi fighters or because the Otomi themselves originally had founded such a group, which had later been absorbed by the Aztecs.

"O Huitzilopochtli, here is your abode! This is the place to which you were sent, it is here where your name should be extolled, on the hill of Coatepec!

"It is now your privilege to rejoice in the gold and silver and all the metals, the precious stones and shining feathers of many colors, rich and precious mantles and cacao and other splendid things found in this new land. From here you will conquer the four regions of the world with the strength of your chest, of your head, of your arm. Here your name will receive glory and honor.

"This is the capital of your kingdom. Command your fathers and your custodians to call the people together. Let them bring an end to the pilgrimage in search of even more peace than we enjoy here, so the Aztecs may now repose and rest from their hardships!"

The god Huitzilopochtli was greatly angered and answered his priests, saying, "Who are they who disregard my will, who object to my decisions and try to contradict them? Are they by chance mightier than I? Tell them I shall take vengeance against them before tomorrow, so they will not dare give opinions in those things that I have determined and for which I am here. They must learn that they are to obey me alone!"

They say that the face of the idol at that point became so ugly and frightening, with its diabolical scowl, that the people were filled with terror.

At midnight, when all was quiet, they heard a great noise in a place called Teotlachco [the Divine Ball Court] and in the Tzompanco [Skull Rack], both sacred places dedicated to this god. When morning came the people found the principal instigators of the rebellion dead there, together with the woman called Coyolxauhqui. All the breasts had been torn open and the hearts removed.[6] From this incident came the

---

[6]Sahagún (*Florentine Codex* 1952:book 3:1–5) gives a different version of the encounter between Huitzilopochtli and his sister Coyolxauhqui. According to this account, Coatlicue, mother of the gods, was sweeping at the temple on Coatepec Hill when she found a ball of feathers that she placed in her bosom. From this miraculous contact Huitzilopochtli was conceived, an act that enraged Coatlicue's other children, Coyolxauhqui (Bells on Her Cheeks) and the Centzon Huitznahua (Innumerable Southerners). They decided to kill their mother and their unborn brother. Led by Coyolxauhqui, the innumerable ones attacked Coatepec Hill. But at the crucial moment Huitzilopochtli was born fully armed, with his magic weapon, the *xiuhcoatl* (fire serpent). Huitzilopochtli fought the attackers, destroyed the Centzon Huitznahua, and decapitated Coyolxauhqui, whose body fell crashing to the bottom of the hill, where it became dismembered. This story of the birth of Huitzilopochtli has become popular in Mexican mythology. It has been interpreted as a metaphoric tale relating to the birth of the sun (Huitzilopochtli), who routs the moon (Coyolxauhqui) and the stars (the Centzon Huitznahua), but is more correctly seen as the triumph of one political

The History of the Indies of New Spain

accursed belief that Huitzilopochtli ate only hearts, and thus was established the practice of sacrificing men and opening their breasts to remove their hearts in order to offer them to the devil, their god Huitzilopochtli.

When the people saw the severe punishment their god had inflicted upon the guilty ones, amazed at the tremendous noise they had heard during the night when this had been executed by their angry, cruel deity, they were greatly frightened. But the wrath of Huitzilopochtli did not end here. In order to demonstrate further his fury he ordered his priests and custodians to destroy the defenses that controlled the lagoon, to open the dam they had made, and let the waters run their former course. The priests did not dare disobey. They removed the defenses and broke the dam, letting the waters run. They did this against their will because these waters had surrounded them and sustained them and had given them tranquillity.

When the lagoon was destroyed the reeds and the rushes began to dry up, the trees also withered, and the freshness of the place disappeared. Fish and frogs and all of the creatures that breed in the water perished, all that the people used for their food. Waterfowl began to fly away until the region became as dreary and desertlike as it had been before. When the Aztecs saw the desolation and barrenness of the place they had thought would be their home, they decided to consult their god as to what he wished them to do. They believed he would now be appeased by the shedding of blood and the destruction, for time dissolves anger and softens hearts.[7]

When the people consulted Huitzilopochtli, he ordered them to leave that site and go on to Tula. This they did presently. The Aztecs reached Tula in the year 1168 and they stayed here a short time. From Tula they continued on to Atlitlalaquian and from there to Tequixquiac. They stayed at Tequixquiac on borrowed land for a few years, sowing the fields for their sustenance. From this place they went on to

and kinship-related faction over another. Interest in this myth has increased following the 1978 discovery of the great relief carving of Coyolxauhqui in the Templo Mayor at the center of Mexico City.

[7]The chosen place for the city of Mexico-Tenochtitlan, the "promised land" described by Durán, reminds one of a number of modern legends still circulating among the people of the country, an example of which is this story from Xaltocan, state of Mexico: "The Aztecs ... arrived in this town and they found the eagle standing upon a stone, which led them to believe that the city was to be founded there. But a little bird sang to them, 'Let's go! Let's go!' Thereupon the eagle flew away, and after it went the Aztecs. The stone is to be seen in the upper part of our village and it is said that when the eagle flew away the water of our lagoon turned salty. Therefore, the city of Mexico was settled where it is today" (oral tradition told to Fernando Horcasitas in the 1970s).

another called Tzompanco, where they wished to stop and repose. But they met opposition from the local inhabitants and had some encounters with them. Men on both sides defended their own factions.

Then the Aztecs continued to the town of Xaltocan. Here, finding the natives more friendly, they planted their fields of maize and chiles and other seeds they had brought with them. Feeling more secure there, they made earthen walls and terraces for greater safety, since they could not be sure that their people would be safe.

After they had harvested their crops, the Aztecs gathered their provisions and went to Ecatepec, and from here to Tolpetlac. Little by little, they entered the territory of the Tepanecs. [The Tepanecs] were the people of Azcapotzalco and Tacuba and Coyoacan, an illustrious nation who at that time ruled over the other groups in the valley.

The Aztecs finally came to rest at Chapultepec [Hill of the Grasshopper], where with much dread they constructed a camp of huts and fortified the place as best they could. When they consulted their god about how they should proceed, he replied that they were to await the change of events, since the deity would know what measures to take and would advise them at the right time. But he added that they should be prepared for what was to come because this was not the place he had chosen for their home. This promised land was near, but first they would meet great opposition from two nations, so they should make their hearts strong.[8]

Awed by this answer, the people chose a captain from the most noble men among them, to command and guide them. This chieftain was Huitzilihuitl [Hummingbird Feather]. He was a skillful man of courageous heart and was capable of leading his people.

After he had been chosen captain general [of the Aztecs] and all of them had sworn obedience to him, Huitzilihuitl ordered the hill terraced with encircling walls of stone. These went up the hill at intervals, one after another, like a great staircase, the steps about two meters wide. At the top these walls leveled off to form a spacious courtyard. Here the people gathered and fortified this high point.

---

[8]The Valley of Mexico, or rather the completely enclosed basin covered in great part by a series of lakes of both fresh and salt water, had been settled thousands of years before the arrival of the Aztecs in the thirteenth century. In Preclassic times (2000–100 B.C.), the valley was teeming with activity of settled groups; during the Classic period (100 B.C.–A.D. 750), Teotihuacan, in the northeastern part of the valley, had become the largest and most influential city on the continent. By the time the Aztecs reached the Valley of Mexico, the great Teotihuacan civilization had been eclipsed for about eight centuries. But cities such as Colhuacan, Tezcoco, and Azcapotzalco had become important centers, and the lake shore was dotted with settlements. It is no wonder that the Aztecs, on entering territory already occupied by others, were not welcome in the area.

They stood guard day and night, placing the women and children in the middle, surrounded by the soldiers. They made ready their arrows, wooden spears, and swords [edged with obsidian blades]. They also carved stone points and shaped stones into round balls for their slings. All these preparations were for their defense.

CHAPTER IV

Which treats of what befell the Aztecs after their arrival at Chapultepec.

fter the Aztecs had come to the hill of Chapultepec and had set up their shelters there, their god Huitzilopochtli spoke to them. He advised them that this place was not the land he had promised them and that they should make preparations for war because these would be needed, as would their fortitude and the valor of their hearts. Although they were fearful, these people then gathered their strength and courage and stood on guard. They built their defense works and prepared their weapons as best they could, seeing that they were in the midst of many unfriendly peoples.

But in order to relate this story in correct order, we must remember what was told in the last chapter where we described a sister of Huitzilopochtli named Malinalxochitl. As she was considered wicked, possessed of evil arts and cunning, Huitzilopochtli had ordered his people to abandon her, leaving her with her followers. So it was that they abandoned this woman, who was totally ignorant of the route followed by her brother. She remained behind but some years later went on to found the province of Malinalco.

This Malinalxochitl, who we have said was a wicked sorceress, later gave birth to a son and taught him all her tricks and witchcraft. When he was old enough, she told him of the offense done her by her brother Huitzilopochtli when he abandoned her, separating her from the rest of the group. The son's heart became filled with wrath and, moved by his mother's tears, he promised to seek out his uncle and with his arts and cunning destroy him and all his followers.

When the mother saw her son's determination, she urged him on and told him that this was also her desire. She helped him prepare to search for his uncle and to incite all the nations to destroy Huitzilopochtli, with their most fiendish skills and cunning. Searching for his uncle, Copil[1] learned of Huitzilopochtli's arrival at Chapultepec.

---

[1]Copil (*copilli*) means "diadem" or "crown"; therefore, in the myth devised by the Aztecs of Tenochtitlan—based on historical fact and probably created after the liberation of Tenochtitlan from Azcapotzalco in 1428 as a justification for the division of the early group—Malinalxochitl's son undoubtedly represents members of an important faction of the Aztecs who migrated from Aztlan but who were overthrown by those represented by Huitzilopochtli. That Copil was Huitzilopochtli's nephew

Copil, as he was called, began to go from town to town, kindling the fire of wrath and provoking the hearts of all the people against the Aztecs, inflaming the other nations so they would destroy them. He claimed that the Aztecs were pernicious men of perverse customs, tyrants and bellicose. Copil said that he had been told these things and he knew they were exactly as he described them. These nations were alarmed, they were apprehensive, they were astonished at this frightening news. They were afraid to admit [the Aztecs] to their lands and were determined to massacre them. A conspiracy was formed among the cities of Azcapotzalco, Tacuba, Coyoacan, Xochimilco, Colhuacan, Chalco, and the neighboring towns, so that all together they would surround [the Aztecs] and annihilate them, not leaving one person alive. This plan was then put into action.

When the evil Copil saw that his scheme had been successful and his plan was about to be carried out, he went up to the top of a hill called Tepetzinco [Place of the Small Hill] at the shore of the lake—at the foot of which there are some famous hot springs—to watch the destruction of the Aztecs. He believed he would rule over all their lands as soon as the annihilation he had planned took place.[2]

But the outcome of the struggle was different [from what Copil desired]. The god Huitzilopochtli discovered his nephew's perversity and warned the Aztecs through his priests. He instructed them to go to that hill before they were surrounded, catch Copil unaware, slay him, and bring the god his heart. In order to carry out this act they were to take an image of Huitzilopochtli with them, to guide them. One of the priests, Cuauhtlequetzqui, took the idol on his shoulders and led [the Aztecs] to the hill. There they caught Copil unprepared and murdered him. They cut out his heart and presented it to his uncle, the deity. Huitzilopochtli then ordered his priest to place himself in the marsh, in the midst of the reeds, in the midst of the rushes, and with all his strength, to cast the heart into the middle of the lake. This he did, and the heart fell in a place now called Tlacocomolco. The Aztecs say that out of this heart sprouted the prickly pear cactus where later the city

proves a kinship tie. And, since his mother and her followers had to be eliminated, it is possible that she stands for a strong matrilineal group that was replaced by a patrilineal one (i.e., Huitzilopochtli's). This myth is one of many that served the Aztecs as justification of the right to rule.

[2] Tepetzinco (Place of the Small Hill), originally in Lake Tezcoco, is now a dry section of eastern Mexico City, near the airport. Tepetzinco was one of the places where children were sacrificed during festivities of the first month of the year in Tenochtitlan, Atlcahualo, or Quauitlehua, which took place beginning February 2 (according to the Gregorian calendar) and was dedicated to the gods of water.

of Mexico-Tenochtitlan was built.³ They also say that in the place where Copil was killed hot springs began to flow. These springs are called Acopilco, which means "Copil's Water."

Although Huitzilopochtli's nephew was now dead, the enmity against the Aztecs continued unabated and the people who had been aroused by Copil wishes to destroy them. Their enemies, burning with ire, surrounded Chapultepec Hill, where the Aztecs were gathered. When the siege began, the Aztecs realized their great peril, but they were so moved by the weeping of their women and children that they took heart and showed not fear but rather great courage and valor.

The men of Chalco, who surrounded the hill, began to attack on all sides, for they wished to massacre the men, women, and children, but Huitzilihuitl, lord and ruler of the Aztecs, urged his people to face the Chalca fearlessly. The chieftain of the Chalcas was Cacamatl Tecutli [Lord of the Tender Ear of Maize]. The Chalca soldiers attacked the Aztecs and in the first skirmish captured Huitzilihuitl, the Aztec leader. His people were not totally routed, however, but gathered the women, children, and old people in their midst and, crying out to their god for help, hacked their way through the enemy ranks until they reached a town called Atlacuihuayan.⁴ They found this deserted, empty of people, so they entrenched themselves here.

³The *nopal* or prickly pear cactus growing out of the heart (or entrails) of a divine being is an ancient symbol in Mesoamerica and probably was adapted to their myth by the Aztecs through oral tradition and/or visual contact with this image. On the back of the Teocalli de la Guerra Sagrada (Temple of Sacred War), a stone monument now in Mexico's National Museum of Anthropology made well after the Aztecs had settled Tenochtitlan (perhaps partly in honor of the founding myth), there is a reclining figure from whose middle (heart?) grows a *nopal*, on which an eagle perches. The supine figure, although much eroded, evidently has a skull instead of a face and is lying in water.

Similar supine figures, possibly symbolizing the earth, from whose abdomen or heart plants grow, are found in the *Codex Borgia*, a pictorial document from the Puebla-Tlaxcala region coeval with the Aztec empire. In Tula earlier representations of a tree growing from a person's heart or head are sculpted on stone balustrades; one of these is also found in the regional museum at Pachuca, Hidalgo. This symbol of vegetation growing out of a divine figure (e.g., fertility, sustenance) was ancient in Mesoamerica by the time the Aztecs reached the Valley of Mexico, as can be seen in Maya relief carvings at Palenque, Chiapas, where a maize plant grows out of a figure, and in the *Codex Dresden*, where a plant comes forth from the chest of an individual whose heart has been removed. Often a bird perches on these plants: a bird atop a tree sprouting from a crocodile-earth monster, though not from the creature's heart, is depicted in a carving from Izapa, Chiapas, dated ca. 300 B.C. (Norman 1976:133).

For an analysis of the myth and symbols of the founding of Mexico-Tenochtitlan, see Heyden 1989.

⁴Atlacuihuayan (Place Where Water Is Caught) is now called Tacubaya, a section of Mexico City.

The Chalcas and their allies, seeing themselves thwarted by so few opponents and feeling ashamed of this, did not attempt to follow them but contented themselves with carrying away the captured king of the Aztecs to Colhuacan, where they killed him. By this act the Chalcas took revenge for all the damage they had received.

The Aztecs renewed their strength and repaired their arms. They then invented a weapon, a type of propelled spear that we call *fisga*.[5] When they were all armed with this weapon, the Aztecs went on to Mazatlan [Place of the Deer], and from here they approached Colhuacan. When they had reached this city, Huitzilopochtli spoke to the priests, saying: "O my fathers, O my priests, I have beheld your toil and affliction! But be of strong heart! Prepare to meet your enemies with your heads, with your chests, for that you have come. Send your messengers to Achitometl, king of Colhuacan, and boldly, without pleading, ask him to show you a place where you may stay, where you may rest. Do not hesitate to approach him fearlessly for I shall soften his heart so that he receives you. Accept the site he shows you, be it good or bad, and settle there until the term required for your comfort and rest is completed."

The Aztecs, convinced by these arguments, sent their messengers to Colhuacan. The envoys then spoke to the king of that city: "The Aztecs beg you to grant them a place where they may stay with their wives and children, entrusting themselves to you as the most benign ruler, confident that in your mercy you will give them land, not only for building but also for sowing and reaping, to ensure sustenance for themselves, for their women and for their children."

---

[5] Among the weapons used by the Aztecs and frequently mentioned by Durán were the following.

Atlatl: "propelled spear" or *fisga* as Durán calls it, a weapon that propels projectile points or short lances, in use for more than a thousand years before the Aztecs. The atlatl is still employed at times by the Tarascans of Lake Patzcuaro in duck hunting, but is fast becoming a weapon seen only in museum exhibits.

Bow and arrow: though introduced in late times by the Chichimecs, these also were used by the Aztecs but were not known by some earlier groups.

Chimalli: a shield of reeds and leather, often covered with ornate featherwork.

Macuahuitl: a wooden sword or club edged on both sides with blades of obsidian, black volcanic glass, or flint.

Tepoztopilli: a lance almost ten feet long tipped by a flint point.

The sling was also an important weapon, woven of maguey fiber. The ball cast was of finely rounded stone or clay.

The blowgun, which shot marble-size clay balls, also played a prominent part in ancient Mexican warfare.

The armor of the Aztec warrior was a fitted, heavily padded quilted cotton suit surmounted by a helmet that could have the form of an eagle, a jaguar, or figures that served as insignia of rank as well as identifications of group and provenience. One aim of the warriors' costume was to terrify the enemy—thus the extravagant decoration.

The king of Colhuacan, favorably disposed to their demands, ordered lodging to be given them and everything necessary for their comfort. This was the custom among the Indians: they accommodated envoys or travelers and always gave them good lodging.

While the Aztecs reposed, Achitometl, lord of Colhuacan, called together his chieftains and elders, exclaiming, "The Aztecs, in all humility, have sent their emissaries to request a place in our territory where they may settle. Look about you and choose the land you think I should give them!"

A thousand contradictions, questions, and answers flew from his council, but, because the king remained favorable to the Aztecs, in the end it was decided to give them a place called Tizaapan. This is the other side of Colhuacan Hill, where now two roads separate in the directions of Cuitlahuac and Chalco. Tizaapan was a wilderness, occupied only by vipers and poisonous snakes that came down from the hilltop. This site was given with malice on the part of the advisers of the king. But [the Aztecs] accepted the favor and occupied Tizaapan, which they still possess today, for all the land around that place, as far as Santa Marta and Los Reyes, is subject to the city of Mexico.[6]

When they reached this place, they began to make huts and shelters. On seeing the great number of reptiles and little poisonous creatures that were there, at first they were horrified and afraid, but later they became accustomed to these dreadful beasts, capturing them in order to eat them. The people, from that time on, ate no other meat except these reptiles, vipers, and lizards found on that hill. They became so fond of them as food that they consumed most of the snakes there, until it became difficult to find even one.

The people of Colhuacan were confident that little by little the reptiles would destroy these people. King Achitometl said to his followers, "Go and see what has happened to the Aztecs and take my greetings to those who have survived. Ask them how they have fared in the place that was granted them."

When the king's messengers went to Tizaapan, they found all the Aztecs untroubled and contented. Their fields were cultivated and in order, a temple had been built to their god, and the people were living

---

[6]Tizaapan, "In Chalky (or White) Water," was clearly part of Colhuacan, as Duran states, but some scholars have confused this site with the Tizapan that is a section of San Angel and is still called by this name. The Tizaapan of the Aztec adventure evidently was located next to the Huixachtepetl, "Hill of the Acacias," today called Cerro de la Estrella, "Star Hill," between Colhuacan and Iztapalapa. Garibay (1967,II: 578, n.1) calls attention to this misconception but prefers the San Angel–Tizapan location.

in their houses. The spits and pots were replete with snakes, some roasted, others boiled.

The envoys went to the houses of the headmen; they greeted them and paid their respects and relayed the message from King Achitometl of Colhuacan.7 The Aztecs, who held this ruler in great honor, answered the messengers and told them how contented they were and how grateful for the favors granted them. But they begged two things of the king: to be allowed to enter his city and trade there and to intermarry with the people of Colhuacan, the sons and daughters of one group with the sons and daughters of the other.

The emissaries, amazed by the vigor and hardiness of the Aztecs, went with this news to their ruler. They described everything they had seen and told him the requests of these people. The king and all his lords were astounded at this incredible news, such as they had never heard before. They again felt a tremendous fear of the Aztecs but decided to grant them their requests. Thus the king announced: "Give them everything they request. I have told you that they are people favored by their god, but they are evil people, of bad habits. Do not anger them, for while you do them no harm they will be tranquil."

From that time on the Aztecs began to go to Colhuacan and deal with the people there, trading freely and becoming related to them by marriage, to be treated like brothers and relatives. But Huitzilopochtli, god of the Aztecs, was an enemy of this quiet and peace and sought unrest and strife. Seeing the few benefits he received from this tranquillity, he said to his priests and the elders: "It is necessary that we search for a woman who shall be called 'The Woman of Discord.' She will be known as 'Our Grandmother' [Toci] or 'Our Mother' [Tonantzin] in the place where we shall dwell. This is not the land where we are to make our permanent home, this is not yet the site I have promised you, it is still to be found. The occasion for leaving this

---

7The name Colhuacan or Culhuacan, "Place of the Culhua people," refers to a city in the southern part of the Valley of Mexico inhabited by a branch of the Toltecs. The term can be translated in a number of ways. It can mean "Curved Place" and is usually represented in pictorial codices as a curved hill; the root in this case is the Nahuatl *coloa* or *culhua*, "to be curved" or "twisted" (Simeon, 1965: 109). Perhaps the most correct interpretation, however, is "Place of Grandparents," by extension "Place of Ancestors," based on *colli* or *culli*, "grandfather," according to the late Nahuatl scholar Thelma D. Sullivan (personal communication).

Culhuacan was a center of great prestige and power, the Culhuas probably the most advanced people in the valley at the time of the arrival of the Mexica-Aztecs. The latter added "Culhua" to their name (Culhua-Mexica), "thus bestowing upon themselves the mantle of tradition and legitimacy that derived from Culhuacan" (Davies, 1977: 25).

Teoculhuacan means "the ancient, sacred, or legitimate Culhuacan," from *teo(tl)*, "god, divine, sacred, old, real."

place where we are now staying must not be peaceful but must be through war, when many die. Let us begin to take up our arms, our bows and arrows, our shields and swords! Let us show the world the valor of our persons! Prepare yourselves, provide yourselves with those things necessary for our defense and for an attack on our enemies. Seek a way to leave this place. Go to the king of Colhuacan, Achitometl, and ask for his daughter to serve me. He will give her to you and she will be 'The Woman of Discord,' as you will see."

The Aztecs, always heedful of the commands of their god, went to the ruler of Colhuacan and asked for his daughter to be mistress of the Aztecs and bride of their god. The king loved the maiden greatly, but he was enthralled by the idea that she should reign and be a living goddess, so he surrendered her to the Aztecs. She was taken away with great honors and everyone, the Aztecs and the people of Colhuacan, rejoiced greatly over this transaction. When they reached Tizaapan and the princess had been given the finest quarters there, that night Huitzilopochtli spoke to his priests: "I have already proclaimed that this maiden is to be 'The Woman of Discord' and the cause of enmity between you and those of Colhuacan. And so that my will be done, you must kill her and sacrifice her in my name. From this day on I take her to be 'Our Mother.' After she is dead, flay her and with her skin dress one of the principal youths, then dress him, skin and all, with the womanly garments of that maiden. Then invite King Achitometl to come adore the goddess, his daughter, and to offer her sacrifice."

After the priests had heard the commands of their god and had relayed these to the entire gathering, they took the young princess of Colhuacan, heiress to that kingdom, and killed her, sacrificing her to their god. They then flayed her and dressed one of the principal youths in her skin, as their deity had willed. Then they went to the sovereign of Colhuacan and invited him to come adore his own daughter and offer sacrifices to her as a goddess, since Huitzilopochtli had proclaimed her his bride and his mother [without telling the king his daughter was dead].

It is she whom the Aztecs worshiped from that time on as the mother of the gods. She is described in the *Book of the Account of Sacrifices*, where she is called Toci, which means "mother" or "grandmother."

King Achitometl accepted the invitation, calling together the dignitaries of his kingdom, recommending to them that they take many offerings for the celebration of the festival in which his daughter was to become the goddess of the Aztecs and bride of Huitzilopochtli, who would then be his son-in-law.

The people of Colhuacan realized that the command of their monarch was just. They adorned themselves regally, embellishing

The History of the Indies of New Spain

themselves as best they could with mantles and breechcloths. They carried offerings of paper, incense, fine feathers, and many kinds of food for the new goddess; they took different types of birds, such as quail and waterfowl, to honor the god of the Aztecs and his goddess. With pomp the king and all his principal men then left Colhuacan and went to Tizaapan.

The Aztecs came out to receive them, to greet them and to make them as comfortable as possible. After they had been accommodated and had rested, the Aztecs put the youth who was dressed in the skin of the king's daughter in the chamber next to the idol, exclaiming to Achitometl, "Lord, if it pleases you, you may enter and see our god and the goddess who is your daughter, and make reverences to them and give them offerings."

The king, with great confidence, arose and went to the temple that had been erected for the occasion. He entered the chamber of the idol and began to perform many ceremonies. He cut off the heads of the quail and the other birds and offered sacrifice by scattering the birds' blood and placing the food before the idols. Then he offered incense and flowers and everything he had brought for that purpose. As the room was dark he distinguished no one, not even those to whom he made the offerings. Taking in his hand a brazier with fire, he threw incense into it fervently and drew close to the figures. Suddenly the room was filled with light from the fire and fresh incense, and the king perceived the priest who was seated next to the idol, dressed in his daughter's skin. This was such a frightful sight that the king was overcome with horror. He dropped the brazier and rushed out of the temple, shouting: "Come here, come, my subjects of Colhuacan! Come avenge the foul deed committed by the Aztecs! They have killed my daughter, they have flayed her and dressed a youth in her skin and have made me worship him! Death and destruction to men so evil and with such vile customs! Let not a trace of their memory remain! My people, let us put an end to them!"

When the Aztecs saw the tumult and heard the cries of Achitometl and saw that his subjects, thus agitated, took up their arms, they immediately retreated with their wives and children toward the water, using the lake itself for protection at their backs. But the men of Colhuacan sounded the alarm in their own city and the people came out in arms. By attacking they forced the Aztecs to retreat farther into the water until they had no place to stand.

Finding themselves so pressed and hearing the incessant weeping of the women and children, the Aztec men regained their courage and began to throw their spears—those *fisgas*, like harpoons, a favorite weapon of theirs—with such force that the Colhuacan soldiers were severely wounded and started to retreat. Thus the Aztecs managed to reach the land and flee to Itztapalapa. They continued to fight their pursuers until they reached a place called Acatzintitlan [Place Next to the Little Reed]. Here they threw themselves into the water. They made rafts with their lances and shields, covering them with grass, and, since the water was deep, they placed the women and children on these. When they had reached the other side, they hid themselves in the reeds and rushes, where they passed the night in anguish and suffering. The women and children wept and begged to be allowed to die there, for they could suffer no more.

Huitzilopochtli, the god, seeing the misery and despair of his people, and that they could no longer bear the torment they had been suffering, spoke to his attendants that night: "Console the people and animate them. They must endure all these afflictions so that later they will find peace. Let them now rest here."

The priests spoke to them, they consoled the people, who then dedicated the entire day to drying the clothes and cleaning their weapons and their bodies. A *temazcalli*, steam bath, was built where everyone bathed.[8] This place was later called Mexicatzinco. The name was given because of a certain lewd happening that I shall refrain from telling in order not to offend the ears of the readers, but because of this [the Aztecs] were driven from the site.[9]

As the Aztecs fled through the marshes one of the main elders, a priest of Huitzilopochtli, drowned. The people cremated him and honored him by giving him a very solemn burial.

---

[8]The *temazcalli* (house of the steam bath) was used for cleanliness and for medicinal and ritual purposes. In his other volume dedicated to the gods and rites (1977:269) Durán calls the *temazcalli* a "bath house with fire," the etymology being *tletl*, "fire," *mozcoa*, "to bathe," and *calli*, "house." He refers to a "diabolical superstition" of the two sexes' bathing together, for otherwise ill fortune supposedly befell the bathers. Durán felt that when a mother took her infant son into the *temazcalli* with her, or a father his infant daughter, this was a way of getting around the punishment threatened by the church (in colonial times), which frowned upon men and women bathing at the same time in this reduced space.

[9]Durán leaves the reader curious about the lewd happening here, which he refrains from telling. In the *Códice Aubin* of 1576 (1979:46), however, in a drawing depicting the Aztecs' stay at Mexicatzinco, an almost nude man is portrayed with a small century plant protruding from his anus. This may be a place glyph, misinterpreted by Durán when he saw it in a pictorial manuscript. This little man is drawn in the space similar to other glyphs: below the date, the scene with people, and the gloss in Nahuatl. *Tzintli* in Nahuatl means "anus" and is usually depicted as the lower part of a body, but refers to a diminutive; combined with the locative *-co*, this forms *-tzinco*, "place of." So the "lewd" image could simply mean "Little Place of the Mexica" or "of Mecitli," another name for Huitzilopochtli as guide of the group's migration. Today Mexicatzinco is called Mexicalcingo.

The History of the Indies of New Spain

By traveling through the reeds the Aztecs came to a place that is now called Iztacalco [Place of the Salt House]. There they celebrated the Festival of the Hills, which was a very solemn ceremony. The people made many hills of dough and gave them eyes and mouths of seeds. Inhibited by their lack of security, they celebrated their festival as best they could.[10]

From there the Aztecs continued on to what is now San Antonio and from San Antonio to a place that we call San Pablo. Here a daughter of one of the principal men of the group gave birth to a child; therefore until this day it is also called Mixiuhcan, which means "Place of Childbirth."

Thus they continued to roam from one place to another, seeking one that would be suitable as a permanent home. And wandering in this way, among the reeds and rushes, they came upon a beautiful spring and saw wondrous things in the waters. These things had been predicted to the people by their priests, through the command of Huitzilopochtli, their god.

The first thing they beheld was a white bald cypress, all white and very beautiful, and the spring came forth from the foot of the tree.

The second thing they saw was a group of white willows around the spring, all white, without a single green leaf.

There were white reeds, and white rushes surrounding the water.

White frogs came out of the water, white fish came out, white water snakes, all shiny and white.

The spring flowed out from between two large rocks, the water so clear and limpid that it was pleasing to behold. The priests and elders, remembering what their god had told them, wept with joy and became exuberant, crying out:

> We have now found the promised land. We have now seen the relief, the happiness of the weary Aztec people. All we desired has come true. Be

[10]Tepeilhuitl (Festival of the Hills) was the thirteenth month, equivalent to part of October. People made images of hills, called *tepictoton*, of amaranth dough (*tzoalli*) with features on their "faces" of seeds and clothing of bark paper painted with designs in rubber. In home shrines these little hills were placed around larger ones representing the mountains Popocatepetl and Iztaccihuatl, great sleeping volcanoes located between Mexico City and Puebla. People also imitated serpents by covering branches of trees with the *tzoalli* dough. Offerings were made to these images and after the ceremony the hills were "decapitated" and eaten, in the belief that the dough had medicinal qualities. It is true that amaranth, native to South and Middle America, is an excellent food, and today is cultivated in many parts of the world. The people of ancient Mexico valued amaranth highly and included it in their basic diet of maize, beans, cucurbits, and chiles. Crippled people who ate the *tzoalli* from the dough-covered twisted tree branches believed that, like the twisted dough that disappeared, their imperfections would also go away.

consoled, sons and brothers! Our god promised us this place that we have found; he told us we would see marvelous things among the reeds, among the rushes: behold them here! O my brothers, let us go, let us return, for we must await the command of our god, who will tell us what we are to do!

So they came to a town now called Temazcaltitlan, where they built a steam bath for the woman who had given birth, for they have the custom of bathing these women in a hot bath five or six days after delivery.

The next night Huitzilopochtli appeared in dreams to Cuauhtlequetzqui, one of his custodians, saying:

"O Cuauhtlequetzqui, now you see that I have told you the truth. In this place where I have brought you, you have seen the things I predicted. But wait, there is still more to come. You will remember how I commanded you to slay my nephew Copil, ordering you to remove his heart and fling it among the reeds, among the rushes. This you have done. Know now that his heart fell upon a stone and from this sprang a prickly pear cactus. This cactus is so tall and splendid that an eagle makes his nest in it. Each day the eagle in his nest feeds here, eating the finest and most beautiful birds he can find. In his lair on the cactus he stretches out his large and comely wings to receive the heat of the sun and the freshness of the morning. You will find the eagle at all times on this prickly pear cactus that sprouted from the heart of my nephew Copil, and all around it you will see the innumerable green, blue, red, yellow, and white feathers from the splendid birds on which the eagle feeds.

"The place where you will find the eagle on the cactus I now name Tenochtitlan [Place of the Stony Prickly Pear Cactus]."[11]

---

[11] The Mexican national emblem as it appears today on the flag and coins consists of an eagle with a serpent in its beak, standing on a prickly pear cactus that grows from a rock. This emblem is based on the founding myth of Tenochtitlan and on early depictions of the eagle perching on the cactus. In Durán's two illustrations of this discovery of the promised place by the Aztecs, the eagle holds a snake in his beak in one, a bird in the other. These drawings were made in the late sixteenth century to illustrate Durán's chronicle. In prehispanic representations (for example, on the back of the Teocalli de la Guerra Sagrada, a stone model of an Aztec temple), the cactus growing from a supine figure has human hearts as fruit, instead of the prickly pears. And in its beak the eagle holds an *atl tlachinolli*, water and fire symbol, a visual metaphor for war. At first glance the stream of water combined with fire looks like a snake and perhaps was misinterpreted as such by colonial observers. The eagle, representing the Mexican people (or Huitzilopochtli, their patron deity) and perched upon the *tenochtli* (stony prickly pear cactus, symbol of Tenochtitlan) bearing images of war and sacrifice (the hearts), gave rise to archaeologists' name for this monument: the Temple of Sacred War.

CHAPTER V

Which treats of how the Aztecs, counseled by their god, went to seek the prickly pear cactus and the eagle, and how they found them. And about the agreement they made for the building of the city.

The next day in the morning the priest Cuauhtlequetzqui, anxious to impart the revelation from his god and to inform the people of what he had seen and heard in dreams, ordered everyone to gather, adults and children, men and women, old and young. Standing before them, he began to extol the great favors they received each day from their god, and revealed especially the happy tidings he had just been told. Cuauhtlequetzqui informed the people that the mysterious and wonderful things seen the day before in the spring had been placed there by the hand of the god: white water snakes, white frogs, white fish, white willows and white bald cypress, everything white. The priest declared that another no less miraculous thing had been disclosed to prove that this was the place chosen by their god for their shelter, where they could rest, where they could multiply, and where the Aztec nation would excel, its greatness becoming renowned. And after stating all these things, Cuauhtlequetzqui cried out:

"Know, O my children, that this night our god Huitzilopochtli appeared to me. Remember, on our arrival in this valley, that we went to Chapultepec Hill where the god's nephew Copil was installed. Copil, having resolved to war against us, used his cunning and deceit to bring our enemies around us and to kill our captain and leader, our lord and king, Huitzilihuitl. Our enemies drove us from that region, but Huitzilopochtli commanded us to kill Copil and this we did, taking out his heart. And standing in the place where the god commanded, I threw the heart into the reeds; it fell upon a rock. According to the revelation of our god when he appeared to me this night, a prickly pear cactus standing upon a rock has grown from this heart and has become so tall and luxuriant that a fine eagle has made his nest there. When we discover it we shall be fortunate, for there we shall find our rest, our comfort, and our grandeur. There our name will be praised and our Aztec nation made great. The might of our arms will be known and the courage of our brave hearts. With these we shall conquer nations, near and distant, we shall subdue towns and cities from sea to sea. We shall become lords of gold and silver, of jewels and precious stones, of splendid feathers and of the insignia [that distinguish lords and chieftains].[1] We shall rule over those people, their lands, their sons and daughters. They will serve us and be our subjects and tributaries.

"Our god orders us to call this place Tenochtitlan. There will be built the city that is to be queen, that is to rule over all others in the country. There we shall receive other kings and nobles, who will recognize Tenochtitlan as the supreme capital. And so, my children, let us go among these marshes of reeds, rushes, and cattails, as our god has indicated. Everything he has promised us has come true; thus we shall now find this place for our city."

When the Aztecs heard what Cuauhtlequetzqui had said, they humbled themselves before their deity. They gave thanks to the Lord of All Created Things, of Day and Night, Wind and Fire. Then, dividing into different groups, they went into the swamp, searching among the reeds and rushes.

Thus they again found the spring they had seen the day before. But the water on that day had been clear and transparent, and it now flowed out in two streams, one red like blood, the other so blue and thick that it filled the people with awe.[2] Having seen these mysterious

---

[1] The possession of "gold and silver, of jewels and precious stones, of splendid feathers and of the insignia" of lords and chieftains is a metaphor for power, for the conquest of other people and for wealth that probably came from tribute—as it did later when the Aztecs became powerful. This manner of speaking also is reminiscent of Tula, where the houses of Quetzalcoatl were referred to as made of greenstone (jade), gold, turquoise, seashells, and precious feathers (*Florentine Codex* 1978:book III:13). This dazzling architecture was more metaphoric than true, although the coral, feathers, and other treasures indicate both Tula conceived of as an ideal place and the Toltecs as merchants, for many of the riches mentioned were brought from far-away places. The Toltecs were great traders; when they settled in Cholula, their deity Quetzalcoatl became the merchant god in that city. In fact, it may have been the search for new markets, the expansion of a commercial network, that caused some of the Toltecs to leave Tula in the twelfth century and migrate to Cholula, Colhuacan, Yucatan, and other places. This move undoubtedly was combined with a change in religion in Tula, an increased settling of the region by other groups, such as the Huaxtecs, and other factors.

[2] The color symbolism in the founding of Tenochtitlan has deep roots in Mexican myth and iconography. The whiteness not only characterizes Aztlan, the ancestral home, and at one point describes the ideal site for the Aztec capital, but also applies to other centers. Cholula, for example, is called Iztac Uexotl Yhicacan (Place of the Stand of White Willows) and Iztac Tollin Ymancan (Bed of White Reeds) (Kirchhoff et al. 1976:162, 240).

The streams of red and blue waters are not unique in the founding myth. Streams of red and blue water can be seen in a mural painting at Tepantitla, Teotihuacan, where they encircle a scene of abundance and earth's fertility. In the 700 years between the

things [where the red and blue waters flowed as one], the Aztecs continued to seek [the omen of] the eagle whose presence had been foretold. Wandering from one place to another, they soon discovered the prickly pear cactus. On it stood the eagle with his wings stretched out toward the rays of the sun, basking in their warmth and the freshness of the morning. In his talons he held a bird with very fine feathers, precious and shining. When the people saw the eagle they humbled themselves, making reverences as if the bird were a divine thing. The eagle, seeing them, also humbled himself, bowing his head low in their direction.

As the Aztecs observed the actions of the eagle, they realized they had come to the end of their journey, so they began to weep and dance about with joy and contentment. In thanksgiving they said, "By what right do we deserve such good fortune? Who made us worthy of such grace, such excellence, such greatness? At last we have fulfilled our desires; we have found what we came to seek [the land we are to possess], the place for our capital. Let thanks be given to the Lord of All Created Things, to our god Huitzilopochtli!"[3] Then they marked the site and went to rest.

The next day the priest Cuauhtlequetzqui told the members of the company, "My children, it is only just that we be grateful to our god and that we thank him for all he does for us. Let us go and make a small temple in the place of the prickly pear cactus, where our divinity can rest. It cannot yet be of stone so let it be of earth and reeds. For the present we can do no more."

The Aztecs went eagerly to the site of the prickly pear tree. By cutting out thick blocks of turf laced with reeds from the marsh next to the cactus, they made a square platform that was to serve as foundation for the shrine, the resting place of their god. On top of this they built a small hut, a humble one, but in the form of a shrine, roofed with grass from the same marsh. At that time they could do no better.[4]

---

execution of the Teotihuacan painting and the mythical founding of Tenochtitlan, the meaning of the colored waters must have changed, but the existence of similar iconographic and mythic themes over the centuries suggests rich oral traditions inherited by the Aztecs from earlier cultures.

[3]Here Huitzilopochtli is equated with Tezcatlipoca, a not uncommon designation, since Huitzilopochtli and Tezcatlipoca are described at times in similar terms, according to the chronicle. Durán and Tezozomoc wrote a great deal of official Aztec history, wherein Huitzilopochtli was supreme. Tezcatlipoca, on the other hand, is featured as the highest god in Ixtlilxocitl's writings (to the extent that he guided the Chichimecs in their pilgrimage, as the other deity did the Aztecs) and also in Sahagún's works.

[4]The squares of turf laced with reeds, formed to increase the land surface, probably were *chinampas*, a system common in swampy parts of Mexico in ancient times and

The Aztecs built these things on land that was not theirs. The land did not belong to them because it was the property of the people of Azcapotzalco and of Tezcoco. The boundaries of their towns met here, and halfway were the limits of Colhuacan. Knowing this, the Aztecs were so pressed and fearful that even the little house of mud for their god was made with dread and trembling.

In the meantime all of them gathered together in council. Some wanted to go to the people of Azcapotzalco and to the Tepanecs, who are the inhabitants of Coyoacan and Tacuba, and, humbling themselves, offer their friendship, in this way subjecting themselves to these towns in order to request of them stone and wood to build their city.

But most of the Aztecs were opposed to this plan. They claimed it could be dangerous and that instead of receiving them well the people [of Azcapotzalco and Coyoacan and Tacuba] would insult them, would mistreat them. Instead, they suggested that on market days in these three towns they and their wives should go sell fish and frogs and other creatures found in the lake, together with waterfowl they hunted. They would go without humility or submission, nor in a flattering way; they would go, not as subjects of any town, but as lords of that place which their god had given them. In this way they would buy stone and wood and everything they needed to build their houses.

Everyone considered this good advice and all went into the lake and along the reed-covered shores and began to hunt ducks and coots and other waterfowl found in that swampy place, among the reeds and rushes. They fished and collected frogs and shrimp and all kinds of edible things. They collected even the worms that thrive in the water and mosquitoes that breed on the lake surface.[5] And, knowing which

---

still used today. The *chinampa* is a rectangular platform made of logs, branches, and reeds, covered with mud brought up from the lake bottom. These organic rafts take root and are used mainly for farming: constant watering underneath and the richness of the silt make an ideal plot for intensive crops. The area of Xochimilco in the southern part of the Valley of Mexico has long been famous for its "floating gardens" as these plots are sometimes called, though they do not float; here many of the vegetables consumed in Mexico City are grown. The Aztecs of prehispanic times, by means of this ingenious system, were able to create numerous small islands that became joined to the major one and eventually reached the mainland.

[5]The lake was important to the Aztec economy and played a basic role in the diet. Mosquito eggs (*ahuauhtli*, water amaranth) are rich in protein. Worms also fill a protein need. Toasted maguey worms taste like nuts and are considered a great delicacy. The historical chronicles refer to a red aquatic worm that must have been popular, since Huitzilopochtli on one occasion said to his people, "This worm from the lake, the *izcahuitli* (*ezcahuitli*), 'little red creature,' is truly my flesh, my blood, my substance" (Alvarado Tezozomoc 1949:33). The sixteenth-century *Historia de los*

were the market days in each town, they went to these market places as hunters and fishermen and bartered the fowl and fish and water creatures for beams and boards, for small wood, for lime and stone.

Although the wood and stone were not sufficient, nonetheless the Aztecs, working hard, began to build their temple with that material. Little by little they filled in and consolidated the site for the city. They built foundations in the water by driving in stakes and throwing dirt and stone between the stakes. Thus they planned their city and founded it. The little shrine for their god was made only of mud, but they covered the outside of this with a coating of small cut stones, then plastered it with a lime finish. So, although it was small and humble, the home of Huitzilopochtli acquired a pleasing appearance.

The night after the Aztecs had finished their god's temple, when an extensive part of the lake had been filled in and the foundations for their houses made, Huitzilopochtli spoke to his priest, saying:

> Tell the Aztec people that the principal men, each with his relatives and friends and allies, should divide the city into four main wards. The center of the city will be the house you have constructed for my resting place. And let each group build its part of the city as it wishes.

These barrios are the ones that still exist in the city of Mexico. They are San Pablo, San Juan, Santa María la Redonda, and San Sebastián. After the Aztecs had separated themselves into these four districts, Huitzilopochtli commanded them to distribute the gods among them and that each barrio choose a special place where these deities might be revered. Thus each neighborhood was divided into many small sections according to the number of idols it possessed. These gods were called *calpulteteo* or district gods. I shall not mention here the names of these gods of the barrios as they are not relevant to this story, but we know that these barrios were similar to parishes in Spain that bear the names of saints.[6]

mexicanos by Cristóbal del Castillo (1908:82) calls the Aztecs of Aztlan "river people, fishermen with nets, those who gather water creatures" and lists some of the lake products, which include the *ezcahuitli, azazayakatl* (cakes formed of dragonfly larvae), *tecuitlatl* ("water excrement" or algae), crayfish, frogs, water flies, salamanders, and the *ocuiltamalli* (a natural "tamale" made of worms). See also chapter I, note 9.

[6]Each member of a *calpulli* had a plot of land he cultivated for a certain time. If he abandoned it for two years it was assigned to another member of the community. The land could not be sold or leased by the holder and its title was carefully recorded on maps in the community house. The right to work a plot of *calpulli* land could be transmitted by inheritance. Some land was also worked by members of the group for the benefit of the community, for the payment of taxes, and for the maintenance of the temple and the priesthood. For a complete discussion of *calpultin*, see Pedro Carrasco (1971).

When this division had been made and the barrios placed in order, some of the elders who felt they deserved more property than they had received, because they considered themselves to be in a more honored position than the others, rebelled. They decided to seek a different place and by going through the reeds and rushes they found a small dry piece of land. They informed their friends and allies and all these people founded a settlement here. This was called Xaltelulli [Sandy Place], which we now call Tlatelolco and which today is the barrio of Santiago in Mexico City.[7]

The elders and principal men who went there were four. One was called Atlacuahuitl, the second Huicton, the third Opochtli, and the fourth Atlacol. These four chieftains separated, left the others, and went to live in that place called Tlatelolco. From what I have heard they were restless and seditious men, of evil intentions. From the day they left Tenochtitlan they were never in peace, nor did they get on well with their brothers, the Aztecs of Tenochtitlan. This lack of understanding has passed on to this day, for between Mexico-Tenochtitlan and Mexico-Tlatelolco there is continuous dissension and rancor.

Some time after this third division among the Aztecs — the first was at Mechoacan, the second at Malinalco, and the third at Tlatelolco — those who had remained in the principal site of the prickly pear cactus held a meeting, they sat in council. They talked about the building of their city and the safety of their people. They did not feel secure from the others who had left them, especially since the latter were multiplying rapidly and expanding their territory.

Addressing the congregation, one of the elders said, "My sons and brothers, you see how our brothers and kinsmen have abandoned us and have gone to Tlatelolco to live. They have left the place designated by our god as our home, like rebels and ungrateful men who do not

---

[7]Tlatelolco's place glyph is a mound of earth. About a mile north of Tenochtitlan's ceremonial precinct, Tlatelolco is now a part of downtown Mexico City. Durán states that Tlatelolco was founded around 1370 by dissidents from the major Aztec group and little by little became an important marketplace. The rivalry between the two cities ended by Tenochtitlan's overpowering Tlatelolco in 1473. However, archaeological excavations have shown that there was a settlement at Tlatelolco far earlier than the one mentioned by Durán. Today the area is distinguished by a large main square, Santiago Square of the Plaza of Three Cultures, with remains of the *tecpan* (the Aztec community house where Cuauhtemoc, last of the native sovereigns, ruled for a brief spell), a sixteenth-century Franciscan monastery turned museum and a colonial church, and modern structures. Within the monastic establishment, Fray Bernardino de Sahagún composed his monumental work on ancient Mexico based upon the data given by his native informants. The modern part of the area consists of the Ministry of Foreign Relations building, still standing, and the gigantic Nonoalco-Tlatelolco Housing Development, much of it devastated in the tragic earthquake of September 19, 1985.

recognize their good fortune; they have abandoned us, they have gone away. I am afraid that with their cunning they will one day wish to surpass us and subdue us. They will wish to raise themselves to a higher position and elect a king and make their own capital, because they are despicable, they are wicked. Before we find ourselves in a situation like that, I believe we should make a rapid decision and choose a king who will rule over us and over Tlatelolco as well. If you feel that he should not be one of us, let us bring him from outside. Azcapotzalco is near and we are on land belonging to that city. Or if you disagree, let him be from Colhuacan or from the province of Tezcoco. Speak, O Aztecs, express your feelings, your ideas, about this!"[8]

When Meci, the elder who had proposed this, finished speaking, everyone was in agreement. They resolved that the Aztecs would not go to Azcapotzalco, nor to the province of Tezcoco [for their king], for they had lived on the lands of Colhuacan and some of their people had intermarried there, begetting children of both lords and peasants, and even had grandchildren there. So they decided to choose a son of their own people from this line, who had the finest blood of both the Aztecs and the Colhuas. And he would reign in Tenochtitlan.

They remembered a great lord who had come with them [on their long pilgrimage] but who had stayed in Colhuacan when they fled that city. He was named Opochtzin. He had married a woman of a principal family of Colhuacan and had produced a son named Acamapichtli, "Handful of Reeds." The Aztecs wished Acamapichtli to come and rule over Tenochtitlan and to be lord of this city.

The people proposed to go to Colhuacan and ask this favor of the ruler of that place, called Nauhyotl. For this mission they decided to take an important gift, the best they could find within their limited resources. Thus, with the gift ready, they chose two esteemed elders who were skillful in the art of speech and who could deliver the message to the king of Colhuacan.

These men went and offered a present, declaring, "O great lord: we, the Aztecs, your servants and vassals, are enclosed in a marshy land and surrounded by a lake filled with reeds and rushes. We are alone and forsaken by all the nations. We were guided only by our god

---

[8]At that time Colhuacan was one of the last surviving centers of Toltec culture in the country. Its royal house claimed descent from the dynasty of the kings of Tula and from the god Quetzalcoatl. It is obvious that the Aztecs, newcomers to this land, found it advantageous to intermarry so as to be able to claim kinship with this line. Any relationship with these ancestors—albeit adopted forebears—was a sure path to prestige. The Colhuacan mentioned by Durán is today San Francisco Culhuacan, in southern Mexico City.

to the place where we now are, which is within your jurisdiction and that of Azcapotzalco and of Tezcoco. Now that you have permitted us to remain here, we must have a ruler to guide us, to direct us, to show us how we are to live, who will free us, who will defend us and protect us from our enemies. Because of this we appeal to you knowing that among your people there are sons of our people related by marriage to yours, who have come out of our wombs and out of yours, of your blood and ours. We have heard that there is a son of Opochtzin here, Acamapichtli by name. He is the son of a daughter of yours, Atotoztli. We beg of you to give him to us for our king, that we may show him all the reverence and respect he deserves, for he is of Aztec lineage and also descendant of the sovereigns of Colhuacan."

The lord of Colhuacan, realizing that he would lose nothing by sending his grandson to rule in Mexico-Tenochtitlan, answered thus: "O honored Aztecs, I have heard your just petition and I find satisfaction in being able to please you. Furthermore, not only is this an honor for me but—what good does my grandson do me here? Take him with my blessings, lead him away, for it is well that he serve your god and be in the place of Huitzilopochtli and govern the creatures whose god is 'He for Whom We Live, Lord of Night and Day, and of the Wind.' Let Acamapichtli rule over the waters and over the lands of the Aztec people. But I warn you that if my son were a woman I would not give her to you, and if this were the case and her mother were alive, she would not allow this either.9 But he is a man, so take him with my consent and treat him as he deserves, as your son and as my grandson."

The Aztecs thanked the king for his liberality, they were grateful to him, and they begged him to give them a woman of his lineage to be their ruler. And so it happened that Acamapichtli was married to a Colhua noblewoman whose name was Ilancueitl. All the Aztec men and women, young and old, came out to receive their king and carried him with great honors to the royal apartments, which, though poor at that time, had been prepared in a regal way. They placed the royal couple on two seats and solemnly declared them to be rulers of Mexico-Tenochtitlan, promising them obedience and loyalty.

And one of the old men arose, saying:

> My son, our lord and king, welcome to your house and city, here among the rushes, here among the reeds, where your wretched ancestors, where your poor grandparents and relatives, the Aztecs, suffered and still suffer what only the Lord of All Created Things knows. Behold, O lord, you have come to be the sanctuary, the shade and the refuge of

---

9This antagonism on the part of the ruler of Colhuacan undoubtedly refers to the flaying of the king's daughter by the Aztecs some time before.

this Aztec nation. You will be the authority, the command. You have come to be the likeness of our god Huitzilopochtli! You well know that we are not in our own country but in a foreign land, and we are not certain what will befall us on the morrow and on later days. Behold that you have not come here to rest, to take pleasure but to endure a new and arduous task. You will labor, you will be a slave to all this multitude, to all the people of this land for whom you must work, whom you must keep happy, contented, since we live within their boundaries, on their land. Therefore, O lord, be welcome, both you and our lady, Queen Ilancueitl.

These words having been said, upon their heads were placed diadems similar to a bishop's miter, which were used for the coronation of kings. Thus Acamapichtli received the kingdom in his hands and promised to take charge of its defense. From this time on, he made decisions regarding the matters of state.

And since I wish to deal especially with the election of this first king of Mexico-Tenochtitlan, his greatness and his way of ruling, of governing (as I consider it an important part of my history), I felt it best to write a special chapter about him and his life and deeds.

But before we begin to deal with him I wish to tell about how some of the Aztecs separated from the others and went to live in Tlatelolco, where they kept their peace but abstained from swearing obedience to their new king. Rather, like rebels and without fear, they remained silent. They paid no attention to the monarch chosen by the Aztecs but acted like a separate nation. This was permitted by the original Aztec group, but I believe it was done from fear, for no kingdom divided against itself can endure. And dreading destruction, yet warring against each other, both groups pretended ignorance [of the reality]. But as time went on—as I shall tell in its place—the Tenochca-Aztecs, unable to tolerate longer the trouble caused by those of Tlatelolco, attacked them many times. They made war on them, they harmed them, they subdued them, they robbed them, they destroyed them. This was all done with too much fury and desire for vengeance.

CHAPTER VI

Which treats of the first king of Mexico, called Acamapichtli, and what took place during his reign.

In the year one thousand three hundred and eighteen after the birth of Our Redeemer Jesus Christ, the Aztecs began to build the city of Mexico-Tenochtitlan, making humble houses and thatched huts on top of earthen mounds they formed, because, as I have said, this was a great lagoon, much of it covered with rushes, reeds, and cattails [with little solid ground].

From this time on the Aztec nation began to consolidate and, compared with their past vicissitudes, the people enjoyed peace and happiness. The land was divided into barrios and property for the temples, then the people began to multiply in large numbers and positions of authority were created. The Aztecs mixed with other nations, dealing with them, conversing with them. Many of the old people who had been left behind during the migration were still alive and were men of much authority and respect. The names of these men were Acazitli, Tenoch, Meci, Ahuexotl, Ocelopan, and Tezacatetl. And with them were Huitzilopochtli's four guardians, who saw him and talked to him; they were first Cuauhtlequetzqui, second Ococal, third, Chachalayotl, fourth Axolohua.[1]

These men were like the fathers, the guardians, the shelter, the protectors of that people. When they saw that their city had been

---

[1] If these men had been left behind they could hardly have formed part of the ruling group in Tenochtitlan. Obviously they were leaders from the time of Aztlan and some of them were god-bearers and/or mythical founders of Tenochtitlan. Four of the *teomamaque*, god-bearers, who carried the bundle of Huitzilopochtli on the migration are depicted in the *Codex Boturini*, also called the *Tira de la Peregrinación*. Here they are Tezcacoacatl (From the Place of the Mirror Snake), who leads the group and carries the god; Cuauhcoatl (Eagle Serpent); Apanecatl (The One from the River), and a woman, Chimalman (Shield Place or Shield Hand).

Durán gives different names for the god-bearers: Cuauhtlequetzqui (He Who Places the Wood in the Fire); Ococal (House of Torch Pine/Lantern); Chachalayotl (Sound Maker); and Axolohua (He Who Owns the Axolotl [tadpole-like creature]). The first place of the *Codex Mandoza* portrays the founder-chiefs. Among these are the men mentioned by Durán: Acacihtli/Acazitli (Reed Hare), Tenoch (Stony Cactus Fruit), Mexitzin/Meci (Agave Navel), Ahuexotl (Water Willow), and Ocelopan (Place of Ocelots). Missing on this place is Tezacatetl (Mirrorlike Stone). Karen Dakin translated the Nahuatl terms.

founded, they were determined to find a king. As was mentioned in the previous chapter, after these men discussed the problem in the council meeting, they brought to Tenochtitlan as ruler a son of Opochtzin, an Aztec lord who, when the Aztecs were living in Tizaapan, had wed a woman of Colhuacan, named Atotoztli. From this union a son, Acamapichtli, was born.[2] The Aztecs had heard that Acamapichtli not only came from the line of their lords but also had developed into a valiant youth worthy of the blood and lineage of which he was a descendant.

After he had been brought to the city, he was elected its king by common consent, in peace, opposed by no one. And Acamapichtli, in all humility, accepted the command, the rule of the kingdom, with the understanding that the Aztecs were subject to, were vassals of, Azcapotzalco. Since they had built their houses on land belonging to Azcapotzalco, they were tributaries of that city.

This king married a woman of high lineage from Colhuacan, named Ilancueitl. She was sterile, she was barren, and because of this the king and his lords were sad. And fearing that the kingdom would be left without heirs, the lords gathered and held council, where they decided that each one would give a daughter to Acamapichtli. These would be secondary wives and from these unions sons and heirs would be born.[3]

When they had come to this agreement, Acazitli was the first to offer his daughter, saying: "O our king, we have seen that after you

---

[2] Durán consistently uses the name Acamapich when referring to the first Aztec sovereign, although this actually is a short form of Acamapichtli, more commonly used. The name means "Handful of Reeds," from the Nahuatl *acatl*, "reeds," and *mapilli*, "handful," and can also be spelled Acamapilli or Acamapichtzin, the latter a reverential form of addressing the king. See Simeón (1965:5–6).

[3] Polygyny existed in prehispanic Mexico. The ruler or a nobleman had a principal wife, wed with all the proper ceremonies, and as many secondary wives or concubines as he wished. These women usually were daughters of nobles, but not always. Itzcoatl was, after all, the son of a slave and Acamapichtli. The offspring of the union between a king and secondary wives were considered *pipiltin* or nobles. The king must have had a large number of concubines. A curious note is found in Dr. Francisco Hernández's sixteenth-century treatise on Mexican flora and fauna regarding an unusual plant and these women. He described the *tetlaxincaxochitl* as a "flower [like] a stone burnisher (possibly referring to the polishing motion), sometimes called adultery flower," whose form was that of a phallus; he said "that large plant [was called thus] because Moctezuma's concubines . . . who were innumerable, used the plant in place of a virile [male] member in order to receive sexual pleasure . . . because of the lack of a man" (Hernández 1959:II:390). Perhaps, however, Hernández's comment may be taken with a grain of salt. Commoners were usually monogamous but could have more than one wife if they could afford them.

married, the Lord of All Created Things, Lord of Night and Day,[4] has not favored you and our lady, Queen Ilancueitl, with children. Therefore, O king, we, your vassals, have decided that each one of us will give you a daughter as a wife. In this way not only will there be a successor to the kingdom when your days have ended but we would be pleased if this successor would be one of our children, one of our grandchildren. Through us, the Aztec nation will be illustrious, it will be renowned. And so, our lord, here I give you my daughter to be your wife and companion, and to serve you."

Tezacatetl, Ahuexotl, Ocelopan, Tenoch, and Aatl followed Acazitli's example. Each one of the great lords and servers of the gods offered one of his daughters to the king as a wife, so in this way there would be descendants from the lords of this land.

However, before I go on to tell about the children born to these women, I should like to mention that the king had a slave, a native of Azcapotzalco, from the barrio of Cuauhcalco, who was so beautiful, of such pleasing appearance, that Acamapichtli fell in love with her and thus possessed her. She became pregnant, then gave birth to a son who was named Itzcoatl. Although he was a bastard, the son of a slave, Itzcoatl, as a young man, was so valiant that he eventually became king, as we shall tell in the right place.

God did not deny the Aztecs their intention and desire but made these daughters of the nobles so fecund that they began to give birth to the king's children. The first son to be born was named Cuatlecoatl; the second, Tlacahuepan; the third, Tlatolzaca; the fourth, Huitzilihuitl. Huitzilihuitl was born to the daughter of Huitzilipochtli's guardian, Cuauhtlequetzqui, whom we have mentioned before; he was the principal one of the four god-bearers.

The fifth of the king's sons was Epcoatl, the sixth Ihuitltemoc, the seventh Tlacacochtoc. I could explain the meaning of these names in our language but it seems to me that listing etymologies is a waste of

---

[4] The Lord of All Created Things, Creator of People, Lord of Night, Lord of Wind, was Tezcatlipoca, supreme deity, god of fate. Tezcatlipoca (Mirror That Smokes) was many things to the Aztecs, both positive and negative. He could bestow wealth and fame upon people or he could take them away. He caused illness and problems and was a sorcerer, a bringer of evil. Yet as Telpochtli (The Youth), eternally young, he was the patron of the *telpochcalli*, a school for boys. As Yaotl (The Enemy) he incited people to war. Yet he was also Teimatini (The Wise One, He Who Understands People), Tloque Nahuaque (Professor of All That Surrounds Us), Pilhoacazintli (Revered Father, Possessor of the Children), Ipalnemoani (He for Whom We Live), the impalpable, the divine. Tezcatlipoca undoubtedly was the most complex figure in the ancient pantheon, one who had to be propitiated, feared, respected, hated, and loved. Yet these same appellations were given to Huitzilopochtli.

time and I could even eliminate naming them if I were not compelled to mention them in the future.⁵

But we must not leave the king's principal wife without telling what happened to her. She was so unhappy, so downcast, at the scorn shown her because she was barren that her eyes were like pools of water, day and night. The king observed her sadness and, because he respected her and loved her dearly, he consoled her as much as he could. And, when she became aware of his great love, she asked a favor of him: that, since the Lord of All Created Things had denied her the fruit of his benediction, and, so that the people would lose the poor opinion they had formed because of her lack of fecundity, the king should concede that, when the children of the other women were born, she be permitted to place them at her breast. Then she would lie in bed and pretend she had given birth, so that when Acamapichtli's subjects came to visit her they would congratulate her for the birth, for the new son. The king, persuaded by her plea, ordered that this be done. Therefore, when one of those women gave birth, Ilancueitl lay in bed and, pretending to be the new mother, took the child in her arms and received the good wishes and gifts from her visitors. And although in truth she had not given birth, the people believed she had. Even today it is believed that this is what happened, although different information contradicts it, and I do not know if it is the truth, because it is contrary to common opinion; yet this is what had been narrated to me. Be that as it may, the common people believed this lady to be the mother of all those children I have mentioned, who were the origin, the issue, the descendants of the nobility of Mexico.

When King Acamapichtli had resolved this matter and all was tranquil, the Tepanecs, people of Azcapotzalco and Coyoacan and Tacuba, seeing that the Aztecs had elected a king, became offended and felt insecure. King Tezozomoctli⁶ then held court and called together his chieftains, exclaiming: "O people of Azcapotzalco, you have seen how the Aztecs have not only taken lands that belonged to us but have elected a king and become independent. What do you think we should do? We have pretended to ignore this problem but it is not convenient to continue to be indifferent in regard to another. For perhaps the day we die these people may not want to obey our sons and

⁵The names of Acamapichtli's sons that Durán does not translate are Cuatlecoatl (Fire Head Serpent), Tlacahuepan (Timber Man), Tlatolzaca (Word Bearer), Huitzilihuitl (Hummingbird Feather), Epcoatl (Serpent of the Conch Shell), Ihuitltemoc (One Who Descends like a Feather), Tlacacochtoc (Recumbent Sleeper), and Matlalxochitl (Green or Deep Blue Flower).

⁶Tezozomoctli is the same as Tezozomoc. The reverential form would be Tezozomoctzin.

successors. They may even want to make them vassals and tributaries and become lords of our own state. Because, according to the way they are beginning, little by little these Aztecs are rising, becoming proud, they are trying to get ahead of us. Lest they rise more, if you are in agreement, let us order them to pay double the usual tribute, twice as much as they used to give us in fruits of the earth, as a sign of subjection."

Everyone thought well of what King Tezozomoc had decided. Taking the matter in hand, they sent their messengers to Tenochtitlan to advise the new king Acamapichtli that King Tezozomoc of Azcapotzalco claimed that the tribute they were paying was too small and that he wished it to be increased. He needed to repair and beautify his city and consequently, together with the usual tribute of fish, frogs, and food plants, they must now add fully grown willow and bald cypress trees, since he wished to plant these in Azcapotzalco. The Aztecs were to construct a raft on the water, sown with all the fruits of the earth, such as maize, chiles, beans, squash, and amaranth.

When the Aztecs heard these commands, they began to wail and show great anxiety. However, on the following night the god Huitzilopochtli spoke to Ococaltzin, one of his priests, saying: "I have seen the affliction and the tears of the Aztecs. Tell them not to be anguished, not to grieve, for I shall bring them peace and spare them all this labor. Let them accept the payment of the tribute and tell my son Acamapichtli to be courageous. Let him take the willows and bald cypress trees that are demanded of him! Let them make the raft, let them sow upon it all the plants that are demanded of them! I shall make everything easy for them, I shall make everything simple."

When morning came, Ococaltzin went to King Acamapichtli and told him about the revelation of the night before. The ruler was greatly consoled and ordered the people to accept immediately the tribute demand, to submit to the command, to carry out the order. And thus they obtained the willows and the bald cypress trees with great ease and took them to Azcapotzalco, where they planted them in the places indicated by the king of that city. And they floated the raft garden, sown with fully grown ears of maize, chiles, tomatoes, amaranth, beans, squash, and flowers to Azcapotzalco.

When Tezozomoc had marveled at all of this, he said to his people, "Brothers, this has seemed to me almost a supernatural thing because, when I commanded that this be done, I considered it an impossible task. And because I wish you to understand that I do not deceive myself in that which I tell you, call the Aztecs here! I want you to realize that they are the chosen people of their god and that someday they will rule over all the nations of the earth."

The History of the Indies of New Spain

The Aztecs were called before Tezozomoc. He addressed them thus: "Brothers, it seems to me that these tasks are not burdensome for you, that you have acquired great strength. My new order is that the next time you bring the tribute you are obliged to pay you do it in the following way: On the raft garden sprouted maize must be growing, together with other seeds and ripe plants and greens, but in the midst of those plants there must be a female duck sitting upon her eggs and a heron hatching her eggs. And at the moment the raft with the tribute arrives in Azcapotzalco [the chicks of the duck and the heron] must come out of their eggs. If this is not done you will all perish."

The Aztecs considered this a very difficult undertaking but they gave the message to their king, telling him what the ruler of Azcapotzalco had ordered, had demanded. The news spread quickly throughout the city and caused sorrow and unrest. However, King Acamapichtli, with faith in his god, ordered the people not to be troubled, not to be grieved, not to feel cowardly. And so all withdrew from his presence in apparent good spirits in spite of their deep apprehension.

And that night the god Huitzilopochtli spoke to his keeper Ococaltzin, saying:

> My father, do not be afraid! Let not the threats daunt you! Tell the king my son that I know what is best for him, I know what must be done. Let him obey me. Let him leave this in my care, let him understand that all demands of the foes will be paid with their blood and their lives! In this way they will become ours. They will perish, or they will become slaves before much time has passed. Let my children suffer and weep now, but their day will come!"

Old Ococaltzin told these things to the king, he related all that the god had said. Thus the king and the people in the city were reassured, were encouraged to fulfill the demands made of them. They prepared the raft and sowed it with all kinds of plants and among them they set a duck upon its eggs and a heron in the same manner. They took these things to King Tezozomoc in Azcapotzalco and, by request of their god, some large loaves made of *ezcahuitli*, a type of small red worm from the lagoon.[7]

When the Azcapotzalco ruler saw the tribute, he was amazed; he realized the truth of what he had said to his nobles the previous year. He now repeated what he had told them at that time [that the Aztecs were the chosen people of their god and one day would rule over all the other nations].

---

[7] Evidently these lake products available to the Aztecs constituted their tribute. Loaves made of *ezcahuitli* must have been an important source of protein, inasmuch as Huitzilopochtli claimed that his body was made of this red worm.

The Aztecs continued to pay the same tribute for fifty years, keeping silent, pretending to be content and feigning obedience, while their numbers multiplied, while they became stronger. King Acamapichtli reigned forty years in the city of Tenochtitlan, ruling in peace, in quiet, in harmony. He built the city, organizing its houses, canals, and streets. He achieved other benefits for the good order of the state. But after forty years of peaceful rule this sovereign became ill and ended his days, leaving the city sad and disconsolate over his death, for he had been much loved and respected by his subjects. On his deathbed he called all his nobles and spoke to them at length, charging them to care for the affairs of state and also for his women and children. He did not name any of these nobles as his successor but indicated that the state should elect someone from among them, or name one from outside, stating that he wished to give them liberty of choice. He also showed great sorrow in not having been able to free the city from subjugation to Azcapotzalco and as tributary to that city.

The city performed many funeral rites and lamented his passing with great ceremony, as was their custom. And I wish to emphasize that the riches, the wealth, with which other people buried their dead, accompanied by slaves, pages, and servants who were killed [as part of the rites], was displayed in a limited manner by the Aztecs because they were still poor, humble, forsaken.

At that time even the king had barely enough to eat. After the death of their sovereign, the chieftains and nobles began to prepare for the election of a successor, as has been said. Acamapichtli began his reign at the age of twenty and ruled forty years; thus he died at the age of sixty. He left valiant sons, men of strong heart. Later some of them became mighty kings, captains and councillors, who will be described later. He died in the year 1404. Three years before his death, in 1402 [sic], the great lord Nezahualcoyotzin[8] had been born, who later became king of Tezcoco. Besides being a close relative of the rulers of Mexico, Nezahualcoyotl was sympathetic to the Aztec nation and a great friend of its people. Very few others, or none, equaled this relationship. In the following chapters will be told the manner and way in which he perpetuated the confederation and friendship of the Aztecs and how he achieved this without letting the other nations know his intentions.

---

[8]Nezahualcoyotzin is both the reverential and affectionate form for Nezahualcoyotl.

CHAPTER VII

Which treats of the second king of Mexico, Huitzilihuitl, and his great deeds and feats.

King Acamapichtli, who had ruled the Mexican nation with wisdom and prudence, who by all means possible had endeavored to give his people greatness, was dead. The Aztecs then determined to elect a new king, consulting among themselves and discussing the matter with the nobles and with the common people. One of the elders spoke:

> O Aztecs, behold that our king and lord is dead! Which [son of Mexico-Tenochtitlan] do you wish to elect as head and ruler of this city? Who will shelter and defend us and have pity on the old ones, on the widows and orphans? Who will be the father of this republic? Let each man speak freely and proclaim the one he favors! He will be in command, he will sit upon the reed mat, the royal seat of this kingdom. He will protect us, he will defend us from our enemies. According to what our god has revealed, we shall soon need courageous hands and hearts. Who, O Aztecs, will have the courage to be the strength of our arms? Who will thrust out his chest freely and fearlessly in order to defend our city and our person; who will refuse to weaken, to defame, the name of our god Huitzilopochtli? This man will be the image of our god, he will defend and lift up his name. He will make known to the entire world that the Mexican nation has sufficient valor and strength to subject the earth and make all peoples his vassals! Now you must elect the man who will be our father, our mother; for we are the feathers on his wings, the lashes on his eyes, the hairs on his face. Speak, O Aztecs, say, name, point out the one who is to hold the staff of authority, who will see that justice is not twisted, who will take the rod and will not pardon the punishment. He is the one who will sit on the left hand of our god. Let him come out, let us see him, let us rejoice on seeing his face! Behold, we the chieftains are old men, without strength. You have many from whom to choose: Among us there are grandsons and a son of the dead king, born of our daughters.

When he had spoken, the heads of the four barrios [that is, Moyotla, Teopantlaca, Atzacualco, and Cuepan],[1] all in accord, answered: "Az-

---

[1] The four barrios in relation to the Great Temple were Cuepopan or Cuepan (On the Road), to the northwest, toward Tlatelolco; Atzacualco (Place Where birds Alight or Place of the Floodgate), to the northeast; Moyotlan or Moyotla (Where Mosquitoes

tecs, we are gathered here in our council; here without offending anyone we speak freely. Our will is that our king, our lord, be the son of our last ruler, Acamapichtli; he is a gallant young man, of good heart, whose name is Huitzilihuitl. He is well bred, kind and peaceable, courageous and of praiseworthy ways. He is the one we select to govern and rule over us. Let him be our lord and king, the very image of our god Huitzilopochtli!"

The election having been carried out, one of the elders appeared before the common people who were outside awaiting the decision. He spoke to them—men and women, old and young, adults and children—in a strong voice: "Brothers, here you are gathered, all those of the Aztec nation. You will now be informed that the heads of the four barrios, chieftains and officials, have elected as king of this nation the youth Huitzilihuitl. He will be your father, your mother,[2] he will be your sanctuary, your protection in your needs. Express your opinion about this, because without your approval the election will amount to nothing."

The people, having heard this—children and adults, men and women, old and young—answered in one voice that they confirmed the election and that it pleased them. They let forth great cries, they shouted:

> Long live our King Huitzilihuitl, image of our god Huitzilopochtli! Our hearts rejoice in him! We give thanks to the Lord of All Created Things, of the Night and of the Day, of the Wind and of the Water.

All the officials, in proper order, went to the place where the new king was standing; and taking him from among the other youths and princes, his brothers and relatives, they surrounded him and led him to the royal palace where he was seated and the diadem was put upon

---

Abound), to the southwest; and Teopan or Teopantlaca (On the Temple), to the southeast.

[2] In the original Durán manuscript in the Biblioteca Nacional de Madrid, the word *madre*, "mother," has been scratched out. This probably was done in the sixteenth century. Yet Durán must have meant "father, mother" to be part of this speech, since it was the conventional way to address a person in a formal presentation. In book 6 of Sahagún's *Florentine Codex* (*Rhetoric and Moral Philosophy*), in the *huehuetlatolli* (words of the elders) the terms "father, mother" and "mother, father" refer to the ruler who watches over his people (1969:12, 45, 54, 58, 61, 63, 67), to a woman about to give birth (1969:144, 145, 146), to the sun (1969:12, 13, 58), to the earth (1969:12, 13, 36, 58), to the god Quetzalcoatl (1969:31), to the fire god Huehueteotl-Xiuhtecuhtli (1969:41), to Mictlantecuhtli, Lord of the Land of the Dead (1969:21, 27, 31, 48, 58, 152, 190), and to the Creator Pair, Ometecuhtli and Omecihuatl (1969:183, 202, 206), among others. "Motherhood and fatherhood" is a designation also found frequently in these orations, mainly referring to protection.

his head. The officials then anointed his whole body with the same pitch used to anoint the statue of the idol Huitzilopochtli.³ After having dressed him in the royal garments, one of the men addressed the new king: "O courageous youth, our king and lord! Do not faint or lose spirit because of this new authority that has been given to you so that you will protect the water and the earth of your new kingdom, which is sunk in the harshness of the reeds, the rushes, the grasses, and the cattails. Your kingdom is here under the protection of our god Huitzilopochtli, whose likeness you are. You well know the hardships, the fear, with which we live because we dwell upon land that belongs to others, for we are tributaries of the people of Azcapotzalco. I tell you this, I remind you of it, not because I believe you are ignorant of it, but so you may acquire new spirit and realize that you have not come to this place [to the throne] to rest but to work. Thus, O lord, you see that we have nothing else to offer you, nothing to give you. You well know in what wretchedness and poverty your father reigned, fulfilling the obligations of his office, suffering with courage and wisdom."

This speech having ended, one by one they came to offer reverence to Huitzilihuitl and each addressed him with elaborate words. Because these talks are long I do not record them here. After the discourses the king was installed upon his throne.

Huitzilihuitl began to reign in the year 1404 after his father died, and, as we have seen, he was elected by vote and the consent of all. This custom had existed since the beginning of this nation: no son inherited through succession or primogeniture as is the custom among us, where the eldest son inherits his father's place. In this Aztec nation it was not thus. Successors were elected, chosen by agreement on the part of the electors and all the people. Though Huitzilihuitl had elder brothers he was chosen to be king of Tenochtitlan.

The lords began to discuss among themselves the problems of their city. Believing that they had now acquired strength and feeling the need for freedom, they stated: "We are weary of being subjects and tributary vassals of the lords of Azcapotzalco. We not only are subjected to the Tepanecs but also are vassals of Colhuacan and Tezcoco. We are not strong enough to resist being dominated by so many

---

³Anointing a body with pitch gave its wearer divine protection. In the case of anointing a new ruler during his investiture with the same unguent or pitch used on the statue of Huitzilopochtli, this conferred upon the man some of the qualities of the god. On other occasions the priests covered themselves with a pitch made of soot from torch pine, combined with mashed spiders, scorpions, centipedes, vipers, and other poisonous creatures. Added to this mixture were ground seeds of *ololiuhqui* (*Rivea corymbosa*), a psychotropic plant. This pitch was called *teotlacualli* (divine food) and was thought to protect its wearer from all evil (see Durán 1977:114–15).

people. Where shall we go? What shall we do? We shall labor to find relief from this intolerable load that is upon our shoulders. Let us rest a while and, as a resolution, perhaps do this: our greatest threat is Azcapotzalco, since the court and king of the Tepanecs are there; we consider that, since our king is young and still unmarried, we should go to Azcapotzalco and ask for the daughter of King Tezozomoctli so that she may be the wife of our king and lord. If he grants us this he may lessen our tribute. How does this advice appear to you, O Aztecs?"

The elders and nobles responded that the idea seemed wise to them. Having determined this, they sent two of the eldest men to Azcapotzalco to beseech the king to grant them his daughter, so that she might become the wife of the king of Tenochtitlan. They entered Tezozomoc's presence and, after greeting him, they spoke: "Our lord and son, we have come before your greatness; we are prostrated upon the earth with all humility possible, in order to beseech you, to beg a favor of you. To whom, O lord, should we go but to you, for we are your vassals and servants. We await your royal commands, the words from your mouth. We are eager to comply with all that your heart and your will desire. Behold, O lord, the embassy that we have brought from your servants, the officials and elders of our city. O lord, accede to our plea. Have pity on your servant, the king of Mexico-Tenochtitlan, Huitzilihuitl, who rules there, among the reeds and rushes and thick grasses, who protects your vassals. He is single, still to be wed. What we ask of you is that you surrender one of your jewels, one of your precious feathers, one of your noblewomen. She will not go to an alien place but will stay within her own land and country, all of which will be under her command. Therefore, O lord, we beg you not to refuse that which we ask of you."

King Tezozomoc, who had listened attentively to the Aztecs' request, and seeing that their petition was just, answered them with affection and benevolence: "O Aztecs, I have been so overcome by your words, by your humility, that I find it difficult to answer. I have daughters and the Lord of All Created Things has destined them for this end. Behold one of most beloved daughters, called Ayauhcihuatl. You are welcome to take her."

They prostrated themselves upon the earth before the king and thanked him profusely. Then they took the daughter of the king together with many attendants from Azcapotzalco and brought her to Mexico-Tenochtitlan, the Aztec capital, where she was well received in the city by all the people, who greeted her with joyful ceremony, according to their custom. The king and bridegroom received her warmly, then she was taken to the palace, where she was greeted with

The History of the Indies of New Spain

discourses of welcome, and where later the marriage ceremony took place. The matrimonial rite consisted of tying the mantles of the groom and the bride together as a sign of union. There were other ceremonies that I shall describe in another chapter further on.

In time, after the king and Ayauhcihuatl, daughter of the king of Azcapotzalco, had been married, she bore a son to him. The city received this news with joy and contentment. The people wished King Tezozomoc, father-in-law of King Huitzilihuitl and father of the new mother, to be advised immediately. Therefore, on the day of the birth, messengers were sent to Azcapotzalco, where they announced to Tezozomoc: "O lord, the king of Tenochtitlan and all his chieftains kiss your hands and notify you that the queen, our lady, your daughter, has given birth to a son, granted to us by the Lord of All Created Things. We have come to gratify you with this news and to calm your heart."

"Aztecs," answered King Tezozomoc, "with great pleasure have I received this news. Rest while I tell my officials and noblemen about it," and he had them notified. The nobles of Azcapotzalco, Tacuba, and Coyoacan appeared before him and he told them that his daughter had given birth to a son, whereupon they congratulated him with great joy. When Tezozomoc asked their opinion regarding the name his grandson should be given, they considered the signs under which the child had been born and, according to their auguries and conjectures, decided that he should be called Chimalpopoca, which in their tongue means "Smoking Shield." This decided, the nobles and allies retired. The messengers returned to Tenochtitlan, bearing congratulations from Tezozomoc on the birth of the prince. They told how the king of Azcapotzalco had sent them back with felicitations for the king and for the queen, his daughter, and notified them that the child should be called Chimalpopoca.

After the Aztec messengers had left Azcapotzalco, the lords of that city, of Tacuba, and of Coyoacan followed them to Mexico-Tenochtitlan in order to congratulate the king and the new mother and to present them with fine gifts. In the name of their king, they asked that the child be called by the name Tezozomoc had chosen. Thus it was done, to the satisfaction of everyone in the city. When the Aztecs had given many thanks to the Tepanecs and had sent their good wishes to King Tezozomoc, these nobles returned home. Immediately they informed Tezozomoc of all they had done, for which he was very appreciative.

Tezozomoc now realized that he had a grandson in Tenochtitlan who would be heir to that kingdom. Soon his daughter brought the child before him and spoke about the great labors and suffering of the city in paying such large tribute. The king, moved by the compassionate plea of his daughter, gathered together his councillors with the intention of relieving the Aztecs of the tribute burden, or, if this were not possible, at least part of it. He proposed this to his advisers and requested they agree to his wish, which was the supression of tribute that the Aztecs, as vassals, had been obliged to pay up to that time.

The officials and noblemen of Azcapotzalco did not show great pleasure when they heard what their monarch asked of them, but in order not to contradict him they agreed that not all but part of the tribute would be remitted. Tezozomoc, having heard this agreement on the part of his advisers, decided to eliminate the heaviest load and to demand of the tributaries only the things that could most easily be obtained. And so he sent messengers to Tenochtitlan who told the king and the authorities there that he had agreed to have pity on them since his daughter and grandson were in that city, and that he would remove the tribute the Aztecs had been accustomed to pay. Because his advisers did not agree to the suppression of all the tribute, from that time on the Aztecs were to pay a yearly tax of two ducks from the lagoon together with fish, frogs, and other creatures that live in the waters. Tezozomoc sent word that he was in agreement with his council and that the Aztecs could now rest and have relief from the problems and distress they had suffered previously. When the Aztec people heard the good news, they went with much humility to thank the lord of Azcapotzalco for the great favor granted to them.

The Aztecs were now relieved, they were content. But after a few years Queen Ayauhcihuatl, who had been their sympathetic protectress, died, leaving Chimalpopoca a child of nine. With the queen dead, it is said that the Aztecs were saddened and distressed, having lost their good mediator, the queen, and they feared that they might have to resume the old tributes. Nevertheless, they had confidence in the child's [influence on his grandfather] and remained calm.

Some say that King Huitzilihuitl married again, this time a daughter of the ruler of Cuauhnahuac,[4] by whom he had many children. Others, though they agree that he married the daughter of the lord of Cuauhnahuac, state that in their paintings [ancient pictorial manuscripts] they find no evidence of his having had other children than Chimalpopoca. Nor have I found notice of other children in the paintings and written manuscripts that I have seen that refer to this king. Furthermore, aside from this lack of reference to other children, I have found information that tells that Huitzilihuitl died one year

---

[4]Cuauhnahuac is the present-day city of Cuernavaca, capital of the state of Morelos, south of Mexico City.

after his wife. He reigned only thirteen years and died young, a little over thirty years of age.

Huitzilihuitl ruled in peace and wisdom and was much loved by both the nobles and the commoners. He began to issue laws for the republic, especially in reference to the cult of the gods. This is what most interested the kings and lords because they considered themselves to be images of the gods and any honor paid to the deities was honor given to them. Therefore, one thing they were eager for, among other important measures, was to enlarge their temple and increase the cult to their god. And they also realized that, though they desired the liberty of their nation, the time of their prosperity had not yet arrived. Other peoples who surrounded them had much more liberty and wealth than they did; thus they felt frustrated and intimidated by this. Though this distressed them, they did not yield to laziness or complaints but, on the contrary, they traded constantly with other nations, moving from one place to another, bringing provisions to their city, and fishing. They also began to make boats and become skillful in activities that had to do with the lake. At the same time they fortified their boats and canoes and began to practice the arts of war upon the water. They knew well that in the long run they must become experts in these arts because, if the truth must be told, all the friendship and flattering words directed to neighboring nations was feigned, founded on malice and treason. All was covered with false friendship so that later their aggressive acts could be carried out safely.

This feigned humility with which they reassured their enemies was so well done that the city began to fill with people from the neighboring towns and from other nations, and the Aztecs frequently joined with these people in marriage. Thus the Mexican nation multiplied and the city expanded.

In this way they won over the people of Tezcoco and of all the other towns they could convince of their goodwill. They treated travelers and strangers well; they invited merchants to come to the markets of Mexico-Tenochtitlan with their goods, for such commerce always enriches a city. And this Aztec nation is famed for its hospitality. A man will go willingly to the towns where he is well received and flattered and given to eat and drink, especially if he sees welcoming faces, which is what most appeals to him.

And so it was that during King Huitzilihuitl's time [who was the second ruler with this name], although there were no notable events except those I have described, this king took great pains to increase the size and population of his city, to please the other nations, to invite them to Tenochtitlan, and to seek their favor for the Mexican nation.

The second king of Mexico, Huitzilihuitl

All this was done with a view to the future, starting, as they say, at the feet in order to reach the head; for this is what happened: in time the Aztecs ruled, dominated all.

The Aztecs were saddened by the death of their king and by the fact that his reign had been so short. During Huitzilihuitl's time they had been content to see his efforts to free the city from domination by other people and to increase the area by obtaining more land for his subjects, plots for farming and for other uses. The people were much distressed, however, and all the king's efforts seemed to have been in vain, for they still lacked sufficient land for growing food; the neighboring people blocked their access to the roads and urged their vassals not to sell them maize, beans, and other foodstuffs. Therefore, most of the Aztecs acted cautiously and with fear.

The council members gathered and discussed the coming election and who should reign. The new king should have the aims and desires of the previous one, namely, the enlargement and liberty of the city. The people felt that they now had the will and the strength to take up arms if necessary, and they only lacked a man who would encourage them, instruct them. This type of leader was vital in order to arouse the spirits and spur into action men who were fearful and cowardly, as the Aztecs were at that time.

And so the members of the council, the advisers, decided to choose as king the son of Huitzilihuitl, Chimalpopoca, grandson of the ruler of Azcapotzalco. Though at this time he was only ten or twelve years old, they felt that this would propitiate the grandfather, Tezozomoc of Azcapotzalco, as I shall relate further on.

CHAPTER VIII

Which treats of the third king of Mexico, Chimalpopoca, and the things that occurred during his time.

The entire Aztec community by common consent had elected Chimalpopoca, a boy of ten years, son of Huitzihuitl the Second, and everyone in the city was well pleased. They placed the child upon the royal seat and, after having crowned him with the diadem and anointed him with divine ointment,[1] they then gave him the royal insignias: in his left hand they placed a shield[2] and in the right hand a sword with [obsidian] blades in it. They dressed him with the garb and weapons of the god they wished him to represent. All of this was a sign that he had sworn to defend the city and die for his people.

In this way Chimalpooca, the favorite of his grandfather, Tezozomoc of Azcapotzalco, was invested, He reigned for some years and during this time the Aztecs visited Azcapotzalco with more frequency, the people of both cities dealing with each other in a more familiar way. One day the principal men went to their king Chimalpopoca and said: "Lord, we all have decided that since your grandfather Tezozomco loves you so well and will listen to you, and since we have become friends with the people of Azcapotzalco, we should ask him to give us some of the water from the Chapultepec springs. We shall use it for drinking and we shall find a way of conveying it to the city. [But we must ask for it first.] Up to this time we have lived in huts and in wretched hovels but now we are beginning to build houses of stone and adobe. We are also beginning to dam up the lagoon and we possess canoes that go about the canals. But we still drink troubled, dirty water. That is why we beseech you to send your messengers to ask for this favor."

Chimalpopoca listened to these words and they seemed right to him. He agreed to send envoys to the king of Azcapotzalco to request

---

[1]See chapter VII, note 3.
[2]If a man is right-handed the obvious way to hold a shield is in the left hand. Nevertheless, the left side was considered the preferred side. One example is found in book 6 of the *Florentine Codex* (chapter IX), when the new ruler addressed the god Tezcatlipoca, stating that those who would become lords would become rulers, would be surrogates of Tezcatlipoca; they would be placed "on the left . . . in obsidian sandals" (1969:41).

that water be sent from Chapultepec to his city. The envoys, carrying presents and the usual gifts of flowers and other things they were accustomed to take on such a visit, soon arrived before the king of Azcapotzalco. After they had made their plea, he told them to rest and feel at ease while he asked the opinion of his chieftains, then he would give them an answer. These officials were consulted and agreed that the Aztecs were welcome to the water since Azcapotzalco received no benefit from this water and in no way would they suffer from its loss.

The Aztecs rejoiced greatly in this and, carefully but quickly, began to take out blocks of earth and make rafts of rushes to create an aqueduct for the water to come through. Very soon, with the aid of stakes and canes, earth and other materials, the water began to come into the city. It was a difficult task because the aqueduct was built on the lagoon and constantly crumbled due to the great impact of the water; also, the conduit was made of clay.[3]

The Aztecs, desiring that matters with Azcapotzalco come to a head so they could become free of their vassalage, a condition they greatly desired, and incited by malice, again sent messengers to the king of Azcapotzalco. They informed him in his grandson's name that the water he had given them was useless, since it traveled in earthen ditches and thus was easily lost, or the clay conduits were destroyed. They also requested him to supply them with wooden stakes, stone, and lime and to order his vassals to construct a conduit of stone masonry that would be solid and unbreakable, through which the water could pass without seeping away.

King Tezozomoc was not pleased at what he heard, though he did not show his anger to the envoys. He told them he would speak to the men of his council and would then tell the Aztecs their decision. Thereupon he called his advisers together and told them of the demand that had been made. When they heard this, they responded: "Our lord and king, what is in the minds of your grandson and of his advisers? Do they think we are to be their slaves, their vassals? Is it not enough that we gave them shelter, that we admitted them to our territory, that we permitted them to build their city, to live here? Have we not given them the water they requested? And now they demand, in a shameless manner, without respect for your royal dignity, that you and all of us serve them, that we build a pipe for their water? We cannot permit this; it is not our will. We would rather lose our lives! Even

---

[3] Clay drainage pipes were not unusual in Mesoamerica. In the archaeological zone of Cholula many of these can be seen, formed of pots open at both ends, fitted one into another. Cholula's drainage system is earlier than Tenochtitlan's, however, and the latter probably was replaced by stone and mortar at a later date, especially in swampy ground.

though King Chimalpopoca of Tenochtitlan is one of us, a kinsman of the Tepanec nation, because of this he has no right to command us in such a despotic way. He is only a child and what he has done has been provoked by his advisers. Let us discover where they have found such daring and insolence."

When they had left the presence of the king, the councillors consulted among themselves. The ruler of Coyoacan, known as Maxtla, was in this reunion, also Acolnahuacatl, lord of Tacuba, and another called Tzacualcatl or Tlacacuitlaua. Lords from these three districts, who disliked the Aztec people, plotted against them. They decided they would not only refuse the demand but would take away the water that had been given the Aztecs, who were then using it. They also agreed to destroy them, doing away with them to a man and leaving no trace of the place called Mexico-Tenochtitlan.

This decision having been made, the leaders of Azcapotzalco, Coyoacan, and Tacuba began to rouse the common people. They armed them and inflamed them against the Aztecs, telling them that these people wanted to make tributaries, slaves, of them. In order to express their anger more clearly and to create war, they gave orders that from then on no one in Azcapotzalco would be allowed to trade or deal in the Aztec city, nor introduce there foodstuffs or merchandise, under pain of death. In order to achieve this they placed guards along the roads so that the people of Mexico-Tenochtitlan could not enter Azcapotzalco, nor the people of the Azcapotzalco region enter that city. They prohibited the Aztecs from using the forests that formerly had been accessible to them and where they had gathered firewood. Furthermore, the Aztecs were denied the use of all the other entrances and exits to the Tepanec territory.

When the king of Azcapotzalco saw that his chieftains were enraged and that they were determined to declare war on the Aztecs, to destroy them, he wished to prevent this. But seeing that this was impossible, he begged the men who had made this decision to kidnap the king of Tenochtitlan, who was his grandson, so that he not be destroyed along with the others. Some agreed with the king but Maxtlaton[4] and Tlacacuitlaua refused to agree, claiming that even though Chimalpopoca came from the lineage of the Tepanecs, this relationship was through a woman, that because on his father's side he was the son of an Aztec, he would always be inclined toward his father's people and not his mother's. The chieftains refused to give in to the king and stated that on the contrary Chimalpopoca should be the first to die.

[4]Maxtlaton and Maxtla are the same.

The king was so distressed when he heard this response, so saddened to see that he could not pacify his people, that he became sick with sorrow and soon died of grief. He died a very old man.[5]

Tezozomoc of Azcapotzalco was dead and the Tepanecs, even more determined to carry out intentions, agreed among themselves to kill King Chimalpopoca by treachery, thereby facilitating the annihilation of the Mexican nation. They sealed this conspiracy by solemnly vowing to carry out this evil plan. At night, when all was silent, they secretly sent men to Mexico-Tenochtitlan, where the murderers entered the palace while the guards, careless, were asleep. Finding the ruler unprepared, they slew him and his son Teuctleuac, who was sleeping beside him.[6]

The next morning, when the noblemen of Tenochtitlan went to greet their king as was customary, they found him and the child dead, covered with wounds. The people became inflamed and set up a great clamor as the news of the disastrous death of the king spread throughout the city, and every man took up his arms. One of the officials, however, tried to control them, to calm them, saying: "O Aztecs, compose yourselves, let your hearts be calm. Behold, rash deeds never turn out well. Do not forget that though our king is dead, the lineage of the nobles and of his generation has not ended with Chimalpopoca; we still have descendants of the past kings who are the princes of Mexico-Tenochtitlan. Which leader, which head of the country, will you choose to guide you with valor? Do not act blindly, with passion! Control your bold hearts. First elect a king to guide you, to give you courage, who will be a shelter against your enemies. Be not deceived by the passion you feel now. You must be prudent: feign tranquillity and prepare to celebrate the funeral rites of your lord and king who lies dead here before you. The time for vengeance will come later!"

Thus, the Aztecs, who had felt this offense so deeply, nevertheless were pacified and showed none of their feelings before their enemies.

---

[5]Tezozomoc formed a great empire by means of intrigues, marriage alliances, and successful military expeditions. The Tepanecs of Azcapotzalco conquered the entire Valley of Mexico and extended Tezozomoc's domains into the Valley of Toluca, to Puebla, and far south toward the Pacific Coast. His reign was one of the longest in history, lasting from 1343 to 1426, a period of eighty-three years. By 1428, when the Aztecs conquered the Tepanec empire that had been formed by Tezozomoc, they acquired a vast domain including hundreds of tributary towns. The sixteenth-century author of the same name (see bibliography) is of course a different Tezozomoc.

[6]Chimalpopoca has been said to have been ten years old, yet here he has a son. The plot to have him killed by assassins of Azcapotzalco must have developed and festered over the years, something Durán fails to explain. Chimalpopoca is said to have ruled from 1417 to 1427 (see chronology of Aztec kings).

On the contrary, they pretended to ignore the offense and feigned friendship while they prepared their plot, the vengeance for the assassination, planning how to manage this. So they invited many guests to the funeral ceremonies of their king, including all the leading men of Tezcoco and Colhuacan.

After the rites had ended, the Tepanecs reproached the envoys of the other communities for attending the funeral, though these envoys had been displeased and offended by the terrible assassination committed by the Tepanecs. The Aztecs begged these people to be calm, not to oppose them or to favor the Tepanecs; nor did they wish favor or help from anyone except from their god the Lord of All Created Things. With the strength of their arms and the courage of their hearts they were determined to avenge the wrong committed against them, to destroy Azcapotzalco or die.

Friendly people of neighboring towns promised not to oppose the Aztec people, or go against them in any way. Since the Tepanecs of Azcapotzalco had closed the roads and routes in the mountains and by water to Azcapotzalco, and had cut off all access to supplies and trading in their city, these other people opened their cities to the Aztecs for the whole time the war was likely to last. In this way the Aztec women and children would be able to go by land or by water to these friendly towns, to obtain necessary merchandise and take it to Tenochtitlan. The Aztecs were delighted with this treatment and gave thanks to their friends. Then with great humility they begged them to attend the election of a new king. The neighbors agreed to this and came to the city for the election.

The Aztec council met to choose the new ruler, and one of the elders delivered the speech that was customary on such occasions. In those times there were great orators and speechmakers who on any occasion could talk lengthily and beautifully and most delicately, filling their addresses with profound rhetoric and remarkable metaphors. Those who speak this [Nahuatl] language will agree with me on the profundity and excellence that it carries within it. I dare to affirm, after many years of studying it, that I still find new things, new words, and most elegant metaphors to learn.

The elder who was to be the first orator stood up in front of everyone and began his talk.

> O Aztecs, you now lack the light of your eyes, though you do not lack it in your hearts. The one who was the guide and light of this Mexican republic is gone, but the fire in its heart is still burning. Although one leader has been killed, there are still many who can fill the void left by him. The noble lineage of Mexico-Tenochtitlan does not end here, nor has the royal blood perished. You can see the noblemen of Tenochtitlan

around you in their correct order. Not one nor two, but many excellent princes, sons of Acamapichtli, our true king and lord. You must choose: this one I favor, this one I do not. Though you have lost your father, here you will find a father, here you will find a mother. Understand, O Aztecs, that for a short time there was an eclipse of the sun, the earth grew dark, and afterward the light shone upon it again. If Tenochtitlan grew dark because of the eclipse of its monarch, let the sun come out again: elect a new king. But observe carefully the one on whom you cast your eyes, the one your heart desires, for the man you elect is the chosen one of your god Huitzilopochtli!

When the speaker had finished, Itzcoatl, a natural son of Acamapichtli, was chosen king by common accord. It will be remembered that we said he had been born of a slave girl from Azcapotzalco, yet he had turned out to be so courageous, a man of such exemplary customs, that he outshone all his brothers. Thus, Itzcoatl was elected, to everyone's satisfaction. The lords of Tezcoco were especially pleased because the father of Nezahualcoyotl, Ixtlilxochitl, who was at that time reigning in Tezcoco, was married to a sister of the new king Itzcoatl. In later times Nezahualcoyotl was to regain his kingdom through the favor and with the aid of Itzcoatl, after having fled from the Tepanecs, who wished to assassinate him.[7]

So it was that Itzcoatl, after the death of his nephew, occupied the royal seat. One of the orators spoke:

"O our son, lord and king, keep up your courageous spirit, be strong and firm. Let not your heart grow faint, do not lose the spirit necessary for the royal burden that had been placed upon you. If you become weak, who do you think will come to encourage you, will give you strength for governing and for defending your state, your kingdom? Do you think, by any chance, that the valorous ones, your mighty ancestors, fathers and grandfathers, will come to life again? O great lord, they have passed from this life and nothing is left but the shadow of their memory, of their strong hearts and of the might of their arms and chests with which they faced affliction and labor. Your ancestors have been hidden away by the Lord of All Created Things, of the Wind and of the Night and Day.

---

[7]Nezahualcoyotl, ruler of Tezcoco from 1430 to 1472 (Alva Ixtlilxochitl 1985:II:135–36), was an extraordinary man. He codified the ancient laws of Tezcoco and founded an immense library. He himself was a fine poet. Several of his compositions, recorded in the European alphabet shortly after the Spanish conquest, still form part of the national literary heritage. As an engineer Nezahualcoyotl was active in the urbanization of Mexico City and in building its aqueduct. On the outskirts of the present-day city of Tezcoco, at Tezcotzinco, Nezahualcoyotl built magnificent botanical and pleasure gardens.

"Will you let your country fall, be lost? Will you let slip from your shoulders the burden that has been placed there? Are you going to permit the old men, the old woman, the orphan and the widow to perish? Would you, perchance, let them suffer? Courage, courage, O valorous prince! Do not gasp, lose breath. Behold that the nations are against us, that they scorn us and have contempt for us. Have pity on the babies who are just beginning to crawl upon the ground. They will die if our enemies prevail against us. Prepare to open your mantle to shelter your children, who are the people, the poor ones. They have faith in the shade of your mantle and in your benevolence. Mexico-Tenochtitlan is joyful and proud of this shelter. The city was like a widow but the husband, the spouse, has been reborn. Let him come back and give it the sustenance it needs. My son, do not fear the work or the burden; do not be troubled. The god whose image, whose likeness, you are favors you and will aid you."

When the Tepanecs, people of Azcapotzalco, Tacuba, and Coyoacan, heard of the new election, they were sorely grieved and angered. Again they placed guards on all the roads. They felt vulnerable so they guarded the causeways to Tacuba, to Chapultepec, and to Tlatelolco. The people of Azcapotzalco were not permitted to go to Tenochtitlan and those of Tenochtitlan could not go to Azcapotzalco. The Aztecs, seeing that the situation was serious, that the Tepanecs of Azcapotzalco openly showed themselves to be enemies, that there was no hope of peace and friendship but that war was imminent, began to arm their men and to prepare for the coming hostilities.

Up to that time the Aztecs had been intimidated and had had litle experience in the arts of war.[8] It was the courage of the king, his valor, that led the common people and the nobles to take spirit. Our Lord decreed that there be at that time a brave man among them by the name of Tlacaelel, a nephew of Itzcoatl, son of his brother. Tlacaelel was to become the greatest warrior, the bravest and the mightiest, that the Aztec nation ever had. He was the wisest, the most cunning, man in the arts and science of war ever found in Mexico-Tenochtitlan. All these things will be described later in this history.[9]

---

[8]It is doubtful that the Aztecs had been both timid and inexperienced in war, since they had once been mercenaries for Colhuacan. The *Codex Boturini* (*Tira de la Peregrinación*) depicts a scene in which the Aztecs, fighting for Colhuacan against Xochimilco, took so many prisoners that they brought back only the ears in large sacks. The Colhuacan ruler was so disgusted at the scene and the smell that he is shown turning his head away.

[9]Tlacaelel must have been a true historical figure, but his long-lived importance as adviser to a number of rulers, as described by Durán, suggests that "Tlacaelel" may have been a title, similar to "Secretary of War."

CHAPTER IX

Which treats of the election of King Itzcoatl and how he liberated the city of Mexico-Tenochtitlan, with a description of other things that occurred in his time.

So it was that in 1424 Itzcoatl was elected to the royal seat and the people of the city were pleased, they were comforted by the choice of the council. The king immediately began to prepare for war, to equip the army with the necessary supplies. It was evident that an attack by Azcapotzalco was imminent; therefore, the people of Tenochtitlan were on the alert, they kept watch with much care. But the common people, aware of the strength of the Tepanecs, were sorely afraid and feared that victory would be impossible. Many of them, filled with dread, filled with timidity, tried to persude the king and his officials to make peace. Their tears and apprehension dismayed the ruler and the members of his council. So they went to the people, asking [these fearful men] what they wished to be done.

The commoners responded that the new king of Azcapotzalco seemed to be a merciful man and the best course would be to carry their god Huitzilopochtli to Azcapotzalco and deliver him there to the new ruler. With great humility they then would offer themselves to this king for him to do with them as he wished. Perhaps in this way he would pardon the people of Tenochtitlan, give them a place to live in Azcapotzalco and mix with the inhabitants of that city. With this plan they were on the verge of offering themselves as slaves to Azcapotzalco.

This miserable suggestion offended the courageous Aztecs. Nevertheless, some of the leading men considered this to be good advice. They claimed that little by little, almost unnoticed, they could penetrate into Azcaptozalco, aided there by friends and some people in that place who already were known to them. Thus they could introduce their gods into Azcapotzalco and take refuge there. They were prepared to carry out this plan and went so far as to call the guardians of their god Huitzilopochtli and order them to take the statue of the deity upon their shoulders and prepare to depart.

In this same way chapter VI of the Book of Joshua in the Bible describes how the priests were ordered to carry the Ark of the Covenant on their shoulders, while all the people were lined up in order, surrounding the ark. At the same time seven priests played their trumpets, the very ones that were played in the year of the Jubilee. This was done seven days in a row until they entered the city of Jericho.

And so the Aztec priests took their god upon their shoulders to go among the enemy with the idea of pacifying the people of Azcapotzalco and of living among them. [They thought that their god Huitzilopochtli] would put fear and terror into the hearts of those people. When they were about to leave, a valiant youth by the name of Tlacaelel, nephew of King Itzcoatl, came forth and exclaimed: "What is this, O Aztecs? What are you doing? You have lost your wits. Wait, stay still! Let us consider this matter more fully. Are you such cowards that you feel you must take shelter in Azcapotzalco?"

He then turned to the king and said, "Great lord, what is this, how can you permit such a thing? Speak to your people. Seek a way to defend our honor; let us not offer ourselves to our enemy in such a humiliating way."

On hearing this, the king turned to the people who had gathered there and addressed them thus: "Are you still desirous of going to Azcapotzalco? This seems to me a slavish act. I wish to have a court that will honor us, not be dishonored. Here you are before me, all the lords and principal men, my uncles, brothers, and nephews, all courageous, all esteemed men. Which of you will venture to appear before the king of Azcapotzalco to hear his decision and that of his people? If they still wish to destroy us and wish not to revoke this decision, they will have no compassion, will not pity us in our difficulties, in our distress. But here you are all present, so whoever wishes to do this, let him rise and be on his way. Lose your fear, O Aztecs."

But although King Itzcoatl repeated these words many times, there was not one among the men present who dared take a message to the king of Azcapotzalco, for fear of being killed by the people of that city.

When the king and his nephew saw that all were afraid to accept this challenge, Tlacaelel the nephew exclaimed in a loud and brave voice: "Lord and king, let not your heart be timorous, do not become disheartened. Although these lords, your brothers, your relatives and mine, are present here, not one replies to your plea, they simply look at one another. Therefore, I offer myself to go to Azcapotzalco to carry your message as you wish, since I do not fear death. If I were to live forever and never die, my decision would still be the same. I well know that I must die someday and it matters little whether it be today or tomorrow. Why should I wait? How could I die a better death than by defending the honor of my homeland? Therefore, O lord, I wish to go."

"I am gratified, my nephew," answered the king, "by your bravery and courage, by your decision. If you undertake this task, I promise to reward you with generous gifts and to make you one of the leading men of my kingdom. And if you die in this mission your children will receive these favors. You will be remembered eternally for this brave act because you will die for your country and for the honor of the Aztec people."

Tlacaelel's daring was received with ill favor since it was obvious that his life was at stake. But the king had singled him out among all those present, considering that by risking the life of one the lives of all could be spared, and although this saddened the ruler he ordered [his nephew] to go. Tlacaelel prepared himself as best he could and departed from the city.

Boldly he approached the two guards at the gate to Azcapotzalco. One was armed and the other, who accompanied him, was without weapons. When Tlacaelel arrived they asked, "Who is this impetuous one who comes? Are you not the nephew of Itzcoatl, the king of Mexico-Tenochtitlan? Are you not called Tlacaelel?"

He answered yes, that he was Tlacaelel.

"Where are you going?" they asked. "Do you not know that we have been commanded to forbid any Aztec, any person born in Tenochtitlan, to enter the city, and that we have been ordered to kill him if he tries?"

Tlacaelel responded, "I well know what you have been commanded, but it is also known that messengers are not to be blamed. And I am an envoy to your king from the sovereign of Tenochtitlan and his chieftains. So I beg of you to allow me to pass. I assure you that I shall return by the same way and if then you wish to slay me I shall put myself in your hands. However, allow me now to present my message and I promise you that you will not be punished because of this."

The guards were convinced and allowed Tlacaelel to pass, whereupon he went straight to the king and made the accustomed reverences. The ruler, who recognized him, was amazed at Tlacaelel's presence and asked him, "How have you managed to enter the city without being put to death by the guards?" Tlacaelel explained the manner in which he had entered Azcapotzalco, and the king asked him what he wished. Tlacaelel relayed his message: that he had come to sue for peace and request mercy for his city, for the old people and the children who would suffer if war were to break out. Tlacaelel besought the king to calm the wrath of his chieftains, for the Aztecs wished to continue to serve the people of Azcapotzalco as they had done up to that time.

The king was inclined to listen to the plea and told Tlacaelel to go on his way with good fortune. He said he would speak to his councillors and try to placate their wrath, but if he failed the matter was no longer in his hands. The courageous young Aztec asked when he could return for an answer and was told come back the following day. Tlacaelel asked for some security in order to pass the guards so they would not kill him, since he was only a messenger. The ruler, however, answered that his only security would be his own cunning.

Tlacaelel, on seeing how little the king could do in this case, went around the city until he reached the guards, now a larger number and more fully armed. He greeted them and spoke these words: "My brothers, I have just spoken to your sovereign and I carry an answer to mine. If you will allow me to pass I shall be grateful. I have come here to talk of peace and I deceive no one. I must return to my city to settle this matter. Whether you kill me today or the next day matters little, since I give you my word I shall place myself in your hands tomorrow." Thus the guards let him pass.

The king of Tenochtitlan and all the people were filled with gladness at the return of Tlacaelel, who then explained what had taken place and said that the next day he had to return to Azcapotzalco for the final answer. Therefore, on the following morning, he went to the king and requested permission to finish these negotiations. The king answered him, "My nephew, I am filled with gratitude for the care and diligence you have shown in this affair, and the way you have risked your life. What you must do now is tell the ruler of Azcapotzalco that I wish to know if his people are determined to abandon us, to forsake us, or if they would admit us again to their friendship. If he answers that there is no remedy, that he must annihilate us, then take this pitch with which we anoint the dead and smear it upon his body. Feather his head as we do to our dead and give him the shield, sword, and gilded arrows, which are the insignia of a sovereign; warn him that I say he must be on his guard since we shall do everything in our power to destroy him."[1]

Tlacaelel, carrying the pitch and feathers, proceeded to Azcapotzalco, where the guards, respectful of him because he was a man of his word, allowed him to pass. Yet they were determined to seize him within the city and kill him there. Tlacaelel went before the king and addressed him in the following way: "O powerful sovereign, your subject and vassal, Itzcoatl of Tenochtitlan, lord of your vassals the Aztecs, wishes to know the decision of your advisers. Are you going to carry out that which you have begun, or are you, O lord, going to favor us, your subjects? Will you abandon us or will you continue to be well disposed toward us, as you have up to now?"

[1] In Aztec times, on declaring war, it was the custom to send messengers to anoint the enemy chieftain for death with unguent and with *tizatl* (chalk) and to exchange weapons as a sign of battle.

"Tlacaelel my son," the king answered, "what can I say? Even though I am the ruler, the people of my realm have decided to wage war on you. What can I do? If I try to oppose them I risk my life and that of all my children. My men are bitter and wrathful against you and demand that you be destroyed."

"Very well, O lord," responded Tlacaelel, "your vassal, the king of Tenochtitlan, sends you this message: take care, be strong, prepare yourself: from this moment on he challenges you and your people. He is now your mortal enemy and either he and his people will be slain upon the battlefield, and some become slaves forever, or this will be your fate. You will deeply regret having begun a thing that you cannot conclude with victory. My sovereign has sent this pitch, which we use as an ointment of the dead, so that it might be rubbed upon you; in this way you can prepare yourself to die. He also has sent you these weapons, the shields and arrows, and has ordered that I anoint you and arm you with my own hands."

The king allowed himself to be anointed and armed by Tlacaelel, and after he had donned the warrior's insignia he requested him to thank King Itzcoatl for his message. He commanded his servants to make an opening in a wall in the back of the palace, through which Tlacaelel could escape. He then said: "Son Tlacaelel, do not go out by the main gate; I advise you that armed guards are waiting there to kill you. I have ordered an opening made in the back of the house, through which you may safely escape and return to your city. However, so that you do not leave without a gift and because of the friendship and bravery you have shown, I wish you to take these weapons, this shield and sword, and defend yourself from those who wish to attack you." Thus the king of Azcapotzalco gave him these things and sent him off to his king. Tlacaelel thanked his protector and escaped through the hole in the rear of the palace. Moving cautiously along secret and little-used paths, he soon left the Azcapotzalco guards behind.

When he found himself within the limits of the Aztec city, he showed himself to the Azcapotzalco sentinels and shouted, "O Tepanecs, O men of Azcapotzalco, how poorly you carry out your task of defending the city! Prepare yourselves, for soon there will not be a Tepanec left in the world! Not one stone will be left upon another, not a man or a woman will be spared. Prepare yourselves to perish in fire and in blood, for in the name of Itzcoatl, king of Mexico-Tenochtitlan, and of all the people of that city, I challenge you!"

When the Tepanec sentinels heard these words they were bewildered and wondered where Tlacaelel had come from. They rushed at him with the intention of killing him, but Tlacaelel faced them all before they could put themselves in order and took the lives of several.

But when he saw other warriors approaching he withdrew, though still fighting bravely, toward the gates of Tenochtitlan, where the enemy abandoned him and returned to the vigil of their city.

War had been declared. The people of Tenochtitlan now knew that it could not be avoided, but the commoners were fearful and requested permission of the king and the lords to leave the city. The leaders reassured the people and the king himself spoke to them. "Do not fear, my children, we shall free you and no one will harm you." But the people replied, "And if you do not succeed, what will become of us?" The king and his men answered, "If we do not achieve what we intend, we shall place ourselves in your hands so that our flesh become your nourishmnt. In this way you will have your vengeance. You can eat us in cracked and dirty dishes so that we and our flesh are totally degraded."

"Let it be as you have said," answered the people. "You yourselves have delivered the sentence. We answer: if you are victorious we shall serve you and work your lands for you. We shall pay tribute to you, we shall build your houses and be your servants. We shall give you our daughters and sisters and nieces for your pleasure. And when you go to war we shall carry your baggage and food and your weapons upon our shoulders and we shall serve you along the way, wherever you go. In short, we shall deliver and subject our persons and goods to your service forever."

The officials, hearing what the commoners offered, what they promised, agreed to this and made the people swear that they would keep their oath. And thus it was done. Then Tlacaelel related to the lords all that had taken place in Azcapotzalco. He also advised King Itzcoatl that there was no time to be lost, since the king of Azcapotzalco had ordered that they were to stay away from that city and going back there would be dangerous.

When King Itzcoatl heard this, he told Tlacaelel to recruit warriors and prepare them for combat. This was done with all possible speed. The sons of past kings were made commanders and so were the brothers and nephews of Itzcoatl together with other relatives of his. When the men were in order, in squadrons, the king spoke to the soldiers, urging them to conquer or die, reminding them of the glorious name the Aztec people had always had in the whole world. He told them that this would be the first great battle in this war and that from it they would bring such honor that other nations would tremble before them. He told them not to be timorous, that the large number of Tepanecs, which reached up into the hills, was unimportant—what really mattered were their own courageous hearts. He ordered them to follow their officers, presenting themselves where they were most needed but in no case advancing without having been commanded to do so. In this way they began to march toward Azcapotzalco in a disciplined and orderly way.

When they reached a spot known as Xoconochnopaltitlan [The Place of the Cactus That Bears Green Prickly Pears], the warriors of Azcapotzalco came out in good order to meet them, carrying shields with insignia richly done in gold, silver, jewels, and feathers, and with splendidly adorned emblems upon their backs.[2]

When the Aztecs saw them coming, Tlacaelel, who was directing the army, suddenly became filled with boldness and courage. He commanded all the officers, the lords, the young recruits who were anxious to do battle, to assemble upon an elevation and to wait for the sound of the drums that was the signal to attack, then to charge against the enemy. The rest of the army, common soldiers who were lacking in spirit, were to remain ready in the rear, waiting for the king's commands, and if the enemy gained ground these soldiers were to approach Azcapotzalco little by little in orderly fashion.

Once all these instructions had been given and the soldiers, with their shields and swords, were lined up against those of Azcapotzalco, King Itzcoatl took a small drum that he carried on his back and began to sound it. At this signal the entire Aztec army let out terrifying yells, whistles, and shrieks, which froze the blood of the enemy.[3] With dauntless spirit the officers and the men in wing formation clashed with those of Azcapotzalco. They struck right and left without order or plan and began to shout, "Tenochtitlan! Tenochtitlan!" In this way they incited all the men, who then began to lose the order in which they had been formed. They struck and wounded with cunning and swiftness, but many of the common soldiers were killed. The Tepanecs were so disconcerted that they fell in confusion; they began to retreat and the Aztecs followed them. The spiritless men who had remained

---

[2] The magnificent back devices can be seen in *Codex Mendoza* (1938:folio 67) or in the *Lienzo de Tlaxcala* (1983:14, 16, 49). Shields with symbolic motifs are shown in the *Mendoza* (1938:27–34 and on other pages), and throughout the *Lienzo*. For mantles or capes with designs referring to the status and provenience of their owners, see *Codex Magliabechiano* (1983:plates 3–9).

[3] The terrifying shrieks emitted by native warriors are described by European eyewitnesses to the conquest, among them Bernal Díaz del Castillo (1939). A particularly vivid account is found in the Conquistador Anónimo (1963:165–81), who writes, "While the natives fight they dance and sing, giving forth the most bloodcurdling shrieks and whistles. Those who are not accustomed to their way of fighting are overwhelmed by their cries and fantastic movements. . . ." These horrifying yells were apparently an excellent psychological weapon, which awed the Spaniards in the early phases of the conquest.

behind, seeing where victory lay, were swept by a desire for glory and attacked the enemy so vigorously that the forces of Azcapotzalco abandoned the field and took refuge in the city.

Tlacaelel, commander of the Aztec army, began to cry "Victory!" and led his men into Azcapotzalco, where they showed no mercy, killing all in their path. King Itzcoatl ordered the soldiers who had remained with him to devastate the city, burn the houses, and spare neither young nor old, men nor women. They were allowed to plunder everything they came across in Azcapotzalco. This was done with no pity but with the greatest cruelty in the world. Not a house was left standing, not a man, woman, or child was left alive, except a few who had managed to flee to nearby fields and slopes.

The Aztecs, following up their bloody victory, like meat-hungry dogs, filled with fury and rage, went after those who had fled into the hills. There they found the Azcapotzalcas prostrated upon the earth. These vanquished men surrendered their weapons, promising the Aztecs lands and service in their homes and fields, and to be their perpetual tributaries. They promised stone, lime, and wood as tribute, as well as foodstuffs such as maize, beans, *chian*,[4] chiles, and all the vegetables and seeds they were accustomed to eat. At this point the Aztecs took pity on them; therefore, Tlacaelel was merciful and ordered the pursuit to cease and his men to assemble. He made those of Azcapotzalco swear that they would fulfill what they had promised. This they did: they swore they would comply with their promise.

The Aztecs returned to their city, victorious and exulting, carrying the spoils they had taken that day. Great wealth had been obtained, for Azcapotzalco was the capital of the Tepanec empire and in the city was concentrated the wealth of that nation. There too had lived the merchants and rich men, all now dead. The Aztecs had lost few men in the battle.

The Aztec chieftains, contented in their victory, reminded the common people what they had promised, that they were not to forget the contract made: that if the nobles defeated Azcapotzalco, the commoners would respect them as lords and would serve them, and inasmuch as they, the nobles, were victorious, this promise must be kept. The people answered that this contract would be fulfilled, that the lords had only to command because they had fought with strength and valor. Therefore, the commoners were ready to serve them in any way they ordered.[5]

[4]*Chian* or *chia* is a type of sage: *Salvia hispanica*.
[5]The Tepanecs of Azcapotzalco already had the type of political system acquired by the Aztecs after the defeat of Azcapotzalco. "Mesoamerican society did not change; all

"Lord," said Tlacaelel to the king, "your noble brothers and cousins who wish such bravery, courage, and fearlessness have gone to war should be rewarded. You well know that the survivors in Azcapotzalco promised us land for our crops. Let us not lose this occasion. Let us go and distribute the land among ourselves since we have won it with the strength of our arms!" The king agreed with this and ordered a count to be made of the nobles who had gone to war and who had distinguished themselves in battle, in order to reward them according to their merits. The count included these men whom I shall mention here, men who were the main cause of the victory.

The first was Cuauhtlecoatl, the second was Tlacahuepan, the third Tlatolzaca, the fourth Epcoatl, the fifth Tzompantli. All these were brothers of King Itzcoatl.[6]

Then a count was made of his nephews: the first was Tlacaelel, the second Huehue Motecuhzoma, the third Huehue Zaca, the fourth Citlalcoatl, the fifth Aztacoatl, the sixth Axicoyotzin, the seventh Cuauhtzitzimitl, the eighth Xiconoc. These were nephews of the king, all descended from Huitzilihuitl the Second of that name. These men were always courageous and strove to win in all the battles in which they fought. They brought glory to Mexico-Tenochtitlan, they conquered much territory though in a cruel way, bearing arms to defend their country. It is admirable that in all the wars in this land the Aztecs never provoked anyone; they were always provoked and incited to fight by others. Generally they asked for peace once or twice before attacking; they were rarely defeated, almost always being the victors.[7]

---

we have is a shift of power from one group and from one city to another" (Pedro Carraso 1971:372). Thus, the Aztecs received a well-established empire on their victory after this war. Whether the nobles and commoners actually made a pact is open to question and the anecdote probably is based on information in the documents Durán consulted. The story of the supremacy of the ruling class in this case may have been used in later times to reinforce a stratified class system. Durán also fails to mention that the nobles were trained as warriors and the commoners were not.

[6]Pedro Carrasco unravels much of the puzzle referring to kinship, family, and marriage (1971:X:349–75). In regard to the ruling lineages, Carrasco points out that marriages between close kin of all types were common. "Moteuczoma . . . married his father's brother's daughter" (1971:370), that is, his cousin. Marriages between members of ruling families in allied cities were frequent. When Durán refers to Itzcoatl's brothers he may mean blood brothers or simply close relatives.

[7]Rewriting history in order to wipe out unfavorable information was not uncommon in prehispanic Mexico. The Aztecs had to be put in a favorable light in order to eradicate their early and probably undistinguished past. The *Crónica X*, official Aztec history, did just that. Also, in Sahagún's *Florentine Codex*, in his description of the Aztecs or Mexitin (1961:book 10:189–97), he tells of a period during which these people were in Tamoanchan: "and how time was recorded . . . The history of it was saved, but it was burned when Itzcoatl ruled in Mexico. A council of rulers of Mexico took place.

But returning [to the aftermath of this war]: the Aztecs went to Azcapotzalco, took the lands, and distributed them among themselves. The largest and best fields were given to the royal government, as the domain and patrimony of the crown. Other lands were distributed among the nobles, and a third group of fields was divided among the barrios, each barrio receiving a certain number of *brazas* to maintain the cult of its gods. These are the lands we now call *calpullali*, that is to say, "lands of the barrios."

In this way the lords of Tenochtitlan and of the provinces came to possess lands as their patrimony and seignory, and thus their children, who followed them, came into possession of these lands, which had been acquired through tyranny and unjust wars. The barrios also obtained property, which is common in these communities.

After the royal house had been given lands, the first one to whom land was awarded was Tlacaelel, commander in this war, who received ten pieces of property, all formerly belonging to Azcapotzalco but in different parts of the empire. But since these are not important I do not mention them here, though I found them named in the *Relación*.[8]

Tlacaelel was awarded all these lands in preference to the others because he was considered responsible for the victory. All the other lords and principal men who fought in that war received two pieces of property each. The commoners who had fought but had been timid and fearful at first and who had sworn to become serfs of the victors, of the nobility, were not given lands or anything else in order to castigate them for their lack of courage. Some, however, who had shown a certain amount of valor and spirit and desire to fight were awarded fields. All the others were treated like people of little daring. They resented this deeply and this discrimination had some bearing on future events.

The barrios were also given one plot each to be used for the cult and collation of the god of each barrio. With the proceeds from tilling the land they could obtain the material most commonly used in ritual, such as paper, rubber, incense, and red ochre paint together with blue and yellow colors, with which they painted the mantles and headdresses of the idols.[9]

They said: 'It is not necessary for all the common people to know of the writings; government will be defamed . . .'" (1961:191).

[8]The *Relación* (history) probably was the *Crónica X*.

[9]While most of the codices or painted manuscripts were written on fine deerskin covered with a coating of white, two types of paper were widely used for ritual purposes. One was made of bark, usually of the wild fig tree, which was soaked for several days in water and then beaten with sticks and the pulp placed on a flat surface to dry. Maguey paper, taken from the leaves of the century plant, was made by a similar method. Most paper was used for ritual purposes: banners, clothing for the

Azcapotzalco was left with so little land that the people could not extend their fields. At this point the Tepanecs of Coyoacan, seeing that their friends and relatives in Azcapotzalco had been ravaged, their houses and fields destroyed, felt grief and anger and a desire for revenge so great that they sent messengers to the surviving lords of Azcapotzalco to tell them of their distress and indignation because of this disaster. They offered their soldiers, their weapons, and everything necessary for a war of revenge.

The people of Azcapotzalco thanked them but pleaded that they be left alone to mourn their disaster, their terrible loss, which "in many years we cannot forget." Thus they dismissed the messengers, who returned to Coyoacan, where they told of the great sadness and distress in Azcapotzalco. They described the burnt, destroyed houses, the temples violated, ruined, the fields covered with the dead, the lands seized and distributed among the Aztecs, the survivors of Azcapotzalco having fled and hidden in the hills and the few who had escaped in the war made perpetual tributaries of the king of Tenochtitlan. The ruler of Azcapotzalco, they continued, having been overthrown, a public edict had been proclaimed stating that from that day on there was to be no king in Azcapotzalco but that everyone was to swear allegiance to King Itzcoatl, who had commanded that never again should there be a king in that city and if this should happen complete destruction would take place again. The people there were to become vassals and tributaries of the sovereign of Mexico-Tenochtitlan.

When the inhabitants of Coyoacan heard this decree, they became fearful. They said to each other, "Let it not be that the Aztecs treat us in this same way, taking our lands and making us their tributaries. Let us be alert, lest moved by their good fortune and by their presumptuousness they attack us." In this they were mistaken, for the Aztecs had no such intentions. They never provoked another nation to war, nor harassed others, unless first they were incited, were aroused to defend themselves, as we shall see in the course of this history.

idols, insignia for priests, and so forth. Bark paper is still made in the traditional manner in certain parts of Mexico (Sandstrom and Sandstrom 1986).

Rubber, native to the New World, was called *ollin* or *olin*. This word also means "motion," because rubber jumps around as if it were alive. Among the people of Mexico it seems to have been used basically for balls in the ritual ball game and for rubber-soled sandals.

The incense referred to by Durán throughout the work is the native *copal*, a resin of a Bursera tree that abounds in the temperate and cool areas of Mesoamerica. As in the Old World, incense was constantly used in religious services in the temples and at the small altars in the homes. In the latter the incense burners may have occupied the position that the candle or vigil light does today. *Copal* is still commonly used all over Mesoamerica, in the cemeteries, on domestic altars, and on pilgrimages.

CHAPTER X

Which treats of how the Tepanecs of Coyoacan waged war on the Aztecs, and how they were vanquished.

The Aztecs rejoiced and were relieved to see their city free and that they now had enough land to work for their sustenance. They also were proud, were contented, with their recent victory. At the same time the lords of Coyoacan had observed and carefully considered (although with little thought to the matter but rather with poor judgment) those dangerous events during which their brothers in Azcapotzalco had fallen, due to their own negligence and obstinacy, like unwise men, without judging the damage they caused or their future danger. These men of Coyoacan, however, failed to take into account the hazards that could befall the people of their city. They were only concerned about retaining their own power, as they saw their kinsmen, their relatives the Tepanecs, destroyed. Therefore, they held a meeting, called the men of the council together in order to prepare their defense against the Aztecs.

The lord of Coyoacan, whose name was Maxtlaton, and his councillor Cuecuech spoke to the people with unbecoming levity: "Friends, Coyoacan has always been famous for the liberty in which its inhabitants have lived. You have seen how Azcapotzalco was destroyed by the Aztecs and how it was stripped of its lands, its dominions. The Tepanecs were massacred, no one was spared, no man or woman, no child or adult, and the few survivors have become vassals and tributaries of Mexico. Would it not be fitting for us to avenge that subjugation lest they conquer us and divide our lands among them, making us their slaves and vassals and the Aztecs our lords? O Tepanecs of Coyoacan, defend your city wisely!

"And if you agree with this," continued Maxtlaton, "we shall make alliances with other nations so that we can destroy the Aztecs. Behold, be aware that the first people we should arouse are the offended ones, the men of Azcapotzalco, by promising them aid and the restitution of their wealth and their lands."

The people received his words with delight, feeling that this was wise advice. They then appointed a messenger, a nobleman by the name of Zacancatl, to become the intriguer, who with trickery and cunning would plant the seeds of vengeance and make alliances with neighboring towns. The first city he visited was Azcapotzalco, where he tried to arouse the spirit of rebellion against the Aztecs, speaking many provoking words in order to incite the people, on behalf of his sovereign Maxtlaton.

They were made angry by his arguments, but the ruler of Azcapotzalco responded, "Behold, Zacancatl, you have made your proposal before all my chieftains and I shall now answer you. What great folly, that of your king and the people of Coyoacan, to ask us to wage war at this point against people as bellicose, cunning, and sly as the Aztecs!

"What strength do I now have after losing my finest subjects, my leading warriors and valiant men, and the old people and the children whose lives were not pardoned? What does your sovereign want now? Are we to see the streets of our city again bathed in blood, covered with entrails, with arms and heads and severed legs? This idea occurs to him now! What ails your king? Why did he not come to our aid when he saw us sword in hand, if he loves our city so much? Why did he remain so still, why did he not send us help? Now that our city has been decapitated, wrecked, destroyed, he finally becomes aware of this, he is full of wrath! Our people have been humiliated and enslaved by the Aztecs, we are their serfs and tributaries. No, we do not wish war or any quarrel with them. Leave us now, take our answer to Maxtlaton your lord: we do not desire involvement, but if he wants to go to war, let him fight without our aid, we are not in favor of this. And come no more with these requests for you will not be welcome."

The noble envoy returned to Coyoacan, where he relayed the message to Maxtlaton, who was disappointed by this reply. Nevertheless, he still decided to go ahead with his aims so he called together all the principal men of his city and addressed them thus: "Go into the streets and proclaim, announce to all that an edict has been issued: without delay all the men of Coyoacan are to prepare themselves and take up arms for the defense of the city and its people against the violent offense the Aztecs plan to launch."

The Aztecs, however, were unaware of this, unprepared, and with no plans for war. But Maxtlaton ordered the roads closed and commanded that no Aztec enter Coyoacan, neither man nor woman, to buy or sell or to carry out any other transaction there. As soon as this command had been announced, soldiers were placed on guard at the three roads that led from Tenochtitlan to Coyoacan, with the order that no Aztec be allowed to pass. This was an unfortunate move: the two cities were neighbors, the Aztecs had done no harm to Coyoacan, and the people of this place were expected to be friends of the Aztecs, help them in their needs, and not intentionally become their enemies, their pursuers, based on no real cause.

One fine day some Aztec women were on their way to the market at Coyoacan with their merchandise, to buy and sell as usual.[1] They had no suspicion that they would be attacked and violated since they knew nothing of Maxtlaton's prohibition. When they reached the place of the guards, the latter came out and, as these men were declared to be enemies of the Aztecs, they robbed the women of everything they carried, then raped them and made them flee. The women, tearful and full of anguish, returned to the Aztec city and told their husbands what had occurred. Everyone was overwhelmed by this disagreeable incident and the king of Tenochtitlan gave orders forbidding the people to go to the market at Coyoacan.

But some persisted, believing that only common thieves had robbed and despoiled the Aztec women. And so, stubbornly going to this market, they continued to be robbed and assaulted by the guards.

The Aztecs realized that this situation had become serious, caused by bad faith, so the king called together members of the council and asked their advice about what measures should be taken. He addressed them: "What is happening? What new thing has Coyoacan invented in order to harm us? They are robbing and insulting our wives and daughters and are stealing their merchandise, and on top of that they do them physical harm. I order that from now on no one, man or woman, go to Coyoacan, on pain of death, and that no one dare do harm to those people of Coyoacan. Leave them alone, they will see what is good for them." After this had been said, no one ventured to go beyond the border into Coyoacan.

When he heard this, the lord of Coyoacan, Maxtlaton, stated to his councilmen, "Observe how the Aztecs no longer come here! They are angry with us. Therefore, be on guard, have your weapons ready for the time when they will be needed. We must fight the Aztecs and these are no ordinary men but are soldiers of great valor. Therefore we shall need not only our own [military] forces but also those of our allies."

He then sent envoys to the people of Xalatlauhco and Atlapulco, who were rough mountaineers, requesting help. The messengers urged them in the following way: "Chichimec brothers, the lord of Coyoacan sends you greetings! He wishes you to aid him against the Aztecs with men, shields, and swords, for both offense and defense. Let the warriors be young, valiant men, capable of facing the foe with daring."

[1] According to Ross Hassig (1985:67–68), "Goods were sold by count and measure, not by weight, and although the Aztecs lacked a unitary system of money, cacao beans, mantas (blankets), quills filled with gold dust, and small copper axes had standardized values and augmented the prevalent barter system. Regulations not only required periodic attendance at the markets but prohibited the sale of goods outside the markets. . . . Of all that was brought into the market, part was paid to the ruler."

The mountaineers of those two towns asked why men and swords and shields were needed. The Coyoacan envoys answered that they were to be used against the Aztecs. But the others asked, "So you wish to fight the Aztecs? Know then that we do not desire this; we are not their enemies, nor do we wish to do them harm. Give this answer, then, to those who sent you and do not return, for this is our final word."

Maxtlaton and the chieftains of Coyoacan heard this firm answer from the mountain people of Xalatlauhco and Atlapulco, and although Maxtlaton was by then sorry he had started something that would have an unhappy ending because on all sides he was being denied aid and reinforcements, he began to console his people, to animate them by asking: what is so important about lands and riches after all? The important thing is to have courage, to forge ahead as best they can. They might end up by becoming slaves of the Aztecs, but in spite of this they have to finish that which had been started.

The king of Coyoacan then followed the advice of his councillors and sent other envoys to Xochimilco, Chalco, and Tezcoco, telling them that he wished to wage war on the Aztec nation and would appreciate their aid in trying to destroy these people, since the Aztecs were the common enemy and all should take up arms against them. He warned his neighbors that the Aztecs wished to conquer the entire land and enslave the other nations, taking away their lands, their dominions, their wealth. [He also stated that] the Aztecs were newcomers, had invaded a land that was not theirs; that they were troublesome and difficult people.

Xilomatzin, sovereign of Colhuacan, the first to answer, replied that he would agree with the decision of the others, but he suggested that all the rulers of the neighboring provinces gather at the palace in Chalco[2] and there deliberate the matter, decide what should be done, so there would be conformity of opinion.

The envoys accepted this decision and took the invitation to participate to Cuitlahuac, Mezquic,[3] and Chalco. There they explained the situation, fervently arguing in favor of the common welfare. All these towns were invited to the meeting that was to be held in the community house at Chalco. All the men promised to attend the gathering on the appointed day in order to form an alliance and pledge themselves against the common enemy, the Aztecs.

[2]The palace or community house was known as the *tecpan* (literally, Place of the Lords). It was used as a meeting house, where policies regarding domestic and external problems were discussed, and maps showing different communal lands were guarded there.

[3]Cuitlahuac today is Tlahuac. Mezquic is now Mixquic. These are two *chinampa* towns in the southern part of the Valley of Mexico, where Chalco is also located.

When Quiztohozin, ruler of Mezquic, received this message from the lord of Coyoacan, he cried out, "I am bewildered, Tepanecs, by your fury against a people who, unless they are provoked and incited, do no harm to anyone. You know that I am of the generation and lineage of the Toltecs of Tula, and according to our traditions we came, we descended, from those Aztecs.[4] Therefore, by no means shall I accept what you propose. I shall not attend that meeting, nor shall I become allied with Coyoacan in such an enormous act of treason. Go with God; do not return, for you will not be well received, and tell your lord Maxtlaton to take care."

Having received this disappointing answer from the ruler of Mezquic, the embassy then went to see King Nezahualcoyotl in Tezcoco. This monarch had recently been made ruler with the approval of his uncle Itzcoatl of Tenochtitlan. The messengers, making the usual reverences before Nezahualcoyotl, made their proposals, distorting the supposed deeds of the Aztecs in many ways. They called them usurpers of Tepanec lands, tyrants, well-known highwaymen, and asked for help in destroying them, in expelling them from the region, since they were an accursed people.

King Nezahualcoyotl, who had listened carefully to all these words, smiled. "Come here, Tepanecs. Are you ignorant of the fact that Huitzilopochtli, god of the Aztecs, fights for them and protects them with all his might? It seems to me folly to try to fight against the gods! I have heard what you plan to do in Chalco and I do not wish to be present at that meeting, nor shall I fight against those who have not harmed me. I wish to observe, to see how you do this and how you come out with this plan. And I warn you that when you find yourselves in difficulties, with your hands on your head, do not complain to anyone except to yourselves. Take this answer to Maxtlaton and do not return here, because you will receive no help from me."

On returning to Coyoacan, the envoys reported to Maxtlaton that, of all the cities they had visited, the people of Chalco, Xochimilco, Cuitlahuac, and Colhuacan had given favorable replies, claiming that the Aztecs should be destroyed and agreeing to meet in Chalco in order to form an allliance. Only Mezquic and Tezcoco had refused this offer and had appeared favorable to the Aztecs.

Maxlaton heard these answers. He hated to lose time so he and his principal men set forth for Chalco. Colhuacan, Cuitlahuac, and Xochi-

[4]Although the Spanish text reads "venimos de esos mexicanos" (we came [or descended] from these Mexicans), the meaning probably is "we came [from Tula] together with the Mexicans"; that is, both groups supposedly descended from the Toltecs. It would have been difficult for the Toltecs to have descended from the Aztecs, inasmuch as their culture was earlier in time.

milco were advised of their departure and all made haste to join them. And so, on a certin day, all gathered in the palace at Chalco. Toteociteuctli and Cuateotl, rulers of Chalco, were present. One of them resided in the principal city we now call Chalco-Atenco and the other in Amequemecan. The representatives of the different cities were received with the great solemnity and honor due their high station. After many polite words, they began to discuss the problem that had brought them all there.

By this time, of course, rumors of this meeting had spread far and wide; the news regarding the possible attack on the Aztecs had reached all the cities and provinces in the region, especially since so many leading men, so many lords, had gathered in Chalco. This congregation awed and frightened the people because nothing like it had been seen before. As the representatives from Coyoacan realized that there was little time to be lost lest the Aztecs obtain help from their friends, they decided to act swiftly in order to win the conflict. All the representatives were gathered, together with the two lords of Chalco, when Cuateotl of Amequemecan spoke: "O Tepanec lords, here we are all together, tell us what you wish, what you seek."

The leaders of the group rose and answered, "Great powerful lords and friends, the reason we are here is this: you know how dangerous the Aztec nation is for us and in the future it will be more so if we do not act soon, if we do not look ahead. Therefore, we ask of you that all act as one, that we surround the Aztecs, destroy them, so there will be no memory of them."

Everyone listened to this short but poorly expressed speech, but no one responded. Finally all turned to Cuateotl, the lord of Amequemecan, requesting that he answer and act as he saw fit. All agreed to do as he said. So Cuateotl addressed the gathering: "Here you are present, O lords of Xochimilco, Colhuacan, and Cuitlahuac, and all the principal men of these provinces. You have heard Coyoacan's proposal, that we destroy the Aztecs. This seems to me to be an impossible task from many points of view, since they have ruled for so many years, they have multiplied and have become united in marriage with the people of all the nations. There are few towns in this region where they have not become our kin, their men marrying our daughters or their daughters our sons. This is one of the reasons why [destruction of the Aztecs] is impossible. Another reason is that their god defends them. And still another: when they are defeated they will beg for mercy and we shall not be able to deny them this. And I should like to know—when they beg for mercy and it is conceded and they become our tributaries—since we are from different provinces, whose vassals will they be? Coyoacan's? No, because my subjects the Chalcas will say that they have waged the war, they were the main cause of the victory, and therefore the Aztecs should serve them and no other people. Xochimilco and Colhuacan and Cuitlahuac will say the same and there will be dissension among us. It seems to me that 'he who has a toothache must take out his own tooth,' as the saying goes. Therefore, I think that those who wish to fight a war should do so independently, and whoever conquers Mexico may keep it. And so, Tepanecs, my opinion is that you should wage your own war by yourselves, and each one here do what is most convenient for him. Take your problem in your own hands, provoke the Aztecs, there you will have your war; we do not wish to be involved."

The other representatives were impressed by Cuateotl's speech; they all agreed with him. They told the Tepanecs, then, that they did not want to help them, to lend them aid. They added that the Tepanecs could wage their own wars whenever they wished to. After this they all returned to their own cities, leaving the Tepanecs sad and discouraged.

When the envoys arrived in Coyoacan and Maxtlaton heard the decision of the council, he said, "O Tepanecs, we cannot turn back now. Must we go into hiding? We have already infuriated the Aztecs and all we can do now is conquer or die. Therefore, take courage, this is the only solution. Lest the Aztecs think we fear them, let us play a trick on them. Let one of our noblemen dress in his warrior's clothing and go spy to see if the Aztecs have guards on the boundary and whether there are signs or rumors of war."

Cuecuech, a great and bold lord, was then dressed in a quilted cotton armor of the kind these soldiers used. He took up his shield and sword and on his head he placed a helmet, also of quilted cotton, in the form of a tiger or lion or eagle such as was customarily worn by outstanding warriors in battle, each insignia according to the fame and glory a man had won. When he reached a place called Temalacatitlan, near Mexico, he looked all around but saw no signs of war, nor did he detect rumors of this. So he took this news to his lord.

Maxtlaton then said to him, "It would be good to invite the Aztecs to the feast of our god. Let them come to honor us and when they are here they will be careless, since they feel we are so inferior, and we shall be able to play a joke on them."

"It would be better, O lord," responded Cuecuech, "if while the feast is going on we kill them all, sparing no one."

But Maxtlaton said that such action was vile treachery and was resorted to only by cowardly men. "We should not consider such dastardly means or act in a perfidious manner, for if we do so the other nations will look upon us as cowards and will have nothing but contempt for us. Let the Aztecs die not through treachery but like men, fighting in the open field." The lord of Coyoacan, though, had another plan: that these men be invited to a feast but that first the Tepanecs prepare themselves, adorn themselves, as best they could. So when the month of Xocotl Huetzi[5] arrived, which was the festival of Coyoacan, the Tepanecs, lavishly adorned and armed, invited the Aztecs to be present. They accepted the invitation and some of the principal men, among them Tlacaelel, went to the feast without fear. Tlacaelel, who was the king's main adviser, said to Itzcoatl, "Lord, we do not want you to go to these festivities, partly because it is not proper that you condescend to a minor chieftain—it would lower the dignity of your majesty and that of the kingdom of Tenochtitlan and partly because we do not know why this feast is being celebrated. In fact, we would not go without weapons of defense, in case they decide to attack us treacherously."

King Itzcoatl was convinced by Tlacaelel's words. He stayed in the city while the leading men of Tenochtitlan went in his place, all on guard in case of attack. These men arrived in Coyoacan, spoke to the ruler and to the noblemen there, giving them as gifts the kind of things found in their lakeside city: fish, frogs, ducks, and greens of different types, all in great quantities. The ruler and the men of Coyoacan were highly pleased thanking them profusely and offering them shelter in the palace. A drum was brought out, a dance accompanied by song began, and many excellent dishes were served. When they had eaten, in place of the flowers that usually were distributed after banquets, each guest was given, by order of Maxtlaton, a woman's blouse and skirt.[6] Placing these before the guests, the Tepanecs said,

---

[5]Xocotlhuetzi, tenth month and festival in the prehispanic solar calendar of 365 days, came at a time corresponding to August and was dedicated to the fall of the fruits, that is, early harvest. The deity honored in this festival was the fire god Xiuhtecuhtli. For a complete description of this fiesta, see Durán's, *Book of the Gods and Rites* (1977:203–9, 444–46), and the *Florentine Codex* (1981:book 2:17–18, 111–17).

[6]Women's garments (the *huipil*, blouse, and skirt) given to the enemy evidently constituted a declaration of war. The commander of the Aztec army, the second most powerful leader (the first being the king), was called the Cihuacoatl in honor of the goddess of that name, and on certain occasions wore feminine clothing. Cecelia Klein (1988:238–278) associates the Aztec cult of Cihuacoatl with the conquest of *chinampa* cities under Itzcoatl; Cihuacoatl was the patroness of Xochimilco and the *chinampa* region. Klein indicates that Cihuacoatl represented a specific sector of the empire (a rich area, a "breadbasket" for Tenochtitlan) whose subjugation marked the foundation of the state. Following this explanation, then, feminine attire worn by men means war, conquest, and subjugation of a people, as well as being a symbol of the goddess Cihuacoatl and the army commander whose title was her name. Wearing her costume "must have been intended to repeatedly humiliate the conquered survivors of the

"Our lord Maxtla orders that we dress you in women's clothing because men whom we have been trying to provoke and incite to war for many days and who are so indifferent to this [seem to act like women]."

The Aztecs allowed themselves to be dressed in this manner, and, wearing the shameful womanly clothes, they returned to Tenochtitlan and presented themselves before their king and described what had taken place. The king consoled them and told them that the insult would in the long run honor them. He charged them not to be sorrowful since he would presently take vengeance, bringing death and destruction to all the Tepanecs. "And inasmuch as you can clearly see that I am determined to avenge you, have guards placed on all the roads and allow not a man or woman, child or old person, to enter our city. And he who attempts this will be killed."

The king continued, "And we shall play a joke on them, as they did on us. Let the guards take ducks, waterfowl, fish, and other creatures from the lagoon that cannot be obtained in Coyoacan. Let them be taken to the gates of that city and there be cooked or toasted in such a way that their rich odor and the smoke that rises from these delicacies will penetrate the city. The women will begin to have miscarriages, the children will become sickly, old men and old women will become feeble and die of longing for the food they cannot have."[7]

The king's orders were carried out: they prepared many loaves of *ezcahuitli*, a type of small red worm that abounds in the waters of the lagoon and is a delicacy for the Aztecs. They threw these loaves into the fire together with ducks, fish, and frogs, and the odor was so strong that it penetrated the streets of Coyoacan. It made the women miscarry out of desire for the food the Aztecs were cooking; it made the children sickly, their mouths watering with craving for those toasted things from the lake; the old men became lax in their bowels from longing, and the women's faces, hands, and feet became swollen. Many became ill and died just from hunger for that food.

Maxtlaton saw the ills that were coming to his city and the harm caused by the smoke from the Aztecs' fires, so he called his councilman Cuecuech, saying, "What shall we do? The enemy is destroying us by making us long for the foods they eat! They have deliberately and with malice come to our boundaries to make this smoke, the odor of which is so appetizing that pregnant women are perishing and children are dying!"

Chinampaneca wars, and thus to intimidate any groups or persons considering rebellion" (Klein, 1988:238–78). See also Brundage 1972:161.

[7]This is another of many references to the importance of lake products in the diet of the people of the Valley (or Basin) of Mexico. See chapter V, note 5.

Cuecuech answered, "What is there to wait for? Let us steal the march on them, let us go into the field. I shall be the first to go." As soon as he said this, he quickly dressed himself in his armor and took up his sword and shield. Unaccompanied, he went to the first place where guards of Tenochtitlan were stationed, a place called Momoztitlan.[8] He challenged the Aztecs, telling them that he had come to destroy them, shouting insults at them, playing with his sword and shield and jumping to and fro.

The Aztecs feared an ambush and not one man went out to confront Cuecuech. Instead, they ordered some laborers and prisoners to build a high scaffold, which was constructed quickly. Then the head of the Aztec forces, Tlacaelel, climbed to the top of it, looked about on all sides, and spied to see if there was an ambush or whether men were concealed anyplace. He saw a little smoke rising out of a field of rushes and suspected that some of the Tepanec army was hiding there. He climbed down and ordered the watchmen to ascend and observe with great care, with caution, to see if anyone left that place and mark where he went. He told his captains not to leave their station, not to move until he returned.

Well armed with his sword and shield, he enterd the rushes and, hidden by them, went toward the place where he had seen the smoke. He emerged from the rushes on a bank that was the boundary of Colhuacan. He spied through the reeds and saw three soldiers, well-armed but careless of their safety. Knowing them to be from Colhuacan and not Tepanecs, he approached them, asking, "Who are you?" They answered, "Lord, we are from Colhuacan and have come to seek our livelihood and to serve you."

But Tlacaelel said, "On the contrary, I believe you to be spies from Colhuacan and that you have come to examine our army in order to attack us from behind. We know that you attended a meeting in Chalco and made a pact with the Tepanecs of Coyoacan."

They smiled and told him, "Lord, we of Colhuacan are not treacherous people but are plain and frank. Treat us as we are."

Tlacaelel inquired their names. One of them said his name was Acaxel, the other Atamal, and third Quilayo. These names were not really theirs; they were false, as they were trying to disguise themselves, being noblemen desirous of gaining glory and becoming distinguished in war. Thus they changed their names, using others, to hide their identity and rank.

---

[8]Momoztitlan means "Place of the *Momoztli.*" The *momoztli* was a shrine placed at crossroads or in marketplaces where some of the gods supposedly sat and rested. Durán (1977:265, 273), says the *momoztli* means "daily place" or shrine and is taken from *momoztlaye,* meaning "every day."

"Well, friends," spoke Tlacaelel, "my name is Tlacaelel, I am the head of the army of Mexico-Tenochtitlan. Since you have come to gain glory I request one thing of you: do not move from this place, do not go away but wait for me until I return. Should soldiers from Coyoacan come here, kill them without mercy."

The noblemen agreed to this and the Aztec chieftain returned to his people, where he found King Itzcoatl exhorting his troops. The sovereign was told how Tlacaelel had met the three men from Colhuacan, young men eager [to aid the Aztecs], using false names, how he had asked them to wait at a certain point for his return and how they had promised to do this.

At that moment the watchmen climbed down from the scaffold and cried out that the troops were approaching in battle formation. Tlacaelel asked the king to remain with his men, then to move toward the Tepanecs and face them, while he took a company of soldiers, led by two captains, to rejoin the three disguised noblemen he had left in the marsh near Colhuacan. The king agreed, telling Tlacaelel to go, to be as courageous as his will and adroitness permitted. So Tlacaelel went among the reeds with his small company, where the three from Colhuacan were waiting. He gave them new swords and shields bearing the insignia of Aztec warriors. With great caution they began to march toward Coyoacan in order to attack the enemy from the rear. By this time a great battle had begun between the Tepanecs and the Aztecs led by their king. The fighting was so fierce, the attack so violent, and the shouting on both sides so loud that it could be heard far away.

In the midst of the battle, in which neither side seemed to be winning, Tlacaelel and his men suddenly broke from cover, shouting, "Mexico! Mexico! Tenochtitlan!" and ferociously attacked the Tepanecs, slaughtering them without mercy. Seeing themselves surrounded, the Tepanecs began to retreat. Tlacaelel and his soldiers performed such bold and courageous feats that no man dared face them but fled before them as though they were wildcats. The Tepanecs, retreating toward their city, intended to use their temple as a last stronghold, but Tlacaelel and the three Colhuacan warriors reached the temple before them and, taking possession of its entrance, ordered one of his men to set it on fire.[9] When this was done, those inside could not defend themselves and were taken prisoner. The inhabitants of the city, having lost heart, went toward the hills, followed by the Aztecs, who took prisoners and then killed all they captured. The Tepanecs fled up the slopes of the Axuchico mountain and from here cried out loudly,

---

[9] A temple on fire in the pictorial codices signifies conquest.

their hands crossed in front of them, begging the pursuers to spare them, since they had already surrendered. They also begged the victors to put down their weapons, to cease fighting, to rest, for their vengeance was complete.

But the Aztecs answered, "We refuse to pardon you, traitors! The name of Coyoacan will be erased from the face of the earth. Today we shall ravage it and cast it on the ground. The names of the treacherous men who call meetings against us, who provoke others and incite them to destroy us, will be forgotten!"

"What will you gain by destroying us?" the vanquished men replied. "You have done enough. We are now your slaves and tributaries forever, to serve you in all ways. We shall furnish you with stone, wood, lime, clothing, foodstuff, lands, workers for your fields, laborers for your houses — everything you may demand."

The Aztecs, insisting that there would be no clemency, told the Tepanecs to remember the women's clothing with which they had humiliated them. The defeated men admitted that they were guilty of this act and again begged for mercy. With tears in their eyes they promised to serve the Aztecs with their persons and with their goods as long as they lived, contributing not only the work but the materials.

The Aztecs, on hearing this, put down their arms, ceased the attack, and saw that the soldiers from Tenochtitlan who still were infuriated against the Tepanecs were sent home. Some of the Tepanecs who had fled reached Ocuila, Xalatlauhco, and Atlapulco. These towns then became full of refugees, who hid in the hills, the ravines, and the caves.

The victorious Aztecs gathered together their men and returned to their city, rich in slaves, gold, gems, precious feathers, shields and insignia, clothing, and many other spoils, all valuable. Tlacaelel and his three companions, who were mainly responsible for that victory, used a trick in this battle in order to ascertain how many prisoners they had taken. Whenever they captured a man, they cut off a lock of his hair, which was given to the soldiers who guarded him, to hold as a record. In this way they could keep an account of the captives each one had taken. In the end it was found that they had captured twice as many as all the other soldiers; thus they excelled above all.

These four were so highly praised, so exalted as brave warriors, that although they received no other reward or compensation this honor was considered sufficient. They were content at that time, especially since later they were greatly favored above the other soldiers, as I shall explain further on. This Aztec nation always took care to praise and reward their courageous men who distinguished themselves in war or who had special merits [for they were examples for the others].

CHAPTER XI

Which treats of how the lords of Mexico requested of King Itzcoatl that he give them titles of honor; and how he awarded these and also distributed the lands of Coyoacan among them.

After the war with Coyoacan had ended, as we have told, King Itzcoatl returned to Tenochtitlan in triumph and was received and honored by the priests and all the people. Old men and old women wept with happiness, showering thanks and benedictions upon the king, for he had liberated them from the possibility of seizure by Coyoacan and because he had exalted the dignity, power, and strength of the Aztec nation. This victory should not be underestimated but should go down in history and the memory of it be glorified because it was such an important episode in adding luster to the Aztec name; and this could lead to great honor and increased prestige in all the republic.

The king thanked his subjects for the reception and for their courtesy. Together with his noblemen and other subjects he addressed the army, thanking the soldiers for the excellent way they had fought: "O lords, princes, all my subjects, I am aware of your great deeds. I have seen the dauntless spirit with which you have resisted our foes. You have concluded your task, for this is your duty: to raise up the fame of our city, to increase its lands and its waters. This is also the task of our god Huitzilopochtli and that is why he came to us, to gather, to draw to him the service of all the nations, with the strength of his chest and his head. Now rest, be at ease, think about how you wish the lands and possessions of Coyoacan to be distributed. They belong to you since you have won them. I rejoice that these will be given to you, be allotted to you, and that you take possession of them as your own."

"O powerful king," replied the commander Tlacaelel, the most distinguished person present, "we who are your servitors kiss your royal hands for your great liberality, for the favor you grant us. This will be a source of great encouragement for those who doubt, for those who are timid. It will stimulate the children who are just beginning to grow. They will be eager to serve you and willing to die for their king and their country, to fight for the benefit of their persons and their possessions. Let your officials go, take the lands and divide them in any way you wish. However, lord, I beg you to forgive me for that which I shall request in the name of all these peers and leading men.

"You well know, lord, that hardships and efficiency are to be rewarded. These men conquered Azcapotzalco at the risk of their lives, suffering the attacks, the resistance of those valiant Tepanecs. You have also seen how many men of great valor went to war against Coyoacan, a city just defeated. Therefore, in the name of all these brave warriors, I beseech you that, as a compensation they fully deserve, you give them titles of distinction according to their merit."

Itzcoatl answered that he would be pleased to award these titles. He called all the nobles and officials together and they went to the king's chambers where the royal seat was found. He ordered them seated in this great hall and asked Tlacaelel to explain the matter to them, which he did in this way: "Friends and brothers, your lord and sovereign King Itzcoatl, my close relative and yours, greets you and wishes to honor you according to your merits. He wishes to give you preeminence, award you titles, as well as distribute among you lands that will support you and your families; for this is your right."

The warriors replied that they were filled with gratitude for the favor granted them. They claimed that these were due to the king's kindness, for they were unworthy of such magnanimity. They again promised to serve the ruler with their lives, their honor, their property, their wives and children, all at his service and for his defense.

Tlacaelel took this response to the king, and they began to consider which titles the noblemen should receive. I do not wish these great and honorable titles to be forgotten and therefore I shall take pains to copy them here in our Spanish language so that their significance be understood. It suffices to say that just as Our Lord, the King of Spain, gives titles to his great men, such as Duke, Count, Marquis, Viscount, Archduke, Master of a Military Order, Admiral, and Governor of a Conquered Province (like the Philosopher, who states that it "is ineffectual to give many reasons for something that can be said with one"), we could say that this also could refer to [the abundance of] titles given by King Itzcoatl to his noblemen, which are the following:[1]

First, the commander Tlacaeleltzin was given the title Tlacochcalcatl Teuctli.[2]

---

[1] The titles granted by the Aztec ruler to his captains should not be compared with modern European titles of nobility. Possibly these distinctions carried more weight in ancient Mexico than a simple title of nobility today.

[2] The -*tzin* as suffix to Tlacaelel's name indicates respect, reverence. Durán explains the first four titles further on in this chapter. The meaning of the others is as follows: Tezcacoacatl: Man from Tezcacoac, "Place of the Mirrored Serpent" or "Place of the Mirror Snake"; Tocuiltecatl: Man from Tocuillan, "Place of the Cranes"; Acolnahuacatl: Man or Person from Acolneuhuac, "Place Next to the Acolhuas" [Shoulders], a bend in the river or curved waters; Huey Teuctli: Great Lord; Temil-

The History of the Indies of New Spain

To Huehue Motecuhzoma was given the title Tlacatecatl.
To Tlacahuepan, the title Ezhuahuacatl.
To Cuatlecoatl, the title Tlillancalqui.
To Huehuezcan, the title Tezcacoacatl.
To Aztacoatl, the title Tocuiltecatl.
To Caualtzin, the title Acolnahuacatl.
To Tzompantzin, the title Huey Teuctli.
To Epcohuatzin, the title Temillotzin.
To Citlalcoatzin, the title Tecpanecatl.
To Tlaueloc, the title Calmimilolcatl.
To Ixcuetlatoc, the title Mexical Teuctli.
To Cuauhtzitzimitl, the title Huitznahuatl.
To Xiconoc, the title and surname Tepanecatl Teuctli.
To Tlazolteotl, the title Quetzaltocatl.
To Axicoyotzin, the title Teuctlamacazqui.
To Yxnauatliloc, the title Tlapaltecatl.3
To Mecantzin, the title Cuauhquauacatl.4
To Tenamaztli, the title Coatecatl.
To Tzontemoc, the title Pantecatl.
To Tlacacochtoc, the title Huecamecatl.5

All of these named here who received titles and distinctions as "grandees," which are, as I have said, equivalent to our titles of Count, Duke, or Marquis, were natives of Mexico-Tenochtitlan, brothers, cousins, and nephews of King Itzcoatl. Not only were these Aztecs given titles for their valor, dedication, and brave deeds, but also the king had stone statues carved of them in order to perpetuate their memory and that of their feats, in order that the Mexican republic honor them. He also had the historians and painters inscribe their lives and deeds with fine brushes and vivid colors in their books.6 In

---

lotzin: Stalwart (Stone) Column; Tecpanecatl: Inhabitant of (or Man from) Tecpan (Tecpan was one of the barrios of Tenochtitlan; also means "palace"); Calmimilolcatl: Man from Calmimilolco, "Place of the Round House"; Mexicalteuctli: Mexica-Aztec Lord; Huitznahuatl: Man from Huitznahua, barrio of Tenochtitlan; Tecpanecatl Teuctli: Lord from Tecpan or of the *tecpan* (palace); Quetzaltocatl: "Plumed Spider"; Teuctlamacazqui: Lord High Priest; Tlapaltecatl: Man of Tlapallan, "Land of Color"; Cuauhquauacatl: Man from "Place of the Wooden or Eagle Heads"; Coatecatl: Inhabitant of Coatlan, "Near the Serpents"; Pantecatl: Man from Pantitlan, "Next to the Flags [or Banners]"; Huecamacatl: Man from Huacaman, "Distant Place."

3Yxnauatliloc is the spelling given by Durán in his sixteenth-century manuscript. Garibay (Durán, 1967:II:99) spells this name Ixnahuatiloc.

4The title is given by Durán in his original manuscript as Cuauhquauacatl. Garibay (Durán 1967:II:99) spells it Cuauhyahuacatl.

5The Durán manuscript spells the warrior's name Tlacacochtoc; Garibay (Durán 1967:II:99) has Tlacochtoc.

6The books were pictorial codices.

this way their fame would grow and spread like the brightness of the sun throughout all the nations. In this same way I have wished this my history to preserve the fame and memory of those heroes so their honor may last as long as my work lasts and may be an example for all those who love virtue. Let their memory be a blessing, since such men are the loved ones of humankind and of God, similar to the saints in Paradise. This is the only type of fame that is worth perpetuating.

After the honors had been given to the Aztec lords and warriors, the three allies from Colhuacan came forth. They were offended by the fact that they had been ignored and complained to Tlacaelel, "Lord, you have not kept your word, your promise. You know that in this war we have not been idle, we showed great courage in serving King Itzcoatl. We should not be defrauded of what our hands have gained for us. We risked our lives in this adventure; do not look upon us as people of low rank. Even though you see we disguised as peasants, we are men of high lineage, worthy of receiving titles like the rest."

Tlacaelel realized that they were right and he took them before the king, together with the two Aztec captains [who had accompanied him when he first met the two Colhuas]. Presenting them to Itzcoatl, he said, "O great, powerful lord, these five men aided me when we attacked our enemies from the rear and destroyed them. Therefore, it is just that they be rewarded like the rest, since they served you as well as the others did. In return for their services they deserve titles so they can be known as noblemen."

The king agreed that this would be fair, that these five were entitled to honors like the others. He awarded one of the Aztec captains the title of valor Cuauhnochtecuhtli and the other Cuauhquiahuacatl.[7] He called the three outsiders from Colhuacan, honored them, and thanked them for their services. He then gave them titles: one was Yopicatl Teuctli, another Uitznahuatl, and the third Itzcotecatl.[8] When these acts were concluded, Tlacaelel dismissed all the lords and warriors gathered there, telling them that the king wished them to go and rest, so they would have respite from the recent toils of war. Pleased and contented, they all went to their homes.

---

[7]Cuauhnochtacuhtli means "Eagle Fruit [Heart] Lord" and Cuauhquiahuacatl Man from Cuauhquiahuac, "Entrance to the Eagle Place." These men may have been awarded entrance into the prestigious Eagle Warriors organization, along with the titles.

[8]These titles can be translated as: Yopicatlteuctli: Lord of the Yopi or Yopitzinco (referring either to the temple or barrio of Yopico in Tenochtitlan or to the Yopi-Tlapanec region in southern Mexico); Uitznahuatl: same as Huitznahuatl—also means "Southerner"; Itzcotecatl: Inhabitant of the Place of Obsidian.

The surviving inhabitants of Coyoacan, seeing the damage they had received, the destruction of their city and their people, the sacking and plundering that had occurred, and the numerous slaves the Aztecs had taken from Coyoacan, were greatly dejected. There was not an Aztec warrior, even of the lowliest rank, who had not taken one or two captives. Inflamed with anger, the people of Coyoacan decided to take vengeance upon Azcapotzalco. Maxtlaton, especially enraged, was determined to deal with that city in a cruel manner. So it would not appear that he was going to make war or cause this to be declared, and because he feared the Aztecs might welcome a situation like that, he sent certain captains of his to Azcapatzalco and ordered them to murder the most important officials there in utmost secrecy.

These perfidious men who were going to commit that treachery left Coyoacan in the afternoon and arrived in Azcapotzalco at sunset. First they blackened and smeared their faces with soot so as not to be recognized. Armed, they then entered the palace of the ruler of Azcapotzalco and did not stop until they reached the place where he and other nobles of the city were assembled. Before these men could defend themselves, the assassins fell upon them, knifing the ruler and other lords and the palace men who tried to defend them. The people in Azcapotzalco began to cry out and make a great uproar; the treacherous men fled the town, stopping for nothing, rushing toward their city.

When King Itzcoatl heard of the murders, he tried to discover the guilty parties but was unable to find out the truth of the matter. Thus were assassinated the highest in office in Azcapotzalco, and from that time on the city lost its importance. It had once been the greatest and most populous city in all the land. It had been the seat of royalty, and it had conquered thirty tributary states long before the Aztecs had dreamed of coming to this land.

But returning to our chronicle: after a few days had gone by King Itzcoatl, mindful of the need to gratify his subjects and all those who had served him, in order to keep them contented, satisfied, and prepared to comply with his service, called his adviser and commander Tlacaelel, who was held almost like the Redeemer of Tenochtitlan as Joseph was [to the Pharaoh in Egypt], for Tlacaelel had animated those who were determined to give themselves up to Azcapotzalco, by encouraging them to resist, with ardor and zeal. The king spoke to him: "Lord Tlacaelel, you know that those who work must be rewarded and paid for their labor. Our men have worked and sweated and it is just that they be compensated. Let them go and receive Cayoacan as their prize, dividing the land among themselves; this is my gift to them." In the name of all, Tlacaelel thanked the king for his favors and told the men, "Go and take possession of the property, this is a valuable gift from the king to you."

When the chieftains heard this, they went to Coyoacan to distribute the lands among them. They were received with honors by the people of Coyoacan, as lords of this place. When they saw that the lands were to be distributed to the Aztecs, the Coyoacan people abandoned the community property so it could be given to the others. The Aztecs then took possession of the lands, saying that these had been won in a just war.

The first to be awarded its share was the royal crown, for the ruler and maintenance of his household. The king and his family, the courtesans, foreigners who came to trade [or discuss state affairs], messengers from other cities—all these would be maintained in part by the fruits of these new possessions. It was customary for the palace to feed the people mentioned here all the time they stayed in the royal house.

After the king and the crown had received property, Tlacaelel was given eleven pieces of land and after him the noblemen were awarded two or three according to their merits. Some received only one, but all were satisfied and felt well compensated. The people of Coyoacan, however, were desolate, they were sad because they were dispossessed of their lands and made tributaries and land workers for their enemies, the Aztecs. Their fate was to become subjects of the Aztec empire, with no possibility of breathing freely, nor hope for well-being, nor for the return of their lands and their possessions. It must be noted that problems caused by one's own arrogance and audacity—without reasoning and forethought—can cause damage through rash judgment as a result of uncontrolled and impetuous passion, and can not only destroy a people but all their followers.

The people of Coyoacan had been tranquil, quiet, well loved by the Aztecs, with only peaceful agreement and communication between them. But provoked by their ruler Maxtlaton (a presumptuous and impetuous man), and on seeing the destruction of Azcapotzalco, they planned to gain more honor than they previously had and win back some of the lost Tepanec property. The Coyoacan people were at that time vain, audacious, thoughtless; they felt it would be easy to conquer the Aztecs. Most of the inhabitants of Coyoacan were seduced by this false opinion, by the mistaken advice; therefore, misfortune fell upon them, as we have seen. Their disgrace was so overwhelming that most of the inhabitants of their city and many from the neighboring towns fled to other places, other cities. Maxtlaton was forced to place guards on the roads and threaten with penalties and punishment [those leaving the city] so that Coyoacan would not be left uninhabited. After that the people cursed him, insulted him with strong words for the harm he had caused them through no fault of their own. Nor had they been forced or driven by the Aztecs, and this was the quarrel the Mexican republic had with them: the real cause of the defeat of Coyoacan by the Aztecs had been the very actions of the people of that city.

And the Aztecs had reached such eminence that now there were lords with distinguished titles in their republic, at the cost of other people.

All the other cities in the region had been greatly troubled at these events, fearing that the Aztecs, self-assured because of so much good fortune, so many victories, could cause harm to them also. Those who most feared were the people of Xochimilco, neighbors of Coyoacan. Among these there were some evil individuals. They disturbed the others, inflamed them against the Aztecs for having had the audacity to create "grandees" and give titles to many warriors, glorifying their republic with lands and fields that had belonged to others. [But before we proceed with the story of] how Xochimilco rebelled against the Aztecs with no motive whatsoever, and before I finish this chapter, I wish to explain something about these titles in our own language, as I promised to do.

First, it must be known that, when a ruler was elected in Mexico-Tenochtitlan, four other lords chosen from among his brothers or near relatives were also elected. They were given the titles of princes and from them was chosen the next king, no others being eligible. Their titles were these:

The first was Tlacochcalcatl, which is formed of the words *tlacochtli*, meaning "propelled lance or dart, or spear," and *calli*, which means "house." It is as if one were to say "Prince of the House of Darts" [or "of the Armory"]. This title was given to a man and his descendants, as in Spain we call a man the Prince of Orange or the Duke of Alba, and those of his lineage are known as the House of Alba.

The second title was Tlacatecatl, from the word *tlacatl*, "man" or "person," which could mean "person from Tlacatlan, Place of People." That is what they called the second nobleman.

The third nobleman was given the title Ezuauacatl, which is composed of *eztli*, "blood," and *uauana*, "to cut or vomit." Therefore, it could be translated as "the one who sheds blood or vomits."

The fourth title given to the fourth nobleman was Tlillancalqui, a word made up of *tlilli*, "soot or blackness," and *calli*, "house." It means something like "Lord of the House of Darkness." It should be known that there was a god of darkness or blackness and that the title of this lord referred to this idol and his house.

These four lords with their titles, having been elected, were made part of the royal council as presidents or judges of the supreme council. Nothing was done without their opinion and if a king died the new ruler was chosen from among them, and from no others. No one could be given the titles and their corresponding positions mentioned above unless he was a son or brother of a king. When one of these had been elected to the royal seat, another was chosen to take his place in the council. It is worth remarking that they did not necessarily elect the son of a deceased king to the throne. As I have said before, the sons did not inherit titles or kingdoms by simple succession but by election. Sometimes it would be a son, sometimes a brother, at other times a cousin who would be chosen king or council member. It was sufficient that he be of the same lineage and a close relative. And thus sons and brothers would succeed one another in irregular succession, if not this time, another time, or still another. The kingship, then, always remained within the same kin.

Each one of these lords had vassals who paid tribute; they had villages, lands that were worked for them and from which they received all kinds of foodstuffs and clothing. I plan to deal with this in a special chapter about the great tributes imposed by the lords of Tenochtitlan on the towns that were subject to them. I shall also tell of the other titles, each one given to a certain lord. These are similar to our Count, Duke, Marquis, court magistrate, *corregidor* or district manager, mayor, councilman, consul, bailiff, officials of the palace, and ambassadors. I shall explain each one, although each title is self-explanatory since the meaning is included in the title; on certain occasions I shall explain some of them more fully.

CHAPTER XII

Which treats of the great discord that arose between the people of Xochimilco and the Aztecs. With a description of how, after much fighting on both sides, Xochimilco was vanquished. And of the great injuries and deaths caused by the Aztecs to the Xochimilcas.

The people of Xochimilco were distressed at the wickedness of the Aztecs in destroying Coyoacan and, fearing a new attack, began to distrust them more each day. The Aztecs gave them no reason for this fear, neither in words nor acts, but rather displayed the same affability and friendliness, pleasant countenance, and agreeable conversation that had been common before this. They came and went to the markets, dealt in trade as they always had. But there are always some who stir up trouble among those whose hearts are already restless, and men of this kind aroused some of the people with evil intentions against the Aztecs. They declared: "People of Xochimilco, we fear that the Aztecs, so confident because of their past victories, will wish to control us also. Without our realizing it they may invade us, take possession of our lands, and then make us farm their fields. It would seem that in order to avoid war and fighting we should go put ourselves in their hands. Let us offer them our city and our property because they will come and possess these anyway."

There were two rulers there, one in the capital city of Xochimilco, called Yacaxapo Tecuhtli, and the other who resided in Milpa [Alta], whose name was Pachimalcatl Tecuhtli. Together they called all the principal men to a meeting and said to them, "What folly is this that has been declared? This thing will not be done or even imagined—that we place ourselves in the hands of the Aztecs! How would we stand, what honor would be left us, if after being rulers and lords we were to turn into vassals, servants of the Aztecs! We shall never sweep the houses or water the gardens of the Aztecs, or be mistreated or serve them water to wash their hands. We shall attempt to keep our dignity! We shall risk our luck and see how we can resist, since something must be done!" All the people of Xochimilco were in agreement with the two leaders. They told these men that they wished this, they desired it, and that steps should be taken in that direction. So this decision was made by all.

Meanwhile, the Aztec women, suspecting nothing, continued to go to the usual marketplaces, which was their custom. And the people of Xochimilco, in order to reassure them, continued to buy merchandise from them: fish and waterfowl. It was at this time that the people of Xochimilco decided to have a meeting and a banquet, during which they planned to perfect their plot against Tenochtitlan. The dishes of food that had been bought from the Aztec merchant women were served at the banquet and then there occurred a prodigious, fearsome thing, which bewildered and frightened everyone. As soon as the people had sat down to eat, the delicacies in the dishes purchased from the Aztec women turned into human hands, arms, heads, hearts, and entrails. In their terror—for nothing like this had ever been seen or heard—the Xochimilcas called their soothsayers and asked what this meant. The soothsayers answered that it was an ill omen for it meant the destruction of the city and the death of many. The lords of Xochimilco, appalled at this, cried out, "Ah, friends, we are lost! There is no remedy for us. People of Xochimilco, prepare to die, because the glory of our city will perish as did that of Azcapotzalco and Coyoacan!"

At this time the Aztecs were not aware that anything was wrong. As far as they knew, the friendship between the two cities continued to exist as it always had. When they needed a small amount of stone and white pine wood for the temple of the god Huitzilopochtli, they were not sure how this request would be received, but they sent messengers bearing gifts to request the stone and wood from the officials of Xochimilco.[1] The envoys, having arrived in Xochimilco, relayed their message in this way, "O, highborn lords! King Itzcoatl and the four council members of Mexico-Tenochtitlan kiss your feet and hands, send you this greeting, and offer you this present. They beg a favor of your lordships, of your greatness, of your generosity. They wish to build a shrine for the god Huitzilopochtli and would like you to permit them to take some heavy stone and some white pine wood from your lands for this building."

Cuauhquechol and Tepanquizqui, two noblemen of Xochimilco, cried out, "What do you say, O Aztecs? What do you seek? Perchance you are drunk? Are you out of your minds that you come here with such a demand? Are we your vassals or slaves, or your servants, that we must provide you with stone and wood and everything you need? Are those who sent you our lords and masters, that we must obey them? Go home, Aztecs, and tell them that we do not wish this, that it is not our will to grant them these things they demand!"

[1] This request was the equivalent of ordering the Xochimilcas to become vassals of the Aztecs. Refusal would mean war.

The messengers returned to their city, where they relayed the harsh reply sent by the Xochimilcas to King Itzcoatl and all the Aztec lords, who were amazed and shocked at this answer. They were sorrowful because they felt no good would come of it. Thereupon Itzcoatl gave orders that no one, man or woman, should trespass upon the lands of Xochimilco lest some unfortunate incident take place, due to the wicked words that had been relayed. And the Xochimilcas were told that they were not to go to Tenochtitlan either.

When the Xochimilcas saw that the Aztecs no longer went to their city as they used to, nor was there communication or trade, some of the lords called a meeting and, after having come to an agreement, said to the other chieftains, "You have seen that the Aztecs no longer speak to us, nor do they come to Xochimilco as before, nor do they wish to see us or deal with us because we have denied them the things they requested. Does it not seem to you that it would be preferable to have peace, to give them the wood and stone they have asked for? This way we would be risking nothing and their friendship would come back to us."

But the ruler of Xochimilco, Yacaxapo Tecuhtli, answered this suggestion, "What are you saying, Xochimilcas? This cannot be, for if we now bow to the Aztecs we would be considered dishonorable. The commoners, the peasants, will rightly condemn us, saying that we failed to defend them, protect them against those who wish to dominate them. If the Aztecs are to conquer us, let it be in a real war, then no one can complain." The nobles were easily convinced by these arguments and agreed.

Thus matters stood, with communication and trade between the two cities prohibited, until one day some Aztec merchants were returning from the Marquesado with loads of cotton that they planned to sell in Tenochtitlan. As they passed through the hills near Xochimilco, soldiers of that city appeared and asked them where they came from. They answered that they were natives of the city of Mexico-Tenochtitlan. Without another word the soldiers attacked them, beat them, took from them the cotton mantles and everything else they carried, leaving them nothing, and having stripped them, robbed them, and wounded them, send them back to their city, Tenochtitlan. The travelers went straight to the royal abode and stood before their king, wounded, beaten, and weeping in distress. They presented their complaint to the king in the presence of all the lords, saying, "Powerful lord, we who stand before you had gone to trade and barter as we always do, and when we came from Cuauhnahuac with the bundles of cotton we usually bring back, Xochimilco soldiers accosted us, robbed us, and beat us as you can see. They said they had been looking for us in order to put an end to us."

The discord between Xochimilco and the Aztecs

When Itzcoatl heard their story, he showed great wrath in his countenance and cried out furiously, "O Aztecs, you have seen how the Xochimilcas have broken the peace without cause. Because of this, have five of your officers and five soldiers, with concealed weapons, go to the biggest maize field you can find on the other side of the boundary of Xochimilco lands and tear out ears or stalks of corn. If people try to defend the field or mistreat you, then strike them, lay blows upon them, but do not kill them. Do, however, devastate the field entirely before armed men come out to attack."

Five officers and five experienced soldiers were then chosen. The ten men went to the first cornfield at the edge of Xochimilco and began to tear out ears of corn and destroy the plants, following instructions. And while they were doing this damage, some Xochimilco men rushed out, tried to defend the field and capture the culprits, whom they knew to be Aztecs. But the Aztecs, turning against the Xochimilcas, clubbed them, severely injured them, and then devastated the fields. None of the corn could be saved. When armed defenders appeared, the Aztecs were already on their way back to their own city. They immediately went to Itzcoatl and told him all about the destruction of the Xochimilco fields.

When Itzcoatl consulted his men regarding this matter, Tlacaelel, the war commander, and the four supreme councillors advised him, "Lord, our opinion is that we should not be responsible for breaking off relations with Xochimilco. Let us send a peace embassy, inquiring of these people if they are determined to wage war or whether they desire our friendship. Let two of our most important young brothers go on this errand."

The king, in agreement with this, called some of his advisers and instructed them to send two valorous and highly esteemed noblemen, Tocoltecatl and Axicoyo, to the lords of Xochimilco with the message. They were to ask the Xochimilcas to advise Itzcoatl of their decision because the Aztecs wished only peace and harmony. If the others did not want this, they were to specify what their final decision was. These two men agreed to go to Xochimilco, as they prepared themselves for this mission. When the two messengers had arrived at a place called Tizaapan,[2] within the limits of Xochimilco, a great number of men from that place, carrying arms and insignia, came out, prepared for battle. The Aztecs were unarmed, unprepared. The Xochimilcas asked them what they wanted and where they were going. The envoys replied that they came from their city and were going to Xochimilco with a

---

[2]Tizaapan, a barrio of Colhuacan, near the Huixachtecatl, now Star Hill, on whose summit the New Fire ceremony was held.

message for the ruler and lords there. The Xochimilcas responded that they would not be allowed to take any message into the city, that anything they wanted to say could be told right there to the guards. The Aztecs, however, insisted on presenting themselves before the ruler of Xochimilco. This angered the other men, who stopped them, threatening them with death, telling them to return to their city and advise their king that the entire land of Xochimilco was intent on destroying them, that they would tolerate no argument. This was the final and only word, they said, and it came from young and old, even from women and children in Xochimilco. The messengers, not daring to insist further, thanked the Xochimilcas, told them they would be happy to relay the answer to their request, but that they would return.

Back in Tenochtitlan, they went before their king and told him how they had met the men on the road, how they were armed and ready for battle, determined to kill the Aztecs, to destroy them. And because they were not allowed to enter the city the messengers were forced to return. King Itzcoatl, amazed, exclaimed, "Is it possible that although you are messengers and unarmed, you were not allowed to pass?"

They replied that in no way whatsoever [could they have entered the city].

Turning to Tlacaelel, Itzcoatl told him to ask the council members to speak to the lords and that the people be made ready for war. The Aztecs were sure of themselves and had no desire to cause harm, but were determined to destroy, to kill the Xochimilcas. The council met and ordered the commanders and captains of the army to gather, together with all the seasoned warriors. They had decided to engage in war and began to make their plans and to arm their men. As the people of Xochimilco were numerous and extremely courageous, these defense measures were necessary. When everything was ready, Tlacaelel took a count of his men in a place called Teyacac. Choosing the strongest and most willing soldiers, he spoke these words to them: "O valiant warriors, the entire land of Xochimilco is against us. They outnumber us, compared with them we are few. But let not this multitude of soldiers trouble you. Strength and spirit are what matter! Be informed that our enemy is very near us, in a place called Ocolco, and the battle will take place there. Therefore, O Aztecs, make your name ring out as you have always done!"

Cheerfully, the soldiers, well ordered in files, each file following its captain, responded that they were ready to vanquish or die; then they began to march. When they arrived in the presence of the enemy, they halted. Then the Xochimilcas let our great shouts, great shrieks, crying, "Come, come, Aztecs! Your end is near!" The Xochimilcas were so numerous that they totally covered the plain, and the gold, jewels, precious stones, and plumes they carried on their weapons, insignia, and shields were so splendid that they shone in the sun as they reflected its rays. What a spectacle it was! Weapons of many colors: green, blue, red, yellow, black, multicolored!

"Oh wretched Xochimilcas," cried the Aztecs as they drew near, "we pity you and your wives and children! Who has deceived you to come to this place where you will soon lose spirit and gallantry? You will soon forget that vain fantasy that has brought you here and soon you will become our tributaries and vassals!"

Having said these words, the Aztecs began to shoot great numbers of darts[3] and arrows with such fury that the arrows darkened the sun. At the same time, so great were the cries of exultation that the valleys trembled. Presently the Xochimilcas began to abandon the field, retreating little by little, though their captains tried to animate them and stir them to hold their ground and keep fighting.

But the cunning, spirited Aztecs, although facing that forest of swords and shields, broke through the squadrons of Xochimilcas and began to push them little by little toward a hill called Xochitepec. When this hill had been taken, Tlacaelel ascended it and, flashing his sword and shield, he shouted to his men, "Hail, my valiant Aztecs, victory is ours! Do not tire yourselves overmuch. Let them die little by little and let perish those who unjustly wished to destroy us!"

Tlacaelel then rushed down the hill and, placing himself before the soldiers who had tired, he began to perform marvelous feats, knocking down all those he came upon. This greatly encouraged the Aztecs, while the Xochimilcas became terrified and fled toward a wall that had been built for the defense of their city. Once they were behind this, they began to wound many of the enemy through certain apertures in the wall. But the Aztecs assailed the wall with swords, clubs, and hoes, and began to tear it down.

The rulers of Xochimilco realized that their city would be sacked unless they quickly came to a decision. The wall had been torn down, the city was almost without defense because its defenders had abandoned most of it, and the Aztecs were laying waste to the city and killing its inhabitants. Therefore, the chieftains came out unarmed, their arms crossed [in front of them]. Making ceremonious gestures, they then prostrated themselves in front of the entire army, saying, "O Aztecs, our lords, here we are, we who are guilty of having provoked your wrath, of having caused you trouble, hardships. Let your ire and rage be vented upon us, but let not the old people and the children

[3]For "darts" Durán gives *varas arrojadizas*, which could refer to the atlatl or propelled spear, the spear being a cross between this weapon and a dart, thrown by the hand-held atlatl.

perish. Do not permit our city to be plundered and destroyed. You have avenged your hearts. Lower your arms and your swords, cast your shields upon the ground! Now you may rest. Tell us what you wish and we shall serve you. From now on the hills and valleys, the waters, springs, lands, and plains that have made this city rich are yours. Stone, heavy and light, wood and firewood, all is yours. Let your hearts be calm. The more of us you kill, the fewer vassals you will have to serve you. Take rest, O Aztecs, let there be no more conflict, for you have overcome us in a just war."

The men of Tenochtitlan, in order to frighten them even further, answered that they wanted to hear no more promises and that they did not need their stone and wood. They said that once the Xochimilcas were dead and their name erased from the earth, they would do as they pleased for all would be theirs, and the Aztecs would settle the city with other inhabitants. Setting up another great cry, the Aztecs picked up their weapons again, as if to attack, and shouted, "Death to the traiters! Let no man be spared!"

The Xochimilcas again bowed, humbling themselves, and begged the attack to cease, considering the greed of the Aztec soldiers and their eagerness to sack the city. "What is it you wish, O lords, valorous Aztecs? If you seek land with which to support yourselves, we shall give it to you in great quantities, and very good land it is. We shall serve you in your homes, we shall give you water for washing your hands, and everything you may need. We shall build your houses. We shall be your carriers and servants whenever you travel, wherever you may go. And should you go to war, we shall supply you with provisions, with food, as well as weapons and soldiers. In a word, we shall be your vassals to the death!"

Tlacaelel then ordered his soldiers to lower their arms, since the enemy had surrendered. He commanded the fighting to cease and everyone to turn back toward Tenochtitlan without entering Xochimilco.

The Aztec soldiers, disappointed and angry, showed their displeasure at this command, and, as they went back to their city, complained that they had not been given permission to loot as had been done heretofore in other cities. They knew that Xochimilco was one of the richest cities in the land and they could have gorged themselves on the spoils, with great pleasure. Tlacaelel, however, promised to compensate the soldiers for what they had lost.

He then turned to the Xochimilcas and ordered the entire city to build a causeway about three *brazas* wide from their town to Tenochtitlan. It was to be of stone and earth and the water was to be held back by a retaining wall wherever the road ran [so it would not flow over it]. Culverts were to be built at intervals so the water could pass from one side of the highway to the other.

The Xochimilcas were depressed, they lowered their heads, but then they went to repeat these orders to the entire kingdom.

Xochimilco had been a great state, with territory covering more than twenty leagues in one direction, as far as a town called Tochimilco, or Ocopetlayucan. The order for the causeway having been given, the entire nation began to build this road and today one can walk upon it from the city of Mexico to Xochimilco.[4]

---

[4] After the conquest of Xochimilco and the *chinampa* region under Itzcoatl, this became an important source of agricultural products for Tenochtitlan. See chapter X, note 7. For the importance of reeds and rushes in the economy, mythology, and symbolism of the people who lived near the lake and in a marsh setting, or on one of the islands, see Heyden 1983b.

CHAPTER XIII

Which treats of how, after the people of Xochimilco and the Tepanecs had built the causeway, King Itzcoatl of Mexico-Tenochtitlan ordered the distribution of the lands of Xochimilco.

After the people of Xochimilco had been defeated and had become subject to the crown of Tenochtitlan, as told above, they were ordered to build the wide causeway that goes from that city to Xochimilco. They requested the aid of the people of Coyoacan in this work, at least in the part that went through their territory. The Coyoacanos immediately agreed to help and thus built the part of the road that crossed their lands. This is the way it was built: it was constructed upon many stakes, stones, and blocks of grassy earth taken from the lagoon. Once this wide avenue had been built, many people began to travel on it.

Itzcoatl called Tlacaelel and said to him, "Tlacaelel, the causeway you ordered the Xochimilcas to build is finished, and they constructed it with goodwill. The time has come for our Aztec warriors to enjoy that which they have won with the sweat of their brows, with the labor of their hands and the strength of their hearts. It is my wish that you go in person, accompanied by two members of my council, and first give each of the leading men, my brothers and yours, a plot of 400 *varas*[1] to keep them contented. And after this I order that the soldiers who distinguished themselves in battle be awarded land in payment for their feats, since they were not allowed to pillage the conquered city. And choose anything you want for yourself, since the blood of our bodies and the lives of many were dearly sold." Tlacaelel and all those present gave thanks to the king. They then advised the officers and the soldiers of the king's orders so that all could pay their respects and thank him, which was the correct thing to do. When all were assembled—a large number of lords, officers, and common soldiers—they left for the city of Xochimilco and the distribution of lands there. They were happy to be able to use the causeway that had been built in such a short time.

When the men of Tenochtitlan reached Xochimilco, the officials of that city came out to receive them with friendship, with honors, and accommodated them in the royal houses. They welcomed the Aztecs

---

[1] See glossary for *vara*.

How Itzcoatl ordered the distribution of lands

to their city and told them to rest, that there would be time to discuss what they had come for. They provided all that was needed: abundant, rich food, fine mantles, jewels and valuable stones, and flowers. They brought a drum and began a fine ceremony in which all danced and sang in the customary way. When the formalities of welcoming and comfortably lodging the Aztecs had been carried out, the Xochimilcas relinquished their lands so that the promise they themselves had made be fulfilled. The division of the lands constituted a judgment against them. The Aztecs, contented, accompanied the Xochimilcas to the places where the land was to be taken and said to their own men, "Sirs, here you see these lands. Take those that our lord and king Itzcoatl has designated, for they are yours, you have won them."

In the order to which they were accustomed, property was first assigned to the Aztec royal house, then to Tlacaelel, and after these the lords and captains were given their share. Each one received two plots each. Then the soldiers who had excelled were also awarded some land. The Xochimilcas, seeing themselves thus dispossessed, were greatly distressed. Unable to hold back their tears, they moaned their misfortune and cried to the Aztecs, "O sirs, now you will be satisfied with having divested us of our lands, of our patrimony. Now it is our ill fortune to be your vassals; we have assumed the burden, the slavery, of being your tributaries. We beg you and our lord King Itzcoatl that you will treat us kindly and that you will be lenient about our weaknesses, our distress, and that you take pity on the old man, the old woman, the orphan and the widow, all of whom put themselves under your protection, confiding in your mercifulness and benevolence."

The Aztecs took pity on the Xochimilcas, consoled them, and tried to encourage them with kind words, promising them their protection whenever it was needed.

The Aztecs then returned to their city and described to their king the correct way in which the Xochimilcas had acted, the honorable manner in which they had treated them, and the generosity with which they had relinquished their lands. The king was amazed and pleased by this and as a result advised the lord of Xochimilco that he would become one of his councillors with the right to attend his meals and to eat in his presence.[2] He was also to take part in council decisions. This

---

[2]Bernal Díaz del Castillo describes Motecuhzoma's dinner: "He was seated on a low stool, soft and richly worked, and the table, which was also low, was made in the same style as the seat, and on it they placed the tablecloths of white cloth. . . . Four very beautiful cleanly women brought water for his hands in a soft of deep basin which they

was greatly appreciated by the Xochimilcas, and it was a favor that had been granted to no other foreign ruler up to that time.

The Xochimilca people had been the third to take possession of lands here, having come out of the Seven Caves, where they had lived for a long time. They had been a great power in earlier times. They had warred with their neighbors the people of Colhuacan over lands and boundaries, over territorial rights. Colhuacan had been the first to elect kings and lords before the Aztecs came to this region and had always competed with Xochimilco because each of these cities had refused to recognize the superiority of the other.

When the Aztecs first arrived in the land, they aided Colhuacan against Xochimilco and achieved some victories. A remarkable battle had once taken place in which the Aztecs had decided to cut off one ear of every Xochimilca who was captured.[3] Thus, every captive taken in that battle was deprived of one ear. I have heard it affirmed, besides having seen it in the painted manuscript, that the people of Colhuacan carried away baskets filled with human ears in their canoes. This victory was so renowned and celebrated by those of Colhuacan that even today they sing about it and celebrate it in their feasts and dances. But, as I have said, this took place with the help of the Aztecs, who at that time had recently arrived in the valley; this victory and the act of cutting off the enemy's ears is attributed to them.

Colhuacan has always possessed great fame as the place of the leading people in the land. Even today it is famous, since it was the place of origin of the kings of Mexico-Tenochtitlan and of many other great princes and governors of other provinces. From here came the women who engendered them. Besides, these people were the first to arrive in this land and take possession of the place called Colhuacan. They were the most important people at one time of all those in the Xochimilca region. Colhuacan was an independent state then; it became the capital and subjected many provinces, notably the people of the *chinampa*, who then became their neighbors and allies. Their goal, and that of the Xochimilcas [who were also *chinampa* people], was to become great.

call *xicallis*, and they held others, like plates, below to catch the water, and they brought him towels.... As soon as he began to eat they placed before him a sort of wooden screen painted over with gold, so that no one should watch him eating. Then the four women stood aside and four great chieftains who were old men came and stood beside them, and with these Motecuhzoma now and then conversed, asked them questions, and as a great favor he would give to each of these elders a dish of what to him tasted best" (1939:I:321–22).

[3] The cutting off of the ears of the Xochimilcas by the Aztecs is seen in the *Codex Boturini*, also called *Tira de la Peregrinación*, preserved in the Historical Archive of the Mexican National Institute of Anthropology.

How Itzcoatl ordered the distribution of lands

The two women who were mothers of the kings and founders of the lineage of lords of this land and of the Aztec nation were called Atotoztli and Ilancueitl, the latter mentioned in a previous chapter. As I said in that chapter, it is the belief that one of these women had been barren and had only feigned having children. It is also a popular opinion that these children had been born to concubines of the king, her husband. I am suspicious of this conjecture because I have seen a painted manuscript in which Ilancueye, who was said to have been barren, appeared as the wife of the lord of Coatlinchan. This ruler had been killed by a tyrant who wanted to conquer that state and who also had wished to kill a child of Ilancueye who could one day inherit the royal power. The widow hid her child and came fleeing with him to the city of Colhuacan, her birthplace. These events had taken place after she had [been the wife and had] become the widow of Acamapichtli, king of Mexico-Tenochtitlan.

CHAPTER XIV

Which treats of how the people of Cuitlahuac rebelled against the Aztecs during the reign of King Itzcoatl and how they were vanquished.

After the Xochimilcas had been subjected by the Aztecs, the people of the town of Cuitlahuac[1] decided that it would be shameful to remain at peace and continue their friendship with the Aztecs, that it would discredit them if they did not demonstrate their valor and force against those of Mexico-Tenochtitlan. The men of Cuitlahuac, who were restless, enemies of peace, felt that being surrounded by water constituted a wall and a defense to their city, that it made them impregnable. They also relied upon their skill in moving their boats to and fro in the waters of the lagoon. In this they were not mistaken, for the Aztecs dreaded meeting their enemies on the water instead of on an open field where they could attack or retreat as they were accustomed to doing.

The ruler of Cuitlahuac was at that time a valorous man by the name of Xochitl Olinqui, of strong heart, who was spoiling to achieve some great feat. Deliberately, then, he and his people began to lose favor with the Aztecs and to abandon their friendship and dealings with them. They did this in a way that was not open, yet it was not so secret that the Aztecs—who were astute, who were shrewd, who did not let things slip through their hands—failed to notice the indifference of Cuitlahuac. The Aztec authorities became suspicious so they used a cunning trick to find out what was happening. King Itzcoatl called a meeting of the dignitaries of the city. It was held so secretly that no one else heard about it. He said to these men: "It seems to me that I have felt a loss of friendship, an antagonism, on the part of the people of Cuitlahuac. Therefore I have thought of a plan: in order to calm my heart and to know with certainty if this is true, I have decided to send two of you to Xochitl Olinqui to extend an invitation to him from me, to attend a solemn feast that will be held in honor of our god Huitzilopochtli. And in order to make the feast more splendid I invite him and the noblemen of Cuitlahuac, together with all their

---

[1] It will be remembered that Cuitlahuac is today's San Pedro Tlahuac, near Xochimilco. The name was changed in the nineteenth century because the prefix *cui-* (from *cuitlatl*, "human offal") was considered offensive at that time. Cuitlahuac originally was an island.

How Cuitlahuac rebelled against the Aztecs

maiden daughters and sisters, so they may sing and dance at these festivities. This is what I have planned. In this way, if he agrees to do what I ask of him, I shall understand that my suspicions have been false. But if he refuses he will be showing his true designs, the evil desires of his heart."

Tlacaelel was the first to answer; he had been chosen to respond, and he said that this proposal was a good one. All the other lords agreed, too. With this agreement two of the leading men present were chosen and sent to Cuitlahuac with the message. When they had come before King Xochitl Olinqui, they presented themselves as envoys and told him, "O great lord, your friend the king of Tenochtitlan, Itzcoatl, wishes to make a solemn feast to our god, and so this celebration will be more notable, he would like you and your principal men to honor us with your presence. He also wishes that the dancers and singers be all the maidens of your city, the daughters, sisters, nieces, and near relatives of the high lords who are of noble blood. Then after the feast the ceremony to the cult of our god will take place. At the same time King Itzcoatl requests that the maidens be accompanied by their duennas, their guardians, so there will be no possibility of any unseeming act occurring that would be a disservice, a dishonor, to the god. And let them bring flowers and reeds to be used in this feast, as is the custom."

When the ruler Xochitl Olinqui heard this message, he showed great displeasure, wrath. He answered sharply, in anger, "Aztecs, do you realize what you are saying? Are our daughters and sisters, the maiden relatives of the lords of Cuitlahuac, toys or buffoons of your god that they must dance and sing before him? Tell Itzcoatl that I respect the virgins of my city too highly, even those of the lowest rank, to send them at his command to be the playthings of his god. He has numerous maidens in his own city; let him make use of them. Neither on this occasion nor on any other shall I obey him. Tell him that if he is trying to alarm us, incite us to war, we are ready for anything he is planning. You may go now." He ordered that no food or gifts be given to the envoys.

The envoys returned sadly to their king, carrying this message. They told about Xochitl Olinqui's anger and the bad treatment they had received. The king, Tlacaelel, and the Aztec dignitaries were indignant and began to discuss Cuitlahuac's rebellion. They saw that Itzcoatl's suspicion of antagonism on the part of that city was true. Among these men, one intervened, saying, "Who do these people of Cuitlahuac think they are, that they do not respect us? They are so presumptuous that they dare send such a negative answer to a sovereign as powerful as you!"

Since all were of one accord, Itzcoatl ordered that immediately, at that very moment, the envoys return with a last message, stating that they demand that Cuitlahuac choose one of two alternatives: either these people serve and obey the Aztecs, become their vassals, be subject to their orders, or they prepare for war. This message was delivered to Xochitl Olinqui. When he heard it, he insulted the messengers and had them thrown out of the palace. He told them to advise the Aztecs that no one was ever to return there, no one was to deliver messages to that city, because he and the lords of Cuitlahuac, on seeing them, became angered, infuriated. And in order to calm their hearts and test their strength and valor, they were determined to destroy the Aztecs or die in the attempt.

The messengers then returned to their city with this answer from Cuitlahuac, which they relayed to their king. They told how the men of Cuitlahuac had made this decision in order to prove the valor of their persons and that their final resolution was to go to war. Already in Cuitlahuac this decision had been made public, the antagonism between the two cities had been proclaimed. Everyone there had taken up arms and was ready for battle.

When Itzcoatl heard this, he cried, "I am pleased, O valiant lords, that you will now have another occasion to show your courage; this is evident in the trouble caused by Cuitlahuac. But never mind, they and their presumptuousness will fall like birds into a net. They will not slip out of our hands." But the Aztec dignitaries were much afraid of the treachery of the people of another city, Chalco, and said so to their king. Therefore a message was sent to Cuateotl and Toteociteuctli, the rulers of Chalco, telling them of the rebellion at Cuitlahuac. They were told that this city had rebelled against Mexico-Tenochtitlan for no reason whatsoever. The Aztecs begged them humbly to reveal if the enemy had asked their aid against his city, because it was unlikely—in spite of their arrogance and self-assurance—that they would rely on their strength alone, their forces being small. What the Aztecs feared was that Chalco might be convinced to send aid to Cuitlahuac. They requested an answer to this because, if Chalco were to help Cuitlahuac, Tenochtitlan would look for allies elsewhere. Not many battle forces would be necessary to combat the Cuitlahuac army, but Chalco [was another story] because it was equal to the Aztecs in the number of warriors, in weapons, and in the courage of its men.

The lords of Chalco responded that they kissed the hands of King Itzcoatl and that he should be told they knew nothing about the matter. They had no news of any war and this was due to the diligence with which the people of Cuitlahuac isolated themselves in their island

How Cuitlahuac rebelled against the Aztecs

kingdom. They also assured the Aztecs that they need not fear any betrayal from Chalco.

When the messengers returned to their city and delivered this answer to the king, Itzcoatl ordered Tlacaelel to form an army of boys younger than twenty-four years, in order to mock and show contempt for Cuitlahuac. The youths were to be given quilted cotton armor, lances, arrows, swords, and shields and were to be trained by the captains. Itzcoatl wished to wage war against the people of Cuitlahuac with these boys and vanquish them. Tlacaelel chose certain diligent captains to guide and teach the youths. The preceptors and teachers in the schools that existed in all the barrios were summoned and were told the will of the king. Great numbers of youths were brought in from all the barrios, all twenty-four years old or younger. They were assigned to captains and immediately showed their eagerness to conquer in war or perish. In this way they were given everything they needed, together with provisions supplied by neighboring towns. When everything was ready, it was proclaimed in the city that all the young soldiers on that day were to go out and meet in a place called Yahualiuhcan. All the boys gathered here and, dressed in their armor, with swords and shields, began to march in good order toward the town of Cuitlahuac. When they arrived at a place called Tecuitlatenco, they called a halt and waited for the arrival of those Aztecs who would attack by water. A thousand canoes were filled with well-armed men carrying large shields, a great number of lances, darts, and arrows. With them came warriors who were to defend the archers and who were experts at deflecting the arrows with their shields. Their skill was amazing; when they saw an arrow coming they would hit it with a shield and make it turn back.

When the canoes arrived, the entire army embarked and passed through a deep part of the lagoon where there was no causeway or road. When they arrived at Cuitlahuac and landed on the bank, the people there came out in highly adorned canoes. The men were richly dressed and armed with fine weapons, and the rowers were also handsomely attired with feathers and great shields. The warriors were well armed and their weapons were covered with white, red, yellow, blue, green, black, and multicolored plumes. On their heads and backs were elaborate feather adornments. From their necks hung many ornaments of gold inlaid with jewels. On their arms were wristbands of shining gold, on their ankles gold bands like short gold stockings. All these things covered them from head to foot and it was as if they were meant to give a final touch to the splendor of the weapons.

As soon as the Aztecs saw the Cuitlahuacas, they signaled to begin the action and a great deal of shouting burst out on both sides. The men began to throw darts, which are dangerous weapons because once these darts have entered the flesh they cannot be pulled out. This is due to their barbs, which make them like harpoons. In order to remove a dart it is necessary to make a large opening or to push it out the other side. Great numbers of these darts were being thrown, on one side and the other, and men in both armies were severely wounded, not only by the darts but by the arrows and stones shot by those on shore, which were returned by the Aztecs who were concealed in the marsh.

The soldiers of Cuitlahuac, hedged in on land and in the water by those tireless youths who seemed to be everywhere, constantly relieving one another, turned to seek help by making offerings to the little aquatic beasts. They invoked the water snakes, frogs and fish, the little shrimp and leeches, and finally the worms and other creatures that live in the water, praying to them in a servile manner and asking their favor and assistance.

But the god of the water creatures reminded them that the Aztecs were bellicose, vengeful people, experts in matters pertaining to the lagoon, and that if the Cuitlahuacas did not wish to perish, to be destroyed totally, they must beg for mercy and surrender. Hearing the answer of the god of the waters, of the fishes, frogs, and water snakes, of the little shrimp and leeches, those who had invoked him returned to the fray. They saw that many canoes were now drifting here and there without their occupants and the lagoon was covered with oars and shields, darts and arrows. Many men were dead and others, badly wounded, were trying to keep afloat on the water.

The officials of Cuitlahuac, led by their sovereign Xochitl Olinqui and laden with gifts of fish, turkey, ducks, and other delicacies, approached the Aztecs and singled out Tlacaelel, knowing that he was a merciful man. Humbling themselves before him, they begged him to calm his heart, [to have pity on them and] to order his men to cease the attack. They told him not only that would they give him their daughters and sisters but that they also would be subject to the Aztecs, become their vassals, disposed to serve them in all ways. Tlacaelel, in the name of all the Aztec warriors, accepted their surrender and then consoled them. He ordered the drum beaten, which was a sign of the end of the battle. The soldiers all put down their arms, for the war was over, then they gathered the canoes that had floated away, and the shields and other valuable weapons that were in the lagoon. They stripped the dead and despoiled them of their finery, each one collecting all he could of that booty.

The people of Cuitlahuac, grateful for the benevolence and mercy shown, led the Aztecs to the community house in their city, where they were given the usual food and drink and fine clothing. Tlacaelel then ordered his soldiers to return home, so they went back in the canoes. On returning the warriors related to their king the events that had taken place, and how the people of Cuitlahuac had become vassals of the royal house of Mexico in the same way others who had been conquered by the Aztecs were made vassals. They had promised to furnish maidens to dance in the feasts to the gods; from now on they would serve the Aztecs for their public works and in their personal service and would pay any tribute that was levied. They no longer had any land that could be divided, but they would give what they could.

Itzcoatl, though ill at the time, was much gladdened by the victory and expressed his gratitude to the lords and princes.

Soon after this his illness became worse and he knew he was about to die. He summoned the king of Tezcoco, Nezahualcoyotl, a close relative of his, and charged him not to war with the Aztecs, his kinsmen and friends, but always to remain on good terms with them. Itzcoatl left orders that from that time on the king of Tezcoco was to be the second ranking ruler of the land and the third was to be the ruler of Tacuba, whose name was Tlaluacpan, which means "the king of the dry land."

As he felt death near, King Itzcoatl had all his lords and courtiers called together and charged them with the cult of the gods. And he requested that the king who would take his place build a sumptuous temple to his god Huitzilopochtli and to the other gods, for he, Itzcoatl, had conquered many cities [and there was now much wealth in the empire. He also ordered] that his image and those of the kings his ancestors be carved in stone for an everlasting memorial.[2] Having thus expressed his last words and will, Itzcoatl died, leaving the city joyless and disconsolate by his death. He had been a dauntless king, of invincible spirit, a man who had made the republic great and who had lifted high the glory of his nation. According to the account most worthy of belief, he died in 1440, having reigned only fourteen years.

According to another curious *pintura*, a painted manuscript, he is said to have reigned nineteen years and to have died in 1445, but I find the first chronicle more truthful. It is also said that this king conquered Chalco, Cuauhnahuac, Huexotzinco, and Azcapotzalco, and that he condensed these kingdoms into only three: Mexico, Tezcoco, and Tacuba. It is also said that Coatlinchan was an independent kingdom and that he subjugated it also. And only those three kings ruled the land from that time on, but the ruler of Tenochtitlan over all the others, like an emperor in the New World.

[2]Remains of portraits of Aztec rulers carved on rocks in Chapultepec Park still exist, although time and weather have made them almost invisible.

King Itzcoatl was buried with great solemnity and a large number of representatives of the neighboring cities were present, noblemen as well as commoners. His funeral rites lasted for eighty days of sorrow and weeping. In those times the funeral ceremonies had not taken the form they were to assume later. However, there was no lack of food of the kind they serve at funerals and the usual gifts of mantles and other clothing were exchanged.

CHAPTER XV

Which treats of the election of the fifth king of Mexico, called Huehue Motecuhzoma, the first of this name, with a description of the pact or covenant he made with Nezahualcoyotl, king of Tezcoco.

After the funeral rites for Itzcoatl had ended, the Aztecs, both lords and commoners, elected a brother of Tlacaelel as ruler. He was called Huehue Motecuhzoma, the first of this name. A cousin to King Itzcoatl, he was one of the supreme council of four, his title being Tlacateccatl, which is similar in Spanish to "Prince" or "Lord High Constable" or some other high title. As I said earlier, the king must be chosen from among these four members of the supreme council—who were like elected princes or officials—and from no other group. And so, when a king died, they chose a new one from among those four and put another in his place in the council, giving him the same title. But he must be of the direct line of the kings, brother or son or cousin of the deceased.

And so Motecuhzoma[1] was elected king with all the customary rites, ceremonies, and anointments used in the election of kings or in certain rites for the gods. Mourning for the dead ruler ceased and the city rejoiced over the new election with dance and song. The neighboring kings came to acknowledge the preeminence of the new sovereign and to acknowledge their subjection, as to a supreme monarch. They brought him great and valuable gifts of rich cloth, weapons, insignia, shields, fine feathers, and jewels, as well as other riches used in those times by the lords to show reverence to one another on such occasions. Nezahualcoyotl, ruler of all the province of Tezcoco, an area comprised of many great towns, was especially generous with his gifts.[2]

As soon as Nezahualcoyotl heard of the election of Motecuhzoma, he gathered the dignitaries of his kingdom and spoke to them sol-

[1] In the original manuscript in Madrid the king's name is spelled differently at times. In the beginning it is Motecuhzoma, and from this point on it is spelled Motecuzoma or Montezuma. Perhaps Durán dictated to different scribes.

[2] The constant exchange of gifts—or the giving of gifts to outstanding persons—was one system of keeping harmony in these societies. Furthermore, the rulers of different states, friends or foes, had a tacit agreement to maintain their position in the hierarchy as well as their luxurious style of living. This understanding between different city-states was based partly on kinship ties; even enemies at times intermarried as a political convenience. Michael E. Smith deals well with this (1986:70–91).

emnly: "I beg of you, lords and brothers, I strongly recommend you to be careful the way you treat the Aztecs. Flee from their enmity and from any conflict with them. Let us keep an eternal peace and inviolable friendship. You know them; I do not have to say more regarding their ways. If you meet them on the roads and they ask you for something you carry, share it with them. Treat them well because in doing so we lose nothing. And should we oppose them we would gain nothing but wars, trouble, deaths, robbery, the shedding of our blood, and the desolation of our kingdom. Therefore, be in peace, be tranquil, and urge the people of the cities in my kingdom, especially the travelers and merchants, to do likewise, for these traders are the ones who go about the roads and move from province to province gaining their sustenance. You and I remain at home and have no reason to cause trouble to anyone, much less to the Aztecs, who never create problems unless they are provoked. It is not fitting that any ignoble act, any lack of respect, come from us. It is the common people who cause war with their ignorance and their recklessness."

The lords kissed his hands [that is, thanked him with all respect] for the favor, for the advice, he gave them. They were intent upon conserving their land, their city, their province, so they requested Nezahualcoyotl to visit the new king and to make a permanent peace treaty, which everyone desired.

Nezahualcoyotl, having made the necessary preparations to go to Mexico-Tenochtitlan to congratulate King Motecuhzoma on the election, provided himself with a suitable rich present. Then he and his officials departed from Tezcoco and went to the Aztec city, where they were well received in that city by all the lords and also by the commoners, who showed Nezahualcoyotl great respect, as a person of his station deserved. When the king of Tezcoco reached the Aztec royal quarters, he was received with great affection by Motecuhzoma, who sat him at his side, an honor it was customary to bestow upon a friend and kinsman.

Nezahualcoyotl offered gifts; these were according to the position of the giver and that of the person for whom they were destined, and although the *Relación*, the written history, does not mention this, these presents were never less than gold jewelry, precious stones, ear ornaments, lip plugs, exquisite featherwork, shields, weapons, mantles, and beautifully worked breechcloths.

After he had delivered his gifts, Nezahualcoyotl explained the cause of his visit, speaking to the king in private, not allowing anyone else to be present:

"Supreme lord and monarch, let not your regal person become weak, let not your heart be anguished over the new burden that is imposed upon you. Keep up your manly spirit according to your true worth. I have come here, O lord, to tell you of the misery, the affliction that reigns in your province of Tezcoco. In your greatness deign to raise it and ennoble it and shelter it with your commands from other nations. You well know, great prince, that all your subjects, nobles as well as the common people, are under your shade for you have been planted here like a great cedar tree under which men wish to rest in order to take pleasure in the freshness of your friendship and love. [Those who need you most are] the old men and women, orphans and widows, the poor and the destitute. All of them are like feathers on your wings, like feathers on your head. Also think of the little ones who are beginning to crawl or are still in their cradles, who do not yet feel, or know, or understand. Their hands cannot defend them, nor do their feet serve to flee from the wrath of the Aztecs.

"All of these, and I in their name, beseech you, implore you, for clemency. Preserve us in peace and concord; at no time allow your people to attack us. If I, without purpose or aim, were to rebel against Tenochtitlan, were to wage a war against your city, I realize that the fury of the Aztecs would be measureless, limitless. This fury pulls the people out from under the earth, it is vindictive, insatiable in its lust to wound, to kill. Therefore, I beg of you to receive my people as children and servants, but without war, without a quarrel. They love you like a father and mother who consoles them, and they hold all Aztecs as friends."

Motecuhzoma, with gladness in his face and kindness in his words, answered that he was grateful for the love that was offered him and that he would be happy to preserve peace and to have them as perpetual friends. He also said that in order that these arrangements be more certain and binding, he desired to communicate all of these things to the officials and dignitaries and that he would later give Nezahualcoyotl an answer.

The king of Tezcoco, with much honor, was lodged in a room within the royal household where he could rest. Then Motecuhzoma summoned all the other lords and principal men. When they were present he addressed them: "The king of Tezcoco, Nezahualcoyotl, a kinsman, a relative, of ours, offers to submit himself and subject his people to the protection of our god Huitzilopochtli. He requests that we keep permanent peace. He and his entire province wish to serve us and be our perpetual friends. He will never permit these people to offend us, to trouble us. Therefore, let all of you who are present answer this request, for I have not wished to respond to it, to say 'yes' or 'no,' without your consent.

"He does mention one drawback: that if war were to be waged against his peaceful, tranquil city, he would fear your fury and that of the Aztecs, who when they make war cut down the forests, tear up the fruit trees and the century plants, destroy the prickly pears, ruin the houses, set the temples on fire. In a word, he says that they burn everything, destroy everything, until their vengeful hearts can rest. Therefore, he asks for perpetual peace and concord."

All the councilmen and lords requested that Tlacaelel answer in their name. So he said, "O powerful king, we accept the peace and goodwill you propose and we are pleased that a truce be made. But let it be on one condition: we are not to lose our authority or rights lest the nations of this earth think it is we who have cravenly and timorously begged for peace. And let not other cities, far and near, wish to make pacts with us and leave us without gain, without authority. I believe that in order for them to understand that we are capable of conquering the entire world, the other provinces should hear that we have overcome the great kingdom of Acolhuacan [whose capital is Tezcoco]. Therefore, let the people of Tezcoco come out to meet us on the battlefield and we shall go out to encounter them on the plain of Chiconauhtla or at Chiquiuhtepec, both of which are part of Acolhuacan. Let the word spread that they have challenged us and there, on one side or another, we shall pretend to fight them. In the first encounter let them turn their backs on us and we shall pursue them without wounding or killing anyone. We shall feign their capture; we shall go after them as far as Tequiciztlan. By then only the captains and lords of our army will be following them. When we reach Totoltzinco, the king of Tezcoco can set fire to the temple and the battle will come to an end. This way our fame, our honor, will be without blemish, and they will not have been harmed nor angered. The common people will be ready to serve us when we need them and the other provinces and cities will be fearful of us, in awe of us, for having conquered Tezcoco and its domain."

King Motecuhzoma and his officials were well pleased with Tlacaelel's advice and ordered him to present these decisions to the king of Tezcoco. So Tlacaelel related all those things I have told here to that king.

Even though it was against his honor, King Nezahualcoyotl simulated content. He agreed to these plans and went to his city, where he communicated the news to his lords and officials, then gave orders that warriors be prepared with great ceremony and show. At the same time they spread rumors of a war they wished to wage against the Aztecs. They forbade the Aztecs to enter Tezcoco by land or by water. The Aztecs, complaining of this, then announced the same prohibitions.

On the appointed day the two armies, having made ready and with a great show of arms, insignia, splendid attire, and rich adornments, met at Chiquiuhtepec and the mock battle began. Many of those who took part in it were ignorant of the agreement to make this a feigned encounter and at the beginning shouted and received great insults as if they were enemies. But as soon as the conflict commenced, the Tezcocans began to abandon the field, retreating toward their city as had been determined, fleeing to a place called Tequiciztlan. Most of the Aztec army remained here, only a handful of their officers following. When they entered a small town called Totoltzinco, at the entrance to Tezcoco, Nezahualcoyotl was ready there and gave orders that the temple be set on fire. Seeing the flames, the Aztecs lowered their weapons, for the burning of the temple was the sign of surrender. Until this happened a city where the temple was would not admit defeat.

King Nezahualcoyotl then appeared before his men, pretending sadness and sorrow, and he begged the commanders of the Aztec forces to lay down their arms and cease their warlike labors, since the Tezcocans had admitted defeat and were now subject to Tenochtitlan.

The Aztec lords put down their weapons, dismissed the few soldiers who had followed them, and ordered the army to return home without harming or injuring anyone, nor stealing anything, under pain of death. Thus, the soldiers, who were not especially pleased with false wars, returned to their city. And the Aztec noblemen were taken to Tezcoco, where they were received solemnly and were given many splendid gifts and valuable objects for themselves and for their ruler.

Nezahualcoyotl in the presence of all his nobles and the people of his city, spoke these words: "O Aztecs, we are now your subjects and we have placed upon our shoulders the yoke of servitude forever. You have won this by the valor of your persons and by the strength of your arms. Therefore I shall give my father and mother, which is Mexico-Tenochtitlan, lands to provide food and drink. And these are for the lords of that city and for the one who commands there, who with only the breath from his mouth can command and also revoke these orders. He is the image of the god Huitzilopochtli and will be served by us. We shall give him water for his hands, we shall sweep and arrange the chamber where his seat of authority is placed, where he receives those who come from outside his city in order to settle disputes and wrongs done to them."

"Lord," answered Tlacaelel, the head of the army, "we are thankful for what you have done to preserve peace between us and your province. But perhaps in the future your subjects will be offended and will not want to accept what has taken place. They may regret that their strength and valor were not tested, and when we ask favors of you they may say they are not our vassals and do not wish to serve us. I warn you of this now."

Nezahualcoyotl assured him that the Aztecs could be at peace, unperturbed. There would be neither rebellion nor complaints. He added that what he had done had been done with the approval of everyone and with the agreement of his subjects and of all the provinces. Never would they rebel against the royal crown of Tenochtitlan.

And so these noblemen left Tezcoco and returned to the Aztec capital, where they informed Huehue Motecuhzoma of everything that had taken place, according to the agreement made between the two cities. They related how this had ended, how the very king of Tezcoco had set fire to the temple and had proclaimed in public that the city had surrendered and the Tezcocans had been made subjects. They had been obliged to agree to all the same terms that were accepted by other cities when they were conquered. Furthermore, Tezcoco had agreed to provide soldiers for attacks, for wars, during which the Aztecs might need them. And they said that the Tezcocans had of their own free will offered lands and people for use by the Aztec noblemen.3

Motecuhzoma responded that everything was in good order and that this pleased him. Nevertheless, they should go immediately to receive lands, lest the opportunity be lost. So the lords returned to Tezcoco, where they were given lands, beginning with property for King Motecuhzoma and continuing with Tlacaelel and the other leading lords and warriors.

This was the first war waged by the first Motecuhzoma after his election,4 and even though it was feigned it was carried out under all the conditions of a real war. Few or none of the neighboring cities were aware of its falseness, since it had been accomplished in great secrecy and dissimulation. This subterfuge of Nezahualcoyotl does not prove him to be weak-hearted. On the contrary, it simply shows the love he had for the Aztecs, who were his kinsmen. In all the histories, in all that can be read about him, he is shown to be a valorous and spirited man. He performed great feats in wars, which he often attended in

---

3Different historical chronicles present different sides to this Tenochtitlan-Tezcoco question. The Tezcocan historian Alva Ixtlilchitl in the sixteenth century describes not one but a number of wars between the two cities; in one Nezahualcoyotl gathered an army of 50,000 soldiers and attacked Mexico-Tenochtitlan through Tepeyac. At one point a young Tezcocan attacked the leading Aztec captain, cutting his body to pieces. The Tezcocans then entered Tenochtitlan, where they sacked the city and burned the temple but spared the lives of civilians. The Aztecs finally recognized the superiority of Tezcoco and saw it is equal to the Aztec capital, according to this account.

4One of the formalities in the accession of a new ruler was his obligation to prove himself in war after his election but before his investiture, as proof of personal valor and the right to rule.

The fifth king of Mexico, Huehue Motecuhzoma

person.⁵ He was especially brave in the long wars waged against the Tepanecs before he was enthroned and after his accession, even though for some years he had been fleeing from the Tepanecs and had been obliged to go into hiding. In the end he made peace with them and reigned with the aid of the Aztecs and his kinsman Itzcoatl. In return for this help he had agreed to the pretended war, with gallantry and nobleness of mind, in order to live in peace with the Aztecs, to respect their authority, to honor them and extol their name. In this way the entire country would fear them and be subject to them because of their fame as conquerors of such a great kingdom. He also favored them by giving them lands to work for their sustenance. These lands were given to the Aztec officials, four plots to some, two or three to others, according to their merit, as judged by Motecuhzoma. The king then gave orders that stewards and overseers be placed on the lands belonging to the crown. They were to be responsible for cultivating them, improving them, gathering the crops and storing these in the royal warehouses. Thus Coyoacan and Xochimilco were ordered to provide stewards. And so it was done: one of the principal men from each city was sent to oversee the royal farmlands, having been assigned certain privileges and wages. The Tezcocans and other peoples responded to this order with men to work for the Aztecs.

When this was done, Motecuhzoma told his men to rest, that with their dedication and work they had shown the valor of their persons and had increased the size of his kingdom. He wished to let his army rest for a few years and not wage any war. He also wished the three kingdoms of Tenochtitlan, Tacuba, and Tezcoco, together with their provinces, to increase and to live in well-being and tranquillity. And he begged all his chieftains to avoid war with any nation or province unless it was unescapable, for he desired to preserve peace for some time.⁶

---

⁵This is a hint as to the actual presence of the ruler in wars.
⁶The Triple Alliance formed by Mexico-Tenochtitlan, Tezcoco, and Tacuba (sometimes spelled Tlacopan) was to be the major force in controlling a large part of Mesoamerica until the Spanish conquest. These three cities, on conquering the domains of Azcapotzalco, automatically acquired a number of tribute-paying provinces that had been held by the Tepanecs, to which they were to add others in later times.

CHAPTER XVI

About how Motecuhzoma the First, known as the Elder or Huehue Motecuhzoma, in times of peace began to build the temple, and how Chalco waged war against Mexico-Tenochtitlan and was defeated by the Aztecs.

For twelve or thirteen years, during the reign of Huehue Motecuhzoma, there was peace and tranquillity. Since there was calm and all was quiet, and he was served and obeyed by the neighboring cities and provinces, he decided to build the temple of his god Huitzilopochtli, like the great King Solomon who, having made peace in all the land, beloved by all the monarchs of the earth and aided by them, built the temple of Jerusalem.

And so King Motecuhzoma, seeing that he and his people were at peace, that he was loved and respected but also feared, was determined to build a house for his god; therefore, he called Tlacaelel and the members of his council and, when all were before him, told them of his desire in the following words: "Lords and chieftains of my kingdom, my heart tells me that I must construct a most sumptuous house to honor our god Huitzilopochtli. You know that he does not yet have a home, even though all of you have dwelling places. Yet he should be the first, in preference to us, the house he has is not worthy of him. Therefore, observe, decide what should be done in this case."

Tlacaelel answered that this was a correct, a just, decision, and that the council also approved the building of the temple. The king proposed that messengers be sent to Azcapotzalco, Coyoacan, Xochimilco, Cuitlahuac, Mezquic, Colhuacan, and Tezcoco, asking that laborers and materials such as lime, stone, wood, and anything else necessary be sent immediately. So envoys went to those cities to advise the lords there of this plan and to request that they send the materials as soon as possible.

"O powerful lord," protested Tlacaelel, "it would be more proper for you to use your royal authority to the full and treat your vassals as a supreme monarch. Every time messengers are sent they are chosen from among the nobility. Where shall we find enough noblemen to act as messengers? Remember also that it is a difficult task for them. It would be more fitting if all the rulers, without exception, were brought before you. Standing in your presence, they would then receive your command to bring their workers, or to send them together with the materials in order to build the temple of our god."

Motecuhzoma agreed with this advice, saying, "Forgive me, lord, even though I am king I sometimes commit errors. That is why it is well that you aid me, giving me advice on things of importance to our city and which are advantageous to us. Let the authorities from those cities be called immediately!"

Four dignitaries then were sent to summon the rulers, in the name of the king of Tenochtitlan. They advised the kings of Tezcoco, Colhuacan, Xochimilco, Cuitlahuac, Mezquic, Coyoacan, Tacuba, and Azcapotzalco. After these lords had arrived and had been accommodated in the royal quarters, as was the custom, Motecuhzoma and Tlacaelel requested their presence. When they had taken their places in the lordly seats they were accustomed to use, Motecuhzoma spoke to them, "O sovereigns of Tezcoco, Xochimilco, Colhuacan, Cuitlahuac, Mezquic, Coyoacan, Azcapotzalco, and Tacuba, you who are present, who have answered my request to come here: you have been brought here because I wish you to consider seriously that our god Huitzilopochtli, father and mother of all, under whose protection we stand, has no dwelling place where he can be worshiped. We have decided to build a sumptuous temple dedicated to his name and to our other gods. You well know that you have pledged to serve him; therefore, you are to do so. I command you that as soon as you return to your cities you order your subjects to come to this project bringing the necessary materials of stone, lime, wood, and anything else that may be required for the construction. All this will redound to your honor and happiness. Let there be no negligence; let every man put his shoulder to the task so that it can be finished quickly."

"O masters, O Aztecs," the rulers of those cities responded, "and you especially, ruler of all the land, you who are obeyed by all, whose city stands in a marsh, in the midst of the reeds and rushes and cattails, do not worry, do not trouble yourself about these things. Care for your health and your life, preserve them. We have heard your command and it will be done as well and as quickly as possible, since it is our duty to obey in this and in all things you wish to command. This work will be done for our lord in whose shade and protection we live and take refuge. Decide what is necessary and it will be brought to you."

The Aztec lords and especially the king thanked them, stating that they were grateful for the goodwill and friendship shown by these men for the building of the temple. They were ordered to bring heavy stone for the foundation and light stone for the building, together with lime and wood. The lords, answering that they were pleased to comply with this request, bid farewell to the king and his councilmen. Then each one returned to his city, where he advised his people to get ready the material for the temple, a task that was done immediately and diligently.

Motecuhzoma called Tlacaelel and said to him, "The rulers of all the provinces have done what we ordered and have obeyed with much willingness. They are preparing for the work and are beginning to bring the material for our construction. Now, if you are in agreement, I would like to send messengers to the lord of Chalco, Cuateotl, and to his coadjutor Toteoci Tecuhtli. We shall not give them orders but shall approach them with great humility. We shall tell them that we wish to build a splendid, a magnificent temple for our god Huitzilopochtli and that we lack large stones to make sculptures and images in order to beautify it. Let them help us with some stones from their hills, the largest that can be obtained and brought here."

Tlacaelel agreed with this and stated that little would be lost [by requesting the stone. He added that if the Chalcas] wished to comply with the request this would be greatly appreciated; if not, there would be no objection. The king, then, sent him to choose the envoys and advise them what they had to do. So Tlacaelel chose four of the leading men and ordered them to go to Chalco and greet the lords and principal officials on behalf of the king and himself. They were to salute the lords and chieftains with great humility and advise them of the work that was to begin, and the fact that some large stones were needed. They were to request some rock from the Chalco hills for this endeavor. The four lords designated answered that they would be happy to carry out this enterprise and prepared to leave for Chalco.

The four envoys, having left their city, arrived in Chalco. They were presented to Cuateotl and Toteoci Tecuhtli, and addressed them thus: "O lords, your servants, the king of Tenochtitlan and his chief official, Tlacaelel, together with all the other Aztec councilmen, send their greetings and wish that your kingdom prosper, and that you yourself prosper. And they humbly beg of you to help us with some large heavy stone and some light stone—which you have an abundance in these hills—for the temple of our god in our city, which we are determined to build."

The lords of Chalco, having listened to this message, to this request, were troubled, they became angry. They answered with arrogant words, irately, "What do you ask, O Aztecs? Do you realize what you are saying? If we did wish to give you what you request, who will compel the people to take out the stone and deliver it to you? Shall I have to do this, or the other Chalco lords? Wait, and we shall explain this to everyone to see what answer is given. And if you do not wish to wait, then go, for this cannot be done without a general agreement and we shall need time to discuss it. So return whenever you wish and we shall give you the answer here."

When the envoys returned and relayed to the king and Tlacaelel the rude answer the Chalcas had given and how they had demanded that the Aztecs return for the resolution, King Motecuhzoma thanked them and told them to rest, to take respite from the difficult task they had carried out. But the king then turned to Tlacaelel and, taking him by the hand, he led him away and spoke to him in private, saying, "It seems to me, Tlacaelel, that it would be better if our messengers do not return to Chalco. Let us drop this request because if the Chalcas cause difficulties with harsh answers, we shall be forced to quarrel with them, to fight them, and this will greatly interfere with our object, our intent to obtain stone."

Tlacaelel responded in anger, "O powerful king, what is this you are saying? Is it possible that you are from a different generation than the rest of the Aztecs? Is it possible that these words have issued forth from your generous heart? Why should our ambassadors not return? Perchance the Chalcas hold us in such little esteem that they will mock us, jeer at us? The envoys must go, O powerful king, they must return to hear the decision, the will, of the Chalcas. And I beg of you, do not contradict me!"

The king was almost ashamed. He answered, "My brother, you know what is best for us. Do what you desire, wish them good fortune and send them to Chalco if this seems best to you." So the following day Tlacaelel summoned the noblemen who had gone to Chalco and ordered them to return immediately for the Chalcas' answer, for their decision. The envoys then went to Chalco and came before Cuateotl and Toteoci Tecuhtli, lords of that city. They asked what decision had been made.

"O Aztecs," the Chalca rulers exclaimed, "we have no need to conceal, to be silent about the answer given by this entire community of jaguars and eagles (for this is what warriors and brave people are called), who respond that definitely they do not want in any way to help or serve the Aztecs, nor is this their desire. Therefore, go and tell your lord Motecuhzoma and his coadjutor Tlacaelel that this is what the Chalcas answer, and that if it becomes necessary to take up the bow, the arrows, and the shield, the Chalcas are here waiting for what may come. Therefore, you may return to your city."

The Aztec lords thanked the Chalca rulers and returned to their city, where they relayed these messages to King Motecuhzoma, to Tlacaelel, and to the other lords. They told how the Chalcas claimed they would defend their faction every time this became necessary.

And they had added with insolence that they were not vassals of the Aztecs, nor were they subject to them, with the obligation to supply them with stone or any other thing. They also said that they were free people and did not wish to give the Aztecs any of the things they had requested. Motecuhzoma told the envoys that they were welcomed home, that they should now go rest, that he appreciated the work they had carried out in coming and going to Chalco.

The messengers gone, the king asked Tlacaelel, "What is your opinion, Lord Tlacaelel, what should be done? What measures should be taken so the Chalcas do not continue to laugh at us? You have seen how they have scorned us, how they have threatened us. If you agree, let us ready our army and go after them, let us try our fortune. Consider carefully the advice you can give me because, although I am the king, I shall abide by the wisest opinion. It is as if you and I were walking and you, as my guide, walk ahead, for in everything I shall follow you."

"For this favor," Tlacaelel responded, "I kiss your royal hands and feet. And regarding what you have asked me about waging war with the Chalcas, we are obliged to go ahead with this, otherwise we shall be branded as infamous and dishonorable people. Furthermore, I suggest this: in my opinion two of the leading captains of your army, very well dressed as for war, should go immediately to the boundaries of Chalco to see if the Chalcas have already placed their guards and sentries there. If they have not done this then they are in disrepute for being careless, for men who have spoken against the Aztecs with such liberty should by this time be prepared for war because they know that the heart of these people cannot be calmed down, nor will it wait until tomorrow."

Motecuhzoma agreed that this was good advice and asked that two captains be chosen to go to Chalco. Tlacaelel then called two courageous captains, one called Tenamazcuicuil, the other Xiconoc. He told them, "Come here! The king orders that you immediately prepare your weapons and your shields, ready for war, and go to the Chalco boundary. Watch carefully all the roads and paths to see if there are guards or sentries or soldiers, if there are any signs of enemy forces or of preparations for war. If you see anything like this, do no more than identify these people or see what preparations are being made, in order to inform us of everything. And if you find nothing at all, then challenge them, call them negligent, warn them that they should prepare to defend themselves because we shall do everything in our power to destroy them."

The two fearless warriors of manly spirit set out for Chalco. When they reached a place called Techichco, they found no one there. So they went on, reaching another place called Aztahuacan, where they also saw no one. But not satisfied with this reconnoitering and being not afraid, they continued on until they came to a place called Cuaxomotitlan. Here they heard the noise and clamor of many people. The Aztec captains advanced to a point from which they could observe and, hiding as best they could, saw that the Chalco army was quartered on that plain. The soldiers were standing in orderly fashion and the Chalca captains were choosing the bravest and most experienced men, placing them in files and squadrons.

After having observed the enemy camp, its order, and the excellent appearance of the soldiers, the spies, these noblemen, returned to Mexico-Tenochtitlan. Here they told the king and Tlacaelel how in Cuaxomotitlan they had seen the whole Chalca army in very good form. They added that the captains there were choosing the bravest soldiers, eliminating the new recruits and the most inexperienced men, and ordering them in files and squadrons. The Aztecs had understood, on seeing all this, that the Chalcas would go into battle little by little and when one squadron tired another would relieve it. They also said that there were vast numbers of people to act as replacements for these squadrons, that the men in the Chalca army were so numerous that they covered the entire plain.

Motecuhzoma said to these captains, "Welcome back, brothers, and now rest."

Then Motecuhzoma, in accord with Tlacaelel, summoned the members of his council and told them that as soon as possible they were to prepare the men, without excluding a single man or youth who was capable of bearing arms. They were to make ready and provide the army with everything they needed. At the same time the suppliers of foodstuffs were to get together all the necessary provisions. The council members summoned the captains and experienced soldiers and ordered them to make an announcement to the people so they would prepare for the war against Chalco that was being declared. The councillors wanted to see the courage and noble comportment of the jaguars and eagles of Tenochtitlan and how they would prove their worth.

The entire city was stirred up. All the men and youths between twenty and twenty-five years of age, and even the older ones of thirty, of forty, came out. There were many, so splendidly dressed, displaying the valor of their persons and their desire to go to war. Some carried lances to be propelled, others bows and arrows, others slings with well-worked round stones, like small bullets carved out of heavy stone in the size necessary for the sling. Still other soldiers carried swords and shields. When everyone was ready, Tlacaelel called out to them,

"Greetings, soldiers! Now you are ready, leave the city and we shall all meet in Aztahuacan!" And the king, directing his words mainly to the noblemen and captains, said, "O lords, you see the pleasure, the willingness, shown by the soldiers, who will be courageous in battle. And there is not a drop of cowardliness or fear in any of you. Go with good fortune, as the brave men you are."

Then Tlacaelel and all his men left the city and marched to Itztapalapa. When they arrived there, they heard the news that the Chalcas were now in Techichco, on that plain which lies between the hills of Colhuacan and Cuitlahuac, at the limits of these two cities. Tlacaelel took up his weapons and with sword and shield in his hands began to encourage his men and ordered all to be prepared, with great care and swiftness. When the army was ready, he cried out to the soldiers, "O Aztecs, behold! Observe what has brought you here, know that you are facing death, that death is your enemy. The Lord of the Earth, your mother, is waiting for you. Sell your lives dearly. You must realize that those over there are not lions who will tear you apart, nor are they demons who will swallow you. They are only men like you and the weapons they carry are the same ones you have in your hands. They are Chalcas and you are Aztecs, both have been chosen for this occupation, for this military profession. Therefore, let us go out into the field and let us show neither fear nor cowardice."

So they all went into the field in orderly fashion, in clear view of the enemy. The Aztec soldiers were splendidly arrayed, their arms and attire magnificent; but when the Chalcas saw them, they raised a great shout and clamor and cried out, "Come, come, Aztecs! Today will be the day, today we shall see, we shall discover who we all are, and it will be seen who the valorous Chalca Chichimecs are! Let us see who will fall first; you have yet to feel the impact of our hands. Before you stand the Chalcas."

The Aztec soldiers in the front line answered with great humility, crying out, "Welcome, Chalca brothers! There is no reason to speak; we must act!" When this was said, Tlacaelel beat the drum he carried on his back, and at its sound the Aztecs let out great cries and attacked the Chalcas with fury, with vigor. They shouted at their own men, "O Aztecs, today we shall take these useless Chalcas as if they were women! Or we shall finish them here, in this place. Let no Chalca be left alive!"

A spirited fight, an angry battle, then took place, which lasted all day, and many soldiers fell on both sides. Nevertheless, the Chalcas fought without resting in such a way that during the entire day the Aztecs were unable to advance. This was because there were numerous Chalca soldiers to relieve others and squadrons to replace squadrons.

When night came, the Chalcas, seeing the fortitude of the Aztecs and the courageous spirit that sustained them, called out to them, "Aztecs, you see that night has fallen, it forms a curtain between us, so go to rest. You surely will need to relax because tomorrow at the same time and place you will find us there. And we shall continue fighting now or for as long as you wish, even though this war lasts a year, for now that we have begun fighting we shall continue without tiring. So now let us break camp for the night."

The Aztecs then withdrew and ordered the captains of the allied troops to gather their men in Tenochtitlan. They feared a possible betrayal by the people of Xochimilco or Cuitlahuac or Colhuacan, Coyoacan, or Tacuba. Therefore, the entire army was concentrated in the Aztec capital, and during the night four spies went to the other cities: Tacuba, Coyoacan, Xochimilco, Cuitlahuac, and Colhuacan. They went in great secrecy in order to see if the people there were gathering in rebellion or if there were rumors of treachery, either secret or public, or if steps were being taken in that direction. The envoys, the spies, went to all these cities and moved around in them, carefully observing if any hostile alliance existed, or any plan to harm the Aztecs. But they found everything peaceful and tranquil, all quiet. They took this good news back to Motecuhzoma.

The king, now calm, summoned his captains and asked them, "What do you think of the spirit of the Chalcas and their valor? How has their strength affected you? Will it be difficult for you to win that victory? Answer me, for I seem to see that you are indifferent, without spirit, and perhaps you feel that fighting them is too weighty a task. Perhaps you feel like facing this enemy is like drinking an unpleasant beverage, a bitter purgative!"

One of the men, Ezhuahuacatl, answered thus, "O lord, our king, you who are here before us: he who is in your presence, who stands next to you, Tlacaelel your servant, should be the one to answer. You must understand this question you ask us, and now we ask: on what do you think the strength of the Chalcas is founded? Perchance it is the sword they carry in their hands? No! Nor does their strength come from the other arms with which they fight, for these are the same weapons used in battle by your subjects! So what is the secret of their might? Their courage? No, because your army has shown more courage than they! Their success is based only upon the multitude of men who relieve their soldiers. In truth this should not be a drawback for us; if we remember our ancestors when they were surrounded in Chapultepec not only by the Chalcas but by all the people on the earth—like a locust plague that descended upon them—they did not fear because of that multitude. On the contrary, with intrepid spirit

The History of the Indies of New Spain

they defended themselves, breaking through all the enemy lines, thus proving their fortitude. And we should do likewise. So there is nothing to fear, O valiant king; yet soon you should place your sentries on guard so that the Chalcas cannot come in through our gates and take us by surprise. And this is how I answer your question, in the name of all the lords and captains."

"I am grateful to you, courageous Ezhuahuacatl," said the king, "because you have spoken like the nobleman you are, like a man of the line from which you descend. You have seen cleearly that the Chalcas are neither jaguars nor ocelots who will eat us."

Tlacaelel, smiling, turned to the king, saying, "Lord, take care regarding what is important, do not waste words. Let the sentries go immediately to stand guard; your subjects know what is best for them. And I believe that as soon as morning comes only three or four squadrons of soldiers should go to skirmish with the Chalcas. When our soldiers have relieved each other during four or five days, this should tire them out. This way, on the sixth day, we shall attack, throwing all our forces against them."

And so for five successive days there were furious battles, where men on both sides fell. The Chalcas, however, received the worst part, but in spite of this they did not retreat. On the sixth day all the Aztec soldiers, somewhat rested, well prepared and ready for action, encountered the Chalcas. Ezhuahuacatl, up in front, cried out, "What is this, O Chalcas? Will you not leave this place, are you rooted to it?"

The Chalcas called back, "We shall not leave it because this is the boundary of our territory and we would rather die than abandon it. You shall not put a foot in our lands, as you have done with others."

The Aztecs responded to this: "Even though it grieves you, you will have to relinquish this land. And you will regret your obstinacy." This said, the Aztecs attacked with such fury that in a little less than half an hour they forced the Chalcas to retreat to a place called Acaquilpan, thus losing a large part of the field. During the second drive an attack they made them withdraw as far as Tlapitzahuayan.

The Chalcas, seeing they were about to be defeated, asked for a truce since they wished to communicate something to the Aztecs. The Aztecs then ceased fighting to hear what this message was. And the Chalcas said, "O brothers, know that five days from now we shall celebrate the festival of our god Camaxtli and we wish to celebrate it with the blood of Aztecs so that our god will be more honored and glorified. Therefore, we ask that on that our god's day you come into the field, in this very place, to join us in battle, because we wish to solemnize our feast with your flesh. Let us offer supplications and sacrifices to Camaxtli and we shall see if he is well honored with these.

Now go and rest. We are not in a hurry, there will be time for everything."

[The Aztecs pretended to understand and accept these reasons], so the two armies disbanded, the Chalcas returning to their city, the Aztecs, having left guards there, to Tenochtitlan. On reaching the Aztec capital, the lords and soldiers told Motecuhzoma what had happened, how they had invaded much of Chalca territory, and the trick played by the Chalcas so they would not be completely routed: seeing that they were about to be defeated, the Chalcas had begged to be allowed to celebrate the feast of their god. And they wished to do this with the aid of the Aztecs since they had promised Camaxtli the feast would be held with their flesh and blood. This was an oath they had made to the god, for which they had beseeched him to help defeat the Aztecs.

When Motecuhzoma saw that the war against the Chalcas dragged on and that the enemy could not be vanquished, and that the Chalcas had promised their deity Camaxtli to celebrate his feast with Aztec blood, he vowed to his own god to honor his festival with the death of many Chalcas. He swore that the Chalcas alone would build the temple of Huitzilopochtli and that he would make a great and solemn fire sacrifice with the bodies of men from Chalco. Tlacaelel and the rest of the officials made the same vow, speaking lengthily and offensively against the Chalcas.

When five days had passed and the truce that Chalco had requested came to an end, the Aztec forces went forth with great eagerness and desire to defeat the enemy. The soldiers were instructed to take the prisoners alive so that the vow might be fulfilled. When the army had left the city, Motecuhzoma ordered that all the boys upward of twelve years of age be called and be armed with bows and arrows, shields and swords. Captains were chosen to accompany them, then Motecuhzoma sent them after the regular soldiers. This was done with the hope that the Chalcas, seeing all these new soldiers, might think that another army had come into the field, and so grow afraid.

The first army arrived at the appointed place, and when the Chalcas saw that these soldiers had reached the slope of the hill at Tlapitzahuayan, they began to shout, "Come, Aztecs, come! Today this matter will be settled! The sacrificial knife is ready and our wives have already put the pots on the fire awaiting pieces of your flesh to be cooked! So to the attack!"

Shouting this, they began to scream even more loudly and attacked the Aztecs. These men fought with such fury that, although they encountered strong resistance, they forced the Chalcas to retreat. At this point the boys, who from afar looked like mighty warriors, arrived. The Chalcas were dismayed and began to abandon the field. Very soon they had withdrawn as far as Nexticpac, that plain which is in front of the resting place today called the shelter of Chalco, and there they tried to regather their forces. However, the Aztecs did not give them time to reorganize and pursued them as far as Tlapechhuacan. The soldiers of Chalco, climbing the hill of Tlapechhuacan, begged the Aztecs to let them rest and catch their breath.

But the Aztecs, ignoring their pleas, answered, "O little girls, do not ask for another truce because we shall not grant it to you. Not even the darkness of night will separate us from you. On this spot you will find out who the Aztecs are, and we shall see who celebrates the feast of their god, the Chalcas or the Aztecs! Let us see how you fulfill the oath you have sworn to your god!"

With these words they continued to pursue the Chalcas until they reached the town of Cocotitlan, near Tepepulla. At this point a great number of soldiers from Chalco were killed; there was not a man or boy in the Aztec army who did not capture one or two of the enemy or kill some. The survivors fled and hid but with such cunning that not one was to be seen.

The Aztecs left a number of soldiers to guard the battlefield in case the Chalcas tried to return and regain it. The Aztec leaders went back to Tlapitzahuayan, where they were received with great fear by the dwellers of that town. There they began to count the prisoners and found that they had captured three hundred seasoned warriors, without counting two hundred others of lower rank. Thus, they had captured five hundred men of Chalco. These were sent to Tenochtitlan and on the day after their arrival, by order of Tlacaelel and the king, they were immediately sacrificed to the god Huitzilopochtli.

In this way the vow that had been sworn was fulfilled, and the temple was reddened with the blood of five hundred men. A fire sacrifice was ordained; this was the most terrible and horrendous sacrifice that can be imagined, as anyone who has read the account I have written about sacrifices will have noted.[1] A great bonfire was built in a large brazier placed on the floor of the temple. This was called "the divine hearth." Into this great mass of flames men were thrown alive. Before they expired, their hearts were torn out of their bodies and offered to the god.

Thus, the steps and the chamber where the brazier was placed were bathed with the blood of the prisoners.

---

[1]Durán refers to his work on the festivals and deities, written before the *History: Book of the Gods and Rites and the Ancient Calendar* (1977:204–5, 213–14).

CHAPTER XVII

Which treats of the cruel attack made by the Chalcas upon the Aztecs between Amequemecan and Tepepulla to avenge the bloody sacrifice they had suffered. And how three brothers of the king of Mexico were killed and the Chalcas finally were defeated.

O nce the sacrifice had ended and the Aztecs were satiated with human flesh and drunk with the victory of which they were so proud, King Motecuhzoma told Tlacaelel to form the army again. As soon as they were ready they departed in the direction of Chalco, following the same road they had taken before. They passed through Tepepulla unafraid and soon reached a place called Tlacuilocan near Amequemecan, which at that time was the capital of that province or kingdom.

The men of Chalco, angered by this boldness, came out of the city of Amequemecan in great numbers. Even the boys who could carry a shield and sword joined them; not one was left in the city. And people from all the neighboring towns rushed to their aid. Having surrounded the Aztecs, the Chalcas fell upon them with such violence that the Aztecs regretted having put themselves in this difficult position. But seeing that they were forced to win or die, the soldiers formed a circle, some in an attempt to rout the Chalcas, others simply trying to survive. The battle raged with the greatest confusion, both sides slaying men right and left. A multitude of combatants covered the field. After some time, weary with fighting the entire day, both sides abandoned the battle, taking whatever prisoners they had managed to capture.

The Aztecs withdrew to Itztonpatepec, and at a place called Aculco they counted their losses among the leading officers in the army and found that three of these, brothers of the king, were missing. They went to look for them in the field and there discovered the bodies of these three warriors, covered with deep wounds, surrounded by many dead soldiers, so they took the three away. One of the brothers was named Cihuahuaque, another Tlacahuepan, and the third Quetzalcuauh. Their bodies were brought before Motecuhzoma and Tlacaelel, who had remained in Tlapechhuacan, confident that their valiant countrymen would be victorious. When the king saw the bodies covered with deep gashes, he and Tlacaelel—both of whom were brothers of the deceased, the most courageous warriors in the army—were greatly sorrowed. The king began to moan and lament over the dead men, wailing, "O valorous brothers of mine: happy are you who died proving your great personal courage. Go now in honor, wrapped in the precious stones and rich plumage of your heroic deeds, performed while fighting for your country and the honor of your brother the king!"

Turning to Tlacaelel, who was still standing there next to the bodies, he asked, "How does it affect you, Tlacaelel, seeing your brothers lying here dead?"

"O my lord," responded Tlacaelel, "I do not marvel at such deaths, nor do they fill me with fear. This is how wars are fought! Remember Huitzilihuitl the Elder, our forebear and king, who died in Colhuacan before we were born; behold how he left behind him eternal glory as a valiant man. The Aztec nation needs bold men such as those who lie before you. This is Mexico-Tenochtitlan, and men who are even more courageous than these will rise here. How long and how deeply must we mourn the deceased? If we stay here weeping we shall not be able to accomplish more important matters."

At this time the day of the feast of Xocotl was due. This was a special feast of the Aztecs and fell on the first day of the tenth month called Xocotl Huetzi [when the god of fire, Xiuhtecuhtli-Ixcozauhqui, was honored by fire sacrifices]. They held the festivities and celebrated them by sacrificing men from Chalco who had been brought as prisoners in the present war.

The Chalcas celebrated in the same way with Aztec captives. But before the sacrifice began, they saw among the prisoners a first cousin of King Motecuhzoma, a spirited young man by the name of Ezhuahuacatl; he was one of the leading noblemen in the Aztec court. Although he was a prisoner, the Chalcas, knowing that he came from the royal lineage of Mexico-Tenochtitlan, consulted with their councilmen and decided to free him and offer to make him king of Chalco. When Ezhuahuacatl heard about this, he laughed and told the other Aztec prisoners, "Do you know, brothers, that the Chalcas want to make me their king and lord? I would be willing if all of you would be given your freedom. But as this is not so, I shall die with you, since I did not come here to reign but to fight and perish like a man. I have already sold my life and with it have bought the Chalcas who will serve my children and grandchildren and all their descendants. And all of you will give your lives the same way!"

When the Chalcas came to Ezhuahuacatl with their decision and made their offer, he feigned he was in agreement. He told them he was honored by their proposal and requested a favor before he was enthroned. He asked that they bring a tree trunk about twenty *brazas* high and that they place a platform at its top. He wished to play and sport on this with the Aztec prisoners. The Chalcas brought him a thick pole, about twenty *brazas* high, and placed at the very top a small platform. When they told him it was ready, he came out surrounded by the other prisoners.[1] A drum was brought out and all began to dance around the pole. After dancing, Ezhuahuacatl said farewell to the Aztecs, crying out, "Brothers, the time has come! Die like brave men!" Having said these words, he began to climb the pole. When he arrived at the wooden platform at the summit, he began to dance and sing. When he finished singing, he shouted in a loud voice, "O Chalcas, know that with my death I shall have bought your lives and in the future you will serve my children and grandchildren! My royal blood will be paid for with yours!" And on this last cry he cast himself off the platform and was shattered to bits.

The people of Chalco were astonished and terrified by this act; they began to worry over what he had said and to be fearful. In spite of their troubled spirit, however, they took the prisoners and, having tied them together, sacrificed them by shooting arrows at them. The Chalcas always sacrificed in this way: as their god Camaxtli was the deity of hunting they killed their victims with arrows.[2]

When the death of Ezhuahuacatl and many other soldiers—the flower of brave and noble men—was known in Tenochtitlan, the Aztecs grieved over this great loss. And since it was also known that the Chalcas had fought with great strength and because of this the Aztecs had lost much of their courage, Motecuhzoma told Tlacaelel, "You have observed the death of our brothers and our kinsmen. It would be unjust if their deaths were not avenged. Therefore, without delay call together the Aztec army once more. Let us go to Chalco, where not a man, child, or adult will be left alive." And all the soldiers left for that city.

Having reached the same place where the latest battle and deaths had occurred, near the houses at Amequemecan, next to a hill called Itztonpatepec, Motecuhzoma and Tlacaelel addressed the soldiers:

[1]This is reminiscent of the *volador* or Flyers Dance, popular in prehispanic times and still practiced today. Four "flyers" dressed as birds climb to the top of the pole while a fifth, also at the summit, plays a small flute and drum in the center of the small platform. The four let themselves go, tied by ropes wrapped around the pole, and descend little by little, head first, "flying" around the pole. They play music at the same time, flute and drum, while the man at the top dances and plays. Thirteen turns bring the men down, thirteen being related to the ancient calendar.

[2]This type of sacrifice, known as the *tlacacaliztli*, was found not only among the Chalcas but also among the Huaxtecs and other indigenous groups. It was also known among the Pawnee of the United States. A depiction of the *tlacacaliztli* can be seen in the *Codex Nuttall* (1975).

"Brothers, we have come to this place from which there is no return if it is not with victory; otherwise we shall remain here, dead. And this time it will not be as it was before, when we came and went. This time it will be 'win or die.' And we shall stay here until this has been resolved; there will be no doubt about it. Therefore, we order that straw houses and huts be made on this same battlefield, where we shall stay, and I shall provide the rations until this business has been concluded. Do not fear, but let no one plan to return to Tenochtitlan unless he has been victorious. And he who has left his mother, his father, know that you may never see them again, or see your homeland. Everything has been left there in Mexico. And so, Aztecs, have courage; each one look after himself and carry out the tasks assigned to him. Think of the great cause that moves us and do not sorrow, do not become angry. I ask of you: do you not miss the dead lords and captains of our kingdom, the flower of Aztec men, our rampart and sanctuary? What has happened to them? Where are they? [It is our duty to forge ahead and avenge them!]"

The entire army then began to weep and the soldiers swore they would not return to their city until they had avenged these soldiers and that they would triumph or die. So they set up camp, making so many houses of straw and mats that it looked like real well-ordered town. Motecuhzoma sent messengers to all the heads of the barrios in Mexico, requesting that they send enough provisions for all the days they would be there, since he did not want to return to his city until the war had ended.

The Chalcas, arrogant and sure of themselves, prepared their men and made any necessary arrangements in their city, fortifying it as well as they could. That night the Chalca and Aztec armies were on the alert. They stood watch through the night, fearful of an attack while asleep. In the middle of the night two owls were heard, hooting to one another, and it sounded as if in their hooting one cried out, "*Tiacauh, tiacauh!*—mighty, mighty!"

And the other answered, "*Nocné, nocné*—alas, alas!" for this was an exclamation used by the people to indicate trouble or a reprimand.

Both the Chalcas and the Aztecs were terrified by these cries, as they took them to be an ill omen. These people are naturally superstitious, all of them. While the Chalcas and the Aztecs still trembled with fear, the two owls continued their song.

"*Tetec, tetec!*—cut, cut!"

And the other answered, "*Yollo, yollo*—hearts, hearts!"

For the third time the owls sang their song, one of them hooting, "*Quachtepol chichil, quachtepol chichil*—bloody red throats, bloody red throats!"

And the other answered, "Chalca, chalca—O men of Chalco, O men of Chalco!"

On hearing this, Tlacaelel arose and went to the king, where many soldiers heard his words: "O Aztecs, listen to the owls, hear how they announce our victory! Some divine thing moves these birds to hoot in such a manner. It is not possible that they are doing it by themselves! Someone moves their beaks so they cry out this way, for it seems impossible that they are hooting these things by themselves! Someone must be moving their beaks so they announce our victory! It is fated! O Aztecs, courage and strength! Let us not in our weakness lose what has been sent to us from above!"[3]

When morning came, the Chalcas, still fearful of the ill omen the owls had brought the night before, when they had heard their names clearly mentioned, decided to make use of a trick. Tlacaelel, however, saw through this. And the trick was this: Cuateotl, ruler of Amequemecan, had three adult sons, already experienced in war. It was decided that these three, feigning fear of death and the ill omen, should pretend to flee from their city secretly and go over to the side of the Aztecs. There they would declare that they had come to serve them and to show them a certain pass through which the city of Amequemecan could be taken. This would be done through the skill of those three.

So it was done. The three sons of Cuateotl, very secretly—pretending to be hiding, to be fleeing—came to the Aztec camp. Having been taken before King Motecuhzoma, they said, "O great lord, we are brothers, sons of Cuateotl, king of Chalco,[4] and we have come to serve you through fear of the ruin of our people and our country, which seems near at hand." "My brothers and I," said one whose name was Teoquizqui, "wish to guide your army so that the city can easily be taken and destroyed."

They were well received by Motecuhzoma, with much courtesy, and were given lodgings. Then Motecuhzoma consulted Tlacaelel, telling him how the three brothers had come with that offer. Tlacalel gave the following advice: "O powerful lord, I believe that in their despair they have come to seek salvation but not to aid us. They wish to guide us into an ambush, or onto rocky cliffs where we shall fall,

---

[3] Book 5 of Sahagún's *Florentine Codex* deals with the interpretation of evil signs. A wild animal at night, an owl hooting, a weasel running across a road, certain dreams, comets—all of these and many others were taken very seriously and affected people's comportment.

[4] Cuateotl was also ruler of Amequemecan, that is, Chalco-Amequemecan (see above in chapter XVII). In chapter XVI two rulers of Chalco are mentioned, Cuateotl and Toteoci Tecuhtli.

where we shall be trapped. Even if what they promise were true, they would say later that they had won the war and would share none of the glory with us. Let these nobles remain here if they wish, and if they want to go, let them. We shall continue with our struggle in our own way and we shall win. Let us show our manliness through our personal acts of bravery, not through the aid and plans of others!"

The king agreed with this. He gave orders that the three noble warriors be served well, that they be given whatever they wished, be treated courteously and given every attention possible. But they were not to be allowed to go into the battle that was to take place that day. When the Aztec army was ready, the soldiers went out in the proper order to a designated place where Tlacaelel exhorted them, animated them, encouraging them to conquer or die. But they were to be careful of their safety, try to protect their bodies from the enemies' blows. Their aim was to capture prisoners and to kill the enemy. It was important to capture soldiers dressed in full regalia, for these were the leading captains, the ones who fought most courageously; it was not desirable to take as captives those weaklings who fled the field.

The Chalcas, ready for battle, saw that their king's sons were absent. Since they knew that these young men should be leading the Aztecs, they understood that the enemy had seen through the trick. The Aztecs launched the attack and Tlacaelel reached the Chalca commander, who was in the front line. Threatening that he intended to wound him, Tlacaelel threw himself at the enemy leader and embraced him, holding him fast. Men from both sides rushed to the defense of their captains. So many Aztecs appeared that they managed to take the Chalca commander captive and lead him before King Motecuhzoma. The Aztec soldiers, greatly animated, captured many prisoners, each one taking his captive, and these were left in charge of the rear guard, while the soldiers went on to wound others. The Aztecs forced the enemy to withdraw, but the Chalcas began to lead them toward a cliff called Cuauhtexcac, which is on this side of the Sierra Nevada. But the Aztecs, not being familiar with that area and fearing an ambush, began to force the Chalcas toward the road that ascends the mountains to pass between the volcano and the Sierra Nevada. They wounded or killed all the people they caught up with, and the old men and old women, the children, the women from Amequemecan, who had already climbed to those heights to watch the battle, saw that their city was being sacked by the Aztecs, that these soldiers were pursuing the people on the hill and were sparing no one. They fled then toward Huexotzinco, where Chalca soldiers had been posted.

When Tlacaelel saw the flight of the women and children, the old men and women, toward Huexotzinco, he ordered one of his captains to cut off their means of escape but not to harm them. He told the captain to calm them and tell them not to flee, not to take refuge in a strange land, that by his command the war would end. They could now return for he did not wish more vengeance than had already been carried out.

The captain, known as Tlacatecatl, went with his forces in all haste and headed off the people who were fleeing toward Huexotzingo. He stopped them and told them that Tlacaelel sent word they were not to fear but were to return to their city so it would not become depopulated. He gave them his word that no further harm would come to them.

The Chalca soldiers returned and, having prostrated themselves before Tlacaelel, they surrendered their arms and cried out, "O Aztecs, we have done everything in our power to defend ourselves and we can do not more! Now that we shall be your vassals we can serve you by providing you with wood for your buildings, stone, loads of earth, carved canoes, laborers to till your lands and masons for your works, brave, spirited soldiers for your wars, and foodstuffs for your campaigns. These are the things we can give you."

In another history I found, which tells about this war, and which I have related as true fact (although I believe it is not so reliable as the one I have been using),[5] it is stated that the war between the Chalcas and the Aztecs lasted thirteen years and that on the day of their defeat the Chalcas lamented, "During thirteen years, O Aztecs, we have done everything in our power to keep from becoming your servants, but since you have finally defeated us, be happy with your victory. Here we are to serve you in everything you command." Then the Chalca noblemen went to Motecuhzoma and offered to give them comely maidens for their pleasure. It is also said that before the Aztecs broke camp the king ordered that all those who had fulfilled their duty in this war should have their noses pierced as a sign of valor. In this way they could enter the city with feathers and golden jewels hanging from their noses, like moustaches. These perforations were made in the cartilage of the nose. And thus it was done.

Tlacaelel also ordered all the Chalcas who had fought courageously, who had done outstanding feats, to be adorned in the same manner, saying to them, "Friends, until this time we have never fought a people who are our equal, as you are. It is just, then, that since we are equal in bravery, you should be honored in this same way." Thus, they also pierced the noses of the Chalcas and placed there the insignia of valor.

[5] "Another history" is evidently not the *Crónica X*, although the "one he has been using" must have been the basic document he refers to constantly, whether the *Crónica X* or not.

The History of the Indies of New Spain

After this Motecuhzoma ordered the lands to be divided. And so they were distributed in this way: first the crown received its share, then Tlacaelel his, and after them each leading warrior was given the land he deserved. No one was offended, for each one was awarded one or two pieces of land according to his position and his deeds. When this had been done the Aztecs returned to Tenochtitlan. After this the Aztecs and the Chalcas remained friends and confederates.

CHAPTER XVIII

Which treats of how the people of Tepeaca waged war against the Aztecs and of how the former were defeated, were harshly treated, and were brought to Mexico-Tenochtitlan to be sacrificed. With a description of the funeral rites in honor of those Aztecs who had been killed in the war with Chalco.

When the Aztec soldiers reached Tenochtitlan, all the inhabitants went out to meet them with much rejoicing. The priests also were festive and appeared carrying braziers and incense burners. Speaking many words of eulogy and singing songs of praise, they led the warriors to the temple, where these men made offerings of the spoils of war and the things they had brought back with them. They also presented the prisoners of war who would later be the sacrificial victims in the festivities.

After everyone had calmed down, was tranquil, and the army had rested from the toils of the recent war, the king ordered that honors and funeral rites be held for all those killed in the war, saying, "O Aztecs, you all know that our brothers who died in the war with Chalco did not lose their lives while offending our god, nor while stealing, lying, or fornicating, nor while committing perjury. They died fighting like the courageous men they were, shedding their blood for the honor and glory of their country, the Aztec nation. Therefore, it is right that as soon as possible we pay them the honors and do the funeral rites that such valiant men deserve."

Motecuhzoma ordered all the old songmakers whose occupation it was to mourn deaths such as these to compose songs that were appropriate for the occasion. So these old men composed chants for the dead, and when they were ready they came out with a drum that was hoarse and dissonant,[1] and began to sing those mournful, sad dirges. Then the widows of the deceased, their sons and daughters, and all their relatives, came out after the chanters. All the women wore their hair loose, hanging close to their faces. They wore their husbands' mantles and breechcloths draped over one shoulder, while the sons and daughters carried in their hands their fathers' ear ornaments, feathers, and labrets, and all their fathers' jewels.

---

[1] Note that the drum had to be off tune, mournful, for this sad occasion.

When all were in order, they began to dance and sing, with a strange wailing sound. The old songmakers stood around the drum; they were dressed in short shirts like albs, edged with fringe, and round gourds hung by special cords from their backs.[2]

All the men who were kinsmen of the dead warriors—fathers, grandfathers, uncles, cousins, brothers—carrying the swords and shields of the deceased, formed a large circle. After they had danced quite a long time, they sat down to rest. While the old singers rested, the others went one by one to console, to encourage each one there, speaking thus: "Courage, brothers, do not be distressed. Respond to the sun, give him thanks, and thank the earth who is our lady, our mother. Bring now the sheath in which your dead ones can be wrapped."

Then each woman brought a mantle dyed red.[3] These they gave to one of the elders, and they also gave him a mantle called *cuachtli* [a mantle or cloth used as "money"], a breechcloth, and a slave who would die at the same time and who would thus go to serve the deceased in the afterworld. All these things were called "offerings to those who must die" and were given to the mourners. Then in the presence of everyone they made mummy bundles out of torch pine, by putting together many strips of this resinous wood. As many bundles were made as there were soldiers killed in the war. These were tied together with cords called *aztamecatl*, meaning "white rope." Those bundles were formed like statues, with faces made by applying eyes and nose and mouth. The space between the eyes was painted black with soot and soot was painted around the mouth. Tied to the neck were a shield and some swords; at the back were insignia formed of little flags and featherwork. Each one was adorned with five of these small banners, then very fine mantles were placed on the statues. These torch-pine figures were then placed against a wall in a room especially set aside for this purpose in the temples. This chamber was called the *tlacochcalli*, [house of darts or arsenal] or *tziuac calli* [house of darts made of cactus spines].

When all these bundles were in order, the old men again began to dance and sing the funeral chants. All the kinsmen of the deceased, both men and women, lined up before these statues made of *ocotl*, which is torch pine, and wept there. The bundles or statues were called *ocoteteuctin*, which means "lords of *ocotl*." Meanwhile, the old men danced.

[2]Gourds hanging on the backs of personages, as seen, for example, in the Teotihuacan murals and in the *Codex Nuttall*, are signs that the wearer is a priest. The gourd probably contained tobacco, which was part of the ceremonial paraphernalia.

[3]In some regions red was the color of death. Archaeologists in Mexico frequently find excavated osseous remains painted red, due to the body having been covered with cinnabrium, which, when the body disintegrates, paints the bones.

When the song had ended, all joined in the playing of the drum by clapping their hands to the same rhythm. Then they took some bones on which marks were cut, like a ladder, and danced to the sound made when these were rasped by other bones. These musical instruments are still used in dances today and are related to ancient superstitions. When the old men danced this dance and sang those songs, they feathered their ears and the place behind the ears. The dancing lasted four days and on the fourth day, after having mourned all those days and having carried out the ceremonies I have described, they set fire to the torch-pine bundles.

After these were burned and before the ashes had become cold, the old men washed the faces of all the relatives of the dead warriors, both men and women, with leaves of wild laurel.[4] After having washed the faces of the family members, the old priests took the ashes from the bundles and buried them. After this ritual washing and burial of the ashes, the old men and all the relatives, men, women, and children, fasted for eighty days. During this time they ate only once a day and they neither washed their faces nor combed their hair. At the end of the eighty days the amount of dirt on their faces, the dirt and dust that stuck to them and streaks from tears, was so great that these people looked like demons.

When the eighty days had passed, the old priests, with their fingernails, removed the crust of dirt that had accumulated on the cheeks of the mourners. They then wrapped this filth in some papers and took it to a certain place called Tzatzcantitlan ["Place Where Wailing (Ends)" or, roughly, "Place Where Sorrow is Left"] and there abandoned those papers that held the dirt of the tears. This ceremony was called "the vestiges of tears."

After these papers had been taken to Tzatzcantitlan, the widows gave clothing—mantles and breechcloths—to the elders. Then the widows were advised that during five days they were to make offerings. So for five days those poor women prepared breads and bowls of toasted maize and took these as offerings to the place where the torch-pine bundles had been burned. At the same time, during those five days, they fed the old men, and when this period was over they took all

---

[4]Plants were very important, both economically and symbolically. In Durán's other treatise, *Book of the Gods and Rites* (1977) he mentions some kind of flora associated with every ceremony. For example, while talking about the ball game, he says that the divisions on the floor of the court were made with "a certain herb and no other, which is a sign of pagan belief" (1977:315) and in the description of the feast of Tlacaxipehualiztli, "All the seats which were used on this day had to be made of the leaves of the white sapote . . . never from other materials, which is another diabolical superstition" (1977:417). See also Heyden 1983a.

The History of the Indies of New Spain

the mantles and breechcloths that had belonged to the deceased and, leaving not one piece of clothing that they had worn, burned them all. And in a rite to honor those mantles and breechcloths they took "wine of the earth" [or pulque] and poured it all over the place where the clothing had been burned.

In this way the funeral rites for those killed in the war were ended. Everyone went home, but the widows were told that the same offerings of food were to be deposited there eighty days later.

When the eighty days had passed and the offering had been placed there, the elders addressed all the relatives but then spoke to the dead warriors thus:

> O you who have died, you who have gone to the resplendent lord, the transparent sun, now you rejoice, take pleasure with him, you call out to him. You stroll through his delightful fields, there in the "scorched lane." You are painted, you are striped, with different hues, with the colors of dawn, before the resplendent sun, where we shall see you no more. Carry out your duty with great care, diligently, with perseverance.

Having finished this address, they again poured "wine" on the ground. And with this the obsequies were ended. Everyone believed that without these rites the soldiers would not find eternal rest.

Shortly after these funeral rites were over, news reached Tenochtitlan that the people of Tepeaca had murdered a number of Aztec, Tezcocan, and Tepanec merchants who had gone together to trade in that city. All their merchandise had been stolen and their bodies thrown to the beasts. When Motecuhzoma heard of this, he called Tlacaelel and all the important chieftains and informed them of these tragic happenings. He stated that he wished to have the lords of Tepeaca captured, brought to Mexico, and be given a cruel death. And if they could not be brought to this city, they should be killed in their own territory. Tlacaelel, however, answered that this was not sufficient punishment and that it would be better to prepare for war and then to destroy them mercilessly, as revenge for the dreadful act they had committed. And so it was decided that four of the principal men would go to Tepeaca to challenge them. These four soon left on that mission.

On reaching Tepeaca, they went before Coyolcue, ruler of that city, saying, "Noble lord, Motecuhzoma and Tlacaelel and the dignitaries of Tenochtitlan send you this shield and sword together with these plumes so that you may feather your head.[5] They also bid you be

---

[5]Sending feathers was one of the ways in which war was declared; in this case they were accompanied by the shield and sword. Balls of feathers on the head usually denoted death by sacrifice.

patient since they will soon visit you, and also they wish us to tell you that, until this problem of the robbing and murdering of the merchants has been settled, all the people who seek a living in the provinces on this side of the Sierra Nevada will not be permitted to go to your city; and the doors of our city will be closed so that no one who is not a friend and ally of the Aztecs can enter, under pain of death. We do not wish any dealings between our province and yours."

Coyolcue and three other lords who were with him answered that they were pleased to hear this for they were ready for anything Motecuhzoma and Tlacaelel might be preparing. The envoys returned and relayed this message to the king from the men of Tepeaca, telling him how those people evidently wished to try their fortune, were much inclined toward war.

The envoys were congratulated and told to go rest.

Motecuhzoma then requested of Tlacaelel that he prepare the men for war and that he obtain from the neighboring cities and all the towns around them great quantities of maize cakes, which are toasted tortillas, toasted grains of corn and maize flour, as well as salt, chiles, pumpkin seeds, and ground beans, with which to prepare cooked dishes. These town were also to provide cooking pots, plates, *metates*—which are grinding stones—and reed mats with which tents and huts are made for use in the field. So envoys were sent to Tezcoco, Xochimilco, Colhuacan, Chalco, Cuitlahuac, Coyoacan, and Azcapotzalco so that all the things I have mentioned, together with shields, swords, and arrows for fighting, would be provided. The rulers of all these towns received the envoys well, saying that were happy and willing to comply with this request, that they desired to lend their services. Then they got together the provisions that had been requested and sent them to the place where the battle was to be held. The messengers returned to Tenochtitlan with the news that all the lords from those cities had fulfilled this obligation gladly and provisions had been sent rapidly to a place near Tepeaca.

This matter settled, Motecuhzoma then commanded the army to leave the city. He and Tlacaelel went with the rest of the soldiers. And when the neighboring cities and towns saw that the Aztecs had set out to avenge the outrage committed against the entire province—because merchants from all these cities had been murdered—they sent soldiers to accompany King Motecuhzoma and the Aztec army, to fight alongside them and to help win the war. Among these allies Tezcoco and Chalco sent outstanding, courageous men. This impressed Motecuhzoma and he stated that he was grateful for this support.

The brave captains and seasoned warriors of Tenochtitlan and its domains arrived at a hill called Coyopetlayo, near the city of Tepeaca.

The History of the Indies of New Spain

Spies were immediately sent into Tepeaca to see what preparations were being made, what supplies were guarded there, and if a wall or barricade had been erected around the city. They also wished to find out the number of enemy warriors. But the spies soon returned to report that they had seen neither barricade nor guards nor soldiers, nor had they heard rumors of war, nor did the people there seem to have any idea of this.

Motecuhzoma and his men were angry that their arrival had aroused so little interest among the enemy. He commanded his soldiers to get ready and then he addressed them: "O Aztecs, do not make haste! Go slowly, for this night, before tomorrow's sun rises, the matter will have been settled. Let the men separate into groups and let us accomplish in one blow what we might have done in many. Let some of our men go to Tecalli, others to Cuauhtinchan, others to Acatzinco, and let us conquer these four capitals so their people will become our vassals." In this way the army was divided into four squadrons.

Before any more steps were taken, they set up camp, putting together their shelters and huts [of reed or palm leaf mats]—for that is what their tents in wartime were made of—in correct order. The quarters of the Aztecs were in a certain section, the Tezcocans on another side, the Chalcas in another place, the Xochimilcas in another, and the Tepanecs in yet another. The soldiers were divided into four companies, each with its own captain and soldiers. In this fashion everyone would receive the glory of the victory that was to come because each company carried its own banner or flag and could be recognized this way: the Aztec banner, the Tezcocan banner, the Xochimilca flag, and that of the Tepanecs, each one was distinctive.

At dusk the companies set out in the direction that had been determined. The history with its account of this war does not mention that the people of Tepeaca were prepared for hostilities, nor that they defended themselves in any way. The history says only that the Aztecs arrived there and challenged the Tepeacas, although they discovered no preparations for war and no defense measures. Near dawn the four companies that had been formed during the night made a surprise attack upon the city, setting fire to the temple, burning the homes of the principal men, and committing robbery and murder. In this way they quickly subdued the four cities so that when the sun rose these were in the hands of the Aztecs, as Motecuhzoma had promised. I do not venture to write here that the Tepeacas fought or defended themselves, nor that they uttered a word of protest [because the source I am consulting does not say so]. I understand that this lack of defense was intentional since they felt their resistance would be futile, and in a cowardly way they allowed themselves to be slaughtered like wild animals. And the history states that the lords of Tepeaca, led by their ruler Coyolcue, all weeping bitterly, their hands crossed as a sign of surrender, prostrated themselves before the Aztecs, begging for mercy and pardon for the offense they had committed by having killed the merchants. The history refers to nothing else in this case, for if the Tepeacas fought and defended their city, the history does not relate these events. My intention here has been only to translate the Nahuatl account into our Spanish language.[6]

The people of Tepeaca pleaded with the Aztecs to stop killing them, stop destroying them. They promised to be perpetual tributaries, paying in maize, chiles, salt, pumpkin seeds, cloth, sandals, palm leaf mats, and deerskins. They also promised to provide labor as workmen on the roads and as carriers for the Aztecs' loads, foodstuffs, and other bundles. And they would build huts and set up tents in time of war. From that day on they would respect the Aztecs as their masters, as their father and mother, as their defenders. From that day on they would be subject to everything the Aztecs wished to command. Then the Aztecs answered, "Come here, Tepeacas. Are you men enough to give us soldiers who will go to war and bring back slaves?" The Tepeacas answered affirmatively, so on top of the tribute already agreed upon an additional tribute was demanded: that every eighty days a certain number of slaves, men captured in war, were to be offered for the abominable sacrifice to the idols.

Now that they were subjects, vassals, of the Aztecs, the latter were taken into the city of Tepeaca to the homes of the noblemen, where they were given rich presents of cloth, skins, sandals, precious stones, jewels, gold, fine plumage, shields, insignia, weapons, and other precious objects. Most of these were presented to King Motecuhzoma, to Tlacaelel, and to the four members of the supreme council. Similar presents were given by the towns of Tecalli, Cuauhtinchan, and Acatzinco, towns as rich and large as Tepeaca. All of these conquered people were given orders to go to Tenochtitlan to acknowledge and adore the god Hutizilopochtli, and to swear obedience to him as their supreme lord. All these people agreed to this, so the captains and soldiers returned to their city.

The priests and elders from the temples came out to receive the victorious army at a place called Acachinanco at the gates of the Aztec city. They all came out in a certain order. It must be explained here that in the temples there was a regular hierarchy among the priests and elders of the temples (each one with his rank and office), such as

---

[6]Another reference to the fact that Durán's basic chronicle was written in the Nahuatl language.

exists in our own churches and cathedrals. There were offices similar to those of archbishop, dean, canon, chaplain, acolyte, and sexton. Thus, in this land and in ancient times, in the temples there were supreme dignitaries and high dignitaries, as well as those of lower rank. The high priest was called by different names; some called him Papa, others called him Topiltzin [Our Lord]. In a word, every province had its own authoritative and high-sounding name for him. Other priests were called Tecuacuiltin, others Cuauhuehuetque, others Chachalmeca, others Tlenamacaque, others Calmecahuehuetque, others Mozauhque, and still others Tlamacazque.[7] There were so many titles and dignities among the priests that I would have to dedicate a special chapter to them in order to avoid confusion regarding these and so that their meanings would be clear. I shall write this explanation when the occasion arises.[8]

All the priestly hierarchy—the dignitaries, old and young—came out to greet the conquerors. They were dressed in cassocks or tunics of different styles and colors. Some cassocks came down to the floor, others were not quite so long, some had fringe along the edge, some had a border in the form of a series of circles, some with tassels—all finely worked with different colors and types of handwork. On their heads were garlands made of paper, or some of leather, and on their foreheads were headbands with which their headdresses were tied. The headbands were in the form of pleated shields, like leaves, and they were painted in various colors. From the backs of the priests called Cuauhuehuetque and Tecuacuiltin hung small gourds strung with leather thongs. These little gourds were called *yetocomatl* [tobacco gourd]. They all carried black staffs in their hands.

The priests came in a procession, some walking on one side of the road and some on the other, but all in proper order. Those called Tlenamacaque, which means "he who handles the incense burner" in our language, came with their braziers in their hands. When all the prisoners had arrived, brought there by the Aztecs—and there were a great many of them—the priests threw incense into the braziers and began to incense the future victims, since they belonged to the gods. Then the priests called Tecuacuiltin (which means "gods" or "images of gods" because *tecuacuilli* means "idol" or "one like an idol")

---

[7]Garibay (Durán 1967, vols. I and II) translates the titles of these priests: Calmecahuehuetque: elders from the school of higher learning (II:584); Chachalmeca: "Huitzilopochtli's sacrificers" or "Sacrificers from Chalman" (I:309); Cuauhuehuetque: "Old Eagles," war veterans who no longer go into battle (II:585); Mozauhque: penitents (I:311); Tecuacuiltin: images in the round, statues (I:313); Tlamacazque: mature men (I:314), priests in the temple (II:589); Tlenamacaque: fire priests, "They who give them incense" (I:314).

[8]Durán never wrote this special treatise, or at least there is no record of it.

arrived and broke pieces of maize bread, which were kept in the temples strung on cords; this was like bread of oblation. They offered these to the captives and the priests then addressed the prisoners in the following way:

> We welcome you to this city of Tenochtitlan, which is in the great lagoon, the great pool of water, where the eagle sang, where the serpent hissed, where the fishes fly, where the blue waters joined the red waters. Here among the reeds, here among the rushes, where the god Huitzilopochtli rules, where he commands; do not think that you have been brought here by mishap, nor that you have come here to seek a living; you have come to die [for Huitzilopochtli], to offer your chests and your throats to the knife. Only in this way has it been your fortune to know and delight in this great city. Only through your death has the door been opened, through which the people of Tepeaca never enter. We welcome you and say to you that you should be consoled that no womanly nor infamous deed has brought you here, but manly feats [have been responsible]. You will die here, but your fame will live forever.

When these words had been spoken, the prisoners were given a sacred beverage to drink that is called *teooctli,* meaning literally "divine wine." After drinking it, they were taken to the temple, where one by one they were made to pass by the feet of the idol, making signs of great reverence to this statue. After this ceremony, which signified that they were offered to the gods, they were taken to the palace, where they were made to perform the same ceremony before King Motecuhzoma, who was on his royal seat in a position of much authority. This was done because the monarchs in this land were adored as gods; thus, the people feared them, obeyed them, and revered them as such.

After this second reverence had been completed, Motecuhzoma ordered that all the prisoners be dressed with mantles, breechcloths, and sandals. When they were thus garbed and had eaten, they were taken to the marketplace, in the middle of which there was a low platform, somewhat like a pillar or pillory; this was the marketplace shrine and great superstition was associated with it. A drum was brought forth and all the prisoners danced to its music on top of the platform. For this dance they were given shields covered with splendid featherwork and other weapons, flowers in their hands, and fragrant tobacco to smoke, which comforts them greatly. Tobacco was generally distributed after meals; they say it is good for the digestion, to settle the stomach. A feast without tobacco was not considered a real feast.

After the prisoners had come to the Aztec capital and had performed the ceremonies mentioned above, all the dignitaries from Tepeaca came to acknowledge and do honor to Huitzilopochtli. Coy-

The History of the Indies of New Spain

olcue, ruler of Tepeaca, and two other lords from the same province, Chichtli and Chiauhcoatl, together with many princes from the same region, went directly to the temple and made offerings to the god of splendid large white fans, rich feathers worked in different forms, bows and arrows, finely painted bracelets made of bone, the tanned skins of diverse animals, and nose plugs of the type worn by the lords. Then they all took out some small blades and drew blood from their tongues and ears with these. Then they "ate the earth" that was at the foot of the idol.[9] Then they went to perform the same rite in front of the king, who was the surrogate of the god, and before his main official, Tlacaelel. And standing before the king, they addressed him: "O powerful lord, you who move the earth simply by breathing, now you can be at ease, now you can rest from the arduous tasks you have performed. Your kinsmen, your relatives, the men of Tepeaca, have come before you in order to honor Huitzilopochtli, he who attracts, who draws to him, all the nations. And I, who am his servant, come to serve him and I bring my subjects, my vassals, so they too will adore him and know him as their lord. They also come with tears, with sighs, to hear from your lips what their duties will be, and to take upon their shoulders the burden, the duties that they are to fulfill."

The king responded: "You are welcome here. You will be given lodgings immediately." Tlacaelel then had these lords shown to their quarters, where they were to rest and to wait for the king's reply. On the next day Tlacaelel went to them and, greeting them on behalf of the king, said:

"Behold, lords of Tepeaca, you have come to this court in this city, you have observed it and found pleasure in its authority and grandeur; this city will now be your mother. You also have come to be told of your obligations and then to inform the people of your land of the commands and instructions you will have received. These are:

"One: You are hereby ordered, since your city is situated in a place through which many pass, to take great care of the travelers from all the provinces, natives as well as strangers. Let none of them be mistreated, robbed, or offended in any way, and be especially careful to protect the merchants who trade with Xoconochco and Guatemala and all the land, since these are the ones who enrich and ennoble the earth. They feed the poor, they maintain the villages, and should anyone mistreat them, harm them, you will notify this court as soon as possible, for their offense is punishable by death.

---

[9]"Eating earth," sometimes called "kissing the earth"—touching the earth with one's finger and then putting it in the mouth—was a sign of reverence, known as geophagy.

"Two: Your lord the king also orders that all those outsiders who wish to may go live in your province. They must be given land where they can dwell. Thus, your city of Tepeaca will be made greater with these people from other areas. The king also wishes that a great marketplace be built in Tepeaca so that all the merchants in the land may trade there on an appointed day. In this market there will be sold rich cloth of all kinds, precious stones and jewels, featherwork of different colors, gold, silver, and other metals, the skins of animals such as jaguars, ocelots, and pumas, cacao, fine breechcloths, and sandals. All this our lord King Motecuhzoma orders you to carry out.

"And so there will be no error or failure in these plans and so they will be done well, an Aztec governor, whose name is Coacuech, will be placed over you and you must obey him and consider him to be a representative of the royal person. And now you may return with goodwill to your cities, for the king cannot speak to you at this time."

The men from Tepeaca were grateful for the honor, for their city having been designated the site for a rich marketplace, over which they would have control and could also control the merchants, according to Tlacaelel's instructions. So they returned to Tepeaca, accompanied by the Aztec governor Coacuech. They were all well received in that city; the governor was paid respect and was given houses to live in and lands to be worked. He was then obeyed and respected as if he had been the king of Mexico-Tenochctitlan. Coacuech was careful to collect the royal tribute every eighty days and send it to the king.

In this way the people of Tepeaca were peaceful and contented, without disputes of wars. They would have had no problems and no harm would have come to them if at the beginning they had done what they finally were forced to do—that is, ask forgiveness of the Aztecs [for having killed the merchants] and offer submission.

CHAPTER XIX

Which treats of the great discord that arose between the Aztecs and the Huaxtecs of Tamapachco, Tochpan, and Tzincoac, and how, after the battle had been fought, the Huaxtecs were vanquished, destroyed.

Huehue Motecuhzoma the Elder (the first of this name) had reigned eleven years when an amazing thing took place: it began to snow daily and so heavily that it is said that in all the towns the snow reached to one's knees. People became so frightened and were so unprepared in their usual light clothing that not a single person could be seen on the roads or streets. The snow fell steadily for six days and the mountains and hills remained covered for many days.

At this time the Aztec nation was at peace, but peace flies away from those who long for it. News came that the Huaxtecs had attacked and killed all the merchants and traders who were active in that area, leaving not one alive. Most of these men had come from Tenochtitlan and its provinces. Having committed this crime and having caused other people to rebel, the Huaxtecs surrounded their towns with five walls, one after another. These were strong adobe walls, reinforced as well as possible [with other materials, and served as defense against other people].

By killing the Aztec and Tezcocan merchants and those of allied provinces, who always traveled together, the Huaxtecs aimed to prove their valor and strength — at the expense of the Aztecs — and thus gain more bellicose fame than other people. This was a foolish, mistaken idea, and a waste of effort, for no rash act, no boldness, was sufficient to destroy the Aztecs. Because besides being numerous they were courageous, so much so that the entire land trembled with fear of them. These Aztecs were so experienced in fighting that even children, the very young boys, played at war and pretended to bring captives home. The youths constantly were preparing themselves with fasts, thirst, and nudity. They would sleep on the ground, they would carry heavy burdens on their backs so they could carry them this way when it became necessary. They followed the leading captains in order to learn from them the military arts and ways. In Tenochtitlan almost nothing else was talked about, except how to act in war. It was also a mistake to begin a dispute with the Aztecs because the main provinces were in favor of them and were commanded by them. At a sign from the Aztecs ten or twelve thousand well-armed warriors responded. And if they wanted twenty thousand, twenty thousand came, or if forty thousand, these too came; the number depended upon the strength of the opponents and the force needed to combat them. And the Aztecs were so powerful that, if they needed to send one hundred thousand men into the field, they could do this simply by commanding it.

The news of the Huaxtec rebellion and the death of merchants, who had been cast from great heights into ravines below, was brought to Motecuhzoma by people of Tulantzinco. The king thanked them and ordered that they be attended well. Then he summoned Tlacaelel and asked him to send envoys to Tezcoco, Tacuba, Chalco, Xochimilco, and all the neighboring towns. Since the aggression had been directed at the people of all these cities, retaliation must be taken by all of them. They were ordered to prepare for war, to obtain provisions and all the necessary arms, tents, and fighting equipment they would need for the conflict.

Tlacaelel immediately advised all the allies of the king's decision. This was heard by the kings of Tacuba and Tezcoco and by the lords of Chalco, Xochimilco, Coyoacan, Cuitlahuac, Colhuacan, and Mezquic, who answered that they were pleased to oblige. With all goodwill they commanded their people to be prepared and ordered that they obtain food supplies, weapons, and tents, as had been recommended. When Tlacaelel heard of the diligence on the part of the allied cities and provinces in making ready for war and complying with these demands, he ordered all the Aztec captains to prepare their men and then leave the city. So they began to depart with their forces for the land of the Huaxtecs.[1]

After these men had left, the wives of the warriors—who had been taught idolatrous beliefs by the old men, who were both superstitious and fond of inventing a thousand strange ceremonies—performed these rites during all the time the war lasted. For example, as a sign of sadness and mourning, they did not wash their faces but left the dirt on them, from the day their husbands left until they returned.

Another custom was that of rising at midnight and building a fire. As soon as the firewood was burning well, a woman would go out into the street and sweep. Once she had swept, she bathed her body without allowing the water to touch her face or head. Then, after bathing, she sat down to grind maize and then prepare some very small, square

---

[1] A description of contemporary Huaxtec culture is found in Laughlin (1969:298–311).

tortillas and other long breads of the maize flour. Then she ground a bit of toasted corn and put it into a deep gourd. After this she entered the shrine where the idols were kept; these were small rooms similar to the ones in which images of saints are kept today. They were used only for this purpose and the same holds true in our times. Having entered this chamber, she then took out the leg bones of the prisoners her husband had captured in war, wrapped them in paper, and hung them from the beams. Next she took a brazier and put fire and incense in it, placing it below the bones. She also burned incense before all the little household idols, which were many, and while the incense was burning she prayed:

> O Lord of All Created Things, of the Sky and the Earth, of the Wind and the Sun, of the Water, of the Night and of the Day, have pity on your servant, on your creature who goes about the hills and the valleys, about the plains and rocky places, offering you his sweat and his panting breath. He is your eagle, he is your jaguar who works incessantly, without rest, to serve you in this woeful life. I beseech you, O Lord, I beg you to lend him life, to allow him time to enjoy this world. Hear me, O Lord!

Having made this petition, she lay down again; and when dawn came, but before it was quite day, she rose and swept the street once more. All this was performed again at midday and then at sunset, and continued during all the time the husband was away at war.

The army meanwhile had reached the province of Tulantzinco, where the men of that place came out to receive the lords and captains of the army, with all the attention to which they were accustomed. With much courtesy and respect they gave them lodgings in their city and provided them with everything they needed. These provisions were so abundant that the Aztecs were amazed at the different breads and savory dishes prepared with fowl, and at the stews and the cacao drinks that they were served. Then the Aztecs were given clothing— finely worked mantles and breechcloths, also sandals. And finally they were regaled with a solemn festival and a banquet.

Later the Aztecs and the men from other cities who accompanied them thanked their hosts, then Tlacaelel ordered all the forces to begin the march in orderly fashion. So the army left Tulantzinco and marched until the enemy was visible. Here they set up camp, each group making its huts and tents. And there were so many that a large, handsome, and well-ordered town was created. An experienced captain then addressed the soldiers:

"O valorous men, you who have come from all the nations and provinces, you who are present here at this time. Consider that by

The discord between the Aztecs and the Huaxtecs

coming here you have abandoned your hearths and homes where you lived happily. You have arrived at a place where you may perish, like dry grass when it is set on fire, or like the navigator on the sea who is snatched from the waves but is sunk into the depths, or is burned like the grass. Contemplate your death and think of nothing else. You have left your fathers and mothers, uncles, aunts, relatives, and you will never see them again. When you face the reason for which you have come here, which is to fight in a dangerous war against a cruel and savage people, whose customs and way of life are completely alien to our own, there is not doubt that the only way to go on is to ignore [to shut your eyes to the suffering of] your own flesh and heart, which after all will die.

"You well know that you did not come here to trade or to seek your living by reselling or bargaining with things you had bought in your own city. You have come to defeat the enemy or to die. Therefore, the bow and arrow, the sword and shield, are what are important to you today. Entrust yourself to them and to the strength of your arms, for these will save you."

[And then facing the new recruits:] "And you, young boys, youths, since you wish to make use of all that for which you were born and educated, you have dared to participate in this war. But be careful that your extreme youth does not make you too rash, driving you on to accomplish more than is possible at your age. Follow the experienced warriors in these things. Do not decide suddenly to jump into the battle and then try to get out. Detain yourself, observe how your captains and experienced soldiers go in and out of the fray. And if you see one who advances because of his skill and courage, then try to imitate him; but if he is not successful, then stay where you are and simply watch. For in the future you will need to have learned these things well since fighting will be our perpetual occupation and this will not be the first war, nor the last.

"Consider also that you will not be fighting jaguars or pumas or demons, nor do they have mouths so large that they will swallow you. They are men of flesh and bones, as we are. But be angry, become impatient, let your hearts be aggravated against a people who have injured you, attacked you. If you are filled with ire, with wrath, you will search for vengeance. Because if you are not inflamed, are not wrathful, you will not show spirit and valor, you will do nothing."

After these words had been spoken, the soldiers were given rations and were told to eat all they wished. When the meal had ended, the officers gave orders to their men in this way: "Listen, soldiers: when you are on the battlefield you can become confused with the enemy and someone might make a mistake when aiming at a squadron [and this way attack allies]. So Tlacaelel orders that the men from each squadron carry a flag on high, with the insignia of its barrio well visible so that all the men of that place will follow their flag and will shout the name of the barrio during the battle, so they will be identified in this way."

Then some seasoned warriors began to marshal the troops and prepare them for battle. These men, who had authority in thus ordering the soldiers, were very well armed and they carried staffs in their hands and wore headbands, long shell earrings, and labrets. The first warriors marshaled into action were those called Cuachic,[2] who were similar to an order of knights. Each one had sworn not to flee if faced by twenty enemies, nor to retreat one step even if this meant death. There was another order called Otomi, whose members were recognized by their hair, which was cut short above the ear, and these had made a vow not to retreat even if faced by ten or twelve enemies but rather to die fighting.

All these soldiers were ordered to lie down upon the earth with their shields and swords in their hands, as if in an ambush. There were about two thousand men from all the provinces, and in this way they were covered with grass until not a man could be seen. Then the captains and seasoned soldiers were formed into squadrons, and next to each experienced soldier was placed a youth, one of those new recruits who had never been to war before. Orders were given to the soldiers to take care of these younger men and give them protection.

The army soon reached the place where the battle was to be fought, when the Aztecs began to yell and shout, "Hear, Huaxtecs, today you will become our slaves and tributaries, from today on you will serve us!"

And the Huaxtecs shouted in return, "We shall see about that! For we shall do everything in our power so that none of you can return to Tenochtitlan to tell about this! We shall kill you and cut off your heads! Don't you know that we possess herbs that can kill you just by touching them?"

The Aztecs called out that they had heard all this and at the same time threw themselves at the enemy. The Huaxtecs also attacked, making a great din with the wooden rattles that hung from their helmets and with the large metal rattles they wore on their backs and feet, all of these making a weird noise. Their heads and bodies were feathered, their faces painted in different colors. Some wore in their noses large, thick, crystal nose plugs, while others had nose plugs of

---

[2]For more information regarding the Cuachic warriors, see Durán's *Book of the Gods and Rites* (1977:198–99).

precious stones. The Huaxtec warriors were so hideous that the mere sight of them terrified the others. They bore shields and carried in their hands darts with sharp flint points.

Once the battle had begun, the Aztecs, seeing this ferocious, frightful enemy, and hearing the ghastly howls that issued from their throats—which made their hair stand on end—pretended to retreat. They went back to the place where the great warriors waited in ambush. When the enemy had entered the trap, the men concealed by the grass stood up and, with great fury, surrounded them, taking many prisoners and killing others. Not one Huaxtec escaped. Even the youths took many captives and all the prisoners were taken to Tenochtitlan. The seasoned soldiers from all the allied provinces also took many captives, both men and women, for they and the Aztecs entered the city, burned the temple, sacked and robbed the place. They killed old and young, boys and girls, annihilating without mercy everyone they could, with great cruelty and with the determination to remove all traces of the Huaxtec people from the face of the earth, so that not one of them remain.

However, many of the leading men came out with their hands crossed, humbly begging the Aztecs to cease the destruction. They promised perpetual subjection and servitude, as well as rich tribute of cloth, cacao, gold, jewels, feathers, brilliantly colored parrots and other tropical birds such as macaws; also both small and large types of chiles, pumpkin seeds, and other foodstuffs; and clothing and jewels that abound in that land. And thus they were spared, for the Aztecs commanded their men to put down their arms, while they instructed the Huaxtecs, "You must comply with these offers." To which these people answered that they would take these things to Tenochtitlan and would serve the Aztecs in every way they were commanded.

When the battle had ceased, the Huaxtecs requested that the Aztecs and officers from the provinces go to the palace, where they were greeted and were given barbecued fish, quantities of shrimp, white honey, turkey, pineapples, and other fruits. They were also given bundles of cloth of many colors, all richly worked. The officers received these gifts and then told the Huaxtecs that in order to find out what they were to do in the future they should all go to Tenochtitlan together. The Aztecs added that they were impatient to leave. The Huaxtecs answered that they would follow later.

The Aztecs and their allies set out, taking the captives and prisoners, all of them with their hands tied behind their backs and collars about their necks. They went along singing sadly, weeping and lamenting. The words of that song told of their fate, since they knew they were going to their death, that they were to be sacrificed.

Whenever the Aztec army arrived in a town, they were well received, lodged, and given food generously. They were served turkey, rabbit, deer, chocolate, maize gruel, fruit, and breads of different types. This was done in all the towns through which they passed. If this were not so, if the people were indifferent or failed to give them the necessary provisions, the Aztecs robbed and sacked the villages, stripped all the people they met of their clothing, beat them, dishonored them, robbed them of all their possessions, and destroyed the crops in their fields. They committed all these outrages, all this destruction. The entire land trembled with fear of them. This ill treatment was often visited upon the people even when they treated the Aztec army well. So anywhere they went they were given everything they needed (and the people had been warned at least eight days in advance to fulfill this obligation). Yet in spite of all this the Aztecs were the cruelest and most devilish people that can be imagined because of the way they treated their vassals, the people who were subject to them—even worse than the Spaniards treated and treat them. One did not dare to question them at any time.

Because in Tenochtitlan it had been heard that the Aztecs were coming with their spoils and prisoners, when their forces reached Coatitlan, Motecuhzoma ordered that on their arrival in the capital they be received with all the usual honors. Therefore, the elders in the temples came out and greeted the army in the same ceremonious way the warriors and captives from Tepeaca had been received, as I described in the previous chapter. There is no need for me to repeat this description here, for I have already told what always took place when the army returned with booty and prisoners. Or when they came back defeated and with great losses, as in the war with Mechoacan when the Aztecs were vanquished; this will be told later.

The army having arrived in Tenochtitlan, the ceremony of the prisoners having passed respectfully before the idol of Huitzilopochtli and then before Motecuhzoma and Tlacaelel, the prisoners danced most of the day. Then Tlacaelel ordered that the captives, who were many, be distributed among the wards. Each barrio was to guard and maintain a certain number of them. Tlacaelel then instructed them: "Take care that they do not escape, take care they do not die. Behold, they are the Children of the Sun![3] Feed them well, let them be fat and desirable for the sacrifice on the day of the feast of our god, since they belong to him!"

---

[3] Although the Aztecs have been called "People of the Sun" (Caso 1958), the "Children of the Sun" were the victims sacrificed to the solar deity. See also Durán (1977:194–202) for "Knights of the Sun."

The heads of the *calpulli* then placed the prisoners in these different barrios, according to their capacity. Here they were treated well and honored as if they had been gods. These captives were called "Children of the Sun," "Children of the Lord of the Earth," and "Gift of the Gods."

When this was done, the king summoned all the soldiers and valiant men who had accomplished great feats in the war. He congratulated them for their actions and then had special clothing given to them: fine mantles, breechcloths, and sandals, all very luxuriant, well made and adorned, the best among these things that arrived through tribute. These mantles were called "shadow of the kings." They were called this because those mantles could be worn only by the kings and noble lords, thus, they were called "shadow of the kings" because only the sovereign could give permission to wear these; this clothing was a special honor for the king and his lords.[4]

After the warriors had been dressed and honored with these mantles, each one according to his rank and merits, the king told them, "Aztecs and valorous warriors from the allied provinces, I do not wish to deceive you into thinking that the wars have ended. They will continue. When you least expect it, when you are not thinking about it, you will see how another occasion arises where your favor, your help, will be needed, and where you will be able to gain great honor. Therefore, do not become idle, occupy yourselves in getting your swords ready, in sharpening your blades, in repairing your shields, and in straightening canes and reeds to make arrows and darts. Behold, you are not just anyone, you are Aztecs, and very valorous ones." Then he dismissed these men, who went home, very contented.

When the warriors had returned to their homes to rest, the elders made ceremonial visits to each of them, beginning with the principal captain. They arrived at his house and congratulated him on his return. The lord received them, gave them food and gifts of mantles and breechcloths. Once the meal had ended, one of the elders spoke: "Lord, you have returned to Mexico-Tenochtitlan, which is your birthplace. You have favored us, you have brought us gifts, and we kiss your hands. Had you died in the war or on the road, we would not be rejoicing in your presence, before you, who are our jewel and precious feather. Let us weep for joy, for we were granted this favor!"

The elders began to weep while the noble warrior consoled them. Then they left, and every day the elders visited a distinguished

---

[4]Feathers were usually called the "shadow of the kings and lords" because of these prohibitions. Even if a commoner rose to the top of the social ladder because of his feats, he still could not wear feathers. See Durán's *Book of the Gods and Rites* (1977:200).

captain by order of rank and merit, and every day they performed the same ceremony, until there were no more of these warriors to be honored in this way. Each day the elders were fed very well and were given so many fine mantles, breechcloths, and sandals that these would last them many years, or until another war broke out. These ceremonies were done so the elders would commend the soldiers to the gods and pray and do penance for them.

CHAPTER XX

Which treats of the cruel sacrifice of the Huaxtecs at the hands of the Aztecs, called Tlacaxipehualiztli, which means "Flaying of Men." And how the lords of all the neighboring states and cities were invited to witness this spectacle and festivity.

Many days had passed after the return of the Aztecs from the war in the land of the Huaxtecs. Tlacaelel then reminded King Motecuhzoma of the work on the temple they had begun to build, and said that a great stone should be carved to serve as an altar or table upon which sacrifice would be made. This Tlacaelel, in addition to being bold and cunning in the artifice of war, also invented devilish, cruel, and frightful sacrifices. Motecuhzoma gave orders that the stone be carved and that on it be sculpted the war of liberation from Azcapotzalco, fought by their forebears, so that it be carved there in perpetual memory. Tlacaelel was pleased with this idea, so he gathered the stonecutters and sculptors, saying to them:

"Master craftsmen, our lord the king wishes you to cut a large round stone that we shall call *temalacatl*, which means 'stone wheel'. On the face of this will be inscribed our wars with the Tepanecs, since this sculpture must be an eternal reminder of that heroic event. I beg of you to excel in this work; let it be well carved and done as quickly as possible, and in this way your names will be glorified and you will be remembered forever." The craftsmen were happy to carry out his orders. They sought a large stone about a *braza* and a half wide; they then made smooth its surface and on it represented in their carving the war with Azcapotzalco. This was very finely done and was finished so swiftly that some days later they were able to notify the king that the sacrifice stone was ready. The king then ordered a base to be made for it to rest upon. And so a platform was made, slightly higher than a man, and the carved rock was placed upon it.

Now that the stone had been set up, they called certain youths who lived in seclusion within the temples—some of those who were outstanding in their duties—and gave them the office of carrying out this sacrifice that the devil had invented and taught them. They were told: "Take care that every day you prepare yourselves to perform this sacrifice, since the lords of all the neighboring cities and provinces will be invited to the festival and you must not put us to shame." The young men thanked Tlacaelel and the king and promised to practice and rehearse according to the instructions that were given to them. And so they did.

When the festival day and the beginning of the month called Tlacaxipehualiztli, "Flaying of Men,"[1] approached, the Aztecs invited the lords from the entire land: the rulers of Tezcoco and Tacuba, of Chalco and Xochimilco, those from the Marquesado, from Couixco and Matlatzinco, and the heads of the Mazahua people. Finally, they invited all the noblemen they could from the surrounding area so they would come and see what took place at that feast and realize what it signified.

Once the guests had arrived, the king had many fine things brought from his treasury and gave these as presents: handsome mantles and breechcloths, rich clothing exquisitely worked, featherwork, wide sashes, sandals, labrets of precious stones, gold ear ornaments, and nose pendants. A great feast followed, with quantities of fowl, meat from the hunt, different breads, chocolate drinks, and pulque. After the guests had eaten and drunk, they were assigned booths adorned with flowers and reeds, within which they could sit and watch. The visitors [sat in the decorated boxes and] awaited the ceremony, which had been unknown to them before that time.

The prisoners were brought out and lined up at a place called Tzompantitlan, which means something like "Mount Calvary" or "Place of Skulls."[2] At this place there was a long low platform upon which stood a rack where the skulls of sacrificial victims were strung and where they remained permanently as reminders of these sacrifices, as relics. The prisoners were arranged in a file and were told to dance; all of them were there, dancing. And all the victims were smeared with chalk, their heads were feathered with down, and on top of the head each wore some white feathers tied to his hair. Their eyelids were blackened and around their mouths they were painted red. Then the men who were to perform the sacrifice came out and stood in a row, placed according to their rank. Each one was disguised as a god. One of them wore the garb of Huitzilopochtli, another was dressed as Quetzalcoatl, another as Toci [Our Grandmother]. Another represented Yopi, still another Opochtzin [the Left-Handed One]; another

[1] Today, many scholars translate Tlacaxipehualiztli as "Flaying of People." I have left it in the traditional way, however, because although women were flayed in religious rites—during the Tlacaxipehauliztli festival only men, captives in war, were skinned this way. This rite is described fully in Durán 1977:172–85, 415–17. See also Johanna Broda de Casas, "Tlacaxipehualiztli: A Reconstruction of an Aztec Calendar Festival from the 16th Century Sources," *Revista Española de Antropología Americana* 5:197–273 (Universidad de Madrid, 1970).

[2] A stone skull altar, possibly a life-size model of a *tzompantli*, can be seen at the Aztec Templo Mayor in Mexico City.

was Totec [Our Lord], and finally one wore the garments of Itzpapalotl [Obsidian Butterfly].[3] Then one warrior was disguised as a jaguar, another as an ocelot, and yet another as an eagle. All carried swords and shields, inlaid with gold and gems, and all these sacrificers were covered with featherwork and rich jewels.

For all these men an arbor, beautifully adorned with flowers and with paintings that bore the insignia of those gods mentioned, had been prepared. This arbor was made of branches and leaves of a tree called *tzapotl* [the sapodilla]; that is why the arbor was called Tzapotl Calli, "House of *Tzapotl*."[4] Within it were seats also made of sapota wood, where all of them sat down according to age and rank. This arbor had been erected on the summit of the pyramid in a place called Yopico.[5]

When the images of the gods[6] who were to perform the sacrifice had been seated, then came the old priests called Tecuacuiltin and the temple singers. A drum was brought forth and to the rhythm of its beat they began to dance and sing. The high priest, in full dress for the rite, then came forth with tall feathers in his headdress, his arms covered with golden bands from which hung large, shining green and blue feathers. Carrying in his hand the great knife of black [obsidian], the knife called *ixcuahualli*, he went to be seated in a place especially arranged for him. After he was seated, they brought out one of the prisoners from the Huaxteca and with a rope that emerged from a hole in the middle of the great round stone tied his foot around the ankle. Thus tied to the stone, he was given a wooden sword and a shield; the

[3]It is interesting that Itzpapalotl, "Obsidian Butterfly," one aspect of the Mother Goddess, is not described in the list of gods given by Sahagún, yet she is depicted in the prehispanic (or early colonial) pictorial *Codex Borbonicus* (1974). She is also described in other chronicles (for example, the *Anales de Cuauhtitlan*) and invariably has a warrior aspect. She is present in Durán's *Historia* in this ceremony, the sacrifice of Huaxtec prisoners, and in the sacrifice of captives from Tliliuhquitepec, both times at the inauguration of a Sun Stone. At these occasions one of the sacrificers is disguised as Itzpapalotl. Since part of her name is *Itzt(li)*, "obsidian"—the material of which the sacrificial knife was made—her association is clearly with sacrifice. For a more complete analysis, see Heyden 1974.

[4]Sapodilla: *Achrae zapote* a member of the family Sapotaceae, whose fruit is edible. The *tzapotl* was one of the most revered trees—for its wood and leaves—used in ritual.

[5]Sahagún states that there was slaying at the Yopico Calmecac: "Very many captives died there, also at night at the time of [the feast of] Tlacaxipehualiztli." See the appendix to book 2 of the *Florentine Codex* (1981:188), for a description of the temples in the sacred precinct, including Yopico.

[6]The fact that the priests were disguised as deities reminds one of ancient Egyptian ceremonies where priests wore god-masks and costumes. As explained by Arelene Wolinski, this costume not only set the priests apart from the crowd and gave them greater prestige, but in the case of the investiture of the pharaoh, who was seen as a living god, only another god could crown him.

The History of the Indies of New Spain

sword was not equipped with blades but was feathered from top to bottom.

At this point the high priest, who for this day was called Yohualahuan [Drinker of the Night] and Totec [Our Lord], rose from his seat and slowly descended the steps until he reached the place where the prisoner was. He walked around the stone twice, sanctifying it, and, having again tied the victim who was upon it, he returned to his seat. Then one of the elderly men, dressed as a jaguar, appeared and gave the victim—or placed next to him—four wooden balls made of torch pine and told him to try to defend himself with them. He wrapped a cloth around the prisoner's body and gave him a little Divine Wine to drink. After this he withdrew, leaving the victim alone. One of the men disguised as a god then approached the stone, dancing, with his shield and sword in his hands, well protected by his [padded cotton] armor. He went up to the stone where the prisoner was tied. The poor wretch threw the balls at him, but these were repelled by the sacrificer (or executioner) if he was skillful. Thereupon the prisoner picked up his feathered sword and defended himself the best he could. Some of the victims possessed such ability that they tired out two or three attackers before others could wound them. But as soon as the victim was wounded—on his leg, on his arms, or on any part of his body—four priests, their bodies painted black, with long braided hair, dressed in garments like chasubles, ascended the stone and laid the wounded man on his back, holding him down by the feet and hands. The high priest then rose from his seat, went to the stone, and opened the chest of the victim with the knife. He took out the heart and offered the vapor that rose from it to the sun. As soon as the heart had cooled, he delivered it to the priest, who placed it in a vessel called the *cuauhxicalli* [eagle vessel], which was another large stone dedicated to the sun. In its center it contained a cavity that was also used for another type of sacrifice.

These ceremonies were performed in the case of all the prisoners, each one in his turn. However, there were some who, on being given the shield and sword, felt the sword with their fingers. When they realized that the sword was not edged with knives but with feathers, they cast it away and threw themselves upon their backs on the stone. The priests then took hold of them, and the high priest opened their chests and extracted their hearts. Some of the victims, such as those mentioned here, were unwilling to go through so much ceremonial and they cast themselves upon the stone immediately, seeking a quick death. Whether one defended himself well or whether one fought badly, death was inevitable. That is why all those priests were required; when one was tired of sacrificing, another would take his place. At the most it means another half hour of life.

After all the sacrificial victims had died, the corpses were taken back to the place where, as live men, they had stood in a row, and the bodies were cast down there. Those who had taken part in the sacrifices entered certain rooms of the temple with the high priest, took off their ritual garb, and, with great reverence, put it away in a place reserved for this.

The lords from other cities and from the provinces who had come to observe the sacrifice were shocked and bewildered by what they had seen and they returned to their homes filled with astonishment and fright.[7]

Motecuhzoma now called those who had performed the sacrifice and thanked them for their skillful work. He had them dressed in fine mantles, breechcloths, and sandals and commanded that they be given maize, beans, *chian* seed, and cacao in large quantities. This was done to encourage others to take part in these exercises, which the Aztecs felt were filled with virtue and honor.

By ancient tradition the feast was followed, the next day, by another celebration. At this time the king gave his noblemen the usual gifts: fine mantles, rich breechcloths, sandals, labrets, ear spools, shields, other weapons, and insignia that were both handsome and valuable. They also received little gold banners. All the men, according to their position and merit, received emblems and insignia, some of more importance than those given to others. In this way no one was excluded from participating in these feasts and ceremonies. Rewards of this type were given to all the noblemen—and even to those who were not of noble birth—who had distinguished themselves in war. Once the rewards had been distributed, those who had been sacrificed were flayed and the Tototectin put on the skins and wore them. Carrying their shields in one hand and rattle staffs in the other, they went from house to house. First they visited the houses of the nobility and chieftains and went to all the other houses after these, asking for alms, wearing the skins all the time. The rich gave them mantles, breechcloths, and waistbands; the common people gave them ears of corn and other edibles. For twenty days these men begged. At the end of this time they had gathered great quantities of clothing and food. The flayed skins had been worn in the manner the god [Xipe Totec] was portrayed.

[7]In spite of Durán's statement that Tlacaelel invented the flaying rite, archaeological examples of flaying exist from earlier periods, for example, in classic Teotihuacan (A.D. 0–750). Much has been written on human sacrifice in Mesoamerica recently, including *Ritual Human Sacrifice in Mesoamerica*, a conference at Dumbarton Oaks organized by Elizabeth P. Benson, edited by Elizabeth H. Boone (Washington, D.C.: Dumbarton Oaks, 1984).

When the twenty days had passed, they took off the reeking skins and buried them in a special room in the temple. In this way ended the feast and the sacrifice of the Huaxtecs, which had been made to solemnize the first use of the carved stone. And here ends the chapter on this subject I found written in the Nahuatl language.

[Durán sums up in his own words:]

This was the solemn ceremony during which Motecuhzoma the Elder, the first of this name, inaugurated the stone called the *temalacatl*, which means "stone wheel." For this inauguration he summoned all the lords of the provinces and sacrificed all the prisoners from Tochpan and those taken in the Huaxtec war. In honor of this festival he made an excessive and costly expenditure, with much generosity and munificence, which both astonished the outsiders and left the nobles and commoners of the city of Tenochtitlan pleased and proud. From this time on all the nearby cities and the provinces ceased rebelling, avoided conflict with the Aztecs, because they saw how these people treated their enemies and preferred to be on good terms with them.

CHAPTER XXI

Which treats of the war with Ahuilizapan. With a description of how the people of those provinces caused an uprising against the Aztecs and how they were defeated and destroyed.

After the festivities [for the inauguration of the *temalacatl*] were over and the terrible, frightening sacrifice of the Huaxtecs had taken place, the Aztecs felt sure that they had intimidated, terrified, the whole world. They then decided to send messengers to Cempoala in the province of Cuetlaxtla (which is next to the sea), asking the rulers there to send them some conch shells, live turtles and scallops, and other curious products that are found in the sea. The Aztecs had heard about these and wanted them for the cult of their god. The king and Tlacaelel had made this decision so they sent their envoys laden with gifts, so the people there would be more inclined to give them what they requested.

According to what the *Historia* says, the envoys or ambassadors — who are called in Nahuatl *teucnene*, which in our language means "royal courier" — left Tenochtitlan and when they reached Ahuilizapan (which the Spaniards corrupted to Orizaba), they asked to be allowed to rest and be given refreshment in that city. Though they were not well received they were given refreshments. And while these envoys ate and rested, the authorities sent a message to Cuetlaxtla [capital of that province], telling the ruler there that the envoys sent by their king and lords had come to ask for large conch shells, turtles, and scallops; thus the people of Cuetlaxtla were informed of this. It so happened that when these messengers from Ahuilizapan arrived in Cuetlaxtla, the lords of Tlaxcala were there celebrating a feast with the high officials of that place. The messengers informed the ruler of Cuetlaxtla, Ce Atonal Tecuhtli, that the Aztecs were going to Cempoala to request these sea products. The Tlaxcalans were alarmed at this news and said to Ce Atonal Tecuhtli, "How is it that the Aztecs dare to ask you for shells or sea snails or any other thing? Are you perhaps their vassals? What contempt, what daring they show you! Kill them, close the roads, do not permit them or others like them to enter your domain!" Ce Atonal Tecuhtli, together with another lord, Tepetecuhtli, agreed with this advice and ordered the people of Ahuilizapan to assassinate the envoys and all the merchants and traders who might happen to be in the region, sparing none.

The royal messengers were then killed by the men of Ahuilizapan, who also murdered all the merchants they could find, not only the Aztecs but Tezcocans, Xochimilcas, Chalcas, and Tepanecs. Not one was left alive. So the Aztec envoys were unable to proceed to Cempoala to present their petition there. From this massacre only two men, from Itztapalapa, escaped and managed to return to their city, where they took the bad news to the king. He received them, thanked them, and gave them the usual gifts of food and clothing.

The men from Tlaxcala realized that they had been the cause of the killing of the merchants and envoys, so they left Cuetlaxtla to return to their city. Before leaving, however, they told the ruler and lords there that, if the Aztecs retaliated, they were to be advised and they would return to help defend that land. The people of Cuetlaxtla thanked them. They then reflected upon the evil act they had committed and realized that because of this the whole world would come to seek revenge. And [a "whole world" soon did appear to punish them for their perverse actions]. Meanwhile, the Tlaxcalans returned to Tlaxcala, laden with splendid gifts from the lords of Cuetlaxtla: gold, jewelry, precious stones, mantles, fine feathers, and cacao. They arrived very contented, feeling no remorse for what they had done.

When the Aztecs heard of these tragic events, the king called Tlacaelel and said to him, "I have been told, Tlacaelel, that the people of Ahuilizapan have killed both our ambassadors and all the merchants and other Aztecs who travel through that region trying to seek a living. It seems to me that we should let them know they have acted in a wicked manner, then if they admit they were to blame we could pardon them, as long as they turn themselves over to us as our vassals. And if they do not agree to this we shall challenge them and prepare for war."

Tlacaelel answered angrily, "In truth, O powerful lord, this will not be done. There must be no vacillation; the death of the messengers, the royal ambassadors, must be avenged, for they were not at fault, nor were the merchants and traders. It was our fault for having sent them and we must vindicate their death."

The king, convinced by this argument, suggested that Tlacaelel do as he thought best. Since there was no further discussion Tlacaelel called the war council to a meeting, ordered those men to ready the people and to explain the reason for these preparations, and to tell them where they would be going. He also summoned the rulers of Tezcoco and Tacuba and the lords of the allied cities and provinces. He told them what had happened in Ahuilizapan and ordered that their people be prepared for war. Soon so many soldiers were called to arms, and with such diligence and speed, that in fifteen days the people of all the provinces were ready and Tenochtitlan was alerted to this. The Aztecs, equally diligent, were by then prepared.

The king, who seldom was seen in public, nevertheless came out and spoke to all the soldiers: "O Aztecs, my sons, this is your occupation. You were not raised by the Lord of All Created Things, of the Sky and of the Earth, of the Night and the Day, so that you would put on skirts and blouses like women, but so you would prove the courage of your heart with shield and sword, with arrow and spear. It must be known that the people of Ahuilizapan and of all those lands along the coast have insulted your god Huitzilopochtli, for whose service we asked for large conch shells and live turtles and other things found in the sea. And these people not only did not allow our envoys to reach Cempoala, but they killed them and all the merchants too, for no reason. Therefore, have courage, go with strong heart and spirit, as is your custom."

All the soldiers thanked the king. They were anxious to vindicate the insult to their god and at the same time wreak vengeance upon the people who had caused the death of those men, who had done no wrong. When the soldiers left the city, the king had them followed by the people in charge of the supplies. Thus, the heads of the barrios sent great quantities of toasted tortillas, ground cacao, corn and beans also ground, pumpkin seeds, and chiles. They contributed tents and huts of the type used in war, together with weapons and war devices; also sandals and thin mantles made of a fiber suitable for the Hot Country. All these provisions followed the army and were destined for the place where camp would be set up. Along the road where the army marched the towns and cities were forced to provide everything that was needed, under pain of death. In this way messengers were sent in advance of the army to warn the people so quarters would be made available and so men from those towns who were able to go to war would be prepared, ready to leave with the Aztecs.

The people of these places responded that their men were armed and ready, that the Aztecs were welcome. And when they arrived they were received with flowers, with tobacco, and with bowls of water for their hands. Then they were given abundant food consisting of deer, quail, rabbit, chocolate, and different kinds of breads. After this they received clothing and sandals and were given sumptuous feasts, as if they were the lords of those cities. The lodgings they were assigned were handsomely decorated [as befitted men of their station]. In the morning the Aztecs continued on the march, and in every town along the road they were treated in like manner.

A day before the Aztecs were to arrive at their destination, the officers in charge of accommodations reached this place, where they then prepared the camp, setting up the lodgings, the huts and shelters for the Aztec soldiers and those of the allied provinces. In this way, when the army arrived, all they had to do was go to the place the billeting officers and local administrators had prepared for them. It was the same when they were marching from one town to another and had to spend the night someplace. When there was not enough room in the towns for the soldiers, they set up their tents and reed huts where a site for these was indicated. They were very careful about these arrangements so that nothing could go wrong.

All along the way they were served and honored as if they were gods, yet people did not dare appear in places where the soldiers were to pass. Everyone hid, none dared come out on the roads because they well knew that the soldiers would rob them of whatever they carried and if they wished to defend themselves they might be beaten, wounded, or even killed. And so the Aztec forces went their way, stealing from the cornfields and killing all the turkeys and domesticated dogs they came upon. They acted in an evil way, just as our own Spaniards do today unless they are controlled. Such is and was the shamelessness of the soldiery. As they felt themselves under their own banner the whole world was theirs. For this reason, when a war was being waged, the people of the towns through which the armies were to pass hid themselves and their maize, chiles, turkeys, [edible domestic] dogs, and all other possessions.

Arriving in Ahuilizapan, the Aztecs found the camp set up, with the quarters all in order. Everyone went to these places and then sentries were stationed all around. Spies were sent to see how the enemy had their defenses arranged, which were seen to be similar to those in other cities.

The following morning food rations were given to the soldiers, each one receiving a large handful of toasted tortillas and another of toasted maize kernels. The usual encouraging speech was made to them, as was made in all the wars. Then they went into the field, the officers in front, all handsomely dressed with fine feather ornaments and insignia, wearing gold bracelets, ear spools, ankle ornaments, beautiful jewels at their throats, labrets of rich stones such as greenstone, rock crystal, carnelian, and amber, and other precious stones these people use. They all carried weapons and shields that were resplendently gilded.

Lined up in an orderly manner, the same way the Aztecs were, the enemy came out. Meanwhile the men of Ahuilizapan had asked the Tlaxcalans [who had instigated them to fight] for the aid they had promised. The Tlaxcalans made great promises but never went to Ahuilizapan, nor did they have any intention of doing so.

The Aztecs, then, seeing the enemy ready for battle, made a signal, upon which their soldiers began the fighting with so much fury that they immediately overthrew many opponents. But the Ahuilizapan soldiers defended themselves so fiercely, refused to give way or to retreat, and were aided by allies from the region, that they also caused much destruction among the Aztecs. Because of this violent attack and the great number of enemy soldiers, for a while it appeared that the Aztecs would lose the war.

But the skill and valor of these men was so extraordinary, their perseverance so great, their dexterity in fighting so inexhaustible, that the soldiers of Ahuilizapan, together with their allies (who were from Chichiquila, Teoixhuacan, Quimichtla, Tzauctla, Macuilxochtitla, Tlacitla, Oceloapan, Totonaca, and Cuetlaxtla) began to desert the field. This infuriated the Aztecs, who, in savage pursuit, followed them and killed everyone they came upon, the old men and old women, the young people and children, sparing no one.

Seeing their cities plundered, ravaged, destroyed, the people of Cuetlaxtla and the other towns, aware that almost no one was left alive, were forced to make the same decision other people had made in similar situations: to ask for mercy and offer themselves as perpetual vassals. Thus, they came out with their hands crossed, weeping, crying out: "O Aztecs, valiant, courageous men. Have mercy on the women and children, feel compassion for them, for the children do not yet know how to speak and have not harmed you in any way. Lower your shields and swords! Cease the injuring and killing! Here we shall serve you, we shall give you gold and silver and precious stones. We shall give you perpetual tribute of all things you desire, with the goodwill and humility you are now witnessing. Let nothing more be asked of us, O lords, for already we have given you lengths of cloth, each ten *brazas* long, richly worked, as well as cacao, feathers, *hueynacaztli*,[1] and pieces of amber. Behold, O Aztecs, your decision will be ours regarding the things you wish, including the products of the sea and foodstuffs for your sustenance. For in this land fish of all kinds are found in the great rivers, also shrimp and crayfish. So stop slaughtering us, Aztecs, calm your hearts."

The Aztec lords lowered their swords and shields and commanded their forces to withdraw. In this way the killing ceased that they had carried out without pity, burning the houses and sacking the cities, leaving nothing standing. The fighting having ceased, the soldiers were ordered to break up camp and collect their belongings, while the

---

[1] *Hueynacaztli: Cymbopetalum penduliflorum*, an aromatic plant used in the preparation of chocolate.

leading warriors from the cities of Tenochtitlan, Tezcoco, and Chalco, and the Tepanecs and Xochimilcas, were escorted to the city of Cuetlaxtla, where they were lodged in the community houses, the palace. They were given water for washing their hands and food in abundance. This consisted of many kinds of delicious dishes, both of meat and fish, as well as chocolate, which is what these people drink. Each warrior was given precious stones: greenstone, carnelian, amber, and bloodstone [or chalcedony]. They also received rich jewels, gold, fine feathers, mantles, and jaguar and ocelot skins.

The Aztecs gave thanks for these gifts and then said, "Brothers, all of you who live in these provinces are now vassals of the king of Tenochtitlan, Huhehue Motecuhzoma. We wish to go give him the news that you are at his service. Be prepared for any orders that he and his official Tlacaelel may want to send to you." With this they left for their city. The men of Cuetlaxtla bade them farewell and requested they give their king their excuses [for not accompanying them].

Leaving Cuetlaxtla, the Aztecs went on to Tenochtitlan, taking with them many captives from that region, all of them tied together. When they reached the limits of the city, the old priests came out in the correct order to receive the warriors and the prisoners. They performed the ceremony of burning incense, of making the accustomed speeches, and of taking the prisoners before the feet of the statue of Huitzilopochtli, where they carried out the rite of eating earth by touching it with the middle finger. From here the captives were taken to Motecuhzoma, and the king ordered that they be dressed and adorned in fine clothing. The *calpixque*, heads of the barrios, were called, and the prisoners were turned over to them. They were told that these men were a gift from the sun, from the Lord of the Earth, who gave them to the Aztecs to be sacrificed. The *calpixque* received the prisoners and quartered them in the community houses of the barrios, or in the house of the priest of each barrio. Here they were given food and drink until it was time to be sacrificed.

The prisoners thus taken care of, Motecuhzoma spoke to his main official, Tlacaelel, and stated that it would be wise to place an Aztec governor in Cuetlaxtla and over the entire province. Tlacaelel suggested a certain prince named Pinotl. When this had been agreed upon, Tlacaelel summoned him and said, "O Pinotl, because of your great personal merits the king has decided to send you to govern and control the province of Cuetlaxtla. There, every eighty days, you will collect the tribute of all that land and you will send it to us, carefully guarded on the road. Go there and perform the duties that are expected of a man of your abilities."

The lord Pinotl expressed his gratitude for the favor that had been granted him, and, gathering his wife, his children, and his household, he set out for that province in order to govern it. The Cuetlaxtecas received him well and with honors, as if he were the king himself. Pinotl addressed them: "O lords, King Motecuhzoma has sent me to this province to take charge of the royal tribute and so that I shall be your father and your protector. I have not come for any other reason. Do not be distressed, do not be troubled, for I have not come to take away your lands, your lordships. It is only that our sovereign, the king, wishes you to respect and honor me in his place."

These people thanked him and promised to serve him with all the goodwill and reverence in their power. Then Pinotl ordered that the promised tribute be collected. The people brought large quantities of gold dust, mantles, feathers, precious stones, jewels, cacao, animal skins, large conch shells, turtles, small shells, amber, and all kinds of dried fish as well as barbecued fish. All these things were delivered to the governor, who then sent them to his king in Tenochtitlan, who accepted them with pleasure.

There is no better governor than one who serves his king in this way. This is evident, also, in the fact that the people of Cuetlaxtla were praised and given thanks for having fulfilled their obligations by sending the tribute quickly as specified.

CHAPTER XXII

Which treats of how King Motecuhzoma warred with Coaixtlahuaca because some Aztec merchants had been murdered. With a description of how that city was destroyed.

The city of Coaixtlahuaca is located in the land of the Mixtecs.[1] The Spaniards now call it Cuixtlahuac, but that is a corruption of the original name, as most of the former names of towns have been corrupted. In ancient times this city was one of the greatest in the Mixtec province; there was a market there where much wealth flowed, and it was attended by merchants from foreign parts such as Mexico, Tezcoco, Chalco, Xochimilco, Coyoacan, Tacuba, Azcapotzalco, and from all the regions of this land. There they traded in gold, feathers, cacao, finely worked gourds, clothing, cochineal, and thread made of rabbit hair, dyed in many colors.[2]

One day when a great number of foreign merchants had been trading in the market, the authorities of Coaixtlahuaca ordered their people to arm themselves and to rob and kill the Aztec traders and the others from the cities who were neighbors of the Aztecs, when they left the marketplace. It is generally thought that in this decision they had been influenced by ill-intentioned persons who wished to cause trouble between Aztecs and Mixtecs.

---

[1] The Mixtecs were far from being the barbarians Durán would have liked his readers to believe they were. On the contrary, strong cultural influences seem to have diffused from the Mixtec region to the Central Plateau (the Aztecs) and the Puebla-Tlaxcala region during the late Postclassic period (Ravicz and Romney 1969). Living in what is now the state of Oaxaca, the Mixtecs, "Cloud People," produced the fabulous goldwork now on display in the museum in the city of Oaxaca. The Mixteca region has always been well known for the great number of pictorial codices produced there. For a history of the Mixtec people in prehispanic times, see Dahlgren de Jordán 1989 and *The Cloud People*, ed. Kent V. Flannery and Joyce Marcus (New York: Academic Press, 1983).

[2] Cochineal is a dyestuff taken from the dried bodies of a scale insect known as *Dactylopius coccus* or *coccus cacti*. This bug was bred in great quantities in ancient Mexico, especially among the Mixtec people of Oaxaca and also in the Gulf region. In spite of its diminutive size it was one of the few domestic animals of Mesoamerica, others being the dog, turkey, duck, and bee. Cochineal insects reproduced upon the leaves of the *nopal* cactus and were the source of much wealth for those who kept them. The reddish or purple dye was exported for hundreds of years to Europe after the conquest and lost its importance only with the appearance of modern chemical colorings. Cochineal is still produced in some parts of Mexico.

The subjects of the lords of Coaixtlahuaca did what they had been commanded. When the Aztecs and their allied merchants left the city, they were attacked, robbed of all they carried, and killed. Not one was spared except a few men from Tultitlan who managed to hide and save their lives. They went to Tenochtitlan in great haste and spoke to Motecuhzoma: "O great lord, all the merchants who were in the Mixteca, making their living by trading, have been killed, some of them cast off high cliffs, and not one has survived." Motecuhzoma asked which men had been assassinated and they answered that one hundred and sixty merchants from Tezcoco, Chalco, Xochimilco, and the Tepanecs [as well as the Aztecs had been the victims]. "Where are you from?" Motecuhzoma asked, and they told him that they came from Tulan.

The king ordered that these merchants be given everything they needed and that they rest for a while, then he sent them on their way to their homes. After this Tlacaelel, the head of the army, commanded that in the name of the king the lords of Tezcoco, Tacuba, Chalco, and Xochimilco be advised of this aggression so they could prepare their men for war. The royal messengers then took the bad news regarding the Mixteca to all the allied cities, telling them of the death of the merchants. They also informed them that the roads to that province had now been closed, so that no one from Tenochtitlan or the other cities was allowed to go there for any reason.

So war was declared and was announced in the cities of Chalco, Tezcoco, Itztapalapa, Colhuacan, Mexicatzinco, Xochimilco, Huitzilopochco, Coyoacan, Tacuba, Azcapotzalco, and all that region, also in Tula and Matlatzinco. So many soldiers were recruited from these places that they seemed to cover the earth. And the amount of war material accumulated for this endeavor was so great that nothing like it had been seen before. The Aztecs, under whose direction this expedition was to take place, prepared their men and equipment, tents and weapons, as well as jars, cooking pots, grinding stones, dishes, and griddles for making bread [that is, tortillas]. Supplies of all kinds were so numerous that it looked as if they were going to settle a new city. The Aztecs made an oath, vehemently, fiercely, not to return to their land until they had defeated those rude, barbarous people, stripping them of all they possessed. And in reality this is what happened.

Tlacaelel was now an old man, unable to direct a war in such a faraway country, so King Motecuhzoma appointed a nobleman named Cuauhnochtli as head of the army, giving him all the authority and privileges that went with this position. He also appointed a second in command, Tizoc Yahuacatl, then orderd the soldiers to be on their way.

Orders having been announced publicly, the armed forces left the city, which then looked so abandoned, so mournful and solitary, that it was sad to see. Mothers wept for their sons and wives for their husbands, others for brothers or relatives, since this war was to be waged in a distant land and no one knew who would return. As that land was immense there was great fear that the many cities would join against the Aztecs and their allies, surround them, and destroy them. Nevertheless, they all left their homes and on the road many people from other towns joined them and also gave them provisions.

All the flower of Tenochtitlan and Tezcoco, the finest warriors from Chalco, Xochimilco, and the Tepanec region, great lords, magnificently attired, took part in this war. They were anxious to win honor and the riches of that land. Marching as rapidly as they could [over those harsh mountain roads], they reached the boundary of Coaixtlahuaca, where they set up an encampment made of tents and huts of straw mats. They fortified themselves as best they could, placed sentinels and spies in strategic places, and kept watch always with sword and shield in hand. They had reason to look out on all sides, as they were in a strange land, surrounded by enemies. They were especially afraid of the Chuchones [or Chochos],[3] a devilish and savage people.

When the camp had been set up and everything was ready, the Aztecs decided not to lose time, so the very next day they ordered all the soldiers to be on guard. All the noble warriors of Tenochtitlan, Tezcoco, and Chalco, as well as the Tepanecs, well armed and dressed in spectacular war attire, with many colored feathers over the quilted cotton armor, thus clothed from head to foot with all the richness conceivable, went into the field. The soldiers went to war attired in this finery, as a sign of their status and valor; the higher their rank, the more precious stones, jewels, and gold they wore. Then, when they were thus embellished and in correct order, one of the older men whose office it was to give exhortation spoke in a loud voice: "O Aztecs, by chance are these barbarians more courageous than our brothers, our kinsmen, the Chalcas? No, they are not! You will remember that the Chalcas held back the courageous Aztecs during ten or twelve years, when the flower of Tenochtitlan and Chalco perished, until finally we Aztecs conquered, subjected them! So if that powerful nation finally succumbed, why should we give in to a barbarous, crude people, such as this? What do these low, uncouth men think of us? Take courage, O Aztecs, forge ahead so that these

[3]The Chocho and Popoloca peoples were organized as a number of small city-states in northern Oaxaca and what is now the southern part of Puebla. They were frequently allied with the Mixtecs. For more on Chocho and Popoloca, see vol. XIV of the *HMAI*.

people will be unable to match us in war, nor will they be able to boast of terrifying us."

When the enemy, disdainful, advancing confidently, came into view, the Aztecs attacked with great cries, shouting, "At them, at them, O Aztecs. Rush them, rush them, let no man stay behind! Break their lines, let no one remain alive!" And thus shouting, they went at the enemy with great fury, mixing in with the soldiers of the opposing side, beginning to wound and kill to the right and to the left, showing no mercy. This was all done so fast that they pursued the enemy through the battlefield, leaving it full of the wounded and the dead, and fought their way into the city. They reached the temple and set it on fire. Not only did the temple burn but all the houses, and when the people fled from the flames they fell into the hands of the Aztecs, who seized them and bound their hands. The old men, old women, and children, whom they could not take prisoner in this way, they killed.

The Mixtec lords, seeing their city destroyed, most of the people dead, others having fled or having fallen into the hands of the Aztecs, came out, their arms crossed and with tears in their eyes. They acted in the accustomed ceremonious way, however, and requested that the killing cease. And although they conducted themselves with humility, expressing regret and sorrow for what had taken place earlier, the Aztecs refused to accept their surrender, stating that there was no reason to pity those people but rather they should kill them all because they were wild and barbarous. Finally, however, the Aztec leaders ordered that the combat end, although it was still raging and blood was flowing. When the fighting did cease and all had lowered their weapons, they addressed the Mixtecs: "What do you say now, Mixtecs?" to which they answered, "O our lords, valorous Aztecs, let your hearts become calm. Observe, whatever you wish us to do in your service, that will be done as you command, as you desire."

The Aztecs replied that they wished only that the Mixtecs agree to become perpetual vassals of their king and to state what tribute they would give. The people of Coaixtlahuaca offered to pay a tribute consisting of lengths of cloth ten brazas long, loads of chiles and cotton, salt from the ocean, and different colors to be used for painting and dyeing. The Aztecs then dismissed them, warning them that they were obliged to deliver this tribute in Tenochtitlan so the Aztecs would not have to send men to the Mixteca to collect it. This condition was accepted.

The Aztecs were offered a great banquet and festival by the lord of Coaixtlahuaca in his palace. Here they were presented with mantles and breechcloths of the finest possible work, then they set off for their homeland. The warriors were contented with the splendid booty they took back, and seeing this, men in Tenochtitlan were so eager to go to war that one seldom saw a soldier in the city. All wished to go to war since the warriors fared so well.

The Aztecs arrived in Tenochtitlan with slaves, people captured in the war. They were all bound and entered the city dancing and singing loudly. As was customary, the elders came out to receive them, dressed for this ceremony in their usual ritual attire. They burned incense before the prisoners as if they were men dedicated to the gods, and gave them to drink the Divine Liquor, as they called it.[4] Then, after having passed before the image of the idol Huitzilopochtli where they "ate earth," they went before the king, who was considered to be the surrogate of the god. It is false to say that they viewed their kings as [representatives of] gods because they truly honored them as deities.

The captives were addressed by Motecuhzoma: "Welcome, O prize of the gods, O gift to him who encircles the earth with his might each day, to the one who passes over our heads, [he who is] Lord of the Earth and of All Things."

Through their interpreter the prisoners thanked him and praised him for having considered them worthy of seeing his face and of having been admitted to his revered presence, though they had not deserved it. Then they were delivered to the heads of the barrios in order to be housed and their wounds cured carefully so that by the day of the feast they might be fat and desirable for sacrifice.

Once the prisoners had been disposed of, Tlacaelel said to Motecuhzoma, "O lord, let us have a stone made that will be the likeness of the sun. Let us put it upon a high place and let us call it the *cuauhxicalli*, "eagle vessel!" In the Nahuatl tongue, *xicalli* means "container" or a type of deep bowl made from large gourds, and *cuauhtli* means "eagle"; that is why it is called *cuauhxicalli*, "eagle vessel." I used to think, like many others, that it meant "wooden vessel" [for *cuauitl* means "tree" or "wood"], but finally I realized its true meaning is "eagle vessel."

---

[4]The Divine Liquor could have been pulque or chocolate, but either one would have contained a narcotic. *Octli* was pulque and *teooctli* was "divine wine/liquor" or "wine of the gods." Captives who were tied to the *temalacatl* stone and fought with dummy weapons during the Tlacaxipehualiztli ceremony first were given a gourd of *teooctli* to drink, to dull their senses (Durán 1977:178). Durán states that "if those who represented the gods and goddesses alive became downcast, remembering that they were to die, it was an ill omen"—therefore, they were amused, made to dance, and eventually given some Divine Liquor. During the feast of Huey Tecuilhuitl the midwives led a young maiden to the summit of Chapultepec Hill, where she was to be sacrificed. "Once she was at the summit, she was forced to dance and sing for half an hour, and if it was noticed that she did not comply with goodwill, the women made her intoxicated with a certain potion, and she became gay . . ." (Durán 1977:232, 439).

The king approved of Tlacaelel's idea and immediately gave orders that the stone be carved so that at its dedication it would be used for the sacrifice of the prisoners from Coaixtlahuaca. Tlacaelel had this stone made, the description of which I shall put in the next chapter in order to discuss it fully, although in the *Book of Rites* I have written I made special mention of the [*cuauhxicalli*] and of the ceremonies held on the day celebrating it. I also told how this stone was recently dug up during the building of our cathedral and now stands by the doorway of the Perdón. It is said that the Mexicans now wish to convert it into a holy baptismal font and I think it would be a good thing for this stone to be used in the service of our God so that the vessel that was a container for human blood, with sacrifices made to the devil, may now be the font of the Holy Spirit. There the souls of Christians will be cleansed and there they will receive the waters of baptism.

And so that the importance of this stone and its dedication can be fully understood, it will be necessary to repeat some of the chapter describing the Order of the Eagle Knights; this was an order of outstanding warriors in Mexico-Tenochtitlan and the men who belonged to it celebrated this festival. And although I have written about this in the *Book of the Gods and Rites* where I tell about the sacrifices,[5] it will still be necessary to repeat some of that description here so that our history will not be confusing and mutilated. All this will be discussed in the next chapter.

---

[5]Durán 1977, chapters X and XI (186–202).

CHAPTER XXIII

Which treats of the sacrificial ceremony performed in honor of the stone called the *cuauhxicalli*, image of the sun. With a description of how the prisoners from Coaixtlahuaca were sacrificed upon it.

Once Huehue Motecuhzoma had determined that a large stone be carved in the likeness of the sun and that a great feast be held for its presentation, the stonecutters were ordered to seek a stone of great size and, first making it round, to carve upon it an image of the sun, also to hollow out a round depression in the center. From the depression or basin, which was to contain the blood of the victims, were to emerge the rays, so that this image of the sun could hold and rejoice in the blood. A conduit would lead from this central basin to the edge, and the blood would flow along this. He also ordered that all around its sides were to be represented the wars the Aztecs had waged up to that time in which they had been victorious through the favor and aid of the sun.[1]

The stone sculptors, having accepted this task, sought and found a massive, beautiful stone and upon it they carved the image of the sun and the wars in which the Aztecs had conquered Tepeaca, Tochpan, the Huaxtec region, Cuetlaxtla, and Coaixtlahuaca. All these carvings were exquisitely done, especially considering that these people did not possess iron mallets or chisels such as those used by our stone workers, but had to carve the small figures—so lifelike—[on the cuauhxicalli] by working stone with stone. This was a marvelous feat. The amazing skill of these stone artisans is worth recording in this history as is their special ability to shape large stones with smaller ones, creating small figures and large ones, producing the sort of realism that is achieved by an artist who uses a delicate brush or by a silversmith with a fine chisel.

[1]This passage could be describing the Tizoc Stone or the recently discovered Arzobispado Stone, both on display in the Mexica Hall at the Mexican National Museum of Anthropology. Perhaps the sun stone with wars represented around the sides was an artistic-political canon, a sculpture done every so often by each ruler to demonstrate his or his forebears' feats, in the same way that each Aztec sovereign added something to the architecture of the Templo Mayor to show his prowess, conquests, and so forth.

The sacrificial ceremony in honor of cuauhxicalli

When the stone was finished and had been seen by the king, he ordered that a platform about as tall as a man be constructed, with four small staircases that would lead up to the stone. These staircases pointed to the four world directions: north, south, east, and west. The whole structure was conceived according to their beliefs, traditions, and demoniac dreams. The monolith was then put upon the platform with ceremonial reverence.

Huehue Motecuhzoma ordered that the sovereigns of the surrounding states be invited to the feast and the ceremony of the image of the sun. Messengers were sent with the invitation to these lords, who were from Tezcoco, Tacuba, Chalco, Xochimilco, Colhuacan, Cuitlahuac, and the Marquesado, saying that the king invited them to this celebration. The invitation was accepted with good grace by all and they sent fine gifts to King Motecuhzoma in gratitude for his attention. They attired themselves with great care and arrived in the city on the appointed day. These men were received with much deference, accommodated in rooms in the palace, and were given everything they needed. The guests were then entertained with dances and songs of the type used by these people in their festivities. After they had rested, the king, Tlacaelel, and all the lords of the court took the guests to see the stone, pointing out the excellent way it was carved and set in place. The visitors admired the stone itself and the figures carved on it. They also were impressed by the ease with which the Aztecs carried out everything they set out to do.

The king spoke to them: "Do you see, do you observe, the likeness of the sun? Do you see the image of him who warms you with his heat and with his fire, most excellent Lord of Created Things? You have come here for the ceremony in which this image will be honored. For that reason have I bid you come."

Humbling themselves before the king, they answered, "O powerful lord, we congratulate you. The city of Tenochtitlan owes much to you, for you embellish it with so many insignia, so many marvelous things. We enjoy contemplating the grandeur, which we do not deserve, of which we are not worthy."

When the day of the festivities arrived, Motecuhzoma and Tlacaelel blackened their bodies with soot, with pitch,[2] and they applied it in such a way that it seemed to be burnished and their faces seemed to shine with this; [the glow could be seen] from far away. [It was

[2]Durán gives a dramatic description of this ritual soot in his other book, *Book of the Gods and Rites* (1977:115–18). He calls it *teotlacualli*, "food of the gods," which was made of soot combined with scorpions, spiders, centipedes, other unpleasant little creatures, tobacco, and the seed of *ololiuhqui* (*Rivea corymbosa*). This mixture was supposed to protect the persons upon whom it was smeared from all dangers.

so dark that] they looked like black people painted black! They placed crowns of fine feathers, adorned with gold and precious stones, upon their heads, and on each arm was worn a sheath of gold reaching from the elbow to the shoulder. On their feet were richly worked jaguar skin sandals, adorned with gold and gems. They also were robed in splendid royal mantles and breechcloths done in the same manner as the capes. From their back hung miniature bowls of finely worked jade. These last indicated that they were both kings and priests. Jeweled nose plugs were placed in the pierced nose cartilage.

Both Motecuhzoma and Tlacaelel carried sacrificial knives in their hands. They now appeared together before the assembly and went to stand upon the stone that was the likeness and image of the sun, one having ascended by one stairway and the other by another. Five priests in charge of sacrificing followed them. They were to hold down the feet, hands, and heads of the victims, and they were painted all over with red ochre, even their breechcloths and tunics. Upon their heads they wore paper crowns surmounted by little shields that hung to the middle of their foreheads, also painted in red ochre. On the top of their heads they wore long stiff feathers that had been tied to their hair, which stood straight up. On their feet were common, worthless sandals. Each of these ornaments had a special meaning and mystery attached to it.

The five priests went down from the platform and chose one of the prisoners who stood in line at the skull rack. This man was led up to the place where the king stood. Then the priests threw him on his back, upon the stone that was the figure and likeness of the sun. One took him by the right arm, another by the left, one by his left foot, another by his right, while the fifth priest placed a big collar around his neck and held him down so he could not move.

The king lifted the knife on high and made a deep gash in the victim's breast. Having opened it, he extracted the heart and raised it up with his hand as an offering to the sun. When the heart had cooled, he tossed it into the circular depression, taking some of the blood in his hand and sprinkling it in the direction of the sun.[3] In this way the sacrificers killed four men, one by one; then Tlacaelel came and killed another four in his turn. And so, four by four, the prisoners were slain, until every last man who had been brought from the Mixteca had perished.

When the sacrifice had ended, the priests took from the shrine of Huitzilopochtli a serpent made of paper coiled about a pole, all made

---

[3]The steam from the heart supposedly carried a message to the sun.

of [red arara] feathers.⁴ Even today I have seen this kind of paper serpent used in certain dances in Mexico City and in the surrounding towns. A priest carried the snake, twisted about the pole. He then set it on fire and walked around the stone, incensing it with the smoke. While it was burning, he climbed to the top of the monolith and threw the still smoldering serpent upon all the blood that bathed the stone. At this moment a great paper mantle was brought and was cast upon the stone. It burned together with the serpent until there was nothing left of it and the blood was consumed or had dried.

Once the fire had died out, Motecuhzoma and Tlacaelel descended, together with the kings of Tezcoco and Tacuba, then all four withdrew to the royal seats. The two royal guests were anointed, were dressed and adorned with headdresses,⁵ mantles, armbands, breechcloths, and nose plugs, all of these ornaments being of the same type used by the sacrificers. These guests and the rest of the gathering then took part in a solemn banquet and festivities to celebrate the inauguration of the stone that was the image and likeness of the sun.

On the next day a second feast was held by the warriors known as the Knights of the Sun, called Cuacuauhtin, that is to say, "Eagles." This was the festival of the sun that these people caled Nauholin [Four Motion], which in the *Book of the Calendar and Gods* I wrote I translated as "the fourth movement of the sun." In this festival, as I have related, a man painted red was sacrificed in the name of the sun. He was handed a staff and a shield, then on his back was placed a bag filled with pieces of red ochre and soot, together with eagle feathers, paper, and many other things. These were messages that he was to carry to the sun, reminding him that his warriors served him faithfully and thanking him for the many benefits with which he had favored them in war. The victim, carrying the bundle of gifts the Knights of the Sun had sent to the solar deity, together with the staff and shield, slowly began to climb the steps of the low pyramid. In this ascent he represented the course of the sun from east to west. As soon as he reached the summit and stood in the center of the great Sun Stone, which represented high noon, the sacrificers approached the captive and sacrificed him there by opening his chest. Once the heart had

⁴This serpent was an image of the *xiuhcoatl* (fire serpent), Huitzilopochtli's magic weapon with which he defeated his brothers, the Huitznahua, and his sister, Coyolxauhqui. The burning of the feathered paper *xiuhcoatl* was one of the most important parts of the Panquetzaliztli festival in honor of Huitzilopochtli, although Durán does not seem to be describing this feast. A complete description of the ceremony is found in the *Florentine Codex* (1981:book 2:147; also in Durán 1977:457–60).

⁵In the Spanish version Durán says "crowns," not headdresses, but it stands to reason that the two kings would already be wearing their "crowns," which were the *xiuhuitzolli* (turquoise pointed adornment) worn by rulers.

been wrenched out, it was offered to the sun and blood was sprinkled upward toward the solar deity. Then, imitating the descent of the sun in the west, the corpse was toppled down the steps of the pyramid.[6]

After the sacrifice, those Warriors of the Sun celebrated a great feast and dance, with so many rich adornments and featherwork displayed that it was an impressive sight. At this feast much human flesh was consumed; there was also fasting and solemn ritual. The curious reader can consult the above-mentioned book I wrote on the ceremonies and rites.

The place where these warriors gathered was called the Cuauhcalli, "House of Eagles," which was a kind of special house where the warriors practiced the use of weapons. No one could enter that house of knightly order unless he was a son of a known knight.[7]

When the festivities had ended, the dignitaries of the neighboring cities returned to their provinces and kingdoms, eager to imitate the Aztecs. They began to build temple-pyramids and sacrifice men in a similar way, to elect and form a priesthood to practice these rites and ceremonies. They organized military orders, practiced with their arms, and created special schools for singing and dancing similar to those in Tenochtitlan.

The Aztecs and others also began to distinguish between the noble chieftains and the warriors, between the warriors and the shield bearers, between these latter and the lower officials who were commoners. Each was to be treated in a manner appropriate to his rank, and thus it was possible to recognize who belonged to one level and who to another. These distinctions were so rigidly enforced that in the palaces there were special rooms for people of different rank, and when one visited the palace one knew his place and went there directly. The common people had no business entering the royal buildings and never did so unless it was their turn to render personal service such as scrubbing, sweeping, and doing other menial tasks. Only the lords, noblemen, and leading warriors wore sandals on their feet. The rest of the people did not dream of doing so since there were grave penalties involved, and if the chronicle is not mistaken, the death penalty was applicable to any common man who dared pass the royal doors or place a foot there. In their trials for misdemeanors,

---

[6]Durán (1977:188–90) describes this ascent of the pyramid steps, where the victim paused on each step in order to reach the summit at noon. The captive not only took a bundle of gifts to the sun but memorized a message that he directed to the sun just before he was sacrificed.

[7]The Eagle Precinct at the Templo Mayor in Mexico City's historical center, where a life-size spectacular eagle warrior made of terra-cotta was found, may have been this "house of knightly order."

each of these classes had its own place or tribunal for obtaining justice. The decision of the judges passed through several tribunals until it reached the supreme council, where the final sentence was then delivered.

The Knights of the Sun had their insignia and distinctive attire by which they were recognized, and which permitted them to be distinguished from other warriors. They were the only ones who celebrated the feast of the sun, who were allowed to eat human flesh, and who could keep as many women as they could support. In this history I am writing I could tell about many things, many privileges, enjoyed by knights and other lords, but since I have written about this in another place where it is more appropriate, it can be read there, if the Lord ever grants it be revealed [that is, published].

When the sacrifice and ceremony had ended and the visitors had departed, Tlacaelel, on the advice of the king, sent a viceroy to Coaixtlahuaca to take charge of that province and to collect the royal tribute. This deputy, who was named Cuauhxochitl, thanked the king for this favor granted and set off for the Mixteca. Every eighty days after this he came to Tenochtitlan in person and delivered the tribute to the king, who received it gratefully.

CHAPTER XXIV

Which treats of how the Province of Cuetlaxtla rebelled again due to the advice of the Tlaxcalans. With a description of how they were vanquished a second time.

The men of Tlaxcala longed to compete with the Aztecs, to subject them, and their hatred was so strong that they began to harass them, molest them, looking for an occasion to demonstrate their enmity, to prove that they would not tolerate the Aztecs' friendship, nor even speak to them. Since Cuetlaxtla is a domain near Tlaxcala, the four lords of the latter state went to visit the principal chieftains of Cuetlaxtla and feasted with them. While they were taking their pleasure, the Tlaxcalans, pretending to sympathize with their hosts, used this occasion to poison their minds against the Aztecs. They said: "How is it that you suffer the Aztecs, allow them to disembowel, to rob your country? From your land they take the gold, cacao, clothing, many colored feathers, fish, sea snails, shells and turtles. How can you consent to such a thing?"

The Cuetlaxtla lords began to be sorrowful, they wept bitterly, but they answered that, since they had been defeated by the Aztecs, they were now vassals and could do nothing about it.

Xicotencatl, one of the chieftains from Tlaxcala, answered, "Do not fear, follow my instructions. We shall favor you, we shall guard your backs. Cease sending tribute! Kill the governor they have placed over you. And should others come to ask for tribute, kill them all! If they come, send us word, then I shall move my people, we shall surround them and not a man will return alive to Tenochtitlan."

The unfortunate people of Cuetlaxtla, forgetting that the Tlaxcalans had abandoned them in the past, now believed their promise and assassinated the Aztec governor. They then gave magnificent gifts to the Tlaxcalans, who returned to their city, pleased that they had stirred up so much enmity.

When the royal tribute ceased arriving and the tribute collectors no longer came, Tlacaelel was advised of this. He communicated the ill news to the king, saying, "O lord, the people of Cuetlaxtla have failed to send their tribute, and the governor has sent no word of this. Let us find out to what this negligence is due." So the king sent messengers, his couriers, who immediately left for Cuetlaxtla. When they arrived there, they were well received and were taken to the governor's house, where they were told to rest while the governor was notified of their arrival. Then the lords of Cuetlaxtla closed the door of the chamber where the Aztec emissaries rested and set fire to a great pile of chile peppers that they had placed next to that room so the smoke would penetrate it. The smoke from the chiles, flowing into the chamber, was so great and so pungent that the Aztec envoys, trapped inside, unable to defend themselves, were suffocated.

Once the Aztecs were dead, the Cuetlaxtla lords and their aides entered and ordered that the corpses be opened through the anus and that their intestines be pulled out and bound around their necks. This was done, then the bodies were stuffed with straw and were dressed in splendid mantles. In order to mock them, they were placed in seats of honor and great quantities of food, flowers, and tobacco were placed in front of them. Doing much reverence before the bodies, the lords of Cuetlaxtla made this speech: "Eat, O dead lords, and take pleasure. Behold, here is food and drink, fruit and flowers. Why is it that you do not eat? What more do you desire? Eat!"

Then the lord Tepetecuhtli, seeing that the cadavers ignored the food, cried, "What! You do not eat? Are you perchance angry? Then throw them out there . . ." So they took the bodies and threw them to the vultures and the beasts and then sent messengers to Tlaxcala to tell them what they had done. The Tlaxcalans answered that they had acted correctly and thanked the men for having brought the message. They told them not to worry about any problems this might involve, that they, the Tlaxcalans, would hear about this and would be alert as to possible danger.

A traveler from Tepeaca who happened to be passing saw the dead royal couriers lying with their intestines about their throats, and entrails and other innards scattered upon the ground. He hastened to Tenochtitlan and told what he had seen. Standing before the king, he said, "O great lord, a terrible thing has happened: your royal envoys whom you sent to Cuetlaxtla were suffocated with the smoke of chiles and their intestines, lungs, and other entrails removed through the anus. All this, thrown onto the ground, is being eaten by the wild beasts."

The king was horrified by this news. He asked the man where he came from and was told "Tepeaca." The traveler was thanked and was treated with hospitality, then Motecuhzoma called Tlacalelel and told him of this dreadful happening. The members of the council were summoned; these words were directed to them by the king: "My desire is that such an atrocious act be severely punished. I want you to have our armies prepared in order to go destroy Cuetlaxtla. Let not a stone be left standing upon a stone, nor one person be left alive. Cuetlaxtla

The History of the Indies of New Spain

must disappear from the earth, as a lesson to those traitors and to anyone else [who might plan similar treachery]. Have the kings of Tezcoco and Tacuba be advised, and the lords of Chalco, Xochimilco, and all the allied provinces, so they will ready their armies with all the provisions necessary."

Messengers went at once to all these places to deliver this request. As soon as the news spread, the men in charge of military preparations ordered that the soldiers and supplies be made ready as quickly as possible. Thus it was done, and with such facility that as soon as the command was given twenty thousand soldiers were available, all with their weapons, swords, and shields. Their enthusiasm and their desire to fight were amazing; this was due to the fact that many ate only when they went to war and could bring back booty. So they were looking forward to fighting like "water in May," as they say.[1]

The kings of Tezcoco and Tacuba and the lords of the other cities went to the Aztec city to present their condolences to Motecuhzoma, to which he replied, "O my friends, what do you think of the Cuetlaxtlas? With what jeering, what mocking, they have insulted us! It was not enough to kill our envoys but they had to offend us further by removing their entrails, their livers, from behind, and then throw these men to the beasts!" He then told them how the envoys had been further ridiculed by having food and drink and flowers and tobacco placed before their straw-stuffed bodies. The other lords, who deeply regretted these vile acts, said that their men were armed and ready and would leave when they were ordered to do so. With that they returned to their cities.

Motecuhzoma then turned to Tlacaelel, saying, "O Lord Tlacaelel, I am determined to see the Cuetlaxtlas totally destroyed, that nothing remain of them."

Tlacaelel, however, answered that instead of removing them from the face of the earth it would be preferable to conquer them, to control them, then to double the tribute paid by them up to that time. In that way they would be castigated. Furthermore, it would be almost impossible to destroy Cuetlaxtla completely and it would be unwise to lay waste to towns where such wealth was found. Also, there were not enough people allied to the Aztecs to repopulate the place, since this is what they would wish to do.

Motecuhzoma was convinced by these arguments and asked what tribute should be imposed. Tlacaelel exclaimed, "If they used to give cloth ten *brazas* long, let it be twenty *brazas* in length from now on! If

---

[1]May is the end of the dry season in Mexico, and everyone is anxious for rain. "Water in May" is the salvation of many crops, and therefore of people.

they used to send us green stones, let them also give us white and red ones. If they used to give us the spotted skins of jaguar and ocelot, from now let them give us white ones. And let them pay tribute of live serpents and a thousand other creatures!" Tlacaelel and the king invented all kinds of difficult tributes, to burden the Cuetlaxtlas and make them suffer as much as possible. Then Motecuhzoma summoned all the captains and officers and told them not to destroy the enemy completely; but when they were beaten and had asked for mercy, they were to be given these orders regarding tribute.

When the Aztec forces reached Cuetlaxtla, they set up camp nearby and put their men in order. The Cuetlaxtlas, observing the strength of the Aztec army and their proximity to the city, notified the Tlaxcalans, reminding them of their promise. The Tlaxcalans sent word that they would prepare their soldiers and would then attack the Aztecs from behind in order to defeat them, that the Cuetlaxtlas were to delay the fighting meanwhile and not rush into battle. But the Aztecs, afraid of some trick, the day after they arrived prepared their army and that of the allies for a rapid attack on the city. When the forces were all in order, the usual address was made to them:

> War is like a field of dry grass set on fire, which while burning is swept away by the wind, and all is consumed. Or it is like a whirlwind that snatches up the dead leaves and with fury pulls them up into the sky. And you can compare all this with your destiny, your fate, with this battlefield where you find yourselves, where your hearts will be set on fire. You must also set on fire, consume, sweep away, those barbarians whom you see before you, the warriors from Ahuilizapan, Quimichtlan, Teoixhuacan, Chichiquilan, Macuilxochtitlan, Tlatectla, Oceoloapan, and Cuetlaxtla.

The men from these latter cities, in battle order, went out to confront the Aztecs. They had not yet seen them when the Aztecs attacked with more fury than savage animals attack gentle sheep. Throwing themselves at the enemy, the Aztecs began to wound them so swiftly and with such violence that the Cuetlaxtla leaders, terrified and showing little courage, turned and fled. The Aztecs, going after them, captured and killed so many that it was impossible to count them.

When the Cuetlaxtla *macehualtin*, the commoners, saw the destruction that was going on and realized that they had no ruler or leader of any kind to guide them, they came out, wailing, "O Aztecs, why do you kill us? What fault is it of ours, we who are simple, ignorant people, who are free of malice and have nothing to gain? Why do you take revenge on us? We have not angered you or offended you or troubled you. And yet you have spared those cursed thieves, our chiefs and lords, who have brought nothing but death to us. Have we not been the ones to pay the tribute? By chance is it a result of the work of the lords? Is not all the result of our sweat and labor? When we gave cloth, did they weave it for you? No, it was woven by us and our wives. If you received cacao, gold and precious stones, rich plumage and fish, were we not the ones who gave it, who offered it to our lords Motecuhzoma and to our masters the Aztecs? Cease, O Aztecs, injuring us, mistreating us; let us speak, hear what we have to say."

The Aztec captains then ordered their men, who were fighting with much spirit, to put down their arms. When this signal was given, the soldiers stopped, lowering their swords and shields, their slings and stones, their arrows and darts, with which they caused so much destruction. Then the Cuetlaxtla commoners were told to speak. They explained: "What we wish is to seek justice against our rulers. We want to see them punished, destroyed, dead, because they have been the cause of all our problems. And listen to us, Aztecs, ask for all you wish, for we are the ones who give the tribute, it is from us that these things come to you. So say what you will, for again we shall give the tribute, all will be sent to you."

"We can well see that you are not at fault," the Aztec lords replied, "and that you have been sent here by your masters. Why do they not come themselves, instead of having you speak for them? Why do they not offer themselves for sacrifice, as is their obligation?"

"You can see that for them our lives have no value," the others said. "That is why we wish you to kill them and let us go free."

But the Aztecs stated that they were not authorized to kill anyone unless it was in war. "Your lords have not appeared in this battle, we have not seen them. But they will not escape; the reasons you have put forth and that which you have asked for will be proposed to our King Motecuhzoma and he will command that our orders be carried out. Therefore, bring these men here before us, safely and without delay."

The common people of that place then sought out their rulers and found them hiding in certain caves. Having bound their hands, they brought them before the victorious general. This officer reprehended them and humiliated them in front of the entire multitude, then he ordered all the people in the city, by public mandate, to hold them prisoners, carefully guarded, and to watch over them well so they could not escape until Motecuhzoma sent word regarding their fate. The penalty for letting the prisoners escape would be the destruction of Cuetlaxtla by the Aztecs still another time. With this warning, the people guarded them well, held them prisoner, at that time.

The Cuetlaxtlas then welcomed the Aztecs to the city, where they honored them, provided them with many things, gave them clothing of mantles and breechcloths, and did all they could for their well-being. The Aztecs gave orders that from then on the tribute was to consist of lengths of cloth twenty *brazas* long, white and red precious stones, double amounts of gold, cacao, fine feathers, and white animal skins of excellent quality. The poor Cuetlaxtlas received these instructions, simulating, a contented aspect and agreeable disposition.

When the Tlaxcalans heard how the Aztecs had conquered Cuetlaxtla and that entire province, they stopped preparing their soldiers and left the Cuetlaxtlas to their fate.

The Aztecs left those lands and returned to Tenochtitlan, where they went before the king, kissed his hands, and reported that the entire region had become subject to him, that it was now quiet and subdued and would be paying double tribute as he had demanded. They also told him that the rulers had been made prisoners, while the commoners asked for justice against them, since these rulers, on the advice of the Tlaxcalans, had been the instigators of that rebellion; the people in general, the commoners, had known nothing of these events. They added that their lords had been encouraged by the Tlaxcalans, who had promised to come to their aid. And believing this, confiding in the Tlaxcalans and their assistance, the Cuetlaxtla lords had done that evil thing: they had killed the royal Aztec envoys and they had refused to give the tribute they owed, as true lords, conscious of their obligation, would have done. These tributes, the commoners said, were paid by them and not by the rulers, who mistreated them cruelly and tyrannized them, abusing them and demanding excessive tribute from them. The only way these lords occupied their time was in eating and drinking at the cost of the rest of the people and by playing and amusing themselves with pleasant pastimes; all those bad habits should not be forgotten. They asked that justice be done, that these tyrants be killed.

Motecuhzoma asked Tlacaelel, his Cihuacoatl—a title he had given him as a sign of renown and grandeur—his opinion, whether the rulers of the vanquished city should be executed, since they were great lords and images of the gods. Perhaps the gods would be offended, perhaps it would be a sacrilege if they were killed. Tlacaelel, however, answered that since those men had rebelled against the supreme deity Huitzilopochtli and his likeness, the king of Mexico, they deserved to be punished. It was also true that the common people were asking for justice and this could not be denied them.

And so it was that Motecuhzoma ordered that the two rulers of Cuetlaxtla be killed by having their throats slit, not at the front of the neck but at the back. Cuauhnochtli and Tlillancalqui, two great Aztec judges of the supreme council, were sent to execute the sentence. The two lords of Cuetlaxtla were then executed by these judges, who, with their own swords, killed them by slitting their throats.

In this way the people were satisfied. New rulers were elected and an Aztec governor was placed over them whose obligation it was to protect those people, to mete out justice, and to collect the tribute and send it to Mexico. And the men who had administered justice [Cuauhnochtli and Tlillancalqui] returned to Tenochtitlan, where they informed the king of the execution. They added that Cuetlaxtla was now tranquil, in peace, with new rulers chosen by the people of that province, and at the same time an Aztec governor had been appointed whose name was the same as the deceased official, who would be able to protect the inhabitants and correct the wrongs caused by their former rulers. He would also send to the Aztec city the tribute Cuetlaxtla was obliged to give.

Motecuhzoma thanked them: "Welcome back, now go rest."

Soon men from Cuetlaxtla arrived, bringing tribute, that which was owed from before as well as the new tribute. They brought great riches in quantity: gold, silver, jewels, rare feathers, precious stones, animal skins, clothing, large and frightening serpents, cacao, cotton, many types of fish found along that coast; that is, everything the Aztecs had demanded. After having delivered the tribute to the king, they addressed him with these words, "O Lord, you see here all that has been won with the sweat of your brow and the strength of your arms. This is what is owed to the god Huitzilopochtli; it is given by the grace of your vassals who have earned it with the blood from their bodies. The men of our city who opposed the royal Aztec crown are now dead, but we shall still continue to serve you with everything at our disposition. They no longer have any control over us, nor did they ever give the tribute we now bring; we were the ones responsible for this and we shall continue delivering it until our death."

Motecuhzoma thanked these men. When they left his presence, they went to the temple and there, kneeling before the statue of Huitzilopochtli, each one placed a finger in the sacred earth and then put it in his mouth. They offerd to the god rich presents of cloth twenty *brazas* long, fine feathers, cotton, jewels and precious stones that were white and red. And taking some of those large, thick serpents they had brought, they sacrificed them there by cutting them in pieces. After the offering and invocation had been made, they returned to the palace. Here they were given fine chambers and all the comforts they could desire, then they were dressed in richly worked mantles and breechcloths. The king spoke to them: "My Cuetlaxtla sons, know that I esteem you greatly, I love you deeply. Now you must be quiet, peaceful, and not listen to what the Tlaxcalans may say. If there is anything you need, that is what we are here for, to help you. Whatever the Tlaxcalans may ask you for, beware that they do not advise you wrongly, deceive you, promise that they will come to your aid. So that you heed our advice, just remember that the Tlaxcalans did not help you, did not favor you, when you needed them." The Cuetlaxtlas were grateful for these words. They then left Tenochtitlan for their city, happy and contented.

When the Cuetlaxtlas had departed, the king summoned the principal men who had fought in this war, the most valiant and courageous warriors, and delivered to them the captured slaves, giving one to each, and distributed among them many things they had brought back from the war except the precious stones, fine feathers, and gold crowns, for these were divided only between the king and Tlacaelel. All the rest was guarded in the royal treasury. The king received fifteen slaves and Tlacaelel five. Everything else was placed in the treasury. In this way everyone was satisfied, pleased with the distribution.

CHAPTER XXV

Which treats of the great tribute and wealth received by the Aztecs from many provinces and cities that had been conquered in war.

The Aztec *Historia* digresses here in order to describe the great tribute and wealth received by Mexico-Tenochtitlan and by those who had won it in war with their labor and sweat and who had shed their blood for their own glory, for the honor of their king and for the defense of the nation. This chronicle makes special mention of the valorous, bold captains who had been a principal cause in the aggrandizing of the nation and who had subjected cities and provinces, people of different tongues and regions—and because of this had been remembered when the tribute wealth was distributed. The mention of those lords, their titles and their feats, reminds one of other distinguished men, such as the Twelve Peers of France, or—in Spain—of the Cid, of Bernardo del Carpio, of Count Fernán González, or Diego de Paredes, or many other courageous and valiant men. Our Spanish books are filled with the skill and bravery of these people.

In the same way the *Historia* tells of the valiant men who labored and suffered, who faced many difficult situations, in order to overcome and subject Azcapotzalco, Coyoacan, Xochimilco, Cuitlahuac, Colhuacan, Chalco, all the province of Tezcoco, Tepeaca, Ahuilizapan, and Cuetlaxtla with its entire province; Coaixtlahuaca and the Mixtec region; the province of Poctla, Guaxaca, Tecuantepeque, Xoconochco and Xolotla, Amatla and Xochtla, Izhuatlan, Cuextlan, Tziuhcoac, Tozapan, Tochpan; Matlatzinco, Toluca, Mazahuacan, Xocotitlan and Chiapan, Xiquipilco, Cuauhuacan, Cillan.

All these densely populated towns, cities, and provinces were conquered and destroyed by the bold men whom I shall name here: the great Tlacaelel, Cuatlecoatl, Tlacahuepan, Tlatolzaca, Epcoahuatl, Tzompantli, Huehue Motecuhzoma, Huehue Zaca, Citlalcoatl, Aztacoatl, Axicoyo, Cuauhtzitzimitl, and Xiconoc. It was because of them that Mexico-Tenochtitlan was exalted, feared, and revered, and the name Aztec respected and obeyed. These men initiated warring as a means of rising in Aztec society, and they did improve their lot this way.

And these were some of the great riches and tribute that flowed into the Aztec city as a result of these wars:[1]

Great quantities of gold, in dust and also worked as jewels.

Large amounts of green stones, of rock crystal, of carnelian, bloodstones, amber, besides many other types of precious stones that these people loved greatly.

Their principal idolatry was the adoration of these stones, together with the feathers that they called "shadow of the gods." These were all kinds of plumes and of all colors: green, blue, red, yellow, purple, white, and multicolored.

Vast amounts of cacao.

Numerous bundles of cotton, both white and yellow.[2]

A bewildering amount of cloth: lengths twenty, ten, five, four, or two *brazas* long, according to the ability of each province.

Fine mantles for the lords, of different weave and design, all richly worked. Some of them had beautiful fringes done in colors and featherwork. Others had insignia on them, others serpent heads, or jaguars, and some were adorned with the image of the sun. And yet others had skulls or blowguns or figures of the gods—all of them embroidered in many colored threads and enriched with feathers of duck and geese, those tiny feathers that are like down. All were beautifully and skillfully worked. Even though silk was unknown in this country, the people were extremely skilled in weaving, embroidering, and painting cotton cloth.

Also mantles of maguey fiber given in large quantities as tribute by the Chichimecs, most delicately worked and painted in different colors, some of them adorned with gilded eagles, a variety of weapons, and insignia.

Live birds, too, sent by these different nations, the most highly esteemed and those of the finest plumage. Some were green, some red, others blue; parrots large and small; other splendid and handsomely colored birds such as eagles, buzzards, hawks, sparrow hawks, ravens, herons, and small and large wild geese.

Wild animals such as ocelots, jaguars, wildcats. All of these fierce animals were brought in cages.

Large and small snakes, some poisonous, others not, some fierce, others harmless.

It was marvelous to see the great variety of snakes and other creatures that were brought in large pots! Tribute was even demanded in centipedes, scorpions, and spiders. The Aztecs felt they were Lords

---

[1] For a study of Mexico-Tenochtitlan's economic system and tribute, see Hassig 1985 (chaps. II–VII and appendix B); also, Berdan 1982 (chaps. II and V).

[2] "Yellow" cotton is the natural brownish-colored cotton called *coyuchi* in Mexico.

of All Created Things; everything belonged to them, everything was theirs!

From the coast came everything that could be found in the sea: scallop shells, large and small sea snails, curious fish bones, shells of giant turtles, other turtles of different sizes, stones from the sea, pearls baroque and smooth, ambers.

Color [for painting and other uses]: red ochre, yellow, green, blue, purple, light green. Dyes of all kinds: cochineal, alum, *nacazcolotl*, *zacatlaxcalli*, which are plants, a mineral for making an ink dye, and red dye from the *brasil* tree.[3]

Other provinces sent gourds as tribute. Some of these were deep, others shallow, some plain, others carved; some were gilded and painted with rich and intricate designs. Some of these have lasted until today and are exquisitely worked. Another type of gourd was wide and flat, and these were used in the same way that we use silver trays or large plates to carry the food to the table or to offer water for the hands. They also had curious gourds with handles, similar to chocolate pots. In sum, this tribute consisted of a multitude of large, medium-size, small, and miniature gourds of different shapes, types, and colors.

Women's clothing was tributed: *huipiles* or loose blouses, also skirts, as well finished and splendid as it was possible to make, all of them enriched with wide borders embroidered in different colors and designs, with featherwork on the front; insignia done in colored thread: and on the back some of them bore embroidered flowers; others, imperial eagles. Still others were covered with flowers that were not only embroidered but were combined with featherwork, and these were a splendid thing to see. Beautiful skirts of great price were richly woven, with excellent skill. All of these clothes were used by the ladies who were wives and concubines of the lords and great chieftains. Another type of female dress arrived through tribute. This was entirely white and was worn by the young women and the old women who served in the temples. There was yet another kind of clothing for women, made of maguey fiber, and this was worn by the servant girls in the homes, where it was allotted to them.

From other provinces were brought mats of different weaves and colors, some of palm leaf, others of water reeds, others of thick shining straw, some of cane, some of rushes from the lagoon. Together with these came seats woven in the same way as the mats, and seats with backs, all finely painted and splendidly worked.

[3]*Nacazcolotl* or *cascalote* is *Caesalpinia coriaria* (Martínez 1987:622). *Zacatlaxcalli* (*Cuscuta americana*), a dye plant that produces a yellow color, is a parasite that adheres to other plants (ibid.:1014).

Yet other lands sent maize and beans, *chian* seeds, amaranth, chiles of many different types that grow in this country and are used in many of the dishes cooked here; each dish had its own name.[4] Another tribute consisted of a great quantity of pumpkin seeds.

From other parts came firewood and the bark of certain trees. The bark was the firewood of the nobility because it makes a beautiful flame. There was also charcoal, and all these things were paid as tribute by the towns that had forests.

Other people paid in stone, lime, boards, and beams to build houses and temples.

From other places were brought deer and rabbits and quail, some uncooked and others in barbecue. As tribute also came gophers, weasels, and large rodents, which thrive in the woods.

Toasted locusts, large winged ants, large cicadas and little ones, and all the little creatures found on the earth. Those who lived next to lagoons sent everything that thrives in the water, such as algae, a certain insect or mosquito that walks upon the water, even arachnids and worms.

From the town where fruit was grown, such as the Hot Country, came products such as pineapples, annonas, mameys, numerous types of sweet fruits, for example, guavas, a wild fruit like a pear, sapotas that are yellow, black, or white, avocados, and two or three kinds of yams. All these came from the Hot Lands.

These provinces also paid tribute every day in great loads of flowers of a thousand varieties, all dexterously arranged. Sweet-smelling flowers abound in the Hot Country, though some are better than others because they have a more delicate perfume. The trees upon which these flowers grow were also brought, roots and all, to be planted in the houses of the lords.[5]

The purpose of this tribute was to show the magnificence and authority of the Aztec nation and so the Aztecs would be held to be Lords of All Created Things, upon the waters as well as upon the earth.

All of this had dealt with food and clothing, but there were also provinces that paid tribute in cotton armor. This armor was stuffed and quilted and was so thick that an arrow or dart could not penetrate

---

[4]For a study of chiles in ancient and modern Mexico, see Long-Solís 1986.

[5]These cultivated plants were brought from every corner of the empire, to be transplanted in the private gardens of the nobility and in the enormous nurseries maintained by the Aztec government. These botanical gardens, for both ornamental and medicinal plants, were later admired and described by European eyewitnesses of the conquest. Among the many parks of this type were Huaxtepec in Morelos, Chapultepec in Mexico City, Itztapalapa southeast of Mexico City, and the gardens of Nezahualcoyotl near Tezcoco.

it. Another tribute consisted of shields made of fire-hardened wooden rods, bound closely together and so strong that a sword could not dent them. The faces of these shields were covered with fine featherwork of many colors, the design being formed by the different shades and colors of the feathers themselves, combined with shining gold. These shields were also decorated with insignia, scenes of great deeds in the past, pictures of their gods and of their past monarchs. Even today they use them or at least keep them put away as a reminder of their ancient history, great deeds, and famous men.

Big thick bows were also paid as tribute, together with arrows of many types and different forms. Finely worked stones in the form of balls for the slings were also sent, and so were numerous slings made of maguey fiber. Blades of white stone or of black [obsidian] for the swords were given in tribute, and flints for arrows and the darts.

Let one try to imagine all the products of this land and he will know what was sent as tribute to Mexico-Tenochtitlan! Honeycombs were sent and even hives with bees inside; also great jars of white honey and others of yellow honey.

Resin from the trees, torch pine to give light, and sooty materials for painting and blackening.

Provinces that lacked foodstuffs and clothing paid in maidens, girls, and boys, all slaves, and these were divided among the lords. The girls became concubines of the lords and bore them children, and their offspring were referred to as "sons of slaves." When people have disputes, the greatest insult is to call someone "son of a slave girl." And these girls were given as tribute by some of the towns in former times.

All these things that I have described here and many more listed in our chronicle—in a confusing manner, in a general way that includes all created things—were paid in tribute to the Aztec king by all the provinces, cities, towns, and villages in the land. And the reason they were obliged to pay this tribute is told [in the *Historia*] in this way:

All the provinces in the land, all the cities, towns, and different places, after having been conquered in war and subjected by the Aztecs, were then obliged to pay tribute. This was because the valorous Aztecs were merciful and lowered their swords and shields, ceased killing, saved the lives of the old men, the old women, and the children. In this way they avoided the destruction of the towns and the spoiling of the lands.

Because of this the conquered people gave themselves as vassals, as servants, to the Aztecs and they paid tribute in all things created under the sky: gold, silver, jewels, precious stones, fine feathers, weapons, mantles, cacao, cotton, maize, beans, amaranth, pumpkin seeds, chiles of all types, flour made from different grains, woven mats, seats, firewood, charcoal, different kinds of pottery, sandals, stone, wood, lime, animals from the hunt, turkeys, fowl, eagles, jaguars, ocelots, wildcats,[6] in fact, all kinds of animals, wild and domesticated, fine tanned animal skins; large and small serpents, poisonous and nonpoisonous; fresh fish and cooked.

There were such vast quantities of all these things that came to the city of Mexico that not a day passed without the arrival of people from other regions who brought large amounts of everything, from foodstuffs to luxury items, for the king and the lords. They had won this with their sweat and work and strength of their chests and heads and arms; they had subjected all those nations and placed them in perpetual servitude and slavery. This vocation of war had been given to them by their god Huitzilopochtli, who promised them his favor and assistance.

Motecuhzoma saw that he was now a great sovereign, that his city was rich and prosperous, that it had increased in size, was filled with wealth, that there were innumerable lords and distinguished men, that the city was bursting with people, foreigners as well as locals and Aztec citizens, to the point that there was no room for more. And he noticed that some of these people offended, insulted, others; they did not observe the expected courtesies. So he decided to establish strict laws, ordinances, statutes, so that everyone who lived in that country would do so with decorum, good manners, harmony, and concordance that should exist in such a large, rich, and heavily populated city. Furthermore, these laws should exist so the authority of his royal person and the lords of the kingdom would be given the respect and reverence that was due them, so they would be known and honored in this way.

Therefore, these laws were established and will be discussed in the next chapter.

---

[6]Throughout his manuscript Durán mentions *leones* and *tigres* when he means jaguars, ocelots, pumas, wildcats, and mountain lions. Tigers and lions did not exist in Mexico. In the same way, Durán calls a flower a "rose," yet roses were unknown there before the European conquest.

CHAPTER XXVI

Which treats of the laws, ordinances, and statutes, and other conditions decreed by King Motecuhzoma, the first of this name, in Mexico-Tenochtitlan.

Although the royal court of Tenochtitlan was now settled, in perfect harmony and order, and the people were at peace, lived in tranquillity, and were careful not to cause disturbances or difficulties, it was the desire of the king to dictate laws, ordinances, and statutes that would help other kings to rule, to govern. Thus would be decreed the laws for the future, the conditions under which the people of each state would live, the rules that would be followed and observed. The country was to be ordered in the best way possible and in accordance with the old customs. To better prepare these laws the king gathered together all the lords of his court, that is, he summoned the general council of all the lords of his kingdom and of the neighboring provinces. Together they established the canons for the honor, respect, solicitude, and reverence in which the kings and great lords should be held; and it was ordered that the sovereigns be regarded as [surrogates of the] gods and be honored as such.

The following laws were decreed:

1. The king must never appear in public except when the occasion is extremely important and unavoidable.

2. Only the king may wear a golden diadem in the city, though in war all the great lords and brave captains may wear this (but on no other occasion). These lords and warriors represent the royal person when at war and thus could at that time wear the golden diadem and royal insignia.

3. Only the king and the prime minister Tlacaelel may wear sandals within the palace. No great chieftain may enter the palace shod, under pain of death. These noblemen are the only ones to be allowed to wear sandals in the city and no one else, also under pain of death, with the exception of men who have performed some great feat in war; because of their valor and courageous deeds they may wear sandals, but these must be common and of low quality. The gilded, adorned ones are to be used only by noblemen.

4. Only the king is to wear the fine mantles of cotton brocaded with designs and threads of different colors and adorned with feather-

work; these will be worked with gold and embroidered with royal insignia. The king is to decide which type of cloak is to be used by the royal person and at which times, in order to distinguish him from the rest.

5. The great lords, who are twelve, may wear special mantles of certain make and design, and the minor lords, according to their valor and accomplishments, may wear others.

6. The common soldiers are permitted to wear only the simplest type of mantle. They are prohibited from using any special designs that might set them off from the rest. Their breechcloths and waistbands must be in keeping with the simplicity of the mantle.

7. The commoners will not be allowed to wear cotton clothing, under pain of death, but can use only garments of maguey fiber. The mantle must just cover the knee and not be worn longer than this. If anyone allows it to reach the ankle, he will be killed unless he has wounds received in war on his legs [then he will be permitted to cover these with the longer length].

(And so it was that when one encountered a man who wore his mantle longer than the law permitted, one immediately looked at his legs. If he had wounds acquired in war he would be left in peace, for in this way he was able to cover those wounds he had been given by being valiant, and if he did not have those wounds he would be killed. People would say, "Since that leg did not flee from the sword, it is just that it be rewarded and honored.")

8. Only the great noblemen and valiant warriors are given license to build a house with a second story; for disobeying this law a person receives the death penalty. No one is to put peaked or flat or round additions [towers? gables?] upon his house. This privilege has been granted by the gods only to the great.

9. Only the great lords are to wear labrets, ear plugs, and nose plugs of gold and precious stones, except for commoners who are strong men, brave captains, and soldiers, but their labrets, ear plugs, and nose plugs must be of bone, wood, or other inferior material of little value.

10. Only the king of Tenochtitlan and sovereigns of the provinces and other great lords are to wear gold armbands, anklets, and golden rattles on their feet at the dances. They may wear garlands and gold headbands with feathers in them in the style they desire; and no one else may use them. These kings alone may adorn themselves with chains of gold around their necks, with jewelry of this metal and of precious stones, such as jade, all made by master jewelers; and no one else may. Other valiant soldiers who are not considered noblemen may wear common garlands and eagle, macaw, and certain other

feathers on their heads. They may adorn themselves with necklaces of bone and of small snails, small scallop shells, bones of snakes, and common stones. (Some of the latter, though, were so well polished, carved, and painted that they were very handsome and looked fine.)

11. In the royal palace there are to be diverse rooms where different classes of people are to be received, and under pain of death no one is to enter that of the great lords or to mix with those men [unless of that class himself]. Each one is to go to the chambers of his peers. A tribunal is to be set up to resolve complaints, disputes, and possible damage caused.

12. An order of judges is to be established, beginning with the judges of the supreme council. After these would come regular court judges, municipal judges, district officials, constables, and councilmen,[1] although none of them may give the death sentence without notifying the king. Only the sovereign can sentence someone to death or pardon him. (Even in this they wished to act like gods.)

13. All the barrios will possess schools or monasteries for young men where they will learn religion and correct comportment. They are to do penance, lead hard lives, live with strict morality, practice for warfare, do physical work, fast, endure disciplinary measures, draw blood from different parts of the body, and keep watch at night. There are to be teachers and old men to correct them and chastise them and lead them in their exercises and take care that they are not idle, do not lose their time. All of these youth must observe chastity in the strictest way, under pain of death.

14. There is to be a rigorous law regarding adulterers. They are to be stoned and thrown into the rivers or to the buzzards.

15. Thieves will be sold for the price of their theft, unless the theft be grave, having been committed many times. Such thieves will be punished by death.

16. Great privileges and exemptions are to be given those who dedicate themselves to religion, to the temples and the gods. Priests will be awarded great distinction, reverence, and authority.

The *Historia* states that Motecuhzoma, the first of this name, acquired such glorious fame, became so powerful, and was so content with the rulership evidenced by such prudent laws and ordinances that the people held him to be more divine than human. They said that those statutes had been ordered more by the gods than by a man of this earth because they had been so beneficial for the nation and for all

---

[1]Garibay (Durán 1967:II:579n. xxvi–1) rightly expresses the opinion that these offices are based on Spanish charges and probably do not correspond to an Aztec equivalent. Nevertheless, it is evident that there was a hierarchy of judges as well as centralized and marginal civil employees.

other regions. This edict was proclaimed throughout all the provinces, cities, towns, and villages, so they would be observed and respected and never violated, as marvelous acts that were necessary for the preservation of the different nations.

[These laws were accepted] as sparks from a divine fire that the great King Motecuhzoma had within his breast and they were issued for the well-being of the entire land. They were like medicine that, given at the proper time and season, will profit the human body and be the cause of its welfare, just as correctly formed laws are necessary for the conservation of the country.

CHAPTER XXVII

Which treats of how King Motecuhzoma the First, now reigning in glory and majesty, sought the place of origin of his ancestors, the Seven Caves in which they had dwelt. With a description of the splendid presents he sent to be given to those who might be found there.

At this point our chronicle tells us that Motecuhzoma, who had become a great monarch possessing glory and wealth, decided to seek out the place where his ancestors had dwelt. He wished to know about the Seven Caves, Chicomoztoc, which his own traditions had so often mentioned.[1] Therefore, he summoned Tlacaelel and said to him, "I have decided to call together some of my valiant warriors and send them, very well armed and provided with a generous part of the wealth we have received through the auspices of the God of All Created Things, of the Day and the Night, the Lord for whom we live, so these riches be offered there at the Seven Caves and be given to those who might be found in that place. We also have been told that the mother of our god Huitzilopochtli is still alive, it is possible that she still lives. Let her be given the presents that are taken there, let her be told that she may enjoy that which her son has won with the strength of his arms and chest and his head."[2]

"O powerful lord," Tlacaelel answered, "your royal chest is not moved, is not governed, by your own reasons, nor is your heart moved by human motives; without doubt this has been proposed to you by some eternal deity, the cause of all that is found in nature and by whose providence, O wise lord, you desire to undertake such an enormous enterprise. Now please forgive me, for it would seem that I always try to impose my arguments upon you, but I wish to tell you this.

[1] The Seven Caves, Chicomoztoc, a mythic place of origin, was common to many groups in Mexico. For Aztlan, Colhuacan, and Chicomoztoc, see glossary.

[2] It will be remembered that Huitzilopochtli was the son of Coatlicue, "She of the Skirt of Snakes," and that according to one myth he was miraculously born on Coatepec Hill, where he defeated his 400 brothers and his sister Coyolxauhqui, who were about to kill Coatlicue. According to Durán in this chapter, Huitzilopochtli was born at Chicomoztoc, the Seven Caves. In the *Codex Boturini* or *Tira de la Peregrinación* (1975) Huitzilopochtli is shown as a sacred bundle that led his people on their migration.

"You must know, O great lord, that what you have determined to do is not for strong or valiant men, nor does it depend upon skill in the use of arms in warfare, for which you would send men of war, captains bearing ostentatious fighting equipment. Your envoys will not go as conquerors but as explorers. They will seek out the place where our ancestors lived, they will try to find the place where our god Huitzilopochtli was born. No, you must look for wizards, sorcerers, magicians, who with their enchantments and spells can discover that place. Our historians tell us that it is covered thickly with thorny bushes and with great brambles. It is in the midst of marshes, of lagoons that are filled with reeds and rushes, and it will be difficult to find except by great fortune. Therefore, O lord, follow my advice and look for those wizards I have described to you, who will go to that place, who will discover it, and who will then bring you news of it.

"When our people lived there it was a delightful land, a pleasant place. There they lived in leisure, they lived long, they never became weary, they never grew old, they never lacked for anything. But after they departed from their home everything turned into thorns and thistles. The stones became sharp in order to wound, the bushes became prickly and the trees thorny, in order to sting. Everything there turned against them, so they would not be able to remember the place, so they could not return there."

Motecuhzoma agreed to accept the advice of Tlacaelel and called the royal historian, an aged man called Cuauhcoatl [Eagle Serpent], and addressed him: "O ancient father, I desire to know the true story, the knowledge that is hidden in your books about the Seven Caves where our ancestors, our fathers and grandfathers, lived, and whence they came forth. I wish to know about the place wherein dwelt our god Huitzilopochtli and out of which he led forefathers."

"O mighty lord," answered Cuauhcoatl, "what I, your unworthy servant, can answer you is that our forebears dwelt in that blissful, happy place called Aztlan, which means 'Whiteness.' In that place there is a great hill in the midst of the waters, and it is called Colhuacan because its summit is twisted, thus it is Colhuacan, meaning 'Twisted Hill.'[3] In this hill were caves or grottoes where our fathers and grandfathers lived for many years. There they lived in leisure, when they were called Mexitin [or Mexicas] and Aztecs. There they had at their disposal great flocks of ducks of different kinds, herons, cormorants, cranes, and other waterfowl. Our ancestors enjoyed the song and melody of the little birds with red and yellow heads. They

---

[3] It has already been mentioned that Colhuacan can mean both "Twisted Hill" and "Place of Ancestors," from *colli*, "grandfather or ancestor," and *colhua*, "he who has grandparents or ancestors."

also possessed many kinds of large beautiful fish. They had the freshness of groves of trees along the edge of the waters. They had springs surrounded by willows, evergreens, and alders, all of them tall and comely. Our ancestors went about in canoes and made plots on which they sowed maize, chiles, tomatoes, amaranth, beans, and all kinds of seeds that we now eat and that were brought here from that place.

"However, after they abandoned that delightful place and came to the mainland, everything turned against them. The weeds began to bite, the stones became sharp and cut, the fields were filled with thistles and spines. They encountered brambles and thorns that were difficult to pass through. There was no place to rest, there was no place where they could settle. Everything became filled with vipers, snakes, poisonous little creatures, jaguars and wildcats, and other ferocious beasts. And this is the story told by our ancestors, it is what I have found [painted] in our ancient books. And this, O powerful king, is the answer I can give you to what you ask of me."

The king replied that this account must be a true one, since it was the same as that related by Tlacaelel. He ordered that all the wizards and magicians who could be found in all the provinces be brought before him. Sixty sorcerers were then brought to Motecuhzoma; they were old men, wise in the arts of magic. The king instructed them thus: "O elders, my fathers, I am determined to seek the land that has given birth to the Aztec people, to discover from whence they came, what land it is, and if it is still inhabited, and if the mother of our god Huitzilopochtli still lives. Therefore, prepare to go seek this place in the best way you can and as soon as possible." He had the sorcerers provided with a large number of mantles of all types, of women's clothing, precious stones, gold, fine jewels, quantities of cacao and *teonacaztli* ["divine ear," a flower added to a cacao beverage], cotton, black vanilla flowers in large numbers, and beautiful feathers, the finest that could be found. All these riches, the most valuable things available, were given to those sorcerers. And so they would carry out this assignment with all possible care, they were also given mantles for themselves and other compensations, as well as sufficient food for their journey.

Laden with rich gifts, the sixty sorcerers departed and some time later reached a hill called Coatepec in the province of Tula. There they traced magic symbols upon the ground, invoked the demon, and smeared themselves with certain ointments that they used and that wizards still use nowadays—for there are still great magicians, men who are possessed, among them. One might ask: how is it that they are not exposed? And I shall answer that it is because they conceal one another and hide from us more than any other people on earth. They have no confidence in the Spaniards and thus it is that these fiendish acts are hidden from us and kept in secret by them; and when by chance some magical practice is discovered, if it happens to come to our ears, there is always someone to cover for the sorcerer and keep him silent.

So it is that upon that hill they invoked the Evil Spirit and begged him to show them the home of their ancestors. The devil, conjured by these spells and pleas, turned some of them into birds and others into wild beasts such as ocelots, jaguars, jackals, wildcats, and took them, together with their gifts, to the land of their forebears.[4]

On reaching the shores of a large lake, from the midst of which emerged the hill called Colhuacan, they resumed their human forms. The chronicle tells us that as they stood on the shore of the lake they saw people going about in canoes, fishing, and attending their little farm plots. The natives, seeing the strangers and hearing them speak the same language as they, rowed to the shore and asked them what they wanted and where they came from. The Aztecs answered, "Sirs, we have come from Mexico-Tenochtitlan and we are the envoys of the authorities there. We have come to seek the homeland of our ancestors."

The people of the place asked them, "What god do you adore?" to which they answered, "The great Huitzilopochtli." They added that powerful King Motecuhzoma and his prime minister Tlacaelel had sent them to find Coatlicue, mother of Huitzilopochtli, and Chicomoztoc, the Seven Caves, from which their ancestors had set forth. They also wished to deliver a gift to Coatlicue if she were still alive or to her guardians if she were dead. The people of that place told them to wait while they went to call the custodian of the mother of Huitzilopochtli. They said to him, "O venerable lord, some men have come to

---

[4]This transformation into animals or birds evidently refers to nahualism, which is the changing of one's form by means of spells; the word comes from *nahualli* (magician). At the same time, a *nahual* or *nagual* is a person's animal epiphany or animal companion. Today, in some parts of Mexico a person is seen as sharing a soul with a wild animal companion, who protects that individual throughout his or her lifetime. If the person transgresses the social norms an imbalance occurs and then the animal *nahual* is set loose and can endanger the person's life (Vogt 1976:86–89). In some beliefs, the *nahual* is the first creature that appears at the time of the birth of a child—be it a snake, a bird, or a deer—and if the human dies, the companion also dies. It may be that Durán's sources, a number of documents written in Nahuatl as well as pictorial documents, did not describe the land beyond Coatepec-Tula; therefore it was necessary for the creators of the *Historia* to draw on oral tradition and myth and thus turn the envoys into wild beasts so they could penetrate this region unknown in written history.

these shores who say they are Aztecs and that they were sent here by a great lord called Motecuhzoma and by another named Tlacaelel. They have brought gifts and offerings to the mother of their god Huitzilopochtli and they were ordered to give these to her in person."

"Let them be welcome," the old man replied. "Have them brought here."

So the fishermen returned with their canoes and took the sorcerers across the lake to the hill of Colhuacan. The top half of this hill is said to consist of very fine sand, so spongy and deep that it is impossible to climb up it. The Aztecs went into a house at the foot of the hill where the old man lived. They greeted him respectfully and told him, "O venerable sir, O elder, we your servants have come to this place where your word is obeyed and the breath from your mouth is revered."

The old man said to them, "Welcome, my children. Who sent you here?"

"Lord," they answered, "Motecuhzoma and his prime minister Tlacaelel, also called Cihuacoatl, sent us."

"Who are Motecuhzoma and Tlacaelel?" asked the custodian. "They were not among those who departed from here. Those who went from this place were Tezacatetl, Ahuexotl, Huicton, Tenoch. These eight men[5] were the leaders of the barrios. In addition to these, there were four custodians of Huitzilopochtli, all great men, two of them being Cuauhtlequetzqui [also called Cuauhcoatl], and Axolohua [Water Creature], and two more god-bearers."

"Sir," answered the Aztecs, "we confess to you that these men are no longer known to us, nor have we ever met them. The men you mentioned are gone from this earth, all of them are dead. We have heard them mentioned, that is all."

The old man was amazed at this and asked, "Lord of All Created Things, who killed them? Why is it that all of us are still alive here in the place they abandoned? Why is it that none of us have died? Who

---

[5]The Durán manuscript in the Biblioteca Nacional de Madrid reads *siete varones*, "seven men," though eight are mentioned. Garibay (Durán 1967:II:579) gives these meanings for the names of the early leaders of Chicomoztoc: *Tezacatetl*: "Mirrorlike Stone Adornment" (from *tezcatl* "mirror," and *tetl*, "stone"); Acacitli: "Hare of Reed" (from *acatl*, "reed," and *citli*, "hare"); could also be "Grandmother of Reed," because *citli* also means "grandmother"; Ocelopan: "Ocelot Banner" or "Banner of Ocelot [Pelts]" (from *ocelotl*, "ocelot," and *pantli*, "banner or flag") or "On the Ocelot"; Xomimitl: "Arrowlike Feet" (from *xotl*, "foot," and *mitl*, "arrow"); Ahuexotl: "Water Willow" (from *atl*, "water," and *huexotl*, "willow"); Huicton: "Little Hoe" (from *huictli*, "hoe" or "digging stick," plus a diminutive); Tenoch: "Stony" or "Hard Prickly Pear Cactus" (from *tetl*, "stone," and *nochtli*, "*nopal* or prickly pear").

Garibay eliminates Ahuatl (which he spells Ahatl). This means "Sharp Thorn" or "Oak Tree" (Simeón 1965:39).

are your leaders now?" The wizards answered that the leaders were grandsons of the men he had named. The old man wanted to know who was the father now, the custodian, of the god Huitzilopochtli and he was told that it was a great priest called Cuauhcoatl, who could speak to the god and then relay messages from him. "Did you see him [the god] before coming here?" asked the old man. "Did he send a message?" The Aztec sorcerers responded that they had not seen him, nor had he sent them; they had been sent by the king and his coadjutor.

The old man then asked, "Why does Huitzilopochtli not let us know when he is to return? Before departing he told his mother that he would come back and the unfortunate woman is still waiting, sad and tearful, with no one to console her. Why do you not go see her and speak to her?"

"Sir," they answered, "we have done what our masters commanded and have brought a gift for the great lady. We have been ordered to see her, greet her, and make a present to her from the riches, the spoils, that are enjoyed by her son."

The old man said, "Then pick up what you have brought and follow me."

They put the gifts on their backs and followed the old man, who began to climb the hill with ease, without tiring. The Aztec envoys went behind him, their feet sinking into the soft sand, climbing with great difficulty and heaviness. The elder turned his head and, when he saw that the sand had almost reached their knees, making it impossible to go on, he said to them, "What is the matter? Are you not coming? Make haste!"

When the Aztecs tried to do this, they sank up to their waists in the sand and could not move. They called to the old man, who was walking with such lightness that his feet did not seem to touch the ground. "What is wrong with you, O Aztecs?" he asked. "What has made you so heavy? What do you eat in your land?"

"We eat the foods that grow there and we drink chocolate."

The elder responded, "Such food and drink, my children, have made you heavy and they make it difficult for you to reach the place of your ancestors. Those foods will bring you death. The wealth you have we know nothing about; we live poorly and simply. So give me your loads and wait here. I shall go call the mistress of this land, the mother of Huitzilopochtli, so that you may see her." He picked up one of the bundles and carried it up the hill as if it was straw. Then he returned for the others and carried them up with great ease.

When all the presents brought by the Aztecs had been taken up the hill, a woman of great age appeared, the ugliest and dirtiest that one could possibly imagine. Her face was so black, so covered with filth,

The History of the Indies of New Spain

that she looked like something out of Hell. Weeping bitterly, she said to the visitors, "Welcome, my sons! Know that since your god, my son Huitzilopochtli, departed from this place, I have been awaiting his return, weeping and mourning. Since that day I have not washed my face, combed my hair, or changed my clothes. My sadness and mourning will last until he returns. Is it true, my children, that you have been sent here by the leaders of the seven barrios my son took away with him?"

The envoys raised their eyes and, seeing the hideous and abominable woman, they were filled with fear. They humbled themselves before her. "O great and powerful lady," they said, "we neither saw nor spoke to the heads of the seven groups. We were sent here by your servant Motecuhzoma and his coadjutor Tlacaelel Cihuacoatl, to visit you and to seek out the place where their ancestors lived. They commanded us to kiss your hands in their name. We wish you to know that Motecuhzoma now rules over the great city of Mexico-Tenochtitlan. He is not the first king but the fifth. The first who reigned was Acamapichtli, the second Huitzilihuitl, the third Chimalpopoca, the fourth Itzcoatl, and the fifth sends this message: 'I am your unworthy servant, my name is Huehue Motecuhzoma and I am at your service.'

"And you must know that the first four kings lived with great hunger, poverty, and suffering and had to pay tribute to other provinces, but now the city is free, is prosperous. Roads have been opened to the coast, to the sea, to all the land, and these are safe. Tenochtitlan is now the mistress, the princess, the leader and queen of all the cities, all of which pay obedience to her. For now the Aztecs have found the mines of gold and silver and precious stones; they have discovered the home of rich feathers. And as proof of all this Motecuhzoma sends you these gifts, which are part of the wealth of your magnificent son Huitzilopochtli, and which the king [with Huitzilopochtli's help] has won, and with the strength of his arms and chest, his head and his heart, and by the grace of the Lord of All Created Things, of the Day and the Night. And this is all we have to say."

Her weeping calmed by these words, the old woman said, "Welcome then, my sons, I am grateful to my children. Tell me, do the elders who took my son away from here still live?"

They answered, "O our lady, they are no longer in this world. They are dead, we never knew them; all that remains is their shadow, the memory of those men."

She began to weep again, saying, "But what killed them? All their friends here are still alive."

She continued, "Tell me, children, what is it you bring? Is it something to eat?"

"Great lady, it is food and it is drink. Chocolate is drunk, sometimes it is eaten, and at times other foods are mixed with it."

"This heavy food is what has burdened you, my sons," she told them. "This is why you have not been able to climb the hill. But tell me, the clothing worn by my son is like these mantles you have brought, with feathers and rich adornment?"

"Yes, O lady, this is the way he dresses and is adorned, is attired, with these riches, with this splendor, for he is the lord of all this wealth," was their answer.

Coatlicue then spoke: "This is all very well, my children, my heart is now at peace. But when you return you must tell my son to have pity on me, to observe the loneliness in which I live without him. Look at me; life has become fasting and penance because of him. Let him remember what he said to me when he departed:

> "O my mother, I shall not tarry, I shall soon return after I have led these seven barrios to find a dwelling place, where they can settle and populate the land that has been promised them. Once I have led them there, once they are settled and I have given them happiness, I shall return. But this will not be until the years of my pilgrimage have been completed. During this time I shall wage war against provinces and cities, towns and villages. All of these will become my subjects. But in the same way that I conquered them they will be torn from me. Strangers will take them from me, and I shall be expelled from that land. Then I shall return, then I shall return here because those whom I subjected with my sword and shield will rise against me. They will pick me up by the feet and cast me down head first. My weapons and I will roll upon the floor.[6] It will be then, O mother, when my time has come, that I shall return for you to shelter me. Until then do not grieve. But I beg you to give me two pairs of sandals, one pair to go on this journey and the other for my return. No! Give me four pairs of sandals, two pairs to go on this journey and two for my return!"

Then the old woman addressed the Aztec envoys, saying, "I told my son to go with good fortune, not to delay, and to return here as soon as he had complied with his obligation. But it seems to me, my children, that he must be content where he is for he has stayed there, and he does not remember his sad mother, nor does he seek her or heed her words. Therefore, I command you to tell him that his time is up, that he must return now. And so that he remember that I wish to see him and that I am his mother, I send him this

---

[6]This prophecy regarding the fate of Huitzilopochtli, venerated in the Great Temple in Mexico-Tenochtitlan, was to be fulfilled in 1520 when Cortés's men cast the sacred idol down the steps of the pyramid.

mantle and this breechcloth of maguey fiber so that he may wear them."

The men took the rough fiber mantle and breechcloth and began to go down the hill. When they were part of the way down, the old woman called after them, "Stop! Wait there and you will see how men never grow old in this country! Do you see my old servant? By the time he reaches you he will be a young man!"

The old, very old man began to descend and the lower he went the younger he became. When he reached the Aztecs, he appeared to be about twenty years old. Said he, "Do you see that I am now a youth? Well look, this is what happens: I shall climb up again and when I am halfway up the hill I shall be older." He ascended again and about halfway up he was like a man forty years of age. Then he went up a little more, about twenty steps, and then ascended more. The farther he went up the older he became—much, much older.

"Behold, my sons, the virtue of this hill: the old person who seeks youth can climb to the point on the hill that he wishes and there he will acquire the age he seeks. If he wants to become a boy again, he climbs up to the top; if he wishes to become a young man, he goes up more than halfway; if he desires a good middle age, he goes halfway up.[7] In this way we who live here live a long time, and that is why none of the companions of your ancestors have died, for we become rejuvenated whenever we so desire. You have grown old, you have been harmed, by the chocolate you drink and the rich foods you eat. They have weakened you, they have debilitated you, they have upset your natural system. You have been spoiled by those mantles, feathers, and riches that you wear and that you have brought here. All of that has ruined you. But so you will not return without gifts, take these things to your lords."

He ordered that they be given all kinds of ducks and geese and herons and other waterfowl found in that lagoon, and every type of fish that bred there. They also were presented with many kinds of plants that grew in that land, and flowers, many of them made into garlands. Also given were fiber mantles and breechcloths, one for Motecuhzoma and one for Tlacaelel. The old man asked to be pardoned for sending those humble gifts but they were all he had. And with this he said farewell.

The Aztec sorcerers accepted the gifts and then, making the magic symbols and incantations they had made before, and anointing themselves with pitch as they had when they began the journey, they were

[7]Here the old man becomes younger as he goes *up*, although he regained his youth by going *down* in the paragraph above.

transformed into the same animals whose forms they had taken earlier and, in this disguise, they traveled to Coatepec Hill. There they turned into their normal human forms, looking at each other, recognizing each other. They arrived one by one, some earlier or later than the others, and after counting their number they discovered that some were missing, that there were twenty fewer than when they had set out, so a third had disappeared. Some said that the savage beasts and birds of prey they had encountered had eaten them.

This must not have been so; the truth is that the devil took them in payment for his help, for according to the *Historia* they made the trip [to Chicomoztoc] in ten days and returned in eight. This is a journey of three hundred leagues and even at this rate they took a long time and could have made it in less.

(He—[the devil]—brought another from Guatemala in only three days because an elderly lady wished to see that face, as the first *auto de fe* celebrated in Mexico by the Holy Inquisition states.)[8]

When they returned to Tenochtitlan, the magicians, the sorcerers, took the gifts to Motecuhzoma and told him, "Lord, we have carried out your order, your word, and have witnessed that which you wished to know: we have seen that land called Aztlan and Colhuacan, where our fathers and grandfathers lived and from where they left on their migration. And we have brought the things that grow and are bred there." They then placed before the king many ears of corn, seeds, and different kinds of flowers, tomatoes, and chiles—foods and plants grown in that land—and the rough fiber mantles and breechcloths, all things that had been sent by people [of Aztlan-Colhuacan-Chicomoztoc]. They told Motecuhzoma everything that had occurred with the mother of Huitzilopochtli and with her old servant, and how they had seen this man change his age, from young to middle-aged to very old. They added that in that place all the ancestors who had stayed there were still alive. And Coatlicue had complained bitterly about her son Huitzilopochtli, for whom she had waited so long. She prophesied that after a certain time he would be expelled from the city of Mexico-Tenochtitlan and would have to return to his original home because, in the same way he had subjected other nations, his dominion and control over them would be wrested from him.

The king summoned Tlacaelel and had the sorcerers repeat in his presence everything that had happened on their journey. He had them show Tlacaelel the gifts those people had sent and describe, especially the great fertility of that land, the freshness of their vegetation, and

---

[8]This enigmatic comment probably refers to a case Durán witnessed when he was an interpreter in the Inquisition (see Durán 1977:45).

the manner in which the people obtained all they needed for their sustenance: how they went about in canoes and made plots of land on top of the water where they sowed and harvested the plants they ate; the abundance and variety of fish, some of which were included in the gifts they brought; the multitude of waterfowl, the melodious song of the small and large birds; the difference in the maize fields, some with ripe corn ready for picking, others nearly ripe, still others with corn just sprouting, and some with grains just planted. In this way there could never be hunger in that land.9

The sorcerers then related that it had been impossible for them to climb the hill because they had sunk into the sand up to their waists, while the old man had climbed up easily. This old servant had then taken all the gifts they had brought up the hill and had given them to the mistress of that place, the mother of Huitzilopochtli. The sorcerers had been told that the reason they failed to reach the summit of the hill was that they ate heavy over-rich foods, such as chocolate and certain plants cultivated here in the Valley of Mexico. Coatlicue and the old man had been shocked and saddened to hear that the people who had left their homeland long ago were now dead.

Motecuhzoma and Tlacaelel wept and were moved, remembering their ancestors, wistful at not being able to see the land of their origin. After having thanked the magician envoys, and ordering fine presents given them for their work, they requested that these same sorcerers take the maguey fiber mantle and breechcloth to the temple, where it would be placed upon Huitzilopochtli, since his mother had sent it to him.

9This ideal situation where there was always corn to eat is also seen in an engraving from 1585 where maize fields were planted in this stepped system among North American Indians (see Hale et al. 1975).

CHAPTER XXVIII

Which treats of how the people of the city of Guaxaca killed the royal envoys who were returning from Coatzacualco. With a description of how the Aztecs warred upon them, destroyed them, and settled the city with Aztecs, Tezcocans, and Xochimilcas.

The wishes of Motecuhzoma and Tlacaelel had been fulfilled; they had learned many things about their place of origin. But they were fearful and uneasy about what the mother of Huitzilopochtli had prophesied—that they and their god were to be driven out of their land in the same way that they had conquered and subjected other people and had divested them of their property and possessions. Thus, their god would return to his place of origin. Motecuhzoma and Tlacaelel wished to find out who would come and triumph over them. So they investigated this as carefully as possible, looking into ancient traditions, studying their old documents, inquiring about prophecies, and on doing this they found an omen that said some Children of the Sun would come from the east and would cast down their god and annihilate the Aztec nation.

This prophecy will be discussed more fully when we talk about the reign of Motecuhzoma the Second, for at that time the prophecy was fulfilled; there were omens and signs and comets, all of which presaged the coming of the Spaniards.

So we return to our present story. At this time Motecuhzoma the First's messengers were sent to Coatzacualco to request of the people there, if they would be so kind, to send some gold dust and some of the fish bones, shells, and sea snails that abound on the coast. For enterprises such as this special envoys were named in the king's court. They were dedicated to no other work but were couriers, messengers, ambassadors. They were given special wages and supplies.

These couriers arrived at Coatzacualco and presented their request. The people of Coatzacualco, in all goodwill, made no objection and on the contrary were pleased to have this favor asked of them. They supplied the envoys with everything that had been requested in the name of the great King Motecuhzoma and made these ambassadors as comfortable as possible in their city. But on their way back the Aztecs, in good spirits and laden with things [from the sea and the gold dust], reached a town called Mictlan, which lies before the city of Guaxaca. The men of Guaxaca, hearing of the arrival of the Aztecs, went out to intercept them on the road, as they were leaving Mictlan. The Aztecs were killed and everything they carried was taken from them: gold and jewels and beautifully worked objects made of shell, fish bones, and other wonderful things that the people of Coatzacualco had sent to Motecuhzoma. The bodies of the couriers were thrown to the side of the road to be eaten by the beasts, and so they were devoured by buzzards.

When Motecuhzoma realized that his messengers were taking too long on their journey and that no news of them had been received, he felt this was a bad sign and wished to send forces to search for them. Meanwhile, some merchants from Amequemecan and Chalco who happened to be trading in Coatzacualco and were coming from there reached Tenochtitlan and went directly to Motecuhzoma, where they informed him, "O powerful lord, we your servants and vassals travel night and day over the hills, over the mountains, to earn our living. And you should know, O powerful lord, that when we were passing by Mictlan we found, at one side of the road, the bodies of some men that had been eaten by buzzards; they had left only the bones. And although they no longer had the figure of men but were just a pile of bones, we could recognize them as your royal envoys. They had been killed by the people of Guaxaca. Those barbarous, ignorant, and evil people had stolen all the things sent to you by the lords of Coatzacualco."

On hearing this news, Motecuhzoma was both saddened and infuriated. But, concealing his anger, he asked the merchants, "Where are you from?" and they answered, "Chalco." The king then had gifts presented to them and sent them on their way to their city. Motecuhzoma then called Tlacaelel and told him of the outrageous events. He was eager to punish the evildoers by declaring war and sought Tlalaelel's agreement.

Tlacaelel, however, insisted that there was much more urgent matter: the building of the new temple of Tenochtitlan, and that the declaration of war must be deferred. After the temple was finished, if the Aztecs were victorious in Guaxaca, all the war captives taken there could serve as sacrificial victims at the temple's inauguration.

Motecuhzoma, convinced by this argument, called his envoys and had them take a message to the lords of all the nearby provinces and to the kings of Tezcoco and Tacuba, requesting their presence. When they had assembled in the city, Motecuhzoma presented his plan to finish the temple of the god Huitzilopochtli as soon as possible and asked for their support in this project. The kings and lords who were present were favorably impressed and were willing to collaborate.

Seeing their compliance, Motecuhzoma ordered the ruler of Tezcoco and his subjects to take charge of the construction of the front part of the [pyramidal] structure, while the sovereign and people of Tacuba were to build the back. Chalco was to erect one side and the *chinampa* area—the Xochimilca nation—the other side. The Otomi people were to work exclusively in bringing sand for the building; these were the Mazahuaque [Mazahuas] and the Chapanecas, Xiquipilcas, Xocotlecas, Cuauhuanecas, and Cauhtlecas. The people of the Hot Country were to contribute lime.[1] Motecuhzoma addressed the representatives of those groups who were present:

> O sovereigns, O great lords, life is short! If while it lasts we do not glorify our own names, we shall be forgotten, for we shall not receive fame for the deeds of our ancestors. Their glory will not follow us, nor can we enjoy fame attributed to our own deeds after we are gone. Which of us, once he is dead, will return to see and enjoy the things on this earth, to know who has become king, who has become lord? Our power, our might, ends with our deaths!

Motecuhzoma then continued: "Therefore, O lords, it is not just that all we can accomplish during our lifetime, won with honor and glory, be exploited by one who follows us. You know that our god, the great Huitzilopochtli, was sent to help us conquer the whole world; and you can see that it has been subjected. Now that you are all here together you can understand that it is only right that we honor our god by building his temple. Therefore, go without delay for the materials—the stone, lime, sand, and wood. And you, Lord Nezahualcoyotl, ruler of the province of Tezcoco of Aculhua,[2] you will be in charge of the construction of the front part of the edifice, and you, Lord Totoquihuaztli, king of the Tepanec province, will construct the back part. And lords of Chalco, you who are present, will see that the right side of the temple is built, while the lady [sic] of all the *chinampa*—Xochimilco and its province—will erect the left side. The Mazahuaque will bring sand, the people of the Hot Lands will be responsible for lime and whatever else they are ordered to provide. This must all be done quickly; it should be finished almost before it has begun. For this is an important project and must be carried out without delay."

---

[1] We doubt that the Great Temple of Tenochtitlan built in honor of Huitzilopochtli and Tlaloc was constructed in this manner. It was built by different Aztec rulers, each level corresponding to a different period. For the chronology and architectural data of the pyramid-temple, see Matos Moctezuma 1988.

[2] Aculhua or Acolhua refers to the region where Tezcoco is situated. Durán's manuscript simply says Culhua, which Garibay (Durán 1967:II:227) wrote as Culhua(can); but Culhuacan is in the southern part of the Valley of Mexico, Tezcoco in the east, so the region should read Aculhua.

Everyone agreed to assist in the building of the temple. They all said they were pleased to do this, that this was expected of them, and for grandiose projects such as this they had been made subjects of the Aztecs and were at the service of the great god Huitzilopochtli. The king then gave them generous gifts and fine clothing, as was the custom. These gifts included mantles and breechcloths, labrets, gold ear ornaments, and valuable jewelry. The kings were given gold bands that are placed on the head in the manner of diadems, with rich feathers hanging down from this to the nape of the neck, tied with a special cord; this was called the *quetzaltlalpiloni*.3 They also were given gold bracelets to be worn on the upper arm and gold leg ornaments that covered the leg from the calf to the ankle. After this they were served food in abundance, then all the guests bade farewell to the king and to Tlacaelel. When they reached their cities or lordships, they advised their people of Motecuhzoma's commands and ordered that they deliver the materials required without delay, each one according to the part of the temple he was to construct. The commoners hastened to carry out their lords' orders—for the latter were always obeyed—and were so diligent in bringing the material (some brought stone, others earth and sand, others lime and wood) that in a short time an enormous amount of building material had been accumulated in the Aztec city.

Master builders were brought to measure the site and to make plans and to mark out the foundations of the structure. These men stated that it was necessary to build a platform about one hundred *brazas* on each side, of rubble and mortar, and this was to be constructed on stakes driven into the ground.4 This plan was accepted by Motecuhzoma and all his council and then, after the one hundred square *braza* space was measured and marked off, the pilings were driven in and over these a foundation of mortar was poured and then the main structure was begun on top of this. The building of the temple grew so quickly that it soon reached a great height. And why should we be amazed at this when our chronicle says that

---

3*Tlalpiloni* was an adornment worn on the head, to bind the hair; *quetzal* means "feather" (Simeón 1965:545). Garibay (Durán 1967:II:587) says that the correct term is *quetzalilpiloni*. This was a bunch of feathers tied to a kind of ponytail at the back of the head, and the privilege to wear it was awarded to leading warriors.

4Remains of these original heavy wooden pilings may be seen at the excavated Templo Mayor in Mexico City. The marshy subsoil of this island city was a problem the Aztecs had to cope with, which has harassed architects and engineers to the present day. The technique used by the Aztecs—sinking long poles deep into the ground in order to support foundations for the buildings—was copied by the Spanish and can also be observed at the Templo Mayor.

people from all the provinces worked like ants in the construction?

Seeing that the temple began to rise so rapidly, King Motecuhzoma desired to honor his god even further and gave orders that all the friendly rulers of the land contribute quantities of precious stones: greenstones, which they call *chalchihuitl*, rock crystal, bloodstone, emeralds, rubies, and carnelian, that is, all kinds of precious stones and fine jewels. At each *braza* this wealth of jewels and stones was to be thrown into the mortar. Therefore, when this tribute arrived, the lords of each city contributing jewels and precious stones and offering these by throwing them into the mixture at every *braza*, each one in his turn, the amount of riches was amazing. But they said that since the god had given them all that wealth it was only just that he receive it in turn because it really belonged to him.

When the building had reached the height of one hundred twenty steps, which was considered sufficient, a chamber was added at the summit in which the image of the god was to be kept. This contained great stone statues and supports in the form of diverse images and sculptures that served as entrance carvings, lintels, corner adornments, and a kind of pediment. All these were placed according to religious symbolism. Some of these statues were called *ilhuicatzitzquique*, which means "those who hold up the sky," and these were placed in such a way that they seemed to support the entire hall.[5] Others were called *petlacontzitzquique*, "those who hold up the divine vessels and insignia"; these insignia were bunches of rich feathers, something like the arms of a cross, whose symbolism indicated that the temple belonged to Huitzilopochtli. Those persons who are interested in seeing these statues today [in 1570] may observe them fixed to the corners of the royal palace.

When the temple was finished and ready to be inaugurated and before the lords from the other cities left Mexico-Tenochtitlan, they were told how the people of Guaxaca had killed the Aztec envoys—who had been returning from Coatzacualco—and had thrown the bodies to the vultures to be eaten. As punishment for such an evil act, the Aztec lords had ordered the temple finished quickly so they could then go to Guaxaca, destroy that city, and with the captives brought from there make a solemn entrance into Tenochtitlan and have victims for the temple's inauguration. With this goal everyone was ordered to prepare the armed forces so that this retaliation could be

---

[5]Elizabeth Hill Boone (personal communication) has suggested that the Coatlicue and Yolotlicue statues in the National Museum of Anthropology in Mexico City may have been supports of this type.

carried out without delay. The entire city of Guaxaca would be razed so it would be completely forgotten. One reason for this proposed destruction was that Guaxaca was so far away that if the people there were to rebel again it would be difficult for the Aztecs to return. Another reason was that this revenge would serve as a lesson and warning to all the cities of that region.

All the allies present accepted Motecuhzoma's announcement and, having returned to their own cities, made it public there. The soldiers, who had been idle and therefore poor, received the news with jubilation, for they went hungry and failed to acquire goods when they did not go to war. When on the march they were taken care of by all the cities, towns, and villages they passed, where they were given food, drink, clothing, and sandals. And where they were not given these things, their superiors allowed them to steal. Furthermore, they held on tenaciously to the booty and slaves they managed to take because these things then belonged to them. And even if the king sometimes did take away the slaves to be sacrificed, he gave their owners, the soldiers, double the amount that they were worth.

The men got ready with such haste that it seemed they took longer to change into their military attire than to get to their proper ranks. A large number of soldiers, led by their captains, left the city and eventually reached Guaxaca, where they set up camp consisting of tents, reed-mat huts, and other shelters, in such a way that Guaxaca was surrounded and no one could leave it by the road that led to Tenochtitlan. When the Guaxaca men saw this great artificial wall [improvised by the soldiers], they were both amazed and fearful at being surrounded by such hostile men, who seemed to be more numerous than the sands of the ocean; they were so splendidly attired that it was a wondrous thing to behold them.

The Aztec captains called the troops to order and made a spirited address in order to encourage them and then prepared the combat plans for the next day. When morning came, the soldiers were given provisions and after they had eaten they were called to order and given instructions regarding the attack. They were to go as soon as they were called, a few at a time. No one was to lose his banner; the insignia was to be held on high so the soldiers from the allied armies could recognize each other. The Aztec captains addressed their own forces and those of the allies, thus: "O warriors, it is the will of his royal majesty Motecuhzoma that this city of Guaxaca be destroyed, be devastated, so that not a living soul remain, and that the trees, the fields with crops, the houses, all the buildings, be torn down, be laid waste. And do not kill the people you capture, but have them placed under guard so they can be sacrificed at the inauguration of our temple and its festival, when the image of our god Huitzilopochtli will be placed there. That is all."

The usual signal was then given and the battle began. The attack was so sudden and so furious that the Aztecs soon gained entrance to the city, although those inside defended it courageously. But the Guaxaca soldiers were forced to abandon it; thus, the Aztecs reached the temples and set them on fire. The common soldiers went about the city causing so much destruction and so many deaths that they tore down every house they came to and killed everyone and everything they found inside: women and children, old men and women, dogs, fowl, and any other creature there. They broke off or ripped out plants and fruit trees. All these actions were disastrous, painful to observe.

When the Guaxaca lords saw the ruin that their city had become, they approached the Aztecs, weeping, their hands crossed. They begged for mercy and asked that their evil deed be pardoned. They pleaded that the great cruelty used against them be ended, for they wished to become subjects and tributaries of Tenochtitlan. But instead of listening to these pleas the Aztecs cried, "Go away, you accursed people! You killed our brothers, our fathers, and you threw their bodies to the buzzards, although they had done you no harm. Know that you will be shown no mercy for the sentence has been dictated: Guaxaca will cease to exist and no memory of it will remain. Therefore, your supplications are meaningless." And shouting this, the Aztecs again attacked them. Unable to defend themselves, the people of Guaxaca were slaughtered. The Aztecs went about the whole city, destroying everything, so that not a man or woman, not a child or bird or dog, was spared. The streets of the city were covered with bodies. The houses and temples and lordly residences were robbed and then destroyed, burned, consumed to the ground. Once this devastation was complete, messengers were sent to Cuilapan and other neighboring cities to advise them to observe the fate of Guaxaca. They were told to live in peace and quiet, to care for their lands and dominions tranquilly, to cause no agitation, for the Aztecs wished them no harm. But if these people were to become rebellious and plan some treachery they would be met with the same savage destruction that had been the fate of Guaxaca. The Mixtecs and Zapotecs humbly replied that they were willing and ready to serve and obey the Aztecs as they would their own lords.

The Aztec army left the region with a great number of captives, of slaves. The prisoners, all lined up and tied together with ropes around their necks, set up such a frightful wailing and weeping that their laments reached up to the sky. The day they left couriers were sent on ahead to take the news to King Motecuhzoma of the successful war, of

The History of the Indies of New Spain

the victory over the Guaxaca army, of the great number of prisoners who were being taken to the Aztec capital to be sacrificed, and how the city of Guaxaca had been destroyed, laid waste. The king was advised that the entire army, consisting of Aztec forces as well as those of the Tepanecs, Tezcocans, Chalcas, Xochimilcas, Cuauhtlalpanecas, and Tlaluicas, had fought bravely. Not one warrior had returned without one or two prisoners, and many of the officers had captured three or four. Motecuhzoma was highly pleased with this information and therefore ordered his stewards to reward the messengers with some of the finest mantles and breechcloths in the royal storeroom. In this way the men were well treated and splendidly dressed.

Motecuhzoma then informed the priests and temple dignitaries of the victory so that they would offer sacrifices to Huitzilopochtli and thank the god for having granted them such favor and aid in the war. They were also asked to prepare the usual reception for the warriors. The priests made themselves ready and offered sacrifices[6] with much ceremony and obeisance. They made lengthy ceremonial speeches directed to the god. These were elegant and eloquent, full of rich metaphors and rhetoric. When the occasion presents itself I shall write these down so it can be seen what excellent orators existed in those times.

Within a few days the leaders of the army arrived, followed by the rest of the soldiers and a multitude of prisoners. The priests, dressed in their special attire and adorned with religious insignia, came out to meet them with incense burners in their hands, intoning hymns to their god. They offered incense to the prisoners, telling them of their fate, and giving them flowers and tobacco. This [formal ceremonial type of reception to the returning army and its captives] was customary. As the captives entered the city, they howled mournfully, they ululated in the way a wild animal cries, whistling, weeping, in such a strange way that those who heard them trembled with fear. These prisoners were taken directly to the temple, but not to the new one, for it was considered ill fortune to enter a new building before a certain ceremony had been performed, and this ceremony had not yet taken place at the new temple. This custom is still used today.

Then the prisoners were taken before the king, where they kissed his feet. One by one they passed before him as they had before the statue of the god in the temple, except that they did not perform the rite of "kissing the earth" here as they had before the god. This consisted of wetting a finger, placing it in the earth, and then eating the earth that had adhered to the finger. [It was a sign of maximum

---

[6]Probably of birds at that time.

respect.] After all the captives had passed in front of the king, Motecuhzoma summoned his treasurers and his assistants and ordered that those Children of the Sun be kept under guard, where they would be provided with everything they needed until the time came for their sacrifice. Thus, they were divided up and sent to the different barrios, where the heads of these wards were responsible for them.

Motecuhzoma then spoke to Tlacaelel, saying, "I believe it would be wise to inaugurate our great temple soon so these Children of the Sun can be sacrificed. And at that time we shall invite the whole world, for an act of such great importance must be known to all, and it is better to make a big display than a little one."

But Tlacaelel answered:

"Lord, the dedication of the temple cannot take place soon because many details are not yet finished. The pointed stone on which the sacrificial victims are to be thrown to have their hearts cut out is unfinished, and so are many statues that will adorn the building and give significance to our rites. Nor is the shining mirror ready, which is to represent the sun. Do not sorrow, O lord, let the temple be finished. There is time for everything. However, if this is your wish, let these Children of the Sun be sacrificed, for we shall not lack victims for the dedication when the temple is completely finished. I have thought of many things that still must be done and it is better to complete these details now than later.

"Our god will not be made to wait until new wars appear. He will find a way, a marketplace where he will go with his army to buy victims, men for him to eat. And this will be a good thing, for it will be as if he has his maize cakes hot from the griddle—tortillas from a nearby place, hot and ready to eat whenever he wishes them. Let our people, let our army, go to this market place to buy with our blood, with our heads and hearts, and with our lives the precious stones, jades, and rubies, and splendid long shining feathers[7] for our wondrous Huitzilopochtli.

"I, Tlacaelel, state that this marketplace will be situated in Tlaxcala, Huexotzinco, Cholula, Atlixco, Tliliuhquitepec, and Tecoac. Because if we place it in remote lands such as Yopitzinco, Mechoacan, the land of the Huaxtecs, or on either coast, it will be difficult, for they are not our vassals, they are far away and our armies could not endure [these long marches into unknown lands]. Those places are too remote and, furthermore, our god does not like the flesh of those barbarous people. They are like hard, yellowish, tasteless bread in his mouth.

---

[7]These treasures are metaphors for the captured soldiers who will be sacrificial victims.

Those people are savages and speak strange languages. Therefore, our marketplace, the fair [where victims will be found], must be in these six cities: in Tlaxcala, Huexotzinco, Cholula, Atlixco, Tliliuhquitepec, and Tecoac. The people from these places will come to our god like warm breads, soft, tasty, straight from the fire.

"I repeat that these cities are near, they are accessible. No sooner will our soldiers have gone there than they will be returning with captives. Not only will they arrive warm, delicious [for Huitzilopochtli], but this will be a relaxation for our soldiers, as if they were just going hunting. And this must not be a real war: we must not destroy those people but they must be left standing so that each time our god wishes to enjoy himself and to eat warm tortillas, we can go to those cities, as one goes to the market to obtain foodstuffs. And so that there will be an agreement regarding this human market you must, O powerful lord, call together your lords and councilmen to ask their opinion of this idea."

CHAPTER XXIX

Which treats of how the king and the nobility decided to wage perpetual war on Tlaxcala, Huexotzinco, Cholula, Atlixco, Tecoac, and Tliliuhquitepec. And how men were to be brought to be sacrificed during the great feasts and how soldiers and the sons of the lords were to practice warfare.

Tlacaelel had now become old and could not go to war in person, though he continued to be the principal adviser regarding war. He also spent much time, however, honoring, exalting, the gods. Therefore, he ordered that sacrifices take place more often. Another reason for this order was that he had acquired a taste for human flesh since the lords ate it frequently. It is also true that Tlacaelel had been persuaded or blinded by the devil and was now inventing a thousand cruel acts, all of which he made into law before his death. He was obeyed so blindly that everything he ordained was done.

So he discussed with King Motecuhzoma the business we had begun to tell about in the last chapter: that the gods were to be given sacrifices of men whenever they desired these and that there be places where the sons of noblemen, enthusiasts in the art of war, be able to train, to practice their skill and show their valor, and to bring in captives.

The king, who agreed with this plan, summoned all his great warriors and when they had gathered he notified them that they were now to fight in a military marketplace, as if they were going to a regular market on certain days, where they would buy honor and glory with their blood and their lives. At the same time the sons of noblemen would be occupied in this way and military activity would not be lost. But the main purpose behind the establishing of this human marketplace was to honor, to revere, Huitzilopochtli. Since he now had his temple it was only just that there be victims to offer to the god and none would be more welcome to him than captives from Tlaxcala, Huexotzinco, Cholula, Atlixco, Tecoac, and Tliliuhquitepec. These six cities had been chosen to serve him and provide him with [human] food, for men of other barbaric nations of alien tongue were not desired by him, nor would he accept them. Inasmuch as most of the land had already been conquered by the Aztecs and no one dared rebel against them, if the god were to wait for some people to rebel, to commit some transgression in order that war be declared and the god be given sacrificial victims, then he might never receive them. But by going to war nearby the soldiers would go happily as if they were enjoying some festivity, going to be entertained.

"And I want all those present to express their opinion about this plan, to come to an agreement regarding it, so it can be put into practice," stated the king. So after much discussion all the noble warriors by common agreement stated that this military marketplace was essential, was indispensable. When the king saw that everyone was in accord, he requested that Tlacaelel describe the privileges granted to men who showed great courage in war and who brought home captives to be sacrificed. Tlacaelel stood up before the others and spoke:

"O sons, brothers, and nephews who are here in the presence of the majesty of our ruler Motecuhzoma, I, Tlacaelel, wish to give more courage to those of a strong heart and embolden those who are weak so the prize for their deeds will encourage them. I wish to compare the strong and the weak and mention their rewards or their retribution. When you go to the marketplace and see a precious ear ornament or nose pendant, or when you see splendid and beautiful feathers or a rich gilded shield, or weapons done in featherwork, do you not covet them, do you not pay the price that is asked? Know now that the king, who is here before you, has willed that labrets, golden garlands, many-colored feathers, ear ornaments, armbands, shields, weapons, insignia, rich mantles, and breechcloths are no longer to be purchased in the market by brave men. Now the sovereign will deliver them as payment and prize for heroic feats, for memorable deeds. Each one of you, when he goes into battle, to perform great feats, must keep in mind that, while he is carrying out these heroic acts in war, he has in reality gone to a marketplace where he will find all these priceless things, for upon returning from the war he will receive them according to his merits and so that he can display these as proof of his worth. [Then Tlacaelel described the fate of a man who would refuse to fight, addressing the soldiers in the usual kind of ritual speech:]

> He who does not dare go to war, even though he be the king's son, from now on will be deprived of all these things. He will have to wear the clothing of the common man, of the man who has no [fighting] spirit. And in this his cowardice, his weak heart, will be known by all.
> He will not wear cotton garments.
> He will not wear feathers, he will not receive flowers like the great lords.
> He will not receive tobacco,
> he will not drink chocolate, he will not eat fine foods.

He will be held in contempt as a man of low rank.
He will be made to do manual labor even though he be of royal blood, even though he be the son or brother of the king or our son or brother, even though he be one of us or a close kinsman.
And let this be the inviolable law:
That he who does not go to war will be scorned, he will not be respected, nor will he consort with, nor converse with, nor eat with the brave warriors. But he will be treated as an outcast, as something putrid, vile. He will be made to wait until the brave warriors have eaten, have drunk, and then he will receive what is left over.

Tlacaelel also ordered that the king eat alone and that when he had finished the great captains be given food from the same dishes that had been prepared for him, considering them remainders from the royal mouth and special honors for these valiant men.

"We also order," continued Tlacaelel, "that if children be born to our sons, or to sons of the king and the other lords, and these children are born of slave girls and servants, even though they be bastards, sons of slaves, they be considered our blood, having been born among the legitimate children of the great lords. And if any of these bastard sons of ours be valiant and courageous in war, and if any of our legitimate sons show themselves to be cowards, let these bastards then inherit our wealth. Let them be lords of our legitimate children and command them as if they were just low vassals. Let them harass them, let neither father nor mother intercede for them, but let them be mistreated as men of low station and weak hearts. And let the honor of being of royal birth, of high lineage, be given to the son of a slave who will inherit these ranks, will take them as his own, while the other, the coward, will lose them. He will no longer be called the son of such-and-such great lord or of a certain noble lady. Therefore, we order that glory and honor and greatness not be inherited simply because one is born of nobles but must be acquired in war, by brave deeds, such as will be won in the wars with Tlaxcala, Huexotzinco, Cholula, Atlixco, and Tliliuhquitepec, which will be fought from now on. And those courageous warriors will be awarded insignia of valor not once but many times and will be given gold and silver, precious stones, jewels, fine feathers. All of these can be used by them always, and by no others. These things will remind them of us after we are dead; we will be remembered by our sons and grandsons and all our descendants.

"These are the royal wishes and will be observed from this day on."

After the king had confirmed what Tlacaelel had said, this new law was accepted by all the lords present. Then the two rulers from neighboring towns were called to Tenochtitlan—that is, Nezahualcoyotl of Tezcoco and Totoquihuaztli of Tacuba—also the lords and chieftains of Chalco, Xochimilco, the Hot Country, Cuauhtlalpan [land of the Otomis], the Mazahuaque [or Mazahuas]. When these were all congregated, having been called to the palace, they were informed of the new law, of Motecuhzoma's and Tlacaelel's decision: that from that time on, when they were called to fight the men of Tlaxcala, Huexotzinco, Cholula, Atlixco, Tecoac, and Tliliuhquitepec, they were to respond without delay in order to win the privileges announced in this new law. Furthermore, they were to make public this ruling immediately in their cities and provinces and all warriors who had performed an outstanding feat and had taken captive some prisoners were to be honored and given awards.

The allied officials and noblemen were delighted to hear that their sons and male relatives could practice their bellicose activities in certain places and thus enhance their reputation. After they had thanked the king and Tlacaelel, the latter said to them: "Sirs, you are all here together and you know that the city of Guaxaca was conquered, destroyed, and ravaged. But it is not right that that place remain devastated, for it is well situated and its lands are fertile. Therefore, it is my opinion that people should gather from all the provinces to settle it once more. Let Nezahualcoyotl bring sixty married men with their wives and children from his province, let King Totoquihuaztli come with sixty families from his province. Let the same be done by those of Xochimilco and Chalco, those from the Hot Country, from the Mazahua region, let them bring all they can to repopulate Guaxaca. I shall be the first to bring settlers and from my city alone I shall send to Guaxaca six hundred married men with their families and I shall make them a land grant that will be distributed among them. My cousin Atlazol, son of my uncle Ocelopan who was killed by the Chalcas during the war, will be governor. Thus Atlazol will be rewarded for his father's merits and great deeds."

After the visitors had returned to their cities, the people who were to be settlers were summoned from the towns under Aztec jurisdiction. These people gathered in Tenochtitlan. The king spoke to them, telling them not to be apprehensive, nor to be sad because they were leaving their homeland. He added that they were going to good lands where they would live at ease and be free from paying tribute. Furthermore, he would command the neighboring towns to provide them with everything they would be needing, for example, jars, dishes, bowls, different types of vessels and grinding stones, and to help them build their houses. Thus they were comforted.

They all kissed the king's hands and responded that they were his subjects, his vassals, and wherever death awaited them, whether it be here or there, in the end it was, after all, the same death. They were happy, then, to go settle that land and were pleased to accept the favors and freedom from tribute given to them.

Motecuhzoma called his cousin Atlazol, whom he made governor of all those people, and ordered him to arrange the city of Guaxaca in such a way that the Aztecs would form a barrio of their own, the Tezcocans another, the Tepanecs still another, and the Xochimilcas and all the other groups also their own quarters. The elders and those men that the governor deemed the wisest were to be made dignitaries and given positions of authority. That city was to be controlled with the order and harmony characteristic of Tenochtitlan: the governor was to be the father and mother of the people, but he must always be prepared and alert because the region to which he was going was surounded by barbarous and evil people. If any problem arose, he was to sound a warning and immediately would receive help.

At this Atlazol was dismissed. A number of men were assigned to him in order to accompany him and lead him and the settlers to their destination. The officials in charge of accommodations went before them so that at each place they passed they were well received and presented with gifts, especially the women and children. In this way every town through which they went gave provisions to everyone and clothing to the men and women, according to their position.

When they reached Guaxaca, these people re-founded and rebuilt the city. Following the instructions of the king each group was given its own barrio. The officials who had accompanied the governor to Guaxaca returned to Tenochtitlan and reported to the king that the city of Guaxaca had been newly built, was now at peace and in good order, and that his cousin had established a successful government. The king was pleased to hear these words. He asked which people had received the Aztecs and their allies well and had provided them with food and other things they needed, and he was told that the inhabitants of Teotitlan, of Tochpan, and Cuauhtochco, and also all those who lived on the coast, had responded favorably. These people had been very helpful in attending them and had given them foodstuffs in abundance. They had received them joyfully with dances and festivities that were customary in those places and had presented them with many kinds of gifts, such as clothing, jewelry, and feathers of many colors. Motecuhzoma thanked the officials and rewarded them, then they were sent to rest.

CHAPTER XXX

Which treats of the great famine that devastated this land for three years during the reign of Motecuhzoma the First. With a description of how this ruler came to the aid of the people of Mexico-Tenochtitlan so they would not perish and so the city would not be abandoned.

In the year 1454, which the Indians called Ce Tochtli, "One Rabbit," and for the next two years the drought was so intense in this land that the clouds remained closed as they did in the time of Elijah, and it rained not at all, nor was there any sign of rain in the sky. And to emphasize this, the *Historia* says that the drought was such that the springs dried up, the streams and rivers ceased to run, the earth burned like fire and, from sheer dryness, cracked in great clefts. The roots of the trees and plants were so burned by the fire that came out of the earth that flowers and leaves dropped off and branches dried up. The century plants ceased to give their sweet juice, the maguey honey. The prickly pear cactus no longer gave fruit; its leaves, once thick and rich, now wilted and became limp, baked by the heat. As soon as the maize sprouted it turned yellow and withered like all the rest of the crops.

People became faint and walked about shriveled and skinny due to the famine they suffered. Others became ill, having eaten things bad for the health. Others in their despair abandoned their city, wives, and children, and departed toward more fertile lands to seek salvation.

When King Motecuhzoma saw that the city, together with the neighboring provinces, was being depopulated and that people came from all parts to implore him, to tell him their sufferings, their want, he called his authorities, the stewards and treasurers, from all the cities in the kingdom. He questioned them as to the amount of maize, beans, chiles, *chian* seed, and other grains and foodstuffs kept in the royal storehouses. All this was collected for the maintenance of the palace and came from the provinces, especially from Chalco, which sent a large quantity of maize as tribute each year and thus was considered an important source. Other foods came from Tezcoco, Xochimilco, and different regions, but in order to avoid verbosity I shall not name them here. Motecuhzoma's stewards answered that there were great quantities of foodstuffs in the granaries that could alleviate to some extent the sufferings of the poor people. Tlacaelel, filled with pity, said to Motecuhzoma: "Sir, let us not lose time because the city is being depopulated and we cannot keep the people from fleeing. We are powerless to stop them, nor would it be just, because we cannot give them what they need. Also, the people become sick because they eat harmful things. My advice is that from the grain that is stored enough maize cakes[1] and gruel can be made every day, be brought to the city in canoes, and be distributed among the poor and needy. The nobility and the merchants will not starve since they have their own granaries, foodstuffs, supplies. The people we pity, who need our assistance, are the old men, the old women, the little boys and girls who live in poverty and who have no place to go."

Motecuhzoma then, having agreed with Tlacaelel's suggestions to avoid the depopulation of the city, ordered the stewards, in certain order according to their cities and provinces, to bring into the city each day some canoes filled with maize and other canoes filled with gruel. The maize dough was to be cooked in the form of large tamales, each one the size of a man's head. He told them not to bring corn in grains and ordered, under pain of death, that no maize be carried away to other parts. From that time on twenty canoes of tamales and another ten of gruel, made from the flour of toasted maize mixed with that of *chian* seeds, began to enter the city. The king put certain authorities in charge, to distribute the food. These men went to the different barrios and gathered the poor people, old and young, children and adults, and distributed the tamales according to the needs of each one. And a large bowl of gruel was given to each child.

One year went by during which the king gave away this food. In the following year the storage had decreased so much that the king could no longer maintain his people. The royal storehouses were almost empty, whereupon he ordered his officials to gather all the people of the city, old and young, male and female, and give them a last banquet with what was left of the maize and other seeds. After they had eaten, he commanded that all the men be dressed in mantles and breechcloths and the the women be given blouses and skirts. He then addressed them with sad words, trying to console them, but when he was finished the people began to moan and shed bitter tears. Motecuhzoma's compassionate words were these: "My children, my brothers, I beg of you that you be patient, that you bear the suffering in this moment! We are not fighting against an enemy in the battlefield. If we were struggling with our foes, we would risk our lives to defend ourselves and we would die fulfilling our duties. No, he who wages war

---

[1]Durán says *panes*, "breads," but since wheat was unknown in prehispanic Mexico this refers to tortillas or tamales.

on us is the Lord of All Created Things, the Lords of Night and Day. Who can fight against him? It is his will that the clouds do not shed rain upon us and that the earth burns and gives forth smoke and the air scorches the crops! This is a thing never seen nor heard by the living or the dead. Therefore, O my children, you know that I have done everything in my power to remedy this situation, but the food supplies have been used up. All that remains is the will of the Lord of the Heaven: that each of you go his way to seek his own salvation!"

Weeping, the people prostrated themselves upon the earth and wailed piteously, their cries reaching to the skies. They exclaimed, "O powerful lord, we have seen the succor with which you have favored us and the loving manner in which you have treated us. We know that you can do no more. Therefore, we kiss your royal hands and accept the liberty you give us to seek a remedy for our misery and hunger. We shall sell our sons and daughters to those who can feed them so that they do not starve to death."

The king, in tears like the others and unable to endure longer the sadness of the occasion, dismissed the people. Weeping bitterly, they began to leave the city in different directions where they hoped help would be available. Many of them found relief in certain places where the inhabitants were wealthy. There, in those towns, they sold their sons and daughters to merchants or to noblemen who could maintain them. A mother or father would trade a child for a small basket of maize, and the new owner was obliged to house and feed the infant while the famine lasted. If the parents wished to ransom him later, they would have to pay for all his maintenance.

During this time the Totonac people had harvested abundant grain; and when they heard of the great need of the entire land of Mexico, and how family members sold one another, they wrought a vengeance upon the Aztecs. They came to Tenochtitlan carrying great loads of maize in order to buy slaves. They also went to other cities—Tezcoco, Chalco, Xochimilco, and the Tepanec center, Tacuba—where they purchased large numbers of slaves with their corn. They placed yokes around the necks of adults and children. Then the slaves, lined up one behind another, were led out of the cities in a pitiful manner, the husband leaving his wife, the father his son, the grandmother her grandchild. They went along weeping and their wails reached the heavens. In this way a great number of people from all these nations became slaves. Others without having been sold went freely to the land of the Totonacs with their wives and children, where they settled permanently and where they remain to this day. Others, in their desire to escape to that province, fell dead along the way, together with the loads they carried. All of this was something never seen before in the land.

The great famine

At the end of the three years of famine that God had inflicted upon these people for their abominations, the clouds began to open up and the sky distilled its dew. It came with such force and the year's crops were so abundant that the people began to revive and regain strength after their sufferings. Men and women began to come to the marketplaces, all of them so shriveled and pale that they looked as if they had gone through some grave illness. But the plenty was such that foodstuffs were more than sufficient and parents were able to ransom their sons and daughters. People could return to their cities and recover their houses and wealth, except those who had gone to the land of the Totonacs. These never returned to their native towns, and even today in that country there are barrios of Aztecs, Chalcas, Tezcocans, Xochimilcas, and Tepanecs, who left during the famine and remained in that region. They were unwilling to return to their native states since they feared a repetition of this suffering and they also knew that the country of Mexico was poor in lands for sowing and that food would have to be brought from other regions. Thus, they stayed in places far away where they had settled.

CHAPTER XXXI

Which treats of how King Motecuhzoma had his likeness carved upon a rock on the Hill of Chapultepec. With a description of his last days and death.

Three years had passed since the famine. The time of abundance had come, but King Motecuhzoma felt that he was now old and that his days were numbered. Desirous of leaving a memorial and image of himself that would last forever, he summoned Tlacaelel his brother, who was no less old than he, saying: "Brother, you have seen the labors and troubles we have gone through in order to sustain this nation and how we have enlarged it and made it great by being victorious in many wars. It is only just that a memorial be set up to you and me; therefore, I have determined that two statues will be carved within the limits of the gardens of Chapultepec. Let the stoneworkers choose the part of the living rock that most pleases them and carve our likenesses upon it. It will be a reward for our endeavors, and our sons and grandsons will see our portraits there, will remember us and our great deeds, and will strive to imitate us."

Tlacaelel agreed with the king's decision and stated that he would see that this project was carried out, since Motecuhzoma's great statesmanship should be remembered.

Tlacaelel at once ordered that the most outstanding stoneworkers and carvers from all the provinces be summoned so that his portrait and that of the king be carved on the rocks. He then spoke to them: "My brother the great King Motecuhzoma, who realizes that he is now old and that his days and mine are numbered, wishes that our likenesses be carved upon the finest rocks to be found in Chapultepec, so this will be a memorial to both of us. This must be done without delay, you must start immediately. And the year Ce Tochtli should be carved on these, for that is the year the great famine began. Go now, and search for the stone that will serve best for this purpose."

The stonecutters and sculptors answered that they were pleased to carry out this command for this was their profession, what they were trained for, and they kissed the king's hands in gratitude. Then, leaving Tlacaelel, they immediately went to the gardens at Chapultepec and, having found the appropriate rock, began to carve on it the figures of the two brothers. These portraits were very exact and were finished almost before the king and Tlacaelel realized it. When they were ready, the sculptors went to Motecuhzoma and addressed him thus: "O powerful lord, we, your servants and vassals, were ordered to portray your royal figure and that of your brother Tlacaelel. These carvings are now finished; we have done them as perfectly as we could, although not with the perfection you deserve. If you would be kind enough to go see them, you could observe them any time you wish."

The king was amazed at the speed with which this work had been executed, especially since he felt it had been a difficult task. Thanking the sculptors, he rewarded them with clothing and valuable gifts and also honored them with titles, which are still used by their descendants today. Tlacaelel said to the king, "Lord, our vassals have done what you commanded and it would be good if we went to see what portraits they have made for us."

So one morning, unattended and unseen, they left the city and went to Chapultepec to admire the carved portraits. They found them to be very lifelike, as much in the features as in the ornamentation and in their attitudes. The king said, "Brother Tlacaelel, I am well pleased with these images! They will remain as a perpetual memorial to our greatness, in the way that we remember Quetzalcoatl and Topiltzin, about whom it is written that when they went away 'they left their images carved in wood and on stone.'[1] The commoners worship these but we know that they were men like us. So let us project our glory into the future."

When they had returned to the city, the king spoke to his brother in private: "Brother, I want to come to an agreement with you. Both of us have governed and sustained this Aztec nation, we have increased its fame, and if I die before you I wish you to become the ruler of the land. From the beginning your deeds have made you worthy of this. I do not want any son of mine, brother, or relative to aspire to this post; only you are worthy of it. And if you should die before I do, let one of your sons inherit this position, the one you choose—and he will sit upon the seat and throne of our ancestors, Acamapichtli, Huitzilihuitl, Chimalpopoca, Itzcoatl, who were kings and sovereigns of this wide world and whom we remember fondly. These forefathers, with much toil and work, founded our city and ennobled it by shedding their blood in this place of reeds and rushes and freeing it from the servitude and tribute in which Azcapotzalco held us. Therefore, you and I are now free, as we have been free in order to wage our own wars

---

[1] Durán speaks of Quetzalcoatl and Topiltzin as if they were two personages, when in reality they were one. Topiltzin was "Our Revered Prince," Quetzalcoatl was the god. Quetzalcoatl, however, was also a title; thus the "prince" would have been referred to as Topiltzin-Quetzalcoatl.

since that time. So it is only just that our children enjoy the results of these labors. And let us direct them correctly so that the Aztec nation, which is truly bellicose, does not dare to deviate from this path after our time."

Tlacaelel then thanked his brother the king for the honor he had bestowed upon him. "Lord," he said, "I wish you to leave another memorial to yourself in this world, and it will be not less worthy of praise than those that you have built heretofore. In the Hot Country, in provinces like Cuauhnahuac, Yauhtepec, and Huaxtepec,[2] I know there is an abundance of rivers and springs, of fertile and rich soil. I am reminded especially of the famous springs that exist in Huaxtepec; they can serve as a recreation place, as a diversion for you and your successors. It will be a delightful place. It will be a good plan to make a large pond or dam where the water may gather and rise to fill up this dam.

"Let us send to Cuetlaxtla, where Pinotl governs in your name, and order him to send the following plants to us: cacao trees, *xochinacaztli, volloxochitl, cacaoxochitl, izquixochitl, huacalxochitl, cacaloxochitl*,[3] and other flowers that grow in the Hot Country near the coast, and see if they will thrive here in Huaxtepec. It will cost little to find out."

The king was pleased with this idea and thought that if these gardens could be made a reality they would bring him glory and praise after his days were done. He immediately sent messengers to Cuetlaxtla, therefore, to have many kinds of plants brought, all with great care. He also ordered that gardeners from there come to plant them with their own hands according to the methods followed in their homeland. Meanwhile the springs were being dammed in Huaxtepec.

When the governor in Cuetlaxtla received the orders from his king, he commanded that these be fulfilled without delay. So all those flowers and plants were brought to Tenochtitlan in great quantities,

---

[2] The famous gardens of Huaxtepec (now Oaxtepec), once sown with luxuriant plants brought from the Huaxteca and other parts of the country, are now a national park and recreational center near the city of Cuautla in the state of Morelos.

[3] The plants mentioned here are: *xochinacaztli*: *Cymbopetalum penduliforum*, sometimes called "ear flower" (the dried flowers are aromatic); *volloxochitl*: *Talauma mexicana*, "heart flower"; *cacaoxochitl*: *Quararibea funebris*, "flower of the cacao"; *izquixochitl*: *Bourreria huanita* or *Bourreria formosa*, an aromatic flower that looks like toasted maize; *huacalxochitl*: *Philodendron pseudoradiatum*, "carrying crate flower"; *cacaloxochitl*: *Plumeria rubra*, "raven flower"; *flor de cacao*: *Quararibea funebris* (same as *cacaoxochitl*). There are many sources to consult for the names and uses of plants in prehispanic Mexico, including *Badianus Manuscript, The (Codex Barberini, Latin 241)*, study by Emily Walcott Emmart (Baltimore: John Hopkins University Press, 1940); Furst 1972; Hernández 1959–84; Martínez 1987; Sahagún, *Florentine Codex* (1963, book 11, "Earthly Things"); Standley 1961.

with the earth still about the roots, wrapped in fine cloth. When Motecuhzoma saw them, when he observed that all the plants were fresh and undamaged and that the gardeners had come to transplant them, he ordered them taken to Huaxtepec and planted around the springs. This was done with all necessary precautions and with all the ceremony that was customary on such occasions.

After the Cuetlaxtla gardeners had taken the plants to Huaxtepec and had sown them there, these men fasted for eight days and slashed the upper part of their ears as a sacrifice, and smeared the blood upon the leaves. They asked their overseers for large quantities of paper, incense, and rubber. They performed a sacrifice in honor of the god of flowers, offering him quail and scattering the birds' blood upon the plants and upon the earth where they had been sown. They did this because they believed that with that rite no plant would be lost and that soon all would burst forth with flower and fruit.

And thus it was that the devil (in order to deceive them and pull them into that false blindness in which some people must believe even today, and that our God allowed to happen because of their great sins) let not one plant be lost. On the contrary, in the third year they gave abundant flowers and the gardeners from Cuetlaxtla were amazed. They said that in their country no flowers bloomed as quickly as here and that Huaxtepec was a more fertile and better land for the plants than their own.

Motecuhzoma raised his hands to the heavens and thanked the Lord of All Created Things for all that he had given them. He and Tlacaelel wept with joy because their plan had been successful, and they considered it a special favor of the Lord of the Heights, of the Day and the Night, since they could now bequeath to Mexico-Tenochtitlan and all the nations in the provinces associated with the Aztecs the refreshment and the delights of the flowers they had lacked until then.

At this time the king became deadly ill; he sickened day by day until he died. He was to be remembered as a most just and merciful ruler. He died in 1469, having reigned thirty years. It is said that in his last illness he made war upon the province of Tlatlauhquitepec and, just before he died, he received the news that it had been conquered. I found this information in a painted manuscript I came across.[4]

After his death, the usual obsequies were celebrated in his honor and all the kings and chieftains of the land came with their offerings and presents, as was their custom. They killed many slaves and people

[4]Garibay (Durán 1967:II:580) refers to this document as one not included in formal annals, since Durán in his manuscript calls this codex *una pintura peregrina*, that is, not a formal historical record. Durán in his works made use of much *peregrina* material he found in outlying villages and in the hands of informants.

who had served him so they could continue to serve him in the afterlife. They buried him with a large part of his treasures in the courtyard of his home. This home was where the royal palace now stands, but [at the time of the Spanish conquest], when the Marqués del Valle, Hernán Cortés, entered the city of Tenochtitlan, he made this his headquarters. However, when Motecuhzoma's palace was later surrounded by the Aztecs, Cortés fled from the city with his people and took refuge in Tlaxcala. Later, when Mexico-Tenochtitlan had been conquered, Cortés chose the site [of Motecuhzoma's palace] to build his own, as we have seen.

CHAPTER XXXII

Which treats of the election of King Axayacatzin and of the events that occurred in his time.

hen the funeral rites for Motecuhzoma the First or Elder had ended, Tlacaelel ordered all the principal people and noblemen of Mexico to come to the place where the council was accustomed to meet. When all were present he spoke:

The death of my brother is known to you. He was like one who carries a load on his back for a time; he bore the burden of being lord of Mexico-Tenochtitlan until the end of his days. He was like a slave subjected to his master, sheltering and defending this republic in all its aspects. What happened to him will happen to me also. His fate will be shared by me and by all of us, for we enjoy life, its pleasures and delights. But these things are only on loan to us for a short time. Observe that all my brothers are dead, I am alone.

Having said this, Tlacaelel began to weep and the noblemen, feeling compassion, went to console him. They extolled his personal valor and the strength of his heart that made possible the endurance of these labors. At the same time they remembered the king's worthiness and they all felt great sorrow. But, controlling his grief, Tlacaelel addressed them: "Lords, you are all here today and you have been summoned so that you will designate the man you wish to be the next ruler, the next head of this nation."

All answered at once that their desire and that of the whole city was that he rule, that he govern them. They wanted Tlacaelel to be their protector, their guardian, since he had been these things even when the other kings had lived. All the people asked that he be the next ruler—all the old men, the young men, the women and the children. They requested that he take on this charge for as long as he lived, be it for a few years or many.

But Tlacaelel answered, "O Aztecs, I thank you for the honor you wish to bestow upon me. But how can I be honored more than I have already been? What further sovereignty could I acquire than that which I have now? None of the past kings has acted without my opinion or counsel regarding all civil and criminal concerns. Now I am too old to carry the burden that you wish to place upon my back. Know that I shall serve you and aid you with the same tenacity that I have always displayed, until the end of my days. And do not be sorrowful, for I shall indicate the one who is to be your king and lord. Go call King Nezahualcoyotl of the province of Acolhuacan. Go call Totoquihuaztli of the Tepanec nation. I wish to consult them, I wish their advice."

All agreed and were confident that Tlacaelel and the two rulers would make a wise choice. When the two sovereigns arrived, Tlacaelel withdrew with them and discussed the selection of a new king. He explained how the council had chosen him but that he could not accept because of his advanced age. He had decided that a young, courageous man should be designated to reign in his place, and he felt that a nephew of his, a son of the last monarch, whose name was Axayacatl, was the best choice.

The two rulers responded: "Most excellent lord, you have just demonstrated the worth of your person and your admirable humility. You could have glorified yourself and your children but you have preferred not to do so. So for the good of this nation the man you designate will be chosen. Nothing will be done without your agreement, in the same way that the former councils followed your advice."

Tlacaelel accepted this decision and stated that although he was well along in years he would continue to fulfill his obligations the best he could. The chieftains and noblemen were called, then all the people were summoned, young and old, men and women. When everyone had gathered, King Nezahualcoyotl of Tezcoco pointed his finger at the young man that he and the other two lords had chosen. He called him forth from among all the other noblemen and had him sit upon the royal seat. He placed the royal insignia upon Axayacatl with all the customary ceremonies. Then he made a long rhetorical address, congratulating him for having been selected, and presented him with rich gifts of mantles, feathers, jewels, and precious stones; all of these had been prepared in advance. The Tepanec king then went through the same formalities [of speech-making and gift-giving]. All the lords present pledged their obedience to Axayacatl, recognizing him as their supreme ruler.

When the rest of the people who were present were informed of the election, they accepted it as a very good thing and gave thanks to the men who were responsible for this. All the provinces were then advised of the choice of the new king. The lords from these provinces came to Tenochtitlan to offer their obedience to Axayacatl and to present the usual gifts. At this time there was much rejoicing as well as dancing and many festivities and songs that were appropriate for the designation of the king.

After Axayacatl had been enthroned, he began to deal with affairs involving the nation. He ordered that the laws formed by his forebears the Aztec sovereigns continue to be observed. But he dared not give any orders without the agreement of his coadjutor, whom he had been told to consult.

In the fifth year of his reign, when all was peace and quiet and tranquillity reigned in the provinces, the city suddenly erupted with problems and some people rose up against him. Trouble had begun between the people of Mexico-Tenochtitlan and Tlatelolco. This made Axayacatl grieve greatly, for the people on both sides were his friends and kinsmen. The cause of the uprising was this: some mischievous youths, sons of noblemen of Tenochtitlan, went to the marketplace in that city one day and met there some maidens, daughters of the lords of Tlatelolco, who happened to be in that market. The young men directed flattering words to them, flirting and joking. The girls answered in the same tone, thinking it was only a game. The boys asked to be allowed to accompany them, and the girls agreed. But before they reached Tlatelolco the youths had dishonored them, violated them. The girls, shocked at the violence with which they had been treated and the unfortunate end of this adventure, went to complain to their fathers, brothers, and relatives, who were highly indignant about the offense.

At the same time—while the Tlatelolcas were digging a canal so that canoes could enter the city—another disturbing event took place. One morning the canal was found broken up and filled in. The lords of Tlatelolco were greatly angered over this and said, one to another, "These Aztecs believe that we are of an alien lineage. Do they not know that we are Aztecs like them, relatives, kinsmen, and friends, who originated in the same place that they came from? What new thing is this with which they want to offend us?"

Among the Tlatelolcas there was a courageous young nobleman by the name of Moquihuixtli. So without seeking advice or asking the people's opinion, the Tlatelolca lords promptly made him their king to show their indignation over these happenings. Although they had always been subjects of the royal crown of Tenochtitlan, they now declared themselves independent [and began to seek help beyond the mountains]. The new king, Moquihuixtli, addressed all his principal men: "What do you think of this, O lords? Are you not sorrowed, are you not angry at the bad treatment given us by our close relatives, as if we were their vassals, their servants? Are we not, perchance, also Aztecs? Are we not possessed of the same spirit that they are? Therefore, O Aztecs, we who live in Tlatelolco, take courage, let us destroy the Tenochcas. In order to accomplish this I shall use a good ruse, a cunning guile that will be to our advantage. I shall send my ambassadors to the people beyond the Sierra Nevada, to incite the Huexotzincas, the Tlaxcalans, the Tliliuhquitepecas, telling them that the Tenochcas have plotted against them and are planning to wage perpetual war against them in order to bring them as victims for their sacrifices and to eat them at their banquets and weddings. We shall tell them that we of Tlatelolco are not in agreement with this conspiracy and that if they decide to wage war against Mexico-Tenochtitlan we shall aid them. We wish only that they back us up in these battles, for we shall be in the front line."

The Tlatelolco envoys immediately took this message to the lords of Huexotzinco, Tlaxcala, and to the other cities that were unfriendly to Tenochtitlan. The ambassadors presented their message to the chieftains of these cities, but all answered that they wanted no conflict with the Aztecs, who had done them no harm up to then. If this came to pass, they said, they would then answer for themselves.

The envoys took this message back to Moquihuix. They reported that the lords of those cities had feared some false plot, and they asked how it was possible that some Aztecs could quarrel with other Aztecs, since they were all kinsmen?

One of the principal men present, called Teconal, said to the new king, "Are we to be frightened by the arrows and darts of the Tenochcas? Are we not men enough to defend ourselves from them? Show me the Tlatelolca youths, let the Tlatelolcas gain control! And if we overcome the Tenochcas, we shall not destroy them totally but the power and rule will be in our hands!" And after this all the youths were summoned and made to participate in war exercises, as we shall describe further on.

CHAPTER XXXIII

Which treats of a fierce battle between the Aztecs of Tlatelolco and those of Tenochtitlan.

When the new king of the Tlatelolco faction of the Aztec people heard the answer from the Huexotzincas, Tlaxcalans, and other people from the region east of the Sierra Nevada mountains [that they refused to wage war on the Tenochca Aztecs]—on the contrary, they reproached the Tlatelolcas for wanting to declare war on their kinsmen—he decided to go ahead with his plans on his own. His wrath was still on fire, his heart was filled with the arduous task he had planned, and he did not wish to lose the time and opportunity to attack the Tenochcas, nor did he wish to abandon the plot. He did, however, ask advice of the council of leading men, this way: "You have heard the answer from the people of the cities on the other side of the mountains, that they do not wish to come to our aid. What do you think we should do? What plan should we follow for this war, which should be begun and ended as soon as possible?"

Teconal, a nobleman, responded boldly and with arrogance: "O powerful lord, why should we be frightened of the Tenochca Aztecs? Are we not men as they are? Therefore, illustrious lord, command your subjects here in Tlatelolco to prepare for war, for you well know that feats the Aztecs boast of are in reality due to the strength and courage of the men of Tlatelolco."

Moquihuixtli realized that this was good advice and they should not waste time, that the present opportunity should not be lost, especially since all the leading men of Tlatelolco were on his side and agreed with his plan. So he ordered that all the young men twenty years old or more be called out immediately. When they had come, he had them gather in the courtyard of the royal quarters, where he addressed them: "Brave Tlatelolca-Aztecs, pay attention to my words. You have come here so that I can ask you to practice the arts of war, and there are some tests you should take for these practices. First, a stone statue will be made and with this you will test your skill with the slingshot. He who aims best at the statue will receive the honor and glory as the most outstanding soldier among you. I wish to be present at this contest so I can reward in person the youth who wins."

All the young men answered that they kissed his hands and that to practice the arts of war was their greatest desire. Without delay, then, a statue in the image and height of a man, carved of stone, was brought and was placed upon a stone block in the square. This statue carried a sword and shield in one hand and appeared to be attacking with these. A great number of young men, more than two thousand, came out. They were all desirous of receiving the prize the new king had promised. They were all sons and relatives of the nobility. With slings and rounded stones in their hands, each competing with the others, they attacked the statue. So many stones hit it that after a little while it fell, broken to pieces.

The king was pleased at the skill with which these young men had destroyed the statue, and, with a smiling face, he thanked all those who had participated with such dexterity in this act. He said that no individual had outshone the others; therfore, all deserved a prize, but he was going to prepare another test to see if anyone was outstanding and thus could claim the reward.

On this occasion a wooden statue was made, similar to the stone one, and was put in the same place. This time the king ordered that the test be made with spears and arrows. The youths, competing with each other, attacked the statue and shortly it had been pierced by so many arrows and spears that the wooden image was covered with them and many had passed through it. The *Historia* mentions that this statue was one *palmo* thick. When the king saw the skill of those youths and their desire to gain glory, he pretended to organize a hunt of waterfowl. Many canoes were put in order and the young men, who had proved so skillful in the test involving the stone and wooden statues, were told that the king wished to see how they would shoot fowl on the wing. Then a large number of the youths entered the water. They were told not to shoot any duck or heron that might be standing upon the land or swimming in the water but only to aim at those that were in flight. In this way their skill would be evident. All were ready with spear in hand and a great quantity of birds that had been in the water were frightened into flight. As soon as they were in the air most of them—ducks, wild geese, herons, and other waterfowl—were killed with the spears and arrows. Our chronicle says that the spears went right through the birds, who then fell down from the sky. The young men spent most of the day hunting in this manner.

Moquihuix ordered that all gather in one place, then he spoke to them: "Tlatelolcas, I have been well pleased to see your ability. You understand that this contest was not carried out merely as a game, but had a deeper purpose. If someday you must wage war against the enemy, you will know that their flesh is not stone, that it is not wood, and that since your intrepid arms break through wood and stone, how much easier will it be to destroy flesh! You will be like ferocious jaguars and pumas! I also want you to know that our enemies are not birds that can fly and can slip between one's hands. Today few flying birds have slipped between your fingers. Therefore, have courage, for soon you will have need of your hands, and Mexico-Tlatelolco will be honored and all the nations will be subjected to us. Tlatelolco will rejoice in all those things that have been Mexico-Tenochtitlan's prerogative up to now."

The youths humbled themselves before Moquihuix and thanked him, though they failed to understand the purpose of his talk, except that he had ordered them to be prepared and ready for any moment when they could be called to arms.

The principal noblemen in whom the king had confided about the affair told him not to hurry or be restless but to keep the matter a secret, and they would give advice when the time came. Their plan was one of treachery: they suggested that Tenochtitlan should be attacked suddenly in the middle of the night. King Axayacatl was still young, they said, and once the leading men in whom he confided were dead there would be no need to worry about him. Tlacaelel was old and he was no more to be feared than a little old woman who spends her time dozing.

However, as this kind of a secret is difficult to keep and some of the nobles failed in this way, it soon became known in some quarters. It happened that some women from Mexico-Tenochtitlan went to the market at Tlatelolco and fell to quarreling with the local women over certain purchases. Heated words were exchanged and the Tlatelolca women yelled that soon the others would pay for their insolence. This made the Tenochca women suspicious, whereupon they went to King Axayacatl. Since he had been advised of the warlike games of the young Tlatelolca men, the suspicions were confirmed and he summoned his council, composed of the principal lords of his kingdom. It was decided that guards be placed secretly in the city and also that certain captains be sent to the marketplace at Tlatelolco. While they pretended to be idling, they would listen and spy on all. This was done. While walking through the market with an air of indifference, they heard many spiteful words against them and above all they noted such phrases as "Behold those who are walking so carelessly! Well, let them, soon they will have to pay!" or "What merchandise have you brought to sell? So you want to sell your intestines, your liver, or your heart?" These taunts were reported to Axayacatl, who then told it all to Tlacaelel. They both feared a rebellion or some kind of treachery prepared by the men of Tlatelolco.

Tlacaelel spoke to the king: "Is it possible that our kinsmen, our relatives, are preparing such a perfidy? Be strong, do not fear, for the

Lord of All Created Things, of the Heavens and the Earth, of the Night and Day, will free you from the hands of the enemy! You cannot flee from that which has been predetermined, you cannot hide, for it is for trials like this that you were chosen from among your brothers. And not only must you suffer these things all the time you live—as I have suffered, before this city had hands or feet and could breathe and rest as it now can—but you must realize that these trials come to you at the beginning of your road to greatness, as a first ordeal to be overcome. And so it is understood that this affair is not of our doing; therefore, send your messengers at once to the rulers of Tacuba, Tezcoco, Chalco, Xochimilco, Coyoacan, Colhuacan, and Itztapalapa. We shall not ask their help, their favor, at this time, but if the Tlatelolcas make war upon us and we defeat them, rout them, it will be known that we were not the cause of this war, for it is shameful that one group of brothers mistreats another and declares war on them. And if we were to be defeated and killed, at least the glory would be ours because we did not begin the war."

The envoys were sent off to the provinces with this message. And when old Tlacaelel had finished speaking he ordered that the young men as well as seasoned warriors be made ready in secret, that their shields, swords, slingshots, and other weapons and paraphernalia necessary in war be prepared, and that they wait to see what would happen.

The ruler of Tlatelolco was married to a daughter or sister of Axayacatl, sovereign of Mexico-Tenochtitlan, and our chronicle says that while she was asleep she dreamed that her private parts spoke, wailing, "Alas, my lady! Where shall I be tomorrow at this time?" She awoke with great fear and told her husband what she had dreamed, asking him to interpret this dream. He answered by telling her what he had decided to do about Tenochtitlan, and said that her dream might be a prophecy of events that could take place on the morrow.

She wept bitterly over her husband's prediction, saying, "Lord, it is a terrible thing, that which you have begun! Have pity on the women and children who will perish because of you! Think of the deaths that will occur on both sides! Remember that you have small children, and consider that you and I shall be needed by them. They will become perpetual slaves if we are conquered."

King Moquihuix arose from his mat and sighed, showing that he repented of his warlike intentions. However, he excused himself by saying that his adviser Teconal had been the instigator of the rebellion and that he, Moquihuix, was not powerful enough to stop it now that it was underway.

The queen answered, "How is it, sir, that being the lord and ruler of these people you cannot calm their hearts? Give me permission to speak to them! They may listen to my womanly words and make peace with Tenochtitlan, then our past friendship will be renewed. Do not be a coward, speak to them. Go see your brother Axayacatl, pacify him and embrace him. Do this for me, give me this satisfaction."

The ruler of Tlatelolco left the room to see if anyone in his house had heard rumors and, passing through the kitchen, he beheld there a very old man whom he had never seen before. The man was speaking to a dog and the animal was answering all of his questions. On the fire next to the man was a pot boiling and within it some birds were dancing. All of these things were considered to be evil omens by the king. It is also said that a mask hanging on the wall began to moan in a sorrowful way and that the king picked it up and dashed it to the floor. Frightened by all these things, Moquihuix decided to consult the gods and make a celebration in their honor so that these omens could be turned against Tenochtitlan. With this in mind he invited his neighbors, the people of Azcapotzalco, Cuauhtitlan, and Tenayuca, and regaled them with a banquet and dances. The adornments for this feast were all weapons: swords, shields, arrows, darts, slings, bows, and with them they performed a solemn dance. And all the presents brought by the lords of those towns, as well as their offerings to the gods, were of the same nature.

When the meal had ended, several songs belittling the people of Tenochtitlan were sung, mourning over them as if they were already dead and their city destroyed. However, their tongues became twisted and though they wanted to say "the Tenochcas" they said "Tlatelolcas"; they had wanted other words to come out of their mouths. But Teconal, who had instigated this rebellion, fearful that they would weaken on seeing so many signs and omens, said to Moquihuix, "Everything is ready. Whenever you desire we shall go kill those wildcats who are our neighbors."

Moquihuix sent his spies to Tenochtitlan to see what was happening in that city and they found King Axayacatl playing ball with his noblemen, apparently ignorant of any trouble. The Aztecs had done this intentionally so as to mislead the Tlatelolcas and convince them that nothing was known about their plans. It was false, though, because the daughter or sister of the king, Axayaca, had notified her father that the attack would be that night. The spies returned to Tlatelolco well pleased and informed their ruler that the Tenochcas were ignorant of their plan. Moquihuix then commanded that his troops be made ready and he entrusted to Teconal the stratagem for the attack, giving him full liberty to carry it out as he saw best.

Teconal ordered half of his men to prepare an ambush, hiding at the city limits of Tenochtitlan. Tlacaelel had placed Tenochca spies, however, who became aware of this and immediately relayed the information to their commander. The other half of the Tlatelolca army was sent to cover the walls of Tenochtitlan and block the roads and paths along which the Tenochca Aztecs might try to escape. But these Aztecs were alert. Everyone was prepared and waiting for the signal that the Tlatelolcas would give when they entered the city to plunge it as they had been ordered. This signal was given at midnight. The Tlatelolca warriors entered Mexico-Tenochtitlan shouting and yelling, but the Tenochca Aztecs came out to meet them and, coming at them from different parts of the city, soon surrounded them. The uproar and slaughtering was so great, men on both sides being massacred, that the Tlatelolco soldiers could barely manage to escape along the roads on which they had entered the city, and those who got away completely leapt into the lagoon and hid themselves under the reeds and rushes. The Tlatelolcas were so humiliated and mortified at this defeat, they were so angry and resentful, that they asked to be able to fight the Aztecs openly on the battlefield. Therefore, everyone was prepared to fight again, not only men but very young boys also, all were made to rehearse for battle.

When the Aztecs heard of the new orders, of the unexpected but obstinate command given by Moquihuix and his principal men, and knowing that these people were traitors who attacked by night, in the dark, they placed guards on all the streets of the city. The people of Tlatelolco took the same precautions, for they feared the retaliation that could be the result of their own treason. These guards, then, were placed in both cities.

King Axayacatzin called his councillors together so they could decide what should be done. They wished to avoid a recurrence of all that killing, also the derision and scorn that the other neighboring peoples would manifest at this war. Agreed on this point, it was decided to attempt to calm Moquihuix's ire, his anger, and that of his advisers, by reasoning with them so they would be obliged to desist. The Aztecs would stress the unions by kinship, by consanguinity and friendship, that had always existed between the two cities. They also would point out that shame would descend upon both when other people heard of the rancor and enmity that existed between these two groups of kinsmen, and these people would laugh at them.

Once this decision had been made, a nobleman named Cueyatzin was commissioned to take the message to Tlatelolco. He was instructed thus: "Go before my brother Moquihuix and tell him to observe, to be aware of what he is doing. Ask him if he considers it a joke to undertake something where so much harm will occur. Tell him that he should be aware of what takes place and not let himself be guided by impetuous men. He should call his people together—the old men, old women, all the men and women—and tell them about this situation, ask their opinion, how they feel [about war with their own relatives], for it seems impossible that they would agree to such confusion and disorder. But if all are in favor of this war then the fault is not directly with Moquihuix, except for some details. He should not then follow his councillors' bad advice."

The ambassador went with this message to the lord of Tlatelolco, Moquihuix, who was amazed that the Aztec envoy had been allowed to enter his city. After hearing the message, he answered, "Tell your lord the king that the answer is that he should be prepared because the people of Tlatelolco are determined to avenge the deaths of the other night. In the name of all the Tlatelolcas I defy him and all his people. I have hopes that the Lord of All Created Things, of the Day and the Night, will ensure that the city of Mexico-Tenochtitlan will become the dung heap and place of excrement for the Tlatelolcas."

CHAPTER XXXIV

Which treats of the second battle between the Aztecs of Tenochtitlan and the Tlatelolcas and how the latter were defeated.

When the message from the Tlatelolco ruler had been heard by the lords of Tenochtitlan and they had laughed and jeered at this arrogant reply, Tlacaelel, so full of wrath that his heart seemed about to leap out of his body, turned to King Axayacatl and declared that he wished he were a young man in order to take revenge upon such arrogant, such insolent men, so he could lower their self-esteem. Rising, he exclaimed with fury, "O powerful king, if I were strong enough to go alone to Tlatelolco to display my person and prove my valor, as I did in Azcapotzalco, even though everyone tried to prevent me [from entering that city at that time], I would convince Moquihuix of his impudence and folly. But, since I cannot do this, please have Cueyatzin return there, taking with him the ointments and insignia that are applied to the dead, and have him do what I did in Azcapotzalco."[1]

This was done immediately. Cueyatzin, having been admitted to Moquihuix's quarters, spoke to this ruler, saying, "O lord, the king of Mexico-Tenochtitlan, your servant, your brother, sends you these funeral insignia. You are to be anointed with this pitch of the dead and you must prepare to die."

Moquihuix rose from his seat, pushed the messenger away, and roughly cast him out of the room, exclaiming, "Tell your master that these ointments are for him!" While he yet spoke, Teconal appeared, sword in hand, and with one blow cut off Cueyatzin's head. This head was then carried to the boundaries of Tenochtitlan, where it was thrown.[2] After that the Tlatelolcas set up a great howling, calling out "Tlatelolco! Tlatelolco!"

Tlacaelel took up his sword and shield and ascended to the top of the pyramid, where the drums began to beat and the shell horns to sound. At this a great number of soldiers, men of war, gathered and Tlacaelel shouted to them: "Sons and brothers, do not be faint, justice

---

[1] See chapter IX of this book.
[2] It is interesting that a sculpture of a head served as a boundary marker between Tlatelolco and Tenochtitlan. This head, however, is carved on the base of a stone cactus and has been identified by Felipe Solís of the National Museum of Anthropology as that of Tenoch, one of the mythical founders of Tenochtitlan.

is on our side! They have killed our ambassador without reason, with unjustified murder. This time we shall not have to go far from our boundaries to fight. Our enemy lies right behind our houses. You will not have to climb mountains or go down cliffs. You will not have to march through valleys. Imagine that you are just brushing flies from your bodies; therefore, cover yourselves with your shields, hold your swords tight, extend your arms strongly. From here I shall watch and I shall rejoice in your bravery."

At this point Axayacatl the king came out, showing valor and self-assurance, dressed with rich adornments and insignia of gold, jewels, feathers, armed with his weapons, the sword and shield in his hands. His noblemen, also splendidly attired, then came out and surrounded him. Tlacaelel addressed the king: "O courageous youth, go slowly, do not rush this. Wait for the signal I shall send you, pay attention, and when I lift my shield on high, that will be the time to attack."

At this the king and his army set out, began to march, and when they reached the indicated boundary point they found that the Tlatelolca warriors were also well prepared and ready for battle, as well ordered and armed as they. Moquihuix and Teconal were in the front line, encouraging and urging on their men.

Axayacatl, keeping his eyes on Tlacaelel, waited for the signal to begin the battle. When he saw the shield and sword raised, he immediately gave the order to attack. His men rushed at the Tlatelolcas with such fury that they put them in a dangerous position. The Tenochcas were making them retreat and were gaining ground, intent upon taking the main square of Tlatelolco, where the market was held and where the great temple was located. This is where the Tlatelolcas had sworn to their god that they would cover the steps of the temple with the blood of the leaders of Mexico-Tenochtitlan. The Tlatelolcas fought with all their strength and power. At this point the resistance of the Tlatelolcas was strong, and a hard-fought battle took place where soldiers on both sides were slaughtered.

It was then that Tlacaelel, from the summit of the pyramid temple, ordered that the drums sound and that the trumpets, shell horns, and other instruments be played for battle. This was done, accompanied by much whistling and hideous howling. At the sound of all this the Tenochcas took courage, they were filled with drive, and pressed forward. They forced the Tlatelolcas to retreat, thus losing the ground they had gained. The Tlatelolcas were surrounded in their marketplace, but they stood their ground and did not allow one Tenochca to enter that place.

Axayacatl commanded his men to stop fighting. They all lowered their swords, their bows, and dropped their slings and spears while the king shouted to the Tlatelolcas, "O brother Moquihuix, behold how we are about to become masters of this marketplace and temple! Surrender! Lower your weapons! Have pity on yourselves and on your children!"

It was Teconal who answered: "We shall do that gladly if you will deliver yourselves with your hands tied so that with your blood we can redden our temple! We have sworn it, we have promised it to our god Huitzilopochtli!"

When Axayacatl realized that his words had no effect, he ordered his men into the battle again and the attack was so furious that they pushed into the marketplace while the Tlatelolcas withdrew in great confusion. When Moquihuix and Teconal saw that they were lost and their people were fleeing instead of continuing the fight, they ascended the steps of the temple-pyramid in order to distract the others while they tried to reorganize their army. To do this they used a feint: a large number of women were gathered, stripped of their clothing, and formed into a squadron. They were made to attack the Tenochcas, who were fighting furiously. The women, naked, with their private parts revealed and their breasts uncovered, came upon them, some slapping their bellies, while others squirted milk at the soldiers from Tenochtitlan. Next to them appeared a squadron of little boys, also naked, with their faces blackened and their heads feathered, making a wailing sound. The Tenochcas, dismayed by such crudity, were given orders by King Axayacatl not to harm any of the women but to take them prisoner together with the children.

The Tenochca men pressed their victory and, having captured the women, the king and some of his warriors began to climb the steps of the Tlatelolco pyramid, though this was done with great difficulty because of the resistance found there. When Axayacatl arrived at the summit where the temple stood, he found Moquihuix and Teconal clinging to the altar of Huitzilopochtli. He walked boldly into the sanctuary where the idol stood on the altar, slew the two men, dragged their bodies out, and cast them down the steps of the temple.

When the Tlatelolcas saw their chieftains killed, their lords dead, they fled from the marketplace and hid in the canals among the reeds and rushes. Some of them were immersed up to the neck, others to the chest. All hid as best they could in order not to be killed by the Aztecs of Tenochtitlan, who were their relatives, their kinsmen. These men, however, pursued them relentlessly, sparing no one.

Now a great nobleman of Tlatelolco, an aged uncle of the king of Mexico-Tenochtitlan, called Cuacuauhtzin, appeared and prostrated himself before his nephew, beseeching him to give orders that his men cease this slaughter because enough vengeance had been wreaked against their offenders. Axayacatl, touched by his uncle's white hairs and the fact that he was prostrated before him, agreed, and commanded his troops to cease fighting. He reproached his uncle, however, for the unfortunate determination that had been taken by the Tlatelolcas [to make war on the Tenochca Aztecs], but the old man excused himself, saying that he had had no part in this.

Axayacatl stated that, since those Aztecs of Tlatelolco had rebelled against the royal crown, from that time on they were to pay tribute to Mexico-Tenochtitlan, like other tribute-paying cities and provinces. All the liberties and exemptions enjoyed by the Tlatelolco Aztecs would in the future be denied them, and every eighty days they must send as tribute mantles, breechcloths, feathers, jewels, precious stones, weapons, and slaves. When these conditions had been fulfilled, the Tlatelolcas would be pardoned. Axayacatl then ordered that the statue of Huitzilopochtli be removed and that the temple become a rubbish heap for the Tenochca Aztecs, just as the Tlatelolcas had sworn to do with the temple of Tenochtitlan. He added that all those who had leapt into the water would not be allowed to come out until the city of Tlatelolco had been plundered and his soldiers had been compensated for their work and were satisfied with the booty they had received.

And in order to abase those who were hidden in the reeds and rushes, the king ordered them to caw like water thrushes, to quack like magpies, and to imitate ducks and wild geese. As soon as they were commanded to do this, the people in the reeds began to caw and quack like water thrushes, magpies, ducks, and wild geese, and the Tenochcas burst into laughter and mockery. Even today the Tlatelolcas are called "quackers" and imitators of waterfowl. They are much offended by this and when they quarrel or say insulting things they are taunted with this name.

In the midst of all the quacking, Axayacatl ordered that Tlatelolco be sacked. The houses were robbed of their contents, even the pots, jugs, plates, and bowls were carried away, and what the soldiers could not carry they smashed to bits, hoping to frighten and humiliate the Tlatelolcas forever. From that day on these people were made to pay tribute, to work in public projects, and to carry messages and even loads to any place where they were destined. In time of war they were forced to carry equipment and food supplies on their backs, although before this they never had to do this type of work or pay tribute. These people also had to go to the royal quarters in Tenochtitlan to sweep and water the gardens and haul water and firewood for use in the palace. They had to give a certain number of work days for service in the royal houses. These Tlatelolcas, then, were treated as subjugated, conquered people, who in this way were made to understand the evil acts they had committed.

And the body of Teconal, instigator of the rebellion, was impaled and placed at the entrance to Tlatelolco as an example and warning to other people.

When this was done, King Axayacatl decreed that the Tlatelolco market and square that constituted the land won by the Tenochca Aztecs (for the Tlatelolcas possessed no more land than this) be divided into lots among the different Aztec lords, and that the Tlatelolco merchants who occupied space here were to pay a tax amounting to one part for every five. In this way the marketplace was divided up among all the merchants, and the tax was collected from each one according to what he had sold.[3]

Eighty days later, when their first payment of tribute was due, the Tlatelolcas did not bring slaves as they had been instructed. They excused themselves, saying that they had been unable to obtain them. The king and Tlacaelel reprehended them and punished them in the following way: the noblemen of that city were no longer to wear splendid mantles. From that time on they must use cloaks of maguey fiber, like people of low rank. And they were not to wear sandals or lip pendants, ear plugs, or fine feathers. Nor were they to be allowed to appear in the marketplace or to rest at the crossroads or at the thresholds of the houses. Like women they were to stay in their houses until eighty days after their second payment had passed.

The people of Tlatelolco, in order not to be punished further, made a great effort to join in the battles against Tlaxcala, Huexotzinco, Tliliuhquitepec, Cholula, and Zacatlan. They took many prisoners and slaves and brought them as tribute to Tenochtitlan, and in this way the interdict they had suffered was removed. But whenever they failed in their obligations it was placed upon them again. The obstinacy of the Tenochca Aztecs was such that, until the Spaniards arrived in this country, the Tlatelolcas were given no liberty whatsoever.[4] They were not allowed to have their own temple but had to worship at the one in Tenochtitlan. Our chronicle tells us that their temple became filled with weeds and garbage and that the walls and dwelling quarters fell into ruins.

[3]It is not clear if the tax was collected from all the merchants, Tenochcas and Tlatelolcas, or only from the Tlatelolcas.

[4]Yet the last Aztec ruler was Cuauhtemoc, a Tlatelolca, and the last stronghold in the resistance against the Spanish was in Tlatelolco. A modern plaque at the Great Pyramid Temple at Tlatelolco reads: "On the 13th of August, 1521, Tlatelolco, heroically defended by Cuauhtemoc, fell to Hernán Cortés. This was neither a triumph nor a defeat but was the painful birth of the mestizo people who are the Mexico of today."

CHAPTER XXXV

Which treats of how the people of Tenantzinco asked the Aztecs for aid against Toluca and Matlatzinco. With a description of how this help was sent and how those cities were destroyed.

I n Toluca and Matlatzinco, cities that actually formed one province, reigned two powerful sovereigns, both valorous men. The ruler of Toluca was Chimaltecuhtli [Lord of the Shield] and the lord of the Matlatzincas was Chalchiuhquiauh [Jade Rain]. The Toluca ruler had three valiant sons, daring young men who were capable of carrying out any great feat, no matter how difficult. The city of Tenantzinco was governed by a lord called Tezozomoctli who had three or four young sons who were also proud of their lineage, their noble background. Among these young men from the two cities rivalries and envies sprang up and they began to form bands and quarrel with each other, all based upon childish disputes. Even though the *Historia* tells about these problems, it is such an unimportant matter that I shall not repeat all the details here. However, it is well known that the young men from Toluca constantly threatened those of Tenantzinco, swearing to wage war upon them and force them to show their strength.

The lord of Tenantzinco was much troubled by this. He saw that Chimaltzin [or Chimaltecuhtli] of Toluca made no effort to control the actions of his sons, but rather encouraged these quarrels and aggressions. Tezozomoctli decided to try to stop all this trouble-making before any serious misfortune could happen. Therefore, following the advice of his councillors, he went to Tenochtitlan in person and, appearing before Axayacatl, he described everything that had happened with those people of Toluca. He told how they had become bad neighbors and how they were trying to take other people's lands, threatening him and his people constantly. Considering that he was a loyal subject of the king of Mexico-Tenochtitlan, Tezozomoctli claimed that those insults and threats were also directed to King Axayacatl, and he begged for help against those of Toluca.

Axayacatl consoled Tezozomoctli and agreed to defend him and his people against the aggressors of Toluca in every way he could. He gave the lord of Tenantzinco a shield and sword and some very handsome weapons, at the same time advising him to be alert, to be prepared for war if Axayacatl called him to arms. Pleased at this assurance,

Tezozomoctli returned to his city in the belief that he had found an ally. And this is exactly what was to happen.

After Tezozomoctli had departed for Tenantzinco, King Axayacatl turned his attention to the building of a place for the Sun Stone that had been carved, at his orders, by the sculptors. Upon it the master craftsmen had painstakingly wrought images of the heroic Aztec dignitaries of the past, scenes of the wars in which they had conquered lands and the remote coastal provinces they had subjected, in which wars they had suffered greatly. They had already brought men from those conquered regions, who had been sacrificed upon this stone. In the center were represented the rays of the sun radiating from a round depression where the victims' throats were slit and from which ran a channel to carry away the blood.

The king was also occupied in the making of the great and finely worked stone upon which were represented the months, years, days, and weeks, all so splendidly carved that it was an amazing thing to behold. Many of us were able to see this stone in the Great Square of Mexico City, next to the canal, before the most illustrious Don Fray Alonso de Montúfar, Archbishop of Mexico, of happy memory, ordered that it be buried because of the criminal acts, such as killings, that had been committed upon it.

Axayacatl had these two stones carved as a kind of altar for sacrifices and offerings and he was in the process of constructing bases for these stones at the summit of the temple. He made this an excuse to wage war on Toluca and Matlatzinco [in order to have victims for sacrifice]. As soon as Tezozomoctli had left Tenochtitlan, Axayacatl sent messengers to the lords of those two cities, informing them that certains rooms had been built in the temple where the sacrificial stones were to be set up and that he wished to request a favor of them: that they send cedar and pine wood in order to finish those rooms. It was not that the Aztecs lacked wood; rather it was on the advice of Tlacaelel, a trick devised by him, so they could have a pretext to invade the others' territory, which is what he desired. The messengers went with this request to the lord of Toluca, who, when he heard it, failed to understand that this was just a pretense and replied, "It would seem that you come to give us orders, not to make a request of us. But I shall consult with my advisers and see what they have to say about this demand."

When the Toluca council met, all its members agreed that there was no wood of the type requested in their hills. They begged to be excused for not being able to supply it. The envoys returned to the

Aztec city with this answer for their king, who, when he heard it, became angry and sent for Tlacaelel. Because he was now very old, Tlacaelel was brought on a litter carried on the shoulders of some assistants. After Axayacatl had told him of the answer sent by Toluca and Matlatzinco, Tlacaelel calmly stated: "My son, do not become so agitated. You must know that since the time of my brother Motecuhzoma I have been convinced that that province should be conquered because I fear that its inhabitants might become allies of the people of Mechoacan, and they could give us an unpleasant surprise some day. See what could happen if we do not subjugate them: they will not obey us or respect us in any way. And, in part, they are right, for we have not been honest with them. And so, courageous youth, before I die I wish to see that province come under Aztec rule, as other regions have been subjugated."

Axayacatl summoned his council of war and the captains and military leaders and ordered them to prepare their men and the necessary provisions for the march to the province of Toluca and Matlatzinco. At the same time he sent envoys to the rulers of Tezcoco and Tacuba, requesting their presence in the city, where he wished to discuss an important matter with them. These two sovereigns responded to Axayacatl's command, together with the chieftains of other nearby cities. He ordered them all to make their people ready for war because he wished to punish the disobedience of the Matlatzincas, as well as bring back captives for the presentation of the two carved stones that had been made for sacrifice in the temple. The two kings and the other lords stated that they were pleased to be of assistance in this matter and as soon as they returned home they ordered their men to prepare for battle as quickly as they could.

At this time the lord of Tenantzinco was also active preparing his army; and when the soldiers were ready, he went to Tenochtitlan and, finding that Axayacatl's men also were armed and ready, appeared before the king, offered his respects, and asked that the army soon attack because he could no longer suffer the insults thrown at him by the Matlatzincas. In answer to this, Axayacatl had his men march out of the city and the third day they arrived at a place called Iztapaltetitlan [Place next to the White Stone]. Axayacatl sent word to Tezozomoctli, lord of Tenantzinco, advising him that they had set up camp there and that the Tenantzincos should be on the alert so that when they saw a great fire consisting of torches, rising from the top of the hill, they should attack with loud cries and shouting. He in turn would attack the city of Toluca from the road. This way the enemy would be caught in the middle. He did not wish any Matlatzincas to be killed; he wanted them all taken prisoner and put in good care in order to redden his temple and the stones of the shrine with their blood in a solemn sacrificial ceremony with the Matlatzinca captives.

Tezozomoctli, on hearing this, sent the envoys back to their king with the message that he would make haste to fulfill these orders. Then he had living quarters prepared where he lodged the principal men from the provinces, providing them with everything they needed, as people of their importance deserved. He ordered the allies to be prepared: the Tezcocans, the Tepanecs, the Chalcas, and the Xochimilcas, with soldiers from the rest of the *chinampa* region. The Aztecs always were in the lead. Since these people were usually victorious or at least victory was claimed by them—even when other nations were actually responsible for the triumph—they were always placed in the most dangerous position during a battle, where their prowess would be seen by all. On this day, in order to distinguish themselves even further, they marched along the royal road [which was open and difficult to protect], while men from the other cities followed whatever path they wished.

When the soldiers were ready and lined up, they all marched in the same order toward the city. On reaching a place called Cuahpanohuayan, they discovered the Matlatzincas marching toward them in the same orderly fashion. The ruler of Toluca was in front, together with his sons and some lords, all well armed with their own type of armor, with swords and shields. When they were a stone's throw from the Aztecs they cried out: "What is this, O Aztecs? What do you seek? Who has summoned you here? Have you come to sell your lives? Someone must have tricked you into coming, for you are not aware of the valor of the Matlatzincas. Some divine being must have directed you here so that all of you will remain in this place. Do you not know that we have no equal, there are no military forces capable of surpassing us?"

On hearing these words, the Aztecs were filled with fear, so the captains and leaders of the army asked Axayacatl to give an encouraging talk to them and to all the soldiers. But since the king was just a youth, he did not feel confident to give this talk, so he asked some wise elders to do this for him. In order to lend authority to the words of the rhetorician, Axayacatl stood next to the man, who made this speech in the usual ritual manner:

> O illustrious Aztecs, Tezcocans, Tepanecs, men of the *chinampa*, and from the four nations of Colhuacan, Iztapalapa, Mexicatzinco, and Huitzilopochco, you who are present, who have come here as a favor to the royal Aztec crown and to lend aid to the Tenantzincas: Know that you have come here to meet with those who deliver death. And if you

were not aware of this when you left your homes, your wives, your children, be aware of it now that [death] is so close and this is your last opportunity [to defeat death], for you are seasoned warriors with experience in similar wars, and you have been victorious in many. Raise your spirits again! What is it that makes your heart beat so, that it seems it will jump out of your body? And why are you so pale? Is it possible that you were more courageous yesterday than you are today? Go now, run, attack! Show that you are brave, spirited men, and not womanly, for what have you here on earth? Sell your lives dearly. What is that you are saying? Are you to live forever? And if you die today instead of tomorrow the labor and misery of this life will end sooner and you will go rest in the next one. Think of no other things, put nothing else in your mind except that now you must conquer or die. And, in order not to die, try to understand your shield and your sword: the one is to protect you, the other is to injure [the opponent], and do not take one step backward. You must realize that these are not jaguars or pumas who will eat you alive, nor are they eagles, who, in flight, fall upon us and snatch us up, carry us off. Nor are they demons rising up out of the earth to terrify us. For they are only men like us. Humble yourselves before the Lord of All Created Things, of the Day and the Night, of Wind and Fire, so he will aid you. And the great lord Axayacatl who stands here before you puts his trust in you and wishes to give strength to your hearts. Act like courageous men, especially if you are a captain, a leader, so that with this bravery your soldiers will be led, will follow you to those places where they are most needed. And they will not let some perish while others are protected, even if the others are from different provinces than theirs.

As soon as this address was finished, Axayacatl ordered the flaming torches raised high on the hilltop. When Tezozomoctli and his men saw this fire, they shrieked, whistled, and yelled so loudly that the clamor reached the sky.

Axayacatl commanded his soldiers to advance slowly and when they met Matlatzincas to demand that they surrender, but they were to spare the old men and old women, and the children.

It was well known that the Aztecs were like fire that burned the fields of grain and the fruit trees, that consumed with its heat the maguey plants and the houses; therefore, the Matlatzincas in order to survive must surrender peacefully and they would be received with benevolence and would become subjects of the royal Aztec crown. Axayacatl advised the captains that he and a chosen group of soldiers wished to remain on the riverbank, hidden among the plants, in an ambush, so that if the Matlatzincas did not surrender peacefully, but retreated little by little until they came to that part of the river where they felt safe and could pass to the other side, the king and his men could catch them by surprise, attack them from the rear, and easily destroy them.

The Aztec army started to cross the river while Axayacatl and his seasoned warriors and some of his bravest men stayed hidden in the ambush, covered by leaves and branches. The same trick that the Aztecs had planned, however, had also occurred to the Matlatzincas. They sent one of their brave soldiers with a thousand men to pretend to retreat, yet their own ambush was set. If the Aztecs were to follow the retreating Matlatzincas they would fall into the trap and the enemy, with fresh soldiers, would catch them and would kill them all. The Matlatzincas, then, were hidden behind the maguey agaves and in the underbrush, and when the Aztecs demanded a peaceful surrender—which was not granted—they came out and a furious battle ensued.

Each army had planned to trap the other, drawing the enemy into the ambush, so the result was not as planned but ended in mass confusion. Nevertheless, the Aztecs feigned weakness and fear and the Matlatzincas, being simpler people than they, believed this and began to follow them, crossing the river to the other side. The Aztec soldiers who were hidden along the banks waited until the Matlatzincas were crossing, then Axayacatl rose up, crying, "Tenochtitlan! Tenochtitlan! O courageous Aztecs, death to those traitors, death to them!"

They fell upon the Matlatzincas and both the men who had hidden and the soldiers who had pretended to flee rushed into battle. Before the Matlatzincas could finish crossing the river, every Aztec had captured one or two of the enemy. King Axayacatl, though still a young man, took many captives from among the hardiest warriors and delivered them to his guards. Then the Aztecs again crossed the river and followed the Matlatzincas, injuring and killing all they could, but in a dispersed, uncontrolled way. Thus, they went straight into the Matlatzinca ambush. Believing that they were victorious, Axayacatl began to sound the golden drum that he carried on his back, which was played when the enemy retreated. As he went running, without waiting for his guards, the Matlatzinca officer in charge of their ambush, who was hidden behind a maguey, saw him running so carelessly, in such a hurry. He realized that this soldier was the king and felt that his own soldiers would follow him, so he suddenly jumped out from behind the agave and drove a knife into Axayacatl's thigh, almost to the bone, right through the king's [quilted cotton] armor. The wounded monarch was on the point of collapse, but he caught his enemy and both fell to the ground, where they fought furiously, neither one yielding. The king's guards and noblemen missed him and began to search for him. They feared for his life and thought that he had either been killed or been taken prisoner by men in the Matlatzinca ambush. But they found him in this struggle, his face covered with dirt, his arms with blood, and, though wounded, he was defending himself bravely like the stout-hearted youth that he was.

The Aztec soldiers and noblemen, when they saw the condition of their lord, rushed furiously at the Matlatzinca with the intention of killing him, but the king ordered that his life be spared and that he be taken prisoner. But the courageous Matlatzinca warrior, Tlilcuatzpal [Black Lizard], managed to defend himself with his shield and sword and, even though he was badly wounded, slipped away from them.

The Aztecs went on ahead, even those who had been injured in the ambush, and entered the city of Toluca. They went directly to the temple that was in the main square, removed the god of that place, called Coltzin, and then burned the sanctuary. This burning was customary in war [and signified that the city where the temple was located had been conquered].

When Chimaltzin and the lords of Toluca saw the destruction, the devastation of their province, they went to Axayacatl and humbled themselves before him, pleading with him to cease the killing. Axayacatl, who because he was injured was being carried on a litter on the shoulders of his noblemen, ordered them to put him down. Tezozomoctli of Tenantzinco, who had been the instigator of this war, came and prostrated himself before the Aztec ruler. Weeping, Tezozomoctli paid his respects, then, continuing to weep, asked forgiveness for having caused all these problems and at the same time thanked the king for everything he had done in his favor. Axayacatl greeted him in good humor and told him to go in peace, that in the future his bad neighbors would no longer bother him.

The Matlatzincas then came to beg the Aztecs to stop looting and destroying, since they, the men of Matlatzinco, finally realized that they had been to blame and now they would subject themselves to any tribute and servitude the Aztecs demanded of them. They said that many things grown in that province would be valuable for the Aztecs as tribute. Axayacatl received them kindly and ordered that the plundering stop. He also ordered the Matlatzincas to go to Tenochtitlan, where they would be told what they were to tribute. A messenger was dispatched to Tlacaelel to relate everything that had taken place and to advise him that Axayacatl would be delayed in reaching his city because he was wounded. The messenger did just that, telling Tlacaelel of the Aztec victory and that although the king was injured he was victorious and was bringing many captives as well as great riches from the sacking of the city. He also said that the god of that province, Coltzin, was being brought to Tenochtitlan, together with all the priests from the temple.

Tlacaelel was pleased with the news of the victory. He gave orders that everyone in the city was to go out and receive the king and the warriors with much festivity and rejoicing. The prisoners, too, were to be received with special ceremonies, for they were captives to be dedicated to the gods. I have told about this many times before.

The priests in all the barrios immediately went to the summit of the temples, where with great joy they made the drums sound and played flutes and shell trumpets. And while the people celebrated with song and dance, men were sent to spy along the roads and in watchtowers to see at what time the king would arrive so he could be received with much ceremony. Those who had remained on guard in the city, the civil authorities and councilmen, went out to welcome him, bearing rich presents. Axayacatl accepted these with gratitude and pleasure. When he and his entourage reached a place called Cuauhximalpan that was under the jurisdiction of Coyoacan, the lords of Coyoacan and Tacuba greeted him ceremoniously and with fine gifts. The chieftains of those mountain towns of Tzaueyucan, Huitzitzilapan, and Chichicauhtla also brought large quantities of deer, rabbits, hare, quail, and skins of different animals, all as gifts to the king. They also welcomed him warmly and told him they regretted his having been wounded.

The next morning Axayacatl's men carried him on the litter to Tenochtitlan. All the people were lined up at the entrance to the city, some on one side and some on the other. All were dressed in festive attire, especially the priests of the temple and the masters of the temple schools. They were all dressed in armor and carried swords and shields in order to receive their king. As soon as he reached the people, Axayacatl greeted them and made a long formal speech, reminding everyone of the great deeds of his ancestors. He was then taken into the city with more festivity and expressions of joy than any other king had received. He went directly to the temple and, before the statue of Huitzilopochtli, gave thanks to this god for having made him victorious and for having liberated him from death at the hands of the enemy. Then, before the god, he drew blood from his ears and calves and shinbones and sacrificed many quails, which he decapitated with his own hands.

After he had gone to the palace, the king of Tezcoco arrived to welcome him home, to congratulate him on the victory and to present him with mantles and jewels. This was also done by the ruler of Tacuba and his noblemen. They stated that Axayacatl's great achievements had honored and glorified his lineage and had renewed the valor of past kings, especially that of Itzcoatl, Axayacatl's father. When they had finished, the lord of Tenantzinco entered, bringing the prisoners he had taken in battle. He also presented many gifts to Axayacatl and Tlacaelel. The guests were then given quarters in the palace.

The king had all the captives he had taken brought before him. He adorned them with his insignia so they would be recognized as his prisoners of war, be seen by all, and so that they would be honored and would dance in the regular festivities that took place every day with these prisoners in the square at Tlateloloco.

CHAPTER XXXVI

Which treats of how the two carved stones were set in their places and how the Matlatzincas were sacrificed upon them during the presentation of these stones at the time of the Tlacaxipehualiztli festival.

In the book I wrote about the sacrifices[1] I described at length the festival of Tlacaxipehualiztli, which means "Skinning or Flaying of Men" and the way in which this was celebrated. A prisoner, naked, was tied by his foot with a rope to a bar in a hole in a round stone. He was given a shield and a sword, but they were only of wood, with feathers attached instead of knives. These were placed in his hands as were some wooden balls, and he had to defend himself with these against four well-armed warriors who came out to fight him. These warriors were the Tlauauanque, the "cutters or gashers of skins." Some of the victims defended themselves against these Tlauauanque in order to prolong their lives a little longer, but others who preferred to end this torment quickly allowed themselves to be killed immediately. They threw themselves upon the stone, where they received cuts from the warrior's sword.[2] Then they were placed upon the stone dedicated to the sun and there the sacrifice was terminated with all the usual ceremony.

When the war with the Matlatzincas had ended and the victorious army had returned to Tenochtitlan with many prisoners, the Tlacaxipehualiztli festival was approaching. Tlacaelel spoke to the king: "My son, you see my white hair, my old age. I beseech you not to tarry in setting up the altars, the stones, for sacrifice, for you know that the feast of the Flaying of Men draws near. And if you delay in preparing these things I may be dead tomorrow or some other day soon, and I shall not be able to take with me the memory of this happy event."

All this was said by that evil old man, who never had enough human flesh to satisfy him. The king then decided to please him; he responded that the stones would be set in place immediately. So people from all the provinces were summoned and a large number gathered in the Aztec city, since many were required to move these heavy stones. Then they were carried to the top of the pyramid.

[1] *Book of the Gods and Rites* (Durán 1977).
[2] Like *touché* in fencing.

How the carved stones were set in their places

When every one was in place and all had been arranged with great care (as they knew so well how to do these things), Tlacaelel spoke to the king: "Now everything is ready; what still needs to be done is that you send ambassadors to invite guests to the rites and festivities." Axayacatl asked him which people he considered deserving of being invited to observe this sacrificial ceremony. Tlacaelel responded that invitations should go to the Nonohualcas, from Cempoala and Quiahuiztlan, two provinces next to each other, which lie near the coast and which had not yet been conquered.[3] "And the reason for this invitation is to see if they obey us and come when they are called, because if they refuse we shall have a pretext to declare war on them and destroy them. This is my intention. But if they do come to Tenochtitlan we shall understand that they are at our service and we shall honor them."

Axayacatl approved of old Tlacaelel's advice and so, not to lose time, he called his ambassadors and envoys in order to send them to the lords of those provinces with the invitations. When the envoys had come before him, he told them to go to the lords of Cempoala and Quiahuiztlan without delay and to request in his name that they be present at the festivities.

The envoys immediately set out for these cities and, having arrived at Cempoala, spoke to the ruler there, Tlehuitzilin, telling him that their sovereign Axayacatl, who governed the great city of Tenochtitlan and all its surrounding regions, had sent them to request that they attend the presentation of the stones to be used in the Tlacaxipehualiztli ceremony and sacrifice. He wished to do honor to Tlehuitzilin at this time.

Tlehuitzilin answered that he accepted with all goodwill because he was and always had been at Axayacatl's service and would be honored to attend. He gave orders that the ambassadors be lodged and taken care of, then he excused himself.

From here the Aztecs went to Quiahuiztlan, where they performed the same mission with much courtesy before the lord of that province, Quetzalayotl. As they had extended the invitation to Tlehuitzilin of Cempoala, they also invited the lord of Quiahuiztlan to the ceremonies in the name of Axayacatl Tecuhtli. When he heard the envoys,

---

[3] In Durán 1977 we read that Huitzilopochtli, tutelary god of the Aztecs, wanted only captives from Nahuatl-speaking regions to be sacrificed to him; people of other tongues were considered inferior. Some derogatory terms used by the Aztecs when referring to other groups were Nonohualca (mute or unable to speak Nahuatl), Popoloca (Barbarian), and Chontal (Foreigner). Durán also says that the Huaxtecs were considered by the Aztecs to be drunkards and sodomites, the Otomi were "brutish and bestial," and the Tarascans were "uncouth and nudist."

Quetzalayotl humbled himself before them and told them that he kissed the hands of their king, that he was prepared to serve him, and that he would be pleased to attend those festivities in which he was to receive much favor and pleasure. He had the envoys given lodgings and treated them with all the attention and honor possible. They were given food and drink in abundance and finally received gifts of rich mantles, breechcloths, and sandals, also gold headbands and labrets and ear plugs of gold. Then amber jewels were placed on their hands and they were given fine shells and other stones and little bones of the kind that are found on the seashore.

The envoys, very contented, returned to their city. They described everything that had taken place to their king, who was pleased with the news. The lords from those provinces visited hastened to come to Mexico, accompanied by their principal men and carrying quantities of rich gifts for the king. As soon as Axayacatl heard of their arrival and that they had been taken to the palace, he went to the main hall, where he received them, with much respect. And they, in the customary manner, placed before him their presents, which consisted of rich cloths, cacao, fine feathers from rare birds, conch shells, large and small shells of many colors, jewels, precious stones, amber—that is, everything found in that province.

The king received these gifts graciously, then had the visitors taken to the home of a nobleman called Cuetlaxtecatl. Here they were given generous quantities of everything they desired: delicious dishes of many kinds, many types of breads, and a beverage made of cacao, which was highly valued in those times.

The guests had been given quarters and their needs taken care of. Then the day for the celebration of the Tlatlauhqui Tezcatl, "Red Mirror" feast, arrived. This is another name for that Tlacaxipehualiztli festivity. When the hour for sacrifice had come, the prisoners were brought out. They were formed in a line at the place of the skull rack [*tzompantli*], as it was called, and were given colored paper breechcloths. They were smeared from head to foot with a white chalk mixture, their heads anointed with molten rubber and plumed with turkey feathers. Their faces were also smeared with the same rubber pitch. When the Matlatzincas had been lined up, the four sacrificers, two Aztecs dressed as jaguars and two as eagles, appeared. They were called the Elder Jaguar and the Younger, the Elder Eagle and the Younger. Then all the gods appeared, or rather their impersonators, wearing the garb of each divinity. They could be recognized by the differences in their dress.

They ascended to the summit of the pyramid, while the singers brought forth a wooden instrument called *teponaztli*, which is commonly played at these festivities.⁴ They placed the drum in the center of the courtyard and began to beat it and sing special hymns in honor of the new stone, all of which had been composed especially for the occasion. On their backs the singers wore round ornaments shaped like millstones, with a hole in the middle, all made of white featherwork. Cords also made of white feathers passed through the holes. The men who sang and danced were called "Singers of the Round Stone."

All wore on their heads decoration made of hair called *yopitzontli*, which means "hair of the divine Yopi."⁵ These wigs are still in use today, as are different hairstyles of the various gods, because each god was represented with a special kind of hair adornment. Wigs similar to those used to help identify each deity in the dances and singing are still worn in festivals.

When they began to play the drum and dance, a man dressed as a jaguar, moving to the rhythm of the drum, approached the prisoners and untied one of them; all had been tied together at the calves. The victim was brought to the stone, was placed upon it, and one foot was bound with a rope that passed through the hole in the center. He was given a shield and a feathered wooden sword with four balls of torchpine to defend himself. His opponent then emerged and came dancing and singing, encircling the stone two or three times, raising and lowering the sword lined with knives while in the other hand he carried his shield. The unfortunate captive then gave forth great cries and shrieks and began to leap into the air, slapping his thighs loudly with his hand and making gestures toward the sky. He picked up his wooden sword and shield, raised it to the sun, and began to fight. [And when he was vanquished, his heart was torn out.] This was all carried out the way I described it in the book of sacrifices: all through this book [of the *Gods and Rites*] the way in which these ceremonies were celebrated is told.

In this way all the Matlatzinca war captives were sacrificed, and there were so many that in order not to be accused of exaggeration or of being one who invents things, I shall not tell the number that died there. It is enough to say that on that occasion the Matlatzinca nation decreased considerably, their people disheartened, since many died in that sacrifice.

⁴The *teponaztli*, one of the several musical instruments played by the Aztecs, was a horizontal drum carved out of a log. The *huehuetl* was a large vertical drum whose mouth was covered with stretched skin. Other instruments were the turtle shell drum, rattle, whistle, single or multiple flute, rasping bone or stone, copper bells, conch shell trumpet, and whistling jar.
⁵Yopi was Xipe Totec Tlatlauhqui Tezcatl, also called Tota, Topiltzin, Yollometl (Father, Son, and Heart of Both, according to Durán 1977:172). Xipe was "Our Lord the Flayed One," god of goldsmiths, associated with agricultural fertility, and probably a native of Yotpitzinco in the present-day state of Guerrero.

The bodies were laid out near the skull rack so each warrior could go identify the captive he had taken in war. The body was given him to be eaten, the bones to be placed on poles in his house as a sign of prestige. In this way these Indian nations lost their fear of the dead and ghosts. Today they are not afraid of sleeping in cemeteries or churches, either accompanied or alone. They do not claim to have seen ghosts or to have heard moans or experienced other frightful things, as some foolish, irrational people do. It is not uncommon to see an old woman or an old man, of those born long ago, squatting all night next to a corpse without uneasiness or fright, or sitting in a cemetery while guarding the place, with only a small light. None of our Spanish people would do these things without great uneasiness no matter how they tried to summon their courage.

The noble guests who had come to the feast and sacrifice were horrified, beside themselves, on seeing so many men killed, sacrificed in this gruesome way. They were so frightened that they dared not speak. They were in a bower handsomely decorated with flowers and branches, the borders covered with designs cleverly made of flowers of different colors. Large fans of rich featherwork protected them from the sun and all were sitting upon high seats covered with jaguar skins, which were well tanned on the inside and whose fur looked splendid on the outside. Before the sacrifices began, the king had given all these guests many fine gifts: rich mantles to wear and garlands of gold for their heads with fine feathers at the temples. They also received gold bracelets, labrets, ear ornaments, and nose plugs, as well as many kinds of flowers and fragrant perfume.

After the ceremonies had finished, the king summoned his guests; and when they had come before him, he said, "You should be very happy to have witnessed and enjoyed the feast and rites for our god, and to have seen this city where he is honored. What I beg of you is that you remain calm, are quiet and tranquil, because while you are so, you will enjoy our friendship and be favored by us. This way you can return to your homeland with our good wishes."

The guests thanked Axayacatl, and after this they returned to their own provinces. They marveled at what they had seen but at the same time were horified by the sacrifices, though they were impressed by the grandeur and majesty of the Aztec city.

Once these lords had left, old Tlacaelel said to the king, "My son, you have now rejoiced in the feast that has glorified your name. You have been painted with the colors, with the brush of honor forever. But now you must go ahead with this greatness, carry on the glorious name you have achieved. You well know that the Sun Stone is finished and that it must be set up and be given the same solemn presentation as this other stone. For this you must send your messengers to Tezcoco and Tacuba and to the kings and lords of the other provinces so they will come help build the place where the Sun Stone is to rest. It should measure twenty *brazas* around, in the middle of which this magnificent stone will stand."

The king of Tenochtitlan, Axayacatl, immediately sent his envoys to those cities with the order that they were to send supplies of stone, lime, and sand for the structure. The kings and lords of the provinces, when they received this message, complied with their obligation and sent the necessary material. So many people came from Tezcoco and from the Tepanec area, and from the other provinces, each with the material that had been requested, that in one day the structure was finished and the Stone placed on top. When the Stone was being set in place, drums and whistles and conch shells were played in all the temples. Many songs were sung in praise of the Sun Stone and quantities of incense were burned in the thuribles by the censerbearers whose only occupation was to do this. These men were called the Tlenamacaque, which means "Those Who Offer Incense" or fire [that is, they were the fire priests].

Once this stone had been put in place, all the principal men who were present discussed the way the festivities would be held for the inauguration of the Sun Stone and where captives could be brought for sacrifice during these ceremonies.

Axayacatl and Tlacaelel requested that their guests stay another day in Tenochtitlan so they could propose to those allies that a war be waged against Mechoacan.

CHAPTER XXXVII

Which treats of how it was determined to wage war against Mechoacan. With a description of how the Aztec army was defeated and most of the soldiers were slain.

The next morning Nezahualcoyotl and Totoquihuaztli, kings of Tezcoco and Tacuba, together with the rulers of other allied nations such as the *chinampa* region and Chalco and the Hot Country, reminded Axayacatl of the decision he and Tlacaelel had come to on the previous afternoon, that is to say, to wage war on Mechoacan. Although they knew from what their ancestors had said that the people there were their relatives, with some common Aztec forebears, the king wished to try out the valor of the Tarascans, test their strength, to see if they could compete with the Aztecs. The main cause, however, for his war was the forthcoming celebration of a great festival at the inauguration of the Sun Stone and the desire to paint the temple red with the blood of those people.

The allied kings agreed with this proposition, saying that they were ready, were prepared, to send their people to aid the Aztecs. On returning to their own provinces, they announced this declaration of war. A multitude of soldiers from all these nations responded and were sent to Tenochtitlan with their necessary weapons and provisions. Old experienced warriors and young recruits all made a splendid appearance. They were anxious to go fight in wars like these because they received much material gain that way, as well as honors that were bestowed upon them.

When Axayacatl, king of Mexico-Tenochtitlan, witnessed the prompt aid sent by the other kings and lords—their warriors and leaders so splendidly attired, as were the Aztecs—he ordered that all his own men and those from outside be counted, for he wished to know how many men made up this army. Once they had been counted, it was seen that there were twenty-four thousand soldiers. Thinking that these were enough men to conquer Mechoacan or even a larger province, Axayacatl commanded the army to depart in the direction of the land of the Matlatzincas. The forces gathered at a point located near the boundaries between Matlatzinco and Tlaximaloyan, next to a lagoon that is near Cinapécora. On the third day all the soldiers and officers were at this site and as quickly as possible set up camp with many tents and houses made of mats. Today these are still used among the merchants, who make a roof or protection for their stalls with reeds and rushes. A great number of tents of this type were set up for the soldiers and a special one was prepared for the king, its walls covered with fine cloth and with splendid seats for the noblemen who accompanied him. Whenever the monarch traveled all his principal men went with him, both from the Aztec city and from the other provinces.

After the camp had been set up, spies were sent to observe the Tarascan army, which was discovered by some Matlatzinca scouts. They came back with the news that the enemy had gathered on a plain near the lagoon. The king ordered the spies to go in great secret and find out how many men were there and in what way the army was organized, since he did not know this nation's manner of fighting. He also wished them to discover what kind of weapons they had and which were the most dangerous.

The spies went very secretly; and when they arrived near the enemy camp, they dug a tunnel that reached the tents of the soldiers from Mechoacan. When they had made a small, hidden crack in the earth, they were able to hear through it and listen to everything that was said by those men. They found out that the Tarascans were forty thousand strong and the arms on which they mainly relied were slings, propelled spears, bows and arrows, wooden swords edged with stone blades, clubs, and other offensive weapons. They also had finely worked shields and insignia made of gold and featherwork.

Axayacatl was not very pleased when he heard about this. He called together his great captains and spoke to them: "I have found out that the Tarascans are forty thousand men, all of them robust, tall, and brave. They have sixteen thousand more men than we! What do you suggest we do?"

On seeing the indecision of the king, the captains encouraged him, made him take heart, thereby giving him the worst kind of advice. They stated that the Aztec nation had never feared any great number of men that had attacked it, that it had never turned its face away from weapons, nor from other arms superior to its own. If they turned back now, having embarked upon this adventure without having been called upon to do so or having been provoked by the adversaries, what would the other nations say? Having come this far, they had no alternative but to attack and triumph or to die.

Upon hearing this argument, the king was convinced so he commanded his men to approach the enemy little by little in orderly fashion. In this correct order first went the experienced warriors called the Cuauh Huehuetque, "Old Eagles," who were in charge of organizing the men. In front were the most experienced and older soldiers, the lords and captains, and those called Cuachic, an order of

The History of the Indies of New Spain

"knighthood" [that is, distinguished warriors] who were sworn never to retreat, but rather to die. Soon the Tarascans were seen in good order, splendidly arrayed, their lords in the front line. They were so covered with gold, gems, and feathers, all so shining, glittering with golden bracelets, ankle bands, ear pendants, labrets, and gold headbands, that as the sun rose (for it was at dawn) the Aztecs were almost blinded by this brilliance.

King Axayacatl, instead of being pleased, was now repentant, but he ordered the usual talk of encouragement be given to the army. This was done by stressing the praise these men deserved, for such words were meant to fill these timorous hearts with courage. When this was finished, the order to attack was given; but our chronicle tells us that at this point some Tarascans, very well armed and attired, came to Axayacatl to berate him, thus: "O great lord, who brought you here? Why have you come? Were you not happy in your own land? Who summoned you here, who deceived you? Was it perhaps the Matlatzincas whom you overcame a short time ago? Consider carefully, O lord, what you are to do, for you have been misled!"

The king thanked them but ordered them to depart since he said he wanted to test their strength, as he had come for that reason.

The Tarascans returned to their leaders with this answer; then the Tarascan army attacked with such fury that soon the Aztecs began to weaken and to turn their backs. When Axayacatl saw the situation, he began to increase his forces with soldiers he had brought from the other provinces, and in this way they managed to continue the battle all day until the sun went down. The Tarascans did not retreat but rather showed valor, skill, and resistance.

When night had fallen, the great lords and warriors appeared before King Axayacatl. Our chronicle tells us that their faces—noses, mouths, and eyes—were so covered with sweat and dust because of having fought the entire day that the king was barely able to recognize them, in order to call them by name. Those in the most unhappy state were the warriors who had sworn not to retreat [the Cuachic]. Many were badly wounded, some by arrows, others by stones, others by sword thrusts, others pierced with spears. The king sorrowed greatly for them and felt much pity for the wounded soldiers, those who were left from the multitude of men from all the allied nations, while the rest lay dead in the field. He had the soldiers called and ordered that they be given a beverage that was used to alleviate the pains of war. This was called *yolatl*, "heart water," which in our language could be translated as "broth of strength."

That night the survivors rested, mending their weapons and preparing to defend themselves again. The next morning the lord of

Matlatzinco came to Axayacatl, lamenting the events of the previous day, trying to console him. He offered the Aztecs a thousand loads of arrows, shields, swords, slings, and other arms of the type they used. He also offered to send Axayacatl his men of war if they were needed. The king thanked him and requested these reinforcements. Many came, well armed and prepared. They were acquainted with the region since it was on their own boundaries.

The king distributed the weapons among those who most needed them, at the same time trying to encourage them, to animate them. So that they would not lack confidence or become faint because of the events of the day before, he insisted that the Lord of All Created Things knew what would happen to them, that if they put their trust in him he would protect them.

The Aztecs attacked the Tarascan army, but the assault was so unsuccessful that they fell into the hands of the Tarascans, like flies that fall into the water. At least, this is what the chronicle says. The massacre was so great that Axayacatl decided to withdraw those men who were still alive in order to save at least a few. In this encounter the Tarascans killed many valiant Aztecs, especially from the military orders called Cuachic and Otomi. Among the fallen was a nobleman who was a close relative of the king and who belonged to the royal council of four from which the king's successor was chosen. When the Tarascans recognized from his insignia that this man was of royal blood, they carried him to the Aztec camp and deposited his body there, in this way showing their boldness and demonstrating their contempt for the Aztecs. Having thus mocked their foes, the Tarascans then returned to their own camp, not wishing to push their victory further.

King Axayacatl had his camp dismantled. Then the Aztec army, in disorderly flight and with broken spirit because of the few men left (most of them wounded and being carried on other soldiers' backs), reached a town called Ecatepec. Here Axayacatl called together the remaining captains and principals from the provinces and told them that they must be prudent, must bear up under this misfortune, since [in better times] the Lord of All Created Things, of the Day and the Night, had given them success and prosperity. All began to weep, all consoled the king with words of compassion, stating that they should not become faint-hearted because of this defeat, nor become cowards. The survivors from Tenochtitlan and from the provinces were then counted. It was seen that of the Aztecs, only two hundred were left; of the Tezcocans, four hundred; of the Tepanecs, Chalcas, and Xochimilcas, four hundred each; of the Xochimilcas and all the *chinampa* region, another four hundred. Only three hundred or a few more of the Otomi forces from Cuauhtlalpan had escaped, and from the Hot Country none had survived. Twenty thousand men had died in the war, perhaps more!

When this count had been made, when the vast number of the dead was evident, messengers were sent to Tlacaelel to inform him of the tragic event, of the sad results of this war. The king dismissed the men from the provinces and sent them home in peace, but promised them that soon there would be an opportunity to make amends for all that had been lost. So these survivors returned to their own lands.

Having received the bad news, Tlacaelel placed guards about the city and ordered drums and conch shells to be played. The gods were invoked and mournful hymns were sung from the summit of the pyramid-temples. The entire city was filled with sorrow and lamentations, mourning and tears.

When the king and his two hundred surviving warriors reached Chapultepec, the elders and priests of the temple came out to meet them. They were dressed and adorned as if the king had returned victorious. He was offered incense in the same congratulatory manner and great speeches were made to him. This was done, I understand, whenever a king returned from an absence from the city of more than three days, even if he had not gone far. For the kings were held to be divine men, likenesses of the gods, and were therefore honored with the same ceremonies offered to the deities. In the city the king went immediately to offer up his lamentation and to spill some of his own blood in sacrifice, together with the usual offering of quail.

On meeting Tlacaelel, they wept together and Axayacatl deplored, "O Lord Tlacaelel, it has been my fate to be unfortunate! Things that did not happen to my ancestors have happened to me! What a terrible loss! What destruction the Tarascans have inflicted upon us!"

The old man answered, consoling him, "Son, do not be faint, let not your heart feel dismay! Have courage: your subjects did not die working at the hearth, nor spinning like women, but on the battlefield, fighting for the glory of your heart and for the honor of their country. They won as much honor in their deaths as, in other times, they gained in their victories. I give thanks to the Lord of All Created Things who has allowed me to see the deaths of so many of my brothers and nephews. But I do not know why I have been spared!" Having said these words, he burst into bitter tears. All went to the old man and tried to console him.

Tlacaelel then ordered that the funeral ceremonies for the dead warriors be prepared. The way in which these rites were carried out will be described in the following chapter, where we shall see how those who died in war were honored and how their obsequies were observed. Much of this will interest the reader.

CHAPTER XXXVIII

Which treats of the long funeral rites with which the Aztecs honored those who had died in war, especially the brave captains.

After the king had been welcomed on returning from the war and had received condolences for the loss of so many men, the Aztec lords requested that the funeral rites for those fallen soldiers be held, with all the solemnity possible. So Axayacatl ordered the men who were in charge of the obsequies to begin as soon as they could, and that not one thing be lacking in the ceremonies but rather that the usual rites be surpassed in every way possible. Though all would be in accord with their ordinances and custom.

The Cuauh Huehuetque, who were like field marshals, went to the homes of the deceased and spoke to each of the widows, whom they already knew, in this formal manner:

> O my daughter, let not sadness overwhelm you or end the days of your life. We have brought you the tears and sighs of those who were your father, your mother, your shelter. We have brought them to your door. Take courage, show your love for our sons who did not die plowing or digging in the fields, who did not die on the road, trading, but have gone forever, for the honor of our country. They have departed, holding each other's hands, and with them went the great lord Huitznahuatl, a close relative of our king, our sovereign. He and the others are now rejoicing in the shining place of the sun, where they walk about in his company, embellished with his light. They will be remembered forever! Therefore, illustrious matrons, distinguished Aztec women, weep [for their memory]!

When these words had been addressed to the widows, the singers whose sole profession it was to sing for men who had died in battle came into the square. On their heads were tied black leather bands. They brought out an instrument and began to play sad and tearful music. The lamentations began with hymns for the dead according to their own special manner. When the playing of the drum and the singing had started, the widows of the dead warriors appeared, carrying the cloaks of their husbands on their shoulders and their breechcloths and waistbands around their necks. The hair of the widows was loose[1] and all of them, standing in line, clapped their

---

[1] Hair hanging loose was a sign of mourning. However, harlots also wore their hair loose.

hands to the beat of the drum. They wept bitterly and at times they danced, bowing their heads toward the earth. At other times they danced leaning backward. The sons of the dead men also were present, wearing their fathers' cloaks, carrying on their backs small boxes containing the lip, ear, and nose plugs, and other jewelry. They clapped their hands like their mothers, and the other relatives wept with them. The men stood there without moving, holding the swords and shields of the deceased in their hands, and joining the women in their lamentations. After having wailed for a long time, the elders said, "Rest a while, let the great resplendent sun, which passes and encircles the world above our heads, console you. To him have you offered your tears and lamentations."

Then certain relatives of the widows, who took charge of laying out the dead, entered and began to weep, showing great feeling. The instruments sounded again and the singers renewed their lamentations. A new period of weeping began. The wailing was so great that it filled one with pity, with fright. And the women clapped their hands loudly to the sound of the instruments. The musicians then ceased to play and there was an interruption in the singing. Those in charge of the funeral arrangements stood in a line and, one by one, they greeted the widows. They expressed their condolences to them and to the elders who were present. They said, "We give you thanks, O lords, O elders, for the honor you pay to the sun, Master of the Earth, Creator of All Things, and to the Children of the Sun, those who have died in the war."

Many other speeches and expressions of gratitude for the honors were made on this occasion.

Four days after the ceremony had taken place, on the fifth day, images of the dead were made from slivers of resinous wood, each one with feet, arms, and head. Faces were made on these, eyes and the mouth. They were dressed with breechcloths, sashes, and mantles. To their shoulders were attached wings of hawk feathers, as it was believed that in this way they would fly before the sun every day. The heads of these images were feathered and pendants for the ears, nose, and lips were placed upon them. The statues were then taken to a room called Tlacochcalco. The widows then entered and each one placed in front of the statue of her husband a dish of a stew called *tlacatlacualli*, which means "food of human flesh." Together with this were offered some special tortillas called *papalotlaxcalli*, "butterfly bread,"[2] and a

---

[2] After death on the battlefield or as sacrificial victims, soldiers were said to accompany the sun across the sky and after four years were transformed into birds with precious feathers or butterflies to return to earth, where they fed on honey from the flowers. The butterfly was considered the soul of the warrior. See the *Florentine Codex* (1978:book 3:49).

drink made of a little flour of toasted maize dissolved in water. After this food had been offered, the drum began to sound again and the singers began their hymns, which told of mourning and of the tears and filth that accompanied mourning. The chanters came dressed in filthy stained cloaks and with dirty leather bands tied to their heads. They called this chant *tzocuicatl* "song of dirt," of filth.

The heads of all those present were smeared with the ground bark of a tree that is used to kill lice. Each one carried a gourd vessel of the white native wine these people drink,[3] which were placed in front of the statues. The vessels into which this wine was poured were the *teotecomatl*, the "divine gourds." In front of the statues were also placed flowers and tobacco and thick straws for drinking. This type of straw is called "sun drinker." The chanters of the dead then took the gourds of wine in their hands and raised them twice, thrice, in front of the statues. After this they poured the wine in the four directions around the image.

At dusk, when this ceremony was over, the widows rewarded the singers with ordinary mantles, breechcloths, and digging sticks. Then the elders ordered that all the statues be placed together and set on fire. Since they were made of resinous firewood and covered with paper, they burned with great fury. All the widows stood around the fire, weeping with great sorrow.

When the fire had consumed the statues, the old men thanked all those present and then addressed the widows in formal speech:

> O sister, daughters, be strong, strengthen and widen your hearts. We have bade good-bye to our sons. They have departed, they who are the jaguars, the eagles. Do not hope to see them again. Do not imagine that this is like the times when your husband left your house sulking and angry, and would not return for three or four days; nor when he departed for his work, soon to return. Understand that these warriors have gone forever![4] This is what you must do now: you must be occupied in your womanly pursuits of spinning and weaving, of sweeping and watering, of lighting the fire and remaining in the house. And

---

[3] Durán says "wine." It was pulque, made from the juice of the maguey agave.

[4] The soul of the dead person was thought to undergo a long and dangerous journey in order to reach the Land of the Dead. Along the way he had to pass through a number of trials: ice-cold wind that cut like obsidian blades, mountains that bumped one another and could crush anyone passing between them, burning deserts, and a great river where a dog awaited him and could help the deceased across the water. A ferocious jaguar stood ready to eat the heart of the individual, but this could be avoided by placing a jade bead in the deceased's mouth at the funeral, which then could be offered to the jaguar in place of the heart. After these trials the deceased reached the ninth underworld, where he offered gifts to the Lord and Lady of the Land of the Dead, Mictlantecuhtli and Mictecacihuatl.

you have recourse to the Lord of All Created Things, of the Day and the Night, of Fire and Wind.

On hearing this, the women wept so copiously that it was frightening, and everyone pitied them. From that day on they went into mourning, not washing their clothes or face or head until eighty days had gone by. Because of that mourning with sadness and tears, the dirt on their cheeks became so thick that after the eighty-day period the elders sent special ministers to go to the homes of the widows and bring the tears and sorrow to the temple. [What was meant was the following:] The ministers went and scratched the filth from the faces of the women, which they wrapped in papers and then took to the priests. The priests ordered that the papers be cast into a place called Yahualiuhcan, meaning "Round Place." Those who went to throw the tears and sadness [represented by the eighty days' filth in mourning] in this place, which was outside the city, were given gifts of clothing by the widows. When these rites had been completed, the women went to the temple, where they prayed and made offerings of paper, incense, and offered ordinary sacrifices. With all these ceremonies they became free of weeping and sadness; mourning was over. They returned to their homes happy and consoled as if nothing had happened. Thus, they were free of sorrow and tears.

With the period of mourning ended and sadness expelled from the city, Tlacaelel sent a message to the king reminding him that he should not neglect all the matters relating to the presentation of the stone that was the Likeness of the Sun. Although the war with Mechoacan had resulted in defeat, not because of this should the proper ceremony and festivities be eliminated. Axayacatl, then, should command that another military action take place in order to obtain men to be sacrificed. The reason is that in this type of ceremony only war captives could be sacrificed.

It was decided, therefore, to go to Tliliuhquitepec for this purpose, since it was one of the towns indicated for this kind of war.[5] The summons was sent to the allies and a large number of soldiers were called up, many of them new, youths, who were sent so they could practice fighting. They were mixed in with the older experienced warriors, who were made ready and were provided with everything they needed. Each company left Tenochtitlan or its own city, with one of the three kings at its head: those of Mexico-Tenochtitlan, Tezcoco, and Tacuba. The lords and soldiers of these places made up the forces.

[5]Tliliuhquitepec was one of the towns in the Puebla-Tlaxcala region where the Flower War was carried out, in an arrangement between both sides.

When they reached the borders of that region, which I believe is where the plains of Otumba and Tepepulco are found, they set up camp. The people of Tliliuhquitepec, having been forced into this war and not being able to excuse themselves every time that one like this was declared, prepared their army and went to take part in the encounter. The Aztec leaders made their usual formal speeches, exhorting the troops. When the fighting started, one side mixed and clashed with the other in such a disorderly manner that they wounded and killed their opponents with much cruelty, each side struggling to capture those of the other.

The Aztecs began to tie up so many prisoners by their hands that they thought that surely they had won the battle, but on counting their own men they saw they had lost four hundred and twenty soldiers. However, when they counted their prisoners they found they had seven hundred. Although they were grieved, were deeply sad, to have lost so many of their own sons and brothers, Axayacatl consoled them by saying that the sun had wished to eat warriors on both sides.[6]

At that moment the lords of Tliliuhquitepec came to Axayacatl, saying, "O powerful lord, we have participated in this skirmish and we have been entertained by it, but if you are leaving this place in tears, we remain here even sadder. However, we can console ourselves that these activities have been those of real men. So now cease, put up your swords and be on your way with good fortune." Axayacatl thanked them and sent his good wishes to their lord, stating that he would go in peace until another time the gods might summon them to another encounter.

A messenger was then sent to Tlacaelel to report to him the results of the battle. Having arrived in Tenochtitlan, he gave the news to Tlacaelel, who, when he heard this, responded in the same way Axayacatl had spoken to his troops at the end: "My son, the sun has wished to devour men from both sides. This is what the Aztecs went for, and they knew they were exposed to great danger." He then had the drum, the conch shells, and the flutes played in the temples.

Everyone was ordered to make ready for the usual reception, except that this time the men who went out to receive the king wore red headbands and the priests had their hair braided with red cord, for these were the signs of victory and gladness. But the other half of this welcoming group left their hair loose, hanging, as a sign of sadness and mourning, because four hundred and twenty of their warriors had been lost.

---

[6]The sun "ate" the dead warriors because they went to live in his house—the sky—and guided him across the firmament each day.

All the usual ceremonies were performed. The prisoners were made to pass before the statues of Huitzilopochtli and eat some of the earth at his feet, and after having walked around the *tzompantli*—the skull rack—they were taken to the royal houses. Here they were given to eat and drink in abundance and were provided with flowers and tobacco. After this the king called his main steward and ordered that these "Sons of the Sun" be lodged in a safe place. They were called thus because it was believed that thanks to the sun the Aztecs had captives to sacrifice.

A little while after the king had entered the city, the regular army arrived. All the soldiers came in correct order, with their shields in their hands and, instead of staffs, they carried their [cotton] armor and wore their insignia, the way men who return from war were attired. The people went out to receive them and the elders greeted them with speeches, welcoming them home. All the soldiers and the captains were taken around the new Sun Stone in order to pay homage to this Likeness of the Sun.

When this circle had been completed, the military men went to the palace, where Tlacaelel greeted them warmly, saying, "My sons, welcome to our city where you have your homes, among the reeds, among the rushes, where you serve your god Huitzilopochtli. Now rest from your labors, refresh yourselves with food. But remember those great lords who died in Chalco and those who not long ago died in Mechoacan, all of them of royal blood. And remember too your brothers, your relatives, who were killed in this war with Tliliuhquitepec or who were taken captive. It is only correct that the customary mourning rites be held."

The obsequies were held in the same way as those described at the beginning of this chapter, except that in these funeral rites the men in charge, after having burned the images of resinous wood, gathered up the ashes and buried them in a special chamber.

The obsequies over, Tlacaelel and the king decided to conclude the ceremonies related to the Sun Stone. After some discussion, it was decided to invite the lords of Huexotzinco, Cholula, and Metztitlan. Tlacaelel chose six of the principal ambassadors to go to these cities, two to each. He told them to take the invitation, presenting it with these words: "On behalf of King Axayacatl we have come before your presence to advise you that the ceremony and festivities of the Sun Stone are about to be celebrated, and the king would be highly honored if you will attend, he begs you to be present."

The envoys left the city to go deliver this message. When two of the ambassadors reached Huexotzinco, they presented the invitation to Quiauhtzin Tecuhtli, who was the ruler of that city. Another two who went to Cholula gave their message to Colomoxcatl. The envoys were well received and provided with everything they desired, with food, mantles, breechcloths, and sandals. While they were eating, the lords of those two cities readied themselves to go to Mexico-Tenochtitlan. Then they said to the envoys, "We are now ready, let us go see what our nephew commands." They left their cities almost at the same time and, having reached the Aztec capital, entered the city at night so they would not be seen. Axayacatl received them cordially and had them well taken care of.

Then the lord of Metztitlan, Cozcatlohtli, arrived, entering at night like the others. This entering in a hidden manner was ordered by King Axayacatl because, since the people from those cities were opponents of the Aztecs, the king did not want their presence known, nor that they had come from those places that were enemies of Tenochtitlan. So all the honors paid to those lords were done secretly, hidden from the people.

After these three rulers had arrived, together with the sovereign of Tlaxcala, both the Stone and those who were to be sacrificed were prepared and adorned. On this occasion the king, finely attired, was to be the main sacrificer, followed by his coadjutor Tlacaelel. After them came those who impersonated the gods: Quetzalcoatl, Tlaloc, Opochtli, Itzpapalotl, Yohualahuan, Apantecuhtli, Huitzilopochtli, Toci, Cihuacoatl, Izquitecatl, Icnopilli, Mixcoatl, and Tepoztecatl, all dressed and ready to act as sacrificers.[7]

The king, who had dressed before dawn, appeared splendidly garbed. Tlacaelel, next to Axayacatl, was also dressed in magnificent clothing. Sacrificial knives in hand, they climbed to the top of the Stone. Then the prisoners came out, all smeared with chalk, their heads feathered and some long feathers in their nose plugs. [Chalk and feather balls on the head were signs of sacrifice.] The prisoners were

---

[7]The surrogates of the gods were thirteen, an important ritual number, for one thing, there was a sacred period consisting of thirteen days, the *trecena*. The gods mentioned here were Quetzalcoatl, god of civilization, patron of priesthood, related to fertility; Tlaloc, god of rain and earth's fertility; Opochtli, an aspect of the sun god, associated with the south; Itzpapalotl, an aspect of the Mother Goddess, associated with the night, darkness, and the obsidian sacrificial knife; Yohualahuan, the "Night Drinker," part of the Xipe Totec complex; Apantecuhtli, water god, one form of Tlaloc, associated with streams; Huitzilopochtli, patron god of the Aztecs; Toci, Mother Goddess, "Our Grandmother," patroness of midwives; Cihuacoatl, "Woman Serpent," one of the Mother Goddesses in her warrior aspect, deity of Xochimilco; Izquitecatl, related to pulque and sustenance; Icnopilli, associated with war and hunting; Mixcoatl, "Cloud Serpent," hunting-war god, another name for Amaxtli, related to Huitzilopochtli and worshiped in the Puebla-Tlaxcala region; and Tepoztecatl, pulque god. See Nicholson 1971.

lined up at the *tzompantli*, the skull rack, but before the sacrifice a fire priest came out of the temple carrying a great incense burner in the form of a serpent, which they call *xiuhcoatl*, "fire serpent," and which was already lit. The fire priest walked around the Stone four times, so the smoke from the incense bathed it, and finally he placed this upon the Stone, where it finished burning.

After this [purification by smoke and fire], the sacrifices began. The king sacrificed many of the prisoners until he tired. Then Tlacaelel took the sacrificial knife and continued cutting out hearts until he too became tired. After Tlacaelel stopped, the surrogates of the gods continued sacrificing the prisoners until all seven hundred captives brought from the war with Tliliuhquitepec had been killed. Their cadavers lay next to the *tzompantli*. The temple and the courtyard were bathed in blood, a frightening spectacle, something that human nature really abhors.

The king then gave his guests rich gifts: mantles, jewels, and precious feathers. After they had been well fed and had received many attentions, they were told they could leave. These men were so amazed, so terrified, at this horrible thing that they had witnessed that they were glad to go home.

Once the guests had left, King Axayacatl became ill from exhaustion in the long ceremony and from the smell of the blood, which had, according to our chronicle, a bad sour odor. Feeling very ill, he begged Tlacaelel to have his image carved on the rocks at Chapultepec next to that of Motecuhzoma before he, Axayacatl, died.

Tlacaelel gave orders that this be done, and when it was finished the king, although very sick, was carried to see his likeness. Having seen his portrait, he said farewell to all his lords because he felt death approaching. The *Historia* tells us that he did not return to the city alive but that he died on the road as he was carried on the litter.

He died young, having reigned thirteen years. Nezahualcoyotl, lord and king of Tezcoco, had died earlier and Axayacatl had been present at his solemn funeral. Nezahualpiltzintli, son of Nezahualcoyotl, was now sovereign of Tezcoco. Axayacatl's reign was a period of constant friction among neighboring nations. There was great enmity and combat between Ocuila and Cuauhnahuac, Ocuila having vanquished the latter. Huexotla rebelled against Tezcoco and waged war against that city. Xiquipilco rebelled and fought against its own brothers and neighbors.

In this way ends this chapter.

CHAPTER XXXIX

Which treats of the gifts that the lords brought to the deceased King Axayacatl and the speeches that were made on this occasion. And of the election of the seventh king, called Tizocicatzin.

King Axayacatl died in the year 1481. After the lengthy funeral rites and ceremonies and the giving of presents were over, it was evident that a new king must be chosen. That same year Tizocicatzin was elected legitimately, by common consent, by the votes of the lords and of all the people. However, before we deal with him, since his life was short and his deeds few, I wish to describe the funeral rites of King Axayacatl, since the *Historia* discusses them in great detail.

Before Tizocicatzin was elected, Tlacaelel sent a message to the king of Tezcoco, Nezahualpiltzintli (although another manuscript says that it was Nezahualcoyotl, that he was still alive at that time), advising him of the death of the king of Mexico-Tenochtitlan. The rulers of Tacuba and the other provinces were also notified. Once the news was known, great mourning and sorrow were prevalent over all the land. The rulers began to weep in front of the messengers and to bemoan the passing of such a young and courageous king.

The lord Nezahualpilli rose from his throne and ordered those of his household to prepare everything necessary so he could go present his respects to the dead king. He came to Tenochtitlan and, having greeted all the authorities, he directed himself to the room where the body lay and offered the dead king four slaves, two men and two women, a labret, ear pendants, a nose pendant, and a diadem, all of gold, also two gold armbands, two anklets of the same metal, and a splendid bow with its arrows. He also offered feathered ornaments of fine green feathers, and others of eagle feathers, a richly worked mantle, a handsome breechcloth, beautiful sandals, and an exquisite necklace from which hung a golden jewel. Having placed these gifts near the body, he stood there weeping, next to the deceased, and spoke thus:

> O my son, O youthful, courageous and excellent Axayacatl Tecuhtli, this is the last time that I shall gaze upon your countenance. You have now gone to the place where you will meet your fathers, relatives and noble ancestors. Like the bird that flies, you have gone there to rejoice in the Lord of All Created Things, of the Day and the Night, of the Wind

and Fire. I have brought you this small gift for your comfort in that other world.

When the king of Tezcoco had uttered these words, the sovereign of Tacuba came in and spoke:

> O my son, you have left your city of Tenochtitlan, your republic, alone and unprotected. It is now in the hands of the Lord of All Created Things, who will decide what to do with that city, tomorrow or another day. You have abandoned your labors forever. Your subjects can no longer appeal to you or seek your shelter as they used to. You have now reached the land of your lordly kinsmen and ancestors. There you lie, there you rest in the shade of the dark fields, of the nine mouths of death, of the glittering house of fire of the sun, together with your ancestors. Let your body rest now, O my son!

And after he had made an offering of slaves, gems, and cloth, as the other king had done, the lords of Chalco came and addressed the deceased: "O mighty lord, may you find yourself in bliss. May your body rest, may your body be calm in death. The Lord of All Created Things bestowed your presence and strength upon us, your Chalca vassals, for a few days." They offered him five slaves, beautifully worked mantles and breechcloths, many jewels, feathers, and a large load of tree bark and resinous wood. This was used to burn the corpses of kings and therefore this type of firewood was much revered.

The delegates from Cuauhnahuac and all the hot country arrived and offered up the same lamentation:

> O powerful lord, unhappy death has cut the thread of your reign, which had been given you by the Lord of All Created Things, of Night and Day. You have left your noble kinsmen alone and disconsolate. You have gone to the place where those who lived before you also have gone. Behold us here in your presence, weeping and filled with sorrow, together with those from our province, for all are in deep mourning. The land has lost a great king and lord, one who was the image of our god Huitzilopochtli. We are all orphans now, we are forsaken.

The men from Yauhtepec, Huaxtepec, Yacapichtlan, and Tepoztlan then entered and, after each one had addressed the dead king in formal rhetoric, gave him four slaves. These slaves were called *tepan tlacaltin* or *teixpan miquiz teuicaltin*, "those who follow the deceased to accompany him." And so we know what kind of slaves these were: they were the domestic slaves who served the nobility, having been obtained by purchase or through a lawsuit. Prisoners of war were used only for the gods. The lords bringing condolences also offered paper, bundles of cloth, feathers, and many jewels and ornaments.

The gifts brought to the deceased Axayacatl

The representatives of Xochimilco then came and spoke to the dead Axayacatl:

> O mighty lord, our hearts are grieved and burn with pain as we see that you have lost your speech and can no longer answer us. You have hidden your face from us and we rejoice in it no longer. All we can do is weep and moan over your departure, since death has taken you away from us forever. Here we have brought you this small gift to serve you in your perilous journey into the other world.

They too offered slaves, mantles, and jewels, then they left and the lords of Tepeaca arrived. They made the ritual speeches and gave presents of slaves, richly worked cloth, jewels, feathers, and women's *huipiles* or blouses and skirts, all of which was to be taken to the other world to be distributed there. The lords of Cuetlaxtla came in and, having spoken in the same formal way, they presented five men and five women, cloth, featherwork, cacao, precious stones, armbands, diadems, labrets, and ear pendants, all of them gold, along with elaborate fans and fine birds of green, blue, and red plumage. They said that all these things were given to be used in the other world, where the Lords of All Created Things had placed the deceased.

After all these noblemen had paid their visits, emissaries from Tlaxcala, Huexotzinco, and Cholula came in secretly at night, in order not to be seen. Going in secret to the chamber where Tlacaelel was, they consoled him and told him that they sorrowed greatly over the death of King Axayacatl. They had brought with them the tears and sadness of their respective states, for this death had affected them deeply. They had also brought things from their cities for the funeral rites. Thereupon they delivered many bows and arrows, cloaks, breechcloths and girdles of agave fiber, animal skins, eagle feathers, little bells for the feet, and other objects.

After the emissaries from all these cities and provinces had made their offerings, lamented, and spoken ceremonial words to the dead king, the Aztec authorities, including Tlacaelel, thanked them profusely, each one speaking in a lengthy and flowery manner, in his turn. This is the way these affairs were carried out. Food was then brought for the large number of guests assembled there, and it was so well served and so abundant that it was not only sufficient for these noblemen but enough was left over for their servants: great quantities of breads, fine dishes prepared with fowl, and chocolate beverages. Flowers and tobacco were also plentiful. After the meal, rich mantles and breechcloths were brought from the king's treasury and were given to all the guests, except the three sovereigns from enemy territory—Cholula, Tlaxcala, and Huexotzinco—who were presented not only with mantles but also with fine weapons. Each one received a shield and sword. All the guests were highly pleased and, having given thanks to the lords of Tenochtitlan, left with their gifts for their own lands.

However, after the noblemen from the other side of the Sierra Nevada, the snow-peaked mountains [that is, from Cholula, Tlaxcala, and Huextozinco], had departed, the others stayed for a while in the city, where a great bower was prepared. This was called the *tlacochcalli*.[1] Within the bower was placed a statue that was the image of the dead king. This figure was made of slivers of resinous wood bound together. Its face imitated that of a human being; its head was feathered with plumes called *ichcaxochitl*, "cotton flowers," and others called *malacaquetzalli*, "spindle-whorl feathers," together with a breastplate of featherwork. The figure was dressed in the splendid garments worn by the god Huitzilopochtli, whom he then represented.

Over these vestments the image of the king was dressed with the garments of the god Tlaloc so that he represented that deity. Upon his head was a crown of white heron feathers mixed with others that were green. In one hand he held a shield of fine quality and in the other a stick carved in the form of lightning, such as that carried by Tlaloc. In this way he also became the image of the god of thunderbolts and rain. He was also attired with a garment like a surplice and was given a spear.

The third garment placed on the figure, over the other two, was that of Yohualahuan, the god associated with the night. With this came a diadem of fine feathers, a shield in one hand and in the other a staff with rattles at the end.

The fourth set of garments worn by the image of Axayacatl were those of the deity Quetzalcoatl. On the head was placed a mask in the form of a jaguar but which had a bird beak like that of geese from Peru. Since Quetzalcoatl was the god of wind he wore flowing garments like wings with rounded edges and a breechcloth with rounded borders. A small cape finished this costume; it was called the [*papalotilmatli*] butterfly mantle.

After the king had been dressed in the manner of these four gods whom he represented, the chanters began to sing hymns and songs of the dead. While they sang, all the deceased's wives, with their hair loose, appeared carrying vessels and dishes of breads and other foods that they had cooked. They placed these in front of the image of Axayacatl together with gourds of chocolate. Then the noblemen entered, carrying flowers and tobacco in the smoking tubes they used.

[1]See glossary for *tlacochcalli*.

The gifts brought to the deceased Axayacatl

These were deposited before the statue of the king. Then came the men with incense, who one by one incensed the statue.

When these rites had ended, the unfortunate slaves who were to serve the dead man in the hereafter were dressed. The women were given fine new blouses and skirts and on their backs were placed the small boxes and baskets in which the king had kept the finery with which he adorned himself: ear pendants, labrets, nose plugs, the elaborate cloaks he had worn, breechcloths, and his other fine adornments. All of these things were tied to the bodies of slaves of both sexes who were to die. Every male or female slave the king had possessed was brought in, and so were the hunchbacks and dwarfs who had served him. All were adorned with jewels, feathers, golden armbands, earrings, and rattles on their feet. They were given the blowguns with which the king had hunted, his bow and arrows, and another weapon that shot pellets.[2] After this the singers began their funeral chants that were special for these occasions. Then all the people of the city began to weep, and wept for some time. Meanwhile priests came, carrying gourds of pulque, which they drank and also poured around the room—at the sides, in the front and in the back, in all the corners of the chamber.

The statue was then picked up by the principal men, who carried it before the idol Huitzilopochtli together with the body of the deceased. Both were set afire, and while they burned those in charge of the cremation went about poking the fire with some sticks so that it burned quickly.

Once the statue and the body had been reduced to ashes, the priests brought in some green gourds filled with water and sprinklers made of laurel branches. Each of the great men—lords, chieftains, warriors, and valiant captains—was sprinkled in the face with that water. They all stood in line and received it, one by one. Also sprinkled with the laurel branches were the widows of the king and the other ladies who were present. After the sprinkling had ended, the noblemen turned to the slaves, saying: "O brothers, go in peace to serve your lord and master, our King Axayacatl. Go along the way consoling him, encouraging him. See that he lacks nothing in the way of jewelry; do not drop any of these things on the way. Serve him with care and see that he lacks nothing, that he always has enough of this food and of his beverage. Take care that you have everything; do not make any mistakes."

---

[2] A burial with rich grave goods is usually interpreted as that of a person of high status, but here Durán tells us that the individual may have been the servant of the sovereign or of another nobleman, simply carrying the fine objects for his master in the afterlife.

The wretches gave thanks to the lords and, weeping, said farewell. The hunchbacks, dwarfs, and domestic servants from the palace were then addressed and were told to take great care in preparing the water for the hands of their master, to give him his clothing and his sandals, as they had done until now. They were advised to hand him his comb and the mirror they carried, and to furnish him with his blowgun or bow and arrows, should he need them. "Take care that nothing be lacking on this road; go and serve your king as best you can."

Next to the king's ashes was placed a *teponaztli*, which is the drum they play when they dance, and on the *teponaztli* the slaves were cast down on their backs, their breasts cut open, and their hearts torn out. The blood was gathered in certain vessels and poured upon the fire where the body of the king had burned. When all the slaves, hunchbacks, dwarfs, and female slaves had been killed (and more than fifty or sixty persons lost their lives on this occasion) and their blood had been thrown on the fire, thus extinguishing it, the buriers took the ashes and, after having made a hole at the feet of Huitzilopochtli, buried them there along with the hearts of the dead servitors and the gems, feathers, and mantles that had been offered. The singers then came with the gourds of water and laurel branches and again sprinkled water on all those present, sparing no one.

These rites having ended, the leading men of Tenochtitlan, who were the four members of the royal council, arose and thanked all the guests assembled there. They kissed their hands on behalf of the council and all the city. They said that the Lord of All Created Things had put out the torch, had hidden the light of Tenochtitlan, and had silenced the voice of the one who had directed and ruled over all with that voice. On hearing this everyone wept anew.

The visitors again gave thanks and then left for their own cities. All the Aztecs, together with the widows and kinsmen of the deceased, fasted for eighty days. At the end of this time, another statue was made and was dressed in the manner that has been described. More slaves, the same number, were killed, and the same ceremonies were performed: the songs and dancing, food and drink, the sprinkling of water, burning the statue, pouring the blood of the victims over the image, and burying the ashes with the hearts of the sacrificed slaves and with all the jewels and riches the king had possessed. This rite was called "the end of the year," as we say here. In this way kings and lords who died were honored long ago, by carrying out these ceremonies.

Four days after these rites in honor of Axayacatl had come to an end, the news spread that Tizocicatzin ("Chalk Leg"), also known as Tlalchitonatiuh, meaning "Setting Sun," had been chosen to be the new king. When this was known in Tezcoco and Tacuba and in the other cities, the lords lost no time in going to Tenochtitlan to pay their respects and swear obedience to the new ruler, since this was the custom. Thus, the king of Tezcoco and his principal men arrived, as did the king of Tacuba with his nobles. Then came those of Chalco and Xochimilco with representatives of the entire *chinampa* region: ambassadors from Cuitlahuac, Mezquic, Colhuacan, Mexicatzinco, and Itztapalapa. The Matlatzincas, Mazahuas, Coatlapanecas, and the lords of all the hot country came. They kissed the Aztec king's hands and presented him with fine gifts of great richness. The king of Tezcoco then gave the official salutation in this manner:

While Tizoc stood, the Tezcoco king took a golden diadem set with green stones and placed it upon the head of the young monarch. He pierced the cartilage of his nose and inserted a nose plug of green emerald, of the thickness of a quill for writing. In his ear he placed two jade spools adorned with gold, on his arms two bracelets of shining gold that reached from the mid-arm to the shoulder, and on his legs were placed two anklets with golden bells hanging from them. With this own hands Tizoc donned his jaguar-skin sandals, which were handsomely adorned with gold. He put on a fine cloak made of agave fiber they call *pita*. The cloth was very thin and resplendent with gold and with [embroidered or] painted designs. His breechcloth was of the same fine material.

The king of Tezcoco then took him by the hand and led him to a throne called Cuauhicapalli, "Eagle seat," also called "Jaguar Seat" [Oceloicpalli]. It was called thus because it was decorated with eagle feathers and jaguar skins. The other chieftains placed him on their shoulders and carried him in the "Eagle-Jaguar" seat to the summit of the pyramid-temple, where they set him down next to the image of the god Huitzilopochtli. They placed in Tizoc's hand a sharp jaguar bone adorned with gold and with this he let blood from the ears, shinbone, and calves. When this penance was ended, they carried him out and brought him to the Sun Stone, which they called the *cuauhxicalli* or "eagle vessel." There he again performed autosacrifice or bloodletting on the same parts of his body and many quail were brought to him, which he beheaded with his own hands upon the stone. He then poured their blood into the depression in the middle of the stone. With an incense burner they gave him he offered incense to the four parts of the world—to the east, west, north, and south.

The new king was then carried to the place where the elders slept. He entered a dark room. This was where the goddess Cihuacoatl was kept. It was called Tlillan, meaning "Blackness." There he again pierced his body in the same places and killed more quail before the goddess. He then offered incense in the dark room where all the statues of the gods were kept.

After this he visited a place called Yopico where the god Yopi was kept, and once more he bled his ears, arms, and shins, killed quail, and offered incense. In this way he visited five of the main gods, where he let blood, sacrificed quail, and incensed the statues and the chambers. When these five visits had ended, he was brought back to his dwelling place, where he was again placed upon the royal seat. The king of Tezcoco, who had given him the royal insignia, then addressed Tizoc:

> O powerful lord, O valiant youth, you have received this royal dais of fine rich feathers, and the chamber of precious stones from the god Quetzalcoatl, the great Topiltzin, and from the marvelous, wondrous Huitzilopochtli; they have left these to you. But this royal seat is only lent to you, not forever, only for a short time upon this earth. This seat was enhanced, was made illustrious by those valorous sovereigns, your forefathers, especially your grandfather Motecuhzoma, he of excellent, supreme remembrance. Throughout his long life he raised this position to heights it had never reached before. Therefore, O lord, take care that these heights are maintained in your time. Do not be careless, be aware of your actions. Take care of the orphan, of the widow, the old man and the old woman who can work no longer, for they are the eyelashes and eyebrows of Huitzilopochtli, they are the palms of his hands. The Eagles and the Jaguars, the courageous, brave men, are these things above all. They are the wall around your land, they are its defense, and they exalt these things with the shedding of their blood. And with this, O lord, my address comes to an end.

The ruler of Tacuba then gave the same kind of formal talk, and after him so did the lords of the other cities and provinces. To repeat these all here, with their elegant speech and metaphors, would give great pleasure and would reveal their manner of ritual speaking and in reality would not be too verbose. Yet I shall refrain from putting down all these addresses because every one ended by recommending that the king maintain a good government, take care of the poor, honor and favor valiant men who were responsible for good deeds, that the king defend his homeland and honor and revere the gods.[3]

Having presented the new king with the same insignia as those given by the lord of Tezcoco, as well as splendid gifts (some more magnificent than others), and the speeches having terminated, these men returned to their own cities, leaving King Tizoc on his throne.

---

[3]Garibay (Durán 1967:II:580) rightly compares these formal speeches to the *huehuetlatolli*, "words of the elders," in Sahagún's *Florentine Codex* (book 6, chaps. X to XVI).

CHAPTER XL

Which treats of how the Aztecs waged war on Metztitlan in order to bring victims for the festivities of the coronation and anointing of their king.

After the kings and lords from the neighboring cities had left Mexico-Tenochtitlan and the Aztecs had evidenced their pleasure and satisfaction with the new king, the principal men of this city decided to make a solemn festival for their ruler, in honor of his coronation and anointment. It was agreed that on the day that the unction was over and the pitch removed, there should be a great sacrifice of men, and that Metztitlan should be invaded in order to bring victims from that place to be sacrificed. This could not be done without war being waged because the sacrificial victims had to be captains taken in battle. These decisions made, messages were sent to Tezcoco, Tacuba, Chalco, Xochimilco, the Hot Lands, and other friendly provinces, as well as to Cuauhtlalpan and to the Matlatzinca people, ordering them to prepare to go to war against Metztitlan so that King Tizoc could be honored. The lords of all those places, on receiving these orders, answered that they were in agreement. The people complied with such speed that in a few days news reached the city of Tenochtitlan that the allies were ready and were waiting for the next commands.

The king, during the period of anointing, while he fasted and did penitence, while he kept a vigil over the royal insignia, did not yet rule in any way. Therefore, everyone went to Tlacaelel for orders. He commanded all the soldiers who were prepared for war to gather in Atotonilco or in Itzmiquilpan and to await there for the rest of the army. This message received, all the soldiers were ordered to march to those places, with no exceptions. And so it was that by the third day not one man who had prepared himself for war, who desired this, was left.

When it was known in Tenochtitlan that all the allies had followed Tlacaelel's orders, the Aztec army was also given orders to leave. All the men, very well armed, left the city. The lords went for Tizoc and took him with them and the rest of the army. Since the king was very young and was not yet experienced in war, Tlacaelel earnestly recommended to the others that they take good care of him, that they not leave him alone but that he always be accompanied by his guards. In this way, then, they left the city and when they reached Tezontepec they found the king of Tezcoco and his men waiting for them. He greeted Tizoc, gave him a comfortable place to rest, and offered him and his officials an excellent and satisfying meal.

After they had eaten, they all left and went to Atotonilco, where the rest of the army waited. King Tizoc summoned the men there and those who had come from Itzmiquilpan and addressed them thus: "Brothers, I have come to test my strength against the soldiers of Metztitlan. Now I want you to do one thing—go into battle by yourselves, because the enemy believes that you alone are waging this war. And if they seem to overcome you we shall come out to relieve you and then capture all we can."

In this way the Atotonilcas and Itzmiquilpas went out to meet the enemy and fought as well as they could, but were unable to defeat them and began to retreat. When Tizoc and his officials were informed of this, all the allied troops attacked. These were the Aztecs, Chalcas, Tezcocans, Tepanecs, Xochimilcas, Tlahuicas, and Mazahuas. The Metztitlan people had requested aid from the Huaxtecs, who, when they saw this multitude roaring at them, nevertheless stood firm and then counterattacked. In this attack three hundred of Tizoc's men were killed, which was a disaster for his army. The Aztecs, desperate and not knowing how to get out of this situation, threw a squadron of young boys into the fray. These were youths of eighteen to twenty years old. Boys of this age always accompanied the regular army to war but just as observers and in order to lose fear of fighting in the future. They were given weapons and were ordered to attack with courage and to do all they could in order to win the reputation of brave warriors. These youths and the soldiers who had come to rest were given a bowl each of *chian* gruel.[1] Then the youths attacked with such spirit that they captured forty valiant soldiers, among those of Metztitlan and the Huaxtecs. When it was seen that these had been captured, most of the enemy troops disbanded. The Aztecs forced them to cross a river called Quetzalatl, while the Metztitlan forces, which had been winning, were made to retreat. This was done by the youths, who achieved what the regular army had failed to do. The Metztitlan men then broke camp and went back to their cities.

When the Aztecs saw that the enemy had fled, that there was nothing left for them to do, they summoned their own men to the Aztec camp. Then the king called the captains from the provinces to his shelter, where he addressed them: "Lords, brave soldiers and captains, we have done everything we set out to do, nothing more was

---

[1]*Chian*, a type of sage used for making a refreshing beverage, *Salvia hispanica*.

possible. I see that three hundred of our sons, brothers, and nephews have fallen. We are subject to this misfortune but we also came with the intention of being victorious. If there is one honor we have won in this war it is that which we owe to those youths, and because of them we are returning home alive. They can glory in this, I honor them for the success of this battle. We have few captives. But I am grateful to all of you for your participation; let each one go with our god to his home. We have done all we can here."

The soldiers thanked the king, and each one went on his way. The Aztec chieftains accompanied their king, left with him. When they reached a town called Chicuauhtlan, they sent messengers ahead to advise Tlacaelel how the war had terminated, how the Aztecs and their allies had met with ill fortune, having lost three hundred men while capturing only forty. And that it had been the young boys who had taken these prisoners—to them was owed the honor and the glory.

Tlacaelel was greatly saddened at the loss of their men. He ordered that the drums, conch shells, and flutes be played and that lookouts be placed at the summit of the temples to observe the arrival of the king and the army so they could be received correctly. When the time came, the elders and priests, all richly adorned, went out in proper order to greet their ruler and the soldiers. They stood in line, on both sides of the road, incense burners in hand. The old soldiers who could no longer go to war, the Cuauh Huehuetque, "Old Eagles," who were tired of fighting and had retired from this activity, went out completely armed, with shields and with swords that served as staffs, their heads adorned with leather bands and eagle feathers. They all lined up in the same order as the priests.

The first to arrive were the prisoners, all tied together, one behind another. The youths who had captured these men came with them, each one next to his captive. After they had been welcomed, the usual ceremonies began. Smoke from the incense was blown over the captives, for they were the gift, the grant, of the sun and of Huitzilopochtli. These prisoners began to sing lamentations and to whistle and cry out. In this way they entered the city and went directly to the temple of Huitzilopochtli, where they came to the image of the god and, standing before the idol, each one took earth with his finger and ate this earth. After all had done this, they were taken to the palace. Here they greeted Tlacaelel and were given abundant food and drink, flowers, and tobacco. Certain officials or majordomos then took charge of them.

Soon the king and his captains reached the city. He was received with ceremony, after which the old men began to weep for the loss the Aztecs had suffered. This weeping was a regular ritual. They addressed the king and the warriors who accompanied him with long speeches, weeping all the while, and in this way they came to the temple. As they went toward the image of Huitzilopochtli, the old men came crying, "O unhappy Aztecs who left your city and will see it no more! But—what can be done? You joined the army of death for the honor of our god Huitzilopochtli. And now all have gone, hands clasped, to see and enjoy the House of the Sun, before whom you will be flying!" Crying out these and many other sad words that made the people weep, they passed before the feet of the statue and then went around the Sun Stone.

The king went to the palace, where he sat upon the royal seat. There the officials who had remained on guard in the city came to pay him their respects. After this the elders went to give condolences to the widows whose husbands had lost their lives on the battlefield or who had been taken captive by the enemy. They made lengthy, wordy, consolatory speeches, one at a time, and when these addresses were over the widows thanked them and gave them food and gifts of clothing. These visits were part of the elders' obligations.

When the city was quiet again, Tlacaelel called the chieftains, saying, "Brothers, let us finish the solemn enthronment and royal rites of our king, since this is our duty, not his. Let us call, let us invite, all the rulers from the neighboring states: Tezcoco, Tacuba, Chalco, Xochimilco and the *chinampa* region, Colhuacan, Itztapalapa, Mexicatzinco, Huitzilopochco, those of the Hot Country, and those of Cuauhtlalpan, Matlatzinco, Toluca, and Coatlalpan." This was agreed upon by all the lords and the invitations for the celebration were sent by messengers. At the same time word was sent to all the towns and cities that were controlled by Aztec governors or where Aztec stewards were posted, requesting them to provide supplies and food from those places that would be required for the festivities. And they were all invited to attend. So the city began to receive great quantities of fine cloth, some more elegant than others, as well as innumerable jewels and feathers, cacao, flowers, fruit, turkeys, many kinds of bread and maize cakes, rabbits, quail, deer, and other game. And from places next to the sea or waterways came such an abundance of fish that it was a thing of wonder. The officials and men in charge of these supplies came with them. Accompanying all the things to be used and consumed in the splendid festivities were the following lords:

> The governor of Cuetlaxtla.
> The governor of Tochtla,
> of Tziccoatl, of Tozapan,
> of Cuauhnahuac and of Yauhtepec,
> of Huaxtepec, of Acapichtlan,

of Couixco, of Uitzoco, and of Tepecuacuilco,
of Tlachmalac, of Youallan,
of Tepetlan, of Nochtepec, of Teotliztac,
of Tlachco, of Tzacualpan, and of Itztapan.

And the lords and governors of the Totoltecas,

of Chiauhtla, of Piaztlan, and of Teotlala,
of Cuitlatenanco, of Cuauhapazco,
of Xochhuehuetlan, of Olinalan,
of Tlalcozauhtitlan,
of Malinaltzinco and Toluca,
of Tzinacantepec, of Tlacotepec, and Calimayan,
of Tepemaxalco, and of Teotenanco.

Then came all those from the mountain regions:

Malinalco, Ocuila, Coatepec, Capuloac,
Xalatlauhco and Atlapulco.

In sum, all the cities and provinces subject to the royal crown of Mexico-Tenochtitlan.[2] The emissaries from these places arrived with wealth and supplies and were lodged in the house of the principal steward, who was called the *petlacalcatl*, which means, loosely, "principal official who is in charge of the royal storehouses, the keeper of the king's treasure." It was he who brought before the king all the representatives of the cities and provinces mentioned above. The king was on his royal seat next to the old man Tlacaelel. Said the Petlacalcatl, "O lord, all your majordomos and treasurers from the cities and provinces have come and they wish to kiss your royal hands." The king ordered them to come before him, which they did, prostrating themselves upon the earth before their ruler, bowing and humiliating themselves as they were wont to do. These people know well how to feign humility and pretend that they are lower than the earth itself when they are in the presence of their superiors.

These men offered gifts of all kinds found in the districts or jurisdictions under their charge (and these men can be called municipal officials because they are in charge of their districts). Some brought gold, others jewels, bracelets, labrets, shields and other weapons, sandals, jaguar and wildcat skins, mantles, and birds. Others offered fine feathers. They presented these gifts to the king, who thanked them. He then asked if everything was ready for the banquet that had been planned. He was told that all was prepared, that nothing was lacking.

---

[2]This list of cities and provinces is a good reference to the extent of Aztec dominion.

The king then ordered that the entire palace be decorated, that every room be adorned with flowers and branches and reed mats and seats, as lavishly as possible. In this way the royal house was prepared, with nothing lacking, with such care and attention that the whole city was stirred up. Everyone was busy with so much activity and with the hubbub of the outsiders who had arrived with provisions, and the decorating of the palace, that the city seemed not to have enough room for all these things. And since these people knew very well how to make preparations for festivities, they adorned the royal houses with flowers and branches in such a way that it could not have been more splendid.

When everything was ready and the day for the public coronation had arrived (and the ritual "lavatory," which was the anointing of the king), as well as the accompanying festivities, the principal men of the city, by order of Tlacaelel, performed the following ceremony: they took a gold diadem, two bracelets and two leg ornaments made of gold, some gold ear pendants, a very fine labret and a nose plug, a handsome mantle and breechcloth. These were placed before the king by the sovereign of Tezcoco, Nezahualpiltzintli, who then said, "O powerful lord, your administrator Tlacaelel sends you these gifts and wishes to tell you that since you, Tizocic Tlalchihtonatiuh, are king of this city of Tenochtitlan, he begs you to come out and dance on this day of your enthronement." And, depositing many flowers and beautiful feathers before Tizoc, Nezahualpilli continued, "The election was a fortunate one, because of that I have come and shall be happy to dance and rejoice."

Then the ruler of Tacuba came, stating much the same and offering another gift consisting of fine garments to dress the new king from head to foot. This sovereign spoke about the election of Tizocic; he requested that his gift be accepted and that the new ruler would come out to dance. The king answered that he was pleased this friend had come to their ceremonies.

In this way all the lords from the different cities and provinces came one by one [and gave presents to the young king]. They were then given gifts of mantles and breechcloths, finely worked and very valuable, ear pendants, labrets, nose plugs, and headbands, all of gold; splendidly adorned sandals, and garlands, some with feathers added. Everyone was given flowers and tobacco. When each one had received his presents, he was reminded that Tizocic was now the king of Mexico-Tenochtitlan, that they should not forget it, and that these presents were given to them so they would enjoy the festivities and dance there, showing their pleasure for all they had received.

Then, before dawn came, the royal singers appeared with a drum, which they placed in the middle of the royal courtyard, called by these people the *tlatocaithualli*. These musicians were handsomely dressed in splendid clothing, with much gold, jewels, and feathers, all in honor of that day. They began to play and sing lordly and solemn songs. When they heard these, the kings and noblemen all went out and danced in a slow, solemn way. About two thousand high-ranking men joined in this dance. All were splendidly dressed and adorned, at the cost of the king and his treasury.

When all were dancing, with no exceptions, the king came out. On his head he wore a gold diadem set with precious stones, with many gold pendants and with fine plumage. He also wore ear pendants consisting of two round green stones in each. These were set in gold and were very striking. His labret was of fine jade also set in gold, and his nose plug was of a fine transparent green that pierced the cartilage of his nose. At each end of this nose plug were set some little blue plumes, similar to peacock feathers, so that combined with the green stone they created a lovely water-like effect. His gold armlets covered the arms from the shoulder to the crook of the arm and on his legs he wore calf-coverings, on his feet jaguar skin sandals. All these were adorned with gold and green and blue stones. He wore two mantles loosely crossed under his arm; they were of the finest work possible, embroidered and woven with feathers. The breechcloth was wide and also beautifully worked, with a fringe that covered the thighs, the legs down to the knees, and the buttocks. In his right hand Tizoc carried a thurible in which incense burned. The leading men of the court followed him, one of them carrying the bag of incense while the others carried quail to be sacrificed, or the royal insignia, and weapons—a shield, a sword, and bow and arrows.

As the king reached the drum, incense was thrown into the burner and he then incensed the drum with this smoke. When the incensing was finished, one of the men took the censer from the king and gave him the quail, which he then sacrificed to the drum, to the god of dance, who was usually painted [or carved] on the surface of the *teponaztli*, or at the bottom of this drum. After having sacrificed the quail, Tizoc returned to his chambers and his royal seat, then he had his finest mantles brought to him. With his own hands he placed these mantles on the shoulders of the lords and presented them with breechcloths and sashes. He told them that they had won these things through their own efforts, that they had a right to enjoy them. "These are yours, won by the shedding of your own blood, so now take pleasure in them." He continued presenting them with these rewards for bravery and placed on their heads gold bands, in their noses and ears and lips labrets, ear pendants, and nose plugs of gold adorned with fine stones and feathers. He gave them flowers and tobacco. Then, thus splendidly arrayed, all went out to dance.

Following this, the king called the courageous warriors who belonged to the Order of Warriors of the Sun (whom we have described: those men who retreated not a foot in war but rather would die) and when they were before him he gave them the finest mantles available. He then addressed them, telling them to enjoy that which they had won with the strength of their arms and by those of their forefathers. At the same time he gave them jewels and precious stones for the ears and nose and mouth, together with flowers and tobacco. The warriors then went out to dance.

Another group of high-ranking warriors was summoned. These were the Tequihuaque [the captains whose special task it was to obtain sacrificial victims for the gods]. The king gave them elaborate mantles and insignia, though different from the others, plus jewels, flowers, and tobacco. Then he ordered them to dance and take pleasure, for their feats and those of their forebears had merited these things. Still another order of warriors came before the king. These were the Otomi and one could recognize them because their hair was cropped short, one or two fingers above the ear, with a round cut done with a blade. These men were given a still different type of mantle, each according to his rank, together with the jewels the men of this rank were permitted to wear. Taking the flowers and tobacco, they joined the other warriors in the dance and festivities. All these military men were responsible for much of the tribute received by the city.

The king then gave clothing and other useful gifts to the priests, the elderly, and the young ones. He gave clothing to the ministers of all the temples, the large temples, and even the small ones, and to all those who served in these, and to the guards. The priests and chaplains of the barrio temples also received these gifts, as did, finally, everyone who served in a temple in any way. Tizoc then had all the old people in the four quarters sought out, and the orphans and the poor, all of whom were presented with clothing. Each person was then given flowers. All thanked the king profusely, then they went to dance and enjoy the festivities. And this dancing went on all day.

On the following day, before dawn, Tlacaelel rose and went to the king's chamber to awaken him and to adorn him in the same way he had been garbed the previous day, then both went out to dance with the noblemen. They said that their days were numbered and that they wished to pass them in contentment and pleasure since in the other world they would not sing or dance or take pleasure in the bouquet of flowers or smoke tobacco, because these activities were denied to those who were deceased.

When they went out, the nobility came to offer garlands of flowers delicately arranged and handsomely decorated pipes of tobacco, to both men, and to the kings of the two provinces.[3] All the lords and principal men of the provinces rose and, in order to make the festival even more solemn, ate wild mushrooms that are said to make a man lose his senses. In that way they then went out to dance. After everyone had danced a while, the king again gave the lords rich mantles and jewels, just as we have already described.

The dancing, the feasting and banqueting, and the presenting of fine cloth and jewels, such as we have mentioned, lasted four days. On the fourth day the king summoned all the ministers of the temples and again gave them clothing, and on the same day presented fine mantles and jewels to all the officials and district leaders of the different towns and provinces. Each one received these gifts according to his rank and the time he had held the office.

On the day called Cipactli, which was the first day of the month, represented as a kind of serpent's head, and which always was the day when kings were enthroned, all the prisoners taken in Metztitlan (even though they were few in number) were taken out and sacrificed on the Sun Stone. After the captives had been killed, the visitors left for their towns and the city was alone with its king. The *Historia* states that this ruler reigned only four or five years and that he spent much of his time in seclusion. He showed no initiative but was pusillanimous and cowardly.

During this time Tlacaelel urged Tizoc to finish the building of the Great Temple because only a small part had been constructed. But before the work could begin, members of Tizoc's court, angered by his weakness and lack of desire to enlarge and glorify the Aztec nation, hastened his death with something they gave him to eat. He died in the year 1486, still a young man. His death was immediately made known in all the reign and his funeral rites were the same as those of the last king. The lords and rulers came from the other cities and towns, bringing with them slaves and gifts. These obsequies lasted four days, then after eighty days — "at the end of the year" — another four days of rites took place with the same solemnity. Many slaves and hunchbacks and dwarfs were killed, with all the slaves of the king's household, so that not one was left and so they would accompany the king to serve him in the other world. All his jewels and wealth were buried together with his ashes.

The remarkable thing about this burial is that after the body had been dressed in the likeness of four gods and had been placed before

---

[3]Durán must be referring to the rulers of Tezcoco and Tacuba as well as to Tizoc and Tlacaelel.

The History of the Indies of New Spain

the statue of Huitzilopochtli, at the time of the cremation, those in charge of the fire appeared naked, their bodies painted black and their faces covered with soot, very black. Their hair was frizzy and also very black. Paper breechcloths covered their private parts. They carried pointed sticks made of oak with which they pushed the king's body to and fro in the fire. These sticks were painted with red ochre.

After them came the King and Lord of the Underworld, dressed like a diabolical creature. In place of eyes he wore shining mirrors; his mouth was huge and fierce; his hair was curled; he had two hideous horns; and on each shoulder he wore a mask with mirror eyes. On each elbow there was one of these faces, on his abdomen another, and on his knees still other faces with eyes.[4] With the shining of the mirrors that represented eyes on all these parts, it looked as if he could see in every direction. He was so hideous, so abominable, that no one dared look at him out of fear. This man who represented the Lord of the Underworld carried in his hand another stick painted with red ochre and he went about the fire giving orders to the others, urging them to hurry in turning the corpse in the flames. Our chronicle says that sometimes he even poked at it himself.

The chronicle also says that at this funeral there was a man with a green gourd in his hand and a sprinkler made of laurel leaves. He went about sprinkling all those present. He was dressed to impersonate the goddess of the waters, Chalchiuhtlicue.

After the ashes of Tizoc had been buried, Tlacaelel and the other Aztec officials thanked the men who had come to the funeral and told them to go home with good fortune, but to be on guard because soon they would have news of a new king. They were to await this news, which would come soon. With that, each lord went to his own city and province.

---

[4]The reference to masks with eyes worn on different parts of the body, including the joints, seems to fit the description of Tlaltecuhtli, Earth Lord or Earth Mother, given in *Historia de los mexicanos por sus pinturas* (1973).

CHAPTER XLI

Which treats of how, after the funeral of King Tizoc, a younger brother of his was elected. And how there was some controversy in this election.

n the fourth day after the death of King Tizocicatzin, there was a gathering in the city of Tenochtitlan. All the lords and highborn men, all the officials of the court, all the chiefs of the barrios, and, in fact, all those who held official positions were present.

This nation had a special functionary for every activity, even minor ones. Everything was so well recorded that no detail was left out of the accounts and registers. There were even officials in charge of sweeping. The order was such that no one was allowed to interfere with the work of another or express an opinion since he would be rebuffed immediately; even today those who can maintain this order still do. As soon as a child is born, he is registered with the heads of the barrios and with the captains. For these services there were centurions, quinquagenarians, and quadragenarians, and this was because one man had in his charge twenty households, another forty, another fifty, and others a hundred. The whole city and all the barrios were controlled this way. He who had a hundred houses in his charge would appoint five or six of his subjects and divide the hundred homes among them. So a person who had charge of fifteen or perhaps twenty households was obliged to govern them, guide them, and collect tribute and men for public works. And so the officials of the republic were innumerable.

All of these authorities appeared on the day of the new election to discuss who would be the successor to Tizoc. This meeting was presided over by Tlacaelel, who had always been second to the king in the court. When the discussion of the choice of a new king for Mexico-Tenochtitlan began, there were many opinions among these authorities and even disputes. Tlacaelel wanted a younger brother of the deceased monarch to be chosen, because he was his nephew and because he was the son of Motecuhzoma the Elder, Tlacaelel's brother. It is said that the succession always passed from brother to brother. Therefore, considering that Axayacatl and Tizocic had reigned, succeeding one another, and that this was the third brother, he had a right to rule. Tlacaelel said that he had promised Motecuhzoma at the time of his death that until his three sons had ruled one after the other he would not permit another to become king. Since two sons were dead, only the third was left and must reign. However, the officials and others present objected, saying that he was only a child, was too young to rule. They believed that the grandeur, authority, and importance of the city were such that a venerable elderly person was indicated, one whom the other nations would fear yet revere, whom they could respect and who had discernment enough to honor those who were worthy and reward those who deserved these distinctions. Furthermore, because of his benevolence and generosity he would attract all those who wished to serve him. He would also help the needy and console the old people, the sad people; he would animate those of weak heart and punish delinquents and evildoers.

When Tlacaelel saw that everyone disagreed with his decision, he replied that this was what he was there for, that divine providence had given him life and had sustained him and that, as he had always been the second in command, with his gray hairs and with his very presence he had been able to compensate for certain qualities that some kings lacked. And he would do the same now.

After much discussion, it was decided to consult the king of Tezcoco and then accept his decision. Tlacaelel summoned his envoys and, while sending them to Tezcoco, told them the following: "Go to the king of Tezcoco, Nezahualpiltzintli, and inform him that I have decided that the next ruler of Tenochtitlan will be my nephew Ahuitzotzin, the brother of the deceased Axayacatl and Tizocic. The only fault my lords find with him is that he is still very young, is but a youth. But I offer to take charge of him and instruct him in all things that are advantageous for our republic. Therefore, we ask your advice and shall abide by your opinion. But you must know that this is my desire, this is what I promised my brother Motecuhzoma on his deathbed—that his three sons would reign, if I lived long enough to help realize this. Well, I am still alive and before I die I want to see my three nephews as kings and rulers of Tenochtitlan, for this is their right."

The envoys appeared before the king of Tezcoco and explained their mission. Nezahualpilli then consulted with his council and advisers. Not wishing to offend the honored old Tlacaelel or anger the Aztecs and these envoys, yet wishing to deliver a correct decision, he answered that in his opinion Tlacaelel should be elected since he was the person who most deserved the position and he had a right to the kingship because he was a brother of Motecuhzoma. The child Ahuitzotzin, his nephew, said Nezahualpilli, could live at his uncle's side and this way would master his statesmanship. Once the old man was dead,

Ahuitzotl could be his successor and by then he would be able to govern.

The envoys took this message back to Tenochtitlan. The council members, the principal men, and the other electors without waiting entered the presence of Tlacaelel, shouting their approval, the way we would say, "Long live the king! Long live Tlacaelel!" But Tlacaelel answered, "I hear you, O Aztecs, I hear you! What shouts are these?"

Then they told him that the king of Tezcoco had claimed he should be appointed king, that this was his decision and theirs too; that this was the desire of every old man and old woman, of the young man and young woman, of the boy child and the little girl, of all the men and women, of the commoners and the noblemen. "That is their wish," they said, "that you rule, govern, that you accept all that is your right, justly yours."

But Tlacaelel responded, "O my sons, I am grateful to you and to the king of Tezcoco. But come here! I wish to ask you, what have I been during the eighty or ninety years since the war with Azcapotzalco took place? What position have I had? Have I been nothing? Why have I not put the diadem upon my head, why have I not worn the royal insignia? When I have been a judge, when I have issued commands, have I been ignored? Have I executed the delinquent or pardoned the innocent without cause? Have I not been able to appoint chieftains or to remove them, as I have done? Have I acted wrongly, have I broken the laws of the republic in wearing the mantles, the breechcloths and sandals, golden armbands, anklets, labrets of gold and jade, and fine ear and nose pendants? Have I broken the law in entering the royal palace and the temple shod, as I have done up to now? For no one can do these things but the king. Have I done wrong in wearing the garments, the symbols, of the gods, showing myself as their image, and as a god taking up the knife to sacrifice men? If I could do these things, and I have been doing them for eighty or ninety years, I am then a king and you have held me as such. What more of a king do you wish me to be? And in this way I shall continue until my death. Why are you disturbed, why are you troubled over the election of my nephew Ahuitzotl? I will always be at his side to punish the transgressor, no matter how high his position may be. I shall place him under the mat at my feet, under my seat, under the throne! I shall be next to Ahuitzotl to honor the virtuous man, to receive guests and strangers and honor rulers and sovereigns. I shall organize wars and command them. Be calm, my children, obey me, for I am now king and king I shall remain until I die. But I want the promise I made to my brother fulfilled, and my sons can also honor this promise. I want all my nephews to rule first and then, should you so desire, you may enthrone my sons. In this way you will compensate me for all I have done for my country and for your persons."

When everyone had heard Tlacaelel's words and recognized the truth and realized that he would be their protector and shelter as long as he lived, all agreed to accept the election of Ahuitzotl. The principal chiefs and noblemen, followed by the masses of the people, went to the school where the sons of the kings and nobles lived and where they were trained and taught morals, the exercise of war, and good manners. When they arrived, they took Ahuitzotl from among his companions and led him to the royal palace, where they seated him upon the throne where the past kings had ruled.

When the boy had thus been given the royal seat, Tlacaelel sent messages to the different regions to proclaim to all that the sun, which had been darkened, shone again in Mexico-Tenochtitlan and the city that had been mute could speak again. All were to come and help seat him upon the royal throne, anoint him, crown him, and recognize him as their king and lord. They were advised that his name was Ahuitzotl and that he was the son of Motecuhzoma the Elder and the brother of the two kings who had recently died.

The ambassadors went out the provinces and delivered this message. Then all the rulers and great lords who were subject to Tenochtitlan and its sovereign left their cities and, taking with them the gifts that were delivered on such occasions, traveled to the Aztec city to be present at the coronation and anointing of their king and ruler, whose subjects they were. When the two kings of Tezcoco and Tacuba arrived, and all the great lords from the cities and provinces, Ahuitzotl was taken back to the place where he had been raised, before the kings and noblemen could see him. All these distinguished visitors went to the royal palace, where they found Tlacaelel in charge, demonstrating much authority. They paid him their respects, then he addressed them: "O powerful lords, for whose very breath your subjects prostrate themselves, you whose power is great: you must know that due to my request a nephew of mine has been appointed king and lord of this land. His name is Ahuitzotl and he is the son of my brother Motecuhzoma the Elder. I realize that he is young, just a boy, and because of this I am here to intervene when necessary, to compensate for his youth. My motive for this has been a promise I made to my brother: that if his sons outlived him they would follow him as ruler, successively. The Lord of All Created Things has allowed me to see this vow fulfilled, and since Ahuitzotl's brothers did not have good fortune, perhaps this one, the youngest, will succeed where the other two failed. They enjoyed reigning for only a short time and, at the height of their rule, death cut the thread of their youth."

The noblemen present thanked Tlacaelel, assuring him that the choice of ruler was an excellent one and had been accepted by all. They wished then to go place the diadem on Ahuitzotl's head, in the chamber where he was at that time. So all went in the proper order, the king of Tacuba carrying the diadem, and they entered the chambers where the sons of the kings and lords were raised. This was the Tlillan Calmecac, the rooms and sleeping chambers in the temple of Tlillan, which means "Darkness, the Black Place." When they had entered, they summoned Ahuitzotl to a large hall there. The first to kiss his hands was the king of Tezcoco, who in a solemn way addressed him: "O my son, on this day these lords and chieftains of all your kingdom place in your hands a little closed chest so that you may open it. You are going to find within it a cloth to wrap up the burden that has been given you. You will put this chest upon your back and you will learn how to carry it from one place to another. Do not become weary, do not be careless, do not let this burden fall. You have been given a key so that you know how to open and close the chest. You will carry the same burden as does the god Huitzilopochtli, which is to provide and maintain this world order, that is, to provide the sustenance, the food and drink for your people. Eyes from the four directions are fixed upon you. You have now been given a sword and a shield so you may risk your life for your country. You have been charged with the responsibility for the mountains, the hills, the plains, caves, cliffs, rivers and seas, pools and springs, rocks and trees. Everything has been commended to you and you must take care and see that these do not fall apart. You may not have to do this with your own hand, but you must give orders, you must command that it be done. Until now your work has consisted of sweeping and washing the place in front of the [images of the] gods. After these tasks you played and enjoyed yourself like a child. But now you must understand and care for all things that exist under the heavens. For this purpose you have at your side the mighty lord Tlacaelel. Follow his footsteps, observe how he rules, and you will not err. He will watch over the way you govern so that you do not let the load that had been given you fall upon the ground. With these words, my son, I end my discourse."

The king of Tacuba came forth, carrying the diadem and pronouncing the same kind of discourse. He differed in some aspects, however, for he called to mind the fine government of the predecessors and mentioned other past achievements in order to animate the young king so that he would abandon boyish enterprises and embark on manly ones. He then presented the royal insignia [in an act of investiture]: he placed the diadem on Ahuitzotl's head, he perforated the septum of his nose and gave him a special nose plug. He gave the new ruler bracelets, ear pendants, and labrets and placed on his arm a fine feather ornament set with magnificent green stones. He draped upon Ahuitzotl's shoulders the royal mantles and on his legs he put gold leg adornments, on his feet splendid sandals. He then gave him a wide and finely made breechcloth.

After Ahuitzotl had been given the royal insignia and the diadem, he was raised to the shoulders of the great lords, who then carried him before the statue of Huitzilopochtli. Here he performed ceremonies and a sacrifice, which were like those described in the investiture of a new ruler in past chapters. After this the young king was taken to the royal palace and placed upon the royal seat. Here all the lords came before him one by one, to honor him and swear obedience. After them came the people in general, bearing gifts.

The elders, the old men, came. They were the masters of the schools, of the places where the king had been raised, where he had studied, where he had slept, where he had been taught correct comportment, good manners. They came to pay their respects, kiss Ahuitzotl's hands. They made long rhetorical speeches, during which they gave thanks to the Lord of All Created Things that a child educated by them, instructed by them, had come to be the *tlatoani*, the sovereign, of such a powerful nation. They encouraged him, told him to take heart so that he would not weaken under the burden of his new responsibilities. The king thanked them and treated them with much courtesy, as if he were dealing with his own father.

The priests of the temples came with their officials and with all the youths who were educated in these temples. They paid their due respects. When the masters and high officials made their discourses Ahuitzotl, quietly and calmly, listened to all of them in a serious and composed manner, not like the child he was but like an elder, a very old and experienced person. And after all these dignitaries, in the order described here, had offered their gifts, made their speeches, and had congratulated him on his election, the king, with unusual dignity, responded to all assembled there: "O powerful sovereigns, illustrious and excellent lords, my fathers and kinsmen: I am grateful to you for the advice and comfort you have given me. I well know that I am nothing, nor am I equal to the honorable position you have given me. What I ask is that all of you, as my fathers, help me, so that in my extreme youth I do not make my country, my homeland, ashamed of me. Nor do I want to do anything to offend my uncles, my kinsmen who are present here, nor to destroy all that which my grandfathers, fathers, and brothers have built up or acquired. Why have I deserved so many benefits? My merits have not been so great as to warrant my sitting here now on this royal seat. Only yesterday I was at my mother's breast and playing in the dirt, making things of mud with the rest of the children."

The king ended his address and those present began to weep. The visitors from distant places bade farewell to Ahuitzotl and returned to their own cities, leaving Tenochtitlan contented and happy because of the new ruler.

When the sovereigns and noble guests had departed, Tlacaelel summoned the lords and described to them the manner in which the coronation ceremony was to take place, so that all the nations would know that Ahuitzotl was the king, the ruler, of that city. They were to find out where victims for sacrifice were to be obtained. The lords answered that no one would know these things better than he. It was decided to wage war against the province of Chiapa where seven powerful towns were inhabited by mountaineers. These were Chiapa, Xilotepec, Xiquipilco, Xocotitlan, Cuauhacan, Cillan, and Mazahuacan. This province was restless, was inclined to be rebellious, was reluctant to obey the Aztecs. The people served them unwillingly and did so because they were forced to rather than because this pleased them. All this irritated and offended the Aztecs. In order to chastise and subdue them, Tlacaelel ordered that war be declared on these people. In this way prisoners for sacrifice could be obtained for the feast of the new king. This decision made, all the allies of the provinces were informed so they could make ready their armies. When these were prepared, they left their own lands and went to a place called Cilucan, where these people gathered: the Aztecs, Tezcocans, Tepanecs, Tlahuicas, Xochimilcas, Chalcas, and men from the four head cities—Colhuacan, Mexicatzinco, Itztapalapa, and Huitzilopochco. Also came the Mizquitecas and Coatlalpanecas, and soldiers from the mountain region of Malinalco and Ocuila, as well as from Tlayacapan and Totolapan, Calimayan, and Tepemaxalco. Also the Matlatzincas, Tzinacantepecas, and Tlacotepecas were represented. Finally a vast army was formed to face those seven cities of Chiapa. Each group of soldiers set up camp by itself, as they always did.

Ahuitzotl was taken to this war by his nobles. He had never fought before. In order to gain time they dressed him and gave him his weapons and royal insignia. He was led before the great gathering of soldiers from all those regions mentioned and, through an interpreter, addressed them, exhorting them. They were all eager to hear his words. When he had finished, the soldiers, in an orderly fashion but highly animated, went into the field and attacked Xiquipilco. They soon subdued, destroyed, and sacked the town. After this they attacked Xocotitlan, which was also destroyed and plundered. Then came Cuauhacan, Cillan, and Mazahuacan. When all these had been

The History of the Indies of New Spain

overcome, beaten, many of their inhabitants slaughtered, others having fled or been taken prisoner, the authorities came out begging for mercy. They carried presents and made promises of service and tribute of all that would be asked of them. With this the Aztecs stopped pursuing and killing them.

When these five cities had been taken, King Ahuitzotl ordered that under pain of death no one dare flee or absent himself from the army. All were to watch one another; and if one was missing, even though he were of high birth, he must be killed as soon as he was found. This was to be done until the war was finished. The two main cities, Chiapa and Xilotepec, had yet to be conquered. No one dared abandon camp because the soldiers were watching each other carefully.

That night the army set out for Chiapa, and when they drew near they were heard by the guards who carried the alarm to the city. The men of Chiapa, thus warned, defended their city and a furious battle took place. But the Aztecs, who had always been crafty and who used a thousand cunning tricks in war, managed to get the Tezcocans, Tepanecs, Xochimilcas, and Chalcas in the front lines, while they secretly followed a path at the edge of the city that had been revealed to them by some of the inhabitants of that province. They entered the city, captured the temple, and made it their stronghold. Once there they took all the priests prisoner, together with the other officials of the temple, youths and elders, and having tied their hands they set fire to the building. When all of this was discovered by the Chiapan army, they abandoned the field and fled, followed by soldiers from the armies of their provinces. The Aztecs and their allies pursued them and captured or killed many who tried to defend themselves in order not to be captured. Thus, the Aztec and allied soldiers were able to enter the city and then steal what they could. Then the high Chiapan officials came with their hands crossed and offered obedience, as men of the other defeated cities had done.

Then the soldiers, with the impetus and enthusiasm [acquired at Chiapa], went on to attack Xilotepec, but in such a disorderly fashion that the soldiers did not wait for their companies to follow their banners. He who could arrive at Xilotepec first hurried to be in the vanguard, for these men were certain of the victory and were anxious for the spoils. As a result, they vied with each other in trying to conquer this town. But the people of Xilotepec, seeing the great wave of soldiers about to engulf them—for these men were like a locust plague that covers the land—and realizing that they could not possibly defeat them, surrendered in order to save lives. So the soldiers of that vast army entered the town freely and began to rob, to plunder, everything in their path. The Otomis of Xilotepec, with tears in their eyes, begged Ahuitzotl to order that the robbing and pillaging cease. Ahuitzotl then commanded his captains and other officers to have the soldiers stop the looting. But the men answered that this was one of the compensations for fighting, this was their pay, and that was the reason they went to war, not just to die; that because of the booty they risked their lives and asked to be left alone to enjoy the spoils of war. When Ahuitzotl heard this, he sent his officers to defend the Otomis. They went into the streets of the town, some from one side, some from another, and forcefully cast the soldiers out of the houses. These men were laden down with maize, beans, *chian*, turkeys, clothing, jewels, feathers—everything they could carry. They were run out of the city, but Xilotepec was left devastated, with many houses destroyed. (When I wrote about this it brought to mind the sacking of Rome and the destruction caused [in Mexico] by our Spaniards.)

Once these seven cities had been captured, they were ordered to pay tribute in maize, beans, many kinds of seeds and vegetables that these people eat, lumber, and other things found in that region. The vanquished people were ordered to bring workers to the capital city for the building of the houses of the nobility, together with slaves—people taken in the war—to be sacrificed when the need for these victims arose. All these terms were agreed upon by the conquered towns. Then people from the seven cities brought fine gifts to Ahuitzotl and to the other lords. These were received with expressions of thanks.

Messengers were then sent to Tenochtitlan to notify Tlacaelel and the city of the victory. When Tlacaelel received this news, he ordered flutes and conch shells to be blown and drums to be beaten and the event celebrated in the usual manner. Guards were placed at the summit of the temples to watch for the return of the army so that it might be greeted with due ceremony.

And so Ahuitzotl, accompanied by his chieftains and by the rulers and lords of the two allied provinces, Tezcoco and Tacuba, returned to his city, where he and the prisoners were received by the elders and the priests. Formal speeches were made to them; they were welcomed and congratulated for their successful venture. Ahuitzotl was taken to the temple and from there to his home, where, upon his royal seat, he received the old man Tlacaelel, who was carried in on a man's shoulders because of his extreme age. He welcomed his nephew and addressed him at length. The same was done by the kings of Tezcoco and Tacuba and the other lords from the provinces who had come with Ahuitzotl. They wished him happiness and success in his reign.

If I were to record here these long, elaborate, and elegant talks, I know they would please the reader but it would lengthen this history too much and would mean too great an expense of paper and time. Perhaps at the end of this book I shall make an epilogue of these, putting down each one as it was said, for the curious reader who would like to peruse them, especially in the [Nahuatl] language. It might be useful for the readers who would be interested in this manner of expression.[1]

After the greetings and lengthy talks were over, the men from the different provinces asked to be allowed to go home. The king, who held these men in esteem and was grateful for their assistance, granted them this permission and they left for their own cities. First, however, Tlacaelel notified them that the coronation was set for Ce Cipactli "One Alligator," the first day of the month, when the ceremony and great festivities would be held. They were all invited to attend and were requested to bring a contribution consisting of products from their region to help cover the expense. These contributions were to be turkeys, fowl, deer, rabbits, hare, quail, and other animals from the hunt, as well as fish from those who lived on the coast, fruit, different kinds of chiles, cacao for making a beverage, cloth, jewels, feathers, weapons, shields, firewood, charcoal, mats, seats—everything that might be needed. As we saw in the coronation of the past ruler, all the sovereigns and noblemen from the surrounding areas or allied regions came from near and far for this ceremony and fiesta.

---

[1] Either Durán did not make an appendix of this type of rhetorical speeches in Nahuatl or, if he did write them down, they have not come to light.

CHAPTER XLII

Which treats of the solemn festival that was held for the coronation of King Ahuitzotl and of the many men who were sacrificed on this occasion.

A ccording to the *Historia* I have consulted, this feast was prepared by the Aztecs with the intention of presenting the king to the people and showing the enemy—those of Tlaxcala, Huexotzinco, Cholula, and the other cities in that region, together with those of Mechoacan and Metztitlan—the greatness of Mexico-Tenochtitlan. It was designed to amaze them, also to fill them with fear, and to make them see the grandeur and abundance of jewels and gifts that were exchanged on such occasions. This was proof of Tenochtitlan's valor and excellence, and of its wealth. All of this was based upon ostentation and vainglory, in order to instill fear in the enemy and to show that the Aztecs were the masters of all the riches of the earth and controlled all the finest lands. This is why they celebrated their feasts so splendidly.

All the great men were invited but were told they must bring provisions. Especially notified were the governors, treasurers, and other high officials of all the cities, who were warned that if they failed in any way they would be deprived of their positions and exiled from their homeland together with their families and relatives. The gem cutters were told to make haste in cutting the precious stones that were necessary for this feast. The same was said to the metal workers and jewelers, to the feather workers who created splendid feather adornments, some of them used in the dances, to the potters who made the necessary earthenware, to those skilled in preparing smoking tubes for tobacco, and to the florists. Everything was to be created in abundance. All of the artisans were cautioned, were threatened with punishment; if they did not fulfill their obligations they would be banished from the city together with their progeny. Certain officials harassed the artisans, not allowing them to rest or pause in their work. These officials were so solicitous and untiring that one would think their lives depended upon this diligence. This was due to the great reverence and fear in which they held their masters. It is true that these people wished to be superior in many ways, and when they inspired fear in others these servitors discharged their duties in such an industrious way that nothing was left undone.

Tlacaelel summoned the heads of all the barrios and ordered them to obtain mats and baskets for the maize cakes that they eat. He had masons and carpenters brought to make seats and to repair those that had been damaged. He ordered those who work with paint and plaster to repair and paint parts that were chipped or badly finished. The woodcutters were told to prepare a large number of branches and sedge. On this day the entire city was so busy providing, repairing, and adorning everything that it was a wondrous sight to behold. And as the king realized that the purveyors and officials of some of the cities responded better than others, he sent his inspectors to ensure that no Aztec official receive any supplies brought for the feast without their being inspected first. When this was known in the provinces, each city took great pains with its contribution to the celebration.

The king met with his officials and all decided that the lords of certain cities must be invited; therefore messengers were sent with invitations to Mechoacan, Metztitlan, Tlaxcala, Huexotzinco, Cholula, Tliliuhquitepec, and Yopitzinco. All of these cities and provinces, which were enemies of Tenochtitlan, had never been subdued. They were constantly warring and making trouble. Nevertheless, the Aztecs said that they did not really wish to conquer them because the soldiers needed places to practice fighting and those cities provided the opportunity and battlefields so that men on each side could win honors and awards in the militia.

These foreign rulers were invited in order to impress them with Aztec grandeur and to instill awe in them with the pomp and ostentation. The sovereign of Tlaxcala answered that he was unwilling to attend the feasts in Tenochtitlan and that he could make a festival in his city whenever he liked. The ruler of Tliliuhquitepec gave the same answer. The king of Huexotzinco promised to go but never appeared. The ruler of Cholula sent some of his lords and asked to be excused since he was busy and could not attend. The lord of Metztitlan angrily expelled the Aztec messengers and warned them to take care, for the people of his province might kill them if they recognized them.

When the lord of Mechoacan received the invitation, he laughed, saying, "What do your masters fancy? Was it a whim to come and make war upon us, to return defeated, with their hands upon their heads, having lost so many men? You must be mad! One day you wish for war, another day you desire peace. [If I go to Tenochtitlan] what security shall I have while I eat and drink among you, after the way we have treated you?"

The envoys answered, "O powerful lord, there are times when one must be an enemy, but there are other times when one must heed the natural obligations that exist between us, and so my lord the king says that enmity and war should now be set aside. Those things have their time and place but due to them certain opportunities should not be lost. Ahuitzotl begs you to come to the feast as a kinsman, as a relative, together with your chieftains to honor his coronation. He also asks that you enter the palace at night, so that the valiant Aztecs do not think your arrival is a trick between the two of you. There he will receive you with all the honor you deserve." The lord of Mechaocan then answered that he sent felicitations for the coronation but that he did not wish to go, nor would any member of his court be allowed to go. The envoys returned to King Ahuitzotl with this answer.

Those who had gone to invite the officials of Yopitzinco brought back the noblemen from that city but failed to bring the ruler himself, who could not be found. The dignitaries of Yopitzinco and those of Cholula were lodged luxuriously and generously supplied with everything they needed. They were treated even better than the two allied monarchs who were in the city at that time. They were given rich gifts, consisting of jewels and beautifully made mantles and breechcloths, also bracelets, waistbands, and headbands of gold, the latter the kind these people wore, with eagle feathers at the sides. These were considered a great honor because when the king gave men eagle feathers or jaguar skins he was signaling them out as courageous men, as people of noble lineage, of strength and valor.

When the day of the celebration arrived, before midnight the musicians began to play the instruments used to accompany song and dance. At that time all the kings present and all the lords and dignitaries were given mantles and jewels and flowers and tobacco, all so rich and magnificent and in such abundance that it was an amazing event. The *Historia* says that before dawn and on four occasions all the nobles and principal men received mantles and jewels, while the rulers were given golden diadems, bracelets, leg ornaments, ear plugs, nose and lip plugs. Each time these were distributed they were told, "This is so you will know that Ahuitzotl is the king and lord of the great city of Tenochtitlan and of its dominions. And also these things are given to you so you may dance and enjoy yourselves."

For these dances and pleasures, as it was nighttime, torches were lit in the royal courtyard and so many people held flaming braziers that it looked like day, and so many people held the torches against the walls that it seemed the houses were on fire.

It was then that King Ahuitzotl, wearing the royal diadem on his head and magnificently adorned with jewels, precious stones, rich bracelets, and other fine pieces of clothing such as have been described, went with old Tlacaelel to the quarters of the Cholultecas and to those of the Yopitzincas, the enemy, and gave them presents of exquisitely made mantles and waistbands, jewels, bracelets, sandals, fine feathers, garlands, bands of gold for the head, flowers, and tubes of tobacco. They requested them to come out and dance before dawn broke. So these guests went out among the other lords but with their identity concealed, because not everyone knew of their coming, nor that they had been invited. Only a few were aware of this.

The feast and dancing lasted four days and four nights. During this time all the lords, noblemen, the chieftains and warriors, the priests and ministers of the temples, administrators, supervisors, and other civil leaders of the cities and of the barrios were presented with a large number of rich mantles and waistbands, quantities of precious stones, jewels, bracelets, leg bands, ear ornaments, nose and lip plugs, all made of gold and fine stones. They were also given innumerable flowers and much smoking tobacco. Food consisted of delicious dishes, with breads and chocolate drink.

I have noticed one thing in all this history: no mention is made of their drinking wine of any type, nor of drunkenness. Only wild mushrooms are spoken of and they were eaten raw. The *Historia* says that people became excited, filled with pleasure, and lost their senses to some extent.[1] It never mentioned wine except as part of sacrificial or funeral ceremonies. Only the great abundance of chocolate drink is spoken of as part of these festivities.

After four days of dancing and feasting were past, a sacrifice was held. The sacrificers were dressed in their priestly garments. These vestments were of special design according to the rite for which they were worn. Prisoners from the seven cities of the province of Xilotepec and Chiauhtla were brought out, and when the multitude of lords and principal men were present (including the enemies of Tenochtitlan, who were seated by themselves in a bower covered with flowers, where they could not be seen) all the victims were sacrificed on the Sun Stone.[2]

---

[1] The *teonanacatl*, "divine mushroom," was a highly important stimulant taken during ritual occasions. The *Florentine Codex* (1959:book 9:38–39; and 1963:book 11:130) describes in detail the effect of eating these mushrooms. Hallucinogenic mushrooms still play an important role in modern Mexican folk religion. They have been studied by many scholars, including Peter Furst (1977).

[2] Although Durán's words here are *sobre la piedra del sol* (on the Sun Stone) we have no way of knowing if he refers to the large carved stone called this (or the Aztec Calendar) on exhibit in Mexico's National Museum of Anthropology. Durán may have had in mind a small painted stone described in some of the ceremonies in his *Book of*

I do not wish to make this story too long, although the *Historia* describes it thus: I understand that almost one thousand prisoners died in King Ahuitzotl's coronation. When this had been concluded, on the next day all the rulers, lords, and chieftains from the provinces bade farewell to the Aztec king and then left for their homelands.

Something I have observed in this chapter and others is that everything that was paid in tribute by the different cities and provinces during the entire year was given to the lords and chieftains in only one day. It was for this purpose that those riches were acquired, were collected, throughout the year, in order to make a grand and magnificent display like the one described here. The same practice was carried out, that of giving gifts to all the ambassadors and envoys who came to the city from outside, and also to those lords who came to visit.

When the noblemen from the provinces had left and the city was free of those visitors, the guests who had been concealed—the lords of Cholula and Yopitzinco—took their leave. They were thanked for their presence in the fiesta and were given rich gifts to take to their rulers and lords, who after all were like kings in their own lands. These gifts were weapons—for each, a fine shield, a *macana* [wooden sword edged with obsidian blades], bow and arrows—a golden diadem for each ruler, golden leg bands, also richly made mantles and royal waistbands. The visitors were instructed to give these presents to their lords together with infinite thanks for having been so kind as to send representatives to do honor to Ahuitzotl. Yet these gifts were sent as a reminder that war and enmity existed between them, and they were not to forget this. These lords received the presents with much humility and promised to give them to their rulers, with respects from Ahuitzotl. The visitors were secretly led to their canoes and then traveled all night long, disembarking at Ayotzinco. From there they went by land to their own cities, safely protected by their guards.

Back in their own lands, and while giving the presents to their kings and lords, they described the grandeur of the Aztec city, its wealth, its excellence in all things, and the king who led them and with whom they triumphed, and the abundance of everything in that city, which so amazed them.

Many days after this feast, Tlacaelel informed King Ahuitzotl that the Huaxtecs and all their province had rebelled again. They had closed their territory, had refused to observe obedience to the Aztecs as they had been accustomed to doing, and had denied entrance to

the Gods and Rites (Durán 1977). Most sacrifices were dedicated to the sun; this could have led to confusion in naming the sacrificial stone.

their lands to merchants and traders who went there from Tenochtitlan. They were like men without a king, who did not recognize any authority. It would be a good idea, said Tlacaelel, to go to the Huaxteca and war with those people, for fighting was the occupation of the Aztecs and for this reason they had been sent here.

The king thanked Tlacaelel and asked that he always advise him of news that had not reached him, the king.

The lords were summoned and Ahuitzotl discussed these events with them, stating at the same time that he favored invading the Huaxteca and the province of Cicoac, Tuzapan, and Tamapachco, because these places had rebelled and no longer observed obedience and recognition of the royal crown of Mexico, as they once had. The Aztec lords agreed with this decision and asked that it be put into effect. When this had been determined, the rulers of the allied cities, Nezahualpiltzintli and Totoquihuaztli, together with the lords of neighboring cities and provinces, were called to Tenochtitlan. Once in this city, they were ordered to prepare their men so that the Huaxteca could be attacked, because that region had rebelled. Furthermore, they had come to the aid of the people of Metztitlan when the Aztecs had attempted to conquer them, and this alliance had been disastrous for the Aztecs. All the rulers and leading men from the provinces and different regions friendly to the Aztecs stated that they would be happy to make ready their armies, that nothing would be lacking that was needed for war, since war was their profession, their calling, by means of which they obtained fame. It was the reason for their existence.

Having returned to their cities, the lords had the call to arms proclaimed. The need to prepare rapidly was stressed so that the enemy would not have time to equip its soldiers, nor to provide defenses. In a short time, therefore, all the allies were ready, with a celerity and promptness that had rarely been heard of. The king of Tenochtitlan was then notified that all these troops were in order. Ahuitzotl replied that the different armies should leave their cities, each one led by its captains and chieftains, and march to Cuauhchinanco so he could see how many soldiers he could count on. They were to wait for Ahuitzotl there because he wished to lead them in this war in person. When it was known in Mexico Tenochtitlan that the armies had left their cities—Tezcoco, Tepanecapan, Xochimilco, Chalco, and the other districts—King Ahuitzotl ordered his own warriors to go out and he, accompanied by his chieftains and other important men, left the city and headed for Cuauhchinanco.

When they reached Cuauhchinanco, the lord of this place came out with all his principal collaborators to greet Ahuitzotl and offer him valuable presents. With great rejoicing the Aztec king was taken into the city, where he and the other lords were given splendid lodgings and everything they needed. They ate and drank well, then Ahuitzotl summoned the lord of Cuauhchinanco, whose name was Xochitl Tecuhtli. When this lord appeared, he was told to round up some men from his region in order to defend it and also to aid the Aztecs. The lord of Cuauhchinanco answered that he would be happy to go to that war himself, together with any of his men who wished to accompany him. He then ordered his men to prepare for war. All the necessary provisions were to be contributed by him. Everything the people from his territory needed was to come from that district. Thus prepared, Ahuitzotl was told of their readiness.

King Ahuitzotl thanked Xochitl Tecuhtli and gave him some of his own weapons, a shield and sword, so that with these he could distinguish himself in the war and use these always as an insignia. The lord of Cuauhchinanco kissed his hands and thanked him for that honor.

All the military men left Cuauhchinanco in perfect order. They reached the limits of Huaxtec territory and set up camp there, each group from its city or province in its own place, in a very orderly manner and accompanied by their rulers and other leaders.

Ahuitzotl ordered his explorers and scouts to investigate the Huaxtec defenses and to ascertain where they could penetrate them. For this task he sent two hundred experienced soldiers from Tenochtitlan, two hundred from Tezcoco, and two hundred Tepanecs, also one hundred Chalcas, one hundred Xochimilcas, and one hundred from each of the four principal cities—Itztapalapa, Mexicatzinco, Colhuacan, and Huitzilopochco. He commanded all these men to spy out that land, to examine it carefully and to look for signs that would reveal where the Huaxtecs could be attacked.

The scouts left all together, divided into groups but with little separation between them so they could communicate one with another. Keeping hidden as much as they could, by twilight they came within view of the Huaxtec city. When they could hear noises made by the people there, they halted and set themselves up to keep watch. When night fell, they left their hidden places and, keeping alert and on guard, the most courageous men entered the city, keeping away from the torches and lights that were in many places, set there by the sentries. They cautiously explored the entire city, discovering the most carefully guarded places where there were guards and barricades. These were the places where the Huaxtecs feared the enemy might try to enter the city. But the Aztecs and their allies saw that the sentries were overconfident, they were lax, so the allies, silently communicating this to each other, attacked the guardians on all sides and captured all of them. Not one escaped. This was accomplished without anyone crying out or shouting, or making any noise at all.

Taking the sentries with their hands tied, the Aztecs passed along the outskirts of the city. All the Huaxtecs who were going to their fields to work in a confident carefree manner were taken prisoner there. Every man and woman, boy child or girl, was captured there. This was done quietly, without crying out or making noise, for fear that the people living inside the city would hear and would come out to investigate. So, at dawn, all these prisoners were taken to the Aztec camp and were turned over to the king, who thanked the soldiers and congratulated them for their good work. It was then decided to put the armies into action, since the places where they could most easily enter the city were now known. Ahuitzotl commanded the alarm to be sounded and in a moment all were in order and ready for combat. The Huaxtecs, taken by surprise and seeing all their defenses overthrown, were greatly afraid but took up arms in anticipation of what would happen next. Ahuitzotl sent word to the allied rulers and lords that since they were in unknown territory each one was to make a supreme effort to win, and anyone who fought carelessly would be deprived of his office for some time. That some soldiers were rulers or noblemen would not be taken into account—the law was for everyone.

The rulers answered that they would do everything in their power to fulfill their obligations, and they kissed Ahuitzotl's hands. They were told, too, that the army of each nation was to follow its own route so that all the soldiers would not be grouped together. Ahuitzotl chose two hundred men and sent them in advance to engage in a skirmish with the Huaxtecs. This they did, but the Huaxtecs counterattacked in such a way that the Aztecs were caught and were losing. Ahuitzotl, who was observing this and saw the advance made by the Huaxtecs, began to send in more men, so that soon a great number of soldiers were on one side or on the other, to the extent that most of the armies were in this battle. Ahuitzotl ordered the remaining soldiers to prepare an ambush. This they did by hiding in the brush and in the woods, then Ahuitzotl commanded the soldiers in the field to retire. As they retired, the Huaxtecs followed them, shouting, whistling, and crying out hoarse wails that these people use. They were howling ecstatically when they reached the ambush, when the Aztecs came out suddenly and surrounded them, some on one side, some on another, others behind them, making those who fled turn against their own men. This was done so fast that the Huaxtecs did not know which way to turn, and many were killed or were taken prisoner.

The city was taken, the temple was burned, and the whole place was plundered, looted to the point that nothing was left. When the

Huaxtecs saw this, they asked for mercy and offered to pay tribute to Tenochtitlan and comply with all the personal services the visitors wished to impose upon them. When Ahuitzotl observed their humility, he ordered all pillaging and killing to cease. When this was done, he and his chieftains were taken to the palace of the local capital and there were given presents of large quantities of clothing, for both men and women, cacao, feathers, parrots, macaws, chiles, pumpkin seeds, and Huaxtec maidens "for their own use." Ahuitzotl accepted all these gifts and divided them among his captains. They were given much food and drink, and an abundance of flowers and tubes of tobacco. After they had rested and had been entertained, the Aztecs decided to return quickly to their city, but first messengers were sent to advise Tlacaelel so that everyone could rejoice in their victory.

The messengers departed and after them came the army, the soldiers proud and joyful, with all the captives before them. The Huaxtec prisoners were linked together by cords drawn through perforations in their noses. Many people had been captured on this occasion and they went along singing in loud voices, moaning over their fate with a pitiful wailing chant. The maidens, daughters of Huaxtecs who had been seized, and the children and little boys who did not yet have their noses or ears perforated wore wooden yokes on their throats, and they were all tied together this way.

The messengers arrived and announced the great victory. The whole city rejoiced with celebrations and expressions of joy (as they always did and as we have described in other chapters), beating drums and sounding horns in the temples, making fires and lighting torches at the summit of those temples. This festival lasted until the soldiers, the prisoners, and the king returned to the city. With the arrival of these warriors and their captives, and the welcome made by the entire city—religious men as well as those in civil duties—the usual ceremonies were carried out by the soldiers and prisoners: eating earth in the presence of the god and walking around sacred rocks and other places. Then they went to the palace, where the prisoners were distributed among the different barrios. The rest of the people bade farewell to Ahuitzotl and left for their homes or for their own lands.

CHAPTER XLIII

Which treats of how King Ahuitzotl finished the construction and embellishment of the Great Temple and of the solemn feast made for its inauguration, and of the many men he had sacrificed.

After King Ahuitzotl, whom we have been discussing, ended this war [with the Huaxtecs], in the second year of his reign, which was the year 1487, "Eight Reed" according to the Indian way of counting, he decided to finish the construction and decoration of the Great Temple.[1] When this structure was completed and embellished, he planned a great and sumptuous feast for its dedication. He conferred with Tlacaelel and when the old man heard of his determination, and being eager to see this work and enjoy its splendor, he told the king he was well pleased with the plans. Giving thanks and weeping many tears, Tlacaelel showed the joy this gave him and added that he wished to see the temple finished before his days ended. The king, seeing that Tlacaelel was pleased, then called his main steward and told him to notify the other administrators in all the provinces that they were to provide cloth and everything necessary that had been stored in the different subject cities and provinces as royal tribute. The steward notified everyone in these places so they would be ready to furnish what had been demanded by their king.

Then he called the stoneworkers and ordered them to finish the temple of their god as quickly as possible. Without delay they began to work on the stones that were lacking and carve the figures I saw in a painted manuscript,[2] which were, in this manuscript, a sharp sacrificial stone and next to it an image of the goddess called Coyolxauh;[3] and on the corners of the temple two statues with cruciform mantles, these made of rich feathers. Also set up on the temple were two large statues that they call *tzitzimime*. Finally the building was finished, with nothing more to be done.

[1] For detailed information on the Great Temple (Templo Mayor) of Tenochtitlan, including history, symbolism, and archaeological excavations since 1978, see Matos Moctezuma 1988.

[2] "Painted manuscript" refers to pictorial codices. Most of those seen by Durán no longer exist. For the story of Mexican pictorial manuscripts, see the *Handbook of Middle American Indians*, vols. XIV and XV (1975).

[3] The stone relief of Coyolxauh was uncovered during the recent Templo Mayor excavations, found at the base of Huitzilopochtli's temple, where it had evidently been thrown in prehispanic times. The sacrificial stone mentioned here also came to light.

When the completed edifice was considered to be perfect, the king sent his emissaries to the provinces and cities to invite all the rulers and nobles there to be present at the solemn festivity for the dedication of the temple. All were asked to bring slaves for sacrifice, as tribute, which was obligatory on these occasions. With these instructions, the ambassadors set forth. The first city and province they reached was Tepeaca, which had jurisdiction over four important cities. These were Cuauhtinchan, Tecalli, Acatzinco, and Oztoticpac. They were subject to the lord of Tepeaca. When the emissaries arrived there, they invited the lord of that province, on behalf of the king of Tenochtitlan, and requested that he take as tribute all the war prisoners that were owed to the royal Aztec crown. The rulers of those cities accepted the invitation and promised to take the prisoners they were obliged to give. Thus, they set out and took many captives with them, natives of Tlaxcala and Cholula.

From here Ahuitzotl's envoys went to Tecamachalco, where they extended the invitation for the festival to the ruler and requested him to send the prisoners everyone was meant to contribute. Then they went to Quecholac, where they carried out the same mission. The men from these two places then sent the prisoners who were part of their tribute, who were from Tecoac and Tlaxcala and Cholula. From here the ambassadors went to Cuauhquechollan and invited the lord of that place, who had authority over six cities. These were Acapetlahuacan, Atzitzihuacan, Yaoteuacan, Hueyapan, Tetelan, and Tlamimilulpan. These were all *cabeceras*, head towns, subject only to the rule and regulations of the lord of Cuauhquechollan, where they delivered the royal tribute and under whose flag and protection they went to war. These towns, having been informed of Ahuitzotl's order, received his ambassadors very well and provided them with everything they requested. The lords said they would attend the feast as they were commanded to and would take the tribute of slaves they were obliged to give. In this way went the slaves, all with collars.[4] They were people from Atlixco and Huexotzinco, with which province Tenochtitlan was always at war in order to extract tribute.

The emissaries then went to Chalco and presented their invitation. From here they turned to Atlatlahuacan, where seven *cabeceras*, the nearest to Atlatlahuacan, were subject to that lord. Among these were Tlayacapan and Totolapan. From here the envoys went to Xochimilco and Cuitlahuac and Mezquic, also to Colhuacan, and to the other four [*sic*] subject cities: Itztapalapa, Mexicatzinco, and Huitzilopochco. Here they made the same announcement and request [regarding the dedication of the Great Temple].

[4]The large wooden collars would have made escape almost impossible.

The History of the Indies of New Spain

The lords of all these cities and territories went at the proper time to the ceremony, taking as tribute captives and slaves for sacrifice. Thus, all the nobility and majesty of the great lords and rulers of the earth were in Tenochtitlan. When the emissaries had concluded their mission in these provinces, they advised the king that they had visited twenty cities and that the lords of all these had arrived, bringing with them as tribute a multitude of prisoners to be sacrificed. The king received the envoys with great affection, had presents given to them, and told them to rest from their difficult task.

Then other emissaries arrived who had gone to the region of Toluca, Matlatzinco, Calimayan, Tepemaxalco, Tlacotepec, Teotenanco, Metepec, Capuloac, Xochiacan, Zoquitzinco, Tenantzinco, Malinalco, and Ocuilan, in order to invite the lords of those cities and to demand the tribute of male slaves that they were to contribute for these solemn festivities. Those lords came accompanied by the prisoners who constituted their tribute. The emissaries gave an account of what they had accomplished. The king was pleased. Then, after these emissaries, the envoys who had gone to the region of Mazahuacan, Xocotitlan, Xiquipilco, Cuauhuacan, Cillan, Chiapa, and Xilotepec, returned with their answer. They told how the lords of that province were coming with their prisoners and slaves for the sacrificial rite.

That day the king of the province of Tezcoco, Nezahualpilli, arrived in Mexico-Tenochtitlan with a large number of his nobles and the leading men of his kingdom, with great pomp and splendor. He was accompanied by the lords of cities and towns subject to him, such as Uexotla, Coatlinchan, Coatepec, Chimalhuacan, Itztapalucan, and, toward the north, Tepetlaoztoc, Papalotlan, Totoltzinco, Tecciztlan, Tepechpan, Aculman, Chiconauhtla, Zacatzontitlan, Oztoyocan, Tecoac, Calpulalpan, Tlatzcayucan, Apan, Tepepulco, Tlalanapan [sic], Tezoyocan, Otompan, Achilhilacachocan, Tzacuallan, Cempoala, Uitzilan, Epazoyocan, Tulantzinco, Tlaquilpan, Tezontepec, Ueitihuacan, and all the other towns subject to the Tezcocan nation. Together with these lords and leading men came King Nezahualpiltzintli, of stately manner. He brought a large number of slaves taken from all those cities and towns, for sacrifice at the feast. He brought them because he was obliged to acknowledge the superiority of Tenochtitlan.

Some have said that the kingdom of Tezcoco was free from paying tribute to the Aztec sovereign and in no way subject to him. But I find this told differently in this Aztec chronicle. Although it is true that Tezcoco did not pay cloth, jewels, feathers, or foodstuffs to Mexico-Tenochtitlan as the other provinces did, I find nevertheless that the Aztecs used Tezcocan lands to sow and reap and that some of the people there were tenant farmers of the lords of Tenochtitlan. I have discovered that, when great feasts took place, Tezcoco paid tribute in slaves and that no one was exempt from this type of tribute. I also find that when war was waged on a city or province the first one called to form his army was the king of Tezcoco. And, as we have seen in this history, the Tezcocan king was called to the Aztec city as often as was necessary. This means that subjection did exist, in spite of his preeminence and the liberties he enjoyed as king and lord of that province Acolhuacan, of which Tezcoco was the capital.

Having arrived in Tenochtitlan, Nezahualpilli went to the royal palace, where he was received by King Ahuitzotl with all the courtesy due to a fellow monarch and kinsman. He was lodged in the place called Tecalli, which means "Royal Palace." He delivered his captives to King Ahuitzotl and spoke to him with elegant phrases, at the same time offering his goodwill and desire to serve the Aztec ruler. Water was then brought for his hands; this was a common custom among the Aztecs, to bring water for the hands of guests and travelers. After he had washed, he was given the usual fare for royalty and a chocolate drink. Flowers and tobacco were given not only to him but also to his followers, great lords and chieftains, who were lodged in other chambers, according to their rank. With great care and courtesy, they were given everything they desired. The captives were turned over to the priests who would take care of them.

Then the king of Tacuba came with all the lords and authorities from his province, which is not smaller than those I have mentioned, and with him came all the captives and slaves he was required to give for this ceremony. As much honor and courtesy were paid to him as had been to the king of Tezcoco. He was given rooms in the same palace as Nezahualpilli, and his lords were lodged in places suitable for them. They were provided with all the aforementioned abundance.

When King Ahuitzotl had received the lords and rulers and had accommodated them in their quarters with the attention and generosity that such high princes and lords deserved, old Tlacaelel spoke to King Ahuitzotl, saying, "You will remember, O mighty prince, how it was that on the feast of your anointment and coronation, the Tlaxcalans and their followers, our enemies, refused to accept our invitation and request, and those of Mechoacan and Metztitlan did the same. It seems to me that it would not be unreasonable to invite them again to this solemn occasion because, even though we are enemies in the wars that we wage, in our festivities we should rejoice together. There is no reason why they should be excluded since we are all one, and in these times it is reasonable that there be a truce and sociable communication among the rulers."

The king thought well of this and immediately had three courageous captains chosen, those of the highest fortitude and valor, who were not afraid to pass the guards and sentinels who day and night watched the frontiers, due to fear of aggression. When these three ambassadors were chosen, they were sent to Tlaxcala, Huexotzinco, Cholula, Tecoac, Tliliuhquitepec, and Zacatlan, to invite the rulers and noblemen of those cities and provinces in the king's name. The chosen envoys stated that they would do what had been demanded of them. Nevertheless, they entrusted their wives and children to the king, indicating the dangers of their mission and the uncertainty of their return. In spite of all this, and forgetting the great peril, they left the city and, having walked all night, arrived near Huexotzinco shortly before dawn. They entered the city secretly and went to the royal houses where the ruler dwelt. Finding the doorkeepers asleep in the outer rooms, they awakened them and asked that the lord Xayacamachan, who was the king of Huexotzinco, be told that some messengers were there who wished to speak to him. They were asked from where they came, but they replied that this information would be given only to the sovereign himself. The doorkeepers went to their master and told him what had happened, but the king gave orders that unless the strangers told who they were and where they came from they would not be allowed to pass. The Aztec envoys begged to be allowed to enter, as they desired to serve him and kiss his hands. They were unarmed and defenseless, being men of peace who wanted only to reveal this to him and deliver their message.

The king and lord of Huexotzinco was fearful. Nevertheless, he ordered that these men be allowed to enter. Once they had come into his presence, they bowed, prostrating themselves before him and performing all the royal ceremonies that were usual when in the presence of a king. After this was done, they told him they were Aztecs, emissaries of King Ahuitzotl of Tenochtitlan, and that they had come to invite him to the dedication of the temple of Huitzilopochtli, whose home had now been finished; therefore, safety and truce were assured. They promised him that he could accept because the courageous Aztecs never used treachery or womanly or cowardly tricks. They fought with their swords in war, on the battlefield, each one demonstrating the strength of his arm. Furthermore, since they had known one another and had been related by blood for one generation, they besought the king to be present at the feast of their god. The lord of Huexotzinco then accepted the invitation and stated that he would be pleased to take part in the ceremony and festivities and that he kissed the hand of King Ahuitzotl for having remembered him and requesting his participation in these formal rites. He ordered that the messengers be given lodging and everything necessary for their comfort, including food and drink at that time and also for their journey, as well as mantles and breechcloths. After having eaten and drunk, the emissaries bade farewell to him and, well content, continued to the city of Cholula.

In Cholula they gave the same message to the lord of that city. They also were well received with much courtesy and benevolence and were refreshed with food and drink and given mantles, flowers, and tobacco, as they had been in Huetxotzinco. They were then given a positive answer, the ruler accepting the invitation with the same gratitude. And so did the ruler of Tlaxcala.

The envoys, having fulfilled their obligation, left Tlaxcala and waited in the forest for the lords and nobles from Huexotzinco, Cholula, and Tlaxcala to arrive. This was done so those lords might secretly enter the city of Tenochtitlan together and to give them certain instructions so they would not be recognized. The entire night was spent watching in order to avoid these lords going by without being seen. Before dawn the rulers and noblemen of these cities arrived. Their customary garments were changed in favor of those of the Aztecs and, in order to disguise them further, they were made to hold flowers, branches, and rushes, as though they were men who were coming to adorn the temple and the royal house. They were also advised not to answer any greeting or to speak, because of the difference in accent that exists among them. The visitors were told that the envoys would answer for them. And so it was that all along the way the Aztecs answered questions asked by people they met. In this way these special guests entered Tenochtitlan secretly.

The visitors were taken to the royal palace, where secret chambers, hidden but splendidly appointed, had been prepared for them. The royal attendant was told of their arrival and at that hour of the night he notified the king, who then called Tlacaelel. He told him how the emissaries who had gone to Tlaxcala and Huexotzinco had returned safely. Having then been called before the king, these envoys gave an account of their mission and of the success of the invitation. The king received them well and gave instructions that they rest and be taken care of. Seeing that the lords of those three cities had been accommodated in private quarters that had been prepared for them, the king instructed the attendant secretly to make royal provisions available to them in the same abundance as they would be for his own person. He also ordered that they be given rich clothing, flowers, and tobacco, and he sent a long courteous message, thanking them for having come and telling them to have no fear, that as soon as the other lords from Mechoacan, Tziuhcoac, Metztitlan, Tliliuhquitepec, Tecoac, and Zacatlan arrived he would visit them in person. In the meantime they

The History of the Indies of New Spain

were asked to rest and enjoy themselves as they did in their own house, in their own kingdom. Ahuitzotl sent them many dishes of fish, frogs, and other lake delicacies the Aztecs were accustomed to eat, also duck, wild geese, herons, pelicans, sea fowl, and other kinds of game, saying that these were things found in his city and were all he had to offer. The visitors were very pleased and gave thanks.

After this, at midnight, the lords of Mechoacan, Metztitlan, and Yopitzinco arrived, together with allies and associates of the Tlaxcalans, who were from Tecoac, Zacatlan, and Tliliuhquitepec. They were all lodged in the same quarters where the men from Tlaxcala, Huexotzinco, and Cholula slept. King Ahuitzotl ordered his steward to provide them with many fine things—mantles, fine breechcloths, flowers, and tobacco. But all this was done in great secrecy. Only those who had gone to invite them were to serve them, and no other person was allowed to enter the secret places where those men were concealed. The reason for this secrecy was that they did not wish the common people or the soldiers and captains to suspect that kings and rulers made alliances, came to agreements, and formed friendships at the cost of their lives and the shedding of their blood. In order to avoid these suspicions and the possibilities of whispers and trouble-making, they kept these foreign kings and lords hidden. This is the reason given in the *Historia*.

After the guests had been lodged, the emissaries who had taken the message to the provinces were called and the king asked one by one how they had been received by the enemy in those cities. Every one of them said they had been well received and had seen only agreeable faces.

But those who had gone to Yopitzinco told about their reception. As soon as they had delivered their message, they had been housed in a splendidly appointed apartment and given water for their hands. Then the king of that province appeared in person with a staff in his hand, followed by his wives and ladies of the court, all beautifully dressed and adorned. These women carried the different kinds of foods and fruits found in that province, which they placed before the emissaries, at the same time greeting them. After them some lords entered with gourds of chocolate that they offered, and then came others carrying different kinds of flowers and tobacco. All this time the ruler had stood with his staff in his hand. He had ordered them to eat, to feel at ease and to rest. When they had eaten, he gave orders that the visitors be clothed with fine mantles and breechcloths, after which a squadron of armed and well-adorned men entered the courtyard and began to engage in a mock battle. They skirmished as if in a tournament, with great cries and shrieks such as these people use when they fight. When this skirmish had ended, the king said to the emissaries, "Do not fear! All of this has been done for your pleasure. Return to your masters; later we shall go to serve them." King Ahuitzotl marveled at the way his emissaries had been received in those parts, claiming that they had been the most successful and fortunate of all the envoys. He ordered all these ambassadors to be dressed in fine mantles and breechcloths and to be given presents and granted special favors for their work well done.

The king gave orders that the visitors be better treated than everyone else so that they would not return to their cities complaining that, because they were enemies, they had been badly dealt with and had been deceived into coming for this reason. So that they would feel more secure, King Ahuitzotl ordered that guards be placed in the palace where they were housed and that no one dare enter. Thus, two hundred soldiers guarded the entrance to those apartments in order that nobody see or know what was inside.

This precaution having been taken, the prisoners and captives brought from all the cities to be sacrificed were formed in lines. Those captured by the armies of Tezcoco were in one line, prisoners from Tacuba in another, and those from Xochimilco, Chalco, and the Mazahuaques and Cuauhtlapanecas in separate lines. This was done so that a precise count of prisoners could be made. It was found that there were eighty thousand four hundred men to be sacrificed in the dedication of the Great Temple of Mexico-Tenochtitlan. They were from Huexotzinco, Tlaxcala, Atlixco, Tliliuhquitepec, Cholula, Tecoac, Zacatlan, as well as men who were Zapotecs, Huaxtecs, Tzinccoacs, Tuzapanecs, and Tlapanecs. Ahuitzotl was greatly satisfied and he sat upon the royal throne, displaying to all the nations his grandeur, the magnificence of his kingdom, and the courage of his people. The two [allied monarchs from Tezcoco and Tacuba] sat next to him, and the enemy rulers were seated where they could see without being seen.

Ahuitzotl then requested that the royal officials have the majordomos, administrators, and treasurers of all the provinces bring the royal tribute to him. One by one these authorities brought the tribute they had collected. The first were those of the very city of Tenochtitlan, bearing tribute and products from different types of assessments, all of great richness. Then came those of Xochimilco from the *chinampa* zone, and the people of Chalco; then the Mixtecs of Coaixtlahuaca, which that province viewed as its capital. And there were tribute-bearers from Tochpan, Tochtepec, Tlatlauhquitepec, Tepeaca, Piaztlan, the Tlapanec zone, Tlacozauhtitlan, Chiapa, Couixco, Tepecuacuilco, and from the Tzinccoaca people. There was also tribute from Uitzoco, Youallan, Tlaxtlan, Teotitlan, Nochtepec, and Tzacualpan. Then came tribute-bearers from the Hot Country: Cuauhnahuac, Yauhtepec, Huaxtepec, Acapichtlan, and the Matlatzinca zone, Xocotlan, Xilotepec, Actopan, and other cities too numerous to mention.

All these men brought tribute in gold, jewels, ornaments, fine feathers, precious stones, all of great value and in quantity. There were countless articles of clothing and many adornments, both for men and for women, of great richness, and an amazing quantity of cacao, chiles, pumpkin seeds, all kinds of fruit, fowl, and game. All this was received in an orderly manner and to show Aztec grandeur and power to the enemies and guests and foreign people and fill them with bewilderment and fear. They saw that the Aztecs were masters of the world, their empire so wide and abundant that they had conquered all the nations and that all were their vassals. The guests, seeing such wealth and opulence and such authority and power, were filled with terror.

All the tribute was delivered to the royal treasurer or to the chief majordomo so that it could be divided according to law. Especially everything the priests requested for the cult to the gods and for the present ceremonies was provided. Then the artisans, silversmiths and lapidaries, and feather workers were given all they needed for making the jewelry, feather ornaments, diadems, and precious objects that the kings and great lords were to be given. In this way not only was the grandeur and sumptuousness of Tenochtitlan made evident, but also these things were available for the great feast and dedication of the Great Temple.

CHAPTER XLIV

Which treats of how the solemn ceremony and sacrifice began, and how Ahuitzotl commanded everyone in the provinces—man, woman, and the elderly—to be present so they would always remember this event.

All the nobles of the entire land had gathered in the city of Tenochtitlan, which was the capital of what is today New Spain. According to what the *Historia* tells us, the three allied kings met with old Tlacaelel. The king of Tezcoco was asked to speak first, as was customary. In the usual rhetorical fashion, he spoke, addressing Ahuitzotl:

> O powerful lords, and ruler of this great land of Mexico-Tenochtitlan, happy and blessed are you! The Lord of All Created Things has permitted you to rejoice in these festivities, and to finish this magnificent, this well-constructed, temple. These things were not granted to King Acamapichtli, nor to Huitzilihuitl, nor to King Chimalpopoca, nor to his successor, our close relative Itzcoatl, nor to Motecuhzoma the Elder, your father, nor to your brothers, Axayacatl Tecuhtli, and Tizocicatzin. All of these have departed from this life. They went away with great sorrow and regret for not having seen what has been granted to you. Therefore, though you are young, you are the ruler of this powerful kingdom, which is the root, the navel, and the heart of all the world order. Take care that the glory of the Aztec nation does not diminish but is increased. I beg of you, then, to call all the lords and officials of this city so that they may be instructed as to the tasks necessary for the completion of the project with which you have entrusted me.

When all the lords and leading men, authorities of Tenochtitlan, and officials of the barrios had come before Nezahualpiltzintli, king of Tezcoco, he reminded them that this was a special day, perhaps a day of triumph, perhaps a day of disaster, and warned them to take special care in all they did. He ordered them to have everything perfectly prepared and all the temples well decorated, newly plastered and painted, everything renovated, the main temples as well as the lesser ones and the neighborhood shrines, schools, and places of retreat, those of men and of women. The reason was that the festival was like a dedication of all the temples and the glorification of all of them. The whole ceremony was directed to this end. The officials replied that thus it would be, and they humbled themselves with much reverence. These orders were then carried out.

After having commanded these things, Nezahualpilli turned to King Ahuitzotl and suggested that he have a message sent to everyone in the region, that the day before the festival all the people of the cities be told to come, young and old, women and men, old people and youths, so that this solemn ceremony would be remembered forever. So Ahuitzotl had this command sent to all the people in the nearby cities, such as Tezcoco, Chalco, Xochimilco, and to the Tepanecs [of Azcapotzalco and Coyoacan], since they were not far away and it was easy for them to come. And so it was that messengers were sent with the order that, under penalty of death, no woman, child, old person, or youth remain in these cities but that all should come and attend the solemn festivities and sacrifice.

Thus, the crowds swarmed through the city. It was an awesome spectacle: the streets, squares, marketplaces, and houses were so bursting with people that it looked like an anthill. All this was done for the purpose of praising the splendor of the dedication ceremony and the greatness of Mexico-Tenochtitlan.

Before dawn on the festival day, when all the people had arrived, the prisoners who were to be sacrificed were brought out and were lined up in four files. One extended from the foot of the temple steps along the causeway that led to Coyoacan and Xochimilco; it was almost one league in length. Another, as long as the first, extended along the causeway to [what is now the shrine of] Our Lady of Guadalupe. In the same way, the third went along the road to Tacuba, and another extended east as far as the shore of the lake. These four lines moved toward the four places where the sacrifice was to take place and where the four lords were ready. The first and principal altar was before the statue of Huitzilopochtli, the dedication and renovation of whose temple was being celebrated. It was here that King Ahuitzotl was to sacrifice captives. The second was where the ruler of Tezcoco, Nezahualpiltzintli, was to kill, and the third was for the sovereign of Tacuba, as sacrificer. The fourth was the Sun Stone, which was prepared for sacrifice by the elderly Tlacaelel.

When all was ready, the three rulers put diadems on their heads, donned their ear plugs and labrets of gold and armbands and leg ornaments, also of gold. They dressed themselves in royal mantles, sandals, and breechcloths. Old Tlacaelel did the same because, as our chronicle states, he was given the same consideration as if he had been a king. Together with these lords, priests put on the garments of all the gods and goddesses. The *Historia* mentions their names, but it is not necessary to repeat them here.[1]

All these men ascended to the summit of the pyramid and each lord, accompanied by the priests dressed as gods, went to the place where he was to sacrifice, holding a knife in his hand. All the lords from the provinces and all the enemies were watching from within bowers that had been built for this occasion. Prisoners from the lines began to mount the steps and the four lords, assisted by the priests who held the wretches about to die by their feet and hands, began to kill. They opened the chests of the victims, pulled out the hearts, and offered them to the idols and to the sun. When the sovereigns grew weary, their satanic work was carried on by the priests who represented the gods. Our chronicle tells us that this sacrifice lasted four days from dawn to dusk and that, as I have said, eighty thousand four hundred men from different cities and provinces died.[2] All of this seemed so incredible to me that if the *Historia* had not forced me to put it down, and if I had not found confirmation of it in other written and painted manuscripts, I would not dare to write these things for fear of being held as a man who invents fables. He who translates a history is only obliged to reproduce in a different language what he finds written in a foreign tongue, and this is what I have done.

---

[1]In his writings Durán occasionally took it for granted that those consulting his works would know as much about his subject as he did and therefore left unfinished some of the information, to the frustration of the modern reader.

Although the names of the deity impersonators are not given here, in the Tlacaxipehualiztli ceremony when Huaxtec prisoners were sacrificed the priests were dressed in the garb of seven gods plus a jaguar, a puma, and an eagle (see chapter XX). When the captives from Tliliuhquitepec were sacrificed at the inauguration of the Sun Stone, the priestly god-impersonators represented thirteen deities (chapter XXXVIII). If the jaguar (*tigre*) and puma (*león*) can be considered one feline symbol, in the first group there are nine supernatural beings, in the second, thirteen. Both these numbers have cosmic symbolism; there were thirteen heavens and nine underworlds. Furthermore, the different gods represent celestial forces, for example, Huitzilopochtli and the eagle, the sun; or Tlaloc, Xipe Totec, Tepoztecatl, and Yohualahuan, water and earth's fertility. Evidently each deity represented in sacrificial rites had astronomical, calendrical, agricultural, economic, or social significance, each step of the rite and each surrogate representing a complex play whose object it was to keep the universe in motion.

[2]The number 80,400 victims given here by Durán has been a controversial subject. Those who believe this to be a gross exaggeration point out the problems in disposing of the huge number of corpses and suggest that the Spanish were always prone to exaggerate the number of sacrificial victims as a justification for the conquest. The Aztecs, of course, also exaggerated. A possible correct number for this mass sacrifice is 20,000 captives.

The streams of blood that ran down the steps of the temple were so great that when they reached the bottom and cooled off they formed large fat clots, enough to terrify one. Many priests went about gathering this blood in large gourds, taking it to the barrio temples and shrines, where they smeared the walls, lintels, and thresholds with it. They also smeared the rooms of the temples both inside and out, and the stench of the blood was so strong that it was unbearable. The *Historia* says it had a sour and abominable smell, to the point that it became unendurable to the people of the city.

After the sacrifice of the captives had ended (and because there were so many it lasted four days), on the fifth day the king sent splendid gifts of clothing to all the lords and rulers, especially to those who were his enemies. These were the lords of Tlaxcala, Huexotzinco, Cholula, Tecoac, Tliliuhquitepec, Zacatlan, also those of Metztitlan, of Mechoacan, and of Yopitzinco. To each one he gave weapons and shields with finely worked insignia, and sumptuous mantles and breechcloths, and magnificent gold diadems, excellently made, and ear plugs and nose plugs and labrets of gold and precious stones, and golden leg ornaments, and handsome sandals. To each guest he gave a tiger [or jaguar] skin, a lion [or puma] skin, and a load of mantles, to be distributed among the followers and allies. The lords of the cities were showered with these gifts, and, after having presented them, Ahuitzotl addressed those men: "O lords, I hold you in good favor for having come to visit and to honor with your presence the festival for my temple. These presents are given to you, they are won by the strength and valor of our powerful arm. They were neither stolen nor acquired in a bad war, but by courageous men dying, facing all dangers and trials with their chests and heads. We possess these things by the grace of our god Huitzilopochtli."

When he finished this address, he bade the visitors farewell so they could freely return to their lands and homes. For this purpose canoes had been prepared so that those men, with all the gifts they had received, could return in secret. The rowers were sworn to secrecy under pain of death and the destruction of their wives, children, and homes, if this incident was discovered or any news of it divulged. The same boatmen who had brought them took them back and left them safe at the borders of their land.

The guests gave thanks for the favor and good treatment they had received and departed happy and safe, yet bewildered by the majesty of Mexico-Tenochtitlan and the amazing number of victims who had died. They were also astonished at the wealth that had been given away so freely during those days. The emissaries from Mechoacan, Metztitlan, and Yopitzinco were also awed by what they had seen. However, they were pleased at the splendid reception that had been awarded them. They also left at midnight, accompanied by guards for their safety. Afer they had gone, men from the other provinces departed, all with gifts of fine clothing and adornments, and all contented.

After all the guests had left, the city continued with festivities and diversions. The king distributed luxurious gifts of mantles and jewels and breechcloths to all the soldiers and captains, to all the majordomos and officials, to all the priests of the temples. To all the old people and poor people in the city he gave a large quantity of mantles and breechcloths.

After gifts had been distributed and the festival had ended, the king ordered that the old skull rack be destroyed and the skulls on it burned. This was done. The eighty thousand four hundred fresh skulls were placed on the newly made rack, all spitted through the temples. Those that had been removed were burned, turned into ashes. Because of this festival no structure, large or small, of those dedicated to the gods was left without having been renovated.

Thus, the king, having taken care of the city, called together all the skilled workmen, those of the city and outsiders, who had contributed to the success of the dedication. These were the silversmiths, lapidaries, feather workers, painters, sculptors, stone carvers, masons, carpenters, potters, mat and seat makers, those who made smoking tubes for tobacco, as well as hunters of fowl and of mountain game, and fishermen. All the artisans and workmen in the city and those from outside were called, as well as the citizens themselves. The king then gave them fine mantles and breechcloths, in accordance with the profession of each one, telling them that he appreciated the services they had given and the great care they had taken in the preparation of the festival. Praising them, the king told these men that they were the ones who maintained the city, they were its hands and feet, without them it was worth nothing. They received their gifts and with much ceremony thanked the king for the favors he gave them. Humbly protesting their little worth, they took their leave and went away, happy for the attention they had received. This way the king won the goodwill of all those in his court and his kingdom, and they loved him and served him willingly and affectionately. His image was that of a compassionate father to his people, liberally distributing his possessions and riches to the rich and to the poor, proving himself to be benevolent and affable.

King Ahuitzotl remembered that the people of the province of Teloloapan[3] had been invited to these festivities but had not attended,

---

[3] In the present-day state of Guerrero.

which made him suspect they might be preparing a rebellion. He sent his emissaries in an attempt to determine the cause of their absence; and when the envoys arrived at the town of Teticpac, they were informed that those of Teloloapan had indeed rebelled and had closed the roads and paths to prevent anyone from entering their region. In order to verify this, the Aztecs followed the royal road and found that it was obstructed with stones, tree trunks, century plants, cacti, and branches and that it could not be used for travel. When the emissaries saw this, they returned to their king and told him that the province was in a state of rebellion, the roads and paths had been closed, and that it was not possible to pass.

Without delay and without asking advice, Ahuitzotl warned his own people and those of the neighboring provinces: Tezcoco, Tacuba, Chalco and Xochimilco, and all the others subject to Mexico-Tenochtitlan. Soon a great army was raised. Ahuitzotl went in person on this campaign, this way encouraging his soldiers. When he came to Teloloapan, he attacked the city, vanquished it, destroyed it, and subdued the region to such an extent that never again did it dare rebel. As punishment for the rebellion, according to the *Historia*, excessive tribute was levied. The people there were ordered to pay the following tribute every eighty days: four hundred loads of cacao, ten loads of cloth, ten loads of women's clothing, together with certain fruits and foodstuffs that are produced in that land and found in that province.

The people of Teloloapan complained that they had been incited and misled by their neighbors, those of Alauiztlan and Oztoman. Ahuitzotl then ordered that these cities be destroyed to avenge that treacherous act, and this was quickly done with the help of Teloloapan. When they reached the limits of those cities, they demanded that the enemy surrender in peaceful fashion so there would be no need for battle. Since this was refused, the king ordered the two cities destroyed completely. They were left desolate, and no man or woman, no old person, was spared but all were killed except the children, the boys and girls, who were brought as captives to the city of Tenochtitlan. So, showing no pity, Ahuitzotl had the two cities destroyed and leveled and the people put to death, with the exception of the children. Forty thousand two hundred little boys and girls, youths and maidens, were then distributed among the provinces and cities of the region of Tenochtitlan. The remaining people of Teloloapan, saddened by the painful destruction, begged King Ahuitzotl to divide up the lands of the conquered territory among them. He answered that when he returned to his city he would decide what to do about those lands, inasmuch as he was extremely fond of the cacao, cotton, and all kinds of fruit from orchards that existed in that region.

With all his army, Ahuitzotl left that province and returned home, stopping at different towns along the way, where the people gave him enthusiastic receptions, giving him everything he required, including large quantities of finely worked mantles with breechcloths, jars of honey, and other valuable presents. Wherever he stopped, he was greeted with long rhetorical speeches and was congratulated for his victory.

When it was known that Ahuitzotl was approaching, the rejoicing began, with the usual torches, bonfires, music with drums, whistles, flutes, and conch shells, also songs and dances. All the priests and elders went out of the city, to Chapultepec, to receive their lord and king, with much rejoicing and happiness, and then accompanied him into the city. Here they made long flowery speeches. As soon as the king had entered the city, all the captives and prisoners from those provinces also began to enter, together with the soldiers who had captured them. After the captives had observed the ceremony of eating earth at the foot of the statue of Huitzilopochtli and had gone in a circle around the temple, they were brought before the king. He ordered that they be well cared for, and then he had clothing and mantles — which I believe must have been the spoils of those cities that were left devastated and deserted — distributed among the militia, those from the city as well as soldiers from the provinces. The latter, contented, returned to their own lands.

The captives were sacrificed during the first feast that came along after they had been imprisoned. This sacrifice was the one called "Flaying of Men."

CHAPTER XLV

Which treats of how Aztec and Otomi colonists were sent to repopulate Alauiztlan and Oztoman, the two cities that had been destroyed.

After some time had passed (six months, according to the *Historia*), during which time King Ahuitzotl was occupied with affairs relating to the royal crown and therefore ignored the requests from the people of Teloloapan [to redistribute the land there], finally, having finished the internal business, he summoned the rulers of Tezcoco and Tacuba to come to the council meeting where decisions were to be made. Without these two lords no resolutions were ever taken.

Although on the one hand this indicates that the king of Tezcoco was in some ways subject to Mexico, it would seem, on the other hand, that he had some authority and voice in this same city. He was always the first to speak, his words were respected, and during elections his vote was decisive. And as proof of this and regarding what will be discussed here, it will be seen that it was his decision that was final, and not that of King Ahuitzotl, nor of his coadjutor Tlacaelel. So when the two rulers, Nezahualpiltzintli of Tezcoco and Totoquihuaztli of Tacuba, came to the city, they met in a council with the king and Tlacaelel. Ahuitzotl explained why they had been called: "O lords, you know that in the war we waged on Teloloapan, Oztoman, and Alauiztlan the last two cities were depopulated. All their fruit, cacao, and cotton plantations were deserted, their fields made barren. It would be sad to see those lands lost, left uncultivated and abandoned forever. Therefore, I have decided to send people to settle that country, to benefit by its riches and make it prosper. I have thought about this and, considering how great and thickly populated those cities once were, I plan to send four hundred men with their families from Tenochtitlan. I also want each of you to send four hundred families so that the total will be one thousand two hundred. From the other provinces should go twenty settlers each, which will make a total of eight hundred. The total will be two thousand families, one thousand for each city."[1]

---

[1] The new settlements founded by the Aztecs remind one of the Inca endeavor to hold together that vast empire by means of new colonies made up of loyal Quec-

King Nezahualpilli of Tezcoco replied that this decision seemed wise to him and that the resettlement of abandoned lands was no new thing, since it had been done many times before. However, he considered it unwise to take four hundred heads of families from Tenochtitlan because it would weaken the city. His opinion was that only two hundred should be recruited and they should be taken from the different barrios so the distribution would be even. Each barrio should give five men and none was to go against his will. The men were to be told about the fertility and richness of those lands and it was to be explained to them that they would be freed from tribute while there and at the same time would be reaping the benefits of the cacao and cotton fields and fruit orchards; they would be masters of all those riches. They were to go of their own will. After the number of families from each barrio was completed, if anyone else wished to go and he was married, he would not be given permission. But if he was unmarried, was a young man who wished to try his fortune, search for a new life, then he would be allowed to leave. Like numbers were to go from Tezcoco and from the Tepanec region. The other provinces were to decide how many settlers they could send. All would go of their own free will; no one was to be forced to migrate.

Ahuitzotl, Tlacaelel, and the king of Tacuba, having listened to Nezahualpiltzintli's opinion, dared not contradict him but remained silent. They agreed with this decision, then, they said it should be so. The principal ambassador was called and told to send his emissaries with this communication to all these places: Chalco, Xochimilco, Cuitlahuac, the four cities subject to Colhuacan, to the Hot Country, and to the regions of the Mazahuaque and the Cuauhtlapanecas. Finally, all the cities subject to the royal crown of Mexico-Tenochtitlan were to be advised. They were to send married men with their families to settle in those two cities that had been left deserted. And, as has been said, they were to be told of the abundance, richness, and fertility of those lands and the possiblity of their becoming masters of all that. No city was to receive fewer than twenty families and any persons above this number who wished to go there would be allowed to do so.

Leaving the palace, the ambassador summoned the emissaries and envoys who were under his orders and without delay sent them to the four directions. They went with their message, some to Cuauhtlalpan, some to the Hot Lands, others to Chalco, or to Xochimilco, to

hua-speaking Incas. This pattern of resettlement was later to be continued in Mexico by the Spanish conquerors, who sent numerous Aztec and other Nahuatl-speaking peoples to the north in an effort to have them merge with nomadic groups there. These colonists found their way to Zacatecas, Saltillo, and other places north of Mexico City.

Cuitlahuac and Mezquic. Other emissaries went to the four cities subject to Colhuacan, while some traveled to Matlatzinco and that whole region. Still other messengers took the news to Cuauhtlalpan, land of the Otomi people, and to Xilotepec, Chiapa, Mazahuacan, Xocotitlan, Xiquipilco, Cuauhuacan, Cillan, and Cocuilan. In all these places that were visited by the emissaries no head town was left before twenty married men had been chosen from each one. They were told that King Ahuitzotl wished them to go to Mexico. Each group of twenty was to be accompanied by its principal man, its leader, so that in those cities where they were to settle they would be established in barrios in an orderly maner, each group with its members under the guidance of its own leaders, recognized by them. In this way they would have someone in authority who could go to the city as the governor or representative of those people.

The emissaries relayed their message to the lords of all the cities and towns, where they were well received. They were fed well and given flowers, tobacco with smoking tubes, and handsome clothing that was typical of each city. After they had been given sleeping quarters and were treated in this generous manner, the people who wished to go settle in those lands were assigned to them. Besides the twenty each town was obliged to contribute, many more asked to go to the lands that were so fertile, so rich, so abundant in everything. Some of these people were allowed to accompany the twenty, others were not.

On their return, the emissaries reported all their activities and claimed to have carried out their task successfully in dealing with the lords of the different cities and towns. They told about being well treated in these places. They also said that a great many people wished to go settle in those faraway lands, especially those who were already acquainted with that region, some having been in the war and having participated in the looting of the cities. Other people wished to help populate that region in order to free themselves from paying tribute and doing personal service, which they had to do in Tenochtitlan.

When all these prospective settlers had come together in the city, Ahuitzotl ordered that new clothing be given to the women and children. This was done immediately. Then everyone was told to go to a certain place where a long, elegant, and consolatory talk was addressed to them by one of the council members. In this way they tried to console those people who were abandoning their homeland, their houses, their fields, their fathers and mothers, their brothers and close kinsmen, and who felt great sadness because of this. Therefore, they were encouraged to anticipate prosperity and consolation and were told that in time they would forget the love they felt for their homeland and for all the things they were leaving behind. They were made to believe that it was the will of the gods and of the Lord of All Created Things who rules over all. Eventually those who remained behind would be envious of those who had found such freedom. In time, it was said, when the settlers had established their homes in peace and comfort, the relatives whom they had left behind would enter their gates, envious of their success and forced to go there also because of the misery that could be found in the city of Tenochtitlan.

In this address all the leaders and heads of barrios, all the protectors of the people who were under their authority, were requested to give a good reception to the ambassadors and envoys who would be sent from Tenochtitlan in the future, to greet them warmly and to treat them in the correct manner that was customary with them. They were to be treated especially well when they went to collect the cacao harvest that was to be set aside for the royal crown of Mexico. The cacao was to be sown collectively, each group contributing whatever labor it could, according to the number of its people. The cacao was to be sent to the capital city in lieu of tribute.

The settlers were also advised to have armed men always ready since they were near the boundary of Mechoacan, which was their worst enemy. It was wise, they were told, to care for themselves with all diligence because the Tarascans were people who abhorred the Aztecs.

After they had been given this advice on the part of King Ahuitzotl, all the new settlers expressed their thanks, but at the same time they cried out loudly because of their apprehension. With much weeping they departed. Twelve elders from the city went before them. These were the most venerable men of Mexico-Tenochtitlan, and the king had ordered them not to abandon the people until they had settled them in their places, had distributed the land fairly, and had seen that the new inhabitants were living in peace and calm in their new homes, the way the royal council had determined this was to take place. The leaders were advised to conduct the people slowly because of the weakness of the women and children. They were told to send men ahead of them to be sure that all things that would be needed had been made ready in the towns through which they were to pass and that all the people of those places would receive and welcome them kindly and make them forget the trials of the journey.

The twelve leading men were dressed in long tunics and from their backs hung small gourds filled with incense in powdered form. Their hair was tied with red ribbons with feathers attached at the point where these ribbons were tied. Each carried a staff in one hand and in the other a fan. Walking in front of the rest, they left the city, thus leading the people who began to follow them. That day they all reached the town of Xalatlauhco, where they were well received by the people here and by the neighboring towns. They were shown every possible kindness and were presented with flowers and tobacco, which pleased these people greatly. They were also given new clothing, each city or town contributing what it could.

Finally they reached the province of Teloloapan, where they were to settle, and there they divided into three parts. The largest group went to Oztoman, another to Alauiztlan, and a third stayed in Teloloapan. The latter were to act as the garrison that guarded the city, for it had not been totally depopulated as had the others. When they had been established in those cities and had been given land, houses, and some furnishings, the people were also given maize, chiles, beans, *chian*, and other seeds and foodstuffs these people eat, in order that they might survive the first year. Everything was taken to those places by order of King Ahuitzotl so that they would have enough to eat until next year's harvest.

The men who had gone as guards and guides with the people, on seeing that they were pacified, were comforted, spoke to them with consolatory words and then returned to Tenochtitlan. Here they related to Ahuitzotl all that had occurred, of how the people had been led successfully to their new homes, how the cities were now resettled and everyone was content. The king was very pleased to hear this.

Not many months after this region had been repopulated, a council was set up and a governor was elected from among the principal men who had settled there. The naming of the governor was communicated to King Ahuitzotl by men who took him rich presents of mantles, feathers, cacao, a great deal of cotton, and many kinds of fruit common to that region. The king was delighted with these things. He received them with much pleasure and then confirmed the election of the governor. He sent this official some fine weapons and insignia that identified him as a nobleman. The other men were given presents of shields and feathers and weapons, all very valuable, in return for the gifts they had brought. Ahuitzotl earnestly implored them to see that peace and brotherhood prevailed and at the same time that the region be well guarded.

In this way those cities were peopled with Aztecs who still inhabit the region and are still subject to the city of Mexico-Tenochtitlan.

CHAPTER XLVI

Which treats of how the Aztecs waged war upon Tecuantepec, also Izhuatlan, Miauatlan, and Amaxtlan. With a description of how cities in that famed province were conquered.

We have mentioned many times that the Aztecs never incited any nation to war against them. Conflicts sprang from disobedience or from crimes perpetrated against Aztecs who were sometimes killed along the roads. This is the excuse they gave, and they give it today. In the *Historia* I find this justification: "We did not seek trouble; they incited us, they provoked us. The fault is theirs and we shall not tolerate affronts from anyone."

The provinces of Tecuantepec, Xolotla, Izhuatlan, Miauatlan, and Amaxtlan were so far away from Mexico, and the people there were so sure of their own greatness due to the multitude of inhabitants in that region and the strength of their armed forces, that they decided to block the way to Aztec merchants who came each year to milk the region of its riches. These riches consisted of gold and jewels, feathers, and many other fine things that the Aztec traders exchanged for foodstuffs and items that were of little value. Each year the merchants returned laden with those fine luxury items. And so many of these people who were trading, exchanging, went to the Tecuantepec region all through the year that they were always to be seen on the road. Not only the Aztecs went back and forth but also the Tezcocans, Tepanecs, Xochimilcas, Chalcas, Tlahuicas, Tlaxcalans, Cholulans, and men from all the area around the Volcano. Not one or two went from each town but one hundred at a time, all carrying things of little value, such as cakes of algae from the lake in the basin of Mexico, patties of little worms, packs of tiny "bones" or eggs of marine flies—called *ahuauhtli*—barbecued duck, and other foods that are not found around Tecuantepec.[1] They also took many toys and little things that they exchanged for cacao, gold, feathers, and precious stones.

The rulers of those cities discussed it among themselves and decided to stop this sacking of their riches that were taken to cities and provinces under Aztec control, leaving behind only the food delicacies and things of little value that had been brought by the Aztec

---

[1] Although Durán places little importance on the lake foods and states that the gold, precious stones, feathers, and cacao from southern Mexico were of true value, in truth the aquatic delicacies were also much desired and had high nutritional content.

traders. Once this agreement was made, those southern cities put guards along the roads who began to attack and kill merchants from Tenochtitlan and from other places who were accustomed to travel those routes. When this news reached the city, it was revealed that the killing of these merchants was so great that at one place after another men had been murdered, had been thrown on the road, and then had been eaten by wild beasts or by vultures. The traders were so terrified by all this that they dared not travel that route.

The rulers of Tenochtitlan, Tezcoco, and Tacuba were sorely worried about this situation, so they met to discuss what could be done about it. It was decided that without delay armed men should be sent to avenge the death of those merchants who mercilessly and without reason had been killed by the people [of the province of Tecuantepec]. As soon as this had been agreed upon, couriers were sent to all the allied provinces to advise them of the decision and to announce that King Ahuitzotl planned to declare war on Tecuantepec and the other cities in that area.

When this was proclaimed, many warriors were excited by the idea of the famed riches from the Tecuantepec provinces. So, well armed and splendidly adorned in the manner customary to these people, the Aztec army set out. The soldiers carried a quantity of provisions, such as toasted kernels as well as maize flour, bean flour, toasted tortillas, sun-baked tamales and others that had a kind of mold, great loads of chiles, and cacao that had been ground and formed into small balls. These was a great deal of everything because, apart from the supplies provided by the rulers from their immense bins and storehouses, each soldier carried on his back his own food, as much as he could. This way he augmented the ordinary rations that were given to him. And tied to this pack were his sword, his shield, and other weapons he would be needing. So many men went to fight in that war that the *Historia* states that, after the soldiers left, the cities and towns were almost deserted. It was rare to meet men on the street; there were only women and small children. Four days after the soldiers had abandoned the city, had gone to war, all the women came out wearing cloths of mourning and with dust and ashes on their hair as a sign that their husbands, sons, and brothers were absent in war. These women did not wash their hair or their faces or their clothes until they had news that the Aztec army was victorious.

Each day the women got up before dawn and made an offering or sacrifice to the gods in a special room in the house. The sacrificial ceremony went this way: first, light a fire in the room, then incense each one of the [little statues of the] gods, place before the gods an offering of tortillas and wine and all kinds of food that were customarily offered at these times, and then, seated before these images, weep and moan and pray in the following manner:

> O great Lord of All Created Things, remember your servant who has gone to exalt your honor and the greatness of your name. He has gone to offer his blood in that sacrifice which is war, to serve you. Behold, Lord, that he did not go out to work for me or for his children! Nor did he go to his usual labors to support his home, with tumpline on his head, or with a digging stick in his hand. He went for your sake, in your name, to obtain glory for you. Therefore, O Lord, let your pious heart have pity on him who with great labor and affliction now goes through the mountains and valleys, hills and precipices, offering you the moisture, the sweat, from his brow. Grant him victory in this war so that he may return to rest in his home, and so my children and I may see his countenance again, may feel his presence.

This prayer was recited every day at dawn by the women until their sons or husbands, brothers or other relatives, returned from the war.

When the army reached the city of Oaxaca, the men were well received by the Aztecs living there and by the people in the valley. Having set up camp, the soldiers rested there a few days and replenished their supplies. King Ahuitzotl, who participated in that war in person, summoned the lords of all the towns and villages of the region. When they answered his call, Ahuitzotl requested that they provide the Aztecs with soldiers and provisions. These lords, then, willingly, sent many well armed men and large quantities of food. Ahuitzotl thanked them for their help and promised to return the favor. But when news of this reached the ruler of Tecuantepec, he threatened the Aztecs with serious retaliation.

Ahuitzotl and his chief advisers met to discuss which cities should be attacked first and it was decided that these should be Izhuatlan and Otlatlan. A public announcement was made that all captives taken in those place would be slaughtered and that no one should bother to take prisoners because there was much work of conquest to be done and the distance from those provinces to Mexico-Tenochtitlan was great; therefore, it would be an enormously difficult problem to take captives from one place to another. So all those captured should be put to death. As soon as these notices had been made known, had been communicated to the soldiers, the army broke camp and marched in an orderly fashion to Izhuatlan. Here they fought and soon destroyed the city. Then they continued on to Miauatlan. Although much resistance was encountered here, eventually the city was conquered. Its people came out with their hands crossed, which is the customary gesture of surrender, and offered themselves and their properties as subject to Mexico-Tenochtitlan. These were accepted by the Aztecs, who offered friendship in return.

Tribute to be paid by the vanquished people was established and a few captives were sacrificed to the gods. Then Ahuitzotl ordered the men of Miauatlan to guide his army to the road that led to Xolotla, to Amaxtlan, and to Tecuantepec. The Miauatlan men agreed and guided them until they were in view of those provinces. Ahuitzotl, informed of this proximity, commanded all his soldiers to be prepared for battle. Since they all greatly feared the Tecuantepec warriors, Ahuitzotl made an encouraging speech to his army, inciting the men to throw themselves fearlessly and with all their hearts into the battle, faced by possible death, for their reward would be given them by the Lord of All Created Things. He goaded them on to accept that sacrifice with their youthful manly hearts, and not to think about returning to their homeland.

When the soldiers heard these words, they all began to weep and feel very sad. They embraced each other, said farewell with great sighs of sorrow, fathers to sons, sons to fathers. But then they all formed in correct order, each man well armed, each group in its designated place. Their faces were blackened with the divine soot, as they call it.

Ahuitzotl was dressed with fine mantles and under these was well armed with blue weapons. He wore gold bracelets, gold leg ornaments, and on his head a splendid crown of rich feathers. On his back was a gold drum, with which the kings signaled the attack or the retreat. In this way the king himself represented the drum — or [in his absence] his general did, when they gave the attack signal or played the sound for withdrawal of the army. Ahuitzotl, his principal men, and all the other warriors were armed and dressed in special attire according to their rank, as their laws permitted them to dress. When they came in sight of the enemy — who were also lavishly dressed, who were also self-confident — they surged forward in a ferocious manner, as did the other side, with the result that both armies fought and mixed together with such fury that for many hours it was impossible to know which side was winning. Nevertheless, the Aztecs were so experienced in similar situations, their courage indomitable, and they were so astute and cunning in their fighting that they began to advance. Soon a number of commanders of the enemy troops were killed on the battlefield. When the Aztecs saw that they were winning, they began to press on in such a way that the soldiers from Tecuantepec and the other towns began to lose heart and flee from the field. They went up into the rugged places, fleeing from the Aztecs, who, wish no pity at all, killed everyone they caught, without pardoning the life of any.

The lords of those cities, seeing this catastrophe and realizing that resistance to the Aztecs had ceased, begged for mercy, prostrating themselves on the ground before Ahuitzotl, who, as furious as his men, was fighting alongside them. But he was moved by these entreaties and so sounded his drum, signaling retreat.

But his soldiers made themselves deaf to the drum, pretending they had not heard it, and with terrifying cries and shouts continued the butchering. They entered all the houses in the city, plundering everything and killing anyone they encountered. The captains, sergeants, and other officers, seeing that the king wished this destruction to cease, ran from one place to another, knives and clubs in hand, trying to interfere and stop the soldiers, who, like wild beasts, were destroying the city. The soldiers became very angry and swore they would never again go to war in such a remote region where, having conquered, they were not even allowed to sack the cities for their own benefit. Only this interest in looting had made them leave their homes, their lands, their wives and children. And after having conquered those four provinces, Tecuantepec being the last one, they had counted on the spoils since the hard work of fighting here had been badly paid and now they were denied that satisfaction. When Ahuitzotl heard these complaints, he promised to compensate his men for all they had lost.

Ahuitzotl very kindly received the lords of Tecuantepec and the neighboring region and granted them all they asked for. In return for these favors and so much benevolence the lords took Ahuitzotl into their city, where they gave comfortable quarters to him and to his allies from the provinces. They also gave the Aztec ruler a rich present and promised to pay tribute every eighty days, in return for Ahuitzotl having pardoned them for their daring [in having crossed him]. They swore, too, to obey him, accept him as their superior, and to be subject to Tenochtitlan.

The king turned the gift over to one of his noblemen and told him to divide it up among the others, since he did not desire anything for himself. Then couriers were sent to the Aztec capital to make known the victories won in those provinces, to announce that all of them had been conquered, though with many difficulties and the loss of some of the Aztec warriors.

This news was received with much joy and exultation. It was then relayed to Tezcoco, Tacuba, Chalco, the Hot Country, and all the other allied provinces, so that everyone could share in the rejoicing and could be prepared for the reception of the king and all the dignitaries of Mexico-Tenochtitlan and the provinces. This welcoming ceremony was as impressive as any that had been held for other rulers, for people from the entire region came with many fine gifts, with much cheer and rejoicing, to celebrate the victory and congratulate the soldiers. The conquest and subjugation of those newly won regions brought many benefits and advantages to the city. And Ahuitzotl's victorious entrance was the cause of jubilation. His arrival set off much rejoicing and festivity, all of which lasted many days. During this time the lords of Tezcoco, Tacuba, Itzucan, Chalco, the Hot Lands, and the other provinces were with Ahuitzotl, who feted them and presented them with many gifts. Each day they received splendid mantles and valuable jewelry and were served an abundance of excellent food and drink.

All of this opulence was directed toward demonstrating Tenochtitlan's greatness and magnificence, also to please the allied lords, to make them favorable to Tenochtitlan, and to have them at this city's orders when the need came.

CHAPTER XLVII

Which treats of how King Ahuitzotl visited all the temples when he returned from war. With a description of the great offerings and sacrifices he made out of gratitude for his victory and the favors he granted to his subjects.

When King Ahuitzotl had rested from the labors of such a long and difficult war and of the wearisome road to Tecuantepec and back, he decided to show his gratitude to the gods and thank them for the favor they had done in granting him this victory. Therefore, he ordered that oblations be prepared and that all the priests in the temples be advised of his decision and that they be made ready. Messengers were sent to Chalco, Itztapalapa, Mexicatzinco, and Huitzilopochco. He had decided to visit these places since some of the most sacred shrines were there.

In this way Ahuitzotl first visited the temple of his city. The priests and guards of the temples were prepared for this visit, all of them dressed in the way that was customary when the kings returned from war. All of them were in their tunics with little gourds hanging down their backs; these served also as ties for a kind of dalmatic. They wore their hair in a braid that hung down the back, much the way women braided their hair. All were painted black and carried flaming incense burners in their hands. These priests formed two long lines on either side of the street, all the way from the door of the palace to the courtyard of the temple, which was adorned with greenery and festively decorated, done with great care. Then the king appeared, preceded by all his guards, who were handsomely dressed soldiers, every one of noble blood. These men carried staffs in their hands but no other weapons. On their heads they wore their insignia that identified them as noble warriors; these consisted of two or three green or blue feathers tied to the middle part of the hair with red cords. Some of the men wore the feathers erect on their heads, while others wore theirs hanging. On their backs were as many tassels as the feats they had performed in battle. These tassels were attached to the headbands or cords that tied the feathers to the hair.

After these soldiers came the great men of the court. They were splendidly dressed and all wore gold headbands, like wreaths. All wore, too, ear pendants and labrets of gold and precious stones. In their noses were nose plugs of white beryl, perforated, so that feathers of the color that most pleased them could be inserted. In this way the translucent beryl took on the color of the feather. Their costume, therefore, vibrated with color. There were great bunches of feathers of many colors on their heads, tied with gold headbands. Other wide, long plumes were attached to gold armbands; jewels and little gold bells were around their ankles, and on their wrists and at the neck were rich jewels set with fine stones.

The king went out after these noblemen. He was dressed in his royal mantle, with a magnificent diadem on his head, and with golden armbands and anklets, golden ear pendants, labrets and nose plugs — all covered with precious stones — and wearing great strings of jewels and fine stones around his neck. These covered him like a cloak. Behind him came many dwarfs and hunchbacks who served as pages to the king and nobility, together with eunuchs who cared for the wives and concubines. The dwarfs carried ornate mantles, armbands and legbands made of gold, rich feathers and fine jewelry, and the skins of jaguars and ocelots that had been brought back from the conquest of Tecuantepec and that region, as well as other objects that were part of the spoils of war.

When the king appeared, the two long rows of priests on either side of the street threw incense into their burners and began to incense him as if he were a god. While this was going on, Ahuitzotl reached the temple and entered the courtyard, where the drums, conch shells, and flutes began to sound. When he reached the top of the temple, the music ceased and all prostrated themselves before him, in a ceremony like that of "kissing the hands." The king received everyone with smiles and greeted all the priests of the gods with courtesy and reverence. He thanked them for the honor they had shown him and asked for an incense burner. A fine one was given him that was intricately made and richly gilded. He filled it with incense and then incensed the wooden and stone images of gods that were inside the temple.

After the incense ceremony was over, many quail were given to Ahuitzotl and with his own hands he decapitated them and poured the blood at the foot of the altar, then tossed the dead quail at the feet of the gods. This was done with special care before the image of Huitzilopochtli, to whom this peaceful sacrifice was offered. When he had finished this rite, the king requested a jaguar bone and a very sharp instrument made of this was handed to him. He drew blood from the top part of his earlobes, from his arms and shins, and this was done in a squatting position, such as the Indians use today, without allowing the buttocks to touch the floor. This position was a reverent one; touching the floor would have been considered disrespectful. This way of sitting was the equivalent of our kneeling. As he squatted there, supported by his heels, Ahuitzotl put his finger to the floor and taking earth with it he put it in his mouth. This ceremony was called "the eating of sacred earth." When this ceremony and the autosacrifice had ended, the king stood up and turned to the people, exclaiming in a loud voice:

> O almighty, powerful Lord of All Created Things, you for whom we live, whose vassals and slaves we are, Lord of the Day and of the Night, of the Wind and the Water, whose strength keeps us alive! I offer you thanks for the help you have given me, for having brought me back to your city with the victory you granted me. I have returned to this great city of Mexico-Tenochtitlan where our ancestors—Chichimecs and Aztecs—with great pains and the sweat of their brows discovered the blissful eagle seated upon the prickly pear cactus. There the eagle ate and rested, next to the springs of blue and red waters, which were filled with flying fish and with white snakes and white frogs. This wondrous thing appeared because you wanted to show us the greatness of your power and your will. You made us masters of the wealth we now possess, and I give you infinite thanks, O Lord, for not frowning upon my extreme youth—for I am still a boy—or my lack of strength or the weakness of my chest. You have subjected those remote and barbarous nations to my power, to my control. You have won all these things, all is yours! All has been won to give you honor and praise! Therefore, O powerful and heroic Huitzilopochtli, in order to honor you and to be successful in war, you have brought us to this place that was only water before, which our ancestors filled in and upon it built our city under your orders. In thanks for these favors I offer you part of the spoils that have been won by the strength of our chests and arms and aided by you, O Lord!

When Ahuitzotl had finished this speech, he aproached the statue of Huitzilopochtli. Here, with much reverence, he removed the garments worn by the god and dressed him with the clothing that the hunchbacks and dwarfs had carried. Then some fine thing brought from each of the conquered provinces was placed before the god so he could share in these acquisitions from war. Among these were jaguar and ocelot skins as well as many jewels, precious stones, and fine feathers, all elaborated in different styles and with excellent workmanship. As soon as these treasures had been deposited before Huitzilopochtli, the king left the temple and returned to his home in the same order and pomp with which he had come.

Ahuitzotl then visited all the temples of the different gods that were in the city, going to one each day. After this he decided to visit the most important temples on the outskirts, in the manner of a pilgrimage. So, accompanied by many of his people, both from his own city and from the neighboring places, he went to Chalco, where there was an imposing, a splendid, temple called Tlapitzahuayan. This was a highly revered and sumptuous temple where everyone in the Chalco area went when there were ceremonies such as offerings and sacrifices. In the temple were statues of Huitzilopochtli and Tezcatlipoca, the two principal gods of the land, although the main devotion was to Tezcatlipoca.

The ruler of Chalco arrived and greeted Ahuitzotl warmly, with the honor and reverence he always received, and this was very great. Ahuitzotl then lost no time in starting the ceremony he had come to perform. With the same solemn order he had followed in Tenochtitlan, the king, accompanied by his guards and noblemen, all attired as has been described and with the same musicians and men with incense burners, went to the temple and climbed to the top. After burning incense to the gods, Ahuitzotl sacrificed a number of quail before the statue of Tezcatlipoca. He then requested the bone of an eagle and with this drew blood from the fleshy parts of his arms and legs. He offered another garment for the statue of Tezcatlipoca, like the one usually used, and many other valuable things from the spoils of that last war. Following this Ahuitzotl made another long, elegant rhetorical speech. After this he went to the royal palace, where, after he was served delicious food, the lords of the Chalco province presented him with splendid gifts of mantles and jewels and numerous things from their towns and treasuries.

Ahuitzotl gave thanks for all this in a most courteous manner, then left Chalco and went to Itztapalapa. This was the second place on his ceremonial route, where the king made the same rhetorical addresses, sacrifices [of quail and bloodletting], and offerings to the gods.

Mexicatzinco was the next city visited, where the same actions were repeated. He ended his pilgrimage in Huitzilopochco, where with great solemnity, perhaps even more so than in Tenochtitlan, he also carried out these ceremonies and offerings.

The king then returned to his city together with all the lords and dignitaries, and with other people who had accompanied him.

The following day the treasurers and factors from the different cities and provinces brought to the king the tribute that had been collected during the year. There were an enormous number of mantles of many designs, bundles and bundles of them, breechcloths, gold, jewels, feathers, shields, weapons, insignia, birds of rich feathers from the coastal regions, and cacao. The tribute, in fact, was so great in quantity, so rich, and so varied that it exceeds the imagination, is impossible to describe. From each city and each province, every eighty days, a million Indians arrived with a third of the yearly tribute, laden with everything the land produced, even tiny creatures.

This is not an exaggeration since we read that Motecuhzoma the Second, with whom we shall deal later, even had lice and fleas brought as tribute. In this the kings showed their tyrannical nature, though they justified these rulings by saying that they were risking their lives for their country in order to have the means to maintain the kingdom.

Among the items of tribute were garments suitable only for the lords and others for people of different stations. The material and designs of each mantle were in accord with the rank of its wearer. After the tribute had been delivered to those who were in charge of storing it, one of the tribute collectors spoke lengthily thus: "O powerful lord, let not our arrival disturb your powerful heart and peaceful spirit, nor shall we be the cause of some sudden alarm that might provoke an illness for you. You well know that we are your vassals and in your presence we are nothing but dirt and rubbish. If we are worth anything at all, if some value is attributed to our persons, this arises from, it emanates from, your power and your will, which are like a spring from which flows all excellence. And knowing this we have come before you to bring tribute from all corners of the earth that your subjects are obliged to contribute. And these vassals—though they acquire these things with hard work, though they sweat doing it, though they have to go, staff in hand, over mountains and through canyons, over great plains and through valleys, with tumpline on the head and digging stick in hand, searching for and obtaining not only food for their wives and children but also the tribute your vassals are compelled to give, all this time eating and drinking badly, sleeping when they can with the bundles of goods they have obtained next to their heads in order to protect them—they are willing to go through all these trials in order to serve you and are very happy that you are pleased with their service."

The king answered that he deeply appreciated all that this man and the other tribute collectors had said and done. He was happy to receive all that tribute.

The treasurers, factors, and administrators from the cities and towns having been well attended, having been given everything they needed, left Tenochtitlan. Ahuitzotl then summoned all the noblemen of his court. When they were in his presence he spoke to them: "It is not correct that although all these riches are won with the toil of your bodies, the strength of your arms and your hearts, the sweat of your brow and the shedding of your blood, it is only I who can enjoy these things." So saying, he led them all to a place called *petaca*,[1] which

---

[1] The word *Petlacalli*, "reed chest," where valuable things are kept, therefore, "treasury." The person in charge of the *Petlacalli* or treasury was the *Petlacalcatl*. *Petaca* in modern Spanish means suitcase, a container where things are carried.

means "treasury," where tribute and wealth in general were kept. He divided up among all those men much of the tribute just received, that is, the fine mantles and breechcloths, jewels and precious stones, weapons, and shields handsomely decorated with feathers of many colors. After making these gifts to the noblemen, Ahuitzotl called the sons of the lords and dignitaries of the court, all the captains and leaders of the army, the seasoned warriors and the other soldiers who had participated courageously in the conquest of those four provinces. They were all awarded part of these riches, each one according to his rank and his feats in battle, as the king had promised them in Tecuantepec when he prohibited the looting and destruction that was going on there. All these men were contented and considered themselves well paid. They thanked their lord and king for this favor. They were most willing to continue serving him, seeing that he was so generous, so magnanimous, in compensating them for their work.

CHAPTER XLVIII

Which treats of the death of Tlacaelel and of how King Ahuitzotl asked the ruler of Coyoacan for water from Acuecuexco. With an account of the excuse that was given to him and how Ahuitzotl therefore had this ruler killed.

Shortly after King Ahuitzotl returned from the conquest that has been described (and to avoid prolixity in this account I did not discuss everything that took place in every province because, after all, the purpose of all these wars was to subject those places and make them tributaries of the royal crown of Mexico-Tenochtitlan); the visits to the shrines and the ceremonies—whose purpose it was to give thanks for those victories over such fierce, such bellicose people—had ended. The king was at peace, all was quiet. But soon the valorous Tlacaelel, who has been mentioned frequently in this history, became ill. Due to the illness and to his advanced age and lack of strength he died, having entrusted his sons to his nephew Ahuitzotl. Thus, Ahuitzotl and these young men were cousins. They were very courageous, very valiant in war, where they had demonstrated their bravery by many feats and outstanding exploits, because of which they had been awarded the insignia and distinctions granted by their laws.

Before Tlacaelel died, Ahuitzotl promised him that he would take upon himself all the responsibility for his cousins and, to prove that he would fulfill this obligation, he summoned Tlacaelel's eldest son and, with the agreement of the noblemen of the court, he gave him the same position his father had held, that of the second in command, after the king. He also ordered that he should be honored with the same respect that always had been paid his father, that all regard him as a prince of Mexico, and that he be given the title of Cihuacoatl that his father had had. This was a title of great distinction and had been bequeathed by the gods. So from this time on Tlacaelel's son was called Tlilpotonqui ("The Black One" or, more exactly, "He Who Smells of Black Pitch"), which was a divine agnomen. And with this the old man died happy.

Tlacaelel's body was cremated and his ashes were buried next to the sepulcher of the kings. His obsequies had been performed as a person of his rank deserved, according to his eminence, in the same way they were carried out for the kings. As has been related, Tlacaelel performed many feats worthy of remembrance, some of which are not told in the *Historia*. One story told by other authors is that after his death the Aztecs embalmed him, set him upon a litter with sword and shield tied to his hands, and carried him into battle. Because of his name and this presence the Aztecs were victorious when fighting with the soldiers of Tliliuhquitepec.

At this time, when the great Tlacaelel had been buried with honors, King Ahuitzotl observed his city and realized that the beauty and fertility of Tenochtitlan depended upon its always being able to receive an abundance of water. The Aztecs had made some plots where on each one they had planted gardens and orchards that provided a pleasant freshness. Here they had sown maize, *chian*, squash, chiles, amaranth, tomatoes, and many kinds of flowers. With all these plants the city was greatly beautified, but their freshness would be lost should they lack water. They would dry up and wither away. In order to preserve this luxuriant verdure Ahuitzotl decided to bring water from Acuecuexco (the same source from which, later, His Excellency Viceroy Don Martín Enríquez wished to draw water for Mexico City but which project, due to certain despicable functionaries, and after a great deal of money had been spent, was found to be defective and was abandoned). This spring was very famous in ancient times, together with another that was next to it, called Tlilatl, which was just as large and also had excellent water.

This fine source of water appealed to Ahuitzotl, especially since in the dry season the water in the canals in Tenochtitlan was so low that the canoes could barely pass. The city then became so parched, so bare of fresh greenery that usually bloomed with the water, that those who took pride in being leading citizens were sorely grieved at this dryness, and the king, above all, was affected by it. Therefore, he consulted with his dignitaries and with the men who governed, whose decisions in government affairs were important. They all agreed that the king's preoccupation was justified. And so it was that, with everyone's approval, Ahuitzotl sent two noblemen from the court to the ruler of Coyoacan with a message requesting that he allow water to be brought to the city. This request was made with all courtesy because Ahuitzotl could have commanded that the water be sent, but he did not wish to anger his subjects, which included the Coyoacan ruler. So he sent those noble envoys to Coyoacan to speak to the ruler and to his council; in this way they could obey his wishes apparently of their own will.

The two envoys went to propose this to Tzutzumatzin, as this ruler was called. After he heard the petition, Tzutzumatzin performed the regular ceremonies of obedience—much the way we conform by nodding the head and kissing with the mouth, they humbled themselves and said certain words that indicated obedience to their lord's commands. After having communicated Ahuitzotl's request to the lords of his city, he answered these envoys that he was ready and willing to send water to Tenochtitlan because he and his people were vassals of that city and were obliged to obey the king's demands: therefore, they must share the water. He said, however, that before the water was diverted he wished to warn them that the springs overflowed once in a while and that this took place because there was no dam or canal to control the overflow and at times it did a lot of damage in the city. Tzutzumatzin feared that if the waters of the springs were forced out of their natural course they would rise too much and would flood the city of Tenochtitlan, causing the inhabitants to abandon their homes. He did not wish this to happen, for then the Aztecs would complain that he had not warned them. The water of the two springs in Coyoacan was plentiful and if the level of the lake at Tenochtitlan was high the water from these springs would have no outlet for its overflow at that point, and the city would be inundated. The Aztecs, he said, should be content with the water that came from Chapultepec and not try to take water from Coyoacan.

When Ahuitzotl heard this answer, he became full of wrath, for he did not consider it a courteous response. He began to speak ill of the ruler of Coyoacan, calling him weak, wretched, a man of low rank. He cursed himself for having been too polite to Tzutzumaztzin, who was but a mere vassal of the Aztecs. He swore he would destroy Tzutzumatzin and erase his entire family from the face of the earth. He would have water brought from Coyoacan in spite of their protests and if the people objected, defended themselves, they would all be killed and their city destroyed, as a result of their insults and contempt.

When the Aztec lords saw their king in such a rage, they tried to calm him with soft words and excuses, speaking of the good intentions of Tzutzumatzin. They referred to the reasons the Coyoacan ruler had given—that he did not object to sharing that water but that it might cause problems in the future. When Ahuitzotl heard these arguments, he calmed down somewhat but ordered two judges from his court to go immediately to decapitate the offender in his chambers or to strangle him with a rope. "He should not have dared answer me in that way," said Ahuitzotl. "This can be an example to others who might give advice when they have not been asked."

Ahuitzotl's advisers saw that the king's commands were irrevocable, but knowing that the lord of Coyoacan was a son of the ruler of Azcapotzalco, who was greatly honored and venerated, they sent a message to Coyoacan telling that lord that he should be on guard since his life was in danger. However, Tzutzumatzin had great faith in sorcery and magical arts. The *Historia* tells us that he was a sorcerer and was an expert in magic spells. Therefore, he remained still and when he was told that the judges from Tenochtitlan had arrived and wished to speak to him, he realized that their intention was to kill him. But he ordered his attendants to allow them to enter. When the judges entered his chamber, they found a great and frightful eagle flying around the royal seat. The Aztecs, surprised by this ferocious eagle, were terrified. They left the room and asked the attendants why they had been deceived. These men claimed they knew nothing about an eagle. The only one in that room, they said, was their master; they had just left him there. On entering the room again, the messenger-judges found a fierce jaguar at the door, threatening to attack them with its claws and fangs. When the envoys saw this, they immediately retreated — and, having been frightened and humiliated by those strange happenings — returned to their city with great haste, where they told King Ahuitzotl everything that had taken place.

The king was much disturbed by this remarkable thing and he also felt he had been scorned, insulted. He gave orders that twice as many emissaries return to Coyoacan on the next day, that they not fear any animal, but if they encountered one they should attack and kill it. So when these men arrived and were announced, Tzutzumatzin ordered that they be allowed to enter, as the envoys had been received the day before. This time, on entering, the envoys saw in the middle of the chamber a huge serpent coiled up with its head twisted around so it lay on top of its back. As soon as the serpent saw them, it began to uncoil and prepared to attack. Even though the emissaries were extremely frightened, they tried to kill it as they had been commanded. But at that moment a great fire appeared within the room. The flames were so strong and so terrifying that they forced the men to flee, as the others had done on the previous day.

They returned and explained to King Ahuitzotl that it was impossible to kill Tzutzumatzin due to his magic powers. This angered Ahuitzotl and made him even more determined. He then sent a message to the royal council of Coyoacan asking that their ruler be delivered to him at once. "Otherwise," he stated, "I shall wage war on Coyoacan and shall destroy the people there for rebelling against my commands."

Tzutzumatzin heard this and, knowing that it was impossible to escape and that because of him Ahuitzotl could destroy Coyoacan and kill many innocent people, he called the messengers and spoke to them, saying, "Behold me here! I am in your hands! But tell your lord Ahuitzotl that my prophecies will come true: that before many days his city will be flooded, much of it will be destroyed. He will be sorry he did not heed my advice." The Aztecs then placed a rope around his neck, strangled him, and cast his body among the rocks. A spring, they say, promptly gushed forth in that place, where it exists to this day.

What I have written here is found in the *Historia*, the chronicle I consult. But another *Relación*, which is that of Azcapotzalco, states that, at the time the Aztecs went in search of the lord of Coyoacan in order to murder him, his father died in Azcapotzalco and he [Tzutzumatzin] was chosen to be ruler. He was taken to that city and ruled in his father's place, governed there, for seven years. Nevertheless, the Aztec *Historia* and the *Relación de Coyoacan* give different information: they say that he was truly killed by Ahuitzotl's men. And this must be the true story, as we shall explain further on.

With the lord of Coyoacan dead, Ahuitzotl sent messages to Tezcoco, Tacuba, Xochimilco, and Chalco in the Valley of Mexico, and to the cities and provinces of the Hot Lands as well as to those of the cold regions, to advise the lords there that he planned on bringing water to Tenochtitlan from Coyoacan. He requested that they send men to work and material such as stone, lime, and wooden stakes with which to dam up the spring and make conduits so water could be brought along canals to the city. When this message reached the provinces, many men came to his beckoning and built a strong mortar dam around the springs, which made the water surge up with great force. The best masons to be found in the provinces were present at this construction, as well as those men whose work it was to enter springs in order to clean them, maintain them, and repair drains and cracks through which the water could be lost.

Workmen from Tezcoco arrived with stone, heavy and light. Also men from the Tepanec region came with heavy stone. Chalco sent poles, stakes, volcanic stone or *tezontle*, and sand made from this, for the foundation. Xochimilco sent instruments to cut blocks of earth and many canoes filled with earth in order to dam the water. People from the Hot Country brought great loads of lime, and the same was done by the Otomis of Xilotepec and Cuauhtlalpan. So many people came to aid in the building of this remarkable work that, though it was two leagues long, it was finished with such astonishing rapidity as had never been seen or heard of before. Each province worked hard at the task assigned to it, each one in competition against the others to see who would finish first, so that in less than eight days everyone was idle. From the spring of Acuecuexco, as the main one was called, to the gates of Tenochtitlan, people from all the cities and provinces labored at different points in the work for which they were responsible, with great contentment and much shouting all the while. It is not an exaggeration to say that the men who built the dam and canals looked like ants on an ant heap.

When this amazing work had been finished and the structure had dried, Ahuitzotl ordered that all the outlets be closed and the water be let loose. He also ordered that children be made ready to be sacrificed at every culvert and the priests be dressed and have the customary offerings to the goddess of the waters prepared. This was all done diligently and rapidly. King Ahuitzotl was finally notified that all was ready and, as he was anxious to see the finished works and the water in Tenochtitlan, since he believed that with this the city would be made more beautiful, would be glorified, he gave thanks to the gods and then commanded a dignitary of his court to dress in the clothing of the goddess of the waters in order to impersonate her. When the water was allowed to flow along the canal, this man was to stand before it and, in his presence, the ceremonies and sacrifices were to take place.

CHAPTER XLIX

Which treats of how the waters entered Mexico-Tenochtitlan and how they were welcomed with much pomp and display. With a description of how the city was flooded and the inhabitants were forced to flee.

The people of Coyoacan were sorrowful over the death of their king because he had been much loved. He had been a brave and kind sovereign to his people. However, they realized it was not the right time to complain of his death; therefore, they dissimulated and feigned as much as they could, waiting for the waters to avenge his death as he had prophesied. The people of Tezcoco and Tacuba also grieved over his death, especially the ruler of Tacuba because Tzutzumatzin had been his closest relative. These people whispered and murmured among themselves, saying that the execution had been unjust, without reason. It was talked about so much that a rebellion almost occurred. However, since all believed there was no remedy for what had happened and the best thing was to keep silent, this is what they did, and no one dared to speak to King Ahuitzotl regarding the matter. All decided to wait for the right time and opportunity [for justice to take place]. Moreover, they wished to protect the children and kinsmen of the dead king from appearing to be traitors or disobedient to the royal crown, but instead they meant them to be rewarded for the valor and merits of their father, as they later were when the truth was known. Tzutzumatzin's offense was not disobedience but his having warned Ahuitzotl that a tragedy could take place, and he did this in order to protect the community. But since his zeal was not recognized by the king, this cost him his life. It also caused much damage to the people and a great deal of work was necessary to rebuild this water project, as we shall explain further on in this chapter.

King Ahuitzotl, however, did not anticipate any failure, so when the day came he ordered that the water be brought in. As it began to run toward the city, a man disguised as the goddess of the waters and springs appeared, dressed to impersonate the deity, in a blue garment over which was a surplice similar to a scapulary. This last was covered with costly green and blue stones. He also wore a diadem made of white heron feathers and his face was stained with liquid rubber. His forehead was colored blue, in his ears were two green stones, another on his lower lip, and on his wrists he wore strings of blue and green beads. In his hands he carried rattles shaped like turtles and a bag filled with flour of blue maize. His legs were painted blue and he was wearing blue sandals, signifying the color of water. This man was accompanied by all the priests of the temples. Their faces were painted black and on their heads they wore paper garlands, on their foreheads large stars that served as ties for the headbands. They were stripped naked, wearing only paper breechcloths to cover their genitals. Some of the priests carried flutes, other conch shells, and they went along before the goddess-impersonator playing their instruments.

Other priests carried cages filled with quail, others bore handfuls of paper, still others carried liquid rubber, and some had *copal* incense. When they reached the spot where the water began to run along the canal, one of the priests began to kill the quail and pour their blood into the gushing water. As the blood was plentiful, the water became reddened and carried the blood with it. The priests who had brought liquified incense and the liquid rubber went along pouring drops of these into the water and into the conduit through which the water was to pass. On top of the water floated slivers of the *copal* incense and pieces of rubber. In their burners they offered incense to the water, and all of this was done to the sound of flutes and conch shells that were being played loudly in front of the others. Once in a while the man who was impersonating the goddess took some of the water in his hand and drank it, then he spilled it on both sides of the canal and, with great reverence, spoke to the water: "O precious lady, welcome to your own road! From now on you will follow this course and I, who represent your image, have come here to receive you, to greet you and congratulate you for your arrival. Behold, lady, today you must come to your own city, Mexico-Tenochtitlan!"

As he uttered these words, he took some of the blue maize flour from the bag and tossed it upon the water. Having cast the flour upon the surface, he took his rattles and, as he sounded them, he went into the canal, where he leapt about and danced in the water. After he had done this, he followed the flow of the water to the pools it formed at different places. All along the way were the singers of Tlaloc, god of Rain and Thunderbolts, and those of the goddess [Chalchiuhtlicue], everyone playing musical instruments, dancing, and singing songs in honor of the water. At the same time old men came up with tubs filled with live fish and water snakes in their hands. Others carried bowls with frogs, leaches, and other amphibia. Every kind of creature found in water was in those bowls and the old men went tossing them into the stream, telling the canal to carry them to Tenochtitlan in order that they might reproduce there; that was the reason for their ceremony.

The procession reached the main culvert, at a place called Acachinanco. Here there were four six-year-old children who were painted black with their foreheads blue. They wore paper headbands with stars knotted in front in the manner of the priests. These children were nude except for paper breechcloths and, around their necks, many strings of blue beads. As soon as the waters arrived, the first of these boys was laid out upon the conduit, his chest was opened, and his heart offered to the water with the blood dripping into the same conduit. A littler farther on another child was sacrificed at a place that is now called San Antonio [Abad]. At this point a great canal had been made and from it water poured into a deposit. The people of the barrios of San Antonio and San Pablo could come along the lake in their canoes and collect water here.

The water continued to flow on with the same ceremonies being performed but with many more people because the entire city had turned out, dancing and singing, and there were many personages in different kinds of attire. The water reached another point, Huitzilan, where it would be both stored and distributed to the residents of another barrio. A third child was sacrificed here.

The water continued to flow on. It reached another deposit at Pahuacan, where the heart of the fourth child was cut out. And from here the water [from Acuecuexco, which had run from Coyoacan to Tenochtitlan along that manmade canal] then emptied into the lake. When this took place, Ahuitzotl, accompanied by all the noblemen and dignitaries, both from the city and from other regions, spoke to them with these words: "O lords, the water has reached its places of distribution in the city. Let us welcome it, let us greet it." He then went out of the palace, wearing the royal garments, insignia, and a diadem on his head, in the manner he was accustomed to be dressed on important occasions. All the noblemen also wore their festive attire, everyone was handsomely adorned, with splendid jewels at the neck. The king went to the place where the water fell into the lake with a great noise and he and his companions humiliated themselves before it by performing the ceremony of eating earth, that is, by placing a finger on the earth and then raising it to the mouth, which was a rite performed before all the gods on coming into their presence. Ahuitzotl offered many flowers to the water, placing them around the canal on the ground. He then offered tubes of tobacco, of the kind these men smoked at banquets and other festivities. Next he decapitated many quail with his own hands and offered these to the water. And taking an incense burner he filled it with *copal* resin and, when it was burning, he incensed the water at the mouth of the canal.

When he had finished with these rites, he stood with his right hand lifted high and spoke in a loud voice: "O powerful Goddess of the Waters, welcome to your city—whose protector and patron is Huitzilopochtli, who is both prodigious and admirable in his acts and deeds. Behold, O powerful goddess, you who come to favor your servants the Aztecs, to satisfy their needs, to compensate for their misery in this transitory existence in which we live. One of our needs is to drink of you, for without you no one could live. Another satisfaction is that with you our crops prosper and our sustenance is assured with the innumerable creatures that are nourished with your unending benefits. All this is just your ordinary activity, it is your duty, and the obligation, too, of the very fish and creatures you create who keep the water in place. So from this day on, carry on with your work."

After he had spoken, he cast into the stream—at the point where the water in the canal joined that of the distribution place—many gold jewels in the form of fish and frogs together with great quantities of stones carved in the same manner. All the nobility did the same, throwing in jewels and stones, each one according to his means.

A few days later the water, captured by the dams and controls that had been made at the source of the springs, began to increase in such quantities that forty days after it had entered Tenochtitlan the water in the lake began to overflow, penetrate the deposits in the city, and flood some of the plots where food was grown. When Ahuitzotl saw the harm that was being done, he remembered the words spoken by the ruler of Coyoacan at the moment he surrendered to the Aztecs. Alarmed at the flooding, Ahuitzotl consulted with his council and then ordered that strong dike be erected so that the water entering the lake should not flow into their city. And so it was that the nearby cities and towns were asked to come help build the dike.

The dike was constructed by these neighboring people at a fourth of a league this side of the Peñol [a knoll on the outskirts of Tenochtitlan]. However, all their efforts were useless. The more they tried to stop the water, the more damage it caused. It began to enter the property of many inhabitants, who, terrified, abandoned their homes and fled from their city. The situation was such that the heads of the barrios came to visit the king and asked him to find a remedy, to stop the harm done by the flood. The water had covered the *chinampas* and the maize fields with their tender cornstalks were lost, and so were the chiles, the tomatoes, amaranth, and fields of flowers. The entire city was saddened to see that what had been luxuriant verdure was now destroyed. The people were so distressed that they left their homes and the city and went to live in nearby towns, they established themselves there. For all these reasons the barrio heads implored the king to find a way to stop the flooding.

King Ahuitzotl, on seeing the distressful situation of the city due to all the water coming into Tenochtitlan, summoned the rulers of Tezcoco and Tacuba, hoping that they could find a remedy. When these two lords arrived and saw that it was not possible to walk in the city but that people had to get about in canoes, they were astonished. They clearly indicated to the king the great danger that he and the rest of the people of the city were in. In view of the enormous damage done by those waterworks and, taking advantage of the disastrous situation in order to speak freely to Ahuitzotl and give his opinion regarding the unfortunate death of Tzutzumatzin, the king of Tezcoco spoke frankly: "O powerful king, too late you have remembered to ask our opinion. Much earlier Tzutzumatzin, lord of Coyoacan, warned you of what would take place. It is now too late to be sorry and alarmed at your own perdition and that of the great city of Tenochtitlan. You could have considered and prevented this before. You can well see that the battle now is not against your enemies who have you surrounded, because with your courageous spirit you could destroy them or force them to flee from your city. You are fighting against water, a fierce element. How can you resist it, what can be done? The great prince of Coyoacan, Tzutzumatzin, gave you good advice and not only would you not listen to his opinion, which he gave you like a loyal subject, but you slew him."

Having said these words, the lord of Tezcoco began to weep and show deep feeling, exclaiming, "What did Tzutzumatzin do? What was his transgression? In what way did he offend? Why did you deprive him of his life so pitilessly? Was he a traitor to the royal crown? Was he an adulterer or a thief? O powerful lord, you must realize that you have offended, you have transgressed against the gods. That lord was the image of the gods and they had entrusted him with the government of his nation. Because of that the Lord of All Created Things is allowing this city to be destroyed, be depopulated. How will it look to our enemies—by whom we are surrounded—when Tenochtitlan is depopulated and you and your noblemen are forced to flee, in this way giving those enemies eternal vengeance? What will they say?—that the city your forebears had built up with so much sweat and labor you have destroyed in only forty days? It is my belief that the dam should be removed from the springs and the water flow as before and that a solemn sacrifice be made to the goddess of the waters so that the wrath she feels against you will be placated. She must be offered jewels and feathers, quantities of quail, incense, rubber, and paper. The outlets made for the canals must be filled in. Let some children be brought for sacrifice also. Perhaps with all of this you will calm the goddess and she will control her streams so they will not flow so abundantly as they do now."

Ahuitzotl and his lords were much moved by this speech. The king then sent his envoys to all the neighboring towns and provinces so they would send the necessary offerings for the ceremony, such as jewels, feathers, quail, and incense, in order that the great goddess of the waters be pacified. She was Chalchiuhtlicue [She of the Jade Skirt]. When the message was received in all parts, people answered at once by bringing many offerings, and divers experienced in going into the water also came. The three rulers of Tenochtitlan, Tezcoco, and Tacuba, dressed in regal attire and wearing diadems, with their lords and all the people from the surrounding region, went to Coyoacan. All gathered around the springs, where they humiliated themselves, celebrated rites, sacrificed children and also quail, and offered incense, rubber, paper, and other precious things. Then divers leapt into the deepest part of the water, carrying on their backs many jewels, feathers, and precious stones. They offered all these riches at the bottom of the springs and buried them in the mud there. Large stone idols were also offered, including a great statue of the goddess. In this way the outlets were stopped up to a certain extent. Once this was done, the king had the dams removed so that the waters might follow their former course. The priests, who up to then had been burning incense and playing their flute and conch shells, ceased these activities. Instead, they began to draw blood from their ears, calves, and shins, in an act of autosacrifice, in order to calm the goddess of the waters. When they believed she was placated and the people of the city were convinced of this also, two more children were sacrificed.

Then Ahuitzotl and the other kings and lords went to Coyoacan to beg forgiveness for the assassination of the ruler, and Ahuitzotl appointed the son of Tzutzumatzin as legitimate heir to this rulership.

The king then commanded that the people from Chalco, Tezcoco, Tacuba, Xochimilco, and the Hot Lands send to Tenochtitlan as tribute canoes and wooden rafts, the largest that could be made, because it was not possible to walk in the city, inasmuch as the courtyards of the temples and houses were under two *palmos* [about half a meter] of water. The palace and the homes of the lords were not habitable. Many homes of the common people were completely under water. A great many canoes and rafts were quickly sent to the city and were distributed to lords and commoners alike. People loaded them with their belongings, everything they possessed, working day and night, since they could not use their houses at all. Meanwhile the king sent word to all the towns and provinces subject to Mexico to come aid him in the rebuilding of the city. This was done rapidly. People from far and near arrived with stakes, stone, earth, and grass plots, with which they managed to seal the places through which the water had flowed into the city, although many of the really old buildings remained below the water level.

Then the city was rebuilt with better, finer, and more splendid structures. Most of the buildings in the city were old and had been erected when the Aztecs were poor and had few resources. So the place had been full of many crude and unattractive structures. But this time the lords (and even those who were not lords) built as they wished because the construction was done by hands that were not theirs; each head man was assigned one or two tributary towns for the building of his house. So they "indulged in wishful thinking" as it is said, each one according to his position. In this way Tenochtitlan became well-ordered, attractive, beautifully finished, with large and well-made houses, full of areas for recreation such as pleasing gardens and fine courtyards. The level of the ponds was carefully controlled and around these were planted groves of willows and black and white poplars. Many defenses were put up where there were water sources so that even when they were full there would be no danger of their oveflowing.

All of these improvements and reconstruction were paid for by Ahuitzotl, to the satisfaction of all the officials and the rest of the community. He distributed mantles, breechcloths, cacao, chiles, beans, all taken from his treasury; he also gave some slaves. This way everyone was satisfied and the city of Mexico-Tenochtitlan was magnificent.

CHAPTER L

Which treats of how news reached Mexico-Tenochtitlan that the provinces of Xoconochco, Xolotla, and that of the Mazatecs had mistreated the people of Tecuantepec because they had become subject to Mexico. With a description of the war that the Aztecs waged on those three provinces.

After the city of the Aztecs had been rebuilt, as was told in the preceding chapter, the Aztecs, whose fortune it was to enjoy little peace and quiet, were advised that the provinces of Xoconochco, Xolotla, and that of the Mazatecs had mistreated the people of Tecuantepec, had done them great harm, because they had allowed the Aztecs to conquer them. They called these people cowards and used many other offensive epithets, referring to them as "womanly." Among the many crimes that the people [of the Xoconochco region] committed was the killing of some merchants from Tenochtitlan who had gone there to trade. Inhabitants of the rebel provinces had formed gangs and had gone about the roads and hills like highway robbers, stripping travelers of their possessions, stealing from them, and sacking the villages that were near Tecuantepec.

When news of these outrages reached the city and the king was informed that the people of Tecuantepec asked for help to make attacks cease—which, they said, were actually caused by the Aztec intervention—Ahuitzotl summoned the members of his council of war and at the same time called together the rulers of Tezcoco and Tacuba and representatives from neighboring towns. Ahuitzotl addressed them this way: "O powerful kings and lords, you can see that it is our fortune to enjoy little peace and happiness. It is obvious, however, that you possess valor and a strong chest for every occasion, as you have demonstrated in other projects of great importance. At this time I am depending upon the strength and vigor of your hearts to face this new situation. And I confide in the support of the Lord of All Created Things, of the Day and the Night, who has always given us victory, not to deny this to us today."

He told them about the harm caused by the people of Xoconochco to those of the region of Tecuantepec because they had subjected themselves to the royal crown of Mexico-Tenochtitlan. He emphasized the importance of that incursion, stressed the self-confidence, insolence, and daring shown by Xoconochco. He spoke lengthily, giving strong reasons in order to incite, provoke, the hearts and will of all his listeners so they would, of their own choice, be moved to join in the war against those aggressors. Ahuitzotl was careful to point out the possibility that other nations subject to them could follow the example of those rebel provinces. From these regions flowed gold and precious stones, fine feathers, cacao, and other riches, with the result that the Aztecs would be deprived of all these things if the rebel region was not subdued, was not punished, as soon as possible. If this control were not exercised promptly, the subjugated provinces of those coastal regions would have an excuse not to send the tribute they were obliged to pay by saying that the roads were closed and they were attacked and robbed by the rebellious groups. Ahuitzotl continued, stating that if they did not go to the aid of the lord of Tecuantepec it was possible that he would again turn against them and would join the others; then reconquering that region would mean double the effort and a possible defeat.

When the kings and lords who had come from all the neighboring provinces heard this warning, they agreed that war should be declared immediately and that a greater number of men should be gathered than had been called to arms for many years past. For this purpose it was ordered that all the young men eighteen years or older should go to the conquest of those provinces. They were to be given weapons of all types that would be needed and that they might request. All this was announced in the provinces as quickly as possible. In response to the proclamation, great numbers of men soon answered the call, and Ahuitzotl was advised of this. Two hundred thousand soldiers gathered; these did not include all the carriers or boys who found it adventurous to go with the army. All of these were gallant men desirous of gaining honor and advancement. The king, seeing that the army was ready, ordered that it leave for the province of Xoconochco and that each group of allies go by itself so it could be seen that men from each region were represented. Thus, soldiers from Tezcoco left on their own, as did those from Tacuba, and soldiers from Chalco, also those from the Hot Country, and from Xochimilco and the rest of the *chinampa* region, and from Cuauhtlalpan. Each company went by itself, all in order, led by their officers. And each one marched by King Ahuitzotl, who was waiting for them at Chalco.

But when Ahuitzotl saw that the allied rulers were staying behind and did not wish to go in person to this war of conquest, he played a trick on them. He took from his rooms several shields, swords, and other fire weapons with royal insignia on them, of the kind used only by kings, and sent to each sovereign his appropriate weapons without telling him whether he was to go to war or not. The king of Tacuba realized what Ahuitzotl meant by this and he sent back his excuses. He said he was too old and that he could not wage war in such a faraway land and on such a long campaign. He begged to be pardoned, as he would have liked to attend and serve the king. However, in his place would go two courageous sons of his and they would give orders to the men of his army. The elder son was given the insignia and weapons that Ahuitzotl had sent.

According to some authors, King Nezahualpilli of Tezcoco took part in this war and showed great bravery. Others say he was not there. The Aztec *Historia* says nothing about this; it states only that the most valiant Tezcocans, directed by their leaders, went to test their forces in this remarkable enterprise and campaign. It would not be strange, however, if Nezahualpilli did not go, because the *Historia* depicts him as a weak, frail, and effeminate man of little strength, more admired as a prophet who could foresee the future than as a warrior. But in a Tezcocan painted manuscript I saw him portrayed with his weapons, sword and shield in his hands, holding a man by the hair. An inscription under the painting read, "Here Nezahualpilli captured this captain in the war with Huexotzinco," and the date was shown. However, since the Aztec *Historia* is not interested in the deeds of other people but in its own, it skips the feats that were not achieved by the Aztecs. The only thing this chronicle tells us is that Nezahualpilli was a sorcerer or a magician, as, too, was a great man from Cuitlahuac, called Tzompanteuctli. This man was honored as a god by the people of Cuitlahuac because he told them of events that would take place in the future. He prophesied many things, including the coming of the Spaniards. This prophecy was couched in confusing language combined with fables and lies.

The army marched along, accompanied by King Ahuitzotl, who went too, in order to animate his men. At every town through which they passed they were accorded an enthusiastic reception and were given food and supplies. The king received rich presents of things produced in these communities, which he then shared with the captains or leaders of the different companies that made up the army. In these things Ahuitzotl was very generous, was magnanimous, therefore was loved and well served by all. The king and the entire army reached Guaxaca, where the ruler of Tecuantepec and the lords of that region awaited him. They welcomed Ahuitzotl in a splendid manner, with gifts of gold, jewels, precious stones, fine feathers, mantles, and animal skins. They made long rhetorical speeches in which they thanked him for coming personally to help them. They also offered the Aztec king admirably made weapons covered with featherwork and shields faced with sheets of gold, all splendidly

How the people of Tecuantepec were mistreated

finished and bearing insignia. Ahuitzotl thanked them warmly, and in their presence he distributed the weapons to his officers so they would be useful to them in that war. All these men were highly pleased and impressed by this action and everyone swore allegiance to the king. They were so honored to be favored thus by him that they claimed they would not return to their lands, to their homes, but if necessary would die in his service during that war. All the soldiers raised their arms high, which among these people was a way of swearing or promising something. This is similar to the way the Carthaginians raised their hands to the gods while making votes or promises to them. The king, expressing his gratitude for this act, ordered the soldiers to depart, which they did in orderly fashion, each faction by itself as they had come from Tenochtitlan. They did not stop until they reached Tecuantepec. Ahuitzotl, seated on a litter and covered with richly woven mantles and jaguar skins, was carried into Tecuantepec on the shoulders of the principal men of that place.

The ruler there came out to greet Ahuitzotl in a dignified and stately manner. He was accompanied by the great lords of that region, who had come to Tecuantepec in order to receive the Aztec king. They prostrated themselves before him, then placed a gold diadem upon his head, gold bracelets on his arms, leg adornments and ear pendants of gold, as well as an emerald labret and a beryl nose plug. They gave him royal mantles such as those used in his own city. When he was magnificently dressed with these garments, Ahuitzotl was taken into the city on a litter covered with jaguar skins, which were tied at intervals with gold fastenings, these adorned with feather ornaments.

Inside the city a long address of greeting was made to Ahuitzotl, who then thanked the ruler of Tecuantepec and had him seated by his side. The Aztec lords served this ruler as if he had been their own king, and Ahuitzotl made him a present of a royal garment as fine and beautiful as the one that had been given to him. The lords of these provinces were highly pleased to see these honors given to their own ruler and thus swore allegiance to King Ahuitzotl and promised to serve him.

Ahuitzotl and his entire army rested there for a few days, even though the soldiers were outside the city in tents or temporary housing. During that time the army was fed and maintained by the people of the region. When the king was well rested, he called the ruler of Tecuantepec and asked him to give him all the men he could. He made the same request of the lords of all the surrounding provinces. They had anticipated this; therefore, a great number of soldiers answered the call. They were armed and ready, dressed in such finery that they were easily distinguished from the rest of the people. This army, consisting of some three hundred thousand men from that whole region, then departed. They went on until they came to the limits of a city called Mazatlan that was subject to Xoconochco. When this city was in view, they set up camp, the Aztecs by themselves, the Tezcocans in another place, the Tepanecs in still another. The men from each nation were with their own group and in their own camp.

All the soldiers were given an encouraging talk, each faction in its own language and in its own camp. They were exhorted to become victorious or, like valiant men, to die in the attempt. They were among enemies, their lives were already given over to this cause, so they should not turn their heads toward that which they had left behind, nor try to flee or go back to their own land, for if they did any of these things they would be transformed into birds! So it was preferable to die like brave men, to sell their lives dearly.

Ahuitzotl then ordered sentinels placed all around the army so that the enemy, during the battle, could not surround them, thus capturing him and his warriors and then killing them. So the guards were thus placed. All day and all night they kept a vigil over the entire camp, going about with great caution in small groups. As soon as it was morning, the king had the call to arms sounded quickly, so that in a few moments everyone was ready. The people of Mazatlan, seeing that multitude of soldiers sweeping over them, were terrified. But since they had no choice but to fight, and realizing that they were responsible for this battle, had forced the Aztecs to declare war on that region, they did all they could to defend their homeland. As a result both sides attacked furiously; and this is typical of these people, that they rush into battle with invincible spirit even in the face of great danger, courageously, tiring the enemy until they collapse. The Aztecs, who were experienced in these actions, who knew these dangers and suffering, attacked with cries and shouting so great that their shrieks seemed to reach the skies, then reverberated from mountain to hill to valley. Yelling and shouting, some called out "Tenochtitlan, Tenochtitlan!" others "Tezcoco!" while the Tepanec men, those of Chalco, the soldiers from the Hot Lands, and those from each nation vociferated the name of their land, their faction.

The enemy shouted and attacked in the same violent way and this charge was so frenetic that men on both sides were badly injured, and many were killed by stones that flew from slings or were cut through by spears and arrows. Some soldiers seized the enemy by the arm, others attacked with obsidian-edged swords; all fought courageously. The Mazatlan army stood up to this onslaught without weakening, but warriors from Tecuantepec arrived opportunely and, since they had been wronged by those people, they were anxious to right this wrong.

They rushed against the enemy with such fury that the Mazatec lines and fighting order fell apart and complete disorientation followed. Although they continued to face the [Aztec and Tecuantepec] armies, they were forced to retreat constantly, and finally were surrounded and locked in their own city, where many were slaughtered. Their courageous stand did them little good, for the city was captured and sacked, its inhabitants either taken prisoner or killed.

Mazatlan conquered, Ahuitzotl's army marched to Xolotla, which they quickly subdued, and then went on to vanquish the Ayotecas. In this way they overcame all the towns and provinces until they reached Xoconochco. This was the last city conquered. By then the Aztecs, who were exhausted, tired because of such long marches and sick of fighting, showed little animation in battle. On observing their fatigue, King Ahuitzotl went before them and scolded them for their lack of valor in battle during those last days. If the Zapotecs had not been there to help them, he said, they would probably have been beaten, would now be dead. He reminded the soldiers of great victories they had won against even more valiant foes. He shamed them by saying that these barbarians had thwarted them. He warned each one and all together that they must show much bravery in this battle, that they must not only win but were expected to demolish many houses, kill the old, the old women and the children, and plunder without pity!

The people of Xoconochco, however, surrendered and offered allegiance to the royal crown of Mexico-Tenochtitlan before the Aztecs could carry out all this destruction, all this disaster that had been their plan. The Xoconochco lords admitted their errors before Ahuitzotl and asked his forgiveness. They prostrated themselves on the ground before him and he received them kindly. He then ordered that his people cease the looting and ill-treatment. The soldiers, however, protested. They pointed out to the king that that region was very far from their home and the people were wicked and treacherous. They requested that the whole province be laid waste and then populated with Aztecs. In that way that whole land would be made safe. But the king chose to be merciful and, contrary to the desires of the soldiers, commanded that the sacking cease. So his men began to break camp and form into their own companies. Ahuitzotl then ordered the lords of all those provinces he had conquered, who had been favored by his preventing the soldiers from robbing and destroying in their cities (who by right should have been permitted to plunder, since they received no pay except what they could steal), to compensate these men in some way so they would not return, disgruntled, to their own land. Those lords, complying with Ahuitzotl's request, brought many loads of clothing consisting of breechcloths and waistbands of many kinds, gold, cacao, feathers, jewels, and precious stones. All these things they deposited before the king, who divided them among the companies, giving each section a share. So much was given away that all the men were satisfied and contented.

Before King Ahuitzotl departed from Xoconochco, he was told by the people there that bordering that region were other large and wealthy provinces, such as Cuauhtemallan, Atlpopoca, Popocatepetl, and Tlatlatepec.[1] These provinces were rich and densely populated and had continually waged war against Xoconochco. The king was told that if he so desired the men of Xoconochco would aid him in conquering those places. Ahuitzotl answered that he did not wish to go farther, in part because those people had not offended him in any way and in part because his men were exhausted and their ranks depleted. He added that he had such faith in the strength of the Aztecs that in time they would conquer the entire world. With this he left that region, leaving its people in good spirits. He and his leading men and all the army marched toward the Aztec capital. Every town they came to welcomed them with enthusiasm.

When they reached Tenochtitlan, Ahuitzotl immediately gave thanks to the gods as was his custom, offering them great riches he had brought from the conquered provinces. At the end of these ceremonies he bled his ears, arms, shins, and tongue. He took a thurible, incensed the gods, and then offered them quail, which he killed with his own hands. This was done the same day he arrived. After these rites, Ahuitzotl left the temple and went to the palace, which was magnificently decorated with flowers, branches, bowers, and triumphal arches, all beautifully worked. Here he bade farewell to all the lords and high-ranking warriors, both those of his city and those of the allied provinces. He thanked them for their participation in that conquest, stating that he and Tenochtitlan had become triumphant and glorious with the victories that had been won because these had augmented the crown with many provinces and abundant tribute.

This vainglory and pride was short-lived, however, for soon Ahuitzotl became gravely ill. When he saw that the end was near, he gave orders that his image be carved next to that of his father on a rock on Chapultepec Hill. Thus it was done and those interested today can see

[1] It is not surprising that Durán should not dwell on the subject of the rich lands to the south since, as he states several times, his chronicle is the history of the Aztecs of Mexico-Tenochtitlan. Cuauhtemallan, Atlpopoca, Tlatlatepec, and Popocatepetl are regions that undoubtedly lie today within the republics of Guatemala, El Salvador, and Nicaragua. Cuauhtemallan is Guatemala, and there is another Popocatepetl, an extinct volcano just east of the Valley of Mexico. I have not been able to identify the other sites.

the carving of that king's figure, which is still there. These images were made in order to perpetuate the memory of the Aztec rulers.

A few days after this work was finished, Ahuitzotl died, leaving many widows, children, and concubines. His city was filled with mourning and sadness. In the following chapter his impressive obsequies and funeral rites will be described in detail.

CHAPTER LI

Which treats of the death of King Ahuitzotl. With a description of the solemn funeral rites performed in his honor and of the many riches that were buried with him.

A few days after King Ahuitzotl returned from the war in Xoconochco, he became ill of a serious disease. It was a strange and terrible illness and the doctors could not understand it. It was thought that perhaps he had been poisoned by some food given to him in that land. This illness was strange because, as we saw in the chapter that dealt with his election, Ahuitzotl was a young man, in good health in both body and spirit. With the disease he withered up, began to lose his vigor, and when he died he was reduced to skin and bones. No one knew which remedy to administer to him, though everything possible was done to restore his health. Everyone was moved to compassion by this and his death caused immense sorrow. Even children lamented, moved by the frightful weeping and moaning that rose in the city. This was done by the mourners, women who were hired to wail at the death of kings and noblemen and for those who died in war. These women had to be of the same lineage as the king. The widows and concubines joined them, also other old women whose task it was to mourn this way. And even though all these women shed not a tear nor felt like crying, it was their obligation to wail and scream, to clap their hands and bow toward the earth, inclining their bodies and raising them continually. I have described this in another section.[1]

The sad news of Ahuitzotl's death spread throughout all the provinces that were subject to the royal crown of Mexico-Tenochtitlan. All the people in the land were saddened by the king's demise, especially Nezahualpilli, lord of Tezcoco, and the ruler of Tacuba. Ahuitzotl had been very dear to them because of his friendliness, his openness, and his extreme generosity. Because of these qualities, if death had not cut short his life, he would have been the most important ruler who ever existed in this land. He would have utilized the tributes received and the royal treasure to consolidate the projects his forebears had not been able to realize—all this as a result of his proud heart and his desire to increase and exalt his kingdom.

[1] In chapter XXXVIII.

After messengers had gone to Tezcoco and there had delivered the news of the king's death, and had been fed, clothed, and attended as was customary, Nezahualpilli and all his noblemen started out for Tenochtitlan, where they would express their condolences. They took with them ten slaves who were called "companions of the deceased." They also took quantities of gold, jewelry, and mantles that they called "the shroud." There were two or three loads of these fine mantles, probably more than one hundred. And part of the offering consisted of many fine feathers, valuable stones, and all the riches they could manage. All this wealth was an offering to the deceased and mainly it served to fulfill the needs he would have in the other life, where he would enjoy these things.

On this occasion everyone gave as many of these sumptuous objects as he could. However, this extravagance was only for the kings and great lords, since the common people lacked the means for such splendid obsequies. Poor widows and relatives could offer only a little food and clay or stone beads of the cheapest kind.

The ruler of Tacuba, Totoquihuaztli, and all his noblemen also arrived in Tenochtitlan in order to console the people of the city and offer condolences to the dead king. They also brought ten slaves who would accompany the deceased to the other world, as well as quantities of jewels, precious stones, and feathers, in order to excel in these offerings. These ceremonial acts were repeated by the lords of Chalco, Xochimilco, and the whole *chinampa* region; by those of the Hot Country, which we now call the Marquesado; by Xilotepec and the entire Cuauhtlalpan, province of the Otomi people; the four lordships of Colhuacan, Itztapalapa, Mexicatzinco, and Huitzilopochco, which at that time were four seigniories of great importance. All those cities and provinces — rather, the lords from those — came to pay their respects to the body of the king, to his kinsmen, to his noblemen, and to his city. They all brought slaves who were to accompany the deceased, as they were accustomed to do, and a wealth of mantles, jewels, precious stones, and beautiful feathers that they always offered in these obsequies. Each lord from each province made a long ritual speech to the king's body, expressing sadness at his death. This speaking to the dead person as if he were still alive was customary. Such a bestial practice![2]

The king of Tezcoco, Nezahualpilli, as soon as he had arrived with his great lords, went to the room where Ahuitzotl was laid out. Here he

[2] In the 1967 Spanish edition of the *Historia*, Garibay (II:581) expresses indignation at Durán's opinion of these ritual talks, the *huehuetlatolli*, which Sahagún, on the other hand, praised. Garibay says they represent an elevation of concepts. They also constitute a fine example of prehispanic oral literature. Probably, however, Durán was shocked at the idea of making a rhetorical speech to a corpse.

offered him the slaves and other gifts he had brought and then, weeping, he took a squatting position next to the boy and spoke to him, thus:

> O my son, valorous youth, lord and powerful king, be at ease, let rest and tranquillity be with you. Now, lord, you have left the difficult task of ruling Mexico-Tenochtitlan and the hardship of that work, where you were obliged to receive and attend all those who came before the grandeur of the god Huitzilopochtli and this illustrious city. You have left as unprotected orphans the lords and great men in your kingdom, you have left the old men, the old women, the widows and orphans and all the poor people who looked to you to remedy their poverty. You have gone to rest with your fathers and grandfathers but you have abandoned the loved ones who helped you bear the work of governing this world: they are your brothers, your cousins, your uncles, your close relatives. Your sons and daughters have become orphans, your wives are forsaken. This city has been steeped in darkness since the sun has gone down, the sun has been hiding since your death. The royal seat is without light because your majesty and grandeur illuminated it, threw light upon it. The place, the chamber, of the omnipotent god is now full of dust, of refuse, the chamber that you ordered swept and kept clean, for you were the image of this god and you governed his state, pulling out the weeds and thorns that appeared in it. Now you have been freed from performing this servile and confining task. The ties with which you were bound have now been broken, those ties that held you to them with the care and sense of responsibility that you always exercised in making decisions about this, about that. Rest then, my son, rest in peace. Here I bring you these creatures of God, your servants, so they will go before you and serve you there in the place of rest.

After this the ruler of Tacuba entered and, addressing the deceased in the same sorrowful and disconsolate manner, as sad and compassionate as the other lord, and speaking as though Ahuitzotl were alive, he offered the same kind of gifts as those already described: slaves, jewels, feathers, fine stones, and mantles.

Then came all the lords from Chalco, who made the formal speech. The dignitaries who followed were from the *chinampa*: Xochimilco, Cuitlahuac, and Mezquic, who formerly were called the Chinampanecas, which in our tongue would mean "the people of fences and borders made of reeds." They too addressed the king's corpse and left their offerings. The men who followed were from Cuauhnahuac and the Hot Country, who brought many slaves, mantles, jewels, precious stones, and splendid feathers. They made their speeches as the others had done. Then appeared the Matlatzincas, with representatives from Cuauhtlalpan, together with the Mazahuas and Otomis of Xocotitlan, the Chiapanecas, Xiquipilcas, Xilotepecas, and men from Tepexi, Apazco, and Tulla. They also came from Cuauhtitlan, Tultitlan, Tenayuca, Ecatepec; and there were the Teptzotecas. All of these representatives, one by one and in the name of their cities or towns, made rhetorical addresses to the body of the king and offered him a large number of slaves. These slaves numbered more than two hundred, all standing around the bier, every one of which must die in order to accompany the king to the other world.

The king was surrounded by an enormous amount of gold jewelry, a variety of precious stones, a great pile of feathers of many colors and worked in different fashions, bracelets and leg ornaments of gold, and diadems of gold and fine stones made in the style they used. There were many vessels, plates and bowls, all of gold, for in this land silver was unknown and gold was the only metal worked. And next to the body there was also a great pile of mantles, exquisitely made in different colors and designs, and each mantle was accompanied by a breechcloth, with which these people covered their private parts and some of the thigh. Together with these there were also handsome sandals in different colors.

When the formal speeches of condolences had come to an end, the mantles and breechcloths the king had worn during his lifetime were brought out along with the jewelry and fine stones he had in his sleeping chamber and with which he had adorned himself. The two hundred slaves who were to die in front of the royal corpse were dressed in all this finery and jewels. The clothes and gems that remained were placed in small baskets and given to the slaves to carry into the other world. These victims were arranged in lines as if for a procession, all of them garbed in royal vestments. According to the superstition of these people, the slaves would go to the other world to become great nobles. There they would accompany the king and have the same occupations and privileges that the chieftains had on earth. This was also believed by the wretched slaves and for this reason they offered themselves freely for death.

All the lords and kings present took Ahuitzotl's corpse on their shoulders and carried it to a place of rest, as they called it, which was like the "first station" [of the cross], as we would say. Here the singers began to play and sing funeral dirges or chants that are used in these funerary rites. When these songs or chants had ended, the lords lifted up the king's corpse and carried it to the second station, called Tlacochcalli. Here the king of Tezcoco placed some special mantles on the corpse, as if this were a royal investiture. Then he placed the diadem on Ahuitzotl's head and tied many feathers to his hair. He put ear ornaments on the king's ears, a nose plug in his nose, placed a labret under his lips, then added gold bracelets, gold leg adornments, and sandals. Then the king's body was anointed with divine pitch; in this way Ahuitzotl was consecrated as a god and took his place among the deities.

After he was covered with this divine pitch, he was put on a litter that the men placed on their shoulders, and then they carried Ahuitzotl up the steps of Huitzilopochtli's temple to the feet of the idol. All the priests of the temple came out to receive them. These priests were dressed in full regalia and, carrying incense burners, they incensed the corpse.

The war captains and officials of the army then came, dressed as if for battle with their war insignia, and, in correct order, also accompanied the corpse. And all the great lords and dignitaries of the Aztec city and from other regions, dressed in mourning clothes, accompanied the dead king too. As soon as the deceased reached the feet of Huitzilopochtli, the musicians whose task it was to take part in these rites played music for obsequies, which is very different from that played in the festivals and usual ceremonies.

At this time the divine brazier, filled with the bark of trees that was the firewood of the gods, had been lighted, and the wood burned with long-lasting beautiful flames. The nobles cast the corpse, splendidly dressed as described, into the fire. At this point the priests picked up their sacrificial knives and, one by one, they sacrificed the slaves that the visiting sovereigns and chieftains had offered. They cast them on their backs upon the wooden drum with which the death music had been played and then they opened the slaves' chests, taking out their hearts. These hearts were thrown upon the burning body and all night the cadaver and the hearts smoldered until they were consumed. The ashes and all the riches worn by the king and by the slaves were gathered and placed in a new urn and buried next to the Sun Stone, the *cuauhxicalli* or "eagle vessel." This is the stone that today stands near the door of the Cathedral in the city of Mexico. Together with this urn was buried all the treasure that had not been burned. This treasure consisted of all that the noblemen had offered to the deceased king and the fine things that Ahuitzotl had in his chamber. These customs were a regular practice among these people.

The solemn obsequies were terminated. All of the rulers and nobility of the country had been present at the funeral and now the king of Tezcoco prohibited them from departing from the city until the election of a new king had been carried out, since he wished this to be done with the approval of all.

CHAPTER LII

Which treats of the solemn council that was formed to elect the new king of Mexico-Tenochtitlan. With a description of how the powerful and great Lord Motecuhzoma the Second was chosen. And which tells of his outstanding deeds.

The day after the ashes of King Ahuitzotl were buried and the obsequies and imposing ceremonies had ended, King Nezahualpilli of Tezcoco, the king of Tacuba, all the noblemen of the cities and provinces subject to the royal crown of Tenochtitlan, and those dignitaries subject to Tezcoco and Tacuba, together with the great lords, met in a council to elect the new ruler of the country. Nezahualpilli of Tezcoco, as principal elector, spoke first, saying:

"O valorous sovereign of Tacuba and great lords of Tenochtitlan! O rulers of the provinces of Chalco, Xochimilco, and the Hot Lands! With your vote and consent we are to choose the luminary who is to give us light like a ray from the sun that shines over us. We are to choose a mirror in which we shall be reflected, a mother who will hold us on her lap, a father who will carry us on his shoulders, and a lord who will rule over the Aztec nation. He will be the shelter and refuge of the poor, of widows and orphans, and he will have pity on those who go about day and night in the wilderness, who, with great difficulties search in the hills and ravines for their sustenance. This is the man you must designate, O mighty lords. Look about you, for there is much to see! You are surrounded by all the Aztec nobles, who are like rich feathers fallen from the wings and tails of those magnificent turkeys, the past kings.[1] They are the jewels and precious stones that fell from the throats and wrists of those royal men. Behold the eyebrows and lashes that have fallen from the courageous sovereigns of Tenochtitlan who ennobled this council. Extend your hands to the one who pleases you most.

---

[1] If calling the past ruler "turkeys" sounds strange to us, it should be remembered that the turkey was a highly respected bird in ancient Mexico. It was one of the aspects of Tezcatlipoca, Supreme God, under the name of Chalchiuhtotolin, "Jeweled Fowl." An offering, possibly to prehispanic Mixtec royalty, was recently discovered in the Puebla-Oaxaca region with fragments of numerous inlaid wooden masks and many turkey bones (see Vargas 1989). Sixteenth-century *Relaciones* from Oaxaca speak of turkeys or turkey bones placed in caves with deceased rulers as offerings.

"The heroic King Axayacatl left sons, as did his brother Tizoc. All of them are highly esteemed princes, remarkable for their courage and boldness of spirit. If these do not please you, turn your eyes to other nobles, among them you will find grandsons and great grandsons, nephews and cousins, of the past kings who founded this city. It will not be necessary for you to leave this chamber where we are all gathered. Extend your hands, point to the one amongst all here who most pleases you, and anyone you indicate will be a strong wall against our enemies."

After Nezahualpilli's address, the Cihuacoatl,[2] son of Tlacaellel, who was presiding over the meeting, spoke:

"O powerful king Nezahualpilli, you have told us what is advantageous for this nation and for all the land. For this we kiss your hands because you seek all that is best for us, you seek the exaltation of our republic. We shall see, O powerful lords, that wherever we turn, wherever we place our eyes, we shall find the precious jewels, the precious stones, that our fathers and grandfathers left us.[3]

"But I ask you, I beg all those present not to elect children or very raw youths, whom we would have to swaddle, and later remove this infants' care. Nor do we want a ruler who is so old that tomorrow it would be necessary to elect another. You all know that my cousin King Axayacatl left six sons. All are now captains in the army and are courageous warriors; already they have been responsible for outstanding feats. Their uncle Ahuitzotl, who was conscious of their valor and bravery, was proud of them. These six are the most promising of Ahuitzotl's nephews, but they are still quite young; therefore, I refrain from naming them here. But if you wish you can choose the one who seems best qualified. And if you do not choose one of these, King Tizocic left seven sons who are cousins of those six. They also are valiant princes and captains. And if you still do not favor any of these young men, Ahuitzotl left three sons, all of them now men of distinction. From these sixteen you can choose one, for all are grandsons of Huehue Motecuhzoma [the Elder], my uncle, to whom this nation owes so much because of his great valor and excellent deeds."

These words were listened to with great care and all those present realized that among the young men mentioned there were many of great valor. The members of the council then began to discuss the

---

[2] The Cihuacoatl, "Woman-Serpent," was the title of the second in command, a kind of viceroy. For a discussion of how this title came to be used, see Klein, 1988:237–78.

[3] The precious jewels and stones, referring to the descendants of former rulers, reminds one of metaphors found in book 6 of Sahagún's *Florentine Codex*, where a child is called a precious bracelet, precious green stone, precious turquoise, precious necklace, and precious feather (1969:141–46).

qualifications of each one. This is customary among people of all nations when elections are being carried out: it is important to dig down to the bones, that is, to discover the good and the bad aspects of the candidates. After they had examined the abilities of this one and that one, they all turned their eyes to the great prince Motecuhzoma, son of Axayacatzin. All the men voted for him, with no exceptions, for they said he was at the proper age, he was mature, virtuous, generous, of invincible spirit, and possessed all the virtues that could be found in a good ruler. His advice and decisions were always correct, especially in matters of war. In the latter he had performed feats that showed remarkable bravery.

When this election was announced among the electors and when Motecuhzoma had been chosen unanimously to be the king of Mexico-Tenochtitlan,[4] the men there looked for him in the chamber where all had gathered, but he could not be found. When Motecuhzoma realized that everyone was inclined in his favor, he withdrew from the meeting. The king of Tezcoco ordered that he be sought and in the meantime the brazier that was kept especially for these occasions was lighted, in order to perform the usual ceremonies next to it. Around the brazier were placed the royal vestments, the diadem, an incense burner containing a large quantity of incense, some bones of jaguar, eagle, and puma, the royal sandals, and a splendid breechcloth. The lords who had gone to look for Motecuhzoma, knowing that he was a religious man, went to the temple, where they found him in the Eagle Shrine, within a room especially appointed for him and where he was often in seclusion. The noblemen greeted him and informed him that the kings and the other lords wished him to join them in that chamber. He rose, greeted them in the same courteous manner, and accompanied them. When he entered the council chamber where they all were gathered, these men rose and did reverence to him. Motecuhzoma, making the same respectful gestures, with his usual calm and serious countenance, ordered them to be seated next to the brazier on a bench that was placed there, next to the royal insignia. When Motecuhzoma had sat down also, his uncle Cihuacoatl, the son of Tlacaelel, addressed him: "O lord, listen to what I wish to tell you, since it is the decision of all here, most of whom are your brothers and close relatives. They and I speak to you in the name of the God of All Created Things, the Lord through Whom We Live, and whose crea-

[4]The illustration referring to Motecuhzoma at this point, in the manuscript in the Biblioteca Nacional de Madrid, has a gloss which, although barely legible, has been transcribed by Garibay (Durán 1967:II:581). It reads: "Moteczuma emperador / tiene por propio apellido / el rey menospreciador, / gran señor esclarecido" (Emperor Motecuhzuma has as his true name the Disdainful King, the Great, Illustrious Lord).

tures we are, the One who with his will and thought moves without being moved! He is the true worker of precious stones and he has chosen you, like a gem from among many others. He has polished you, he has refined you so that you may be a jewel for his arm, a precious stone for his neck. This has also been done by all the lords who are present since they too are true lapidaries or goldsmiths who know the value of gems and of gold. They have thus discovered a precious vessel, a splendid jewel, picked out from all the others of the earth. All these present have, in one voice, declared and proclaimed that you, because of your virtue, are to reign over Tenochtitlan and over its grandeur. They have all acknowledged your supremacy and so it must be. This is your lot: leave the low seat that you now occupy! Take the royal seat that has been assigned to you and rejoice in that which the Lord of All Created Things has granted you!"

Then the two kings of Tezcoco and Tacuba rose, and, taking Motecuhzoma by the arm, they seated him on the royal and supreme throne. They cut his hair in the way their kings wore it and, piercing the cartilage of his nostrils, they placed into this opening a thin tubular stone that must have been made at least of jade or emerald. Then they placed a labret below his lip and some magnificent ear ornaments in his ears. He was given the royal mantles that are reserved for investiture, together with a handsomely made breechcloth, the royal sandals, and, finally, a golden diadem was placed upon his head.

Motecuhzoma, having been ordered to take charge of the position for which he had been appointed, then rose and, taking the incense-filled burner that was next to the brazier, began to incense the gods. He did this while walking around the brazier and paid special attention to incensing the god of fire. When this rite was finished, he took the three perforating instruments made of bone and with the jaguar bone he let blood from his ears, with the puma bone he drew blood from the fleshy part of his legs, and with the eagle bone, from his shinbones. After this he was given many quail, which he decapitated and gave as an offering to the fire. The new ruler then left the chamber and was led to the temple, where he was taken up to a stone called the "eagle vessel." On this stone he again drew blood from the same places on his body with the same three pointed bones, then he sacrificed more quail.

From here Motecuhzoma went to the palace, accompanied by the noblemen. All the people were waiting for him there. Also waiting were the officials and magistrates of the city and the heads of the barrios. When Motecuhzoma was seated on his throne, these men came one by one to greet him and to swear obedience. They congratulated him on the election and expressed their pleasure at this. After everyone had greeted the new ruler, Nezahualpilli, king of Tezcoco, spoke thus:

"O most powerful of all the kings of the earth! The clouds have been dispelled and the darkness in which we lived has fled. The sun has appeared and the light of the day shines upon us after the darkness that had been brought about by the death of your uncle the king. The torch that illuminates this city has again been lighted and today a mirror has been placed before us, into which we are to look. The high and powerful Lord has delivered his kingdom to you and he has assigned the royal seat to you. Therefore, my son, you will now begin to labor in the fields of the gods like the farmer who works his lands. Cast out weakness from your manly heart, do not be faint, do not be careless in your duties. Remember that all of this has not been given you to sleep away in idleness and pleasure. From now on you must be alert. Be aware of sleep; because of the cares of the kingdom you must be wakeful. You must rise early and go out to watch the stars in order to observe their movements, signs, influences, and omens. You must be ready to see the morning star as soon as it appears so that when it does so you will take your ritual bath, purifying yourself and anointing yourself with the divine pitch. You will then bleed yourself and, taking the incense burner, you will offer incense and sacrifice to the gods. Finally, you will contemplate the hidden places and the nine folds of the heavens.[5] You will descend to the place of the abyss, to the center of the earth, where stand the three houses of fire. You will go to the hills and the wilderness where the sons of God do penance and live in the solitude of the caves, and you will also contemplate the divine springs and streams.

"I entrust you with all these obligations; you must remember them all, especially those connected with the divine cult and reverence of the gods and honor of the priesthood. You must see that the priests continue with their penance and you will give them courage and all the assistance they need. With these words I end my discourse."

When Nezahualpilli had finished speaking, Totoquihuaztli, king of Tacuba, addressed Motecuhzoma with a flowing speech:

"You have heard, my son, the explanations given you by the king of Tezcoco. But many other responsibilities are entrusted to you in this

---

[5]The nine heavens were considered to lie one above the other, with the ninth at the summit. Anything that was placed in layers—a pile of tortillas, stacked plates, heavens, or folded things such as cloth, for example—was expressed in a certain way in Nahuatl, especially when counting. "Nine" would be *chiconauhtlamantli*, the suffix *-tlamantli* expressing the folding or layering. See Molina 1944:119; also the *Codex Vaticanus Latino 3738 (Rios)*, plate 1, for the nine celestial tiers (Kingsborough 1964, vol. III).

position you have accepted, in this burden you have placed upon your back. You should keep in mind the old men and the old women, whose youth was spent in doing service for the republic, and now, their hair white, they are unable to work and die of hunger. Remember, too, the poor commoners, who are the wings and feathers, the hands and feet of the cities. Be careful to see that they are not mistreated or oppressed, nor that justice for them dies because there is no one to speak for them.

"Remember always to honor the lords, for they represent the strength in opposing Tlaxcala, Mechoacan, and Metztitlan, and all the other enemies on the borders of Aztec lands. As protection from these you must always be mending your weapons, straightening your arrows, and taking care of your shields. Guard against becoming idle, always be watchful, alert, so this way you will be a true lord. You must understand everything, yet many things will give you pain, will make you feel pity. And for everything you must give thanks to the Lord of All Created Things.

"This is the royal position in which you have been placed, where neither food nor drink will have a pleasurable taste. You will continue to lead your life with the care that has always been typical of you because now you realize that the whole face of the earth depends upon your government.

"Do not be restless, do not become troubled. Go slowly, feel your way little by little. Experience will teach you what you have to do and how you should govern. You should be poor when you are with the poor people, you should be powerful with the powerful ones, austere with the transgressors and evildoers, and compassionate and merciful with those who come to humiliate themselves before you. And I say that you even must take care that the roads are kept clean. Watch over the schools and places of learning in the city where the youths are instructed in the arts of war or are prepared for divine service.

"This, then, is the end of my talk."

When Totoquihuaztli had finished speaking, the lords from the provinces came, in order of age and length of service, each one bringing greetings from his region and giving a formal speech. They stated the obligations they were expected to fulfill and the honor it was to perform these tasks. Motecuhzoma heard all these noblemen with a serene and quiet expression on his face (although his usual expression was severe, grave), especially since this was the day of his election. He answered those men: "O powerful lords, why have I deserved to be the cause of the opening of that precious treasure that has been enclosed within your breasts? Why is it that you have poured into my ears—like precious stones and valuable jewels—the wealth of words with which you have adorned me, which have flowed into my ears with a constancy that has pierced my heart? Happy am I, fortunate am I if I could take these words and embrace them to me!"

The *Historia* states that, after he said this, Motecuhzoma began to weep, his emotion stemming from the heart, and he invoked the Lord of All Created Things, and, also straight from the heart, asked the Lord's divine favor. He turned to the people assembled there, whom he thanked, bade them farewell, then he retired to his own secret chambers.

All the noblemen went out and departed for their homes, their cities, or their more distant provinces, leaving Tenochtitlan comforted because of the new election. And this was justified because Motecuhzoma was a very great ruler and enhanced the whole Aztec nation in his time, more than it had ever been. This king was revered and also feared, to the point that it took only hearing his name for them to prostrate themselves on the ground. I shall tell about this further on.

CHAPTER LIII

Which treats of the order and harmony decreed by King Motecuhzoma for his personal service and that of his household and of other things commanded by him that were deserving of such a great lord.

As soon as Motecuhzoma was enthroned and placed on the royal seat of Mexico-Tenochtitlan, he decided to show the loftiness of his thoughts regarding the way a king should be treated and the esteem due to his exalted person. Even though it is true that in supernatural and divine matters these people lacked the light and knowledge of God, in secular matters and in good government they surpassed many other nations and were far superior to them.

After this great prince had been elected, as we have described, he called in his main councillor, who was his uncle Tlilpotonqui, the second in command [the Cihuacoatl]. Through his hands passed all things connected with the government. When Tlilpotonqui appeared, he and the king withdrew to the royal chambers, where they discussed Motecuhzoma's plans regarding the service to be given the king and the authority with which he would rule. He wished to place new officials in the service of his household, in the city, in the provinces and all the kingdom, and remove those his uncle Ahuitzotl had appointed. He said those men were of low rank or children of commoners. It was undignified and unworthy of a king to be served by lowly people, and Motecuhzoma wished to be attended by persons as high-ranking as himself. This was to be done in part because he wished to be revered and in part because if these sons of noblemen, his cousins and brothers, were always at his side, always in his presence, he could teach them the virtue of courtly manners and the art of ruling. In this way, when their turn came to govern, it would not seem difficult to them. The removal of people from the positions they now had should not be done in a harsh or cruel manner because Motecuhzoma wished those who served him to do so willingly. He also wished to begin governing the nation according to his own rules, then guide the country in the way he saw fit and in a direction opposed to the ruling carried out by his predecessor.

Motecuhzoma then asked Tlilpotonqui to go to the places where the sons of the nobility were educated, both to those in Mexico and to those of Tezcoco, Tacuba, and other provinces. Most of these boys had been reared under the care of guardians and tutors in the schools in Tenochtitlan, where they were raised and where their fathers had sent them to be educated. The king ordered that these youths be brought to him, to serve him, for he did not want the lowly people who had served his uncle. Orders were given that no illegitimate boy be brought before him, even though he be his own brother, son of his father, Axayacatl. He would admit only legitimate sons, for he considered that anyone born of a lowly woman or of a slave might take after his mother and be, therefore, ineligible for his service. All of those who served Motecuhzoma were to be sons of lords. All must be legitimate and children of ladies of noble blood.

"I wish to educate these youths," spoke the king, "to train them as I see fit, according to my customs, my wishes, as my heart dictates. And neither do I wish them to be grown men. They should be young boys because it is easier to give them good advice; they have greater facility to do what they are ordered, to accept what they are taught. And because I know you will ask me the reason for these new rules, I shall explain this to you. You must know that to anyone who has served under a great lord and king such as my uncle Ahuitzotl, any change that I wish to make, anything I order or command, more or less as my uncle had done, will seem wrong. Then these people will murmur, will resort to calumny, they will condemn my ideas, will say that the lord Ahuitzotl would not have done things this way. I would always be living in a state of apprehension and because of this I do not want those people with me. And so I beg of you that you do as I say. The men who served Ahuitzotl who are still here will not hear my words, accept my doctrines and the changes I plan to make with the same spirit and kindness with which I shall present them. And since the royal words are of great value, to be respected, and are pronouncements of majesty, it is not correct that these words be in lowly mouths and fall on servile ears. Those who use them, who pronounce them, should be as estimable as those from whose mouth they issue.

"Just as precious stones lose their value when mixed with common, inferior stones, people of royal blood do not look well when they are among those who are of low birth. As worthless feathers look even more despicable when they are with precious plumes, the feathers [that is, the children] that come from the great lords can acquire a lowly appearance when they are among laborers and workmen's children. And as finely worked mantles and breechcloths are different from those of low quality made of coarse fibers, there is also a vast difference between people who are noblemen and people who are not. Therefore, I wish these men of nobility to serve me so that my royal precepts, my royal words, will be in the mouths of lords like vessels of

395

grandeur, and will come forth in illustrious and excellent breath. They will not be pronounced in low, base mouths, for they will be directed to noblemen, to great lords.

"One reason for all this is that the clumsy rustic, with his awkward way of speaking, can change the meaning of words he is supposed to say, thus altering a sentence by adding or removing part of what he has been told. So I desire my pages, chamberlains, stewards, chief waiters, majordomos, porters, and all those who serve in the royal house and appear in my presence to be sons of great lords, well chosen, of known noble lineage. Even those who sweep and clean the palace chambers, and the persons who light the fires and feed them in the rooms of the palace must also be children of lords. You will choose these youths with your own hands."

Prince Cihuacoatl, seeing that this was the king's will and amazed at this new concept, and realizing that any opposition to it was useless, answered, "O powerful lord, your ideas are so correct that I dare not contradict any of the orders you give me but shall immediately comply with your commands."

After he had left the king, Cihuacoatl summoned all the lords and principal men of the court and, explaining to them Motecuhzoma's wishes, ordered them to bring their sons or brothers or nephews to perform service for the royal majesty. He sent the same command to the instructors in the schools where the sons of the noblemen, both from Tenochtitlan and from the provinces, were educated. These orders were obeyed without delay, with the result that numerous sons of noblemen were brought in. The king's plan was explained to them this way: "My sons, you are fortunate, you will be happy, to know that the king our lord wishes you to be in his service. He says he wishes you to be the hands and feet of his person. You are to attend him in his presence, to do the things that he in his position cannot do, nor would it be correct for him to attend to himself. He wishes you to learn how to rule, to govern, and the way in which noblemen receive and bade farewell to people. For you will succeed others in the affairs of the kingdom and King Motecuhzoma wants to show you, to instruct you, as a teacher, as a father."

While Cihuacoatl was speaking to the youths, a member of the council appeared carrying a staff that he placed in Cihuacoatl's hand, saying, "Sir, the king our lord sends you this staff for measuring so you can measure the height of all those who are to enter his service. He does not want them to be taller or shorter than this."

The boys' heights were measured this way and all those whose measurements were as they were supposed to be were set aside. There were one hundred of these sons of great lords, all of them exactly the same height. They were taken to the palace and, before the king, they were told: "O my sons, behold, open your eyes. Do not neglect your duties in any way, do not be responsible for some carelessness that could offend the eyes of the great lord. Understand that the object of his summoning you here is to honor you and occupy you in the things of his personal service and of his household. It is advisable that you attend to these with all the diligence possible. They are: the care and cleaning of the king's clothing and his footwear, some of you will take charge of this; for others, service at his table, the serving and removing of the dishes for those to whom they are destined; sweeping, washing, and dusting the royal chambers and the royal seat. You must also learn to compose the expression of your face correctly when in the presence of the king and the noblemen. You must learn modesty and humility in speaking and in answering anything you might be asked, and to walk calmly and quietly."

When all had been given instructions for each task, and had been filled with fear since the penalty for negligence or transgressions probably would be death, King Motecuhzoma was informed that the sons of lords he had called for were there. He ordered that they be led to the first chamber and there he went in to meet them. When they saw the king, they prostrated themselves on the ground before him and thus greeted him. Motecuhzoma knew them all because most of them were his nephews, cousins, or uncles, and among them were sons of prominent lords. He explained to them why they had been brought to the palace, how he wished to be served by people of his own blood, by his kinsmen, and how he would communicate his affairs to them and trust them with his own person and with the royal treasury. This should be done with care and consideration and with good manners. They were to serve nobles and strangers who might appear in the palace with such meticulous attention that no one would ever depart from the court displeased. This was to be true for ambassadors and envoys who came.

Motecuhzoma also insisted on the respect these young men must show to the queens, wives, and concubines, also to the other women in the palace and in his service. They were to respect the modesty of these women and observe the comportment among the women themselves. The household was to be kept clean and in good order. The new courtiers were told to be heedful of the commands and messages they were charged with and to beware of any alteration of the words or meaning of the messages. They were told to speak without stuttering, without nervousness or haste. They were to talk in low voices, calmly, slowly, and gravely. They were to walk with dignity and never were to tell lies to the king or bear false witness against anyone. If Motecuhzoma heard any complaints against their comportment, he would have them pierced with arrows or burned alive. The youths responded with much humility. They thanked the king for having offered them the opportunity to enter his service and promised that they would obey all his commands.

Each youth was then given his assignment. The *Historia* tells us that every day the king summoned these young men to his quarters, where he instructed them in the ways of virtue, giving much advice, placing much emphasis on dealing with people and the correct way to speak. In this way they all were so subdued, so modest, so well bred, so courtly, that they appeared to be completely different from the people who had preceded them.

As soon as Motecuhzoma had given the young men their instructions, he dismissed all the officials that his uncle Ahuitzotl had employed, not sparing one of them. He also changed all the officials dedicated to the royal affairs in the city and replaced them with noblemen. The heads of the barrios and the captains of hundreds of men were also changed for new commanders. And if the information in another chronicle I saw in the city of Mexico is true, it is said that all these officials were put to death, that no one who had served under Ahuitzotl was allowed to live. It would not surprise me if Motecuhzoma really did this cruel deed because, from the moment he started to rule, he showed himself to be the greatest butcher that ever existed, in order to be feared and held in awe. From what I read in this chronicle, I shall say that, if any commoner dared to lift his eyes and look upon him, the king ordered that he be slain. He said that men of low birth should never gaze upon the one who represented the deity. Therefore, he was honored as if he were a god and when he passed everyone prostrated himself on the ground.

I wish to relate here that once I questioned an Indian about the facial characteristics of Motecuhzoma, about his height and general appearance, and this is how he answered: "Father, I shall not lie to you or tell you about things that I do not know. I never saw his face!" When I asked him why this was so, he responded that if he had dared to gaze upon the monarch he would have been killed in the same way that others who had looked upon him were slain. When someone committed a fault within the royal household, the deed was doubly serious because—how could this error have taken place in the house of the god? Motecuhzoma called his palace "the house of the god" and the punishment for any irreverence was death.[1]

---

[1]Motecuhzome was probably the surrogate of Huitzilopochtli, tutelary god of the Aztecs, but this could also refer to Tezcatlipoca, supreme deity among late central Mexican people, or Xiuhtecuhtli, fire god, who was also the patron of rulers.

In disagreement with this description of Motecuhzoma II, from an unknown source,

The order and harmony decreed by Motecuhzoma

This powerful sovereign began his reign in the year 1503, the same year the Spaniards attacked and conquered the island of Cuba. In this same year, also, the great Turkish sultan Selim was crowned.

When King Motecuhzoma had put his household and court in order, as stated above, the noblemen in the court discussed the ceremonies and festivities that would take place in the public coronation and during the divine anointment, all of which were required by law. Victims must be obtained for sacrifice in these ceremonies because the anointment and coronation could not take place without the killing of many men. We have seen this in the same kind of rites dedicated to the investiture of former kings.

At that time it happened that the provinces called Nopallan and Icpatepec had rebelled against the royal crown of Mexico-Tenochtitlan. A great number of Aztec soldiers as well as Tezcocans, Tepanecs, Chalcas, Xochimilcas, and some from other provinces, were sent to combat those people. Motecuhzoma went in person on this campaign, together with as many of his leading warriors as he could gather. Since the king was informed that the cities in those two provinces were surrounded by high wide walls made of stone, earth, and wood, all strongly compacted, he had many kinds of ladders made, some of wood, some of rope. He also called for a great number of *coas*, which are the hoes they use for working the earth, and a kind of pickax they have to break down the defenses. These implements were obtained so quickly that the destruction of the walls presented little difficulty. The conquest of these cities was carried out easily in this way: Motecuhzoma, who was astute, ordered his explorers and spies to approach when night had fallen. That way they found the guards at the main wall sleeping and cut off their heads, which they delivered to the king. The ladders were then brought; and while some soldiers climbed the walls, others went about breaking down the barriers. So many men swept over the walls and into the city—more than sixty thousand carrying their swords and with the shields tied around their necks—that they did what they always did, steal and kill without pity, shouting and howling so loud that the sound reached the heavens. The soldiers who had wrecked the walls did so with such skill that in a little more than half an hour they had leveled all of them or had made enormous openings.

So the city was captured and the people of the others surrendered, their hands crossed. When the principal center was conquered, the smaller towns fell easily. All the people the Aztecs could capture had

Cortés and Bernal Días del Castillo describe the Aztec ruler as the most gentle of men. It is possible that Durán's harsh picture of Motecuhzoma is colored to some extent by the traditions that had grown up after the Spanish conquest, viewing everything prehispanic as evil or diabolic.

wooden collars placed on them, while the soldiers caused tremendous damage in the fields, in the orchards, in the cacao plantations, felling everything and stealing all they could. The king commanded that all this looting cease, that the Aztec camps be taken down, and that the men stop invading the village and other places, inasmuch as the lords of that land who had surrendered made that request.

The king and all his noble followers were received in the royal houses of the city. They were regaled and treated well, as the royal personage deserved. After these provinces had been conquered and had been warned that if they again rebelled they would be so thoroughly destroyed that they would be completely forgotten, a governor was installed there. Motecuhzoma then left for Tenochtitlan with his army, with the prisoners going before them. There were five thousand and one hundred of these prisoners, captured by the different companies in the army. The spoils as well as the gifts received were divided among the lords and the soldiers.

On his arrival in the Valley of Mexico, Motecuhzoma was given an enthusiastic reception, the people almost honoring him as if he were a god. He was carried on a litter by the lords until they reached the province of Chalco. Then, when they came to Tlalmanalco, he sent word to the guards at Tepepulco (which is still a hill where there was a recreation center, now called "Hill of the Marquis," and where much light stone for buildings in the city was and still is mined), saying that he wished to rest there. When the guards and administrators of that hill received this message, they decorated the whole place well in order to greet their ruler, thinking he would stay there a few days. They sent news of this visit to the city. When the governor of Tenochtitlan, Cihuacoatl, was informed of this, he sent reinforcements of nobles and other high lords, also many commoners, to welcome the king at Tepepulco. When the king reached Tlapitzahuayan, all the leading men of that community came out with fine gifts of waterfowl, land birds, and a wide variety of fish and other creatures from the lake, from both the salt and the sweet waters.[2] Fishing and breeding these things is the way the people who live near the lake make their living.

The king accepted these gifts and gave thanks for them. Then he summoned all the old men, old women, widows and orphans who lived on those lake shores and he gave clothing to all of them, as he would to the poor. Not one of those people was left without clothing, which had been given to the king's forces in the cities and towns through which

---

[2]The five lakes in the basin of Mexico, which in reality formed one, held salt water in some parts and fresh in others.

the army had passed. From here Motecuhzoma was taken in a canopied canoe to the hill, where he enjoyed himself for a few days with those lords and rested from the arduous work of the conquest. He also offered thanks and sacrifices in the shrine there.

Returning to the road on dry land, Motecuhzoma again left for his city, carried on the litter. When he arrived at the city, the people and slaves were waiting for him, with all the order and harmony that have been described when other kings and warriors returned from war. The captives came, shouting and singing as was customary in the city. They were given flowers and tubes of tobacco and were incensed by the priests as the divine victims they were considered to be. All went to the temple, where they performed the ceremony of eating earth by placing the middle finger [in the earth and then in the mouth]. The king did the same. He also let blood from his ears, the fleshy part of his legs, and thighs, as an expression of gratitude. Motecuhzoma then went to his home, where he was greeted with the usual dignity and majesty. He ordered the captives to be guarded well, distributed in the barrios, each barrio receiving a certain number to maintain and to fatten up. The officials there were told that they would be responsible to see that no captive became ill or died. Nor should they lack anything they might need, and those in charge had to be careful so that none escaped.

The king then dismissed the people and the lords from the different cities and provinces, giving them thanks for their aid, for their support in the war. He rewarded them well. Then, highly contented, they bade farewell to him and each one left for his homeland. The city then turned to the business of the king's investiture.

CHAPTER LIV

Which treats of the solemn festivities that were held at the coronation and public anointment of King Motecuhzoma and of the many men who were sacrificed.

The powerful King Motecuhzoma returned from the war of conquest and was welcomed with joyful celebrations, as was correct and due to a man of his prominence. The glory and honor of the victory were attributed to him. The officials then determined that the public coronation festivities were to take place and that these acts were to be clearly manifest to all men and all women so they would be made aware of that personage from whom, when necessary, they should solicit aid for their needs. Also, as was customary on these important occasions, everyone was waiting anxiously to witness the spectacular event. There was a certain urgency for this, for there were now plenty of victims for sacrifice. So the king of Tezcoco and the king of Tacuba were summoned (the latter recently elected due to the death of Totoquihuaztli; the new ruler was Tlaltecatzin). Together they sent word to the other princes and lords of the provinces so they would come and enjoy the feast and be present at the public investiture of the king, their lord. All these chieftains soon began to arrive, to enter the city, together with all their noblemen. The king knew that all the great men were coming to the palace and he was aware of the fact that the different councils were discussing his enthronement. He called his advisers to his chambers in secret and requested that they send invitations to his enemies the Tlaxcalans, Huexotzincas, Cholultecas, and to those of Mechoacan and Metztitlan. Seeing that this was the king's wish and was evidence of his courtesy, they stated that it was their pleasure to do this. So emissaries were sent with invitations to all those nations, requesting that their representatives attend the coronation of Motecuhzoma, that they honor him with their presence. They were assured of safety measures and a truce during the time the festivities would last. It was stated that wars have their time and place and that between the Aztecs and these other cities there was no real enmity. But that the flower war that did exist had as its purpose recreation for the army, on the one hand, and, on the other, pleasure and food for the gods. They all knew, it was said, that in everything else they were brothers, kinsmen, all related to each other. The king beseeched them to accompany him at that time, to feel no apprehension or fear, for he gave them his word in good faith that they would be well treated, would be served in the same manner that he was served, because the majesty and quality of their persons deserved this.

For this mission Motecuhzoma chose some of his leading men. They were not only lords but they were courageous men who put little value on their lives, and they were full of spirit and fortitude. It was important that these emissaries have those qualities because they would be traveling among enemies, with their lives in danger.

On the borders that separated these cities or provinces one from another each nation had established important lookouts, watchtowers, where there were garrisons with many soldiers constantly on guard. They were changed every eighty days. These men were always keeping watch. Not a bird could fly past without being seen by them. All this care was taken because it was known that the Aztecs were fond of ruses, of treachery, and their enemies did not want to be surprised suddenly because of their own negligence. These guards were expressly commanded by their kings to let no Aztec enter any of the cities. Nor could any Aztec be permitted to cross the borders without being registered, examined, and asked what his mission was. If he did not comply with this he would be killed. And the men of Tenochtitlan also took the same precautions against the enemy.

Thus, Motecuhzoma chose men who were brave and daring but also were cautious. They must, furthermore, be able to speak different tongues so they could pretend to be foreigners from some of the other cities and provinces, without it being known that they were Aztecs until they had appeared before the lords and had revealed to them that they had brought a message from their king. This is what they did when they went to Tlaxcala: arriving at dusk, when it was just getting dark, they were seen by the guards, who asked where they were from. The emissaries responded in the Cholula dialect, stating that they were envoys from that city and that they brought a message from their lord to the rulers of Tlaxcala. (There were four who governed that province.) The guards, believing that these men were friends, did not question them further but announced them to the lord of Tlaxcala, who happened to be governing at that time. He ordered that they be sent in. When they were alone with him, the Aztecs first placed flowers and gifts before him, then they removed their Cholultec attire and stopped speaking the Cholula dialect, reverting to the speech of the Aztecs. They addressed the Tlaxcala ruler thus: "O powerful lord, do not be perturbed, do not be upset. The purpose of our coming here is not to alarm you. We have used cunning in order to enter your household because we felt that your guards would not allow us to come before you. But, by being astute, we have managed to be here and we now invite you, on behalf of the powerful, the majestic, lord Motecuhzoma, to his investiture. He humbly requests that all enmity be put aside and wars left for their proper time and that you be present at his coronation, where he assures you that security will be guaranteed. He wishes only to honor his person with your presence, and his word [ensuring your safety] will be kept until you have returned to your own royal seat."

The lord of Tlaxcala was astonished at this statement and responded, "Your daring has been great; it is obvious that you Aztecs are powerful enough to go after anything you want." He then told the emissaries to disguise themselves as Cholultecs again and he sent them to rest in some chambers, where they were given food and drink. The next day he summoned the men of his court and, in secret, told them about Motecuhzoma's message and asked their opinion about what his actions should be. They advised him not to go to the Aztec capital in person but to send one of the leading dignitaries from that place, accompanied by other noblemen. The ruler thought that this was a correct decision, so he called the Aztec emissaries and asked them to tell the lord Motecuhzoma that it gave him great pleasure to be remembered by the Aztec king on that occasion. He would attend the coronation, he said, if he were able to, and, if not, he would send in his place one of the most important lords, who would be accompanied by his own noble assistants. They would go to serve Motecuhzoma.

The Aztec ambassadors then left Tlaxcala, disguised as they had been on entering the city. They went to Huexotzinco and gained entrance with the same ruse, pretending to be Tlaxcalans and carrying a message from the lord of Tlaxcala. They presented the same invitation to the ruler there. And from here they went to Cholula, pretending to be envoys from the lord of Huexotzinco. The same was done in Tliliuhquitepec. All were asked to join in the festivities in Tenochtitlan and all accepted the invitation.

These same actions were carried out by the emissaries who went to Mechoacan, Metztitlan, and the Huaxteca region. They pretended to be foreigners and spoke a strange tongue in order not to be molested by the guards. In this way they all returned safely, bringing good news, for all those who had been invited to the royal coronation had accepted and had promised to come and had offered to be at Motecuhzoma's service.

Motecuhzoma was contented, was well pleased. He had many riches assembled for the ceremonies, in order to demonstrate the grandeur of his city. He also had a hall in the palace adorned handsomely with many paintings showing the magnificence of Tenochtitlan and of the provinces where his quests came from. The seats and mats woven of rushes were beautifully adorned and special seats were set aside for the great lords who were to come. This hall was arranged in such a way that the people there could see and enjoy the festivities and sacrifices without being seen by the people of the city.

When the day appointed for the coronation arrived, the foreign kings and nobility began to enter the city, accompanied by men from their court. Some came in person, others sent distinguished men to represent them. All were accommodated in those chambers, which were adorned with flowers, reeds, and rushes, magnificent shields hanging on the walls, and splendid featherwork. All these things the people appreciate, really love greatly, and at times feel that their happiness depends upon them. The guests, well lodged and provided with all necessary things in abundance, requested the steward who served them to tell his majesty that they desired to see him in order to kiss his royal hands. They wished to be given permission to enter into his presence. Motecuhzoma, through his steward, bade them enter. A secret door, made especially for this occasion, was opened and all of them were allowed to come before the king. Representatives from each province went in and their lord, who went ahead of the others, made a long oration and offered Motecuhzoma fine presents and riches. They also congratulated him on his election and the beginning of his reign. All this was done with reverence but in an imperious manner. The great king, his countenance peaceful and happy, thanked them one by one. He received each of the lords with courtesy and seated them next to him by order of their seniority. When all had been seated, he addressed them in a florid speech, for he was an excellent orator. His style was so fine that he could attract and win over others with his reasoning and all were delighted by his pleasant talk.

Cihuacoatl then led them back to their chambers. The king ordered that the guests be given splendid mantles and breechcloths, rich sandals that they called "royal shoes," fine jewels, necklaces, and precious stones. Each guest was given a special mantle according to his rank. All this was done without the knowledge of the kings of Tacuba and Tezcoco because, as the *Historia* relates, they knew nothing about the coming of the enemy to Tenochtitlan. King Motecuhzoma ordered expressly that no one dare disclose their presence or reveal it to the other foreign rulers who had filled the city. In this way the enemies remained unnoticed and they were provided for and served in complete secrecy. The people of the city were also ignorant of these visitors' presence. When the night of the ceremonial dances came, they attended, dressed in the royal vestments, diadems, precious jewels, and feathers that the king had given them. When they appeared in the royal courtyard, all the torches and lights in the palace were put out while they danced, although up to that time there had been so much light that it had seemed like midday. The torches were dimmed at the moment the dancing began so these guests would not be recognized. When they finished dancing, they retired to their chambers and the torches were relighted, giving the courtyard the brilliance it had earlier. This was repeated on the four days and nights of the feast.

The rulers of Tezcoco and Tacuba were also given royal attire with gold diadems, bracelets, ear ornaments, labrets, and nose plugs. These raiments were given to them during the four days of the festivities, each day a new set. Motecuhzoma also made presents of mantles, breechcloths, jewels, precious stones, bracelets, and ear pendants to the lords of Chalco, Xochimilco, and the region of the Hot Lands. Each day every lord received different attire and different adornments. The same gifts were given to the lords of Tenochtitlan and Tlatelolco.

Motecuhzoma was just as generous, just as splendid, with those of his household. He distributed valuable presents that reflected the benevolence of his person. And he was splendid not only in these things, but also in the abundance of food. The *Historia* states that every day a thousand Indians came into the city laden with deer (which was the meat they ate most), rabbits, hare, quail, turkeys, and all kinds of animals and fowl that these people consume, both water creatures and those of the land, both domesticated and wild. Everything was brought in great quantities, as were loads of chiles and certain seeds for preparing special dishes. There were quantities of cacao for making a beverage. Fish from lakes, rivers, and from the coastal regions were brought, as were a wide variety of fruits. All kinds of provisions from one hundred and fifty leagues around came into the city. These were all indispensable for such a notable banquet where such a large number of outstanding noblemen and dignitaries would be present.

On the fourth day, after the festivities had ended, Motecuhzoma was anointed and crowned in public by the two kings of Tezcoco and Tacuba and by the high priest. All the rites and ceremonies and splendid acts that were indispensable according to their laws were performed. These culminated with the anointing of Motecuhzoma, the applying of the divine pitch to his body—which was like consecrating him as a god—during which he promised to take care of the divine things and defend the deities and the law. Motecuhzoma was dressed in the royal garments, a diadem was placed upon his head, and other insignia of kings were given him. He promised, he swore, to observe the civil laws and statutes and watch over the preeminence and glory of his city. He would support the wars and defend the republic or die in the attempt.

When the festivities had ended, Motecuhzoma seated himself in the supreme place, the Divine Seat, the Place of the Gods, and the war captives were brought out. All of them were sacrificed in honor of his coronation (a painful ceremony), and it was a pathetic thing to see these wretches as victims of Motecuhzoma. It had become as common among these people to sacrifice men on feast days as it is for us to kill lambs or cattle in the slaughterhouse. I am not exaggerating; there were days in which two thousand, three thousand, five thousand, or eight thousand men were sacrificed. Their flesh was eaten and a banquet was prepared with it after the hearts had been offered to the devil.

When the sacrifice was finished and the steps and courtyard were bathed in human blood, everyone went to eat raw mushrooms. With this food they went out of their minds and were in a worse state than if they had drunk a great quantity of wine. They became so inebriated and witless that many of them took their lives with their own hands. Under the strong influence of these mushrooms they saw visions and had revelations about the future, since the devil spoke to them in their drunken madness.

When the mushroom ceremony had ended and all had recovered, the lords from Tlaxcala, Huextozinco, Cholula, and Tliliuhquitepec asked for royal permission to depart. This was granted to them and they were given jewels, sumptuous and rich gifts, weapons and shields with their insignia done in fine featherwork. They left the city accompanied by a large number of Aztec guards so that no one would dare molest them in any way. They departed at night and went along hidden paths in order not to be seen—and if seen, not to be recognized. The guards accompanied them until they were safely at their own boundaries and these guards then returned to their own city to report to Motecuhzoma. This same procedure was carried out with the men from Mechoacan and Metztitlan, and with the Huaxtecs and Yopitzincas. Care was taken so that they would not be offended by the people subject to Tenochtitlan whom they might meet on the way.

From this day on, says the *Historia*, Motecuhzoma invited the enemy rulers with some of their lords three times a year to great feasts. One of them was known as the Feast of the Lords, another of the Banners, and the third, when they ate mushrooms, was called the

Feast of Revelations. A description of these feasts discussed at length will be found in the second part of this book.[1]

The reason for Motecuhzoma's decision to invite his enemies to the celebrations is not explained in the *Historia*. Nevertheless, I shall say that Motecuhzoma did extend these invitations to his enemies, which is something not done by the former kings, with the exception of his grandfather, Motecuhzoma the Elder or the First. This custom continued during the entire reign of Motecuhzoma II. The Tlaxcalans also invited him to their solemnities, and when he attended or sent representatives it was without the knowledge of his own people, nor did the people of Tlaxcala know anything about it. However, according to the *Historia*, he seldom attended these feasts in person.

After the festivities were over, Motecuhzoma ordered that gifts of clothing be given to all the priests, guards, and attendants of the temples, to all the majordomos, administrators, stewards, heads of the barrios, and all the officials of the city, as well as the old people, the orphans and widows, and all the poor people in the city. This way Motecuhzoma performed all these generous acts in honor of his coronation.

---

[1] Durán, in his *Book of the Gods and Rites* (1977:434), calls Tecuilhuitontli, seventh month of the Aztec year, the "Little Feast of the Lords," beginning June 29, which was a prelude to the eighth month, the "Great Feast of the Lords," Huey Tecuilhuitl, which fell twenty days after the end of the "Little Feast" (1977:436). During this time everyone presented flowers to friends. The Feast of the Banners refers to Panquetzaliztli, fifteenth month, whose name means "Raising of the Banners" in honor of the god Huitzilopochtli (1977:457).

Book of the Gods and Rites, however, does not describe a specific feast dedicated to the eating of mushrooms and to revelations. In the present volume there is mention of the frequent eating of mushrooms when the noblemen gathered on important occasions. Sahagún (1959:book 9:33–40) describes the feast held by the merchants in honor of Huitzilopochtli and other gods, when the participants ate mushrooms with honey but no other food except chocolate, which was drunk on the previous night. When the hallucinogenic effect of the mushrooms had passed, the men at this banquet discussed their visions and the prognostications revealed at that time. Durán briefly describes the festivities held by the merchants in Cholula, dedicated to Quetzalcoatl, where the "diabolical custom" of spending all one's savings in order to offer the god a lavish banquet is told (1977:139). This may be one of the feasts referred to by Durán.

CHAPTER LV

Which treats of how Motecuhzoma conquered the provinces of Cuatzontlan and Xaltepec. With a description of how he ordered the slaughter of all the old men and the old women, though he spared the young.

Icpatepec and Xaltepec are towns, or rather large and populous provinces, whose inhabitants, on hearing that there was a new king in Mexico-Tenochtitlan, thought that he was not the bellicose, cunning, or rigorous man that he really was. Therefore, they decided to become independent of that city. The Indians will test anyone who has been appointed to a high office and feel his pulse to determine his spirit. In this they are clever and sly, and when they discover a man of good heart and soft entrails—as they say—they pay little heed to him. Instead of pleasing him they make him drink gall. In this way those provinces wanted to try out Motecuhzoma's spirit when he began to reign, and they ordered that all the Aztecs within their borders be murdered. And so it was done; not a single man was spared. Then, as was the custom, they blocked the roads and paths, closed all the gates, and placed a roadblock. They encircled their towns with high walls and prepared to defend themselves as best they could. These rebels believed that they could sustain themselves, be free of the Aztecs, as did Mechoacan, Tlaxcala, Metztitlan, and the Huaxtecs. They did not remember, however, that Motecuhzoma had explained to all that he did not wish to subject Tlaxcala and the other provinces because they served to give warlike practices and honor in these exercises to his men, so the soldiers would not lose their dexterity. And in this way food would always be provided for the gods.

The men of Icpatepec, believing that they could avoid becoming vassals of Tenochtitlan and feeling that the time was ripe for an insurrection, rebelled against the Aztecs. When news of this reached King Motecuhzoma, he wished action to be taken, so he called the two kings from the neighboring cities and other allied lords. When they had arrived, he informed them, in a council meeting, of the problem at hand. This type of council was always held, because without the agreement and support of all those lords and their domains Motecuhzoma and his people were worth nothing. When the meeting had ended and all had agreed to declare war, Motecuhzoma ordered that the soldiers be advised of this and be prepared. As many men who could be called to arms were needed, and as large a quantity of supplies as possible. It would be necessary to carry as many provisions as they could manage because those cities were far away from Tenochtitlan and the allied regions— although the towns the army would go through would provide food and other things, and when these were not offered the soldiers would search for them. (Therefore, these people are not too shocked when the Spanish soldiers steal and cause damage because they know that part of a soldier's occupation is to rob and commit outrages.) And this is the way it is with these Indian people: if they are not always provided with food they do not work well, and since Motecuhzoma was aware of this weakness he took care that sufficient provisions would always be available so the men would not lose heart. The army had a certain order in war: the soldiers were divided into squadrons; and while some squadrons were fighting, others were eating. And when the first groups tired, they rested and ate what had been prepared for them, while the others went into the field. This was called "taking a breath" and was done when the enemy resisted for a long time.

After the council had taken a decision to declare war, the allied kings and other lords returned to their cities and began to recruit men. So many wanted to go to this war that it was necessary to reject some; otherwise the cities would have been depopulated. Not only did the Aztecs and their friends and allies prepare for this war, but they were joined by some soldiers from enemy places—Tlaxcala, Cholula, and Huexotzinco—some who went for the practice in fighting, others for the spoils. They filtered into the companies of soldiers, disguised in any way they could manage. Thus, the *Historia* never gives an exact number of men who went to war but says in a general way that they were "innumerable," or at times compares the soldiers to sands of the sea, or to an anthill. So I rarely mention the number of combatants who went to war for their king, in order not to give false information where the chronicle gives no numbers or facts. And the reason so many men volunteered for war, aside from their main interest in winning honor and possessions, was that they placed little value on their lives and considered that those who died in war were fortunate, were blessed.[1]

War was called *xochiyaoyotl*, which means "flower war" or "war of flowers," and death in battle was called *xuchimiquiztli*, "rose-colored death, happy and blissful."[2]

---

[1] For the destination awaiting men who died in war and who went to the house of the sun—after which they became birds or butterflies whose pleasant occupation was to flit from flower to flower, sucking the honey—see the *Florentine Codex* (1978:book 3:49).

[2] This is a metaphor, comparing death in war to a flower (*xochitl*, "flower"; *miquiztli*, "death") that blooms brightly.

The soldiers left Tenochtitlan and the other cities on a certain day. They went in excellent spirits and happiness as the *Historia* states, and their contentment grew with each mile they marched. Motecuhzoma went with the army, as did the king of Tacuba. The *Historia* mentions him, but says nothing about the king of Tezcoco. The Tacuba ruler must have gone on this adventure because he, too, was recently elected and wished to win honor and demonstrate his courage and valor. Cihuacoatl, son of Tlacaelel and prince of Mexico-Tenochtitlan, accompanied Motecuhzoma, and all the chieftains also went along. At the end of the first day, Motecuhzoma ordered Cihuacoatl to return to the city, entrusting him to take charge of the government. He was also told to behead all the tutors of his [the king's] children and the duennas of his wives and concubines so they could be replaced by new ones. Cihuacoatl would have preferred to go to war and so it was that he returned to the city in sad spirits. He went back accompanied by the royal councillors, judges, and warriors who were no longer obliged to wage war. On his arrival he immediately carried out the king's orders, beheading all the tutors, duennas, and other court ladies who lived with Motecuhzoma's queens and concubines. Motecuhzoma sent certain spies after Cihuacoatl to see if his orders had been fulfilled. The spies saw that the executions had taken place and returned to inform the sovereign. This was typical of Motecuhzoma; all the orders he gave had to be obeyed immediately without any discussions, never admitting pleas or supplications. His reason for slaughtering these tutors and court ladies is not explained in the *Historia*; it was something the king kept secret.

At that time, before Motecuhzoma proceeded on the march, he ordered that the lords of Tlatelolco, now the barrio of Santiago in the city of Mexico, appear before him. "You will remember," he said, "that my father waged war on you and subjected you to the royal crown of Mexico-Tenochtitlan. He demanded that you pay a certain tribute because of your rebelliousness. However, you have not complied with this as you should have, especially for this war and for the past one. You know it is your obligation to bring arms and other provisions."

The Tlatelolcas answered that it was true that his father had commanded them to give that tribute but that the previous rulers, Motecuhzoma's uncles, had relented, as they recognized the people of Tlatelolco to be kinsmen, to be relatives, who had not been charged with that tribute. Motecuhzoma responded, "If my uncles feigned ignorance of your obligations, I do not wish to do so. I want to carry out what my father ordered since he won your tribute in a good war. Therefore, I command that before I leave this place you bring me what you are obliged to pay. You are fortunate that I am not asking you for all the back tribute. I order you to comply with this now and, if you fail, I shall bring judgment upon you."

The Tlatelolco men had come to this war well prepared and so, before leaving the king, they delivered the provisions and goods they had brought. These were immediately placed before Motecuhzoma: many sacks of ground cacao, of toasted maize, maize flour, bean meal, loads of maize breads, loads of chiles and of pumpkin seeds. They also deposited many pairs of sandals and fine, sheer mantles made of a certain fiber, which they call "mantles for the sun." Then, too, there were weapons: arrows, shields, swords, slings, as well as special shields made just for the lords, and all kinds of arms and war instruments these people used. And, as if this were little, they said that if the king needed anything else they were prepared to serve him.

When Motecuhzoma saw the liberality with which they had paid their tribute and still offered to contribute more if he so desired, the king masked his harsh words with kind ones, stating that he was extremely grateful to them. As a special favor he ordered that the officers of that company be lodged next to his tent from that time on, and that they be given all the same provisions that he himself received. He ordered that they be given clothing and he gave them back their titles, which, as the *Historia* gives us to understand, until that day had been taken away from them together with other distinctions enjoyed by the lords. According to their laws, these Tlatelolco people had been traitors. All honors won by the Tlatelolcas in that war also would be viewed permanent, said Motecuhzoma. The king also permitted them to rebuild the temple at Tlatelolco, which had lain in ruins and had been used as a dung heap since the conquest of that city. In our own Spanish nation a custom exists that is to destroy the houses of traitors and to sow salt in their fields. A similar custom was this one of leaving the temples of traitors in ruins, since they believed that the advice to rebel, to betray, had come from these houses of the gods.

The men of Tlatelolco were also allowed to take their own companies to war, as separate entities, as their own city and provinces. Motecuhzoma was very generous with them, showing them affection and friendship, treating them like relatives, like kinsmen, like friends. However, they were forced to continue to pay tribute, for this was something he never pardoned.

After this Motecuhzoma and his armies continued on to the territories he planned to conquer. When they arrived, they set up camp in view of the enemy's defenses. Motecuhzoma divided the forces into three parts so each of the three would fight on its own. He did this so he could observe which company fought best and had the bravest warriors. The Aztecs formed the main group, with Motecuhzoma at its head. A second company was formed of men from Tezcoco and all that region, with the most courageous warrior leading it. The third company was that of the Tepanecs. Their ruler led them. When these three sections had been formed, Motecuhzoma sent explorers and spies in secret to discover how prepared the enemy was, and the condition of those cities and their inhabitants. The spies were so skillful and they entered these cities so cautiously, with such discretion, that, after night had fallen, they managed to steal some grinding stones and dishes from the very houses. Our chronicle says that they even managed to kidnap some children who were asleep next to their mothers. All these things were brought to Motecuhzoma. When the king saw this, he announced that because of the negligence of those people the lives of not one old man or woman over fifty years of age was to be spared. He claimed that these were the ones who committed treason and caused rebellions because they incited the younger people, they gave them bad advice.

So the different cities began to be conquered. The armies covered that whole land, some in one direction, some in another, according to their orders. They killed any man or woman who seemed to be over fifty. They robbed and sacked the houses and villages, leaving them bare. After a few days, the land was subjected to the royal province of Tenochtitlan and, whenever King Motecuhzoma was received in a city, he was recognized as sovereign and was paid homage and was offered gifts.

The people of Tecuantepec had been waiting to see the outcome of the war. They saw that Motecuhzoma had prevailed, and when they remembered that they had not yet gone to the Aztec capital to acknowledge the new ruler, to congratulate him, the officials went to visit him. They saluted him and welcomed his arrival in those parts. They offered him gifts and informed him of their great desire to see him. They asked him for a daughter of his to be the wife of the heir to the kingdom of Tecuantepec. He granted them this request. Later she was brought to that place and was married to this lord with many honors, feasting and rejoicing. The people of Tecuantepec considered themselves fortunate in having obtained a lady of such high lineage. This princess some time later was to free that city and her husband by revealing to him an ambush of ten thousand Aztecs who had hidden in the province of Tecuantepec, sent by Motecuhzoma to destroy it. The ruler of Tecuantepec, who had married the Aztec king's daughter and later had an heir, stopped recognizing his father-in-law, which he had previously done. He thought of himself as a fellow ruler and whatever tribute was to be paid he decided to keep for his son, grandchild of Motecuhzoma. The ambush, discovered by the queen, was revealed to

The History of the Indies of New Spain

her husband and the latter gave secret orders that each inhabitant kill any stranger who might be in his house that night. No visitors were to be left alive. This was done, and during the night ten thousand valorous, courageous Aztec soldiers who had entered the city surreptitiously, little by little, were slain.

But, going back to our story of that war, the army, Motecuhzoma with them, left for Tenochtitlan. The lords of Tecuantepec accompanied them and were showered with attention and favors, which were reciprocated later in the form of fine gifts for Motecuhzoma. Chieftains and principal lords on both sides also went along, including the lady who was going to be the wife of the ruler of Tecuantepec, the queen. It has been said that she was not the daughter of Motecuhzoma but his sister, but this is of no account. It is enough that she was mentioned. According to the *Historia*, because of Motecuhzoma greatness, from the time he left the province of Xaltepec until he reached Chalco, and every day his people were on the march, the leading men and the rest of the inhabitants of the cities and towns through which they passed placed themselves on both sides of the road as if they were in a procession. They were so massed together, one pressed against another, that not a single thing could be passed between them. This mass of humanity, all standing in an orderly but humble manner with their heads lowered, depicted such great numbers of people that it seemed there was not another soul alive. When Motecuhzoma passed, everyone humbled himself while greeting him. And so, as the king and the army went by, the great human wall disintegrated after the king and the warriors had passed. Motecuhzoma, on his litter, was carried on the shoulders of his warriors and noblemen. As they reached each town, the people there came out to greet the king, then carried him on their shoulders to their homes and special chambers, which were ornately decorated. After he and his dignitaries and the rest of the company had been lodged and provided with everything they needed, with food and drink, and after they had dined, the king was presented with gifts of gold, fine stones, jewels, precious feathers, mantles, breechcloths, golden bands for the head, bracelets, leg ornaments, ear pendants, labrets, and nose plugs. All these were of excellent quality and in great quantity. It was amazing to see how much wealth existed in those places.

In this triumphant way Motecuhzoma reached Chalco, where he was received with much rejoicing and splendor. The *Historia* says that the governors of Chalco, who were almost like kings of that province, went out to greet Motecuhzoma and gave him a receptacle with water for washing his hands. I had not noticed this detail when the chronicle talked about past kings. After he had dined and had been treated splendidly, Motecuhzoma was given a great quantity of riches from that whole region. He thanked the lords profusely and sent word ahead to the rocky Hill of Tepepulco, where he had a home and pleasure gardens. This was built on the hill and also took advantage of the concavities in the rocks there in the way it was constructed. It was a fine thing to see. Motecuhzoma said that he wished to rest there a few days, as he meant to await the arrival of the prisoners who had been captured in the war. These were to enter the city of Mexico-Tenochtitlan with the soldiers as proof of their valor and as trophies of war. Motecuhzoma sent a message to the governor of the city, Cihuacoatl, to receive the great chieftains and to treat them royally, as he, the king, would be received, according to the decrees that had been ordained.

The king then went to Tepepulco while the warriors and the chieftains continued on to Tenochtitlan. The dwellers of the lagoon began to arrive in their canoes, bringing offerings of many kinds of waterfowl, fish, frogs, and all kinds of creatures that are found near the shores and in the waters of this lake. Their leaders made elaborate speeches of welcome. The king received them with much kindness. They were then dismissed, though they were very contented since Motecuhzoma first had provided food and drink for everyone and had given clothing to the old people, to the children, the orphans and widows. This custom of giving food and drink to everyone who came to greet them was so common that at any time people arrived to greet the king or his lords (even the less important ones) at any hour, or to deliver messages, at that precise time they were to be fed and given to drink. For this purpose there were special attendants who had to have provisions ready to be served when any one of these visitors or envoys arrived. This was to be done without exception, on pain of death.

Once these people had gone and Motecuhzoma had retired to his chambers, he summoned his assistant and ordered him to prepare a canoe with six rowers. As soon as it was night, in great secrecy and without anyone being aware of his actions, he entered the boat and went to Tenochtitlan. He ordered that no one be notified of his arrival since he wished to see how the men returning from the war were being received. He wished to know if there were deficiencies in the ceremonies when he was not present. The reception for the officials was carried out with all the usual solemnity and ceremony and the king, disguised, was able to watch and notice all that occurred without being seen. These officials, having been welcomed with much rejoicing, went to the temple and performed the usual rite of thanks to the gods, that of touching the earth next to the feet [of their statues] with the finger, then eating it. And before they had completed this ceremony, they were advised that the powerful Lord Motecuhzoma had arrived at the royal houses.

So they went directly to the palace from the temple to greet the king and to perform the ceremony that was customary when a king returned from war, which was this: after honoring the idol and thanking him for the victory, they honored the king as the image of the idol [the god], because due to his skill that victory had been won. This ceremony having ended and the rhetorical addresses having been directed to the king, the guest lords were thanked for the splendid reception of the army and the order and harmony that reigned in the city. Then they were dismissed and Motecuhzoma retired to his chambers.

In this city there was a custom. It was this: when warriors returned from battle, some poor man and some old man went to their houses to greet them and congratulate them on their return. In adulatory speeches they extolled their great feats. These eulogizers were then given on that day food and drink; clothing consisting of mantles, breechcloths, and sandals, and something from the spoils the soldiers had brought back. This was a grand gesture on the part of those noble warriors and was a very common ceremony among them. Thus, every time the lords went to war, the men in the city who were poor made special supplications to the gods for victory to be won by the Aztecs, both for their own benefit and for the goods they might receive, which would be lost if the Aztec armies were defeated.

When Motecuhzoma's arrival in Tenochtitlan was made known, all the lords from the nearby provinces went to the city to felicitate him on his success.

CHAPTER LVI

Which treats of the reasons Motecuhzoma had for warring against the provinces of Quetzaltepec and Tototepec. With a description of the strong resistance he met in subduing them, and how he conquered them.

At this time the lapidaries of the city of Tenochtitlan, of Tlatelolco, and of other cities heard that in the province of Tototepec and Quetzaltepec there existed a type of sand that was good for working stones, together with emery to clean them and polish them until they became bright and shining.[1] The stone workers told King Motecuhzoma about this and explained the difficulties in obtaining the sand and emery from that province and the high prices that were asked. Motecuhzoma, after consulting with his council, decided to send envoys to Tototepec and Quetzaltepec to ask as a favor that this sand be sent to the master lapidaries. He stated that he would send in return things they desired, since he wished this to be an exchange. (In this land the manner of buying and selling was the exchange of one thing for another.) For this purpose one hundred principal men were sent on this mission, and with them went many fine mantles, jewels, and precious featherwork as well as shields. These were to be presented to the lords of those two cities, and they were to be offered goodwill and friendship from the Aztecs forever.

The envoys arrived in Tototepec and went to the royal houses, where they asked the guards to inform their lord that some Aztecs had come to speak to him in the name of the king of Mexico-Tenochtitlan. This lord, who understood that they were just messengers, bade them enter. When they came before the lord, the Aztecs greeted him with the respect and reverence that was customary with them; because in matters of good breeding this nation was outstanding in honoring their superiors and showing respect to one another, and in giving shelter to travelers and pilgrims. They presented half of the gifts they carried to this lord, then they stated the request for sand and emery made by their king. The Tototepec ruler, having heard this request, told the envoys that they were welcome, they were to rest, but that which they requested had to be decided by the lord and the republic of

---

[1] From this chapter on, the manuscript appears to be written in a different hand, as discussed in the introduction to this book.

Quetzaltepec. He added that he would speak to those people and would give the Aztecs the answer. He then sent a messenger to Quetzaltepec, telling the lord of that city that Motecuhzoma had sent envoys to request sand and emery for working stone. What did the other ruler think of this? The second lord sought advice of his officials, who felt that they should concede nothing to Motecuhzoma, nor should they subject themselves in any way to another ruler, neither freely nor in exchange for goods. And in order that this answer to Motecuhzoma be delayed, it was decided to kill all the envoys. So this could be done, fifty of the Aztecs were to be sent to Quetzaltepec and fifty would remain in Tototepec. As soon as the first fifty reached Quetzaltepec, they would be killed by men waiting and prepared to do this, and at the same time the other fifty would be murdered.

When the lord of Tototepec was informed of this decision, he was displeased by it but, after all, could do nothing to counteract it. So he sent fifty of the noble Aztec envoys to Quetzaltepec. They took the other half of the gifts they had brought, delivered them to the lord of Quetzaltepec, and stated their mission. This lord became very angry and exclaimed: "Does Motecuhzoma think he can subject the whole world? He commands us as if we were his vassals. It is obvious that he has not tested the courage of the Quetzaltepecas, nor have the Aztecs waged war against us! Do not dare come to us with this impertinence!"

At this the Quetzaltepec ruler commanded that the envoys be killed, which they were, right there in his presence. Their bodies were thrown into the rushing torrents of the Quetzaltepec river. At that same time the other envoys who had remained in Tototepec were assassinated and their bodies thrown into a ravine. The death of the Aztecs, however, made their killers fear for what might happen in retaliation, so they decided to surround their cities with walls and defensive barricades. This was done as soon as possible. Tototepec was protected by a great river, but the people there also built five walls, as strong as could be made, of tamped earth, stone, strong wood, and all kinds of material for the fortification. When these walls were finished, the one surrounding the city was six *brazas* high and four wide, while the others were four or five *brazas* high. Guards, sentinels, and armed men were placed on each wall. The main road was blocked with tree trunks, rocks, thorns, and thistles, so that no one could walk there. For their own use these people found paths and hidden entrances to the city. This way no one could know when they went in or when they went out. Tototepec built the same kind of defense measures, reinforcing their city as best they could. They feared the fury of the enemy, the Aztecs, who made the whole earth tremble.

Motecuhzoma awaited the return of his ambassadors; when they did not come back, he feared that something tragic had happened, so he sent men to investigate. They found what has been described: the roads closed or blocked and, as they looked in different directions, the Aztecs saw vultures attacking the dead bodies. They then followed the path of these birds and discovered the disintegrating bodies of the envoys, eaten by beasts. Furthermore, the guards in the region had frightened off most of the merchants who were accustomed to trade there.

All of this was reported to Motecuhzoma, who was highly indignant at the news. He sent a message to the neighboring cities requesting that they prepare their armies to go avenge the great offense committed by those people. He then called the wives of the dead envoys and showed them the men's mantles and breechcloths, which the women recognized, saying that those were the clothes their husbands had worn. They wept bitterly but were consoled by the king, who then gave them many gifts.

Motecuhzoma was not content with the news his messengers had brought, so, while the men in the nearby cities were preparing for war, he sent other spies. He gave them strict instructions to walk day and night without stopping, to see and explore the region, to go around the cities, examine them carefully, and calculate the strength of their walls, to measure them. And if it was possible to enter each city, to ascertain everything that had been done as defense, and to find out all they could to help the Aztecs in case of war, and the way to enter those cities. These messengers, anxious to comply with the commands of their king, walked day and night and finally reached Quetzaltepec. Driven by the desire to discover those facts the king wished to know, they managed to cross the river; and when they were about to reach the first of the series of five walls, some guards of the wall jumped out of the brush and tried to seize them. But the Aztecs explained that they were only merchants who came to trade, as they always did. The guards believed them; however, they ordered them to go back and not to cross the river again, under pain of death. This the spies did, for they were more frightened than ashamed [of not completing their mission]. They were afraid to return to Motecuhzoma with such bad news, fearing that he would have them killed, and decided to spend the night in that enemy territory. However, on seeing that so much surveillance was being kept, they preferred to return to the city. Here they told the king what had happened.

When Motecuhzoma heard this, he issued a proclamation that within three days all the army was to march from the city, leaving only the old and the weak, the sick and the children. No young man older than eighteen was to stay home; all were to go to war. On the third day, then, all the divisions of the army from all the friendly cities and provinces went out. Tenochtitlan was almost emptied; it seemed that there were no people in the city. So many men went to this war that they seemed to blot out the sun. There were more than four hundred thousand soldiers, all magnificently attired and armed. In this Motecuhzoma took more pains than his predecessors. He was careful to see that his officers and soldiers carried splendid weapons and insignia that were very showy.

The army reached Xaltianquizco,[2] where the men rested and waited until all had arrived, and where they revised their equipment. Motecuhzoma in person called a meeting of all the lords of the allied cities. It was decided that some would attack on three sides while the soldiers from Tenochtitlan would charge from the front and fight in that position, while the Tezcoco forces would attack on the right side and those of Tacuba on the left. Motecuhzoma always wanted to see which forces were weak or deficient, and this could not be observed well when all the soldiers were fighting together in one tightly packed group. And so, because of this trick of Motecuhzoma's, each faction tried to excel, for fear of falling into dishonor and disgrace. Motecuhzoma first sent out scouts to reconnoiter, to look for trails and ways the army could penetrate, for the roads were all blocked and covered with rocks, tree trunks, branches, and thorns. Some of the scouts went one way and others another way. They passed rivers and ravines until they found some paths and ways to go in, though these were of difficult access. The scouts returned to the camp that was set up and then they guided the soldiers. They reached the banks of the river Quetzalatl, which was swollen and raging and poured into the sea with great fury. The soldiers were much frightened by this [since it was their first encounter with the sea]. They arrived at this point an hour before sunrise because Motecuhzoma had made them march all night. Camp was set up on the riverbank while the people of Totoltepec and Quetzaltepec appeared on the other side, making ferocious gestures with their bodies, faces, hands, and feet, meanwhile shouting offensive and obscene words.

Motecuhzoma, who was an enemy of lost time, ordered the captains immediately to make balsa rafts and bridges out of the roots of trees and reeds. These rafts were called *acatl apechtli*, "bed of reeds."

[2] I suggest the possibility that Xaltianquizco may be the Xaltianguis of today, which lies north of Acapulco in Guerrero and is next to the Papagayo River, which empties into the Pacific Ocean. In this case the Papagayo would be a new name for the Quetzalatl "Feathered River" or "River of Fine Plumage" (*quetzalli*, "beautiful feather," or *quetzal*, "quetzal/handsome bird"; *atl*, "water").

The bridges, which were formed like large nets, were made of a root called *cuauhmatlatl*. Everything was done carefully and an entire day was employed in these preparations. When night came, Motecuhzoma ordered that the bridges be set in place and the rafts placed in the water, and in a very short time the entire army had crossed the river. The inhabitants of Tototepec had been free of worry since they trusted the river, swollen and furious as it was, to prevent the Aztecs from crossing. When the Aztec soldiers saw that they were on the other bank of the river, they lost no time but immediately attacked the first wall by surprise. The sentinels sounded the alarm, but, although the people in the city reacted rapidly, by that time the Aztecs had made many openings in the wall. They poured into Tototepec, where they burned the temple and the palace and slaughtered all the men they could. They looted and destroyed the city to such an extent that finally only the women and children were left. Motecuhzoma gave orders that they were not to be harmed.

The looting and killing had lasted until daybreak, when Motecuhzoma ordered his men to gather in one place. However, many of them had gone off to neighboring villages and farms to steal and at midday they had not returned. Motecuhzoma was told that some were returning now and others would be along in about an hour. It took the whole day to gather the soldiers together. When they did come, they were laden down with spoils and brought captives wearing wooden collars—some of them injured, some well, some half dead—and all being treated with such cruelty that it was sad to behold.

With his men together, Motecuhzoma summoned all his captains and those from the other allied cities and asked their opinion about attacking Quetzaltepec, which was the second city. It was decided to use a ruse in order to take that place. Many ladders were to be made so the soldiers could climb the walls and many wooden digging sticks were to be prepared in order to dig into the adobe and thus destroy the walls. But the people of Quetzaltepec, having seen what happened to Tototepec and having learned from others' unfortunate experience, sent out spies who learned what Motecuhzoma's forces were doing. Therefore, they covered the top of the walls with stones and chunks of wood, and men armed with spears were placed there. All during the night these men sang and shouted so the enemy, the Aztecs, would understand that they did not sleep. The great Lord Motecuhzoma realized that his plan had failed, so the next morning he summoned his soldiers and encouraged them by saying, "Courageous Aztecs, Tezcocans, Tepanecs, and all the men from the provinces: there is nothing we do here but conquer or die. For this we have come. Our enemy shows valor and a brave heart and has decided to defend the city. I beg of you to demonstrate bravery in this endeavor, for to die is to live forever in perpetual honor and glory."

While he was speaking, the Quetzaltepec army came out from one side of their city, all in correct order, the soldiers splendidly attired. They arranged themselves in position next to the first or outside wall of their city, the wall being four *brazas* wide and three high. All these men were outside of the city, in the fields. Motecuhzoma ordered that only the Aztecs, the Chalcas, and the Tlahuicas attack, while the Tezcocans and Tepanecs be on guard until he gave them orders. The Aztecs charged the enemy soldiers, who received them with great courage. A cruel battle ensued, the Aztecs trying to scale the wall and the others attempting to defend their city. Many men were killed on both sides. The Aztecs were severely harmed by the stones and spears thrown at them from the top of the wall and thus were forced to retire. The battle lasted almost the whole day, and in the end the Quetzaltepec forces were, in a way, victorious. The following morning these men left the city and went into the field, where, showing the same courage and spirit as before, they began to fight. Motecuhzoma gave orders that the Tezcocans and soldiers from their province, one hundred thousand strong, face the enemy alone. The fighting was intense and lasted all day, but with neither side marking a great advantage over the other. The Tezcocans tried to reach the wall but failed to do so and returned to their camp. They had lost some men but not many.

The next day the Tepanecs and a great number of soldiers from their province went into the field and fought with such spirit that the Quetzaltepec army could not resist them and had to retreat toward the wall. When Motecuhzoma saw that the Tepanecs fought so courageously that they made the enemy retreat, he had the signal for attack sounded. At this sound the Aztecs and the Tezcocans rushed into the field, attacking all together and crying out (the Aztecs), "Tenochtitlan! Tenochtitlan!" and (the Tezcocans), "Tezcoco! Tezcoco!" Each group carried the assault with its own men, thus dispersing the enemy forces. Although the allied armies suffered greatly from the stones and pieces of wood that were thrown at them from the wall, many men managed to reach it and place ladders upon it, which they climbed as if they were cats. Other men, chopping at the first wall (which was three *brazas* wide and four high) the defense by the enemy was strong and it took the Aztecs three days to conquer it. The leading men of Quetzaltepec then came out to speak to Motecuhzoma and plead with him to go away with his armies, to leave their city. They stated that before surrendering they would rather die and lose their wives and children. Motecuhzoma answered that if, when he left his city, he had planned to return without victory, he never would have left at all.

Since he was there in Quetzaltepec, he was bound to triumph or die. The men from Quetzaltepec could choose not to let this trouble them and could even ignore his existence if they wished, but the two sides had been fighting for six days and, even if the war was to go on for six years, he had enough spirit to resist that time and even more and had no intention of leaving.

That day the Aztecs captured the second wall and little by little advanced until they reached the fifth wall (which was six *brazas* high and six wide). Next to this they dug a hole and enlarged it by excavating farther on all sides. At night they crept through this opening and entered the city, where they set fire to the temple. When the people of Quetzaltepec saw that their temple was burning and that they were being attacked, and while the men tried to defend themselves from the soldiers coming in through the openings in the wall, they got their women and children away safely by having them flee to the hills. Those who were defending the city fought until they collapsed, then they abandoned the wall and the Aztecs with the entire army went into Quetzaltepec. Here they began to roam through the houses, which they found deserted, empty. The principal men and the elders of that place then approached Motecuhzoma, requesting peace and mercy. They accepted subjection to the royal crown of Mexico-Tenochtitlan, promising to pay tribute and to become vassals of that city. Motecuhzoma listened to their pleas, then pardoned them and ordered that the sacking by the Aztecs be stopped. The people of Quetzaltepec presented him with valuable gifts that Motecuhzoma, without taking a single mantle for himself, distributed among the Tepanecs and Tezcocans. In this way he demonstrated his great generosity and true grandeur, since he gave them to understand that they were the real conquerors in that war. When Motecuhzoma had come to an agreement with the men of Quetzaltepec, the rest of the people returned to the city, which again became populated. After this Motecuhzoma was well served by the inhabitants of that place.

The Aztec king left this region subdued, pacified, and the people willing to serve him. He traveled with his army to Izucan, where he was cordially received by the lord of that place and of the surrounding towns. They gave him fine presents of great value, which he distributed among the Aztec soldiers, keeping nothing for himself. From Izucan Motecuhzoma and his men went on to Chalco. There he named all those who had accompanied him "Caballeros" or "Knights" and honored them with insignia and emblems that identified them as lords. Then Motecuhzoma and his retinue continued on to Itztapalapa, where the lords who had remained in Tenochtitlan awaited him, including the governor of the city, Cihuacoatl. He had left orders in the city regarding the reception that was to take place when the king entered the city. This has been described earlier and was customary on such occasions when not one detail could be lacking. This was protocol and a rule when men returned from war.

And so they came into the city, greeted by those ceremonies and festivities that have been described, except on this occasion Motecuhzoma, when he entered the capital, had his body painted with a yellow pitch called *axin* and wore ear pendants, a nose plug, and a labret. Prince Cihuacoatl was attired in the garb of the goddess Cihuacoatl. These were female clothes, which were called "eagle garments." In this way they entered Tenochtitlan and went to the temple, where Motecuhzoma bled his ears, arms, and shins as sacrifice and gave thanks to Huitzilopochtli for the victory he had granted.

CHAPTER LVII

Which treats of the cruel battle waged between the Aztecs and the men of Huexotzinco in the Valley of Atlixco. With a description of how the flower of Mexico-Tenochtitlan and Tezcoco perished and the Huexotzincas triumphed.

Many days passed after the two cities, Tototepec and Quetzaltepec, had been conquered, and no news of importance had reached King Motecuhzoma. He became weary of so much idleness and of the fact that there was no war in which his soldiers could practice their arts. Therefore, he decided to provoke the people of Huexotzinco, and he called the two neighboring kings and their chieftains to the city. He proposed to them what he had in mind. He told them that many days and months had gone by and that there had been no campaigns or military exercises. He was desirous of waging war against Huexotzinco and testing its strength. When the rulers and lords heard his plan, they agreed with him and said that it pleased them very much, since for that very reason the cities of Huexotzinco, Tlaxcala, Cholula, and Tliliuhquitepec had been exempt [from conquest and tribute]. With this decision made, Motecuhzoma immediately sent his messengers to challenge the cities, telling them he wished to join in some entertainment with them for a few days on the battlefield and to give the men some practice in skirmishing. He proposed to them that they go to the plains of Atlixco, where he would meet them so they could all disport this way.

The men of Huexotzinco, on hearing this challenge, accepted it with goodwill. They sent a message saying that they were well pleased and that three days later they would wait for the Aztecs in the valley and there would show them why they were so eager for this encounter.

When Motecuhzoma heard this answer, he gave orders that anyone in the three allied kingdoms who wished to gain honor should present himself on the plains near Atlixco within three days. As supreme commander of the army he appointed a brother of his named Tlacahuepan, presenting him with the device of the god Totec, and with splendid weapons and a shield of gold. He urged Tlacahuepan to be courageous and to win honor in the battle, as his only risk would be an exercise in warfare and the gaining of honor. Tlacahuepan kissed the king's hands and he and two other brothers—who also wished to fight with him—went to consult soothsayers to find out what would happen to them in that war. They were told the omens were bad. Tlacahuepan went to bade farewell to his royal brother, saying, "O mighty lord, I believe that I shall never see your face again. Take care of my wives and children!" In this way he and his brother left the city and on the third day they arrived at the appointed place, a small village called Atzitziuacan, subject to Papayecan.

One hundred thousand soldiers, the finest and most illustrious men of the three kingdoms, met upon the battlefield, all of them in splendid array. The Huexotzincas then appeared, no less finely attired and in equally good spirits, looking as if they had come to a festival. The Aztec commander ordered two hundred chosen soldiers to go out and begin the skirmish and he told the rest to remain still until they received new orders. These two hundred warriors went into the field and began to fight the Huexotzincas. Both sides went into the battle with such spirit that men began to fall on either side. The Aztec commander, who was watching carefully, began to send in Tezcocans, and as more men entered the field, more were killed, since the Huexotzincas were fighting with great boldness and invincible spirit; they stood their ground courageously. When the Tezcocans had gone into the fray and had suffered severe losses, the commander, observing this and realizing that these forces were exhausted, ordered the Tepanec soldiers to relieve them. Those Tepanecs rushed in and began to perform great feats among the enemy while the men of Tezcoco withdrew to rest. But the Huexotzincas were alert and also sent in new troops, and a great slaughter took place, the men on both sides behaving like ferocious mountain lions drenched in blood.

At this point Tlacahuepan embraced his two brothers, saying, "Behold, my brothers, the time has come to go to the help of our friends!" After giving a signal to the Aztecs, they then threw themselves into the battle with frightful shrieks, knocking down and killing men. It was a terrible thing to see!

The Huexotzincas did not retreat, however, but continued to send all their men to the aid of the companions, and with these new arrivals a most cruel battle developed. Tlacahuepan, in his eagerness to gain glory, hurled himself against the enemy with such fury that he seemed to have lost his mind. He behaved so rashly that when he wished to retreat he was unable to do so, surrounded as he was by more than one hundred soldiers. When he realized his situation, he began to do marvelous things with his sword. Soon he had around him and at his feet over fifty dead. But now his strength had been drained from the great feats he had performed and, seing that he could not defeat the many enemies who surrounded him (though he was unwounded), he dropped the arm that held his sword and his shield, exclaiming,

"Cease, O Huexotzincas! I see that I am yours and that I can no longer defend myself. Let the combat end here! You see me here, now do what you will!"

The Huextozincas seized him, planning to carry him off alive to their city, but Tlacahuepan took hold of the fallen bodies, shouting that he would not go, that he would die there! His sacrifice was to be on the battlefield, upon those corpses! And so it was that since they could not pull him away they killed him, tore him apart, and carried away his body in little pieces, which were then saved as relics. Not a bone or hair of his was left.

The commander was dead. The Aztecs began to withdraw, but in those moments the Huexotzincas killed Motecuhzoma's two other brothers, who had also accomplished great feats. In addition, they captured many other lords and chieftains from Tenochtitlan, Tezcoco, and Tacuba, and in this way the Huextozincas returned to their city victorious and boastful.

Motecuhzoma was notified of the death of his brothers and his noblemen. He was also told how his army had been routed. When he heard this sad news, he began to weep bitterly for the loss of his brothers and the other warriors. The tidings spread throughout the city and everyone sobbed in sadness and despair. When it was known that those who had survived the war were about to return, broken and wounded, Motecuhzoma ordered that they be received in a manner suiting the occasion. Their reception was a sad thing. The priests who usually went out on those occasions with their hair braided with colored cords this day appeared with their hair loose and unkempt. The elders and officials who generally showed themselves wearing feathers tied to the hair at the crown of the head were seen without their feathers and with the insignia of mourning. The priests who at times of triumph offered incense this time brought no incense but instead were full of tears and affliction. The conch shells, trumpets, flutes, and drums, which usually sounded victory, on this day were mute.

In this way those who returned from war entered the city, going to the temple, where, instead of prayers and thanks, there were long lamentations and complaints against the gods, to whom no sacrifice was offered. From the temple they went to greet the king in his palace. Here they found him sunk in despair. He ordered that the wounded be cured and that those who had returned naked, their belongings destroyed, be dressed, and that they all be comforted in every possible way. He also ordered that the funeral ceremonies for his brothers be prepared and that three statues of them be made. These statues were formed of resinous wood [which was used for torches]. They were covered with paper and faces were painted on them. These images were dressed in mantles and fine breechcloths, which bore their insignia as noble warriors. They were given weapons, featherwork, ear pendants, nose plugs, and labrets, and swords and shields were placed in their hands. When the statues had been put in the place chosen for this purpose, people began to come from all the villages, cities, and provinces to offer their condolences to Motecuhzoma. They brought presents and slaves to be sacrificed for the dead and in this way the funeral rites began. I shall not stop to describe them since I have already told about these ceremonies in previous chapters and it would be tedious to repeat them here, even though the *Historia* narrates them again at length. Once the obsequies, the weeping of the women, and the funeral chants had ended, the officials of the city and of the provinces took the images on their shoulders and carried them before the statue of Huitzilopochtli. There they were set on fire and the slaves who had been offered were killed and their bodies burned with the statues. The ashes were gathered and buried in the Altar of the Eagles (as they called it), next to the Sun Stone. With this the foreign rulers and lords who had come for these rites bade farewell and went home, Motecuhzoma having thanked them for the honors paid to his brothers.

When news of these disasters became known in the land of the Mixtecs, it was believed that the Aztecs would be unable to take up arms soon, and the rulers of Yancuitlan and Zozola sent a challenge to Motecuhzoma. As part of a plot against Tenochtitlan they closed the roads to the Aztecs. Motecuhzoma sent couriers to Yancuitlan and Zozola with the message that the obsequies for his men killed in the war had just taken place and that the soldiers' wounds were not yet healed. Therefore, he requested that there be peace. The war with Huexotzinco, he stated, was different from the hostilities the Mixtecs sought because one was a means of exercise for the soldiers while the aim of the other was to try to convert the Aztecs into perpetual vassals and payers of tribute. The Mixtecs were to consider these things carefully.

The messengers set out for Yancuitlan. On the road they met some Tezcocan and Xochimilca merchants who were naked and badly hurt, all bathed in blood. When the envoys questioned them, the merchants responded that the people of Yancuitlan and Zozola had robbed them and mistreated them. The envoys went ahead, nevertheless, although they were advised to proceed cautiously. When they reached Yancuitlan, they found there was almost no way to enter. The city was surrounded by four walls, all protected by many guards. These guards would not allow them to pass, nor would they receive any message. So the Aztecs returned to the city to relate to Motecuhzoma all that had taken place. They took with them the wounded merchants from Tezcoco and Xochimilco who had been robbed and told the king about their plight. The king promised that he would avenge this affront, then he had their wounds dressed and the men were given good clothing and anything else they needed.

This done, Motecuhzoma called his advisers and reminded them that the solemn feast of the Flaying of Men was near. He told them to prepare for war with Yancuitlan and Zozola so that captives from these places could be sacrificed in the Tlacaxipehualiztli festival. Orders to that effect were also sent to Tezcoco and Tacuba and the declaration of war was announced in Tenochtitlan and its provinces. As soon as the army was ready, the soldiers went out under the leaderhsip of Cihuacoatl, prince of Mexico, since Motecuhzoma remained in his city. Cihuacoatl gave orders that everyone was to make a stop in Zapotitlan on the fifth day. At that time two hundred men from all the provinces, splendidly attired and well armed, were at that place. Then, marching in correct order, they reached the boundaries of Yancuitlan. Here they fought, looted, and destroyed with so little opposition that the chronicles barely mention any defense made by the Mixtecs but simply say that they were defeated, their people taken captive, and the city sacked, burned, destroyed.

Having achieved this victory, the Aztec lords, led by Cihuacoatl, ordered the soldiers to rest. Three days later they attacked Zozola, but first explorers had been sent to observe the state of this town. When those men arrived, they found Zozola abandoned, without a man, woman, or child to be questioned. The houses and huts had been burned, the people of Zozola having set them on fire themselves. The scouts returned to Cihuacoatl and told him what they had seen. He ordered that a search be made for these people in the mountains and ravines. For four days the Aztecs sought everywhere but found no trace of them. When the commander, Cihuacoatl, saw that the search was fruitless, he ordered his men to return and no longer pursue the enemy. The battle of Yancuitlan was sufficient to justify their victory.

The army returned to Mexico with the spoils, consisting mainly of the Yancuitlan captives destined for the coming sacrifice. They were welcomed with all the customary ceremonies and rejoicing for the victory. Many offerings and sacrifices were made to the gods amid much contentment and joy. When it was time for the feast of the Flaying of Men, the captives brought from Yancuitlan—and there were more than a thousand—were sacrificed. Their death marked the end of the ceremonies.

To this feast were invited the lords from the other side of the Sierra Nevada, who were from Tlaxcala, Huexotzinco, Cholula, and Tliliuhquitepec. Also men came from Mechoacan and Metztitlan, as well as the Yopitzincas and Huaxtecs. These people were present during the ceremonies and they were well attended and presented with many gifts, as I have described on other occasions. They went back to their own lands, well pleased with everything and laden with presents from Motecuhzoma.

CHAPTER LVIII

Which treats of how Motecuhzoma had the Temple of Coatlan built within that of Huitzilopochtli. And how it was called Coateocalli or Temple of the Serpent, also meaning the Temple of Many Gods. And about the solemn festival that was held, where many victims died.

Motecuhzoma had come to feel that there should be a shrine where all the gods revered in all the country could be adored. Moved by religious zeal, he ordered that one be built. This was constructed as part of the Great Temple of Huitzilopochtli, in the place where the house of Acebedo now stands. It was called Coateocalli, which means "Temple of the Diverse Gods," and it was called thus because in it were housed many gods from the different towns and provinces. They were all placed within one chamber and there were great numbers of them, all of different types, faces, and forms. These things will have been noted by those who today see them lying about on the street or in the houses, others embedded in buildings. They have done much harm (and still do) by recalling memories of Amalech[1] among the old people and natives of this land.

But returning to our subject, when this shrine was finished, as perfectly as the king had desired, Motecuhzoma began to consider its dedication. He wondered where victims could be obtained for sacrifice and he remembered that the province of Teuctepec was in a state of rebellion against the royal crown. This was a province close to the sea. He then summoned to Tenochtitlan the rulers of Tezcoco and Tacuba and all the neighboring lords and heads of subject people. When they had assembled, Motecuhzoma described the building of the shrine to them and explained its purpose [having images of all the gods in one place], and they were shown the temple. He told them he wished to have a solemn festival for its dedication and, since they knew that the province of Teuctepec had rebelled, men could be brought from there for the sacrifice to the shrine. And because Motecuhzoma wished to declare war upon this region in order to conquer it and subject its people, bring them to serve him, his allies were to order their armies

---

[1]Amalech refers to that tribe, the Amalekites, mentioned in the Old Testament as enemies of the Israelites. Amalech (or Amalek) fought with the Hebrews during the exodus from Egypt (see Exodus 17:8–13). Actually, Durán refers to paganism or the enemies of Christianity.

to be ready. The men who were present all agreed with this proposal, so they returned to their own cities, where they announced the coming war and gave orders that everyone be prepared. In the Aztec capital as well as in the other provinces this preparation was done without delay.

The soldiers left their respective cities, displaying pomp and making themselves audible, which was customary with them, and in this way they reached the borders of Teuctepec, where they set up camp next to a great river on the outskirts of the town. The river's current was fast and rushing and joined the sea with a great uproar. The soldiers looked for a way to ford the river on all sides, but they failed to find it. The leaders then ordered the Aztecs to make two wide rafts of tree roots and branches, the Tezcocans another two, and the Tepanecs two more. This way the three groups could pass their soldiers to the other side. It must be said that three formal armies always went to war together: the Aztecs, the Tezcocans, and the Tepanecs, for each king sent his own troops. The reason the Aztecs gave for each group to have its own rafts was that if any one of the rafts capsized and some of the men were lost there would be no possibility of one blaming the other for the accident, trying to place the blame where it did not belong. So when the rafts were made they were put into the water and the men held onto the trees along the shore in order to pass. Although the people of Teuctepec defended against this invasion they were not strong enough to prevent some of the brave soldiers and their captains from crossing the river. At least four thousand soldiers from the three armies managed to reach the other side. They began to skirmish with the men there and soon so many well-armed soldiers came out of Teuctepec that they seemed to cover the whole land. The Aztecs, seeing them, feared they might be defeated, so they decided to trick the enemy. The commander ordered that an ambush be prepared with many men next to the river on the side opposite Teuctepec. All the soldiers who had not yet crossed the river were placed in the ambush. Then word was sent to the soldiers on the other side to retreat, showing weakness as if they were fleeing, and to cross the water on the rafts carefully so as not to fall in. When the Aztec, Tezcocan, and Tepanec captains received this message, they realized there was an ambush. They started to retreat, apparently vacillating and showing fear of the enemy that was engulfing them. The enemy soldiers, believing that the others were in reality retreating, began to follow them, shouting and crying out proudly, believing themselves to be the victors, and went after the Aztecs on thier own rafts.

After a great number of those soldiers had crossed, the Aztecs decided that there would be enough men for the sacrifice, so they withdrew from the riverbank. And seeing that so many of the enemy were falling into the trap, the Aztecs in the ambush cut the rafts off [from the tree branches that guided them], thus making the enemy fall into the water. The rafts had been covered with soldiers and the men in the ambush poured out and captured and killed many of those who had managed to pass.

The city of Teuctepec appeared to be impregnable since it was surrounded by four high, stout walls, and its inhabitants were extremely bellicose. The Aztecs, therefore, decided not to attack the city but, placing collars on the two thousand three hundred captives taken at the river and roping them together, they made these men march ahead of their own soldiers; thus, they were well guarded. The Aztecs dared not detain themselves further but set out for Tenochtitlan. Here the *Historia* states that some of the conquered soldiers who fell into the water turned into alligators or fish or other water animals. All of this amazed the Aztec army and filled them with terror.

News of these events reached Motecuhzoma, who was disturbed because the city itself had not been taken. However, since the army had been victorious and sacrificial victims, who at the moment were indispensable, were being brought to his city, he became calm. The soldiers reached Chalco Atenco, where each faction left for its own province. The soldiers were not very happy because they had not been able to do much plundering in this war. But Motecuhzoma gave orders that they should be present the day of the festival, especially those who had distinguished themselves in taking captives or killing enemy soldiers.

In all the cities and provinces the usual reception was made for the returning warriors. There was much playing of drums, conch shells, flutes, and whistles. There was singing and dancing, smoke from the incense burners, and groups of people handsomely dressed went out to receive the victorious men and adorn them with flowers. After this welcome, the soldiers gave thanks to the gods and kissed the king's hands, then, the prisoners having been put in a safe place, each man went to his home. Motecuhzoma let the soldiers rest for a few days, then he sent word to all the neighboring people requesting that they attend the festivities and presentation of the temple. At the same time he sent an invitation to the enemies of the Aztec nation. As we have stated before, these were the people of Tlaxcala, Cholula, Huexotzinco, Tliliuhquitepec, Mechoacan, Metztitlan, and Yopitzinco. All of these accepted and when they arrived were received and treated splendidly, as has been described in other chapters. And since it will not be necessary to repeat this as often as the *Historia* does, it will be said only that when the lords from those enemy cities were invited to

The History of the Indies of New Spain

Tenochtitlan and accepted, they came and went in such a hidden way, were so concealed, that neither the people of the city nor those from outside who attended the festivities were aware of their presence. There were strict rules about this because the rulers feared that uprisings and fighting could break out if the people knew. This was as if our own king [of Spain] were to invite the Great Turk to his ceremonies and festivals. In that case the grandees would not be pleased, nor would they enjoy themselves, nor would the different realms and provinces see this as correct, for the Turkish are our mortal enemies. The same would be true in this country if it were known that the principal enemies of the Aztecs had come to the city and had participated in the fiestas. Therefore, Motecuhzoma had secret chambers for these occasions where only certain trusted persons were allowed to enter in order to deliver the necessary provisions.

When the day of the fiesta arrived, before dawn the king presented clothing to all the lords from the enemy cities and gave them rich gifts. All this was done early so it could take place in secret. When the lords were dressed in that clothing, they were taken to a terrace that faced the temple. It was decorated with branches, covered with a canopy, and so highly adorned with latticework, decorative masonry, reeds and rushes and flowers, that it seemed like a place for women.[2] From this point the visitors could observe the sacrificial rites.

When it was mid-morning, the king of Tezcoco arrived, accompanied by his lords and the soldiers who had done great feats in Teuctepec. Motecuhzoma went out to welcome them with due courtesy. Then the king of Tacuba came with all the noblemen of his province. With him came the soldiers who had distinguished themselves in the recent battle, in answer to Motecuhzoma's command. The Tepanec king was lodged with the same attention given to the king of Tezcoco. After these the Aztec lords, led by Cihuacoatl, Motecuhzoma's coadjutor, arrived at the palace, together with the noblemen from Chalco, Xochimilco, Colhuacan, Mezquic, Itztapalapa, Mexicatzinco, Huitzilopochco, and the Hot Lands. They were all illustrious and valorous men. Also came the regular soldiers from these places who had shown great bravery in the recent war. Motecuhzoma went out to greet them and, giving all those brave soldiers special titles as a reward for their feats, he personally presented them with arms, with splendid swords and shields, and with insignia of distinguished warriors. He then gave them fine devices such as headdresses made of

---

[2]Durán may have been thinking of Moorish architecture, where women observe festivities on balconies, from behind latticework, so they can see without being seen.

exquisite featherwork. All these things came from his own treasury. Once his men had been honored and given titles, he sent to the king of Tezcoco as many insignia, weapons, swords, and shields as there were men who had been outstanding in this war. He requested that with these things the Tezcoco ruler give titles to those courageous warriors. The same act was performed with the king of Tacuba; these three rulers gave high ranks to the warriors who were present at that time and who received weapons and insignia. They were given these honors and from that day on could enjoy the privileges that were part of the honors.

These privileges were to be allowed to dress in cotton clothing, wear sandals, enter into the palace, eat of the royal food, drink cacao, use flowers and tubes of tobacco, have all the wives a man could support, take part in the royal dances, eat human flesh, drink wine, build a house with more than one story, vote in meetings that deal with war, be exempt from paying tribute, taxes, or any other tithe or imposition or personal service, and meet with the Warriors of the Sun, whom they call Eagle Knights.

When these privileges had been explained, the powerful king went out and addressed the men. He told them that he was the dispenser of those titles and insignia; therefore, he was bestowing these upon them since they had won them by their personal valor and thus deserved them. They were to enjoy them. Then Motecuhzoma, dressed in royal garments and with a diadem on his head, took a staff in his hand and went before them, in the place of the captain. With all of the soldiers armed and in proper order as if for review, having been lined up by their officers and, as I have said, with Motecuhzoma carrying his staff at the head, they left the palace and went to the temple where the dedication ceremonies were to take place. The priests and ministers of the temple came to greet them, carrying incense burners and playing musical instruments such as conch shells, flutes, whistles, and drums. On reaching the shrine, Motecuhzoma was dressed in the garments of the high priest, then his body was anointed with the divine bitumen, and Cihuacoatl did the same. Both men placed gold diadems on their heads, then Motecuhzoma took a gold brazier in his hands and entered the chamber where all the images of the gods had been gathered, brought from all the nations and representing all created things. Having incensed them and having performed the ceremonies that were usual when a temple or house was to be used for the first time (and this is still done today), he and Cihuacoatl went to the place of sacrifice, which was at the entrance to the shrine, outside.

The prisoners taken at Teuctepec were brought out. Motecuhzoma and Cihuacoatl began to sacrifice them, slicing open their chests and extracting their hearts. First they raised the hearts to the sun, then they threw them into the shrine before the gods. This sacrifice began at midday and ended at nightfall. Two thousand three hundred men were killed, and their blood bathed the entire temple and its stairway. Each time the priests cut out a heart, they rolled the body down the stairs. Every time I describe this my whole body trembles with horror. This is something that nature itself abhors.

When these sacrifices had ended, the enemy visitors from other regions, shocked at so much cruelty and such inhuman acts, bade farewell that night and left for their cities. The friendly kings and great lords went home to their own cities and provinces. The men from Huexotzinco and Atlixco, proud and boastful about their past victory over the Aztecs, repaid the splendid attentions they had received in Tenochtitlan in an unjust manner: when they came to the boundaries of Cuauhquechollan and Atzitziuacan, which were at the limits of the places where the Aztecs had their garrisons, they wrecked the cotton fields, tore out the corn in the corn fields, trampled on all the other plants, and in general did a great deal of damage. The people from Cuauhquechollan went to Tenochtitlan to complain to the king there, where Motecuhzoma consoled them and promised to avenge them. He then sent word to the neighboring cities, telling them of this outrage, and ordered them to ready their armies.

When the lord of Tula, Ixtlilcuechahuac, heard of this transgression, he asked Motecuhzoma if he would be allowed to take care of this undertaking, since he and his men wished to try their fortune with those of Atlixco and Huexotzinco. Motecuhzoma was grateful for this offer and conceded the enterprise to the ruler of Tula. Nevertheless, as he was aware of the strength of the enemy, he prepared his soldiers so that if help was needed they could offer it. All the armies left shortly for the valley of Atlixco. Ixtlilcuechahuac of Tula had the main forces, all splendidly attired and in excellent order. They fought the enemy very courageously for two days, but neither side was ahead of the other, and there were casualties on both sides. But on the third day the lord of Tula wished to prove his valor, so he went into the field in advance of the rest and, finding great resistance on the part of the Huexotzincas, he rushed into their ranks with such fury that he performed marvels with his weapons, all by himself, until finally he was captured and cut into pieces by the enemy.

On seeing this capture and dismemberment, his men began to weaken, so the Tezcocans went to their aid, forming a rear guard. But the Tula men, having become fearful, paid little attention to this succor and the Atlixcas and Huexotzincas resisted the onslaught, almost eliminating their opponents. The Tepanec armies, including

Azcapotzalco, however, stood firm and put up great resistance that whole day. Many people were killed on both sides, though, including officers and important men. On the following day, each army went into battle with the intention of ending the war. The Tezcocans and the Tepanecs together entered the fray and battled for a long time but eventually tired, so the Aztecs and the Chalcas, seeing that they might be beaten, went in again to help and thus reinforced the armies. In this new clash the Huexotzincas killed three very courageous cousins of Motecuhzoma, who had been fighting at the side of the Chalcas. The Chalcas, when they saw this killing, were so enraged that they threw themselves at the enemy and forced them to retreat, although they tried to hold their ground. But the Huexotzincas and Atlixcas soon realized that the Chalcas had vanquished them, so they surrendered and pleaded for the battle to cease. And so it ended.

The news of the death of his cousins saddened Motecuhzoma greatly and he complained to the gods. Full of grief, he and his people went out to receive the soldiers who returned from war. In Chalco, however, since their army had been victorious, the soldiers were given a great, solemn, and joyous reception and were covered with many kinds of flowers that were given to the victors. At the reception of the army in the Aztec city, meanwhile, Motecuhzoma appeared carrying his sword and shield. On his face there was no sign of sadness or lack of courage, and he consoled his men, having greeted them warmly, then he sent messengers and gifts to Tula so that the funeral honors for their lord could be performed as soon as possible. The Toltecs were grateful to him for this attention. Motecuhzoma also ordered the funeral rites for his cousins to be held with all the ceremony possible. Great lords from all the districts came to be present at these obsequies.

In Huexotzinco—although the men had fought courageously and had defended themselves with great bravery—there was much weeping and sadness for the death of the many leading warriors who had perished in that cruel battle.

But the people on one side and on the other consoled each other by saying that this was an honorable death and they were obliged to dedicate themselves to these wars. According to the *Historia*, when they went to these wars there never was a time when some of the great lords from all the provinces were not killed or taken prisoner. And the same could be said of the opponents. This type of death was considered blessed, was considered magnificent, and thus was called "happy and fortunate death."[3]

---

[3] Perhaps referring to the flower war between the Aztecs and the people of the Puebla-Tlaxcala region.

CHAPTER LIX

Which treats of how the city of Cholula defied the Aztecs on the road to Atlixco, with a description of the battle that took place three days after the challenge.

After the great Motecuhzoma had been chosen king, the people on the other side of the snowy mountains began to have conflicts with the Aztecs. This happened with great frequency, more so than at any time in the past, when previous monarchs had ruled. The reason for this is not known, but it is to be suspected that Motecuhzoma himself secretly provoked them in order to give his men practice in war. Or perhaps the inhabitants of those regions were anxious to humble the pride of Motecuhzoma and his nation and therefore caused these conflicts. Whatever the reason, the *Historia* states that during the time of Motecuhzoma Tlaxcala, Huexotzinco, Cholula, and Tliliuhquitepec were always declaring war, never allowing the Aztecs to rest. Our chronicle also relates how the Chalcas and Matlatzincas routed the Huexotzinca army, thus avenging to some extent the harsh way they had treated the Aztecs, the Toltecs, the Tezcocans, and the Tepanecs, when some of the leading valiant men of these four armies were killed and the rest were about to retreat because the Huexotzincas were winning—and would have triumphed if the Chalcas and Matlatzincas had not intervened. The soldiers from Cholula, however, who had never met the Aztecs on the battlefield, wished to test their strength and their valor. They sent messengers to the neighboring cities of Cuauhquechollan and Atzitziuacan, which were on the borders between Tenochtitlan and the cities beyond the snowy mountains, bidding them notify Motecuhzoma that they wished to have the pleasurable experience of skirmishing with the Aztecs in battle. In this way they would please the Lord of the Earth, the Lord of the Battles, and the sun. They asked him to send his men because in three days they would be waiting for them there. The envoys took this message to the Aztec capital, where they relayed it to Motecuhzoma. Since he was forced to accept the challenge, he sent the messengers back, telling the Cholula men to prepare their army well, for in three days they would meet on the field. At the same time Motecuhzoma sent his own messengers to the king of Tezcoco and the king of Tacuba, ordering them to have their soldiers go to the plains of Atlixco. They were to be very well armed and alert because the Cholulans had challenged them, had asked for battle, and with very little warning had stated that in three days all the men would meet for that purpose.

The two kings sent word that they would obey his commands. Motecuhzoma ordered the soldiers be prepared in Tenochtitlan and in the provinces. He also ordered them to leave immediately and march all night without stopping until they reached the valley of Atlixco where the battle was to take place. They dared not oppose Motecuhzoma, so, leaving the city, they marched all day and all night—the Aztecs, the Tezcocans, the Tepanecs, the Chalcas, the Xochimilcas, and the other *chinampa* people, and men from the Hot Lands. At dawn they reached Cuauhquechollan and Atzitziuacan, where they were welcomed and their supplies replenished. Towns on the borderland were always provided with plentiful supplies for such occasions.

The Aztec forces were called to attention, then the soldiers set up camp. The commander ordered them to be prepared, as some of them would be sent out for the first confrontation. He chose courageous, valiant men from the three allied nations. They went into battle against the Cholulan soldiers who were waiting for them. Beginning to skirmish, these Cholulans soon started to fight seriously, with great courage, and the Aztecs and their allies did the same, exhibiting no less valor and skill. Both sides took captives and some soldiers were killed. Then the armies attacked each other with terrible fury and the battle lasted the entire day. It was fought with such rage that when the Aztecs withdrew that night they found that they had lost eight thousand two hundred soldiers including men from the allied nations. Among the fallen were three most valorous captains, close relatives of King Motecuhzoma. However, the Aztecs had performed similar feats against the Cholulans and the fields were covered with dead bodies. And many prisoners had been taken. It was obvious that great damage had been done to the Aztecs, so an envoy was sent to Motecuhzoma to tell him of the happenings of the day and of their significant losses. They waited until the next day to see if Cholula wanted to fight again. While the Aztecs were preparing to avenge the deaths of their own lost warriors, the Cholulans sent a message saying that they had had enough practice and recreation. They bade the Aztecs go home in peace.[1]

When the Aztec commander heard these words, he departed in the direction of his city, sad and mournful. No less sad was Motecuhzoma,

---

[1] Durán actually says, "Go with God"; this is the Dominican friar speaking, not the Cholulans.

who, when he heard the news, wept bitterly and complained about the gods. He cried that he did not know how he had offended them. In this he did not take into consideration that fighting with Tlaxcalans, Cholulans, and Huexotzincas was like Spaniards warring against Spaniards. According to the native histories, all these people were of the same origin and the only difference was that they belonged to different factions. However, other nations such as the Mixtecs, Zapotecs, Huaxtecs, and the coastal peoples were to them as the Moors, Turks, heathens, or Jews are to us. "Chichimec," a name of which the Aztec nation was so proud, is similar to our use of the word Castilian or Goth and the above-named people did not use this title. Only those around the snow-capped volcanoes bore it, and these people were the inhabitants of Tlaxcala, Huexotzinco, Cholula, and Tliliuhquitepec. All of them called themselves Chichimecs before they came to possess these lands. So it was that Tlaxcala and Tenochtitlan fought in order to practice war and not because of enmity. We shall talk about this further on.

When the soldiers who had managed not to be killed in the war returned, they were received with sadness, the people wearing insignia of mourning, the priests with their hair loose, their faces not painted with the pitch that designated victory. There were no incense burners; the conch shells and flutes were silent. There were no flowers, there were no festivities, there was only weeping, there was only sadness. The wives of the soldiers who had been killed or who were wounded or maimed went to the entrance of the city, their hair hanging loose, where they howled loudly and slapped themselves with their hands. Motecuhzoma was at the door of the temple wearing a mantle of eagle feathers. Cihuacoatl, wearing the same kind of mantle, stood next to him. Both carried swords in their hands but wore serene expressions. All the men returning from the war passed between them without greeting them, then, inside the temple, they performed the usual ceremonies of giving thanks and eating earth before the image of the god. From there they went to the palace, where Motecuhzoma was on his royal seat. They kissed his hands and informed him of everything that had taken place in the battle. He responded that fighting was their occupation and just because of this defeat they should not abandon their calling, the use of arms, since their goal was to win or die. If this day the enemy was victorious, on another day the Aztecs would be. They should not be upset at this loss, although they grieved due to the death of their brothers, for having lost such valiant men. When men died in honor for their homeland, the defense of that homeland, they were colored and adorned with the color of their excellent blood, of their valor, they were adorned with the precious stones and fine feathers of their deeds and brave feats.[2] That kind of death was the end they and all the others should desire, for they did not die like women beside the hearth fire, cooking at the stove, but with sword in hand, painting with the rosy hue of their blood and the blood of others, glorifying in the flowers of the field and the rays of the sun. They were proud of this, they gloried in it.

With this Motecuhzoma ordered the obsequies carried out for the men who had died in that battle, and that they be held with all the customary solemnities. These were then performed with the formal ceremonies that have already been described when speaking of funeral rites, especially those involving the men who died in war.

Motecuhzoma observed that the Tlatelolcas had not held any funeral rites for the Aztecs killed in the war and asked why they failed to do so. The answer given was that no Tlatelolca soldiers had died there, so there was no reason for them to observe the obsequies. Motecuhzoma became very angry at this answer and exclaimed: "How can this be? While my brothers and kinsmen die, fighting courageously for the love of our country, and at the same time lords from the provinces and their valiant soldiers perish, the Tlatelolcas return without having lost one man, so they wash their hands of everything! Why do we have to endure their laughing at us and delighting in the harm, the injuries, that we have suffered? Do not those traitors know they are my vassals? Are they satisfied only to give me a low, civil tribute? They are my tributaries, and after I had again become lenient with them, have they returned to their former loathsome habits? From now on I command them to give slaves as tribute as the other provinces do and when we go to war they must go by themselves, fight by themselves, and not be attached to our forces, nor be protected by us. If the Tlatelolcas fail to obey these commands, I swear by all the gods that I shall again destroy them, that I shall wreak my wrath upon them! Go immediately and inform them of all this."

When the lords saw Motecuhzoma so angry, everyone feared his fury, so with great humility the responded: "O powerful lord, humbly we beg of you to calm your wrath, which could cause some sudden danger to your health, and we wish you to conserve that health. You have given your commands, their negligence deserves your punishment. These commands will be carried out as you have ordered."

Two officials from those of the highest level in the court went to carry out the sentence, to notify the Tlatelolcas. Summoning all the elders of that city and the lords and councillors, they pronounced this

---

[2]The stones, feathers, and colors were metaphors for excellence, for courage. For a brief study on metaphors, see Heyden 1986a.

rule set by his majesty King Motecuhzoma: that no Tlatelolca would be allowed to enter the palace in Tenochtitlan until he had performed an outstanding feat in the first war that was declared from then on and had brought back captives. The Tlatelolcas, humbling themselves and recognizing their culpability, made a great show of regret, weeping and expressing sadness at least on the surface, since some of the older men had been alive when Motecuhzoma's father had destroyed Tlatelolco, and they remembered this. So they sent a message to Motecuhzoma promising, with all humility possible, to correct their ways in the future. The Aztec officials returned to their city, where they told the king that they had followed his orders and had gone to Tlatelolco, where the men had received them submissively and had admitted their fault. What had depressed them most about Motecuhzoma's sentence was the prohibition to enter the palace and royal houses. But they would observe this restriction until the royal personage lifted this banishment. They looked forward to this as they would [to a nullified ruling] from a devoted mother or father.

Once the Aztec officials had left Tlatelolco, the men there called a council meeting to decide what was to be done. Some were in favor of trying to free themselves from Aztec control, but others gave a different opinion, stating that Motecuhzoma's power was so great that they had neither the intelligence nor the courage to confront him. It would be better to placate him by excelling in some important way, thus recuperating his friendship and goodwill. This second proposal was agreed upon and would be done when the opportunity presented itself. This exile from Motecuhzoma's court, then, lasted exactly one year. The Tlatelolcas did not enter the palace, they did not look upon the face of the king, nor did Motecuhzoma wish to admit them or pardon them or lift the restrictions he had imposed upon them.

During this time war with Teuctepec occurred. The people there had not been completely conquered but rather had been taken by surprise by the trick the Aztecs had prepared and, fooled by this when they had been made to cross part of the river (as was described earlier), did not want to swear allegiance to Motecuhzoma. Prior to this they had attacked merchants and travelers who came their way. Now they had built a new wall on the other side of the river in order not to be surprised so easily and felt themselves invulnerable. When Motecuhzoma heard of this, he called to arms men from all the allied regions—so many that they seemed to blot out the sun—ordering them to go to war against Teuctepec and not return until that province had been subjected to his royal crown, or destroyed if the people there resisted. The armies were to win or die in the attempt.

After these armies had left for the war, the people of Tlatelolco, believing they could be pardoned for their past failings, brought to the Aztec capital a great quantity of supplies of all kinds for the war, as well as many weapons and similar things necessary for the armies. With these provisions and gifts they presented themselves before the lords of Tenochtitlan, who informed Motecuhzoma of their presence. But the king, furious at what he considered an affront, refused to accept anything they had brought and had the men thrown out of the city. So, rejected and feeling insulted, they returned to Tlatelolco with all the provisions they had brought. Convinced, then, that they could only gain through war what gifts had not brought them, the Tlatelolcas called their people to arms and, forming the largest army they could, they marched day and night until they reached Teuctepec, arriving there before the Aztecs. Putting the men in order and dividing them into squadrons, the Tlatelolcas began the attack and, having captured the first wall, the only one that was newly made on the side of the river across from the town, they forced the Teuctepec soldiers to retreat across the river. The Tlatelolcas, however, could not cross, but at that moment the Aztec troops arrived and together they all managed to pass. All fought bravely and in this way they tore down the five defense walls. They set fire to the city and captured a great number of men, women, and children, thus leaving Teuctepec depopulated. Those who remained were turned over to Motecuhzoma's forces for the king's service. Few people, however, were left there as subjects to Mexico-Tenochtitlan because so many had been captured or killed in reprisal for their rebellion, for having refused to become Motecuhzoma's vassals.

Motecuhzoma was advised of these events as soon as possible. He was especially informed of the outstanding exploits performed by the Tlatelolcas. He was told, too, that two thousand Teuctepec soldiers had been captured and were coming as prisoners of war. Aside from these there were women and children who were now slaves. And many of the young recruits who had never before gone to war had performed marvelous feats. These men were marked with a special sign such as their laws demanded. And there was no count of the dead who had remained on the battlefield. When Motecuhzoma heard all this, he gave thanks to the gods, especially to the Lord of All Created Things. He then gave thanks to his captains who had fulfilled their obligations diligently. Seeing that the army and prisoners were about to arrive, he had his lords go out to welcome them with the customary ceremonies. All were very contented, very pleased. They greeted the captives with the usual solemnity because, as I have already stated, these men who were to serve as sacrificial victims were treated with great respect and reverence, in a way similar to that of the priests of the Mosaic Law, who honored and revered the calves and lambs that were sacrificed in the temple.

On entering the city, the Tlatelolcas came first, with five hundred captives that they presented to Motecuhzoma. The king, in agreement with his principal lords, welcomed them courteously and accepted their gift of the prisoners. They then were reconciled with the royal crown and Motecuhzoma lifted their banishment from the court, allowing them access to the palace and returning the privileges they had before. He then ordered that the captives be cured of their wounds and treated with great care.

It should be known that Motecuhzoma, on seeing that any nation or faction from his provinces demonstrated cowardliness in war, was accustomed to punish them in the same way he punished the Tlatelolcas: he deprived them of access to the palace and he removed them from all the royal posts until they changed that cowardice for some great deed. In this way they placated the king and returned to his good graces and affection. He often used these same tactics with his own kinsmen and with other Aztecs, as we shall soon describe.

CHAPTER LX

Which treats of the enmity and war that arose between Tlaxcala and Huexotzinco. With a description of how the Huexotzincas asked the king of Tenochtitlan for help and how this plea was granted.

The Aztec people were remarkable for the way in which they counted the years, and there existed among them old men who were specialists in the division of time: in the hebdomads and the number of these, of the Olympiads and the number of years in each Olympiad. Their cycle [which we could call a "century"] was one of fifty-two years, though some say it consisted of eighty but I think the latter are mistaken. Some people remember the number of years it took to celebrate a jubilee, others remember the count of the hebdomads, and some talk about the ages of the world. In their old chronicles they tell of five ages of the world, including the one we live in now. The count of these began from the time the world was created and we should be in the sixth now, based on the time Christ the Redeemer died. But since these people lacked any knowledge of Christ in those times, their count was based on the five ages or eras, as I find here in the *Historia*, where they are called the Five Suns. And there is a reason for my telling about this: the *Historia* tells us that a cycle ended at this time after the Teuctepec war and that it was called *toxiuhmolpilli*, the "binding of the years." The elders who were in charge of these things advised Motecuhzoma that it was the year of the end of the cycle. Besides the solemn festivities that were to take place, the elders pretended that the sun and the moon were to be hidden for four days and that everything would be enveloped in darkness. Thus it was ordered that in all the provinces around Mexico-Tenochtitlan the fires should be put out and no one dare light a fire in secret until, four days later, on the hill of Huixachtlan, a great fire was rekindled from which the inhabitants might ignite their own fires. This hill, which we call the Huixachtecatl, stands between Itztapalapan and Cuitlahuac, next to the road that leads from Cuitlahuac to Itztapalpa. And on this hill the New Fire ceremony was held the day the fifty-two year cycle ended and the new one was about to begin. After having been in darkness for four days, not because the sun had failed to shine but because of lack of fire, the rites of the New Fire were performed. These were similar to our ritual of the Paschal candle, where other candles are lighted from this one. At the end of the ceremony on the hill at Huixachtecatl, then, everyone took new fire.

This ceremony was celebrated with great solemnity and the priests of all the temples were present, led by the high priest dressed in his sacerdotal vestments and finery. There were offerings and incense, together with the sacrifice of many human beings on that hill who died as victims to the god of fire. So it was that on that day the two thousand captives who had been brought from the destruction and conquest of Teuctepec (which I have described) were sacrificed there. This sacrifice began at midnight and lasted most of the next day. Triumphant and joyful, the priests were bathed in blood, and the vessels filled with human blood were sent to smear the lintels of the doors, posts, and altars of the temples, and to sprinkle the statues of the gods. This smearing with blood was always done when there was a sacrifice.

After these rites had been concluded, two high officials from Huexotzinco came to see Motecuhzoma in representation of their lord, Tecayehuatl, prince of that city. With great distress they spoke of how the Tlaxcalans had antagonized them during the past year, but for unjust reasons. They had been very bad neighbors and had destroyed the planted fields belonging to Huexotzinco, thus causing the people of that city to suffer hunger and privation. Their lord begged Motecuhzoma to aid them in driving the Tlaxcalans out of their lands and to favor them with some food supplies. Motecuhzoma felt sorry for them so he had them given lodgings and then he called his councillors, telling them about the request of the Huexotzincas. His advisers suggested that he not make a decision without consulting the rulers of Tezcoco and Tacuba, his neighbors and allies. These lords were summoned and, when consulted, it was decided that they would help in this endeavor since they had always been favored by the Aztecs, and all were as one. The Huexotzinca envoys were then told to take a message to their lords telling them that if they so wished they were welcome to take refuge in the city of Tenochtitlan with all the people of their court including the women and children, to rest there where everything they needed would be provided while Motecuhzoma would send his ambassadors to talk to the Tlaxcalans. When everything was settled, the Huexotzincas could return to their homes and land.

The envoys, amazed at Motecuhzoma's generosity, returned to their city, where they relayed the Aztec king's offer to their lord. Tecayehuatl was overcome with gratitude. He proclaimed this message in his city, and many of its inhabitants immediately took advantage of the offer. Such a great number of people left for Tenochtitlan— women and children, old men and old women, people in need, those

The war between Tlaxcala and Huexotzinco

who would otherwise die in the war, and even the lord and his chieftains—that Huexotzinco became depopulated. When Motecuhzoma heard of their arrival, he went out to welcome the lord of Huexotzinco, who was like the king in his own land. Motecuhzoma received him and his noblemen affectionately and gave them chambers in the palace, where he ordered that they be served with all the same attentions he received. The Huexotzinca nobles were lodged in the houses of the Aztec lords, each one receiving one or two guests and treating them as if they were his own person. The rest of the people, the women and children, old men and old women, were distributed in the different barrios of the city, among its inhabitants. The city became so swollen with people that there was not one Aztec who did not have two or three guests in his home. They were so careful to give these visitors everything they needed each day and to take care that they lacked nothing, nor complained about anything, that it seemed a strange situation. Any negligence on the part of those in charge could be punished with death.

When the Huextozincas had been settled in the city, it was announced that all the Aztec soldiers were to be prepared to go to war against Tlaxcala in favor of Huexotzinco. They immediately made ready. Motecuhzoma did not allow one man from Huexotzinco to go to this war but sent his own people, commanding them to remain in the battle until they triumphed or died, or until they were losing and thus were forced to retreat. He was especially interested in capturing the commander of the Tlaxcalan army, whose name was Tlahuicole, a most valiant man who had become famous for his outstanding exploits and whose greatness resounded among all the nations. The Aztec forces set out for Tlaxcala, and when they were in sight of this city Tlahuicole was informed of their coming. He was much pleased, thinking he would gain glory in fighting these people. He led his troops into battle and fought with the enemy twenty days without interruption. During this time neither side could claim the victory they so desired. The Aztecs, tiring because of the constant attacks by Tlahuicole and his people, sent word to Motecuhzoma saying that the Tlaxcalans were reinforced each day with fresh troops from neighboring towns and that they, the Aztecs, were now exhausted. They requested that soldiers from allied cities and provinces be sent so that the Aztecs could rest. Motecuhzoma then formed new troops and called on Tezcoco and Tacuba for aid. Since that war was a serious one and not just a skirmish prepared to give the soldiers practice, and the honor of Tenochtitlan was at stake for having offered to defend the Huexotzincas, Motecuhzoma ordered that everything possible be done and with utmost care.

The History of the Indies of New Spain

When the reinforcements reached Tlaxcala, the soldiers who had been there returned to their city. The fresh troops fought so well that within a few days they captured Tlahuicole, the Tlaxcalan commander, together with many of his officers. The Tlaxcalan army was disbanded and driven out of Huexotzinca territory. Then the allied armies returned to Tenochtitlan with their prize. Motecuhzoma was highly pleased at this and had Tlahuicole brought before him so he could see what kind of man had made the entire earth tremble. When the captive entered the presence of the Aztec king, he kissed his hands with humility and reverence and begged pardon for his offenses. Motecuhzoma received him well, consoled him, and said that these were things of war and that all warriors were subject to such conditions. He told him not to be sorrowful and gave orders that he be lodged comfortably and all his needs be taken care of. He added that he greatly admired Tlahuicole and he dressed the Tlaxcalan warrior in royal garments with the weapons and insignia of a nobleman, thus honoring him in all ways possible.

After Tlahuicole had been in the Aztec city for many days, he began to remember his wives and children, being moved by the natural desire to see them. Every day he was found weeping, sighing for his family. Motecuhzoma was informed of this because it was considered an ill omen if a captive became sad. The king was both depressed and angered and sent a message to the captive saying he thought that a person like Tlahuicole, capable of scorning life itself, would not be worried about wives and children. However, since he was so cowardly and fretted in such a way over the absence of his wives, he would be given his liberty. He was held in contempt and would be allowed to go back to his city and retire with his women. It was also ordered that he not be given food or things from the palace and that the soldiers who had accompanied him as custodians leave him immediately. They were to pay no attention to him.

When Tlahuicole heard the king's message, he became mute with sadness, he became dejected. From that day on his food was taken away from him and so was his guard. He went from house to house begging for food and finally in despair he set out for Tlatelolco. There he ascended to the summit of the pyramid and cast himself down the steps. In this way he sacrificed himself to the gods, fulfilling the purpose for which he had been brought to Tenochtitlan, to be sacrificed at the right time and for the right reasons. He did this because he was humiliated at being so despised and he knew that if he returned to his country he and his descendants would live under a cloud of shame forever. After his death he was offered to the gods with all the usual ceremonies and solemn rites, and the other prisoners who had been brought from Tlaxcala were also sacrificed. After this the Tlaxcalans stopped persecuting the Huexotzincas.[1]

The disputes and antagonism between the Tlaxcalans and the Huexotzincas having ended, after many days the lord of Huexotzinco asked permission of Motecuhzoma to return to his homeland. He thanked the king profusely for all that he had done for him and his people and offered to be at his service always in return for the special treatment they had received. Motecuhzoma was sad to see them go but since he understood that they were determined to return to Huexotzinco he gave Tecayehuatl many gifts of jewels and other valuable things and, providing many soldiers and noblemen to accompany him, he ordered them not to abandon the Huexotzinco ruler until they had left him in his city and in his home. In this way Tecayehuatzin left with all the people he had brought—women and children, old men and old women, some of the commoners and the poor ones. All gave thanks to Motecuhzoma and praised his greatness and magnificence. However, on that occasion many Huexotzincas remained in Mexico-Tenochtitlan, settling in that city, for they had become accustomed to the splendid way they had been treated there. According to the *Historia*, from that time on the people of Tlaxcala did not dare anger those of Huexotzinco, in view of the friendship that had been forged between them and the people of Mexico.

Nevertheless, this friendship was short-lived. The Huexotzincas, having been convinced by the Cholulans, again made enemies of the Aztecs and warred with them as they once had. I shall tell about this enmity here.

Motecuhzoma sent an invitation to the lord of Huexotzinco to attend a festivity that was about to take place in Tenochtitlan, request-

[1] Diego Muñoz Camargo (a mestizo, son of a Spanish father and an Indian mother), the greatest of sixteenth-century Tlaxcalan historians, tells the story of Tlahuicolli or Tlahuicole in a different way. He states that the captive warrior from Tlaxcala ingratiated himself with the Aztecs and was made a commander in the army. Motecuhzoma II placed Tlahuicole at the head of the forces that invaded Mechoacan. The Tlaxcalan commander returned with a record of such glorious deeds that Motecuhzoma gave him his freedom. However, Tlahuicole seems to have realized at that time that his life had come to an end; he could not continue to fight for the Aztecs because they were the enemies of his own people. Nor could he return to Tlaxcala, for he knew he had betrayed his own nation by fighting on the side of their enemies. Therefore, Tlahuicole asked Motecuhzoma to allow him to die upon the *temalacatl*, the round stone of sacrifice. The Tlaxcalan was given a few days of rest and then was allowed to fight on the gladiatorial stone. According to Muñoz Camargo, Tlahuicole managed to eliminate eight Eagle Warriors by killing them and wound some twenty others before he collapsed upon the surface of the stone. Then he was sacrificed, his heart cut out by the high priest. For Muñoz Camargo's account, see his *Historia de Tlaxcala* (1966:125–28).

ing him to honor them with his presence. The messengers who carried this invitation, on going over the mountains and reaching the borders of Huexotzinco territory, met some guards who had patrolled these lands before friendship grew up between Huexotzinco and Tenochtitlan. When they saw that the messengers were Aztecs, they closed the road to them. The Aztecs, who had been completely off their guard and going in a carefree manner, were startled at this new treatment. "What is happening, brothers?" they asked. "What is this? Do you not know that there is peace between us?"

The guards answered, "No, we do not."

"Well, then, we are messengers from the Aztec lords," these men responded. "Have you forgotten the excellent treatment you received when you were staying with us? Kindly let us reach your city so we can speak to your lord and hear the answer to our message from his lips."

The guards allowed them to pass; and when they were in the presence of Tecayehuatl, they were well received and accommodated as honored visitors. But when the invitation was presented on behalf of Motecuhzoma, requesting that he attend the solemn feast that was about to take place, Tecayehuatl began to weep. He spoke to them thus: "Tell your lord that it is my will to serve him all my life in return for the fine treatment he gave me and my people in his city but that my very people, voluble, fond of change, have joined with those of Cholula. They have asked that I reject your friendship, that I refuse to accept peace, under the threat that if I disobey they will take away my rule and destroy my entire family and progeny. But in spite of this I shall send my principal noblemen to attend the feast in my place."

The messengers returned with Tecayehuatl's answer, which they presented to their king. He was amazed at this but ordered that those noblemen who were coming be received in the usual place. When they arrived they were taken in secret into the city and then went before the great lord Motecuhzoma. Weeping, they spoke to him, "O powerful lord, the fear that has been instilled in the Cholulans by your great deeds and the feats of your people has been the cause of their making overtures to our people, to our soldiers, and of having persuaded the officers of our armies, advising them against friendship with the Aztecs. They have given them many reasons for this distancing and, thus convinced, these men have asked your servant Tecayehuatl to abandon his friendship with you and once again have the practice in war that we used to have. Therefore, he begs you to pardon him since necessity obliges him to be ungrateful for all the benefits we have received from you."

Motecuhzoma responded with a cheerful countenance: "My brothers, I would be pleased to have your friendship, have us treat each other as brothers, but since you do not wish this, it will be as you command. I am prepared and ready for everything." He then ordered that the Huexotzinco lords be provided with all they desired and presented them with rich gifts of clothing and jewelry. He did not wish them to be present at the festivities, however, so he gave them weapons, a shield and sword, to be taken to their lord Tecayehuatl. These were like insignia of a challenge, of perpetual enmity. They remind us of what we read in some stories that when noblemen challenged each other they cast a glove. So sending these arms was a sign of hostility and a permanent challenge.

The Huexotzinco lords returned to their city, where they presented to their sovereign the gifts sent by Motecuhzoma. They told him of the Aztec king's serenity in receiving them and dismissing them. They related that he had not wanted them to attend the festivities and that he paid little attention to the animosity that existed between them. So the two cities again became enemies and once again fought the regular wars that they had been accustomed to fight, and sacrificed men on both sides.

CHAPTER LXI

Which treats of how Nezahualpiltzintli, king of Tezcoco, informed Motecuhzoma that the Spaniards would soon arrive and that the Aztecs would have few victories over their enemies.

Often have I spoken of how the king of Tezcoco, Nezahualpilli, was considered a necromancer or sorcerer and the most common opinion I find among the natives was that he had a pact with the devil, who revealed to him many things regarding the future. These things he then proclaimed as if they were his own conjectures and as if he had knowledge of their causes.

One day when King Motecuhzoma was at ease, it was announced that the ruler of Tezcoco had come to see him. Greatly surprised at this unexpected visit, he came out of his private chambers to receive him. When they had greeted one another with the usual courtesies, they spoke in private in Motecuhzoma's chambers. When he was asked the reason for his visit Nezahualpilli answered:

"O powerful and great lord! I do not wish to trouble your peaceful spirit, but the obligation I have to serve you forces me to reveal a strange and bewildering thing that I have been permitted to see by the Lord of the Heavens, of Night and Day, and of Wind, something that is to happen in your time.

"You must be on guard, you must be warned, because I have discovered that in a very few years our cities will be ravaged and destroyed. We and our children shall be killed, our subjects humbled. Of all these things you must not doubt. In order to prove to you that I speak the truth, you will see that whenever you wage war on Huexotzinco, Tlaxcala, or Cholula, you will be defeated. You will always be overcome by the enemy and will suffer great losses of your officers and soldiers. I shall add this: before many days have passed you will see signs in the sky that will appear as an omen of what I am saying. But do not be cast down because of these things, since one cannot turn one's face from that which must be. One consolation is that I shall not see these calamities and afflictions because my days are numbered. That is why I wished to warn you before my death, O my most cherished son."

Both men wept and Motecuhzoma cried out to the gods asking that his days end soon so he would not have to see what had been foretold — all those calamities that were to happen in his time. However, he thanked Nezahualpilli for having warned him and the Tezcocan king left Motecuhzoma afflicted and fearful, remembering everything that had been prognosticated, but revealing this secret to no one else.

Since he wished to discover whether Nezahualpilli's words were true, Motecuhzoma ordered his soldiers and allies to prepare for war against Tlaxcala. Messengers were sent out with the request that the armies be readied. The soldiers then left the cities and reached a place called Auayucan, where a camp was set up. A fierce battle took place here and the Aztecs were thoroughly beaten, some killed, some captured. All of the commanders were taken prisoner by the Tlaxcalans.

When news of this defeat was told to Motecuhzoma and when he heard that the Aztecs had taken only forty prisoners during the entire time the battle had raged against Tlaxcala, the Tezcocans had taken only twenty, and Tacuba had only fifteen and Tlatelolco five, Motecuhzoma rose from his seat, shouting to the men who had brought the message, "What is this you say? Do you know what you are telling me? Are not the Aztecs filled with shame? Since when have you lost your vigor, your strength, like weak women? Are you just learning to take up the sword and the shield, the bow and the arrow? What has happened to all the skill acquired since the founding of this renowned city? How has it been lost, how has it become effeminate, to the point that I stand in shame before the entire world? How is it that so many courageous lords and captains, seasoned in war, went to the battlefield—yet is it possible that they have forgotten how to command their squadrons in order to fight the whole world? I can only believe that they were deliberately heedless in order to mock me, to insult me!"

Motecuhzoma then called his doorkeepers, telling them to summon Cihuacoatl and the members of his council. He described what had happened and how he felt offended. He ordered that those who returned from this war should not be given a welcome. No conch shells or other musical instruments were to be sounded and neither men nor women were to receive them at their entrance to the city. No sadness or sorrow was to be shown because of their losses and no gladness for those who had come back. Therefore, when the return of the armies was imminent, a strange silence spread over the entire city, where not a man, woman, or priest was to be seen anywhere, not even in the temples. No one was seen who could explain this unusual phenomenon. When the soldiers arrived and had worshiped in the temple with the ceremonies that were customary for the returning army, they went to render homage to the king, but the doors were closed in their faces. They were ejected with scorn from the royal household and in shame they went to their homes and cities.

On another day the great "Angry Lord," for this is what the name Motecuhzoma means, gathered his councillors and, in great anger, he told them that he was disillusioned with the army and that he wished to punish, to give a lesson to the captains, officers, seasoned soldiers, and famed warriors. He wished them to be humiliated eternally because he believed they were all becoming very lax in matters of war. Everyone approved his decision, and the judges and those who enforced the rules were called together. These justices were ordered to go immediately to the homes of the officers and to shear their hair and take away from them the insignia that distinguished them as brave warriors. At the same time those men were to relinquish all the weapons and emblems that he had awarded them when he gave them the title of lord. And, under pain of death, they were forbidden to wear cotton mantles. From now on the officers were to wear cloaks of maguey fiber like those of the common man. They were not to use the sandals of the nobility and they were to refrain from entering the palace for one year.

With great sadness, with sorrow, the justices, who had no alternative, carried out the sentence and commands of their king. Some went to Tlatelolco to do this, others executed the orders in Tenochtitlan. In both places many people were affronted by this action. I understand that the reason these men were so humiliated when, as a punishment by judges, their hair was sheared off can be found in an old custom. That is, the way their hair was cut, in this way or that, was proof of their great deeds, was an insignia. When this certain hairstyle was removed as a sign of degradation, they lost all the prestige they had won. The justices returned from having performed their duties and informed the king of the weeping and sadness that these actions had caused, and how the city seemed empty and lonely with the captains and lords locked up in their houses, not daring to go out [since they had been stripped of their insignia]. There was no one in the streets, no one enjoying himself, no one enlivening the city as was customary. But the king showed no regret, no sorrow, but rather feigned indifference and ignored the soldiers during all that year, treating them as despicable men of low birth, who should be disgraced.

After a year, however, Motecuhzoma ordered that another war be declared on Tlaxcala so the warriors who had suffered could go of their own accord and thus again win their emblems. These men were not commanded either to go to war or to stay at home. No attention was paid to them, as if the idea of war was independent of them. So they enlisted with the others like rank soldiers, like adventurers, in that war. They did everything in their power to regain their former positions and fought bravely against the Tlaxcalans, although neither side was ahead of the other, and when the battle ended it was seen that the Tlaxcalans had lost as many soldiers as the Aztecs. They both had shown great valor.

Motecuhzoma was much pleased when he heard this, was contented with the news of the battle. Dressing in a mantle whose design was that of many eagles, he then summoned Cihuacoatl and the other lords and told them that they should all be pleased because the Aztecs had fought courageously against the Tlaxcalans and there had been a kind of reconciliation between the two armies because neither one fought more valiantly than the other. The Aztecs had brought back many Tlaxcalan prisoners, although a number of Aztec, Tezcocan, and Tepanec soldiers had died. They had enjoyed a happy, flowery death.

The news of this battle caused much rejoicing in the city and in the temples, with the sounding of drums, conch shells, flutes, and all the musical instruments that these people played on joyful occasions. The Aztec army was welcomed in Tenochtitlan with all the ceremonies typical of a victorious entrance, with singing and dancing and incense, with many long, formal, elegant speeches congratulating the men for their valor. They went to the temple, where they performed the usual rite of eating earth and then every one of them went to greet the Angry Lord. He welcomed them warmly with a cheerful and benign expression on his face. He then called all the officers who had been castigated for a year and gave them back their privileges, ranks, insignia, and arms. He praised them and thanked them for all they had done and for their valor in the desire to recuperate the honors they had lost. And this was especially notable because so many men had lost their lives in that war. This is something that takes place frequently and almost always with those who have fallen from the state of honor that they had held: they die while striving to regain that which has been taken away. And those people in their pagan belief placed great importance on honor and were greatly affected when they fell from the heights they had enjoyed, to the extent of risking their lives in order to possess that honor again.

King Motecuhzoma, after having restored the privileges to his officers with joyful and agreeable festivities, had the funeral rites held for those brave and notable warriors who had died. He also ordered that when the obsequies ended all the captives brought from Tlaxcala be prepared for sacrifice at the feast of the Mother of the Gods, which would soon be celebrated. This sacrifice will be seen in the next chapter.

CHAPTER LXII

Which treats of the cruel sacrifice of the Tlaxcalan victims on the feast of the goddess Toci. With a description of how the Huexotzincas were angered by this and how they burned her temple at night.

The time for the feast of the goddess Toci, Our Grandmother, now arrived. This feast was celebrated with great solemnity and many ceremonies each year. These celebrations are described in the second part of this book.[1] The reason for such ceremony is that Toci was considered to be the mother of the gods. In case it has been forgotten, she was the daughter of the king of Colhuacan whom the Aztecs, shortly after their arrival in this land, had requested of her father to be married to their god Huitzilopochtli. She had been killed, flayed, and then her image adored as a goddess. From this had come enmity and war between the Aztecs and Colhuacan.

When this important day came, King Motecuhzoma ordered that the prisoners from Tlaxcala be prepared for sacrifice. All the preparations for the ceremonies were made, and when the time came some of the Tlaxcalan captives were sacrificed in the ordinary way. Their chests were cut open, their hearts extracted, and their bodies rolled down the temple steps.

Men in a second group were sacrificed by fire. They were burned in the divine brazier and half dead, almost unconscious, they were pulled out of the embers where they had been buffeted about and their hearts were torn out. This was the fire sacrifice.

A third group of prisoners was taken to the temple of the goddess that was on the outskirts of the city where the first cross now stands on the road as we leave Mexico City. In front of the little temple was erected a scaffold of boards and poles, all very thick and tall, where the statue of Toci was placed. It was there that the victims were tied to the poles and cruelly shot with arrows. This was the special sacrifice in honor of this goddess and it was performed in memory of those who had been wounded with arrows when the Aztecs fled from Colhuacan and had hidden among the reeds and rushes in order not to be slaughtered. In memory of the wounds inflicted by arrows, caused by

---

[1]Durán's, *Book of the Gods and Rites* (1977:chap. XV).

that goddess, they now offered her men killed in an arrow sacrifice, who had been tied to those poles.[2]

The sacrifices and other solemnities of the feast having ended, Motecuhzoma was satisfied, and the news of the sacrifice by fire spread throughout the land. But the people of Huexotzinco were angered because of the cruelty with which the prisoners had been treated, though it is true that when the Aztecs fell into their hands they were no kinder to them. However, the Huexotzincas were now friends of Tlaxcala and had forgotten their ties with Tenochtitlan. So one night they came and burned the temple of the goddess and the four poles where the platform and the image of Toci were found. The *Historia* says, as does the account of rites and sacrifices in the second part of this history that I have written, that those four poles were the thickest and tallest trees that could be found in the woods.

Dawn found the structure in cinders, and when the Aztecs realized what had happened the city was thrown into a state of confusion and terror. Motecuhzoma was filled with wrath, for he considered it a personal offense and an ill omen. Therefore, he ordered that the priests of the temples be taken prisoner and cast into cages. The floor of these cages was covered with small sharp blades and fragments of sharp stone and the prisoners had to sit upon them and sleep upon them until their deaths. They were given food in very small portions (as we say, "by ounces") until they starved to death. Every day, though, Motecuhzoma sent messengers to upbraid them, telling them that it had been their duty to watch the temple of the gods day and night, the way a captain in war and his soldiers keep watch so as not to be surprised by the enemy. These priests had gone to sleep and had been so neglectful that they had not even been aware of such a frightful thing as the burning of a paramount goddess. Because of this Motecuhzoma was angry with them. The unfortunate priests received the rebuke with humility and patience, realizing that they had offended by their carelessness.

Motecuhzoma sent inquiries to the cities of Tezcoco, Chalco, Xochimilco, the Hot Lands, and all the Tepanec nation to try to find out who had committed such a great sacrilege. This message went out with great speed, and finally the truth was told by a Tlaxcalan prisoner held at Tlatelolco. The Huexotzincas, he said, had burned the temple and had gone to Tlaxcala to boast about it with the idea that the Tlaxcalans

---

[2]According to Durán 1977 (234–35), men were sacrificed at Tocititlan, the shrine of Toci, by forcing the victim, who wore a paper hood over his head, up the 180-foot ladder to the platform at the top, where he was then pushed off, being crushed on the floor below. For a study of human sacrifice among the Aztecs, see González Torres 1988; and Inga Glendinnen, *Aztecs* (1991).

would be grateful to them. When Motecuhzoma was informed of this, he had other poles, taller and stronger, put in place of the burned ones and the shrine renovated, made larger and more splendid. In this shrine were placed great riches and many fine adornments, with guards to take care of them who were paid to do so, and there were new priests.

Motecuhzoma then commanded his own soldiers to be made ready and sent orders to the allied cities to prepare their armies. He wanted to make war on Huexotzinco and bring captives from there to be sacrificed at the dedication of this temple. He wished the Huexotzincas to be the victims since they had offended him so deeply and had committed such an enormous sacrilege. Therefore, the Aztecs must take revenge. The armies prepared, the soldiers looking their best, and the war declared, the men were promised many awards and privileges if they carried out the king's plans. They marched out from the different cities and came to the valley of Atlixco, where the battle took place, lasting many days. Both sides took many captives and killed many men, but the Aztecs did not want to stop then but forged ahead—in spite of threats from the Huexotzincas—with the idea of taking prisoner as many Huexotzinca warriors as they could until they had a sufficient number for the sacrifice. Thus they would please the Angry Lord. Every day that this war lasted the Tlatelolcas excelled in the fighting. Not once did they go onto the battlefield, alone or accompanied by others, without bringing back prisoners while leaving some of the enemy dead or wounded. When the Aztec commander saw that the number of captives was sufficient to satisfy the hunger for prisoners of the Angry King, who was so anxious to kill, to sacrifice men, they broke up camp and left for Tenochtitlan. The king and the whole city there welcomed them warmly and the wounded were sent to be cured. The Tlatelolco people gave one hundred and twenty captives to Motecuhzoma to do with as he wished. He thanked them and told them to hold those captives until he asked for them. In this way Motecuhzoma had innumerable slaves entrusted to different cities and provinces so that when a great lord died or when an important festival took place in a neighboring city he could send slaves as a gift to the lords or as an offering to the deceased.

The same was true of the kings of Tezcoco and Tacuba, because in their own way they were as great kings as Motecuhzoma was and in their cities there were temples as splendid, as beautiful, as those of Tenochtitlan, and even more so. These rulers celebrated their feasts and sacrifices with the same order and ritual, with the same ceremonies and sacrifices, and with the death of as many men as took place in Tenochtitlan. Nezahualpilli of Tezcoco excelled to such an extent in his kingdom that the Aztec ruler, Motecuhzoma, showed respect and almost submission before Nezahualpilli. (At least a history from that time and place insinuates this.) I understand that this was because Motecuhzoma considered him more than human since he could predict the future, understand the phenomena of the sky, and with all this knowledge communicate to others the things that were revealed to him.

The Huexotzincas were waiting to see what happened to their men who had been captured. And what did happen was that some of them were flayed alive or when they were half dead, and their skins were worn by certain men who wore them for forty days and went from door to door, begging for food, until those who bore them could no longer tolerate the stench. Other prisoners were burned alive, and still others were killed by arrows. These sacrifices were performed in honor of the dedication of the temple of Toci. After they had learned of the frightful sacrifices of their soldiers, the Huexotzincas invited the king of Tenochtitlan to a feast they wished to hold for their god Camaxtli (for this was his name), but since Motecuhzoma did not wish to attend he sent some of his principal lords. In their presence and in honor of their god the Huexotzincas flayed many Aztec captives, cut out the hearts of others, burned some alive, and shot arrows into others, with the same cruelty the Aztecs had shown with their prisoners. Among the Aztecs who died this way there were many valiant warriors, which was a sad thing.

When Motecuhzoma was informed of these sacrifices, he said, "Why are you amazed by these things? For this fate we have been born, for this we go into battle, and death in this manner is fortunate. That is the blessed death that our ancestors extolled."

With this he summoned the Tlatelolco soldiers in order to reward them for the outstanding way they had fought. When they were in his presence, he had them given shields bearing certain insignia, arms of different colors, jewels, mantles, and other valuable presents. The Tlatelolcas were very proud and happy; they thanked the king profusely. When Motecuhzoma dismissed them, he said that he had not done these favors so they would relax, slacken, but so that in the future they would be more dedicated and carry on with even more valor. They promised the king that they would serve him with more dedication, with all their power. Then they left the city.

CHAPTER LXIII

Which treats of how a comet appeared in the sky and how it troubled Motecuhzoma. With a description of how he consulted the king of Tezcoco in order to discover its meaning.

At this point the *Historia* tells us that in each temple of the gods there always lived a man who represented the image of the god in that particular sanctuary. He lived in a special room where he was like the idol itself and was revered and served as such. He had his own servants and gods who were changed every year. These were called Mocexiuhzauhque, which could be interpreted to mean "those who do penance." For one year they abstained from women and did not offend the god. This took place as well in the temple of Huitzilopochtli.

One of these Mocexiuhzauhque was a virtuous young man who represented the god Huitzilopochtli and his name was Tzocoztli. One night around midnight, when he rose to satisfy bodily needs, he happened to look into the sky and in the east he saw a great comet with a large tail that seemed to advance in the direction of Mexico-Tenochtitlan. This youth was frightened so he went to his servants and guards, saying, "Awaken, for you will behold a marvelous and terrifying thing never seen before in this land." Everyone looked toward the east, where all saw it. None of them went to sleep again, but all waited in order to discover where the comet would be when dawn came. At the moment of sunrise it hung over the city and with the light of the sun it disappeared.

That morning the image of the god and his attendants left the temple and went to the palace, where Motecuhzoma, when informed of his arrival, bade him enter, and, honoring him like the surrogate of the deity, invited him to be seated and asked him the reason for the visit. The king was told of the strange thing seen in the sky, as I have described it. Motecuhzoma was sorely frightened, yet he did not completely believe it and asked the god-image if he had not perhaps dreamed of this apparition. The young man responded that not only he had seen the comet but also all those in his service had witnessed it, and if the king wished to ascertain this he had only to call them. So the king did call them in and asked what they had seen. These servitors told him the same thing he had heard from the god-image, then they left. Motecuhzoma, however, was still concerned, so when night came and everyone had retired he went to a terrace on the roof. Having watched there until midnight, he saw the comet appear with its brilliant tail, whereupon he was astonished. Then he remembered what Nezahualpilli had said, and he was so filled with fear that he thought his death would arrive within the hour. When dawn came, he summoned the representative of the god Huitzilopochtli and informed him that he too had observed the comet during the night, since he had wished to see for himself that which the young man had described. He asked to be told what this phenomenon meant. The young man replied that he was just a poor ignorant youth, with no knowledge of things of the sky because he was not an astrologer, sorcerer or seer. He suggested calling in the astrologers and diviners and asking those who study the night sky, for that was their occupation.

Motecuhzoma then summoned the priests, sorcerers, presagers, soothsayers, and astrologers, all who could be found in the city and consulted them. When they had come before him, he asked if they had observed the new sign that had appeared in the sky, but they claimed that they had seen nothing. The king, indignant at this reply, cried, "But how is that possible? Is this the care with which you watch over things that pass in the night? Why do I have in my kingdom astrologers, sorcerers, diviners, and soothsayers? In what way do you serve me? Speak, answer me! Have you not seen the sign that has appeared in the sky?" Again, they answered that they had not seen it. The king, now carried away by his anger, cried, "Since you live so carelessly, I shall see that you no longer sleep!" and he called his justices and gave orders that these diviners be thrown into some special cages they have that are like jails. Here no one was to feed them, under pain of death, but these men were to be left there until they starved to death. So they were cast into those cages, where, weeping, they begged to be killed right away so they would not die in such a terrible way.

Then Motecuhzoma called the king of Tezcoco and asked him to come to the Aztec palace and explain what he had seen in the sky. Having arrived in Tenochtitlan, where he was welcomed with the usual courtesy, Nezahualpilli went before the king, who told him of the strange thing he had seen in the sky and the care he had taken [to investigate its meaning]. He pleaded with Nezahualpilli, since he possessed the faculty of divining, which was a divine gift and a natural quality, to explain the meaning of this mysterious new thing. The Tezcoco ruler said to him, "O lord, your subjects the astrologers, soothsayers, and diviners have been careless. That sign in the heavens is ancient, has been there for a long time, yet you describe it to me now as if it were a new phenomenon. I thought that you knew about this, that your astrologers would have explained it to you. Since you now tell me you have seen it I shall answer you that that brilliant star appeared in the heavens many days ago. It comes out of the east and is directed toward Mexico-Tenochctitlan and this whole region. It is an ill omen for our kingdoms; terrible, frightful things will come upon them. In all our lands, in all our provinces, there will be great calamities and misfortunes, not a thing will be left standing. Death will dominate the land! All our dominions will be lost and all of this will be done with the permission of the Lord of the Heights, of the Day and the Night and of the Wind. You will be witness to these happenings because they will take place in your time. For my part, as soon as I leave your presence and depart from this city, I go to die. You will never behold me again; this is the last visit in which we shall see each other in this life. I long to hide, to flee from the labor and afflictions that await you. Do not be faint, do not feel anguish or despair! Make your heart wide, strengthen your spirit and manly chest against these predestined troubles!"

Motecuhzoma wept bitterly, saying, "O Lord of All Created Things! O mighty gods who give life and death! Why have you decreed that many kings, many powerful lords, shall have ruled proudly but that my fate is to witness the unhappy destruction of our city? Why should I be the one to see the death of my wives and children and my subjects, and the loss of my powerful kingdoms and dominions and of all the Aztecs have conquered with their mighty arms and the strength of their chests? What shall I do? Where shall I hide? Where shall I conceal myself? Alas, if only I could turn into stone, wood, or some other earthly matter rather than suffer that which I so dread! But what can I do, O powerful monarch, but await that which you have predicted? For this reason I kiss your hands and thank you. Alas, I cannot at this moment become a bird in order to fly into the woods and hide in their depths!" With these words, says our chronicle, the two kings said farewell to each other with great sadness.

After Nezahualpilli and Motecuhzoma had said their farewells, the Tezcoco ruler having gone to his city and the Aztec ruler remaining in Tenochtitlan, Motecuhzoma called his justices and all his noblemen and addressed them thus: "You all know that the other day the temple of the goddess Toci was burned because the priests were not vigilant; they did not watch over the shrine with the care they were supposed to exercise. They did not attend the penitential ceremonies at night, which is their obligation, as they are obliged to do, to keep a vigil in the temples and refrain from sleeping. Therefore, they were negligent, and all this carelessness could lead to great danger in the city, for we could all be surprised and killed, or the city could be burned since no one is on guard against these possibilities. It has also happened at this time that because the astrologers, diviners, sorcerers and prognosticators here have failed to be on guard they have not advised us of a remarkable, a prodigious phenomenon that appeared in the sky some days back. I believe that you all are ignorant of this since no one has told you about it, nor has anyone taken the trouble to observe it. Because of all this delinquency I order that without delay every one of the astrologers, diviners, sorcerers, and prognosticators be killed. Go to their houses and take away all the children you find there, let their houses be robbed, be stripped of everything in them, and their wives and children be given as perpetual slaves to anyone who wishes to take them. Their houses will be razed to the ground and no memory will remain of them because it seems that they have mocked me, have paid little attention to the things I have recommended and to the demands of their occupation. All this is the result of not having the respect for me that I deserve."

This sentence having been pronounced by Motecuhzoma, the justices went out and carried out his commands. Each one of the astrologers or diviners had a rope placed around his neck and this way was dragged through the streets of the city, where they suffered a bitter and painful death. Then many boys were taken out of school and were ordered to sack the houses of the dead men. Shouting wildly, the boys plundered, looted the houses until nothing was left in them. The leading men took the wives and children of the dead men and divided them up among themselves, making them perpetual slaves. The houses were torn down so there would not be even a memory of them left. This was the terribly cruel punishment that Motecuhzoma gave to anyone who failed to conform with his commands, who did not carry out his orders. Therefore, he was feared and obeyed with such diligence and care that everything ran smoothly, to the minutest detail.

After these men had been judged and executed, Motecuhzoma was told that his orders had been carried out, that those who had failed to serve him as they were obliged to had been punished with death. The king responded to this: "Observe, my brothers: to die is natural, you and I must die and I know that well. These men who have died have just disappeared a year or so before we shall go to our death. But I do this [execution] because just as I reward those who fulfill their obligations well, I give them the compensation, the prize that their services merit, then the evil ones, those who shirk their duties, must be eliminated, must be erased from the face of the earth in such a way that no one will ever remember that they existed. These traitors pretended to be astrologers, diviners, soothsayers, they deceived us, they tricked us with their lies and falsehoods. It is only just that they pay for their false prophecies so that others do not dare to pretend to be that which they are not."

Motecuhzoma then ordered that new astrologers, diviners, soothsayers, and prophets be found to take the place formerly held by those who had been killed. Many were designated who from then on took great care in observing the stars at night and they prognosticated regarding the comet. Some augured plagues, famines, wars, killings, and death. Others predicted that princes and great lords would die. In short, each prophesied what he understood or what the devil gave him to understand because in truth all these things were determined more by the devil than by the natural sciences.

Although truly there were great astrologers and people who had knowledge of the stars and of time periods, the majority were sorcerers, tricksters, enchanters, magicians, and people possessed by the devil. According to the *Historia*, when news of the comet spread through all the provinces of those kingdoms, the people were filled with such fear, with such fright, that as each day dawned they all got together and their wails and laments were so loud that they reached up to the heavens and there was such terror and anxiety that it seemed the world was coming to an end.

CHAPTER LXIV

Which treats of the death of Nezahualpilli, king of Tezcoco, and the election of a new ruler called Quetzalacxoyatl.

The *Historia* deals little with the king of Tacuba, mentions no great deeds of his or famous happening in that Tepanec kingdom. I myself am amazed to see that it glosses over everything that does not concern Motecuhzoma and the previous Aztec kings. It tells only how they called that Tepanec ruler for council in war, to obtain soldiers, or to take part in an election. He is never mentioned aside from these affairs. All of this I consider strange since I am sure that if I went to Tacuba to ask about their glorious deeds the people there would tell me that they had been greater than Motecuhzoma's. This situation has tied my hands and has made it impossible to fulfill my desire to write a history of each city, state, and town. There is no village, small as it may be, that does not take credit for all the grandeur of Motecuhzoma. All of these towns claim that they were exempt from tribute, had royal insignia, and were the victors in war. I speak from experience because in a certain town in the Marquesado I asked about their power and preeminence in ancient times and they exaggerated to such an extent, raising this superiority to the skies, that before they reached the stars with their tales I was forced, with soft words, to get them to admit that they had been subjects of and had paid tribute to Nezahualpilli of Tezcoco, who had subjected them in a fair war. And this is one of the finest towns in the Marquesado.

I explain all these things because I do not wish to be called a liar. If there is any falsehood in what I write, it is not to be attributed to me. I simply wish to record what the *Historia* narrates and, as I stated, it glosses over many things. However, I note that it often describes great things regarding the kingdom of Tezcoco and the power of King Nezahualpilli. Sometimes it suggests (and I have mentioned this previously) that Motecuhzoma in some way owed recognition and subordination to him, since he did not contradict any statement made by the Tezcocan ruler.

At this point the *Historia* speaks of Nezahualpilli's death with great sadness and states that he was mourned in Tenochtitlan as well as in Tezcoco. The chronicle says that, when news of Nezahualpilli's death came to Motecuhzoma, he wept in anguish and donned the garments of tears and sorrow, exclaiming, "He has now drained the cup that we must all drink from. He who was my father and true friend has gone to rest with his ancestors in the place of repose in the other world and has forgotten the cares and worries of this one." Weeping, Motecuhzoma called the messengers and asked them to thank the lords of Tezcoco who had sent him the sad news, saying that his men would go to Tezcoco later. Ordering that the messengers be well provided with anything they might need, he then dismissed them.

Motecuhzoma advised Cihuacoatl and the other lords of the court of Nezahualpilli's death. He ordered them to be present at the funeral rites, so they went to Tezcoco with twenty slaves, much jewelry, many rich mantles, a gold diadem, and other jewels consisting of ear pendants, nose plugs, arm and leg adornments, fine feathers, and everything that was usually offered in these obsequies of kings and the nobility. In the presence of the deceased, the great prince Cihuacoatl took Nezahualpilli's hand and addressed him in a most solemn way, offering him all the jewels and mantles and other fine things they had brought, as well as twenty slaves so they would serve him in the afterlife. Then the other leading men of Tenochtitlan, one after another, made sorrowful speeches to the body of the Tezcoco king, expressing condolences for his death but speaking to him as if he were still alive. Each one presented jewels and other gifts, according to his possibilities. The king of Tacuba also sent slaves and gifts of royal mantles and jewels, as did the ruler of Chalco and the lords of Xochimilco and of the Marquesado. Noblemen of all the land came with quantities of jewels and gifts and with many slaves. This was the greatest, the most solemn, funeral ever held for a king or for one of the nobility, the Tezcocans excelling in wishing to demonstrate in these obsequies the love they had had for their ruler. Nezahualpilli had governed them in peace and tranquillity for forty-one years and two months, more or less.

All the funeral rites known to them were performed for this king. The ritual weeping, the fasting of the deceased's wives, children, and all his kinsmen, lasted eighty days. The Tezcocan nation made an enormous expenditure in honor of the distinguished men who were present at the obsequies and the incineration of the body. Together with the king there died many male slaves, female slaves, hunchbacks, and dwarfs, to go serve him in the other world. These slaves and the other servants were deceived into believing that in this other world they would be lords and officials of the king; therefore, they went to their death willingly and contented. And they were going to enjoy the infernal flames *in aeternum* with their lord!

The funeral rites and the burial having ended, the Aztec dignitaries returned and informed Motecuhzoma of the impressive obsequies that had been held, and now Tezcoco had been left alone and in sadness, their people grieving because they now had no lord, no head [of state], to console them. Motecuhzoma sent his envoys to Tezcoco in order to call the principal lords of that city and its environs to Tenochtitlan to consult with them and to find out whom they favored in the coming election. When these lords had arrived and been welcomed with all the usual courtesies, he asked them how many of Nezahualpilli's sons had grown to manhood who could reign, governing that nation. He was told that there were five that they favored and who were capable of ruling. They added that they wanted one of these five to be designated, that they would accept no other.

Motecuhzoma asked the names of these five young men. They were Tocpaxochiuh, Coanacoch, Tlauitol, Ixtlilxochitl, and Quetzalacxoyatl. Motecuhzoma asked which one they preferred and they responded: His Majesty Motecuhzoma should choose, should indicate the successor. Everyone would be content with this choice, especially since it had been made by him. In view of their great consideration Motecuhzoma requested that Prince Quetzalacxoyatl be designated the next king, since he preferred him above the others. He pointed out this prince's many virtues and his noble character. The Tezcoco men promised that he would be chosen because they already had decided in his favor. This decision having been made, they returned to Tezcoco, where they communicated Motecuhzoma's decision to the council there. The lords of all the provinces subject to Tezcoco were notified that they should be present at the new election. When they arrived in Tezcoco, they named Quetzalacxoyatzin, son of Nezahualpilli, as king.

All the important men of Tenochtitlan and Tacuba were present at the coronation. They enthroned him, they anointed him, and they cut his hair in the fashion that a royal person, a king, wore it. This coronation took place next to the divine brazier, in the same way that Motecuhzoma had been made supreme ruler and that has been described. One of the leading Aztec lords made a long rhetorical speech, entrusting him with the affairs of the government and with the care he must have with his nation. He was to follow the steps of his father, to keep the love and brotherhood that Nezahualpilli had shown for his collaborators so they would love him and obey him. He was told to keep watch over all the things necessary for the welfare of the country, to care for his subjects, for the poor, the ophans, the widows, the old people. Above all he was to fulfill his obligations with the divine cult, to revere and honor the priests. The speaker told him he was to take care of the fields and the farmers, the hills and valleys, the springs and rivers, the roads. Finally, Quetzalacxoyatzin was urged to see that everything a good government required was taken care of. He should forget nothing, should anticipate everything, should provide for all possibilities.

The accession ceremonies over and Tezcoco having been made happy and contented with its new ruler, the Aztec lords returned to Tenochctitlan and described these ceremonies to their king and also told him that the people of Tezcoco were pleased with Quetzalacxoyatl as the head of their city and province. Motecuhzoma received this news with pleasure and sent thanks to the electors. He also sent the new king of Tezcoco many gifts of jewels, mantles, and feathers, all of which were very valuable, and congratulated him on his election. He and all the city of Tenochtitlan, he said, were delighted with this news.

According to the *Historia* and histories of Tezcoco that I have consulted, however, this new ruler lived only a short time. He accomplished no great deeds and no remarkable events took place in his days. I have seen a painting showing him dressed in a white mantle without insignia or any other mark such as was worn by the other rulers. After his death, his brother Tlauitoltzin was elected, but he too lived only a short time and was succeeded by another brother named Coanacochtzin; during his reign the Spaniards came to this land. Those lords of Tezcoco who were sons of Nezahualpilli were unfortunate and died young without having been able to enjoy their power. This is very clear because the *Historia* states that Nezahualpilli died ten years before the arrival of the Spaniards and during this decade three sons of his were made ruler. When Cortés came, the fourth son, Ixtlilxochitl, had succeeded his brothers. We know this because the Marqués del Valle rewarded him for some outstanding feats he had performed with a sword given to him by the Marqués, Cortés, in the conquest of Mexico. Even though he was not responsible for these feats he had a right to the throne by being the son of Nezahualpilli.

Be it one way or the other, in those times the sons of the king were the heirs and passed this right from one brother to another—although I have noted that, according to the *Historia*, there was no inheritance or direct succession; but the council that elected a new ruler did so by choosing only from those who were either sons or brothers of the deceased, or from among nephews or second cousins. I believe that this order is observed in all elections, so the many persons who now claim to have rights through inheritance because in former times their parents were kings or lords do not, I understand, deserve these rights. According to ancient law, these things were decided by elections and not by inheritance. In only one case do I find that in the old laws some men were heirs to positions that had been their father's, and this is the position of a civil authority that they call *tepixqui* or *tequitlato*,[1] and all those regular occupations necessary for running the country. As I understand it, a father was obliged by law to teach his son his own profession so there would always be sufficient officials in all areas. In relation to other men of high birth I find control only through election and the will of the electors. In this way there would always be a king of the ruler's lineage even if they followed it to the end of the world, because if today a brother was elected, another day it could be a grandson and another time a nephew—and so it could continue forever, without that lineage ending.

---

[1] *Tepixqui* and *tequitlato*: see glossary.

CHAPTER LXV

Which treats of how the people of Coaixtlahuaca were bringing their tribute to Mexico-Tenochtitlan and how the men of Tlachquiauhco attacked them on the road and robbed them. With an account of the war Motecuhzoma waged against the latter and how they were later sacrificed in Tenochtitlan.

At this time, the *Historia* tells us, a daring undertaking was carried out by the people of Tlachquiauhco. This would have been an unforgettable event if those people had known how to finish that which they had started. But those people, always bold, were strangely rash in rushing into any difficult task, yet toward the end they weakened, they lost heart. This is evident in the *Historia*, which states that those Tlachquiauhco people, with much audacity, killed the messengers sent by the different rulers to that region and destroyed the merchants who went out from the Aztec provinces to make their living on the road. With much vigor they closed the roads and then retreated to their own cities and rebelled against Tenochtitlan and Tezcoco and Tacuba. Yet later, when it was time to show force and bravery, they weakened, they let themselves be killed or captured like animals, without showing the stamina they should have, since all this had been their fault. This stamina, this opposition, was found, from what I can see, only in the Tlaxcalans, the Huexotzincas, and the people from Atlixco, as well as those from the provinces of Mechoacan and Metztitlan. All of these, when they challenged the Aztecs or were challenged by them, stood firm courageously, defending themselves with all their might, and in this way there was a certain balance or equalizing in the wars. And when one side was suffering more losses than the other at least they did not let themselves be destroyed or captured in the first battle like those other barbarians who, in the first encounter, turned their backs, then came with their hands crossed to surrender, to offer to pay tribute, to become vassals, prostrating themselves on the ground, as we shall see in this chapter.

When some men from Coaixtlahuaca were leaving that province and going to Tenochtitlan with the tribute they were obliged to pay to Motecuhzoma, which was of great quantity and immense value, they were going by the boundaries of Tlachquiauhco when a number of soldiers with their captain came out from that place and asked what they were doing. They responded that they were on their way to the city of Tenochtitlan with their tribute. The soldiers warned them not to continue and tried to convince the Coaixtlhuaca men to join them, to remain there with those riches, saying that they would be their bodyguards, would protect them. They urged them to rebel against the Aztecs. When the envoys from Coaixtlahuaca heard this, as did the Aztec *calpixque* or tribute collectors who accompanied them, they reprehended the soldiers for this bad advice. They knew that in that region there was little resistance against the Aztecs. In answer to the negative response the Tlachquiauhco men took away that tribute by force, injuring the others in the act. Some of the envoys even died from the injuries on the road. In this way, wounded and bloody, the rest reached the Aztec capital and immediately went before the Angry Lord, who, when he saw them, was moved with pity. He asked what had happened. They answered that they were delivering the tribute as they always did, when soldiers from Tlachquiauhco had assaulted them, beaten them, and robbed them of all they carried. Motecuhzoma consoled them, gave them lodgings and had their injuries treated with all possible speed and care, and ordered that they lack nothing.

Then immediately, and without even advising the council, Motecuhzoma summoned the kings of Tezcoco and Tacuba, whom he consulted about this case. He ordered that they prepare their armies to put down that rebellion. He asked that the bravest men be sent in view of that daring attack, for he feared more opposition than in reality the allies found. The kings of Tezcoco and Tacuba returned to their cities, where they formed armies of the most courageous men that could be found. Some of the most fearless, intrepid captains went with them to Tenochtitlan, where they informed Motecuhzoma that their forces were ready. The Aztec army was equally well prepared. Motecuhzoma informed his commanders that, if they meet with much resistance, in order to severely punish the people of Tlachquiauhco, they should kill half of the inhabitants of that province, women as well as men. This way the rest would be filled with fear. And if they surrendered right away, the soldiers were to bring back only enough people to sacrifice in the coming feast, which was that of the Flaying of Men.

With this definite command the Aztec army left, together with the soldiers from the other cities. They reached the borders of the principal city of the Tlachquaiuhco province, where they set up camp. Every night they heard such loud singing and dancing coming from the city, with the sound of drums and shrieking and shouting. When the Aztecs heard all this, they understood that it was a way of keeping watch over the city, of guarding it in order not to be surprised by the

Aztecs, whose tricks they knew. But the commanders of the army decided to send spies in secret. So, finding some soldiers who were experienced in this kind of reconnoitering, they sent them to investigate all that noise and clamor. These spies were quite fearless and, going some on one side and some on the other, they reached the place the sounds came from without having been observed. They arrived in time to see that the priests of the temples and some of the elders and principal men, all covered with blood from terrible and cruel self-sacrifice of letting blood from their ears, tongues, thighs, and shins, were begging their gods to free them from the Aztecs. They were making great supplications and entreaties while they danced, sang, and wailed, thus crying for victory. All the rest of the people were sleeping, everyone senseless, out of his right mind, completely intoxicated, which is common when these people are seeking a prophecy.

On seeing this, the Aztecs returned to the other soldiers and in the midst of laughter and mockery they told what they had seen and boasted that they alone could take the city if they wished. The commanders of the army heard this and felt that those Mixtecs of Tlachquiauhco had tried to outwit them, so they gave orders that as soon as dawn came the army be prepared to attack. This done, the soldiers went into the city, where some entered the temples and others the houses of the lord of Tlachquiauhco. They found not a sign of war, nor a man armed, but in the palace all the lords and officials were dancing happily, with much contentment. The Aztecs captured all those who danced and set fire to the palace and the main temple. Then the soldiers began to sack the city and capture and kill some of the people. This was done with great cruelty, and the soldiers continued the looting in the neighboring villages. There was much plundering and despoiling by the Aztecs in all that land.

The Mixtec lords and captains, seeing so much destruction and wretchedness, came out and quite openly sought the officers and, prostrating themselves before them, with their hands crossed, begged that their soldiers be ordered to stop the damage and destruction they were causing. The Aztec officers, in view of this humility, commanded that the robbing and destruction cease. As they always did when they heard their officers give this order, the soldiers stopped the looting and laid down their arms. All returned to the main city of the province and were lodged by the people there, who attended them splendidly, giving them everything they desired. This was done more through fear than because of integrity, however. Then the victors asked that the tribute the Tlachquiauhco guards had robbed from the Coaixtlahuaca people be returned to them. This was done with all diligence, for it had been put away and not a thing was missing. When all had been brought, the Aztecs, in order not to spend too much time there, asked what the Mixtecs could contribute as tribute. They answered that this could consist of weapons, shields, feathers, jewels, and many kinds of precious stones. They were told what they should send to Tenochtitlan. They accepted this and promised to carry out those orders.

Leaving behind a number of tribute collectors and one main official to administer them, the Aztecs left Tlachquiauhco with many prisoners wearing wooden collars and bound together with ropes. Four of the leading officers went on ahead to tell Motecuhzoma how all the houses there had been leveled, how the stolen tribute from Coaixtlahuaca had been recovered, and how the troops were bringing many prisoners and many valuable things. They also meant to tell Motecuhzoma that his soldiers were rich and contented with the results of that war and that they had lost not one soldier because they had found no one to fight. They planned to describe to their king how everything had taken place and the ridiculous joke the Mixtecs had thought to play on them; because of this the Aztecs had found them dancing and singing, all of them intoxicated, all of them contented and happy. And apparently they were barbarous and stupid because it had been easy to capture them, rob them, kill them. The messengers, on arriving, told all this to Motecuhzoma, who marveled at it and was delighted. He then ordered the usual rejoicing and welcome for victory to take place. As I have stated, this consisted in the playing of drums and conch shells and flutes and whistles, which were a sign of joy and happiness. All the prisoners were to be given flowers and tubes of tobacco on entering the city and they were to come dancing and singing, expressing joy.

Everything was done this way. When the army reached the Aztec city, it was welcomed in a solemn and festive manner by the priests, with songs and smoke from the incense ladles, and music from many instruments. The prisoners were given flowers and canes of tobacco already lighted. They sang and danced as if they were rejoicing. The soldiers with their captives went to the temple, where they performed the ceremony of eating earth before the gods, then they went to the palace, where they greeted the Angry Lord. He received them with his customary serenity and grave manner, thanking the soldiers and congratulating them. He then told them to go rest but first put the prisoners in a safe place, carefully guarded, for there were a great number of them.

Since the feast called the Flaying of Men was approaching, Motecuhzoma gave orders that everything necessary for this ceremony be made ready. So preparations were made and all those who were to take part were taught their role and were made to practice what they had to do. As I have already mentioned, one of these rites was the tying of a captive by one foot with a rope to a bar in the middle of a round stone. The captive was nude, armed only with a painted paper shield and a sword that was but a stick, and with these he must try to escape death at the hands of the fully armed warriors whose aim it was to kill him on top of the round stone that was special to that sacrifice. Four warriors, two disguised as eagles, two as jaguars, fought with this unfortunate captive. On the day of the ceremony one thousand Mixtec prisoners were sacrificed in the way I have described [the Tlacaxipehualiztli festival] at length in the *Book of the Gods and Rites*. Many lords from the region and from allied provinces attended this feast, as well as noblemen from cities that were enemies of Tenochtitlan, for example, from Mechoacan, Metztitlan, Tlaxcala, Cholula, Huexotzinco, and others. There was a great outlay and expenditure, an abundance of everything, in view of Motecuhzoma's greatness, for on these occasions he was very splendid. He excelled in showering his subjects with favors and gifts, so although he was feared by them at the same time he was loved and revered.

The *Historia* tells us that when these festivities had ended, when everyone was satiated with human flesh and had seen enough blood flow from those miserable captives, Motecuhzoma ordered that all his men who had taken part in that war be brought there, especially those who had performed outstanding feats and had brought prisoners to be sacrificed at that time, thus honoring the gods. For this purpose a proclamation was made, it was announced all over the city, and as a result a large number of soldiers and officers gathered in the appointed places, each one designated for the men according to their rank and record. When Motecuhzoma heard that all the soldiers were in their correct places, he sent for splendid riches from his treasury: mantles, jewels, feathers, weapons, and shields. Each man was presented with gifts suitable to his position, because great care was taken to give each man the objects and insignia according to his deeds and to the lineage from which he was descended. So Motecuhzoma rewarded them for what they had done in that war and for the honor they had paid the gods and the pleasure they [the noblemen] had received in being given human flesh to eat. In those days the bellies of the lords were gorged with that human flesh. It is said of that king that not a day passed since he began to rule that he did not eat human flesh. For this he had many slaves and each day had one killed so he could eat that flesh, or so his guests could, or those who usually shared his meals.

After these favors had been distributed to his own soldiers and to all those who had taken part in the war, Motecuhzoma ordered that a speech be made to them so they would understand the reason they had been given those presents and had been awarded insignia and titles of nobility. So this was done. They were told that all those honors were bestowed upon them not so they would become arrogant or be exalted, but so they would always be ready, be prepared in case they were called to arms. When this happened, they were to go to war without delay, making no excuse, and risk their lives for their city, for their king, to defend their country. The men were in agreement with these conditions and considered themselves fortunate, well rewarded by their king. And this king showed them great affection, displaying much fondness for them, but did so only if they were dedicated to him and would serve him well in war. These rules were in effect since Nezahualpilli had pronounced the bad news, the evil omen, which predicted that rarely would the Aztecs triumph over their enemies. Because of this Motecuhzoma was always in a state of alarm and gave instructions that every time the soldiers went to war there were to be consultations with the oracles, lengthy and verbose orations to the gods, abundant sacrifices and offerings, and bloodletting [on their ears and other body parts] by the priests and by the king himself. When a war was declared, Motecuhzoma climbed up to the temple and, sometimes with his hands raised to the sky, other times with his hands crossed, or at times squatting on his haunches — which was their way of kneeling — he made supplications to the gods, making offerings of mantles, jewels, and feathers, while he sacrificed innumerable quail by decapitating them with his own hands. He told the gods that he knew those offerings were not his but belonged to the gods themselves and were only on loan to him. But he offered these things because he realized that they were his true gods and he expected them, in return, to give him success in war.

After the king had made these supplications and had expressed his desires, he had the elders and old priests eat green mushrooms and drink some strange concoctions so these ecstasy-causing substances would reveal to them whether or not their army would be victorious. And woe to those who predicted defeat, for they were immediately put to death, with no reprieve. Thus, the terrified priests and old men and presagers, having learned through experience, never told him the truth about the things the devil said to them or revealed to them in dreams, for they feared death at the king's hands. Another thing this tyrant, the Angry Lord, did: if some of those prophesiers or sorcerers were mistaken in what they said, or admitted that they knew nothing, or that the devil had refused to reveal future events, the king had them killed at once because he said that the devil, or the gods, paid no attention to these seers, nor did they wish to tell them anything because of their bad habits and evil way of living. Therefore, Motecuhzoma had them murdered and their families and homes destroyed.

The recent festivities having ended and the guests having left, Motecuhzoma called the lords of Tenochtitlan and told them that during all those ceremonies he had been troubled because the sacrifice stone was very narrow, that it was just barely possible for the men performing the rite to circle around the prisoner. He had determined, he said, to have another larger, wider one made, so there would be enough room for the victims and the sacrificers. The lords agreed with the king, thinking this was a good plan. This decision made, they all left after orders had been given to search for the finest stone in the entire region. This stone was found, as we shall see in the next chapter.

CHAPTER LXVI

Which treats of how Motecuhzoma ordered that the largest stone that could be found be brought for the sacrifice of the Flaying of Men and of what occurred while it was being brought to Mexico-Tenochtitlan.

Motecuhzoma was always anxious to have his accomplishments well known throughout the entire land, and all the feats of earlier kings seemed of minor importance to him, from his own point of view of grandeur and fame. He considered that the sacrificial stone his grandfather had set up was too small and banal and that it did not conform to the magnificence and authority of his city. Therefore, he called a meeting of the chieftains of his council and spoke to them of making another stone, the widest and largest that would be found in the entire region, for the feast of the Flaying of Men. Having heard their agreement in this matter, he summoned the stone sculptors of the city and told them of his decision, requesting that they search for the largest and finest stone in all the province, with all the diligence possible. This was to be carved carefully and made into a great *temalacatl*, which means "round stone," to be used in the sacrifice of the Flaying of Men, since the present stone no longer pleased him.

The stonecutters, obeying his orders, went off to different places where they knew good stone existed and in the province of Chalco, at a site called Aculco near Tepepulla, next to the river that flows down from Amequemecan, they found on a hill a great rock that seemed suitable for what the king desired. When he had been notified of this, Motecuhzoma ordered that the men of Xochimilco, Cuitlahuac, Itztapalapa, Colhuacan, Mexicatzinco,[1] and Huitzilopochco bring ropes and stout poles so that all together they could carry the stone. They were told where to go and Motecuhzoma ordered that all the stone workers be provided with food for the entire time it would take to convey it. They were thus given ample provisions.

The stonemasons went to the indicated site, scraped the rock clean, and prepared to pull it out from the place in which it was stuck. When it was ready to be removed, Motecuhzoma was notified so he

[1] I am indebted to Jorge de León, official historian of the city of Itztapalapa, for having called my attention to a line in Torquemada stating that before the Spanish conquest Mexicatzinco was called Acatzintitlan (Torquemada 1975:I:132).

could send his men. A great number of these men arrived, together with more people from the above-mentioned towns, all carrying ropes, poles, and other instruments they might need. Anxious to have propitiatory rites performed [that we call] superstition and idolatry, Motecuhzoma ordered that the priests of the temple go to that place with their incense burners, paper, incense, little balls of rubber, and many quail. Together with them were to go chanters of the temples to sing and dance in front of the stone when it began to be moved along the road. Jesters and clowns were also sent to perform buffooneries before it, celebrating it and rejoicing, since it was a sacred thing to be used for divine rites.

A great number of men who were to drag the rock arrived and the priests, having donned their sacerdotal garments, took the paper they had brought and covered the whole rock with it. Going around it many times, they incensed it with much ceremony, pouring molten incense and rubber upon it, killing quail, and splashing the blood upon the stone. The chanters began to sing pleasant, joyful songs and the clowns and jesters performed little skits and buffooneries, all of which provoked laughter and pleasure. While this was being done, the Xochimilcas tied a long, stout rope around the stone and the same was done by the men from Cuitlahuac, Mezquic, Colhuacan, Itztapalapa, Mexicatzinco, and Huitzilopochco. With great enthusiasm, these men began to pull with so much shouting and yelling that the noise went up to the heavens. After having persisted a long time, trying to wrench the stone from its bed but without success, the ropes snapped as if they had been made of tender cotton. The officials in charge of the operation, seeing that the stone refused to move, sent word of this to Motecuhzoma. He then begged the king of Tezcoco to give him more men to help bring in the monolith. This was done and, when the priests again had performed the same rites as those of the day before, new ropes were tied to it by the Tezcocans. At last the stone began to budge, and the men managed to drag it as far as Tlapechhuacan. They rested there, and at dawn the next day the men again went back to work, tying new ropes while conch shells and other instruments were played, the priests performed their ceremonies, and the singers sang while quail were killed. Shouting, the men began to pull at the ropes with all their strength, but for two days they were unable to make it move from that place. Our chronicle says that it seemed to have sprung deep roots and had no intention of moving. In spite of enormous efforts by so many men, even the stoutest ropes snapped. When Motecuhzoma heard this, he summoned the Otomis of the province of Cuauhtlalpan and they, with their strong ropes and poles, went to help those who were struggling with the rock. These Otomis also tied their

How Motecuhzoma ordered a large stone

ropes around the stone, on top of those that already were there, and as they began to pull, shouting and howling all the time, a voice was heard coming from within the stone. It spoke: "O wretched people, O unfortunate ones! Why do you persist in your desire to take me to the city of Tenochtitlan? Behold, your work is in vain for I shall not go there, it is not my will. But since you insist so much, pull me and I shall go as far as I wish, but it will be to your misfortune!"

The voice was then silent and everyone was bewildered and frightened by this extraordinary event, something never before heard or seen. The men began to pull again, and the stone moved with such ease that they barely felt its weight. In that way it was carried that afternoon as far as Tlapitzahuayan. From this point messengers were sent to Motecuhzoma to inform him of the amazing things that had taken place and what the stone had said. When the king heard this, he had the messengers thrown into jail, for he felt they were joking. He then sent one of his officials to inquire of the people there in Tlapitzahuayan if this information was correct. When the official saw that it was true, he told this to Motecuhzoma and informed him that everyone at the site had heard the stone speak. So the king released those men he had incarcerated. He then sent a message to the ruler of Azcapotzalco requesting men from there to help move the stone. When they arrived with ropes and devices to do this work and tried to move the stone, it refused to budge but spoke these words: "Poor wretches! Why do you labor in vain? Have I not told you I shall never reach Tenochtitlan? Go, tell Motecuhzoma that it is too late. He should have thought of this before, it occurred to him too late. Now he no longer will need me; a terrible event, brought on by fate, is about to take place. Since it comes from a divine will, he cannot fight it. Why does he want to take me? So that tomorrow I be cast down and held in contempt? Let him know that his reign, his power, has ended. Soon he will see what is to come upon him, and this will happen because he has wanted to control things more than the very god who determines everything. Therefore, leave me. If I go farther it will cause you harm."

All this was told to Motecuhzoma, and although it filled him with fear he did not really believe it. He was angry with the messengers, he was furious with them, he threatened them and commanded them to return and bring the stone, thus fulfilling this obligation. So the men again pulled at the ropes, and the stone moved so easily and so rapidly that it seemed that at least twenty were tugging at it. That day it arrived at a place called Techichco, next to Itztapalapa, and the following morning the men pulled it so easily that they were most contented. They were accompanied by people who sang and danced, by the music of conch shells and whistles, by the buffoons who acted out farces, and by the priests who burned incense and sacrificed quail. When the stone reached Tocititlan—which is the place where today there stands the first cross as one leaves the city of Mexico—Motecuhzoma was informed of its arrival. He ordered everyone in the city to go out and welcome the stone with quantities of flowers and with incense and to adorn and honor it as much as they could. This was done with all the care, solemnity, and festivity that is correct for a divine thing. Motecuhzoma remembered what the stone had said to the masons and other officials, its bad omen, that it would never reach Tenochtitlan, but since the king was obstinate, insisted on having his own way, he again ordered that great ceremonies, sacrifices, and offerings be made in the stone's honor in order to calm its ire, if it still was angry. After these ceremonies had been performed, Motecuhzoma ordered that the stone be taken into the city. When the men pulled it, it moved with such ease and speed that it reached the place that is now the irrigation gate of San Antón, where Motecuhzoma had built a strong bridge with many stout beams especially for this occasion. When it reached the middle of the bridge, with a tremendous crash the stone broke all the beams, falling into the water—which then was very deep—and carrying with it numerous men who had been attached to it by the ropes. Most of these drowned, while others were severely wounded.

The people were terrified by this accident and because the words the stone had spoken, that it would not enter the city, had turned out to be true. Motecuhzoma, informed of the events, went with his officials to the place where the stone had fallen. When he saw the destruction of the bridge and heard of the death of so many men, he immediately called for divers from Xochimilco, Cuitlahuac, and Mezquic. These divers were brought to Tenochtitlan and were ordered to go into the water without delay and seek the stone. If it was in the place where it had fallen, Motecuhzoma wished to try to pull it out again, all because of his stubbornness and stern will. The divers went into the water and searched all over for it, from noon until night, but, unable to find it, they went to the king and informed him that they had not been able to locate it in all that water, not even in the very bottom of the canal. They wondered if it was not there at all, since it had said that it was being moved against its will, and perhaps it had gone back to its original place. Motecuhzoma, considering that this was possible, sent some of his people to go seek it where it had first been extracted. The envoys found it there, all covered with paper and with signs of the sacrifices it had been offered. It was still bound by the ropes just as it had been when it fell. The bewildered and frightened envoys returned in great haste and told Motecuhzoma of the astonishing thing they had seen. Terrified, the king went in person to see the rock, accompanied by all the lords of his court. The king made offerings to it, prayed, and sacrificed some slaves. Having done these things, he returned to Tenochtitlan and spoke the following words to his principal followers: "Truly, O brothers, I now believe that our labors and afflictions will be great and that our lives are about to end. And I am determined to allow death to come just as my brave ancestors did. Let the will of the Lord of All Created Things be done!" He called his stonecutters and ordered that his statue be carved on a rock in Chapultepec, in the place where portraits of his forefathers had been carved. Motecuhzoma was portrayed with the insignia and arms that he was accustomed to bear. When the work was finished, he wept to see his image and, observing it, moaned, "If our bodies were as durable in this life as this carved effigy is upon the rock, who would be afraid of death? But I know that I must perish and this is the only memorial that will remain of me!"

Turning to the stonemasons, he then thanked them and gave orders that they be paid for their work. They were given many loads of maize, beans, and chiles, also mantles and clothing for their wives and children. Some loads of cacao were also given, to be divided among them, and each sculptor received a slave to serve him. The stoneworkers were happy with these compensations and considered themselves well paid, both for their help in trying to bring the stone from Chalco to Tenochtitlan and for having carved Montecuhzoma's effigy on the rock at Chapultepec. When Motecuhzoma returned home and was seated with his officials and noblemen, he told them what Nezahualpilli of Tezcoco had said, the omen of evil he had pronounced, and what he had explained about the comet. And because of what had happened with the stone and what the stone had said, he began to weep bitterly. The other lords wept with him and since he wished to console them he said: "O my brothers! How can I find consolation when I am surrounded by worries and anguish? Am I greater than Nezahualpilli, who was a prophet and who could tell of things to come and who died in spite of all his knowledge? Am I greater than my kinsman the great Tzompanteuctli of Cuitlahuac, who was also a prophet, knowing six hundred and ten sciences, all of which he could explain with the greatest of ease? He also died. What shall become of me, then, I who am ignorant, knowing no science? How am I to avoid the calamities and ills that await me?"

The lords consoled him as best they could, advising him to have faith in the Lord of the Heights and the other gods, whose seat on earth he occupied and whose [terrestrial] kingdom he possessed and over which he ruled. They would favor him, the lords said. Motecuhzoma was somewhat consoled by these words, although this consolation lasted only a short time, as will be seen in the following chapters. The officials and lords took their leave, saying good-bye and then going to their homes.

CHAPTER LXVII

Which treats of how Motecuhzoma decided to abandon the city and hide himself where he could not be found. With a description of how he did this, and an ill omen that appeared before these events.

M otecuhzoma was so greatly disturbed, his heart so agitated, that each time he saw the comet or, when he went out of the palace, heard the wailing of the people, he could not calm his heart or tranquillize his breast, although he was a courageous and virtuous man. One day, in a thoughtful but sad mood, he called the hunchbacks and dwarfs who served him in the palace and, first warning them that they must keep secret what he was about to tell them, under pain of death, he said, "You must know that I am very sad and frightened, for I fear that what has been predicted about me and my time will take place. Because of this I have decided to go hide in a cave in the hills, and I shall disappear forever. If you would like to go with me I should be very pleased to have your company." The hunchbacks and dwarfs answered that he was their lord and could send them wherever he wished, that they would obey him and would accompany him anyplace he decided to take them. The king, seeing their willingness to serve him, thanked them and told them to wait while he searched for the proper place to hide. When the time came, he would advise them. However, while he was looking for that place they were to guard the secret.

Meanwhile, while Motecuhzoma was looking for his hiding place, a strange thing happened. This is described in the *Historia*. A farmer who was a native of Coatepec in the province of Tezcoco was calmly plowing his fields (which they call *milpas*) when a mighty eagle descended upon him, took him by the hair with its claws, and carried him into the heights until he was lost from the sight of those who had been with him. The farmer was carried to a high mountain, where he was then taken into a dark cave. There he heard the eagle say, "O powerful lord, I have obeyed your command. Here is the peasant you ordered me to bring." The farmer heard a voice saying, "Bring him here! Welcome!" The man saw no one, but he was taken by the hand into a lighted place and there he saw Motecuhzoma asleep or perhaps unconscious. The farmer was made to sit next to the sleeping king. He was given flowers and a tube of tobacco that those people light and then smoke, and he was told, "Take these things, be at ease, and behold that wretch Motecuhzoma, unconscious, intoxicated with his pride and haughtiness! He feels nothing but scorn for everyone and if you wish to see how his pride has blinded him, burn him on the thigh with the tobacco you carry and you will see that he does not feel it." The man was afraid to do this but he was told, "Burn him, do not fear!" The farmer then touched him with the fiery tobacco and Motecuhzoma did not stir, did not feel the burn.

"Do you see," asked the voice, "how he is unaware of everything? Do you see how entranced he is? Know that for this reason you have been brought here by my command. Go now, return to the place from which you were brought, go tell Motecuhzoma what you have seen and what I had you do. That he may know what you say is the truth tell him to show you his thigh and point out the place where you burned him with the smoking tube. There he will find the sign of fire. Also tell him that he has angered the God of All Created Things and that he himself has sought the misfortunes that are to fall upon him. His reign is coming to an end. Let him enjoy what little remains of it! Let him be patient since he has been the cause of his own ruin!"

When these words had been spoken, the eagle was told to transport the farmer back to the field. With his talons, the eagle then picked up the man by his hair and deposited him in the place where he had been found. As he flew away, the eagle said, "Behold, peasant and common man that you are, do not fear! Go with spirit and a strong heart and do what the lord has commanded. Do not forget any of the words that you are to say!" With this the eagle soared into the sky and disappeared.[1]

The poor farmer seemed to be awakening from a dream, frightened as he was by what he had seen. However, with his digging stick still in his hands he came before Motecuhzoma and begged permission to speak. Humbling himself before the king, he told him this story: "O powerful lord, I am a native of Coatepec and while I was working in my field an eagle flew down and carried me to a place where I saw a great, a mighty lord, who told me to rest. And as I looked into a clear and pleasant place, I saw you sitting next to me. That lord gave me flowers and a tube of tobacco that was lighted and ordered me to burn you with it on your thigh. I burned you with that fiery tobacco tube but you made no movement, nor did you feel the fire. And saying that you had

---

[1] This curious story is found perpetuated in stone on a Christian monument in front of the church of San Hipólito in Mexico City. It was on this site that hundreds of Spaniards found their death in the confusion of Cortés's midnight flight from the city in 1520. Tenochtitlan was finally taken by the Spaniards on August 13, 1521, feast day of Saint Hippolytus, whereupon the Spanish conquerors made him patron saint of Mexico City.

no feeling, were arrogant to the extreme, that your reign was about to end and trials and hardships brought about by our own hand, the result of your bad deeds, were near, that lord ordered me to return to my place and then come tell you all I had seen. The eagle, lifting me by the hair with his talons, returned me to my field from which he had taken me and now I come to tell you what I was commanded to say."

Motecuhzoma remembered that the night before he had dreamed that a commoner had wounded him in the thigh with burning tobacco. He then looked at his thigh, where he saw a mark and felt such pain that he dared not touch the burned flesh. Without asking the peasant any other questions, Motecuhzoma called his jailers and ordered that the man be thrown into jail without food and left there until he starved to death. The man was then cast into prison and forgotten there.

The pain in the king's thigh became worse and he had to spend several days in repose while the doctors cured him with great care. After he was well, he called his hunchbacks and had them summon the magicians and conjurers, who were called *tequitque*. He told them to flay ten men and bring their skins to him, for he needed them. When the skins had been brought to the king, he gave them to two of the hunchbacks, telling them that he had finally discovered a place where he could hide. This place was called Cicalco, which means "Place of the Hares," a place of joy and pleasure where men live forever.[2] According to what Motecuhzoma had been told, it was a land of clear, crystalline waters, it was a place of great fertility where all kinds of foods grew and where there was the freshness of many flowers. Though the king had already decided to go there, he wished his servants to precede him to greet the lord of that place, Huemac, and to give him the human skins as a gift. They were to tell him that King Motecuhzoma wished to be received as his servant, to accompany him, for he greatly desired to avoid the fate that had been announced to him by Tzompanteuctli, the lord of Cuitlahuac, and by Nezahualpilli, king

---

[2]Cicalco, "Place of the Hares," undoubtedly should be Cincalco, "House of Maize," possibly another name for Tlalocan (House of Tlaloc), a layer of rich vegetation lying immediately underneath the earth's surface. Tlalocan was also the paradise of Tlaloc, water-earth god, where those who had died by drowning went after death. In Mexican mythology caves were often seen as storage places for grain and other foodstuffs, watched over by *chaneques* or dwarfs, all of which reminds us of the paradisiacal refuge for Motecuhzoma, which was also a cave. It seems to have been part of the underworld too, guarded by Huemac. It is strange that Huemac, a historical personage and last ruler of Tula in the twelfth century, should be described here as lord of the underworld. Generally the latter is called Mictlantecuhtli, Lord of the Land of the Dead. The placing of Huemac in the scene may have been meant as a reference to the Toltecs—considered by the Aztecs to be their ancestors—in their last days, as these were also the last days of Motecuhzoma's Mexico.

485

of Tezcoco, before he died. And also he, Motecuhzoma, wished this because he had seen so many signs in the sky and omens and premonitions on earth that he was certain of this fate. He asked that Huemac grant him the favor of admitting him to his service. He told the dwarfs and hunchbacks to keep all this in utmost secrecy. They were then given supplies they might need on the road.

    The hunchbacks went out with the *tequitque* to seek the cave of Cicalco, following the instructions given by Motecuhzoma. According to some opinions, this cave was situated in a place called Atlixucan between Tenochtitlan and Coyoacan, where, say the old men, a ghost used to appear every night, kidnapping the first man it encountered, who was never seen again. Therefore, everyone avoided this place at night. It was to this place, though, says the *Historia*, that Motecuhzoma sent his messengers. As soon as they entered the cave, they met a black man[3] who held a staff in his hand. This man was called Totec. He asked them what they wanted and they answered that they had come to speak to the lord of that cave, Huemac. Totec took them by the hand and led them into the depths of the cave until they were in the presence of Huemac, whose appearance was terrifying. Humbling themselves before him, they presented him with the ten human skins they had brought and repeated Motecuhzoma's message. But Huemac answered: "Ask Motecuhzoma why he wants to come here. Does he think he is going to find jewels, gold, precious stones, feathers, and rich mantles like those he now possesses? Tell him that he has been deceived! Let him rejoice in what he has and let him be calm. That which has been fated cannot be avoided. Tell him that those who accompany me here were also men like him. They too enjoyed the things that Motecuhzoma enjoys; now they suffer, as you can see. Behold them and observe how different they look from the way they did when they were alive. There is no happiness or joy here; all is toil and sorrow. We did not come to this place of our own will but were brought here by force and reside here because of the desires of the Supreme One. Therefore, why should he join us here?"

    The hunchbacks and sorcerers then left the cave and went back to Motecuhzoma, where they gave him Huemac's answer. When the king heard this message, he became furious with those who had brought it and immediately had them put to death. He then sent other messengers with ten more human skins, but they brought back the same answer, so he had them killed also. He called two of his closest collaborators and told them everything that had happened, swearing them to secrecy. He promised to grant them and their children great

[3]Aztec priests painted their bodies black.

privileges, many favors, if they would go to that cave with his request, insisting to Huemac that he be allowed to enter there and serve him.

These men obeyed Motecuhzoma's command and went to that place, where they questioned the devil (for it was he who spoke, incited by those magicians), who then answered that they should console Motecuhzoma by telling him that if he wished to come to that place, if he wished to fulfill his desires, he should do penance for eighty days. He was not to eat the royal food or drink those delicious beverages they were accustomed to imbibe, but only amaranth seeds dissolved in water; and all water he drank was to be hot. He was not to be intimate with his wives or even be near them. During those eighty days, he was not to sit on the royal seat or in any place relating to ruling, nor was he to wear the royal mantles or any jewel or fine thing, but was to dress in the rough clothing that penitents wear. When these eighty days had ended, the messengers were to return to that place and he, Huemac, would tell them what was to be done. The men went back to their king with this message. He welcomed them warmly and was so overjoyed that he gave them gifts and bestowed titles upon them and had them take the place of some of the dignitaries who were in the council.

When he began his period of penitence, Motecuhzoma, in a very harsh manner, ordered that his wives and all the elders who were their guardians and all the women who attended the wives be denied access to his chambers. But if any of the wives wished to marry and someone asked for them, they were to be allowed to wed, and husbands could be found for them. Motecuhzoma then shut himself up in his chambers, where he spent eighty days in harsh self-humiliation, not eating or drinking anything that tasted good, nor drinking water that had not previously been heated. After these eighty days of penance, he again sent the two envoys to that place where Huemac was, to tell him he had obeyed his orders. What did Huemac command now?

Huemac responded that Motecuhzoma had acted well, that he was to wait and be watchful. Four days from that time, Huemac would go to the hill at Chapultepec; and when Motecuhzoma saw this, he was to go in a canoe to a place called Tlachtonco. Huemac would meet him there and would take Motecuhzoma with him. The king was to adorn Tlachtonco as elegantly as he could. When Motecuhzoma heard this, he again appeared in public, took up his usual activities, and put in order the affairs of his country. He also began to prepare for his flight. All of this was done cautiously and secretly and, having given gifts to his attendants and relatives, he ordered his slaves to prepare a place at Tlachtonco for his arrival. They did this, adorning the place with branches from the sapodilla tree and arranging seats made of bunches of its leaves.

When everything was ready, Motecuhzoma entered his canoe with much secrecy and began his watch. On Chapultepec hill he saw a cave so brilliantly illuminated that it gave light to all the city, to the hills and trees, as if it were midday. Knowing then that Huemac had come for him, he ordered his hunchbacks to row quickly and soon he reached Tlachtonco. There he and his hunchbacks and dwarfs dressed themselves in royal garments and Motecuhzoma put on his arms and leg bands, feather headdress, and necklaces of gold and rich stones. He sat down on one of the seats surrounded by his attendants and awaited the coming of Huemac. However, it was fated that he was not to escape his destiny.

That night, in the city of Tenochtitlan, the *texiptla* of the temple, who was the image of the god, heard a voice in his sleep saying, "Awake, *texiptla*! Behold, your king Motecuhzoma is in flight and goes to the cave of Huemac!" The *texiptla* awakened and saw light as if it were day. The voice again told him that Motecuhzoma was fleeing, was waiting for Huemac in the place called Tlachtonco, and that it was the *texiptla*'s duty to make him return to the city. He was to tell Motecuhzoma to become aware of what he was doing and to reprimand him for such enormous capriciousness. The god-image left the temple alone and entered a canoe he found at the edge of the water. With great haste he rowed as far as Tlachtonco, where he found Motecuhzoma and his hunchbacks with him. All, as I have said, were splendidly dressed and adorned. Approaching Motecuhzoma, the *texiptla* said, "What is this, O mighty lord? What folly is this in a person of such courage and valor as you possess? Where are you going? What would the people of Tlaxcala say of this cowardly flight? What would those of Huexotzinco, Cholula, Tliliuhquitepec, Mechoacan, and Metztitlan say? Think of the contempt they will have for Mexico-Tenochtitlan, the city that is the heart of the entire world. Truly, it will be a great shame for your city and for all those who remain behind you when the news of your flight becomes known. If you were to die and they had seen you dead and buried, it would be a natural thing. But [how can one explain flight]? What shall we say, what shall we answer, to those who ask about our king? We shall have to reply, with shame, that he has abandoned us. Return, O lord, to your city and your royal seat and forget this folly, for you dishonor us!" Removing the feathers from Motecuhzoma's head, he forced him to rise.

Greatly ashamed, Motecuhzoma sighed and, on looking back toward the hill of Chapultepec, he saw that the light that had burned there—and for which he had waited—had gone out. He implored the *texiptla* not to reveal this folly and then he returned to his city, entering his house with great secrecy. The *texiptla* went to the temple and was seen and heard by no one. Waking the guards there, he reproached them: "It is evident that you guard me well! And since during this whole night you have not been with me, some disaster could easily have occurred to me!" The guards were very upset and begged him not to tell Motecuhzoma, for he would have them killed.

At dawn, when the sun had risen, the *texiptla* left the temple and went to the palace, where he asked for the king. The guards and doorkeepers told him that Motecuhzoma was not yet awake. The *texiptla*, smiling, said, "He must be tired from the bad night he had." The guards, not understanding what this meant, just looked at each other.

But Motecuhzoma did not wish to appear before anyone for four days. During this time he shut himself away and was ashamed to face the *texiptla* because of the folly he had committed. But on the fourth day the *texiptla* entered the king's chambers and begged him to go out and see his officials, who were waiting for him, anxious to greet him. So he went out and, having spoken to the lords, he then returned to his chambers with the *texiptla*, who consoled him with comforting words and reminded him of the grandeur of his forefathers and all their great dees. Motecuhzoma wept and implored the *texiptla* to guard his secret, which the man promised to do. In this way, every day when the king was to have dinner, he summoned the *texiptla*, who then ate with him. This same thing happened when Motecuhzoma desired to relax in the pleasure gardens: he called the *texiptla* to accompany him. Any time that Motecuhzoma wished to converse or just take pleasure, he wanted the *texiptla* to do these things with him, from the day this man of the temple had found him in the lake. Motecuhzoma also confided all kinds of secrets to him. Such a close friendship grew up between them, the king showering such affection upon the other man, that it seemed they shared one heart and one will. But all this was founded upon the king's interest in having his secret kept, regarding the time he tried to run away from his kingdom. Motecuhzoma now felt that he had committed a vile, low action.

The *texiptla* also was prudent, was cautious, because, in view of the honor paid him by the king and in order not to fail from his grace, he never revealed the secret. I believe, however, that he did this more due to the fear of being killed and the possibility that his entire family would be destroyed.

CHAPTER LXVIII

Which treats of how Motecuhzoma ordered the authorities of the city to investigate the dreams of the old people regarding the coming of some phenomenon that they might have anticipated, and of other wondrous events that would affect him. With a description of how he had many killed because they revealed dreams contrary to his desires.

Motecuhzoma was so distressed that he could not calm his heart, and he was inclined to hope that the events that had been predicted would take place immediately and in this way he would know what the future held, then be less preoccupied. Because of these worries he called the chieftains of the barrios, asking them if they had dreamed anything regarding the arrival of the strangers whose coming he so feared or what might happen in the future. He told them to reveal these dreams even though they might be contrary to his desires, since he wished to know the truth in this much-talked-on matter. He wished to know the evil threats that had been predicted. His only reason for investigating these things was that he wished to put his children in a safe place, for they were the ones for whom he feared most. That is why these omens preoccupied him.

The heads of the barrios told him that they had dreamed nothing, nor had they seen or heard anything about this affair. Motecuhzoma answered, "Then I beg you, my friends, to tell all the old men and women of the barrios to inform me of whatever dreams they may have had or will have from now on, be they in my favor or against me. Also, tell the priests to reveal any visions they may see, such as ghosts or other phantoms that appear at night in the woods and dark places. Let them ask these apparitions about things to come. It will also be good to give this advice to those who wander about in the late hours. If they encounter the woman who roams the streets weeping and moaning, have them ask her why she weeps and moans.[1] Tell the priests

---

[1] The woman to whom Durán refers is La Llorona, "The Weeping Woman," a character found in many Mexican legends. Even today she is said to appear to those who wander about in the late hours, as an ill omen. She dresses in white and has long, flowing hair, and her fearful moan—*Ay, mis hijos!* (Alas, my children!)—is a sign of impending death or other misfortune. She is also looked upon as a seductress of men who are unfaithful to their wives. The theme actually is a universal one.

to find out everything they can until they are satisfied with the information."

The men promised to carry out these orders, so they went to the barrios, where they told the old men and women what the king wished to know. This message was also given to the people who were known to dream and those who kept vigil during the night and the priests whose custom it was to go into the hills or caves by night or by day in order to make their supplications. From that day on everyone was careful to be aware of the dreams and to remember them so they could be told to the king in case they referred to those things he wished to know.

Because the old people, the priests, and the presagers had been carefully informed of the king's orders regarding their dreams, some of the old men and women went to the barrio heads and the *tequitlatos* to tell them that they had had frightening, astonishing dreams that had filled them with fear, and they wished to communicate these things to the king. The authorities then went to Motecuhzoma and notified him that some of these people, in answer to his command, wanted to describe their strange dreams to him if he would so permit. He was anxious to hear these things, so the old people were brought before him. Humbling themselves, with much reverence, some old men said, "Powerful lord, we do not wish to offend your ears or fill your heart with anxiety or make you ill. However, in compliance with your command and since we are obliged to obey you, we shall describe our dreams. Know then, that these last night the Lords of Sleep have shown us the temple of Huitzilopochtli burning with frightful flames, the stones falling one by one until it was destroyed. We also saw Huitzilopochtli himself fallen, cast down upon the floor! This is what we have dreamed."

Motecuhzoma told them to wait at one side and he then asked the old women about their dreams. Seated before him, they said, "My son, do not be troubled in your heart for what we are about to tell you, although it has frightened us greatly. In our dreams we, your mothers, saw a mighty river enter the doors of your royal palace, smashing the walls in its fury. It ripped up the floors from their foundation, carrying beams and stones with it until nothing was left standing. We saw it reach the temple and with the same violence demolish this too. We saw the great chieftains and lords filled with fright, abandoning the city and fleeing toward the hills. This is what we have dreamed."

Motecuhzoma listened attentively to what the old men and women had described. When he saw that it was not in his favor but that it confirmed the earlier ill omens, he became infuriated, enraged, and ordered that the dreamers be cast into jail. There they were to be given food in small measures until they starved to death. The priests in the temples had also been ordered to relate the dreams they had dreamed and the visions they had seen in the hills, in the woods, in the caves, in the rivers and springs. When they saw what had happened to these old people, however, and since they had dreamed many strange things and seen and heard others through their prophecies and at the places of sacrifice, they agreed among themselves not to declare anything to Motecuhzoma, for fear that they would meet the same fate that the old people had.

The king, seeing that the priests had failed to go tell him their experiences, summoned them and with gentle words asked, "Is it possible that you have dreamed nothing, have seen nothing?" When they answered negatively, Motecuhzoma told them that they had fifteen days in which to report what they dreamed, saw, and heard. But the priests decided among themselves to continue denying everything, even though they were threatened with severe punishment. When the fifteen days had passed, the king called these men and they, full of fear, appeared before him. "Is there anything you can inform me about that which I commanded?" Motecuhzoma asked. They answered, "O powerful lord, if by breaking your law we deserve death, to be annihilated by your powerful hand, how much more we would deserve this if we offended your ears by telling you lies! What we can truthfully say is that we have not seen, hear, or dreamed anything related to your person, nor to any of those things you wish to know."

Possessed by anger, Motecuhzoma cried, "This is not possible! Either you do not wish to tell me the truth or you have contempt for my orders or you are not efficient in your work, which is to observe the things that take place during the night." Then, calling the jailers, he ordered the priests be tied up and thrown into cages, where they would die of hunger. They wept and threw themselves before him, imploring him to kill them immediately instead of subjecting them to slow torture. This action caused Motecuhzoma to feel pity for them, so he gave orders to have them untied and locked up in a room. They were not to leave that place until he wished it.

The people of the city, terrified by these actions, dared not speak or declare that they had dreamed, fearing the cruel reprisals and death ordered by Motecuhzoma when the dreams did not favor him. When he realized that no one in the city would speak about anything, the king sent his messengers to all the coastal provinces to summon the governors there. He also called the chieftains of the cities and villages of the Marquesado to come before him. When they were in Tenochtitlan, having come in great haste, he asked them to search for all the magicians, seers, and sorcerers that could be found in their region. They were to be told that he wished to know of any omens, prophecies, or divinations found by any of these means: by studying the stars or divining by water, fire, or wind; by casting [maize kernels] or by any other method or science; but principally through dreams or visions. The governors and leaders returned to their cities and towns and with great care searched for the people Motecuhzoma had asked for. They sent him diviners, magicians, sorcerers, and prophets, who then presented themselves, saying, "Lord, here we are in answer to your call, to serve you and to discover what it is you wish of us."

"Welcome," answered Motecuhzoma. "You must know that the reason I called you is to discover if you have seen or heard or dreamed anything regarding my person and my reign, for you study the night sky, you go into the hills and divine in the water and observe the movement of the celestial bodies, the course of the stars. I beg you not to hide anything form me, but to tell me all."

The sorcerers answered, "O lord, who would dare lie to you? We have not seen, heard, or dreamed anything that refers to your questions."

Motecuhzoma, furious, cried, "It is your position, then, to be deceivers, tricksters, to pretend to be men of science and forecast that which will take place in the future, deceiving everyone by saying that you know what will happen in the world, that you see what is within the hills, in the center of the earth, underneath the waters, in the caves and in the earth's clefts, in the springs and water holes. You call yourselves 'children of the night' but everything is a lie, it is all pretense."

Still in great anger Motecuhzoma called his justices, who threw these people into cages that they surrounded with guards so the sorcerers could not escape. Thus jailed, the diviners and other magicians showed no sorrow but on the contrary appeared to be contented, happy, and joked and laughed among themselves. On hearing of this, Motecuhzoma sent one of his main advisers to beg the sorcerers to reveal anything about which he had questioned them, and in return he promised them their freedom. They answered that, because Motecuhzoma insisted so much in knowing his misfortune, they had seen in the stars and by all the other sciences that a most astonishing and prodigious thing, never before experienced by man, would befall him. One of the old men who had been incarcerated exclaimed irately and loudly so that everyone heard him, "Let Motecuhzoma know in one word what is to become of him! Those who are to avenge the injuries and toils with which he has afflicted us are already on their way. Let him anticipate that which is about to happen. I say no more!"

All this was reported to Motecuhzoma, who, instead of being troubled, seemed to be serene and content. This was because he intended to extract all the information possible from the prisoners [through kindness]. He instructed the attendants: "Go there and question that man again. Ask him what kind of men are those who are coming, what road they will follow, and what their intentions are." However, when the attendants tried to comply with his command, they found that all the prisoners had disappeared from the jail. The jailers, fearful of the wrath of the king and seeing that the prisoners had escaped but had left the jail closed as it had been, with locks and stones, went and prostrated themselves before Motecuhzoma. They swore they were innocent and claimed they were not responsible for the escape but that it had been achieved through the prisoners' own magic. Motecuhzoma ordered the jailers to rise, stating that he would not punish them but instead they would have to go to the towns of all those who had prophesied evil things, and, "Tear down their houses," he cried, "kill their wives and children and dig in the places where their houses had been until you reach water. All their possessions are to be robbed or destroyed. And if any of these men are discovered or are seen in a temple, they are to be stoned and their bodies thrown to the wild beasts!"

All this was done, and the wives and children of the offenders were dragged through the city with ropes about their necks. Their homes were looted, their possessions taken from the places where they had resided. Their houses were destroyed and the sites excavated until water appeared. Motecuhzoma was informed of all those things, but the sorcerers and magicians were never seen or heard of again, although the search for them was carried out assiduously.

From that day on, Motecuhzoma's heart was filled with such sadness and affliction that he was never seen with a smiling countenance. He fled from all contact with others and locked himself up in his secret chambers with the *texiptla*, to whom he communicated all that the propheets and magicians had told him. He was greatly distressed and sad that they had disappeared, believing that, if they had been detained a little longer, they would have been made to reveal the events to come. He also regretted having killed the wives and children of these men, since they were not at fault and had offended no one.

CHAPTER LXIX

Which treats of how a ship from Cuba arrived in this land and how Motecuhzoma, having been notified of this, sent emissaries to investigate what people had come. With a description of the events that followed.

A few days after the wizards, soothsayers, enchanters, and magicians had disappeared from the jail, the Angry Lord Motecuhzoma was very troubled because of the threats he had received, and at that time a man came before him. Having greeted the king with reverence, he said he wished to speak to him. Motecuhzoma observed him and saw that he lacked ears, thumbs, and big toes. He hardly looked like a human being. When the king asked him where he came from, the man responded that he was from the Infernal Mountain [or Mictlancuauhtla].[1] When he was asked who had sent him, he answered that he had come of his own will in order to serve the king and narrate the things he had seen. The king asked what these had been. The stranger described how, while he had been walking next to the seashore, he had seen a round hill or house moving from one side to another until it had anchored next to some rocks on the beach. He had never seen anything like this, which was both wondrous and terrifying.[2] Motecuhzoma told the man to rest while he sent someone to see if this story were true. Meanwhile he called his jailers, who threw the man into jail.

Motecuhzoma then called one of his officials, who was named Teuctlamacazqui, giving him orders to go to the sea and take along a slave of his whose named was Cuitlalpitoc. He was told to find out the truth or falseness of what had been told to him. He was also to

---

[1] According to Garibay, referring to other historical accounts (Durán 1967:II:581), "Infernal Mountain" is a name invented by Durán. It should be, says Garibay, Mictlancuauhtla, which could mean Forest of the Land of the Dead.

[2] Durán's account may refer to the first Spanish expedition to Mexico, but this man's report seems to lie in the realm of myth.
Francisco Hernández de Córdoba led a group of Spaniards to Yucatan and certain points on the Gulf in 1517. Juan de Grijalva captained a second expedition from Cuba, which at that time was the headquarters of the Spanish in the New World. Grijalva's voyage in 1518 reached as far as the island later named San Juan de Ulúa, facing the modern port of Veracruz. It was there that the first contact between the Aztecs and the Spaniards took place. The third expedition was that of Hernán Cortés, who arrived at Ulúa on April 21, 1519.

reprimand the rulers and governors of the province of Cuetlaxtla and the coastal region because of their carelessness in not being alert and not watching for things he had recommended to them. The official and the slave left Tenochtitlan and soon arrived at Cuetlaxtla, where they presented themselves to Pinotl, the governor there. Teuctlamacazqui chided Pinotl for his negligence and ordered him, in the name of Motecuhzoma, to send some men to see if truly a hill had appeared upon the waters near the rocks on the coast.

The lord of Cuetlaxtla sent messengers to the seashore to see if there were truth in this. They soon returned, greatly frightened, saying they had seen a terrible large round thing in the midst of the waters. It moved to and fro and within it there were men who appeared from time to time. Teuctlamacazqui and his companion Cuitlalpitoc said they wanted to go see for themselves in order to give an account to their master, Motecuhzoma. Having arrived at the rocks on the beach, they concealed themselves so that the Spaniards could not see them, and soon they realized that everything that had been said was true. In order to observe the strangers better the two men climbed a large tree and from there they saw a boat being lowered into the water. Men entered it and went fishing near the shore. Later the boat returned to the ship, carrying the fish that had been caught. When the Aztec emissaries had seen these things, they departed for Tenochtitlan with great haste to tell their lord what they had observed.

On reaching Motecuhzoma's presence, Teuctlamacazqui said, "O powerful lord, you may kill us or have us put in jail to die, but what the man who is your prisoner said to you is the truth. I myself, O lord, with my own eyes wished to find this out, and with your slave Cuitlalpitoc I climbed a great tree in order to see better. This we saw: in the middle of the water a house from which appeared white men, their faces white, their hands white. They have long thick beards and their clothing is of all colors—white, yellow, red, green, blue, and purple. On their heads they wear round coverings. They put a rather large canoe in the water, some of them jump into it, and they fish all day near the rocks. At dusk they return to the house into which they are gathered. This is all we can tell you concerning which you queried us."

Motecuhzoma lowered his head and, without answering a word, placed a hand over his mouth. In this way he remained for a long time. He appeared to be mute or dead since he was unable to give any answer. After a long time had passed, he gave a mournful sigh, saying to the official who had brought him the news, "Whom shall I believe if not you? Why should I send another envoy if with your own eyes you have beheld the things you have described to me? The best thing to do now is to decide what measures must be taken."

Having stated this, Motecuhzoma called an attendant, telling him to liberate the man who was a prisoner, the one who had come from the coast and who had said he was from the Land of the Infernal Mountain. When the assistant reached the jail where the man had been, he found the cage empty and the prisoner gone, leaving no trace of his means of escape. When the king was told this, he stated that the man must be a magician, a sorcerer, and he was glad that he had escaped, since he had spoken the truth, although the king had planned to recompense him. Motecuhzoma then called one of his officers and told him to bring two goldsmiths, two lapidaries, and two feather workers. This was to be done in utmost secrecy, under pain of death, and that of the official's wife, children, and kinsmen, and the destruction of all his possessions.

The official took care in carrying out these orders. When the artisans arrived, they were given gold, stones, and feathers. They were told to create jewels of gold in different forms as swiftly as possible. The lapidaries were told to cut all kinds of precious stones, while the feather workers were ordered to make splendid ornaments. All of these were for a certain purpose and had to be done in secret, without anyone hearing a word about it. So, all precautions having been taken, in the very palace the goldsmiths made many jewels of gold—bracelets, leg ornaments, labrets, and ear pendants. The lapidaries worked green stones into many forms and cut other stones, and the feather workers made some fine ornaments. Motecuhzoma was satisfied with these splendid things and paid the artisans with mantles, food, and other basic items, which was the way he always remunerated those people who served him satisfactorily. He reminded them that all this was being done in secret. Then he called Teuctlamacazqui, who had returned from his trip to the coast where he had verified the coming of the Spaniards, and spoke to him thus:

"I have had jewels, precious stones, and featherwork made and I wish you to carry them as gifts to those men who have arrived in our land. I want you to find out who their commander is, since he is the one to whom you must give all these presents. You must discover with absolute certainty if he is the one our ancestors called Topiltzin or Quetzalcoatl.[3] Our historians say that he abandoned this land but left word that he or his sons would return to reign over this country, to recover the gold, silver, and jewels that he left hidden in the mountains. According to the legends, they are to acquire all the wealth that

[3] Although Durán suggests that Motecuhzoma thought of Hernán Cortés in terms of a returning Quetzalcoatl and had the Spanish biscuit taken to Tula in a ritual procession in honor of this god, this interesting story may be a post-conquest revisionism, as suggested by L. Burkhart (1989).

we now possess. If it is really Quetzalcoatl, greet him on my behalf and give him these gifts. You must also order the governor of Cuetlaxtlan to provide him with all kinds of food such as cooked fowl and game. Let him also be given all types of bread that can be made, together with fruits and gourds of chocolate. Have all of this placed at the edge of the sea, and from there you and your companion Cuitlalpitoc, who will go with you, will take it to the boat or house where they are lodged. Give these things to their captain so that he, his children and companions, may eat them. If he eats and drinks he surely is Quetzalcoatl, for this will show that he is familiar with the foods of this land, that he ate them once and has come back to savor them again.

"Also tell him," continued Motecuhzoma, "that I beg of him to allow me to die, to do me this favor! After my death he will be welcome to come here and take possession of his kingdom, for it belongs to him. We know that he left it to be guarded by my ancestors, and I have always considered that my domain was only lent to me. Let him permit me to end my days here. Then let him return to enjoy what is his! Do not go with fear or anxiety and do not fear death at his hands, since I swear to you, I give you my word, that I shall honor your children, give them much wealth, land, and houses, and I shall make them members of my council. If by any chance he does not like the food you give him and is desirous of devouring human beings and wishes to eat you, allow yourselves to be eaten. I assure you that I shall fulfill my promises regarding your wives, children, and relatives."

Teuctlamacazqui said he would be pleased to go and he and his companions, laden with the jewels and featherwork, left the city secretly. They arrived in Cuetlaxtlan, where they ordered the governor and officials to prepare all kinds of fowl and game, made into delicious stews, together with white maize cakes and all the fruit they could gather. Many Indians, carrying these loads, set out for the coast where the Spaniards were anchored. They deposited the food close to the shore without being seen. Teuctlamacazqui bade the carriers depart and he and Cuitlalpitoc remained alone. They climbed the same tree from which they had spied before and saw that the Spaniards were fishing from their small boat. As it was late, the two Aztecs did not wish to disclose their presence but decided to wait until morning. One hour before dawn Teuctlamacazqui and his companion took all the food and placed it upon the rocks near the place where the strangers came to fish in their boat. The two sat down to wait, and when the sun rose men from the ship began to appear upon the deck. They saw the two men sitting on the beach and swiftly lowered the boat into the water. Four Spaniards soon were rowing toward them. When they were face to face, however, the Spaniards and Aztecs were unable to understand each other and it was only through signs that Teuctlamacazqui told them to put the food and drink into the boat, as he and Cuitlalapitoc wished to be taken to the ship. The Spaniards understood them and with the help of the Aztecs they placed the gifts in the boat. Teuctlamacazqui and Cuitlalpitoc stayed in the boat and made signs that it was to go to the ship.

The Spaniards rowed toward the ship and when they arrived they delivered the food to it. The Indians boarded the vessel and were amazed at such a powerful structure with its many cabins, decks, and other spaces. It seemed a thing more divine than human, a work of genius, and they asked to be shown the chief or head of those men. Through the Indian woman[4] the Spaniards had brought with them, who was a speaker of both Spanish and Nahuatl, they were told that the leader was the man she was pointing to. Teuctlamacazqui then prostrated himself before the man, presenting him with the jewelry, precious stones, and featherwork that he had brought. The *Historia* states that when the sacks were opened the Spaniards gazed upon the contents with great joy. They passed the objects from one to another; and after they had scrutinized the wealth, the Indian woman asked who had sent it. The Aztec emissary answered that it came from the great king Motecuhzoma, his lord, who sent them greetings from his city. The Indian woman then asked where he came from and he responded that his home was in the great city of Mexico-Tenochtitlan. Then she said, "What is it that you want?"

"Lady," answered the emissary, "I have come to ask this lord why he came here, where he is going, and what he seeks."

She responded, "The leader of these men says that he has come to greet your master Motecuhzoma, that his only intention is to go to the city of Mexico-Tenochtitlan to salute him and thank him for these presents and the honor he pays us."

[4]Durán often confuses dates and the role of certain individuals, as we have seen. Malinche, Malintzin, or Marina, as she is referred to in different documents, Indian interpreter and mistress of Cortés, came to Veracruz for the first time with Cortés in 1519. One of the most remarkable figures in the conquest of Mexico, Malinche is not given her proper role by Durán, while other historians, such as Bernal Díaz del Castillo, emphasize her key position in the subjection of the Aztecs. Malinche was born in the tropical area of Tabasco or southern Veracruz and belonged to a Nahuatl-speaking group. As a child she was sold to merchants who carried her south, where she apparently learned the Maya language. As a young girl, Malinche was given to the Spaniards together with other slave women when the invaders reached a certain point on the Gulf of Mexico. As Lockhart points out (personal communication), she knew Nahuatl and Maya before the arrival of the Spaniards. Then a Spaniard who had been among the Maya interpreted between Maya and Spanish. Thus the three languages had to be used for the final translation into Spanish. Little is known regarding the extraordinary woman Malinche after the conquest.

Teuctlamacazqui answered that Motecuhzoma would be much pleased by this but that he wished to be left in peace until his reign ended and that after his death their leader could return. Then he could recover his lands and his kingdom just as he had left them. He added that the Spanish captain should eat of the presents his master had sent. The Indian woman answered in the following way: "These gods say that they kiss your hands and that they will eat. But since they are accustomed to this kind of food they wish you to taste them first and then all of us will eat them."

The two men tasted the different foods and when the Spaniards saw them eating they too began to eat turkey, stews, and maize cakes and enjoy the food, with much laughing and sporting. But when the time came to drink the chocolate that had been brought to them, that most highly prized beverage of the Indians, they were filled with fear. When the Aztecs saw that they dared not drink, they tasted from all the gourds and the Spaniards then quenched their thirst with chocolate and realized what a refreshing drink it was. Having eaten and drunk, the leader of those men told the Indian woman to ask the Aztec emissary his name. The answer given was that his real name was Tlillancalqui, but that his title was Teuctlamacazqui, and his companion's name was Cuitlalpitoc.

"This lord says," the interpreter explained, "that he and his men have enjoyed your food and that they desire that you now eat some of their own, even though it is very different from that which you have brought." Biscuits, bacon, and jerked beef were brought out and, when Teuctlamacazqui and Cuitlalpitoc had consumed part of the biscuit and the other foods, they saved what was left in order to take it to Motecuhzoma. After they had eaten, wine was served and they were made to drink it. Their hearts were gladdened and they said they kissed the hands of the Spaniards since that drink was good and fine. The Aztec emissaries slept that night on board, because with the wine they had drunk they could not get off the ship. The next morning they asked permission of the captain of the ship to return to their master and inform him of the things they had learned. The captain produced a string of glass beads together with trinkets and gave them to Tlillancalqui so that they could be delivered to Motecuhzoma. Another string of beads was given to the emissary to keep for himself and still another to Cuitlalpitoc. By means of the translator a message was sent to the Aztec ruler saying that the Spanish captain kissed his hands and that he would do what Motecuhzoma had requested—they would go away now and leave the king free to reign peacefully for a long time. The Spaniard added that he had come from a distant country but that in time he would return and that he hoped to find Motecuhzoma still alive in order to reciprocate his kind actions and gifts.

Having bowed low and said farewell with much courtesy, the two Aztec envoys left the ship and were brought to shore in the boat. Once they had been left there, they consulted between themselves and decided to climb the tree again to observe. Here they watched carefully in order to describe everything to their lord. They saw great sheets of cloth being hoisted on poles coming out of the ship and when this had been done the ship sailed away. They watched it go and remained in the tree to observe these strange happenings. They saw the craft move without anyone pulling it upon the waters. They did not leave the tree until the Spaniards were out of sight. Then they came down and went to Cuetlaxtlan. Here they were welcomed warmly and given food and gifts by the lord there. Then they continued on to the Aztec capital to inform their king of all these events.

When the two men arrived before Motecuhzoma, they told him what they had seen and described how they had been given jewels, food, and drink. They told of what they had eaten and drunk and said the drink was so good and easy to swallow that they had lost their senses with it. They described how the Spanish captain had promised to go away, leaving the king to finish his reign, that he wished Motecuhzoma rest and tranquillity, and that he had sailed back to his country, which was far away. Even if he did return, it would not be soon. After this the two Aztec envoys had left the ship, but they had brought back some of the food given to them so the king could see it. When some pieces of biscuit were given to him, Motecuhzoma tasted a tiny bit and said it seemed like tufa stone. He ordered that a chunk of tufa be brought in and he compared one with the other and, seeing that the tufa weighed less than the bread, he called in his hunchbacks and asked them to taste the latter. They found it to be sweet and soft. However, Motecuhzoma was afraid to eat it, saying that it belonged to the gods and that to eat it would be a sacrilege. He instructed the priests to carry it with much ceremony to the city of Tula and to bury it in the temple of Quetzalcoatl, for those who had arrived here were his sons. The priests took the biscuit, placed it in a golden gourd wrapped in rich cloth, and made a long procession to Tula. Along the way they incensed it and sang hymns honoring Quetzalcoatl, whose food they said they carried. Once it had reached Tula, it was buried in his temple with great honors.

Motecuhzoma asked Tlillancalqui if he and Cuitlalpitoc had seen the Spaniards depart. They answered affirmatively, saying that they had not left the tree until the strangers were out of sight. Then they had left the tree and had gone directly to report to the king. They produced the string of beads that had been given to them, saying that it was the only present the Spanish captain had sent since he had no other. Motecuhzoma accepted this, considering it a wonderful and divine thing. He said, "I accept the favor and gift that the god has given me." He gave orders that the necklace be buried at the feet of the god Huitzilopochtli, as he was not worthy to wear such a sacred thing. And so the beads were buried with much solemnity in the midst of the burning of incense and the sounding of conch shells and other rites.

When these events were over, Motecuhzoma thanked Tlillancalqui for what he had done and gave the slave Cuitlalpitoc his liberty. He had both of them go home to rest, but soon he sent them gifts of mantles, women's blouses, and skirts, together with cacao, cotton, maize, beans, and three slaves, one male and two female, to serve them. The two men received these gifts with much gratitude and thanked Motecuhzoma for his generosity.

Motecuhzoma was now anxious to find out who the strangers were and where they came from, so he decided to investigate in every possible manner, seeking out old and wise people. All of this was done in the utmost secrecy because what had just taken place was known to no one in the city, not even to the great lords. The few who had heard of the arrival of strangers on the coast had been threatened with death and the destruction of their families and possessions. Because of fear everything was kept secret, hidden, silent, as if nothing had happened. This secrecy prevailed until Don Hernán Cortés returned to this land with three ships some time later, on his final trip to Mexico.

CHAPTER LXX

Which treats of how Motcuhzoma ordered an artist to paint pictures of the Spaniards according to the description given by Tlillancalqui Teuctlamacazqui. And how the Aztec king was desirous of knowing what kind of people had arrived in this land.

After Tlillancalqui had told him all the details described in the last chapter, Motecuhzoma became even more worried and attempted to discover what kind of people had come to his land, their place of origin, their lineage, and, above all, whether they planned to return. For this reason he called Tlillancalqui and conversed with him in private. He said that he wanted to know more about those men who had just departed and that he wished to have a painting made of them. He wished this to be painted in his presence but said it must be done secretly.

Tlillancalqui answered that he would be happy to comply with the king's wishes and have the painting made, whereupon he ordered that the best artist in the country, an old man, be brought. Motecuhzoma warned this man that he must not reveal anything that might happen, under pain of death. The painter was cowed but exclaimed that he was not a man to uncover secrets of such a great and mighty lord. His paints were brought to him and Tlillancalqui began to describe to him what he should depict. The artist drew a picture of the ship the way it had been seen, showing the Spaniards with their long beards and white faces. He painted their clothing in different colors, their hats and caps upon their heads and their swords in their belts. When Motecuhzoma saw this, he marveled and gazed upon the painting for a long time. Finally he asked Tlillancalqui, "Were those things like the ones that have been painted here?" And the answer was "Yes, O lord, they are exactly so. They are identical." Motecuhzoma paid the artist for his work and said, "Brother, I beg you to answer this question: by any chance do you know anything about what you have painted? Did your ancestors leave you a painting or a description of those men who were to arrive in ths land?" The painter answered, "Powerful lord, I shall not lie to you, tell you an untruth, or deceive you, for you are the image of the god. Therefore I shall tell you that I and my ancestors never were dedicated to any arts save those of painting pictures and other symbols. My forebears were merely the artists of past kings and

The History of the Indies of New Spain

they depicted what they were ordered. Thus, I know nothing of that which you ask. If I said I did my answer would be a lie."

Motecuhzoma then ordered him to question with much caution the other artists of his profession, asking if they possessed some picture or [oral] account that had come down from their forebears regarding those who might come to this land and possess it. The artist agreed to do so and, excusing himself from the presence of the king, went and inquired for several days. But he was unable to find out anything certain, so he returned to Motecuhzoma and told him that he had discovered nothing exact regarding these things.

Seeing that his attempts had been ineffectual, Motecuhzoma summoned all the oldest painters of books from Malinalco, those from the region that is the Marquesado or Hot Lands, and those from Chalco. When the men from these places had arrived, he begged them to tell him if they knew anything about strangers who were to arrive in the land, asking them what kind of men might come, from where, and what they looked like. He also wished to know if the ancestors of the painters had left information regarding these things or painted manuscripts or images. When all this had been asked of them, the Malinalcas brought a picture and showed it to him. It portrayed men with a single eye in their foreheads like Cyclops. They said that their forebears had told them that these were the ones who were to come to this country and possess it. Other people in this picture were one-legged. The painters from the Marquesado displayed a drawing in which men appeared who were fish from the waist down, explaining to Motecuhzoma that they were to come to this land. Others showed the king creatures who were half man, half snake. But in the end, none was able to present anything that looked like a painting that would clarify Motecuhzoma's doubts.

Having dismissed those painters, Motecuhzoma sent for others from Cuitlahuac and Mezquic. He reminded them that they were descendants of the Toltecs, great wise men, and that they should be able to tell him about those strangers. He then asked them the same questions. These men had brought their ancient paintings with them. They informed the king that their ancestors had left a tradition that the sons of Quetzalcoatl were to come to these lands and take possession of them, and they would recover that which had been theirs in ancient times. They were also to acquire again that which [the Toltecs] had hidden in the hills, in the woods, in the caverns. They showed Motecuhzoma in their old manuscripts what kind of men those sons of Quetzalcoatl were, but they did not look like the ones Motecuhzoma's artist had painted; therefore, he bade them depart, thanking them for what they had told him and described.

Motecuhzoma was about to call the painters from Xochimilco, but the noble Tlillancalqui, the Teuctlamacazqui, said to him, "Powerful lord, do not tire yourself or waste time in questioning so many men. None of them will be able to tell you what you desire to know as clearly as a very old man from Xochimilco whom I know well. His name is Quilaztli; he is very learned and is well informed in all matters that concern ancient history and painted books. If you wish I shall bring him to you. I shall explain to him what you wish to know and shall ask him to bring his ancient paintings." The king thanked him and requested that he bring the old man immediately. The next day he returned with the man, who brought the painted manuscripts that seemed to describe the coming of the strangers. He appeared before Motecuhzoma, the Angry Lord, who received him well because he was a venerable old man and of fine appearance. The king asked him what he knew about the people who were to arrive in these lands and Quilaztli answered: "O mighty lord, if because I tell you the truth I am to die, nevertheless I am here in your presence and you may do to me what you wish!" Before showing him the paintings he narrated that some men would come to this land in a great wooden hill. This wooden hill would be so big that it would lodge many men, serving them as a home. Within it they would eat and sleep. In the rear of this house they would cook their food and in it and on the surface they would walk and play as if they were on firm land. They were to be white, bearded men, dressed in different colors, and on their heads they would wear round coverings. Other men were to arrive with them, mounted on beasts similar to deer and others on eagles that would fly like the wind. These men were to possess the country, settle in all its cities, multiply in great numbers, and become the owners of the gold, silver, and precious stones. "So that you may see," continued Quilaztli, "that what I say is the truth, behold it drawn here! This painting was bequeathed to me by my ancestors." He then took out a very old painting on which were depicted the ship and the men dressed in the same manner as those which the king had already seen in the painting his artist had made. There he also saw other men mounted on horses or on flying eagles, all of them dressed in different colors and wearing their hats and swords.

Motecuhzoma, on seeing the similarity between what the old man described and what appeared in the king's painting, almost lost his senses and began to weep and to show anguish. Baring his chest to the elder, he cried out, "O brother Quilaztli, I now see that your ancestors were verily wise and well informed. Only a few days ago the men that are shown on your painting arrived in this land, coming from the direction where the sun rises. They came in the wooden house that you have described, dressed in the same style and colors that appear in the painting that was made for me. And as proof that I had them portrayed—behold them here! However, one thing consoles me; I have sent them a present and begged them to go away in peace. They have obeyed me, departed, though I do not know if they will return."

"Is it possible, O powerful lord," the old man Quilaztli asked, "that they came and went away again? Listen to the words I shall say to you, and if I lie I am willing to have you annihilate me, to wipe from the face of the earth my children and my descendants, to kill all of us! Behold, before two years have passed, or at the most three, the strangers will return to these lands. Their coming was meant only to discover the route to this country, to find a way to return. Even though they said to you that they were returning to their own country, do not believe them! They will not go that far but will turn back when they have gone half way."

On hearing what the old man said and though these words did not please him, Motecuhzoma said to him that he did not wish to let such a wise man return to his city but that he should remain in Tenochtitlan at the king's side. He then gave orders that the wise old man was to be rewarded with property and houses in the city, for him, his children, and his kinsmen. From then on Motecuhzoma always had Quitlaztli at his side, paying attention only to his advice. Thus, he sent messengers to all the cities on the eastern coast with orders that great care be taken in observing the sea, and if anything was seen moving upon the waters, Motecuhzoma was to be advised at once. From this time on, great watchtowers and bulwarks were set up along the coast, from which the sea was constantly observed.

But when a year had passed, and then another, and the strangers had not returned, Motecuhzoma again became possessed of his usual fiendish spirit and to become so arrogant that he feared not the gods. He began to tyrannize the people of the towns and cities, to take away lands from their rightful owners and give them to his own relatives. In this way he placed a nephew, Oquiz, the son of one of his brothers, in Azcapotzalco as lord there to govern that city and region, having deposed the true ruler. Another member of his family, named Uanitl, was made lord of Ecatepec; another, Omacatl, in Xochimilco; and in Tenayuca one of his own sons, called Yacamapich, was made ruler there and the people of that province swore allegiance to him.

Motecuhzoma had become careless in regard to the possibility of the return of the Spaniards; in fact he had forgotten about it. And so he destroyed and tyrannized and killed people everywhere. But God put a stop to these wicked acts. For the *Historia* tells us that three years later, when Motecuhzoma had almost forgotten these things, news came that on the sea a hill was moving to and fro upon the waters again. Then the king was told that there were two hills or houses, and then three, but they were unable to reach the shore or remain still upon the water. Motecuhzoma, astonished at this news, again began to grieve and to fear what might take place. We shall tell about this in the next chapter.

CHAPTER LXXI

Which treats of how Don Hernán Cortés, of happy memory, disembarked at the port of Chalchiuhcueyecan, for that was its name, and how, when news came to Motecuhzoma regarding their arrival, he ordered provisions to be sent to Cortés.

Motecuhzoma was negligent about these things I have mentioned, for he firmly believed that in his time the Spaniards would not return to this land, [later called] New Spain, and that they had gone away, never to come back. But after three years they returned, appearing in the same port. The governor of Cuetlaxtlan, who had maintained spies and lookouts on the coast in order to observe anything that might appear, as his king had commanded, was told by the lookouts that the ships were tossing on the waters, attempting to reach land. The governor went to see these things in person and, on observing that the wooden hills did exist, he immediately sent messengers to Motecuhzoma, advising him that the ships of the gods had returned, that they were floating on the sea, here and there, trying to find a harbor. The emissaries soon arrived in Tenochtitlan, since they did not stop to rest night or day. In four days they were in the city, where they communicated their news to Motecuhzoma, who, according to the *Historia*, almost died of fear and was unable to speak a word. After some time in this numb silence, he finally composed himself and spoke to the messengers: "You will tell the governor that I thank him for this news. He is to be watchful, and if those men descend from their ship he must advise me immediately with other messengers. He must put post stations all along the road so I can be given the message without delay."

The messengers, returning to Cuetlaxtlan, warned every town they passed that the people there must prepare posts, and quickly, so that as soon as news was passed to them they in turn could relay to Motecuhzoma this news about the strangers who had appeared upon the sea. The messengers reached Cuetlaxtlan with these instructions from Motecuhzoma. The very day the ships arrived at the port of Chalchiuhcueyecan, the lord of Cueltlaxtlan sent word to Motecuhzoma to say that they were anchored there. The stations along the road to the Aztec city relayed this news one to another with such speed that Motecuhzoma received it on the third day. He immediately sent word that if those men went on shore they were to be given all kinds of

How Cortés disembarked at Chalchiuhcueyecan

provisions, food as well as any other supplies they might need. There was to be no lack of turkeys, fish, eggs, maize bread, or fruit, and everything was to be provided in abundance. The people in the way stations, because they had been impressed by the need for speed, went as swiftly as possible to Cuetlaxtlan, where they repeated the commands of the king. The lord of Cuetlaxtlan received them well and ordered that all necessary provisions be gathered, in great abundance. So large quantities of turkeys and game were brought, also tortillas and tamales, eggs and many kinds of fruit, and cacao that had been ground to make a beverage. All the towns in that province were told that they must prepare provisions and be ready for the day they would be called upon to serve and feed the Spaniards, whom they called gods.

After having been assured that the gods were well provided for, Motecuhzoma called Tlillancalqui, the Teuctlamacazqui or high official who had met with the Spaniards before, and said to him, "You should know, Tlillancalqui, that the gods have returned to this land and are anchored at the port of Chalchiuhcueyecan. This worries me, I am apprehensive about it, and I do not know whom to send, in whom I can confide to investigate the matter as you did."

"O powerful lord," Tlillancalqui responded, "do not be distressed by this, for I am here to serve you: I shall go and shall carry out your every command because by chance you could send someone who would dishonor you, not act with due respect as your royal person deserves or in accord with your royal commands." Motecuhzoma thanked him and asked him to go on this mission, to give orders on Motecuhzoma's part to the lord of Cuetlaxtlan to prepare all things that would be needed. And when these provisions were ready he should go and present himself to the gods who had come and ask if they intended to continue on to Mexico, for in that case Motecuhzoma would have a welcome prepared that was proper for such high gods. And if the gods answered affirmatively, saying they did wish to go to Tenochtitlan, Tlillancalqui was to give orders that all the roads be cleaned and to warn all the towns and cities on the way that they must be prepared with ample supplies of fowl, game, breads, fruit, and anything else that might be needed such as firewood, charcoal, and resinous wood that is used for torches. The lodgings and houses where the gods could rest and sleep were to be swept and adorned, and these guests were to be welcomed with kindness and goodwill, provided with every comfort, and men were to be prepared to carry their loads for them.

Tlillancalqui departed from Tenochtitlan and, walking rapidly day and night, he came to Cuetlaxtlan, where he was well received. Here he

The History of the Indies of New Spain

gave orders that the governor prepare food for the strangers. The governor stated that everything was ready, so he departed for the port with numerous men who carried food and drink. When he arrived there, he saw that the Spaniards and their horses had already disembarked. Then he approached Don Hernán Cortés [later called the Marqués], whom he recognized to be the leader, greeting him and placing around his neck a gold necklace set with many jewels and precious stones. Cortés greeted him and ordered that Marina be called, for that was the name of the interpreter who accompanied them. She said, "O father, this god wishes to know who you are."

The Aztec answered, "Lady, have you forgotten Tlillancalqui, also called Teuctlamacazqui—which is the title of my position—who came here to see you three years ago on behalf of my lord and king, Motecuhzoma of Mexico-Tenochtitlan? Now he has sent me on the same errand. I am to serve you food and provide you with anything else you may need."

This emissary then ordered the food be placed before the newcomers and their horses, and in their naiveté they gave one turkey to each soldier and another to his horse, a basket of tortillas for the master and another for the animal. This was done until they were told that the beasts ate only corn and grass. Soon the Aztec envoys provided the animals with these things.

All this food was given to the Spaniards in abundance, all that was necessary for the three hundred men who had reached these shores, without counting servants and blacks, and all ate with great pleasure. After they had eaten and rested, the Marqués told the noble emissary Tlillancalqui through the interpreter that he was grateful and that he should carry his gratitude to Lord Motecuhzoma. Tlillancalqui answered that his master had sent a question: was it Cortés's will to journey to Tenochtitlan, where Motecuhzoma already ruled that city and its environs in his name? If so, the king wished to be notified since it would be necessary to have the throne of the kingdom prepared for him. It belonged to Cortés and Motecuhzoma was his vassal, and this throne was waiting for its rightful master. The translator spoke to Cortés, who answered through the same interpreter. Marina said, "This god asks you to tell your master Motecuhzoma that he kisses his hands many times and that it is his will to go to Tenochtitlan to see him and enjoy his presence. However, he will not be able to do so immediately as he must first organize his men and unload the ships. 'As soon as I am able,' he says, 'I shall journey there, and I request that you be so kind as to send some chieftains to show me the road that I must travel.'"

The noble Tlillancalqui bade farewell to Cortés and hs men and carried the news to the Aztec ruler. Whenever he passed through

How Cortés disembarked at Chalchiuhcueyecan

towns the Spaniards were to visit, he gave orders from Motecuhzoma that everything be prepared for the gods who had arrived. Under pain of death no one was to be neglectful of the food for the Spaniards or for their horses, of good lodgings for both and for the *tamemes* or carriers of their supplies. This was all done as diligently as possible, all these orders were fulfilled. Even the very Spaniards, ungrateful and thankless though they were, admitted that all along this road they received good treatment and hospitality. They were served with everything the Indians had, even with their daughters and sisters as we shall tell further on. This was all done in compliance with the commands of the great and powerful Lord Motecuhzoma, who, until he died, always desired peace and harmony. Thus, he subjected himself in matters spiritual and temporal to the Catholic faith and to the service of his Spanish Majesty and, because of this, put himself in the hands of the Spaniards with a sincere and friendly heart, with no duplicity at all.

Tlillancalqui gave his news when he arrived in the Aztec capital, telling Motecuhzoma how all his orders had been carried out, how ample provisions had been given to the strangers, how those who had come a few years before had returned in larger numbers, and how the same Indian woman who had spoken to them previously was now the interpreter. He added that it was the will of their leader to go to Tenochtitlan, that he desired to enjoy Motecuhzoma's presence and see his kingdom. But because he could not come soon he begged Motecuhzoma to send him two of his principal officials to guide him, to show him the road.

When Motecuhzoma had heard what Tlillancalqui had to report, he said to him, "I am grateful for what you have done, although it would please me more to hear that the strangers had returned to their own country as they did before. However, my fate has been decided and the Lord of All Created Things is venting his ire against me. Let his will be done since I cannot escape it!" Motecuhzoma began to weep, then continued, "I beg of you that after the gods have come and I have received death at their hands, and I know they will kill me, I beseech you to take charge of my seven children, help them and conceal them from the hands of these gods and from the Aztecs since you know how evil and perverse our people can be. In the belief that I have surrendered the nation to the strangers, they will take vengeance on my wives and children. Therefore, I beg you to safeguard them, to protect them from these gods, and remember that I have always considered you my own son, placed all my trust in you, and honored you during my reign. Then too," continued Motecuhzoma, "undoubtedly all of us will die at the hands of these gods, and those who survive will be made their slaves and vassals. They will reign and I shall be the

The History of the Indies of New Spain

last king of this land. Even though some of our descendants and relatives may remain, even though they may be made governors and given states, they will not be true lords and kings but subordinates, like tax collectors or gatherers of the tribute that my ancestors and I have won. Our descendants' only task will be to comply with the commands and orders of the strangers. And so it was fated that I should be the one to be cast from the ruling seat given to me by ancestors and leave it in ruins. None of my children or kinsmen will be able to recuperate it or sit on the throne." Having said these words, Motecuhzoma could not control his tears and his bitterness.

Tlillancalqui tried to console the king as best he could, assuring him of the kindness of the gods who had arrived and the affability they had shown. He spoke of how they had embraced the emissaries and shown them affection, insisting that they would do no harm. Even though Motecuhzoma might be distrustful, said Tlillancalqui, he should find a way to ingratiate himself with the newcomers in order not to anger or displease them in any way.

Motecuhzoma thought he would honor the Spaniards in a way that would please them and therefore he ordered that soon ten slaves be taken to be sacrificed before Cortés, their hearts presented to him as if he were a god, for they did believe those men were divine. And so that was done, in this way: The Marqués was first offered many jewels, feathers, and other splendid things on behalf of Motecuhzoma, then certain dances were performed before him. But when it came to the sacrifice of the slaves, Cortés and his men prevented it. In another chronicle or painted manuscript it is stated that Cortés ordered the death of the sacrificers who were ready to perform their task. This is not mentioned in our *Historia*. It says only that the priests were prevented from sacrificing and I consider this last version the true one. Even though the act of sacrificing was reprehensible, appalling, the intention in this case was to please and honor the newcomers.

At this time the Spaniards were established in the town of Cempoala, in the palace and in the houses of the principal citizens. Here they had been well received by the officials and the rest of the people. Motecuhzoma meanwhile still persisted in that which bothered his heart: in trying to discover by his oracles and divinations whether he would be deprived of his power and then assassinated. Since these fears never left him, he called his minister Tlillancalqui and said to him, "I do not know what measures to take or what to do with all my power—which I am obliged to exercise in this case—to prevent these gods from reaching the city or seeing my face. The best solution I can think of is that there be gathered enchanters, sorcerers, sleep-makers, and those who know how to command snakes, scorpions, and spiders, and let them be sent to bewitch the strangers. Let them be put to sleep, let them be shown visions, let the little beasts bite them so that they will die. I have decided to send messages to Yauhtepec, Huaxtepec, Malinalco, and Tepoztlan, to invite their wizards, the ones trained in those arts, to come here and then I shall ask them to destroy the strangers with their enchantments."

"O powerful lord," responded Tlillancalqui, "your decision seems wise to me, but if they are gods who will be able to harm them? However, nothing will be lost in the attempt. Perhaps those magicians will be able to achieve something and their magic may have some effect."

Motecuhzoma immediately had all the sorcerers from those towns brought to him. When they had arrived, he ordered them to go to Cempoala. They were to pretend that their sole reason for coming was the desire to serve the Spaniards but they were, instead, to use their tricks and arts to kill the strangers. He ordered the sleep-makers to put them to sleep and the wizards to create frightful visions and images. He told those who had the power to control animals to send serpents and scorpions to bite those men while they were asleep, together with spiders, centipedes, poisonous lizards, and other deadly creatures. He also ordered the enchanters to bewitch the Spaniards, to make them lose their reason, and to create infections in their bodies.

Thus commanded by their king the wizards departed for Cempoala, where they used all their devilish and fabulous arts to the utmost. But after a few days of trying to kill the Spaniards with their magic tricks, they returned to Motecuhzoma, saying that the Spaniards were gods and that their sorcery had been ineffectual. They had done everything in their power to put those strangers to sleep, but they had been on guard all night and therefore the sorcerers had been unable to enter their living quarters and send in the poisonous creatures. Those who knew how to enchant had tried to cast a spell on them, but it had not worked. The Spaniards had been shown visions, but they had paid no attention to them. In fact, if a flea bit them they would get up immediately to look for it and then kill it. These men did not stop talking all night and before day had dawned they were up, had mounted their horses, and had taken up their arms. These people were of a different manner and disposition than the Aztecs. The flesh of these gods was so tough that no magical device could penetrate it, and their hearts were impossible to locate. Their entrails and chests were so dark, so obscure and hard to find, that the magicians had been unable to explore their flesh in a way that would cause them harm. No matter how much slumber the wizards had wished to cast upon the Spaniards they had not been able to put them to sleep. They had attempted to catch the Spaniards in order to throw them into the river or into a ravine, but like the birds in the trees the strangers had immediately awakened, opening their eyes. While some of them slept at night, others spent all their time moving about. After four nights of intense effort [that resulted in failure], the magicians returned to Tenochtitlan, where they told Motecuhzoma that they had done all they could but had been unable to accomplish their purpose, but they were the king's vassals and because of their nonfulfillment they deserved death.

Motecuhzoma was greatly afflicted to see that his plan had failed, but he said to the conjurers, "You have done everything in your power, you may rest now. Perhaps when the strangers arrive here your enchantments and control over dreams will be more effective. Let them enter the city, since it is here that we shall find a way to destroy them totally. Here my desires will be fulfilled. Not one of those strangers will be left alive and no news of them will be carried back to their native land. Therefore, I charge you to keep up your knowledge and to continue to practice your arts." Having heard his answer, all the wizards went back to their towns, where they awaited the moment when they should be called.

CHAPTER LXXII

Which treats of how Motecuhzoma sent a chieftain to bring Cortés and how he guided the Spaniards along a difficult path to a cliff. With a description of how two horses fell and two Spaniards were killed, and of how the chieftain fled and later was executed by Motecuhzoma.

When Motecuhzoma saw that the sorcerers and wizards had been unable to harm the Spaniards, he tried to make his heart strong, as they say, though his determination was even stronger not to allow the Spaniards to enter Mexico-Tenochtitlan. He decided to put obstacles in their way and he could have done this easily had God not blinded his reason, whereupon the Divine will was fulfilled. But in case the Spaniards should arrive, he said to his sorcerers, "Be prepared for when they are here in the city, for here it is not possible for them to escape death at your hands or at ours. So please come to the city." But in spite of these threats he was so fainthearted and cowardly that he was not astute enough to invent some special treachery, although he was as cunning and as full of ruses as anyone. But on this occasion he was torpid in planning evil actions. He summoned an official named Motelchiuh, whose title was Huitznahuatl, and ordered him to go to Cempoala to receive Cortés. He was instructed to return with him from wherever he might find him, to see that Cortés lacked nothing, and to tell him, through the woman who was his interpreter, that Motelchiuh had been sent by Motecuhzoma, to attend him, and that he was welcome to come to the city of Tenochtitlan, where the king would await him. "Add nothing to my message," said Motecuhzoma. "Let us see what he answers."

Huitznahuatl Motelchiuh left the city with haste, accompanied by other great lords who were desirous of seeing the famous and fearful gods. They soon arrived at a place called Chichiquila, where they found Cortés together with his men. When Motelchiuh arrived, he went straight to the Spanish leader, greeted him with due reverence, and gave him the usual presents of flowers and other things. For when the Indians go to welcome someone or to visit a person it is not their custom to go empty-handed because this would be considered offensive. This is customary with the hosts as well as with the guests.

After Motelchiuh had greeted Cortés in his master's name, he said, "O lord and true god, welcome to this, your country and kingdom!"

The History of the Indies of New Spain

Cortés answered through his interpreter, asking the emissary where he came from, whereupon Huitznahuatl Motelchiuh answered that he had journeyed from the city of Tenochtitlan by command of his great master Motecuhzoma. This great ruler kissed the stranger's hands and welcomed him, advising him to travel slowly and to watch his health. Motecuhzoma was expecting him and was waiting for his arrival in that city. Marina repeated to Cortés all that the emissary had said in the name of Motecuhzoma and then addressed the Aztecs: "This god asks, O my father, what is your name?" He answered, "O lady, my name is Huitznahuatl Motelchiuh."

"Well, lord," responded Marina, "this god says that he thanks your master Motecuhzoma for the interest taken in sending you to visit him and to favor him so much. He says that he is on his way to Tenochtitlan to enjoy the presence of the king who has treated him so well and thus has put him under obligation."

"Lady," answered the emissary, "tell this god to rest assured that all his desires will be fulfilled since King Motecuhzoma wishes to serve him and has ordered all the towns and provinces, under pain of death, to receive him and his divine companions. He will be greeted with festivities and good feeling since all are Motecuhzoma's subjects. He will be given provisions for all his needs in a way that has not been done before. I wanted to assure myself of all these things so I could communicate this to my lord and king."

"Huitznahuatl," said Marina, "this god who is present thanks you and your master for your courtesy and attentions and for inviting him to travel little by little to Tenochtitlan. He begs you to return to your city and tell your lord of his gratitude. He does not need men to guide him as we have people here who can indicate the way for us."

Huitznahuatl Motelchiuh, seeing that he was not needed as a guide, as his master had ordered, returned to his city. On the way he cautioned the towns to be provided with everything the Spaniards might need and to welcome them warmly and with festivity. When he reached Tenochtitlan, he informed Motecuhzoma in these words: "O powerful lord, I have carried out your orders. I presented myself to those gods and through the woman who is their interpreter I told their leader that you kiss his hands, that you wish to see him, and that you are expecting him here, that he will be welcome. He answered that he kisses your royal hands and that he is on his way here. He thanks you for the care you have taken in having him welcomed and for the gifts you sent. He is coming slowly in order not to trouble you or cause difficulties to those who are carrying the supplies. He will be happy to be in your presence and to enjoy a visit with you. This is what he answered."

Motecuhzoma responded, "Let him be welcome, let him come when he so desires. We shall be waiting for him, there is nothing else we can do, because we have not managed to convince him and his men to return to their country as we did when they arrived here three years ago."

Meanwhile Cortés had journeyed to a town called Nauhtlan, where the local ruler Coatlpopoca received him well and lodged him in comfort. Cortés thanked him for the good treatment received and presented him with a necklace of blue glass beads, which the chieftain greatly appreciated. That night Cortés asked him the most direct way to the city of Tenochtitlan. Coatlpopoca, however, disregarding the gift of the necklace and the good treatment and kind words of Cortés, said that he would lead him and his men along a short and quick route to the city. This was done with malice, as he wished to guide the Spaniards to their destruction by having them fall off a cliff, and in this he was guided by the devil. Cortés believed that this man spoke with honesty, he trusted him, and ordered his men to depart before dawn in order to reach their destination, where they could rest from the sun and the trials of the journey. Having prepared themselves, the soldiers left the town near dawn. They were guided by Coatlpopoca, who gradually led them into rough country of rocks and cliffs that was so harsh and difficult that the horses and foot soldiers were soon exhausted. As it was not yet light, they could not see the way. When Cortés realized how rough the path was, worse than any they had ever followed, he asked the guide why he had brought them along such a bad route. Coatlpopoca answered that it was simply a shorter way and that it would not last long. But he led them straight toward the cliffs. When they tried to descend, two mounted men who were in front fell over the edge and were killed, together with their horses. When Cortés saw the malice of Coatlpopoca and the harm he had caused, he ordered him taken prisoner. But when that man realized that he would be punished, he fled and concealed himself and was not to be found. Having waited until morning, Cortés and his men returned the same way they had come and then were guided by other Indians on the true road to the Aztec capital.

Cortés sent messengers to Motecuhzoma, against whom he now felt resentment, for he thought that the chieftain's daring and outrageous treason had been at the command of the king. His message stated that he had had a better opinion of Motecuhzoma and that the king should take care because two of the Spaniards had been killed on the cliffs. Cortés added that Motecuhzoma should order the capture of Coatlpopoca; only in this way would he understand that the treachery had not been due to the king's orders.

When this news and Cortés's message, which insinuated that the king was to blame, was delivered to Motecuhzoma, he became very angry and ordered that Coatlpopoca be captured and surrendered to Cortés so the Spanish captain could punish him in a way that fit the crime. The chieftain was sought assiduously and when found he was turned over the Cortés. When he confessed his evil intentions and admitted that Motecuhzoma had had no knowledge of his act, Cortés had him put in chains. He gave orders that the traitor be brought with great care so that he could deliver him in person to Motecuhzoma. Then the king could decide upon a fitting punishment. When Cortés arrived in Tenochtitlan, later, this was done and Motecuhzoma had Coatlpopoca torn to pieces. In this way the Aztec king showed his innocence in the whole matter.

Meanwhile, Cortés arrived at Tecoac, a town near Tlaxcala, belonging to the jurisdiction of the latter city. Before he arrived, however, messengers had gone to notify the inhabitants that the gods would be spending the night there, that the people were to come out to welcome them and provide them with everything they needed. Tocpacxochiuh, lord of Tecoac, was told how he must receive the Spaniards and their horses, feed them, and have prepared turkeys, eggs, breads, fruit, and maize, and also grass for the horses. The rooms of the houses where the strangers were to be lodged were to be well swept, also.

On hearing this the Tecoac ruler rose from his seat with great anger, crying out, "Are we vassals of the gods who are coming? Are we vassals of Motecuhzoma? Are they to command us as if we were their servants? I do not wish it! It is not my will to receive them in my city or give them provisions and living quarters!" He called his officials and all his subjects and addressed them, "O Chichimecas, bold men of Tecoac! Take up your arms, your swords and arrows to defend your nation. Let us destroy, let us annihilate the gods who have come here, who create such fear and awe among all the people who lay eyes upon them. Let us test the strength of these strangers who have come to our land. Let us discover whether we are really their vassals or their tributaries. Let us see if we must provide for all their needs. Prepare yourselves to go out to meet them. Let us rout them, let us destroy them, let us prove ourselves to be valorous men!"

Having thus been commanded, everyone in Tecoac was put on guard and the entrance to the city was defended against the arrival of the Spaniards. Rapidly the fields were covered with Indians, all of them armed for war. Cortés, who was always prepared, ordered his three hundred men to form in squadrons in order not to be surrounded or attacked from the rear. But when he saw the enormous number of men facing him, he was filled with fear. And when the enemy formed itself in wings, their squadrons arranged in their customary way, he saw that in the front lines there were many gallant men, splendidly arrayed, covered from head to foot with their military ornaments inlaid with gold, as were their shields. On their heads and over their backs they wore rich feathers and insignia that indicated that they were spirited and courageous warriors. Filled with contempt, they made scornful signs and faces at the Spaniards. Once these men had been formed in ranks, two valiant Indians came forward. With their gilded and elaborately adorned shields and swords in hand they defied the Spaniards, ordering them to depart.

The Spaniards were greatly confused and frightened. The native army was so large that it seemed to eclipse the sun, and this was the first battle the strangers had to fight. The Spaniards were few in number, not well equipped, and were fearful at finding themselves in this strange and barbarous realm. They were confronted by men as numerous as the sands of the sea, who could have killed them with the greatest of ease. In fact, I heard a conqueror who is now a monk and who was then a layman and was present in that battle[1] say that many Spaniards shed tears and wished that they had not been born, cursing Cortés for having brought them to this fearful end. But the brave captain, who never lacked spirit in any tribulation of this type, ordered two horsemen to charge wildly and kill the two Indians who had placed themselves in front of the army, since it was obvious that all were depending upon them. Courageously the two cavaliers raised their arms ready to thrust their lances against the two opponents who awaited them, but at the moment of the kill one of the native warriors lifted his right hand and with amazing skill slashed at the horse with his sword and severed its hoofs, whereupon the horseman fell upon the ground. The other Indian leaped to one side and managed to avoid a blow that the other Spaniard aimed at him, and he hit the horse with his sword in such a way that its severed head hung from the reins and master and beast were left lying on the ground.

Seeing that the Tecoac men were anxious to attack again in order to take them alive, Cortés ordered that a small cannon be fired. All the Indians in the front ranks were killed by this and others scattered. This allowed the Spaniards who had fallen to rise from the ground. Taking hold of their swords, they tried to defend themselves from the Indians. Shrieking while horns, drums, conch shells, and other instruments sounded, the Indians attacked with slings, propelled darts, and other weapons. The Spaniards managed to penetrate into the enemy

---

[1]This undoubtedly was Fray Francisco de Aguilar (see Aguilar 1977), mentioned many times by Durán.

lines, where they shot the small cannon, fired their arquebuses, and sent arrows from their crossbows. Little by little land was won from the Indians until the Spaniards had reached a small village on a hill near the city, which probably was a pyramid on whose summit was a temple, because they say that a house was there that contained large, spacious chambers. There the Spaniards took refuge and the Indians, having surrounded them, attacked every day. It is said that this assault lasted ten or twelve days.

During this time Motecuhzoma kept sending food to the Spaniards. Cortés tried desperately to break the siege, asking the enemy for peace many times and telling them to cease fighting and subject themselves to His Majesty. He told them that he had not come to harm them or kill them. But seeing that they were unwilling to do what he desired, Cortés decided to set up an ambush and finish them off.

Night came, and the Indians believed that the Spaniards had gone to sleep, as they usually did at that time. But it was not so, since they were all awake. The Spaniards waited until the fires of their sentries had gone out, and when everything was quiet Cortés and his men abandoned their shelter and came forth in groups of ten, some on one side and some on the other, according to the plan and cunning of the good captain. They found the Indians sleeping, notably the captains, in some large houses in the village. They were fast asleep, completely relaxed and unaware of any danger. Cortés gave orders that no one harm or kill any of them but that the captains be taken prisoner and tied up. When they were brought to the Spaniards' camp, none of them was killed, not even their sentinels and guards. Cortés reproached the captains through Marina the interpreter. He asked then why they were rebellious, why they made trouble, since he had not come to harm them. He asked them to examine and judge him according to their experiences: though he had been able to massacre all of them, he had not wished to do so or cause any harm. He also said that proof that he wanted them as friends would be shown by his freeing all the prisoners at dawn.

So it was that, when morning came and the Tecoac army wished to renew the battle, the men saw that their commanders, the leaders who guided them and encouraged them, were not there. Cortés then brought out these captains, exactly as they had been captured and tied up, and told the soldiers of the difficult situation in which he had placed their officers. He repeated that, though he could have killed them, his mission was not to kill or to destroy. He besought them to allow him and his men to enter the city to rest, and he freed all the prisoners. When the Indians saw his generosity, they lifted the siege, coming in peace to lead Cortés to the city.

How Motecuhzoma sent a chieftain to guide Cortés

All that I have narrated here I heard from a conqueror who was an eyewitness to these events. But the *Historia* tells us exactly the opposite. It says that the Spaniards entered by force, killing numerous Indians. In a way one account is not contrary to the other, since it is clear that during the siege a great number of Indians were killed with the cannon and muskets, as a battle took place every day.

And so it became known throughout the land that the gods possessed lightning of fire and with each shot many men perished; therefore, the natives became quiet with fear. Their terror and cowardice were so strong that they fled from the Spaniards, in their flight hiding in caves, in the woods, in caverns. They even threw themselves off cliffs in order not to face the Spaniards. This situations continues even today, for they hide from the friars as if they were their mortal enemies, although the friars live among them, love and cherish them.

In order to illustrate the terror that took hold of those people, I wish to relate what the Tlaxcalans did when Tecoac surrendered to Cortés and to the Spanish crown, which Cortés represented.[2]

---

[2] The story of the Spanish conquest of Mexico is related quite differently in Sahagún. See book 12 of the *Florentine Codex*, "The Conquest of Mexico," and a revised account of the conquest by Sahagún in Cline 1989.

CHAPTER LXXIII

Which treats of how the Tlaxcalans held a meeting and decided to receive Cortés in peace and deliver the city to him. With a description of the great reception held in his honor.

Tecoac and its people were not subject to the king and to the Marqués, who had made them swear they would never again rebel against him.[1] The *Historia* says that Cortés took with him as a prisoner the lord of that city, Tocpacxiuh. After leaving Tecoac, they soon came to the limits of Tlaxcala, arriving at a town called Tzopachtzinco. When the Tlaxcalans heard that the gods were approaching, they called together a gathering of all the rulers of the province.

Tlaxcala was a great and populous nation, governed by four lords representing four different regions. During the meeting one of these nobles spoke lengthily, exclaiming, "O Chichimec lords, natives of the great Tlaxcala! You have heard that certain gods have arrived in our land, coming from the place where the sun rises. They appeared among the mists and the darkness of the sea, living in wooden hills or houses. All of this was a great mystery, it came from above and was permitted by the Lord of All Created Things, of the Sky and the Earth, of the Night and the Day. You must know, too, that little by little they have been penetrating into our country. Therefore, decide what we must do, decide if we should or should not defend ourselves. You have seen how the people of Tecoac were restless and tried to protect their city, to keep those gods from entering it. You have also witnessed the deaths of all those who perished from the fire shot out by the invaders. This all could have been avoided if other actions had been taken. If you wish to hear my opinion I shall give it to you: have pity upon your children, brothers, the old men and women and orphans who are to die, all of them innocent, perishing only because we wish to make a defense. All of this will profit us nothing, will be of no use. Therefore, I believe it will be better to receive them in peace, bring them into our city and furnish them with food and other things for their needs."

Everyone agreed with this position and they decided to prostrate themselves before Cortés, offering him their services as well as many

---

[1] On the original manuscript in Madrid, this chapter and the following five (LXXIII to LXXVII) are full of revisions; words and lines have been crossed out.

presents. And so it was done. Gathering many of their chieftains, the Tlaxcalans departed with the finest gifts that could be obtained and appeared before Cortés. When they were in his presence, they did much reverence to him and offered him the gifts. Among these were many garlands of flowers that they hung around his neck. Having greeted him, the Tlaxcalan emissaries delivered a long speech that Marina translated for Cortés. In this speech they offered their persons and wealth for the service of the Spanish captain and of His Majesty, whose name Cortés always extolled to these nations. He always begged them to submit themselves to his king and to our Catholic faith. These people then did subject themselves to His Majesty and agreed to be his vassals; they are his subjects to this day.

Then Cortés asked the emissaries about their country. They responded that they had come from Tlaxcala to serve him, receive him as their master, and provide for his necessities. After this they presented him with a great quantity of food: fowl, maize bread, fruit, and other edibles for which Cortés thanked them courteously. He then asked if they were subjected to Mexico-Tenochtitlan and if they paid tribute to Motecuhzoma or to some other ruler. "O great lord," they answered, "we are free men! We do not pay tribute, nor are we vassals of anyone. That great sovereign you mentioned is the king of Tenochtitlan, our mortal enemy, with whom we wage a perpetual war. Those Aztecs and their allies come to our lands to die and we go to theirs to perish at the hands of their sacrificers! Our enmity is so great that all their pleasure and ours has been reduced to providing men for sacrifice and the killing of one another!" Cortés had now found that which he desired: discord. He allied himself with the Tlaxcalans against Tenochtitlan in case he should need them later.

On entering the city, Cortés was welcomed by the Tlaxcalans with dances, farces, and merrymaking. He was given rooms in the best palace, which according to the *Historia* was that of Xicotencatl, one of the lords of the city. After he had rested, Cortés asked Xicotencatl for men to carry the Spaniards' possessions. He also asked the officials to give him guards to accompany them, together with women to grind corn and to cook. The Tlaxcalans willingly and rapidly gave the Spaniards a number of soldiers as well as carriers for their belongings and presented them with women to serve them. The latter were accepted by the soldiers with pleasure. Our chronicle narrates that from that time on, wherever the Spaniards arrived, they were given young, beautiful maidens, daughters of men of high position, to serve them. A notable case of this was in Amequemecan, a city on the way to Venta de Chalco, where Cortés passed after leaving Tlaxcala.

The people of Amequemecan came out to welcome Cortés and regaled him with rich presents of gold jewelry, precious stones, feathers, splendid armbands, clothing, blouses, and ornate skirts. He was also offered many young girls, all beautiful, well dressed and handsomely adorned. On their backs they wore magnificent plumage, their hair was loose, and their cheeks were painted in a way that enhanced them greatly. The soldiers received them with thanks, being grateful for this gift.[2] Filled with gratitude, Cortés lingered a few days in the province of Chalco and during this time people from all the surrounding towns came to greet him, to swear allegiance and to present him with gifts. He and his men accepted them with goodwill, especially the jewels, gold work, and precious stones. All of these whetted their appetite.

When Motecuhzoma heard that Cortés was approaching, he sent messages to the kings of Tezcoco and Tacuba, asking them to come so that all three might be there to welcome the gods who were now near the city. They acceded to his petition and came to Tenochtitlan, where they were received in Motecuhzoma's royal abode. After they had been given quarters in this palace, they formally greeted one another as was their custom, then Motecuhzoma addressed them, weeping: "O mighty lords! It is fitting that the three of us be here to receive the gods and therefore I wish to find solace with you. I wish to greet you now and also bid farewell to you. And I wish to comfort your

[2] In a study based on data from sixteenth-century sources (Heyden 1976), I have stated that when a young girl's cheeks were painted red, and when her arms and legs were usually feathered with red plumes at the same time, she was a virgin and was either about to be married or about to be dedicated to the service of a god. In fiestas honoring Tezcatlipoca or Huitzilopochtli, for example, young girls associated with the temples danced with the red feather adornments and with their cheeks painted. There is a clear sexual association with this rouge and with red feathers. Bernal Díaz del Castillo (1939:I:262) says that the old ruler of Tlaxcala told the Spaniards that they all wished to be brothers; therefore, they were giving them their daughters, adorned as described above, as brides. Paradoxically, harlots also painted their cheeks and lips red and left their hair loose; both were sexual symbols. In the advice given to daughters by their fathers, the girls were told never to use these beautifying measures unless they were about to be married or were dancing in a festivity for the gods (Sahagún 1969, Book 6:101). Xochiquetzal, however, who was the goddess of vegetation and flowers, was portrayed with red cheeks, as were some of the other figures of the Mother Goddess. This is because vegetation, agricultural fertility, was related to human fecundity: Xochiquetzal was also the patroness of prostitutes. Other characteristics of the Mother Goddess were also associated with love, fertility, and therefore sex.

In the Durán manuscript in Madrid's Biblioteca Nacional, two words—half a line—were crossed out in the sixteenth century in this paragraph that mentions the girls with red cheeks and were replaced by one word, "soldiers." We do not know what was originally written here.

How the Tlaxcalans received Cortés in peace

trobled breasts. How little we have enjoyed our realms that our ancestors bequeathed to us! They, mighty lords and kings, went away in peace and harmony, free of sorrow and sadness. Woe to us! Why do we deserve calamity, this anguish? In what way have we offended the gods? What has happened? Who are these men who have arrived? Whence have they come, who showed them the way? Why did this not happen in the time of our ancestors? There is only one remedy: you must make your hearts strong in order to bear what is to happen. They are at our gates!"

The other two kings wept in their anguish and tried to console one another. Afer they had said farewell and embraced each other with feeling, Motecuhzoma, the *Historia* tells us, went to visit his oracles and in front of the gods he uttered terrible reproaches. He complained bitterly to them for having brought him to this frightful end. He told the gods that he had served them with all possible care and that he had pleased them and had promoted their cult and increased the reverence paid to them. All of these laments to the gods were pronounced by Motecuhzoma in the presence of those two kings and before the people. With abundant tears he cried out to his people that he was terrified because of the arrival of the strangers. He begged the gods to have pity on the poor, on the orphans and widows, on the children and the aged. Many other prayers did he utter, accompanied by sacrifices, pious offerings, and tears. He performed autosacrifice, drawing blood from his arms, ears, and shins, doing all this in an attempt to prove his innocence and to demonstrate his sorrow over the coming of the Spaniards.

When Motecuhzoma returned to the palace, he bade farewll to his wives and children with sorrow and tears. He charged all his attendants to care for his family, for he considered himself a man about to die, a man who saw certain death staring him in the eyes.

It was at this time that Cortés reached Coyoacan, where he was well received, welcomed with much ceremony and esteem, more than he had been shown in any other part of the land. The entire Tepanec nation, led by its rulers, came out to see and salute Cortés, presenting him with gifts of mantles, jewels, stones, feathers, all rich and fine things. They offered their allegiance and promised to serve him in the name of His Majesty. In this way Cortés was gradually taking subjects and obedience of the people away from Motecuhzoma and the Aztec nation. They were all turning against the latter and joining Cortés, promising to aid him. At this time the Tlaxcalans, Tepanecs, and Chalcas, who had subjected themselves to His Majesty, warned Cortés not to trust Motecuhzoma or his people as they were traitors, and also evil, tyrannical, and bellicose. The Spaniard was told to beware when the Aztecs acted most amiably and affably to him, for that was the moment to trust them the least. Cortés thanked them for the warning and asked these new allies for some of their people to accompany him in order to guard his own person. The men of Coyoacan gave him guards to serve him.

When Motecuhzoma and his people saw that everyone was abandoning them, was becoming an enemy, they were much saddened, for [their former allies] went over to the Spaniards, leaving the Aztecs alone. However, these allied cities actually remained neutral, for they dared not profess their enmity toward the Aztecs, nor show themselves to be true friends of Cortés. Nevertheless, they served the Spanish captain and gave him provisions that were needed. They showed obeisance to him and treated him with much respect.

When Motecuhzoma heard that Cortés was in Coyoacan, he prepared a solemn reception to welcome him to the city of Tenochtitlan. He ordered that all his noblemen be present, including those of the neighboring cities. But Cortés, who was a sly, cunning man, always managed to stay a few days in the important towns where he had arrived, resting, making friends with the people, flattering them, showing them great affection, warning them against the Aztecs, persuading them to be his friends. He said that he had not come to do them harm but to liberate them from the tyranny and oppression of King Motecuhzoma, promising them freedom from the servitude in which they lived. After he had persuaded them, he would depart with his men and go on to the next town.

When Cortés was told that he was now not far from the city of Tenochtitlan, he sent messages to Motecuhzoma telling him that he was near and wished to meet him; and he asked what the king's orders were. The sovereign received the messengers well and answered that Cortés should consider that his home was here and that he, the king, longed to see him, to greet him. He was welcome to come when he so desired. Only one thing worried Motecuhzoma and that was that Cortés was coming in the company of the Tlaxcalans, who were his foes; he was fearful that they would enter the city. They were the mortal enemies of the Aztecs and his people had become agitated and afraid that the Tlaxcalans might cause trouble. Cortés responded that he was not bringing soldiers but carriers who bore his provisions, the equipment of his own soldiers, and the presents of cloth and other fine things he had been given in the towns that he had visited. These things were plentiful, well worked and with rich designs. There were ornamented mantles for men together with exquisite women's garments. A great number of Indians accompanied the Spaniards in order to carry all this wealth.

How the Tlaxcalans received Cortés in peace

Cortés was planning to distribute all these fine things among his soldiers and other friends, which he did, in the city. And this was to prove fatal to the recipients, since later and because of their greed in carrying this wealth during their flight from the city they lost everything, including their lives. And perhaps—no, I should *not* say perhaps—they lost their souls *in aeternum*!

CHAPTER LXXIV

Which treats of how Hernán Cortés, the Marqués, was welcomed in Mexico-Tenochtitlan by Motecuhzoma and his dignitaries with much solemnity and rejoicing. With a description of how he was lodged in a palace in the city and was well served there. And how King Motecuhzoma was taken prisoner.

It has never been my intention or my will, nor is it now, to write a new history of the coming of the Spaniards to this land. It is not my desire to tell of their daring and heroic deeds or to set them up on a pinnacle or give them the praise they deserve. They were worthy of being remembered forever. Their chests and hearts were more than human and showed the spirit of the Spanish, which has been lauded, praised, and renowned throughout the entire world. And these traits were necessary for them to have undertaken such daring feats as those we shall be describing.

As I have said it is not my intention to deal with their greatness or their fantastic deeds, nor to reminisce over how Cortés entered the port and scuttled his ships in order to remove any hope that his men might have of fleeing from this land and, because there was little possibility of their returning to Spain, he wished to inspire them to risk their lives like spirited men. Nor shall I describe how his own men at one time decided to assassinate him, nor the humility he showed and the diplomatic words he spoke that saved his life. All this is well known and has been recorded by many authors.

Since I must tell the truth according to the stories and traditions of the Indians, I should have to describe, together with good and heroic actions, the frightful and cruel atrocities, the inhuman acts carried out by Cortés and his men. In this way, however, I may offend those whom I am desirous of serving and who would wish to read these passages with pleasure. Many of these barbarous acts were committed on the way to the city of Tenochtitlan, but about these I have been silent. Nevertheless, I shall describe one of these. It took place in the city of Cholula and was a sorry affair. There, in the courtyard of the temple where Cortés was staying, he slaughtered a great number of men who had come to serve the Spaniards. These people had carried water, firewood, and grass for the horses, together with other provisions. But Cortés thought that they were chieftains in disguise, come to harm him, because there were so many of them, and therefore he had them massacred, sparing no one. I could cite many other cases, but since this is not my intention I shall only describe the events that led up to the death of Motecuhzoma, as it is his life I am narrating. I shall tell about the end, the death, of a monarch so powerful that he had been feared, served, and obeyed in all of this New Spain. This ruler came to such a low, disastrous end that, even at his funeral, there was no one to speak in his favor or to mourn over him. In fact, surrounded by his enemies as he was, he—whose name had made the earth tremble, who made people quake simply on hearing "Motecuhzoma"—was not even interred.

Let us continue, for we are nearing the end of our story. It must be noted here how Cortés departed from Coyoacan on his way to Tenochtitlan. He was accompanied by many great lords, some of these natives of Coyoacan, others from the whole Aztec province and different areas such as Tlaxcala, Xochimilco, Tacuba, and Chalco, all of whom went along to serve him. Aside from the nobles there came many plebeians who wished to observe the spectacle. When Motecuhzoma was notified of the coming of Cortés from Coyoacan, he surrounded himself with the nobles and kings who had been with him and all his other officials and, seated on a handsome litter that was covered with splendid cloth and that he always used, he was carried out of the city on the shoulders of some of his great men, in this way showing his grandeur and power. Many of the nobles went ahead while others walked behind, carrying flowers and rich presents that were to be given to the Spaniards, who were thought to be gods. When Motecuhzoma reached a place called Tocititlan (which was almost next to the place where there is now the first cross on the road at the [southern] entrance to the city), he ordered his men to let him descend so all could await the arrival of Cortés.

When Motecuhzoma heard that the Spanish captain was approaching, he again ascended his litter and then, carried on the noblemen's shoulders in the same way he had come, he went out to meet him. On seeing Cortés, he descended. When Cortés saw this, he climbed down from his horse and went to embrace the Aztec sovereign, treating him with much reverence. Motecuhzoma did the same, paying homage to the other with humility and words of welcome. From one of his noblemen he took a splendid necklace of gold, inlaid with precious stones, and placed it around Cortés's neck. Then he put in his hands a magnificent piece of featherwork, done in the form of a flower. He also placed a garland of flowers about Cortés's neck and another on his head. Then, holding each other by the hand, the two men walked to the shrine of the goddess Toci, which was near the road, and there the mighty king and Hernán Cortés seated themselves on special seats that had been prepared for them. The rulers of Tezcoco and Tacuba then came up to pay homage to Cortés. They also offered necklaces and flowers befitting their status as rulers. After this all the great lords came and performed the same courtesies and ceremonies that were done for their god Huitzilopochtli.

When this long ceremonial salutation had been completed, Motecuhzoma spoke to Cortés through his translator, Marina. He welcomed Cortés to his city, telling him that he was overjoyed to receive him. He added that he had been ruling in the other's place, governing the kingdom that his father, the divine Quetzalcoatl, had abandoned. Upon this seat Motecuhzoma had sat, unworthily, reigning over the vassals of Quetzalcoatl. If Cortés had come to rule, he was at his service and the kingdom was now his, because the written prophecies and the accounts of his ancestors had foretold these events. However, if the Spaniard had only come to visit him, he considered this a great favor and felt joy in his heart. The Aztec king told Cortés to rest and make known his needs, which would be provided for in great abundance.

Having removed his hat to show reverence and gratitude, Cortés answered courteously, saying that he had come in the name of a powerful king, whose servant he was. This monarch lived in Spain and was the ruler of a large part of the world. Cortés urged Motecuhzoma to swear allegiance to him as this would bring him many favors. He also asked him to receive the Catholic faith of the one True Lord and God, under whose rule and power heaven and earth are governed. When Motecuhzoma recognized these two lords, he was told, especially the Supreme Lord, and subjected himself to His Faith and then to the earthly lord, Cortés would become his friend and servant forever. He would never be mistreated, nor would his people, for Cortés had come to do no harm. Motecuhzoma agreed to all these things, placed himself in Cortés's hands, and offered his subjection to His Majesty at that hour, asking to be instructed in things related to the Holy Catholic faith.

After having spent some time in that small shrine, both men entered the city of Tenochtitlan, Cortés on his horse and the powerful Angry Lord on his litter, carried on the shoulders of his officials as he had come. But according to traditions and to paintings kept by certain elders, it is said that Motecuhzoma left the sanctuary with his feet in chains. And I saw this in a painting that belonged to an ancient chieftain from the province of Tezcoco. Motecuhzoma was depicted in irons, wrapped in a mantle and carried on the shoulders of his dignitaries. This seems difficult to believe, since I have never met a Spaniard who will concede this point to me. But as all of them deny other things that have always been obvious, and remain silent about them in their histories, writings, and narrations, I am sure they would also deny and omit this, one of the worst and most atrocious acts committed by them. A conqueror, who is now a friar, told me that though the imprisonment of Motecuhzoma might be true, it was done with the idea of protecting the lives of the Spanish captain and his men. Also taken prisoner were the kings of Tezcoco and Tacuba, and the ruler of Xochimilco, who was as great a lord as the others and a favorite of Motecuhzoma, who often advised him.

They entered Tenochtitlan preceded by dancers and merrymakers and were greeted by the priests who came out to meet them, carrying incense burners and blowing horns and conch shells. They were painted with pitch and decked in their priestly garments. Behind them came the old men and warriors who had retired from war, dressed as eagles and jaguars and carrying their staffs and shields. In the midst of this ceremony and ovation Cortés entered the city. The Spanish captain was given rooms in the royal palace that Motecuhzoma's grandfather, also called Motecuhzoma, had built.[1] These royal houses were large, divided into numerous chambers, and stood where the viceroy's palace now stands. There, together with his men, Cortés was lodged and provided for splendidly by the people of the towns that surround Tenochtitlan, each in its turn, all having been ordered to do so by Motecuhzoma.

During this time, however, Motecuhzoma and his allied rulers, together with other lords, were held prisoners in chains in a room guarded by three soldiers who were changed every other day. It is said that in the eighty days during which the Aztec ruler remained there he was instructed in the things of the Faith by a cleric whom the Spaniards had brought with them and that he received the waters of the Holy Baptism. The *Historia* makes no mention of this; if I record this event it is only because I have heard certain trustworthy persons speak of it. In order to ascertain the truth I questioned the friar who had been a conqueror and whom I have mentioned before. In a hesitant way he answered that he had not been present at the baptism but he believed it had taken place at that time. He also stated that the soldiers and Cortés, who were residing in the palace, were more interested in seeking Motecuhzoma's treasure (the pious cleric among them) than in converting Motecuhzoma to the faith. My reasons for believing the latter rather than the former are based upon the descrip-

[1]The building described by Durán stood on the western side of the Zocalo, main square of modern Mexico City, and occupied the space of what is today the National Pawn Shop. On the eastern side of the square the "House of Motecuhzoma" was built, where the National Palace is today.

tion given to me by the friar who had been a conqueror. He told me of the intense search that was made for the secret treasure chambers of Motecuhzoma. One day the Spaniards' eagerness and hunger for gold led them to a small low door that had been filled in and recently plastered, a mystery that intrigued them. They were ordered to open it and when they passed through a narrow door they found a spacious chamber in the middle of which stood a pile of gold, jewelry, and rich stones, the whole pile as high as the tallest man. If we wish to know what this pile of riches was, we see that according to the *Historia* the treasure did not consist of things acquired by Motecuhzoma, nor were they objects for his own use. This was the treasure that had belonged to all the kings who were his ancestors, which they had deposited there but which could not be used by the present ruler. When a king died, on that very day all his wealth in gold, gems, feathers, and weapons and his entire wardrobe were placed in that room and guarded as if they were sacred or divine things. The king who was about to reign would then begin to acquire wealth so that it could not be said he used the treasures of his ancestors. So it was that the treasure was guarded as a testimony to the greatness of the city of Mexico-Tenochtitlan.

In this room there were also heaps of fine mantles as well as clothing for women. On the walls hung many shields, weapons, and insignia of fine workmanship and colors. There were piles of golden vessels, of plates and dishes made in the style of these people, which the kings used to eat from. The most remarkable were four large platters made to represent fountains, all beautifully worked in gold, as big as shields and so covered with dust that it was plain that they had not been used for a long time. There were also golden vessels for drinking chocolate, made in the shape of gourds, some with supports and others without. In the corners of the chamber lay quantities of uncut stones. In sum, this chamber contained the most amazing wealth ever seen, and the bewildered Spaniards took the gold platters to Cortés as proof of these great riches.

The captain entered the room and, after seeing the beauty and richness of the objects, and having realized that they had now achieved what they so desired, he ordered that under pain of death no one should enter the room again. He commanded that the chamber be closed and that everything be guarded in the name of His Majesty, as here was the best part of the treasure from which the royal fifth was to be taken. And so guards were posted there and the door was again sealed as it had been, so no one would dare try to enter.

But the Spaniards, still possessed of that unsatisfied hunger for riches, did not leave a corner or chamber unsearched or undisturbed. In this way they discovered a secret apartment where the women of

Motecuhzoma were kept, together with their ladies and duennas who served them and looked after them. These women had hidden in those chambers out of fear of the Spaniards. Others say, however, that these were no other than the cloistered maidens of the temples, who lived like nuns, fulfilling their vows under the orders of the duennas, who were like abbesses. They had been concealed in that house in order not to be mistreated and violated by the Spaniards, who already were giving signs of incontinence.

I have heard it said, though I do not find it in this *Historia*, that Motecuhzoma and the other rulers offered to give an enormous amount of wealth to Cortés if he would return to his own country— enough to sink a ship.

But the good Hernán Cortés, like a true Christian, was only interested in saving souls! He and his men scorned everything but the extolling of the faith of Christ and the conversion of these blind and idolatrous people! They also wished to acquire more prestige and wealth in any way possible, their aim being that this wealth would last and thus be enjoyed. This may be said about the conquerors, that "that which has been won honestly is often lost, and that which has been gained wickedly is also lost, together with its possessor."

And so it is that I have seen the conquerors become wretches, their children dying of hunger while their wealth was possessed and enjoyed by others. In order to prove this I wish to refer to a familiar sight in these unfortunate times: the sons of many conquerors are so poor that they are almost driven from door to door begging for food, for they often do not have enough. The secret of all these things is known only to God.

CHAPTER LXXV

Which treats of how Pánfilo de Narváez arrived at the port of Veracruz and how Cortés captured him and sent him away. With a description of how Cortés returned to Tenochtitlan with his men and how a rebellion broke out among the natives against the Spaniards.

We have already seen how the Spaniards discovered the great treasure of Tenochtitlan and how they entered the secret, hidden chambers of the maidens who served the gods. Even though the *Historia* does not speak of this, I do not believe that the virtue of our Spaniards was so great that they insisted that these women persevere in their chastity, modesty, and seclusion. If they were Motecuhzoma's wives, it is difficult to believe that they would remain faithful to a prince who, although he had treated them so well, was now a prisoner in fetters.[1]

The Spaniards at this time were living comfortably, eating and drinking without worry, when Cortés was notified that Pánfilo de Narváez had landed in Veracruz and had established his headquarters in Cempoala with his men and artillery. He had entrenched himself there and was preparing to take Cortés prisoner because the latter had left Cuba without permission, not awaiting the commands of his superior officer.

Cortés was disturbed at this news but, astute and cunning as he was, he left Don Pedro de Alvarado in command of the men in the city and departed toward Cempoala with one hundred soldiers. They marched day and night, wearing disguises and hiding when they could, so news would not spread of Cortés's coming, since he was so well known to the Indians. Disguised in this way, no one recognized him. When Pánfilo finally heard of his coming, he was not worried; he had faith in his own valor and in the bold men he had brought with him. Narváez had all his artillery ready at the doors of the buildings in Cempoala, and his men were on the alert. However, Cortés was so determined to succeed in this enterprise that he did not even sleep, nor was he careless at any time.

And so it was that when Pánfilo de Narváez thought that Cortés was

---

[1] At this point in the original manuscript, eleven lines are crossed out.

just leaving Tenochtitlan, he had already arrived with his men at the doors of the buildings in Cempoala—but I shall shorten this account because it is well known. When Cortés saw their lack of vigilance, he waited until the artillery man—who should not have abandoned his post—left the cannon for a moment. In that instant ten soldiers jumped upon the cannon and took possession of it. This was done so swiftly that Narváez's men were unable to make use of the cannon. At that same moment Cortés, leading his men, jumped over the walls of the buildings, all with sword in hand. Others picked up pikes and halberds that Narváez's careless soldiers had left lying next to the walls. Immediately they began to strike left and right, injuring, wounding, and, when Narváez and his men tried to defend themselves, he was hit in the eye with a pike and the eye was torn out of its socket. After this he was taken prisoner.

Immediately Narváez's soldiers, believing that their end had come because Cortés had his whole army with him, fled—some over the walls, others through the doors, and others hid in the different rooms. Those who did not manage to flee threw themselves at Cortés's feet, begging for mercy. And so we should not be surprised that the local Indians came with their arms crossed and also pleaded to be spared. Cortés received them all in a kindly manner and when the soldiers who had come with Narváez saw his friendliness they gradually joined his army in the name of His Majesty, placing themselves under his flag. Narváez's feet were chained; he was placed in a ship and sent back to Cuba, from whence he had come.

Once Narváez had been defeated and sent away, Cortés gathered his army and returned to Tenochtitlan, leading one thousand more men than he had brought with him. If we were to praise these men in that case and the attitude they took toward their captain [Narváez], we could compare this to similar circumstances involving Gonzalo [sic] Pizarro and his lord and king in Peru. How true are these words: "When greed and self-interest appear, friendship and justice depart!" In this way the soldiers set out for the city with Cortés, but soon there came news that his men there were in trouble and that the Indians had slain some of them. This was false news, a lie, sent by Don Pedro de Alvarado so that he could carry out his own plan, which was a cruel, tyrannical atrocity.

When Cortés returned to Tenochtitlan, triumphant and accompanied by so many men, he apparently feared no unexpected problems such as he had encountered up to that time. And so, with that self-assurance and daring, he followed the advice given by Don Pedro de Alvarado and others, which was to kill all the lords and captains and great men of the Aztec capital. Therefore, they planned a treacherous act; our *Historia* calls it "treachery" in our language [Spanish], although this was written by an Indian.[2]

It must be noted that the Indians were about to celebrate the solemn feast of Toxcatl, during which the idol of Huitzilopochtli was transferred from one place to another. This was a very important festival and rites were held before and after, like our octaves after a religious ceremony. I have dealt with this in the *Book of Rites*.[3] Every day the natives came out to dance in preparation for their feast, and Cortés asked Motecuhzoma to explain to him the meaning of those dances and ceremonies. [He was afraid of a rebellion and] he warned the Aztec king not to stir up trouble since neither he nor his men wished to harm him. Motecuhzoma reassured Cortés, saying that a rebellion was not their intention. He added that he was a prisoner and that he and his people had no hostile plans.[4] He begged Cortés to be calm as the dances and songs he heard meant only that the feast of the god was approaching and that certain ceremonies must be performed before and after the great day. Cortés then asked him as a favor to order that all the rulers and lords of the city and province gather to dance in the courtyard of the temple, together with the most courageous men, for he wished to take pleasure in observing the grandeur and nobility of Tenochtitlan. But all this was a cunning plan to massacre all those people, which is what happened.

This plan had been communicated to Cortés by Pedro de Avlarado, who had been instigated in turn by the Tlaxcalans, who hated the Aztecs, and who said that the object of this feast and the dances was to stir up a rebellion against the Spaniards and murder them. It is also possible that Alvarado in his cruel nature was desirous of making himself ruler of the land, even though it be at the cost of the lives of many. I have read much about him and his cruelties, and how he boasted about these. Motecuhzoma, who was naive and sincere and did not suspect malice, nor did he realize that such treachery was being planned, called together his dignitaries and told them that the Spaniards wished to enjoy the spectacle of the grandeur of Tenochtitlan and its nobility.

When the day for the Toxcatl feast arrived, when Tezcatlipoca and Huitzilopochtli were honored, the Aztec lords and warriors, unsuspecting, came out to worship their god and to show the splendor of

[2]Other authors stress the fact that the massacre of Aztecs in the Great Temple during the feast of Toxcatl took place while Cortés was in Veracruz fighting against Narváez and was carried out by Pedro de Alvarado. See *Florentine Codex* (1955:book 12:12–49).
[3]The feast of Toxcatl is described in Durán's *Book of the Gods and Rites* (1977), in chapter IV and in "The Fifth Month of the Year."
[4]Here one line is crossed out in the original manuscript (fol. 212r).

Mexico-Tenochtitlan. Wearing all their finery, their splendid clothing and adornments, they wished to please Cortés in performing their dances and ceremonies before him and the others—although their performance was not appreciated and they received a treacherous attack in compensation, as we shall soon see. Motecuhzoma's order had been heard all through the city, so the principal men and captains prepared themselves with their most magnificent attire in order to participate in the Toxcatl feast.

The day for the festivities having arrived, some eight or ten thousand men of the highest order and purest lineage appeared, wearing all their finery as we have said, and formed a great circle in the temple courtyard. While they were dancing, all with contentment and pleasure, Cortés, instigated by Alvarado, ordered ten soldiers to be placed at each of the four gates of the courtyard so that no one could escape. He sent ten others to stand next to those who were beating drums where the most important lords had gathered. The soldiers were told to kill the drummers and after them all those who surrounded them. In this way the "preachers of the Gospel of Jesus Christ," or rather, disciples of iniquity, without hesitation attacked the unfortunate Indians, who were naked except for a cotton mantle, carrying nothing in their hands but flowers and feathers with which they had been dancing. All of these were killed; and when the other Aztecs saw this and fled to the gates, they were slain by the soldiers who were on guard there. Others tried to take refuge in the rooms of the temple, fleeing from those ministers of the devil. As they were unable to do so, all were slain and the courtyard was drenched with the blood of those wretched men. Everywhere were intestines, severed heads, hands and feet. Some men walked around with their entrails hanging out due to knife and lance thrusts. Verily it was a terrible thing to behold, the saddest thing one could imagine, especially when those dreadful screams and lamentations pierced the air! And no one there to aid them!

The entire city became frenzied, and the frightful wails of the women and children resounded in the mountains and were enough to make the stones burst from pain and pity. Eight or ten thousand men, the entire nobility of Mexico-Tenochtitlan, torn to pieces in the courtyard of the temple! They had done nothing to deserve this fate, unless they were being punished for having given of their possessions in abundance to feed and quench the thirst of the Spaniards.

When the priests saw the cruelty with which their own people were being treated and when they realized that the Spaniards were trying to ascend the steps of the pyramid, they knew that they too were soon to be massacred and that the image of the god was to be cast down the

The History of the Indies of New Spain

steps. They prepared to defend themselves and, on seeing the ascent of three or four Spaniards whose names I shall not record here, these Aztec priests brought out a large heavy beam and sent it rolling down the steps. But it is said that it stuck on the topmost stairs and its flight was arrested. This was held to be a miraculous thing, and so it was, for divine mercy did not wish those who had committed that wicked and cruel massacre to go straight to Hell but was desirous of giving them an opportunity to do penance—that is, if afterward they really did it. However, they were so lacking in sensitivity that they did not recognize the mercy of God in liberating them from this great peril and continued up the steps, killed all the priests, and cast down the idol of Huitzilopochtli. Many other barbaric acts were committed by them, always in the belief that they were serving God.

At this point [in the *Historia*] it says that some of the captains,[5] hearing the clamor of the women and children and the moaning of the entire city, began to sing the ballad:

> From the Tarpeian Rock
> Nero watched Rome on fire.
> Not even the tears of the women
> His pity did inspire . . .

All of the above I discovered in certain writings,[6] which tell that this was the most atrocious act ever committed in this land. It was the end of the flower and nobility of Tenochtitlan, where so many illustrious and courageous men died.

Motecuhzoma, seeing the treachery and deceit of the Spaniards, wept bitterly and asked the men who guarded him to kill him, for he knew that the Aztecs were wicked, vindictive people who might believe that he had advised the Spaniards to commit that evil act and who might slay him his children and his wives. He and all the others who were prisoners begged to be slain, and their wishes were to be granted later.

After this the Aztecs and the Tlatelolcas confederated and raised Cuauhtemoc, lord of Tlatelolco, to the kingship.[7] He was a youth about eighteen years old and a nephew of King Motecuhzoma. Everyone conspired against the dethroned Motecuhzoma and killed his wives and children. However, certain people had pity on his family; it is said that they managed to take them out of the city in secret. They were

---

[5]"Some of the captains" (*algunos capitanes*) replaces half a line that is crossed out and is written in a hand different from that of the rest of the manuscript (fol. 212v).

[6]A little more than a line is inked out here. Perhaps originally the "certain writings" (fol. 212v) were identified here.

[7]Cuitlahuac was made ruler in 1520, before Cuauhtemoc, but soon died of smallpox.

taken to towns in the country, where they remained concealed until the land was at peace again.

The new king, Cuauhtemoc, had grieved sorely over the death of his kinsmen in the massacre, so he gave orders that all the remaining men take up arms and prepare to attack the houses where the Spaniards were lodged. These houses were then surrounded by a great number of Indians with spears, stones, and arrows, and the attack was so fierce that the Spaniards did not dare appear in the doorways or on the roofs. The courtyards were filled with round stones that had been shot by the slings and that destroyed some of the walls. These courtyards were also filled with spears and arrows and the bonfires and torches lit by the Indians at night were so brilliant that it seemed like day. In this way they did not let the Spaniards rest or sleep and they could no longer obtain food supplies. Their plight was so desperate that they and Cortés repented having followed such bad advice [given by Alvarado].

During all this time Cuauhtemoctzin placed garrisons around the entire city, as he was determined that the Spaniards must die. He ordered all the neighboring towns, especially those that had not yet seen Cortés and his men, to be ready to be called to arms. Some of these towns were Tenayuca, Cuauhtitlan, Tula, Tulantzinco, the province of Xilotepec with all of Cuauhtlalpan and the Otomi towns, as well as those of the Matlatzinca region and people from the many towns in the Tezcoco province. He ordered them all to be prepared for war when they might be called. So great was the number of men who answered this call that, if God in His Mercy had not seen the tears of those who invoked Him, none of the Spaniards would have escaped with their lives. Their need for food was so great and their hopes of obtaining any help so slim that they were like men staring into the eyes of death. Among them there were different opinions. Should they go out and die fighting? Escape from the city was impossible! The metropolis was made up of canals with narrow bridges from house to house. These ditches were so deep that horses could not traverse them. Risking their lives, the foot soldiers tried several times to leave, but the rain of stones, darts, and spears was so furious that they were forced to return rapidly. Any barbed dart that entered the body could not be extracted save by pushing it through the flesh. All those who were wounded were in great danger.

During these days when the Spaniards were in deep affliction and dared not leave, the new ruler of Mexico, Cuauhtemoctzin, realized that the Aztecs were unable to force them to leave their quarters, nor could they enter those places because of the artillery that had been placed at the doors. Therefore, he called all the old men of the province and the enchanters and sorcerers and asked them to frighten the Spaniards by showing them nocturnal visions. In this way the Spaniards were to die of fright.

The wizards came and every night they conjured visions and frightful things. Sometimes the Spaniards would see human heads jumping about in the courtyard. At other times they would see a foot still attached to the leg, walking around. Or they beheld corpses rolling on the ground. At other times they heard screams and moans. At length the tension became unbearable. Before I read about these visions in the *Historia*, I had already heard of them from the lips of the conqueror who is now a friar, who had been greatly frightened by the mysterious apparitions.

So it was that the Spaniards became weary of so much sorrow and affliction, but no one knew what to do since Cortés came to no decisions. He said that he was waiting for the right moment. He encouraged his companions, promising them that they would soon find relief, and prayed to Our Lady of Remedies to alleviate the situation. Having great faith in this Virgin, Cortés decided to make Motecuhzoma appear in public and with his own lips command his people to be calm and cease their attacks. One day while the Aztecs were attacking fiercely, almost demolishing with stones the house where the Spaniards had taken refuge, Cortés and one of his soldiers (one carrying a leather shield and the other with a steel one) took Motecuhzoma to the flat roof of a housetop, next to the place where the Indians were fighting most fiercely. Protecting him with the shields, they led the Aztec lord to the edge of the roof, where Motecuhzoma made signs with his hands that the people should stop yelling since he wished to speak to them. There was silence and the assault upon the house ceased. The two shields that covered him were removed and in a loud voice he implored the people to stop attacking the Spaniards.

The Aztec captains who were in the front line, therefore the closest to him, began to insult him with ugly words, telling him that he was a mistress of the Spaniards and, as such, that he had helped them plan the massacre of the great warriors and brave lords. The Aztecs, then, no longer recognized Motecuhzoma as king; he and his children and wives, his whole lineage, were to be killed, erased from the face of the earth! With them would die the wicked Spaniards who had perpetrated such evil among them! Having said these things and before Motecuhzoma could be protected by the shields, one of the Aztecs threw a stone that struck Motecuhzoma high on the forehead. Although he was wounded, it was only a glancing blow that did little harm. Others say that at the same time he was injured by an arrow in one foot. This is mentioned by different authors though our chronicle says nothing about it. It is said to have been an account by a certain Indian. Motecuhzoma, wounded, was then carried down into the palace. His appearance before the crowd had no good effect because the people were possessed by a raging fury against the Spaniards.

The valorous young Cuauhtemoctzin appeared every day to encourage his people and to fight with them. Whenever a Tlaxcalan was captured by them, his life was not spared. The soldiers of Tlaxcala were in the same difficulties as the Spaniards and later were to suffer greatly. Few of them returned to Tlaxcala, as we shall see later on.

CHAPTER LXXVI

Which treats of how Don Hernán Cortés fled from his quarters and how the Indians were aware of his departure. With a description of how many Spaniards and Indians were killed in that flight.

We have already seen the difficulties in which the Aztecs placed Cortés and the other Spaniards. As they say, "where there is much misery there is little reason." And so Cortés struggled to find a way of escaping and freeing his companions from the plight they were in. To die and to be eaten by those who, with such fury, surrounded them now seemed their fate. Every day they were threatened, were told that their flesh would be devoured and that not one of them would escape. Many soldiers including some from the neighboring regions wept bitterly and complained of Don Pedro de Alvarado, who was to be blamed for the cruel massacre of the flower of Mexico-Tenochtitlan.

The killing in the temple courtyard was attributed solely to Alvarado, and a certain conqueror told me that, while Cortés was in Veracruz fighting with Narváez, in his absence Alvarado committed this atrocious massacre. However, I believe that this account may have been invented so that such an appalling act would not be attributed to a person who deserves to be praised and honored as one of the most valorous men among those who are distinguished by their integrity, in the entire world. What makes me think that in truth Cortés was not absent from the city at this time is that immediately after the massacre the Indians rebelled against the Spaniards and surrounded them, and not even a bird could have penetrated the city without having been seen, much less Cortés with Narváez's men who had increased his ranks. All of Tenochtitlan was up in arms at that time. Even if Cortés had returned at that moment with more men than he had when he left, I doubt that these would have been of much help because the Indians were so infuriated, so desirous of revenge, that life meant nothing to them.

Tenochtitlan had been founded on an island in the lake, the canals serving as streets, and small narrow bridges going from one house to another, thus making the city almost impregnable. The conqueror who was telling me this continued, saying that the day Cortés arrived, or maybe the next day, before the Indians rebelled against the Spaniards, they were and had been in peace, the Spaniards eating and drinking, being idle and enjoying life—but now after these tragic events they were in great danger. They were dying of hunger, were surrounded by so many Indians that they looked like swarms of ants, who had threatened them with a cruel fate, and who all day and night did nothing but wail and project strange visions. It was impossible for the Spanish soldiers to leave, nor could they use their weapons or their horses. They thought they were destined to die, for they considered the nightly visions to be bad omens, foretelling their death.

But Our God in his kindness and mercy sees not our evil acts but with pious will and open arms goes to the aid of those who call Him. This will went especially to those who had not been in agreement with such a great malevolence, such an enormous cruelty, nor had they given permission for those wrong deeds. Furthermore, divine will had been meant to save those miserable nations, to free them from pagan idolatry and bondage, therefore He went to the aid of the good captain. Cortés and his men had beseeched Him with all their hearts and especially had implored the blessed mother of sinners, our advocate, she who is the Queen of Angels, Our Lady of Remedies, to intercede in their behalf. Cortés begged for her help, and she responded, being truly one who remedies, as is her name. And so, through her intervention, when God had been placated by Cortés's prayers, one night He sent a great thunderstorm, precisely when it was needed. The storm was so intense, with tremendous winds, rain, and hail, that the Aztecs were forced to lift the siege and the sentinels' fires went out. All the people, fleeing from this terrible tempest, returned to their homes. When Cortés saw that this phenomenon had been willed by the great and pious Lord and by Our Lady of Remedies, to whom he had prayed, he ordered that everyone be quiet and that all leave the palace in order and silence. The Tlaxcalans and other friendly Indians would be their guides. On seeing that the torrential rains and the darkness favored them, the men began to go forth. Cortés ordered them not to carry any of the treasure or to be greedy in taking gold and jewels that might hinder their flight. He realized that anyone carrying these things would be unable to flee, and he told them to leave all the treasures since they would find them when they returned. He did, however, instruct them to carry all the bread they could as a provision until they had escaped across the boundaries of Aztec lands. This would be more useful than all the gold and riches they might take with them.

With this advice Cortés, in the utmost silence and secrecy, led his soldiers in orderly fashion, laden with bread and provisions. A number of men, though, did not carry provisions but loaded themselves and their horses with all the gold and jewels they could carry, which was a vast treasure they had found there. Some of the Indians and some of the Spanish soldiers were laden, then, with all that gold. When they departed from the buildings where they had been lodged, because of that treasure they were unable to move silently. An Indian man and woman happened to appear on one of the roofs and, seeing this, cried out, "Come out, Aztecs! The criminals are escaping! Come forth, the traitors are fleeing!"

When these cries were heard, all the Aztec men of war who were still in the city, together with those who had come in from the provinces, emerged, giving chilling cries, frightful enough to trouble the strongest heart. The Spaniards most shaken were those who carried no arms but were laden with gold. Their panic was such that many of them turned back toward the palace from which they had emerged, where they tried to entrench themselves again. Others, having already passed some of the bridges, tried to turn back but found the bridges lifted. The Indians fell upon both groups, rabid with anger, and killed every one of them, both the Spaniards who tried to flee over the bridges and those who had taken refuge in the palace chambers. On this occasion Cortés lost seven hundred men, all of them cut to pieces mercilessly. The canals were filled with corpses, with horses, and with dead Indians, both men and women, together with gold and gems, mantles, feathers, and other riches that the wretched Spaniards had tried to carry with them.

Leading the six hundred survivors, Cortés managed to pass the last of the bridges swiftly and gain safety. There he organized his followers, the natives and Spaniards who had escaped. The Aztecs were still following them, yelling and shooting stones, arrows, and darts. Little by little but in good order the Spaniards retreated as far as a place now called Our Lady of Remedies. They arrived there exhausted, wounded, and filled with affliction. Many of them had lost their shoes along the way and they wet the earth with blood from their feet. Others had lost their hats and their heads were exposed to the burning sun. Some had been severely wounded by the stones and spears thrown by the enemy.

Cortés was filled with sorrow over the men he had lost. He almost resolved to go back to save those who might be alive but realized that all must have perished. However, the *Historia* relates that many of the soldiers who took refuge in the palace held out bravely for a few days but finally, lacking direction, advice, and above all the presence of their courageous leader, they died at the hands of the Indians. I pray to God that these men were not those who had planned the vicious massacre of the Aztec lords and that He did not blind them in their flight in order to punish them for this atrocious act.

The *Historia* tells us that once the Spaniards had fled from Mexico and those who had remained behind had been killed, the Aztecs entered the chambers of King Motecuhzoma in order to treat him with the same cruelty that had been inflicted upon the Spaniards. There they found him dead with a chain about his feet and five dagger wounds in his chest. Near him lay many noblemen and great lords who had been held prisoner with him. All of them had been slain shortly before the Spanish soldiers abandoned the building. If it were not that the *Historia* states all these things and a certain painted document verifies them, I would find it difficult to believe. However, I am obliged to record what the authors tell, write, or paint, therefore, I put down what I find written and painted. I wish to avoid being blamed for having stated something false that the conquerors had not said or written, since it was generally believed that Motecuhzoma had been stoned to death. In order to clear up this point to my satisfaction, I again asked my informant and insisted that some writers had said Motecuhzoma had been killed with stones. But I was told that the wound from the stone had been nothing, the head wound had healed quickly, and that in truth he had been found knifed.

This was the tragic end of Motecuhzoma and of the other rulers and lords who had been captives with him in the palace.[1] In this way the omens and prophecies that he himself had revealed were fulfilled—an amazing thing, only permitted by the Most High. It seems that He wished to inflict a rigorous punishment on Motecuhzoma for his intolerable tyranny, cruelty, the abominable and unspeakable vices in which he lived, more than any man in the history of the world.

Some say that the dead king was given a rich and solemn burial and that the funeral lasted many days and was attended by numerous lords and dignitaries. However, according to the *Historia*, the cadavers of Motecuhzoma and all the others were burned and turned to dust, without honors or solemnity of any kind. It adds that in order to make the vengeance complete his children and wives were sought out and killed. This powerful Angry Lord, this unfortunate king, ruled sixteen and a half years. His death took place in the year in which the Spaniards reached this land.

Because Motecuhzoma was imprisoned and then killed, his nephew Cuauhtemoc, son of the lord of Santiago Tlatelolco, became ruler.[2]

[1] Durán uses the word *calpules* instead of *palacio* or *casas reales*. *Calpules* or *calpulli* would refer to different neighborhoods, that is, the "other lords" would have been held captive each in his own barrio, but it makes more sense that they were imprisoned together with Motecuhzoma and all killed at the same time by the fleeing Spaniards.

[2] See chapter LXXV, note 7, regarding Cuitlahuac.

The History of the Indies of New Spain

Due to the death of his father, he also governed Tlatelolco at that time. When Cuauhtemoc saw that the siege had been fairly successful because more than half of the Spaniards had been killed, he nevertheless rebuked the carelessness of the guards for having sought shelter indoors on the night of the storm, without having left other guards to keep the Spaniards from escaping. In order to prevent further flight of the Spanish soldiers, he sent messengers to all the neighboring towns asking that they send men to join the Aztecs on the plain of Otumba. There they would cut off the retreat of the surviving Spaniards and kill them as they passed on their way back to Tlaxcala. When this message was heard in towns of Otumba and Teotihuacan and in the Otomi settlements in that area, so many Indians appeared upon the plain in order to cut off the Spaniards' retreat that they eclipsed the sun.

The Spaniards—sad, distressed, disconsolate, and fearful, many of them ill, wounded, without shoes, and dying of hunger and thirst—left what is today the shrine of Our Lady of Remedies. Cortés gave this name to that place to show that by that Lady's blessed hand they had been saved. The captain and his men and allies believed that with their departure from the city and province of Mexico they were safe. But as they approached the plain of Otumba a multitude of Indians appeared suddenly, covering those plains, making grimaces and furious signs at them and leaping about, shaking their swords and throwing spears and stones. When the Spaniards saw this great throng, they almost lost their senses, believing the end had come. But the courageous Don Hernán rebuked them for their cowardice and fear and showed once more his spirit that was more than human. He reminded them that he[3] had saved them from past trials and promised them that he would do so now. He encouraged and consoled his followers with spirited words. The Spaniards formed a close-knit group, facing the enemy on all sides, more on the defensive than the offensive because they were surrounded and were being constantly attacked.

It was at this moment that Cortés saw a banner flying on a small hill in the plain and next to it an Aztec captain who, judging by his insignia and weapons, was a man of great valor and rank. This man spurred on his soldiers from the hill and inspired by him the Indians found their strength, attacking and greatly harming the Spaniards. Cortés then leapt on a colt that one of his soldiers had brought along. This beast had been barely tamed and was strong and spirited. With a lance in his hand, crying out to Our Lord with invincible faith, Cortés alone—in what the other soldiers saw as a rash action—charged against the

[3]In the 1967 edition of Durán, Garibay (p. 557) capitalizes this "he," making it a reference to God, but in the manuscript (fol. 215v) it is not capitalized; therefore it must refer to Cortés.

Indians. He passed through their ranks and reached the place where the man stood with the banner. The other Aztec had not been able to stop him, so when Cortés reached this point he struck the man with his lance. The enemy captain fell to the ground dead. When his followers saw this, they all dispersed and began to abandon the field. But Cortés attacked them again, indicating to his horsemen that they should follow him. These men then rode about the field, attacking and killing many of the Indians who had fled. A great number of these were killed, including Otomis and others from Tula, Otumba, Cuauhtitlan, Tenayuca, and Tlalnepantla, all of whom had faced the Spaniards.

It is certain that if Cortés had not performed this feat the Spanish army would have been in grave danger. Cuauhtemoc had commanded the Chalcas, Tezcocans, and Tepanecs, on pain of death, to send reinforcements to the soldiers of Cuauhtlalpan and all the others who were fighting the Spaniards. This command was so severe that the Chalcas, Xochimilcas, Tepanecs, and Tezcocans prepared themselves for war and could not avoid going to join the fighting. But, just when they were about to leave for the battle, news came that their allies had been routed and the Spaniards were firmly entrenched in Otumba, together with the Tlaxcalans, who had aided them greatly. Therefore, the different armies dispersed, each one returning to its own city.

Cuauhtemoc was crowned in Tenochtitlan with solemn rites and the inhabitants of the city swore allegiance to him as king. However, this was not done with the rejoicing and solemnity that had been usual in the past, for the city was filled with sorrow, the entire land was troubled and divided against itself. Some wished to make peace with the Spaniards, while others wanted war. Some wished to destroy the strangers and were preparing their fighting equipment and were building walls and dikes. But others remained passive, asking only for peace, quiet, and the preservation of their lives and possessions.

For a long time the Spaniards remained in Tlaxcala, healing their wounds, making plans and seeking a way to return to Mexico-Tenochtitlan as conquerors. This lasted for more than one year, and meanwhile more ships filled with Spaniards arrived in Veracruz. During this time Cuauhtemoc, who felt great hatred toward the Spaniards, tried to gain the support of his people. He devoted himself to making the canals deeper, building wide, tall dikes, and inciting the natives against the invaders. His activity was so furious that he went to the extreme of sending messages many times to the rulers of Tlaxcala, asking them to forget their friendship with the Spaniards and rebel against them in order to expel them from the land, or to kill them. He was so insistent that one of the lords of Tlaxcala became persuaded and instigated the others to join in this plan, to heed

Cuauhtemoc's plea. Cortés, however, discovered the plot and denounced them all, whereupon the three other Tlaxcalan rulers delivered to the Spanish captain the man who was most inclined to kill him and his companions [and who had stirred up animosity against them]. Cortés put him in prison and, I believe, finally had him executed.

When Cuauhtemoc realized that he was unable to convince the Tlaxcalans to slaughter the Spaniards and that all his diligent pleas brought no results, he sent threats to Tlaxcala telling the people there what he would do to them if he were victorious. He also attempted to attract the people of Chalco, Xochimilco, Tacuba, and Tezcoco, but Cortés, too, was busy making allies among these nations. He sent word to these cities, saying that he had come to liberate them from the tyranny of Mexico-Tenochtitlan and the oppression in which they had lived. When he added that their friendship with the Aztecs had not been of their own choice but had been forced upon them, they decided to become friends with the Spaniards, and not their enemies. All believed that they would be given their freedom and be liberated from the servitude of Tenochtitlan.

At this time Cuauhtemoc learned that the Spanish forces were multiplying and that Cortés had sent for help and that all these men were readying themselves, preparing to return to the city. The news also came that the Tezcocans had declared themselves allies of the foreigners and that Chalco, Xochimilco, and Tacuba had also done this. Cuauhtemoc therefore filled the city with soldiers, the most valiant and brave men he could find. He explained to them that now the Chalcas, Tepanecs, Xochimilcas, and Tezcocans were enemies, so it was no longer wise to wait but they must triumph or die.

Cuauhtemoc sent for help to other cities and soon Tenochtitlan swelled with brave warriors. They came from the province of Cuauhtlalpan and from towns in the area of Cuauhtitlan, which alone remained antagonistic to the Spaniards. Other soldiers were of the Tlalhuica people of the Hot Country (today the Marquesado) and they came from the towns of Yacapichtlan, Huaxtepec, Yauhtepec, Tepoztlan, Cuauhnahuac, Tlayacapan, and Totolapan, with their subject towns. All these were hostile to the Spaniards, though Cortés later subjected them one by one. Those towns did not yield to the Spanish forces until Cortés entered their country, killing and destroying all those he encountered. They then abandoned their homes and fled into the hills.

All that happened in the Hot Country, however, took place after Tenochtitlan had been conquered and the people subjugated. In the next chapter we shall see how Cortés, after he had gained the goodwill of most of the people in the land and more men had joined his ranks, returned to Tenochtitlan and captured that city.

CHAPTER LXXVII

Which treats of how Cortés came from Tlaxcala to Texcoco, with a description of how he built brigantines there and then went on to Tenochtitlan. And how King Cuauhtemoc defended himself with great valor.

Cuauhtemoc now saw that the Spaniards were determined to return to Tenochtitlan. The vigilant ruler discovered this through his spies and messengers. While he instigated the other nations and asked for their aid, he and his people also offered sacrifice to the gods. They beseeched the gods to succor them and give them victory against the Spaniards and their other enemies. But it was too late. Even their gods were silent, the oracles became mute. It was the general opinion that the gods had become mute or had died since the new divinities had taken away their strength; they now had no power. The Aztecs wept bitterly. Nevertheless, they had not given up their intentions to defend their city or die in the effort.

This is an example of the Indian way. Once an Indian decides to achieve something and begins to look with scorn upon life, he loses all fear and does not give up until he accomplishes what he desires. It would be easy to prove my assertion because in our own courts we deal with such cases every day. If one town has a lawsuit against another, or a small town against its capital, or a peasant against his master, each will fight to the death or until he has accomplished what he wants. It does not matter if the objective is unjust or unreasonable. The Indian is headstrong and stubborn. In cases such as these he does not respect his father, brother, kinsman, or friend.

So it was that Cuauhtemoc, anxious to reign and to show his courage, decided to defend his city to the death. He was unwilling to listen to the messages and pleas of Cortés—which were sent many times—asking him to surrender in the name of God and His Majesty, begging him not to be the cause of the destruction and death that would follow his resistance. When Cortés realized that his pleas went unheeded, he decided to journey to Tezcoco to build the ships that could enter Mexico by way of the lake. This decision was a wise one. I believe it was the principal reason for his subsequent conquest of the city, which was surrounded by water, canals, and great pools, in which horses were of no use. In this way Cortés left Tlaxcala with his men and followed by large numbers of Tlaxcalans, Huexotzincas, and Cholulans, all of them enemies of the Aztecs. Along with them came the Tezcocans, now friends of the Spaniards, bringing cargo and the wood with which the brigs were to be built. Between the carriers of wood and equipment there were more than ten thousand natives.

Cortés arrived first at a place that is now caled Tezmeluca, near the White Mountain and not far from the boundary of Chalco. The Chalcas received him again with honor, offering him jewels, mantles, fine feathers, and food supplies. They also made a pact with him, promising to aid him in the assault on Tenochtitlan. The Spanish captain thanked them and told them they would be recompensed. He stated that he was on his way to Tezcoco to build the brigantines and that he would be grateful if they would send him men to carve the wood in order to carry out that task quickly. They promised to furnish him with carpenters and this they did. Cortés then departed for Tezcoco, where he was welcomed with honors and ceremony. Here he rested and had time to admire that remarkable and populous city with all its fine and beautifully fashioned buildings, palaces, homes of the lords, great pyramids and temples, all very splendid; also the pleasure gardens with their pools and marvelous groves. All of these belonged to the previous rulers and noblemen of Tezcoco, who delighted in them.

In Tezcoco Cortés was welcomed and given quarters and was served with respect and reverence, especially by Ixtlilxochitl, son of Nezahualpilli and brother of King Coanacochtzin. Ixtlilxochitl pleased Cortés and served him so assiduously that the Spaniards took a strong liking to him, kept him near them, and honored him in a way befitting a son of the great Nezahualpilli and brother of one who was as honorable and valiant as his father and who was said to be one of the greatest rulers of Tezcoco. Cortés valued Ixtlilxochitl's friendship and took him to Tenochtitlan after having given him a gilded sword and a shield. During the conquest the Tezcocan performed great deeds, so daring that on hearing the name "Ixtlilxochitl" the Aztecs fled as would the devil on hearing the name of Christ. Later, when Cortés had seen his remarkable feats and the enormous aid he had given in the conquest, he made Ixtlilxochtil lord of Tezcoco after the death of his brother Coanacochtzin. According to the rulings the people had in those times it was Ixtlilxochitl's right to rule anyway, for he was then the legitimate lord [after his brother's death].

Cortés lingered in Tezcoco until the brigs of war were completed. During this time a number of Spaniards arrived in Veracruz and this was a great satisfaction to him because he needed assistance. When the ships had been finished under the direction of Martín López, Cortés prepared to attack. He divided his men into four companies: the first he himself was to lead and was to attack by way of Coyoacan;

the second was to be commanded by Don Pedro de Alvarado and was to proceed by the road that went by Our Lady of Remedies, which is the causeway to Tacuba; the third was to travel by way of the road of Our Lady of Guadalupe; and the fourth company was to go aboard the brigs. In this order the march toward the city began. The allies were attached to the four companies and they came from Tlaxcala, Huexotzinco, Cholula, Tezcoco, Chalco, Xochimilco, and Tacuba. All of these soldiers were well equipped and they marched in good order. They were to fight against those people who had subjected them, whose vassals they had been, and they knew that if the enterprise failed their destiny would be perpetual and cruel misery.

Cuauhtemoctzin, sovereign of Mexico-Tenochtitlan, on seeing that the entire country was beginning to rise up against him and that the moment had come when not only his hands were needed but that his spirit and heart were perhaps more useful, spoke to his people: "O courageous Aztecs, you have seen how all our subjects have rebelled against us! Our enemies used to be the people of Tlaxcala, Cholula, and Huexotzinco, but now we must contend with Tezcoco, Chalco, Xochimilco, and the Tepanecs. All the latter have abandoned us and have gone to join the Spaniards; now they come against us. I charge you now to remember the bold hearts and spirits of the Mexica-Aztec-Chichimecs, our ancestors. Though they were few in number they arrived in this land and dared to enter this territory. They appeared in the midst of many millions of people and with their powerful arms conquered this great new world and all its nations. Not a distant coast or province was neglected by them, all fell into their hands! They risked their lives in order to glorify our names. That is why the Aztec name has reached the renown and excellence that it now conveys and is feared throughout the world. Therefore, O valorous Aztecs, do not be dismayed, do not be cowardly. Strengthen your chests and hearts in order to embark upon the most important enterprise that has ever been presented to you. Behold, if you do not succeed in this, you, your wives and children, will become slaves forever. And your possessions will be stripped from you. Have pity on the aged, on the children, on the orphans! If you do not defend them with the valor of your persons and the love of your country, they will be left unprotected and in the hands of your enemies, to be torn to pieces or cast into slavery. Do not scorn me because of my extreme youth, but consider that what I am telling you is the truth. It is your duty to defend your city and your homeland, and I promise you I shall not forsake them until I win back freedom or die."

With great zeal all promised to follow his example, and the valorous youth, in his invincible determination to die rather than be enslaved, filled the city with his followers. However, he did not foresee the need to provide food in order to maintain so many men and, as the Spaniards and his other enemies blocked all the entrances, by water or by land, food was very soon lacking. So it was that more people died of hunger than by the sword. I have heard it said that a handful of golden jewels or of precious stones was exchanged for a handful of maize. Certain noblemen from nearby provinces managed to enter the city secretly in order to exchange maize for the jewels of Tenochtitlan. Men from Cuitlahuac, Colhuacan, Mezquic, and the city of Xochimilco became rich in gold, jewels, stones, and feathers because of the hunger caused by the above.

In this way the greatest enemy of the people was hunger and the impossibility of acquiring food supplies. Some of the soldiers were forced to flee from the city and return to their lands, leaving King Cuauhtemoc alone with the Aztecs. These were few, and they were feeble from starvation. It is to be noted that these Indian people become thinner than any other people on earth when they lack victuals.

Cortés and his captains were now at the gates of Tenochtitlan, each one having come along the road that had been agreed upon. The dikes were covered with armed Aztecs, however, and the canals with warriors in canoes, all awaiting the Spaniards without showing the slightest sign of cowardice. King Cuauhtemoc, who directed the maneuvers like the general of the entire army, divided his people into four parts so that they might meet the Spaniards at any one of the causeways and thus defend the entrance to the city. The king, in his small canoes, flew from one place to another to observe the activities of his men.

The Spaniards began to attack the city by tearing down the dikes that had been built next to the canals. They gained land by filling in the water with earth, blocks of mud, and stones, together with adobe bricks from the houses they demolished. But the diligence and hard work of the Aztecs to counteract this was extraordinary: as soon as a canal was filled in by the Spaniards to be used as a bridge for the horses, they opened it again. Each morning the canals would be found free of rubble, deeper than ever, and all the solid land that the Spaniards had gained the day before would be lost.

Now it is time to tell how the Aztecs, surrounded and harassed by a multitude of men, decided to build a trap for the enemy. And the main reason for this trap was to obtain an outlet through which they could seek help and provisions. They realized that the best place to set it would be on the Tacuba causeway, since on that side there were people who would help them. There they placed a false bridge so that, when the Spaniards and the other enemies passed, the bridge would collapse and the Aztecs could then fall upon them and slaughter them all. So they set to work to construct this trap. The false bridge was set up in the place where the shrine and hospital of Saint Hippolytus now stand. There was a wide and navigable canal at that place that the Spaniards had filled in so they could pass over it. But that night the Aztecs opened it again, made it as deep as possible, and built over it a false bridge made of wooden beams and boards. It was set up in such a way that the enemy soldiers would think that it had been unchanged since they had left it the day before. The Aztecs prepared an ambush of numerous men, all in canoes that were hidden by the reeds and rushes. All were well equipped with swords, shields, and spears, and many of them carried swords and lances they had taken from Spaniards who had been killed. On one side of this false pass many warriors gathered, calling to their opponents on the other side and provoking them to attack. They made faces at them, yelling offensive words and mocking them with gestures and motions of their bodies.

Cortés had ordered that no one move or attack until he commanded and the trumpet was sounded. But Don Pedro de Alvarado, whose heart rebelled against the contempt and scorn shown him by the Indians, did not wait for the signal. He immediately gave orders that his Spaniards and the Tlaxcalan allies attack the bridge. The Aztecs pretended to flee and the Spaniards followed them, forty foot soldiers, all of them spirited youths, together with a few horsemen and their captain Alvarado and many Indians. When the bridge was laden with men and horses, the Aztecs who lay in ambush pulled the false bridge from their canoes on which it had rested and which had supported the structure. The entire thing collapsed into the water, together with the Spaniards and Indians who stood upon it.

Shouting "Tenochtitlan! Tenochtitlan! Fight, valiant Aztecs!" the natives fell upon the invaders, and those who tried to return across the bridge found that it had fallen into the water. A multitude of Aztecs were attacking and they spared no lives. All were in canoes, and none of the Spaniards were able to escape because they were trapped in the canal and there was no one on either side who could help pull them out. Therefore, they were taken prisoner.

Don Pedro de Alvarado was able to escape by sinking the point of his lance into the bodies of the dead who lay in the water and leaping to the other side of the ditch. This is what is called the famous "Leap of Alvarado."

The forty Spanish soldiers who had been taken were immediately stripped and led up the steps of the great *cu* in front of the entire Spanish army. No one could aid them in any way and they were sacrificed there. Their chests were cut open, their hearts were torn out and offered to the idols, and finally their bodies were rolled down the steps of the temple. The Spaniards who witnessed this sacrifice wept aloud and screamed to God that He take pity on their companions and save them, but this did not happen.

When Cortés heard the cries and uproar, he hurried with some of his men to the place where the bridge had been, and he did this risking his life. The Indians who moved about in their canoes were, with great fury, killing the Spaniards who still were in the canal. Cortés tried to help a wounded soldier who was still defending himself in the water when two enemy soldiers came up to him. As Cortés turned to face one of them, the other sprang at him from behind and held him by the back, while the first one tried to wound him from the front. Both the Aztecs struggled with him, trying to drag him into deeper waters. It was at this point that a Biscayan page of Cortés rushed up with his sword drawn and, striking at the Indian who held the captain, cut off his arm at one blow. When the other Aztec saw himself attacked he let go of the captain, who managed to escape. However, the page was attacked by many of the native soldiers, who tore him to pieces, Cortés not being able to save him.

When the Spanish captain beheld this bloody and dangerous skirmish, he gave orders that his men retreat, while the Indians remained triumphant. Cortés felt like hanging or decapitating Alvarado because of his rash attack without waiting for the signal.

Thus ended the battle and both Spaniards and Indians withdrew. The Indians, however, managed to keep as prisoners several of the Spanish soldiers whom they had pulled out of the canal during the battle. Among them was a young gentleman who, according to what the conquerors have told me, was a handsome Sevillian who always fought with his crossbow in his hands. The next day the Aztecs brought him out with their warriors. He still carried his crossbow and was made to shoot at his countrymen. However, with a demeanor, he shot in such a way that every arrow whistled harmlessly through the air, not one of them touching the Spanish soldiers. When the Aztecs realized what he was doing, they ripped him to bits then and there. Because of him a shrine was later built on the spot by the conquerors, and it was called "The Martyr," the walls of which are still standing. Whether the martyrdom of this youth was acceptable to God or not, only His Divine Majesty knows! But my own opinion is that it is an evil thing to preach the faith, sword in hand, taking by force what belongs to others.

I wish to return to my subject, as my topic is the Aztec nation, its great deeds and its tragic end. And I shall not stop to tell of the tragic events that occurred during the eighty days it took the Spaniards to conquer Tenochtitlan. However, I shall mention two things. The first is that the *Historia* states that, when Cortés saw that the Aztecs were resisting so fiercely and holding out so long, he asked the Tlaxcalans to bring all the fighting men they could. When they arrived, he commanded them to enter the city in order to expel the Aztecs. But, though they fought an entire day, they were unable to enter Tenochtitlan. On the second day he ordered the Tezcocans to attack, but they failed also. On the third day Cortés called the Chalcas to him, and Marina addressed them in Cortés's name: "O valorous men of Chalco, you have now seen how neither Tlaxcalans nor Tezcocans have been able to enter the city and displace the Aztecs. I beseech you to take charge of this enterprise today and do everything in your power so that we may capture the Great Temple of Huitzilopochtli and entrench ourselves there. I charge you to be men of bravery and great spirit."

The Chalcas were encouraged by these words and, leading the army together with Ixtlilxochitl of Tezcoco, who carried his golden sword in his hand, they attacked the Aztecs furiously. In this they were aided by the Spaniards, who used their arquebuses, artillery, and crossbows. Having rapidly filled in some places where bridges had been, they made an entrance and managed to take the Great Temple of the city. It was there that they established themselves, and they also gained the palace that had been abandoned before.

Having occupied the temple, the Spaniards placed guards in order to avoid being surrounded again. Cuauhtemoc now lacked men and strength to defend himself and the city, but, enraged over the death of so many of his people, because so many of his allies had abandoned him, had fled the city, and because of the great hunger they had suffered, he decided not to show weakness or cowardice. He pretended that he did not lack warriors to fight for him and therefore had all the women of the city take up shields and swords. Early in the morning the women ascended to the flat roofs of the houses, where they made gestures of scorn to the Spaniards. Leading the allies from Tlatelolco, brave Cuauhtemoc brought his few remaining men to face the enemy.

When Cortés saw the great number of people covering the flat roofs and filling the streets of the city, he became afraid and feared that he would not be able to conquer Mexico without causing harm to his Spaniards and friends. But he urged the Chalcas, Tezcocans, Tlaxcalans, and Tepanecs of Tacuba to take courage and finish with the enterprise. All the men returned to the combat and at this time they realized that the warriors who stood on the roofs were women. They sent word to Cortés about this and then began to ridicule and insult the enemy and attack and kill many of them. However, the men of Tlatelolco did everything in their power to defend themselves and killed numerous enemy Indians and some Spaniards, among them a lieutenant from whom they snatched the banner, tearing it to pieces in front of the entire army. This took place in a barrio now called San Martín. In another document I read that they destroyed four Spanish flags and killed a captain by the last name of Guzmán and that the Tlatelolcas won much glory in this battle.

In the end, though, the Spaniards, greatly aided by their Indian allies, vanquished the Aztecs and made the courageous King Cuauhtemoc flee. Cuauhtemoc boarded a small canoe, covered himself with a straw mat, and was rowed out of the city by only one man. He was taken prisoner, however, by some Spanish soldiers who saw him from their brig and then brought him before Cortés. When Cortés faced this youth, a man of refinement and handsome appearance, he said to Marina, the interpreter, "Ask Cuauhtemoc why he permitted the destruction of the city with such loss of lives of his own people and of ours? Many were the times I begged him for peace!"

The young king answered:

> Tell the captain
> that I have done my duty;
> I have defended my city, my kingdom,
> just as he would have defended his
> had I attempted to take it from him.
> But I have failed!
> Now that I am his captive,
> let him take this dagger
> and kill me with it!

Putting forth his hand, Cuauhtemoc took a dagger that Cortés carried in his belt and placed it in the captain's hands, begging to be slain.[1] Cortés was greatly troubled by these words and, though he did not rise from his seat, he spoke soft and consoling words to Cuauhtemoc and made him sit next to him.

The entire city then surrendered to Cortés, and when he took possession of it he went to live in the principal palace of Motecuhzoma, which now belongs to [the heirs of] the Spanish captain. He put guards about the city and gave liberty to Cuauhtemoc to go where he wished, telling him to ask for whatever he might desire, that it would be granted him. Cuauhtemoc asked him to free the men, women, and

---

[1] Eduardo Matos Moctezuma (personal communication) notes that Cuauhtemoc insisted on being slain by Cortés at this point because, according to Aztec tradition, this was the only honorable way for a soldier to die: if the enemy killed him on the field or sacrificed him after his capture, he would spend his time in the afterlife escorting the sun across the sky.

children whom the Spaniards had captured, many of whom had fled the city because of the famine. Cortés then made a public announcement that, under pain of death, all his men must liberate those who were being held captive. So it was done and all the refugees, men and women, returned to the city and resettled in it.

But the dead on that day were over forty thousand men and women, who, rather than fall into the hands of the Spaniards, knowing of the cruel death they could meet at the hands of those men and their Indian allies, threw themselves and their children into the canals. The stench of the corpses was so great that, even though bodies were continually disposed of outside the city, many were left and the evil smell was unbearable for a long time.

CHAPTER LXXVIII

Which treats of how Don Hernán Cortés, Marqués del Valle, after having conquered Mexico-Tenochtitlan left that city in good order. And how he set out to conquer other provinces, sending people to many different regions. With a description of the death of Cuauhtemoctzin.

Valiant Don Hernán Cortés conquered Mexico-Tenochtitlan on the feast of Saint Hippolytus, three days before the Assumption of the Most Blessed Virgin, Our Lady. It is said that She appeared during the conquest in order to aid the Spaniards. It is also told that the glorious patron of Spain, Santiago [or Saint James], appeared also, just the same as his image is now seen in the church of Tlatelolco. The Indians claim that they saw him in the fiercest of the battles when the Spaniards were losing and their banners had been taken from them and were being destroyed, to their great shame. At that moment the glorious Saint James appeared, frightening away the Indians and favoring the Spaniards through divine intervention.

Once the Aztec capital had been taken in the name of His Majesty, Cortés ordered that the temples be demolished, the idols broken, the city razed, and the canals filled in. He divided the land into lots, having ordered the people of Chalco, Tezcoco, Xochimilco, and Tacuba to bring stakes, stone, earth, and other materials to fill in the lagoons and pools that existed. He also laid out streets and had houses built to the best of his knowledge. He considered it safer to found a city where Mexico-Tenochtitlan had been, within the lake instead of outside it, for the strength of the country was concentrated in the capital and all the people were ruled from there. He was afraid that if the site of the city was to be changed there might be a rebellion.

While the new city was being planned and Cortés rested, the Spaniards began to seek the treasure that had been found in the secret chambers. The Tlatelolcas, by command of their leader, had concealed it in a deep pool in the city that the Aztecs feared, due to a certain religious superstition. It was believed that this spring was the place discovered by their ancestors, where the red and blue waters flowed, where lived the white fish, the white frogs, the white snakes. This pool was never seen by the Spaniards, nor has anyone ever discovered its exact location.[1] In order to find it Cortés ordered that many Indians be hunted down by dogs, others hanged, and yet others be burned alive so that the secret might be revealed. However, it never came to light, nor has it been discovered in our times. In fact, it never will be found, as those who might have known about it are no longer alive. If this secret is in the possession of anyone, it would belong to the lords of Tlatelolco, to whom it was entrusted. For this treasure the conquerors wept more tears than for the wicked deeds they had committed. They also searched in the canals where many Spaniards laden with gold had lost their lives. But as the Indians had cleaned out and deepened the canals in order to defend their city, all the gold had been removed. It is also true that the Spaniards who had been most heavily burdened with gold had fled back to the palace, where they had hidden before, in order to entrench themselves.

One curious case tells of a horseman who in his flight carried a coffer of jewels and gold on his saddle. He embraced this box with more fervor and desire than he would have embraced the Cross of Christ. One of the conquerors told me that, in spite of the danger this man was in, the conqueror saw him weep when the Indians attacked because the other Spanish soldiers had called out to him to drop the coffer and take hold of his sword to defend himself. He did not want to let go of the gold, however, so he placed it under one arm while he took his sword with the other. But with this impediment he could not fight and, still embracing the treasure, he was killed by the Indians. It may be said that greed was the cause of his perdition. All the gold was recovered by the Indians, who concealed it and divided it among themselves. And it reminds one of the proverb: "In a troubled river the fisherman catches many fish."

After the city had been leveled, after the Spaniards had begun to build their homes in it, the most Christian Don Hernán, Marqués del Valle, saw to it that the natives were instructed in the things of the faith. He indicated sites where churches were to be built, where crosses and images were to be set up, and he ordered that the Indians be taught the doctrines of our Holy Catholic faith. All this was begun by a cleric whom Cortés had brought with him, though it

[1] Expression in prehispanic Mexico was full of metaphor and symbolism. When the chronicles refer to red (or yellow) waters and blue waters, these have ancestor value, a legitimation of power, inasmuch as some of the roots of this image are found in Teotihuacan. Also, these waters of two colors are metaphors for government, for rulership, according to the *Florentine Codex* (1969:book 6). Although most modern editions of Durán's *Historia* say that the Tlaxcalans had concealed the Aztec treasure, the Madrid manuscript clearly states that the *Tlatelolcas* did this, a logical statement since the Tlatelolcas were Aztecs defending the twin cities while the Tlaxcalans were the invading enemy.

is my opinion that this man should have been suspended or excommunicated since I heard that he was more eager to wash his hands in the blood of innocents than Pilate to wash his hands at the death of Christ.

But let us forget my moralizing. The conversion of the natives was beginning and, in order to carry this out more efficiently, a ship was sent to Spain to inform his Catholic Majesty, the Emperor Charles V of happy memory, then king of Spain, that this land had been conquered in his most serene name. I have heard a trustworthy person say, however, that some advised Cortés not to send any messages to Spain but to crown himself king of New Spain. These persons promised to pay allegiance to him and obey him; but like a true subject of His Majesty, he refused to commit such an act against his oath of obedience.

Cortés also asked that friars be sent to administer the sacraments, and these were chosen carefully and dispatched to Mexico. So it was that twelve friars of the Order of the glorious Saint Francis arrived in this land three years after the conquest. The "Twelve Apostles" [as they were called] gained many converts because of their religious and holy lives, like the original apostles whom they imitated in everything. They preached and baptized in all the provinces with apostolic zeal, filled with spirit and divine fervor. Each barefoot friar went off on foot to a different region and each was such a perfect example of virtue that in this way they drew the nations to them. These natives were much moved by the words, labors, and abnegation shown by the Franciscan friars.

Two years after these saintly friars had come (or five years after the conquest), men from the Order of Our Glorious Father Saint Dominic also arrived, and they were no less holy or zealous in promoting the honor of God and gaining souls. These friars came from the island of Santo Domingo, which is also called Hispaniola. They took charge of the work of conversion (after all, that is why they had come) and obtained privileges and exemptions in order to protect the natives. They fought the great cruelty and inhumanity that the Spaniards had discharged upon these natives, although most of those evil deeds had already been committed.

After Cortés had conquered the Valley of Mexico, he went forth to subdue other provinces, especially those we now call the Marquesado, the hot country. This land defended itself for many days, its ruler being the lord of Yacapichtlan, who was a son or grandson of the great Tlacaelel, of whom the *Historia* speaks many times and whose great deeds I have described. The lords of Yacapichtlan are of his lineage. The inhabitants of that land fled to the rocky cliffs of Tlayacapan,

Totolapan, and Tepoztlan; but when the artillery began to be active and the natives fell from the cliffs, the Indians disbanded and fled into the hills. As Cortés conquered these towns, he divided them among the conquerors in the name of His Majesty.

Here is a story I was told about a woman who accompanied Cortés's army and who later was married to Martín Partidor. As Cortés was leaving Huaxtepec after having subdued the entire hot country, he passed through Ocuituco, where he was received in peace. After this he ascended to a town called Tetela, where the Indians were lined up in order to fight, having much confidence in the rugged nature of the place. Other Indians from Hueyapan, which faced Tetela across a deep ravine, also appeared in warlike manner. When Cortés saw these forces, he ordered his men to prepare themselves. But this Spanish woman, advised by certain soldiers, mounted a horse, took a lance and leather shield, and asked the Spanish captain for permission to attack the Indians and demonstrate her personal valor. Cortés granted her this, whereupon she came forth and, spurring on the horse, she attacked the enemy, shouting, "Saint James, and at them!" The foot soldiers then followed her; when the Indians saw them all coming, some fled and others fell into the ravine. The town was taken and all the leading men came with their hands crossed to surrender to Cortés. When he realized the bravery of the woman, Cortés granted her the control of the two towns of Tetela and Hueyapan in the name of His Majesty.

In this way, I understand, the Spaniards went from conquest to conquest, subjecting the land. They went here and there, from town to town, conquering and pacifying. After each town was taken, a Spaniard would ask Cortés to grant it to him and he then received it as an *encomienda*. So it was that *juste vel injuste*, justly or unjustly, men, women, and children were taken, branded on their faces, and sold as slaves for the mines or as servants. In those times they even loaded ships with slaves to be carried away from New Spain. I myself met some of them in the home of my relatives, and they were marked in the face with the name of the man who had sold them. These slaves had not come from nearby towns but were brought from more than ten leagues away. Most of them were brought to the city from the province of Guatemala and from the coasts that were distant from the capital. And even though I did not actually see slaves being branded on the face with hot irons, just like horses in a corral (as the Indians now are confined in *repartimientos*), I did see those men who had been branded, later liberated through the intercession of the friars in the time of the most Christian Viceroy Don Antonio de Mendoza.

At this time Cortés journeyed to a place called Las Higueras,[2] taking with him many principal men from Tenochtitlan, Tezcoco, Tacuba, Xochimilco, and Chalco, that is, from all the land. And among these chiefs went the heroic Aztec king, Cuauhtemoc. He was taken along as it was feared that he might cause trouble if he remained in the city, which had been left unprotected [by the Spaniards] and in which there were few people at that time.[3]

It seems that after a few days' journey Cuauhtemoc was accused of rebelling against the Spaniards and of trying to assassinate them. Several witnesses appeared to denounce him, and Cortés had the Aztec king hanged. In this way perished the great Cuauhtemoc, who had ruled over Mexico three or four years. That he might not depart this world alone—and the conquerors used this as a pretext—the other chieftains from the different provinces whom Cortés had brought along died there also. Some died a natural death; others, against their will, were also hanged or were run down by hounds; and still others died in different ways. Some Spaniards who had attempted to kill Cortés and steal his ship were also hanged.

When Cortés returned from this campaign, the Christian religion began to grow and the Indians took to it with love and willingness. After the Christian fathers had preached to them, they began to abandon their idols. They broke them, mocked them, stepped on them, and demolished the *cúes* where these images had been. Turning to God, they accepted the True Faith in One Deity. With great fervor they begged to be baptized, and it was an amazing thing to see the millions who came for this baptism and who gave up the blindness in which they had lived.

Twelve years after the conquest of New Spain, the fathers of the Order of Saint Augustine arrived and took up the work of conversion with no less devotion and fervor. With their lives and example they dedicated themselves to this divine work and began to convert these poor nations. The Augustinians dispersed in all directions and, like the apostles of the two previous Orders, they brought forth great fruit in this vineyard of God. In order to present a good example before the

[2]In the manuscript, an illegible word is crossed out and "Higueras" written above it (fol. 220v).

[3]Revision in Durán's time has blocked out two lines right after this. The original (fol. 220r) reads "viendo la ciudad con tan poca gente [crossed out] . . . y a que a pocas jornadas después quessa dió de México." Possibly the censored lines referred to Cuauhtemoc's death, which is mentioned immediately following.

In the third paragraph in chapter LXXVIII, Durán states that the Tlatelolcas, by command of their leader, had concealed the treasure. Garibay's version says the Tlaxcaltecas concealed it, but this is a mistake; the original manuscript says "Tlatelolcas."

Indians, the most Christian Don Hernán Cortés would kneel and kiss the hands of any friar he happened to meet, no matter what Order this friar pertained to. When Don Antonio de Mendoza, the viceroy, ruled in Mexico, he treated the friars with the same respect and reverence.

But let us return to our purpose and speak again of the Indians, who have been the subject of my book. After the country had been conquered, a plague of smallpox broke out. This had been brought by a black man who had come with the Spaniards. A multitude of Indians died from this disease because there were no doctors and the illness was new to the people. They had never seen it. So it was that thousands died, men, women, and children, and the pestilence was attributed to the Spanish men who had brought it.

I have been ordered to write another treatise on past events from the time of the plague to the unhappy present, when this most fertile and rich land together with its capital, Mexico, has suffered many calamities and has declined with the loss of its grandeur and excellence and the great men who once inhabited it (for it is now full of the misery and poverty that have invaded it). Because of this order I shall conclude this work by honoring and glorifying Our God and Lord and His Blessed Mother, the Sovereign Virgin Mary, subjecting the book to the correction of the Holy Catholic Church, Our Mother, whose son I am, and under whose protection I promise to live and die like a true and faithful Christian.

This work was finished in the year 1581.
LAUS DEO SUMMA

APPENDIX

DURÁN'S *HISTORIA* AND THE *CRÓNICA X*

By Ignacio Bernal

A book, written by a Dominican friar, a kinsman of mine, which was the most exact account based on ancient records that I have ever seen," writes the scholar Juan de Tovar in his famous letter to Father José de Acosta in reference to Fray Diego Durán's *Historia*. This letter is undated but must have been written between 1586 and 1588. It is, therefore, the first reference, though indirect, to Durán's work and his first praise. "This is the finest in its field that I have ever seen" is the opinion of Agustín Dávila Padilla, who would one day be Archbishop of Santo Domingo. It is probable that these were the only two men within a period of three hundred years to see the *Historia de las Indias de Nueva España e Islas de Tierra Firme*. Tovar was related to Durán and undoubtedly was the Jesuit most versed in "things about the Indians." Dávila Padilla was, like Durán, a Dominican. Therefore, one being a relative and the other a member of the same religious Order, it might be suspected that they had personal reasons to exaggerate the value of the unpublished chronicle. Today it is believed and it is my own opinion that both these scholars realized the extraordinary importance of Durán's work, since they were the only ones among those who saw it, capable of evaluating it.

During the following two and one half centuries other authors— León Pinelo, Alonso Franco, Eguiara, Clavijero, Beristáin, etc.— mentioned the *Historia* without being familiar with it. Frequently they went so far as to alter the name of the author: Eguiara calls him "Pedro" and Clavijero refers to him as "Fernando." Durán is a remarkable case of the incomprehension or ill luck that sometimes falls upon the historian. His work, finished in 1581, was seen by only a few contemporaries; afterwards no one seems to have known the manuscript, which was preserved in Spain until the nineteenth century.

Appendix

We do not know with precision the date on which the learned José Fernando Ramírez discovered the existence of Durán's manuscript in the National Library of Madrid, but we know that in 1854 an exact copy, made under orders, was finished. This does not mean, however, that it was published immediately. Ramírez, like many other Mexicans then and now, combined historical research with administrative and political occupations. He was eventually to become Mexican Minister of Foreign Affairs. These activities consumed valuable time and his adventure-filled life prevented the termination and publication of many manuscripts and studies. The historical archives of the National Museum of Anthropology in Mexico City preserve numerous volumes containing the unpublished manuscripts of this scholar. For this reason the first volume of Durán's chronicle which contains the *Historia* up to Chapter LXVIII did not appear until 1867. According to an unpublished letter to García Icazbalceta of April 13 of that year, Ramírez had left Mexico on January 20 en route to Europe, during the last throes of the Empire of Maximilian. Never to return, he died in Bonn on March 4, 1871. In the letter we have just mentioned, he speaks of the publication of the first volume of Durán and one receives the impression that he saw the printed edition before he left Mexico. Therefore, the printing of it must have taken place at the end of 1866 or during the first days of the new year. In any case, Ramírez, now ruined and far away from his native land, was unable to continue his great work. The remainder of the manuscript together with the plates (which had already been reproduced, but not distributed) were considered lost at the end of Maximilian's rule, with which Ramírez collaborated. Years later Alfredo Chavero removed these papers from a mouldy storehouse in the College of Mines, where they were rotting along with many other treasures which had been "put away" in order to avoid their loss in the confusion of the times. The director of the museum, Alcaraz, had taken no pains to rescue these precious documents. Therefore, it was not until 1880 that Chavero released the second volume in which the *Historia* is completed, and in which are included the other two books: *The Rites* and *The Calendar*. Chavero's edition, however, did not contain Ramírez's study, announced in the first volume, which had been lost. It was also at this time that forty-nine plates of the *Atlas*, bearing water stains from the storehouse, were also released.

The Ramírez-Chavero edition modifies the spelling and very bad punctuation of the original manuscript to some extent, but it does not correct these sufficiently to make easy reading. Durán's paragraphs are interminable—at times they cover an entire chapter—and his antiquated form of writing makes reading difficult. Furthermore, this cannot be considered a critical edition as numerous notes and indexes—essential in these cases—are lacking. In spite of all these defects this edition not only definitely saved from oblivion one of the most important documents on ancient Mexico that exists, but also made it available to scholars. In 1952 a re-edition appeared, but it contributed nothing new; a genuinely critical edition of this book, basic for the study of Aztec history, is indispensable. Because of this we are happy that Durán's *Historia* is appearing in this translation. This magnificent text may be called one of the principal keys to the roots of Mexican culture.

We do not know the title Durán gave his work. On the reverse of the first plate of the *Atlas* can be read an inscription written by a copyist: "Historia de las Indias de N. i islas y tierra firme." These words seem to be taken from the title of the first chapter to which the copyist added "Historia" and completed the "N" to mean *Nueva España* (New Spain). Even so, this title is inexact, as Durán not only dealt with history but with many other things. He did not discuss the islands (we assume that this means the Antilles) nor "Tierra Firme" (the mainland which later would be the Audiencia of Panama). Ill luck, which has pursued Durán, does not stop there, since because of an inexplicable confusion, in Ramírez's edition the work is called "Historia de la Nueva España i Islas de Tierra Firme," or "History of New Spain and of the Islands of the Mainland." It is difficult to imagine "islands" on the mainland; therefore I suppose that this must have been simply an error.

This translation covers the entire *Historia de las Indias* but does not include the books dedicated to rites and the calendar.

We know little about the life of Fray Diego Durán. Through a written accusation which he presented before the Inquisition in 1587 we discover that he was born in Seville fifty years before, which means that the date of his birth must have been around 1537 . . . After having spent his childhood in that Tezcoco which had been "the Athens of America," he entered the Dominican Order on May 8, 1556, in the monastery of Saint Dominic in Mexico City. In September of 1559 he was ordained a deacon in this establishment and in 1561 was sent to the province of Oaxaca, an area of great importance to the men of his Order. The length of his stay in that region is unknown; he is never mentioned among Dominicans who labored in Oaxaca at that time. Durán himself never speaks of his stay in that province. I believe that he must have remained there a short time, and it is probable that ill health prevented him from gaining fame there. What little information he gives on his work as a missionary mentions the area surrounding Mexico City. There is no doubt that his knowledge of the Nahuatl language (which he had learned as a child in Texcoco) would serve him better in this region. His book was begun at least by 1574, although one must admit that Durán's entire life since 1542 was a subconscious preparation for it. The *Historia* was finished in 1581 and our chronicler died in 1588.

Two important facts may be deduced from these scant biographical data: Fray Diego Durán was exposed in an intense manner to Indian culture in Tezcoco, one of its principal centers, and his thirty-two years of life as a Dominican were spent in intimate contact with these people. We also know that he had a relative especially important in the field of ancient history, who lived in Texcoco and who later became a Jesuit, Father Juan de Tovar, whom we have already mentioned. Durán was also able to work at the Indian school at Santiago Tlatelolco, near the heart of Mexico City, perhaps collaborating with the Franciscan Bernardino de Sahagún, the foremost authority in his time on pre-conquest Aztec culture.

It is as part of this world of Spanish friars devoted to research on the ancient civilizations of Central Mexico that we must place Durán, in one of the most important periods of Mexican historiography. Only thus can we understand the intricate relationships that exist between the writings of Durán and those of his contemporaries.

Durán's entire work, though it forms a single corpus, actually is divided in three treatises; "the first contains seventy-eight chapters on the history of Mexico from its origins to the Conquest and complete subjection of the country by the Spaniards, ending with Cortés' expedition to Honduras. . . ." At the end of this book can be read: "The present work was finished in the year 1581." The second treatise contains twenty-three chapters on Mexican deities, rites, feasts and temples. The third, divided into two sections, consists of nineteen chapters on the Mexican calendar. This third part is in reality, according to Durán himself, a continuation of the second treatise. It was finished in 1579. Therefore, even though it appears at the end of Ramírez's and Chavero's edition, it is really the first. Actually, the entire order of the edition is incorrect. As Garibay has pointed out, this is a serious defect in the Ramírez-Chavero edition. Beauvois has reorganized the text in a more logical fashion, in the manner planned by Durán. Actually Durán had planned to write a fourth book (or third, if Two and Three are to be considered one work). This was to contain *huehuetlatolli*, ancient Aztec speeches and sermons, plus other matters which had been omitted in his previous books. Unfortunately our chronicler died before this work could be written.

Fray Diego Durán lived in a golden age of chronicles written on ancient Mexico—the second half of the sixteenth century. The fury of warfare had passed and it was possible to approach the Conquest as an historical episode. However, the pre-Hispanic epoch was still sufficiently close and there not only existed individuals born before the arrival of Cortés and bearers of the ancient civilization, but also many groups who for all practical purposes were living a pre-Spanish life. The Franciscans, Dominicans, the descendants of the Indian rulers, and even aged conquerors filled reams of paper which described the ancient Indian ways as reported by the "elders" of Tula, Tezcoco, Mexico-Tenochtitlan, and numerous other cities. Many chronicles were produced—some of them superb. This corpus is unique in the Americas. All of this marvelous production of material on the native cultures, however, is not only due to the activities of the friars of the latter half of the sixteenth century, but also to the fact that great libraries of painted books had already existed before the Conquest. These books today are called "codices" and even though they are sadly diminished in number they constitute a highly valuable mass of original material. The codices were commonly used by the missionary and Indian chroniclers for their writings as they themselves often attest. All these historians utilized two basic sources: the pre-Hispanic manuscripts in picture writing and living informants. Bernardino de Sahagún seems to have used live informants more extensively than historians such as Durán and Ixtlilxochitl of Tezcoco, who based their chronicles on written sources. Often, of course, these manuscripts had to be explained by informants. Ixtlilxochitl tells us that in ancient times "there were writers for each branch of knowledge. Some composed the historical annals, setting in order the events that took place every year, stating the day, month and hour. Others recorded the genealogies and descendants of the kings, lords and personages of high lineage; they would make note of those who were born and cancel the dead. Others painted the limits, boundaries and border stones of the cities, provinces and villages, and of the fields and plantations, indicating their owners. Yet others made records of the laws, and the rites and ceremonies performed in pagan times. The priests made records regarding the temples of the idols, of their idolatrous doctrines and the feasts of their false gods and their calendars. And finally, there were philosophers and wise men among them who recorded in picture writing the sciences they were versed in. They also taught the chants which dealt with these sciences and with their historical traditions." A number of these documents have been preserved. They are few compared to those which perished but they suffice to prove to us that such books did exist and that there were different schools of scribes just as Ixtlilxochitl affirms.

But how did these pictographic documents, so difficult to interpret for the European mind, become well-organized history books, such as that of Durán? One must remember the manner in which the ancient books were conceived. Because of the nature of native hieroglyphic writing, these codices could only serve as a sort of *aide-mémoire*. Essentially they were only lists of events which certain well-trained individuals in special schools learned how to "read" out loud, elaborating on the action of events, which could not be described adequately by picture writing; they added adjectives and reproduced conversations or any other pertinent commentaries that had been memorized. So it was that the pictures were only a guide which allowed the commentator to narrate a story which was to be told to a group of listeners. Poems, speeches by historical personages and many other things—in prose or poetry—were memorized and the skillful "reader" would include them as he went along in his narration. Tovar, in his letter to Acosta, explains the procedure followed by missionaries, probably since the time of Father Olmos: "It is to be noted that even though the Indians had different figures and characters with which they wrote, these were not so perfect as our own letters. However, they did not omit a word when they quoted what was written. Each reader kept an accurate account of this oral tradition in his mind and had memorized the words and the general order of these speeches. The latter were composed by the orators and recorded in picture writing. That the texts might be preserved with the exact words that their orators and poets had used, they would be taught to the young nobles who were to succeed the speakers. With this continuous repetition the oral versions were memorized word for word. The natives preserved the most famous orations which were composed in each generation by teaching these to the young men who were to become eloquent speakers. In this manner many discourses were passed on exactly from generation to generation, until the coming of the Spaniards. The latter wrote down many of these speeches or chants in our alphabet, and I personally saw these. In this way the ancient traditions have been preserved."

So it was that European writing was used after the Conquest in order to record earlier history and form a permanent and fixed corpus of documents. To this praiseworthy task the friars and the indigenous historians dedicated their lives. Among them the role of Durán is outstanding. "Its main value," writes Garibay of Durán's *Historia*, "is that it is the first and only chronicle of the sixteenth century that gives us a harmonious view of Tenochtitlan."

Since the seventeenth century there has been much discussion regarding the relationship between Durán's *Historia* and those of the other chroniclers.

The most superficial observation shows us that there are a number of chronicles, all of them written in the second half of the sixteenth century, which are very similar—sometimes almost identical. Besides the *Historia* there exist Tezozomoc's *Crónica Mexicana*, the *Códice Ramírez*, the *Historia de la venida de los indios* by Juan de Tovar, and Chapter VII of the *Historia natural y moral de las Indias* by Joseph de Acosta. There is no doubt that there is a direct relationship among these documents, which, incidentally, are nearly all of first-rate importance. In this introduction we shall not discuss all the details of the problem, as they would be of interest only to specialists in this field. However, in order to grasp the *Historia* of Durán more fully, it is necessary to understand the general outline of this confusing situation, which began during the early part of the seventeenth century when Dávila Padilla stated that Acosta based his Chapter VII on the work of Durán. Over the centuries affirmations—some correct and some false—were made regarding this problem. But, in general, all of them are of little importance before the manuscript of the *Historia* was published. When, in the middle of the nineteenth century, the first edition appeared, the problem began to be understood. Recent scholarly studies such as those of Barlow and Sandoval have been based on profound knowledge of all the documents mentioned above together with others that shed light on the situation. Thses studies have revealed much to us, although there are still many enigmatic points.

It is evident that Acosta—he himself says so—used the manuscript of Tovar as a basis for his Chapter VII. This is not a problem. It is also evident that the *Códice Ramírez* and the *Historia de la venida de los indios* by Tovar (only part of which has been published) are the same document, recorded, however, in two copies with slight variations. Both of them are, therefore, the *Historia* by Juan de Tovar. Tovar himself states, in his famous correspondence with Father Acosta, that he based a large part of his writings on Durán's *Historia*. It could be thought then that we have only two basic sources whose origin and relationship should be studied—Durán and Tezozomoc.

Nevertheless, the problem is more complex, as Tovar states that the *Historia* to which we have referred is the *second* that he wrote and

Appendix

we will call it *Tovar II*. *Tovar I*, therefore, is missing. We must keep this in mind. Further investigation reveals that Tezozomoc and Durán are derived from a common source, even though they are far from being identical, as they both used new material apart from their original source. It had been thought that their similarity was due to their both having used *Tovar I*, which is not extant. It is a fact that Durán mentions with complete honesty a "Chronicle" that he followed. Tezozomoc also used it, even though he does not say so clearly. With this information the problem again might appear to have been solved: Tovar wrote a first chronicle (*Tovar I*) which has been lost, and it served as a basis for Durán on the one hand, and for Tezozomoc on the other, even though both utilized additional oral and written material. The *Códice Ramírez* (*Tovar II*) served as a basis for Acosta but not for Durán or for Tezozomoc. Tovar himself says that as he had sent his first book to Spain, he did not have it available to consult and therefore wrote his second version from memory, making use of information furnished him by his kinsman Durán (who, in turn, it has been said, had taken them from *Tovar I*). In a scholarly article, Barlow indicates a certain doubt that events took this course, mainly because of some inconsistency in dates in the Indian calendar that appear in the *Códice Ramírez*. Barlow suspects the existence of an earlier chronicle which would not be *Tovar I* and which he names the *Crónica X*, and from which he thinks the other histories—in their different forms—are derived.

The Indian date of the *Códice Ramírez* as studied by Caso could only have fallen between 1536 and 1539 in the Christian calendar. Tovar could not possibly have written his work at this time as he was born in 1543. Therefore, it is evident that we are dealing with an earlier chronicle, called by Barlow the *Crónica X*, that cannot be the same as *Tovar I*. So it is that we are dealing with two lost chronicles. However, we must remember that there are different schools of thought as to the interpretation of the native calendar and that Durán did not have an understanding of it. It is probable that Tovar did not have a grasp of this either. It is also possible that the date given by the *Códice Ramírez* is an error. In spite of the fact that the date may be erroneous, there are other aspects of the matter that lead us to think that the *Crónica X* did exist, independent of *Tovar I*.

Tovar, in his letter to Acosta, after mentioning that he had been unable to recover his first *Historia*, writes, "... as I then looked deeply into these matters and spent much time on them, a great deal remained in my memory. Aside from that I consulted a book, done by a Dominican friar, a kinsman of mine, which was the most exact account based on ancient records, that I have ever seen. This refreshed my memory in order to write my chronicle (*Tovar II*), which now Your Reverence has read." Is it not unlikely that Tovar would fail to mention that the book of his "kinsman" Durán is based upon Tovar's own first work?

It could be expected that when Tovar wrote to Acosta, sending him *Tovar II*, indicating that he had written it from memory, and based on Durán, he would have revealed that Durán's chronicle had been based on *Tovar I*. This revelation would not necessarily have been made because he wished to belittle Durán or even less to boast that Durán had written his chronicle based on *Tovar I*. Rather, he might have done so because he wished Acosta to be advised that Tovar's second work was trustworthy and not only composed from memory. For, had it been based on Durán (and if the latter had been practically the same as *Tovar I*), this meant that *II* was fundamentally *Tovar I*. Let us remember that what Acosta sought was to be sure that his sources were accurate. It seems to me that all of this leads to a belief in the existence of a *Crónica X*, which is not *Tovar* but the original source used for *Tovar I*, Durán and Tezozomoc.

However, there is another problem involved, and that is the fact that Tovar, in his letter, explains clearly to Acosta the manner in which he wrote his first chronicle. He did not take it from another similar document but from several painted manuscripts and written accounts which he tried to organize into a history of the events in their consecutive order. To achieve the latter, he found it necessary to use a number of indigenous informants. Therefore, it is probable that Tovar's work is not based on the *Crónica X*, or at best Tovar used the latter as only one of his sources.

I feel that the painted manuscripts and written accounts mentioned by Tovar as the basis of his first *Historia* could be part of the material gathered by Olmos. This Franciscan missionary arrived in Mexico in 1528 and we know that he was concerned with Indian history at least since 1533, as he had been commissioned to study it by Sebastián Ramírez de Fuenleal and Fray Martín de Valencia, high civil and religious authorities, as is narrated by the early ecclesiastical writer Mendieta. Olmos gathered numerous documents. Perhaps these are the "ancient records," some of which have been preserved, even though his own history has been lost.

Be it as it may, Garibay, the eminent Nahuatl scholar and critic of ancient Aztec literature, has demonstrated the immense importance of Olmos's work, which, unfortunately, for the most part has been lost, but whose pioneer research methods set the standards for all the important scholars of the sixteenth century—not excluding Sahagún. This gathering of material included "interviews" with informants, in

Appendix

the manner of the modern ethnologist. Besides these, the scholar then gathered and examined all available written material. Is it possible that these documents, compiled by Olmos, were in part those used by Tovar and Durán? To prove this would require an enormous comparative study which would be out of place here. I have only tried to indicate briefly the antecedents of the great *Historia de las Indias* of Durán.

It may be wise to point out to the reader that when Durán refers to the ancient "crónica" the translators have used the term *Chronicle*. This *Chronicle* signifies to them the unrecorded or lost documents which I have just identified as perhaps being those collected by Olmos.

It is important to discuss the source material used by the ancient historians in order to evaluate their statements, to see whether we may draw trustworthy conclusions from the information contained in them. However, it is not necessary to fall into what the historian Edmundo O'Gorman has rightly called "the excessive quest for originality in information." Much less are we concerned with the problem of plagiarism which has been so thoroughly discussed in past times. It matters little that one historian reproduced the words of another, as long as the source that he used was a good one. From a moral point of view it would be absurd to try to apply our modern ethical standards to an age when no such standards existed and the restating of what a previous writer had recorded was no sin.

The profound knowledge of the mind of ancient Mexico shown by Durán is not to be found even in Sahagún. A good example of this is given to us by Garibay when this scholar refers to certain difficulties in the understanding of the esoteric meaning of the ancient Aztec poems. While Sahagún "sees visions and demons . . . another writer, Durán—with more profound knowledge, with more human sympathy— had listened to ancient traditions told by the natives, since childhood." These natives were still permeated with the ancient culture of Tezcoco. Durán writes that "all these chants are filled with metaphors so obscure that very few persons can understand them unless their significance is studied and discussed. I have listened with great attention to what they sing and after hearing the words and metaphors, which at first seem nonsense, I find them to be meaningful thoughts, after I have examined them and meditated upon them. . . ." Durán's authority is definitive.

It is this sensitive perception of the Indian soul which makes Durán unique among the Dominicans. The Order of Preachers, more intellectual than the Franciscans, believed—as Garibay has clearly expressed—in the total renovation of the Indian world, in "erasing the past in order to instill the new faith of Christ." Though Durán did not forget the principles of his Order, he had an enormous sympathy toward the indigenous culture, toward the native ways of life and even toward the landscape of the Valley of Mexico, the scenery of Tezcoco of his infancy.

The truth is that Durán, though a Spaniard by blood, was in reality a mestizo or hybrid. His childhood gave him a fluent knowledge not only of Nahuatl but also of the indigenous culture. It is evident that though he writes in Spanish, he seems to be thinking in Nahuatl. Rather—he mixes both cultures in such a way that they are difficult to separate. Fundamentally this is what places Durán at the very roots of Mexican culture and explains the historiographical climate in which he achieved his work.

We would like to be able to answer this question: Why did Durán write the *Historia*? What was his aim? Durán was not a professional historian, as Antonio de Herrera was to be later. He was a Dominican missionary whose task was the conversion of the Indians. His interest in history and ethnography was merged with the aims of his profession. The sixteenth century linguists who left us excellent dictionaries and grammars of many Indian languages did not learn them as an intellectual pastime. Their aim was to make themselves understood by the natives to whom they preached, so their writings were to facilitate the task of later friars in learning the languages. In like manner historian-ethnographers *needed* to understand the indigenous culture, grasp its present and past in order to reach the soul of their flock, thus converting it to Christianity. When Durán produced his works, fifty years had passed since the Conquest. The conversion of the Indians, at least in Central Mexico, should have been accomplished by then, and the basic obstacles eliminated, if it is true—as has been said—that the conquered Indians came in hordes, anxious to receive the new faith. Is it not possible that Durán, like many other alert men, realized that the conversion had been superficial, that in reality under the slight veneer of Christianity the ancient religion was still thriving? Ramón Iglesia is of this opinion. He believes that because of this situation Durán throws himself into "the study of the ancient religion, not in a cold impartial or simply descriptive way, but using this study as an indispensable weapon in order to uproot the old faith. That is why his book condemns not only the deeds of the nonclerical conquerors who wished to impose the Gospel at sword's point but also the complacent attitude of many friars who had allowed themselves to be deceived by the apparent success of their missionary labor."

Durán himself clearly explains the principal aim of his work: to destroy "ancient idolatry and false religion." But this will not be possible, he adds, "no matter how hard we work, if we do not understand the old religion profoundly." Therefore, he looks upon his chronicle as a basically pragmatic work which will be an aid in the labor of proselytism.

Durán, like almost all the historians of his century, is of the opinion that the purpose of history is to analyze the eternal struggle between God and the Devil, between good and evil, and that the role of man is to take part in this struggle in order to achieve the triumph of God on earth. However, in this there is a contradiction which Durán does not express clearly but that is nonetheless present. We do not know how he solved this. Since the conversion of the natives is the work of God, and God is the direct mover of history, the evangelization should have been successful, judging by the large groups of Indians that came running to receive baptism. Durán understood the Indian soul only too well. During his childhood he had lived too close to the native not to realize that baptism in many cases was an empty ceremony which changed the mentality of the neophyte little or not at all and that the Indian continually returned to his ancient practices. The solution to this problem evidently consisted in intensifying the preaching, but well-instructed preaching, an evangelization that does not rely exclusively on the zeal of the missionary. The latter must fully understand not only the ancient tongue but also the religion and culture in order to fight them with more effective weapons.

All of this may explain another interesting aspect of Durán: his open sympathy for the Indians which cannot be reconciled with his bitter criticism of them at times. The truth is that while he loves them in many ways he detests them as recalcitrant idolators. He cannot understand in reality how there may exist virtues in those who are without or only apparently within the flock of Christ. Let us not forget that he is a Dominican and that the Order of Preachers was precisely the organization that wielded the weapon of the Inquisition, attacking the heretic and, above all, the relapsed convert. But Durán was not the Inquisitor as shown in melodramas, nor was he a fanatic, blind to things of the world. As Garibay expressed with clarity, "he was an enthusiast of the Indian way of life even though he did not abandon the moderation of his own intellectual manner." In Durán, as in many other men, there exists a duality which forces him to be strict and almost inexorable in matters of the Faith, but which permits him to feel and understand a culture which he does not wish to destroy but to evangelize.

In this he is a typical product of his age. Durán, who lived in the second half of the sixteenth century, could not have had a completely medieval mentality. He belongs to the Renaissance and no matter how he may react against some new ideas, he realizes that the heathens, though lost spiritually, possess valuable things. Pagan Greek and Roman culture was fashionable in that time. Man had discovered what those peoples learned, how they progressed, and had realized the greatness of their art and of their deeds. In the same way the ancient Mexicans had obviously been mistaken in their religion but this did not mean that they had lacked admirable traits worthy of being studied and preserved. Durán believed that the study of ancient history—history is a teacher—could uproot the diabolical arts and show at the same time the positive aspects and the innate goodness of the ancient peoples.

Mexico City, 1964

CHRONOLOGY OF AZTEC KINGS

Acamapichtli, "Handful of Reeds" — 1376–96
Huitzilihuitl, "Hummingbird Feather" — 1396–1417
Chimalpopoca, "Smoking Shield" — 1417–27
Itzcoatl, "Obsidian Serpent" — 1427–40
Motecuhzoma Ilhuicamina, the Elder (I),
    "Angry Lord, He Who Shoots into the Sky" — 1440–69
Axayacatl, "Water Face" — 1469–81
Tizoc, "Chalk Leg" — 1481–86
Ahuitzotl, "Water Monster" — 1486–1502
Motecuhzoma Xocoyotzin, the Younger (II),
    "Angry Lord" — 1502–20
Cuitlahuac, "Lord of the Kingdom of Cuitlahuac" — 1520
Cuauhtemoc, "Descending Eagle" — 1520–25

GLOSSARY

Acolnahuacatl: Public official in charge of caring for the level of the lake's water and seeing that it does not overflow. Also, ruler of Tacuba during the time of Chimalpopoca of Tenochtitlan.
ahuauhtli: "Water amaranth," eggs from marine flies deposited on the lake surface, appreciated as a delicious food.
ahuexotl: *Ahuehuete* (Nahuatl *ahuehuetl*: *Cupressus disticha: Taxodium mucronatum*) is another tree frequently mentioned in the chronicles. This coniferous tree similar to the cypress grows near water or needs watery soil. The root is *atl*, "water," and *huehue*, "old." It grows to a venerable age; one in Oaxaca is said to be more than 1,000 years old. There are also many in Chapultepec Park in Mexico City.
amaranth: See *tzoalli*.
amatl: Bark paper, usually made from the bark of the wild fig tree, *Ficus padifolia*. *Amatl*, or *amate* as it is called today, was not only used for pictorial documents or codices, but formed part of rituals as banners or as clothing for images of the gods. In ceremonies to the rain gods *amatl* was sprinkled with liquid rubber, a symbol of water.
anecuyotl: One of Huitzilopochtli's insignia.
Atamalcualiztli: "Eating water tamales," a major ceremony held every eight years in the month of Tepeilhuitl or in Quecholli, in honor of vegetation deities. For seven days people fasted, eating only maize tamales made with water.
atlatl: Spear thrower, used to propel a dart or spear.
Atlcahualo: "The Water Ceases," first month in the eighteen (twenty-day) month prehispanic year, corresponding to February 14–March 5. Also called Cuahuitlehua, "Raising of Trees," and Xilomanaliztli, "Offering of Tender Young Ears of Corn." Deities of water and earth's fertility were honored in this period; offerings of maize were given to maize deities in the Great Temple precinct, and children were sacrificed to the *tlaloques*, water gods.
atole: Gruel made with a maize base, then sweetened with honey and flavored with fruit or chocolate.
Atzacualco: One of the four original barrios of Tenochtitlan.
axaxayakatl: Edible cake of dragonfly larvae from the lake.
Azcapotzalco: City "In the Anthill," a multitude of ants referring to a multitude of people.
Aztec: Person or people from Aztlan (see chap. II, note 1).
Aztlan: "White Place" or "Place of Herons." Mythical original home of the Aztecs (see chap. I, note 9).
barrio: A subdivision in a town, a territorial unit. See *calpulli*.
braza: Fathom, about six feet.
calmecac: School for children of dignitaries where they were taught astronomy, religion, the calendar, history, moral comportment, and other subjects that

Glossary

would permit them to belong to the ruling class or the priesthood when they were older. The *calmecac* were attached to temples, and priests were the teachers. Some children of plebeian families attended the *calmecac*.

calpixqui (pl. *calpixque*): Administrative official whose major duty was collecting taxes as well as receiving provisions paid as tribute from the different provinces. These *calpixque* were members of the *pilli* or noble class and were in close communication with the sovereign in regard to the country's possessions, the condition of roads and public buildings, and the maintenance of the palace.

calpullali: Land belonging to the *calpulli* for maintaining the cult of its gods.

calpullec (pl. *calpulleque*): *Calpulli* headmen, elected by members of the ward but usually related to their predecessors. They were tribute-free, kept land records, and represented the barrio members before higher authorities. They kept records in the form of pictorial manuscripts, codices, or *lienzos*.

calpulli (barrio or ward): The name means "big house." According to Pedro Carrasco (1971:364–68) a *calpulli* was a territorial division and the people in it, a landholding group, a political and administrative subdivision. A *calpulli* member had the right to work a plot of land, which could be transmitted to heirs; but if he died without heirs or failed to cultivate the land for two years he lost his plot, which then was acquired by another person. The *calpulli* could rent out lands to members of other wards. The *tecuhtli* or *calpullec*, head of a *calpulli*, possessed a plot that was worked for him by other members of the group. There was a certain amount of kinship relation within a *calpulli*, as there was association with craftsmen, but this was not the main basis. Each *calpulli* had its own temple and patron deity, as well as a *telpochcalli* or school where youths were trained in the arts of war. Another type of barrio or ward existed, composed of *mayeque* or *terrazgueros*. The colonial chronicler who discusses *calpulli* in full is Zorita (Keen 1971; Vigil 1987).

calpulteotl (pl. *calpulteteo*): Guardian god or gods of the *calpulli*.

casa real: "Royal house," whose function was something like that of a town hall; sometimes called the palace.

Cemanahuac: "In a circle of water" or "In the center of the world" or universe.

Centzon Huitznahua: "400 Southerners," the innumerable brothers and sisters of Huitzilopochtli and Coyolxauhqui. Also "the innumerable ones of the south," a group of stars.

Centzon Mimixcoa: "400 or innumerable ones of the north," a group of stars.

chacmool: Sculpture of an individual in supine position with a receptacle on his abdomen, probably for offerings. These sculptures are typical of the Toltec culture but also are found in the Maya area and are sprinkled throughout the center, north, and west of Tenochtitlan. A spectacular Aztec *chacmool* with Tlaloc characteristics is displayed in the Mexica Hall in the MNA; another is at the summit of the Templo Mayor.

chalchihuitl: Jade. Symbol of that which is precious and of water.

Chalchiuhtlatonac: "Glowing Jade," an aspect of Tlaloc, rain-earth deity.

Chalchiuhtlicue: "She of the Jade Skirt," goddess of groundwater such as springs, rivers, lakes. Consort of Tlaloc. The skirt of jades (*chalchihuitl*) symbolizes something precious, in this case water.

Chalmecatl: "Lord of Jade Lineage," from *chalchihuitl*, "jade," and *mecatl*, "rope, line, or lineage"; "person from Chalma(n)."

Chapultepec: "Grasshopper Hill," park in today's Mexico City. In Aztec times the place from which spring waters flowed and where the Aztec rulers had their portraits carved on rocks.

chia or *chian*: A type of sage (*Salvia hispanica*), whose seeds are used for making a refreshing beverage. Oil for paint is also obtained from the seed.

chichimecatl (pl. *chichimec*): No two scholars agree on the definition of this word. It comes from *chichi*, "to nurse or suckle," and refers to young groups. The Spaniards called people in northern Mexico Chichimecs. The Aztecs called their ancestors Chichimecs.

Chicomoztoc: "Seven Caves," the legendary birthplace of seven groups, one of them the Aztecs. In myth Chicomoztoc is often confused with Aztlan, the Aztec homeland, or with Colhuacan, Place of Ancestors.

Chiconaumictlan: Ninth region of the Land of the Dead, where the "soul" of the deceased had to cross the Chiconahuapan River on the back of a reddish-yellow dog.

chinampa: Agricultural plot formed artificially by making rafts of branches and piling lake mud on it; then it takes root. Because it is constantly watered from underneath, it is very fertile and can produce more than one crop a year.

Cholula: Originally Chollolan. City in the present-day state of Puebla, east of Mexico City.

Churubusco: Originally Huitzilopochco, "Place of Huitzilopochtli," now part of Coyoacan in southern Mexico City.

Cicalco: "Place of Hares," undoubtedly meant to be Cincalco, "House of Maize." The latter was a cave, a mythological storeroom for people's sustenance.

Cihuacoatl: "Woman Serpent," goddess of the *chinampa* region. After the Aztec conquest of this rich agricultural region during Itzcoatl's time, the title "Cihuacoatl" was given to the ruler's main adviser (Klein 1988).

Cihuatlampa: "Place of Women," the west, mythical home of women who died in childbirth.

Cipactli: Crocodile (*Crocodylus* sp.). One of the day signs in the prehispanic calendar.

Cipactonal: The first man, husband of Oxomoco. They were the creators of the human race and in *Codex Borbonicus* 21 are seen as old sorcerers divining with maize kernels. He was commanded by the gods to work the land. The count of destinies was initiated by Cipactonal and Oxomoco, with the aid of the first human couple. Some sources state that Cipactonal was the first woman, Oxomoco the first man.

Citlalco: "Place of Stars," the second tier in the level of heavens.

Coateocalli: "Serpent House" or "Temple of Divine Gods" according to Durán. Statues of gods from many regions were housed here. Etymology: *coatl* means "serpent" and *cocoa* means both "serpents" and "twins," by extension, "many." *Teocalli* is "temple."

Coatepetl, Coatepec: "Serpent Hill," site near Tula, Hidalgo, where Huitzilopochtli was miraculously born, fully armed, of Coatlicue, in time to war against and defeat his 400 brothers the Huitznahua, who, led by their sister Coyolxauhqui, tried to kill their mother Coatlicue. It was at Coatepec that Huitzilopochtli decapitated and dismembered Coyolxauhqui, an event commemorated at the Great Temple in Tenochtitlan, which is a symbolic reconstruction of the Coatepetl.

Coatlicue: "She of the Serpent Skirt," Mother Goddess, patroness of florists. Mother of Huitzilopochtli, Coyolxauhqui, and the 400 Huitznahua. Her spectacular statue is in the MNA in Mexico.

Colhuacan, Culhuacan: The name Colhuacan or Culhuacan, "Place of the Culhua People" (a branch of the Toltecs who inhabited this city in the southern part of the Valley of Mexico), can be translated in different ways. It can mean "Curved Place" and is usually represented in pictorial codices as a curved hill; the root is the Nahuatl *coloa* or *culhua*, "to be curved" or "twisted" (Simeón 1988:123). Another interpretation is "Place of Grandparents," by extension "Place of Ancestors," from *colli* or *culli*, "grandfather." Colhuacan was a center of great prestige and power and the Culhuas probably were the most advanced people in the valley at the time of the arrival of the Aztecs. Teocolhuacan means "the ancient, sacred, or legitimate Colhuacan," from *teo(tl)*, "god, divine, sacred, old, real."

Copil: Son of Malinalxochitl, one of Huitzilopochtli's sisters. Copil was born after his mother's expulsion from the Aztec-Mexico group because she was a sorceress; when Copil tried to avenge her by murdering his uncle, he was killed instead. His heart, thrown into a swamp of reeds, marked the spot where the *nopal* (prickly pear cactus) grew and indicated the place for the foundation of Tenochtitlan.

corregidor: Spanish district administrator.

Coyoacan: "Place of Coyotes," in prehispanic times a Tepanec settlement, today a part of Mexico City in the southern area.

Coyolxauhqui: "Bells on Her Cheeks," sister of Huitzilopochtli, leader of the other 400 brothers, the Huitznahua; all were children of Coatlicue. Coyolxauhqui was an aspect of, or associated with, Chantico, goddess of the hearth fire.

cu (pl. *cúes*): Temple. Pronounced "coo."

Cuachic: Order of distinguished warriors.

Cuatecpan (or Cuauhtecpan) Tecutli: "Lord of the Eagle Place." From *cuauhtli* (*quauhtli*), "eagle," and *tecpan*, "meeting house, palace.

Cuauh Huehuetque: "Old Eagles," experienced warriors.

Cuauhnahuac: Today Cuernavaca, capital of the state of Morelos.

Cuauhtlequetzqui: One of Huitzilopochtli's priests, to whom the god revealed in dreams commands for the Aztecs. It was Cuauhtlequetzqui who threw Copil's heart into the reeds and rushes, which marked the site where Tenochtitlan was to be founded.

cuauhxicalli: "Eagle vessel," where hearts of sacrificed victims were deposited.

Cuepopan: "Place Where the Causeway Is," *calpulli* north of the Great Temple of Tenochtitlan. One of the four original divisions of the city.

Cuicatlicac (Quauhuitlicac): One of the 400 Huitznahua who did not agree with Coyolxauhqui's plan to kill their mother, Coatlicue, and therefore advised her of the attack so Huitzilopochtli could be born and defeat the offenders.

Cuicuilco: "Place of Many Colors," Preclassic archaeological site in southern Mexico City.

Cuitlahuac: "Water Excrement," name of a city in the southern part of the Valley of Mexico, today called Tlahuac. Also, name of the tenth *tlatoani* of Tenochtitlan.

Culhuas: Group of people of Toltec lineage. Their capital was in Colhuacan or Culhuacan in the southern Valley of Mexico. The lineage of the rulers of Mexico-Tenochtitlan could be traced back to the Culhuas.

Ehecatl-Quetzalcoatl: "Wind-Feathered Serpent." An aspect of the god Quetzalcoatl, Ehecatl was the wind that swept the roads before the rains.

encomendero: Holder of an *encomienda*.

encomienda: The Mexican *encomienda*, based on prototypes in Spain and the West Indies, was a system of private labor and tribute jurisdiction. An *encomendero* originally was granted no landed property but received tribute and labor from the Indians on the *encomienda* lands during his lifetime. In the *encomienda* system the Indians initially were required to perform labor services and pay tribute to their *encomendero*, while the latter was obliged to protect and Christianize his charges. The Crown thus intended to reward deserving Spaniards and to place the natives under the tutelage of responsible colonists (Vigil 1987:297). The New Laws of 1542–43, concerned with good treatment of the Indians, included the regulation of labor and tribute and the prohibition of the possession of *encomiendas* by public officials and ecclesiastics (Vigil 1987:83). However, after the partial repeal of these laws (which had prohibited new *encomienda* grants; existing ones were to revert to the crown upon the death of the holders), the right of inheritance by an *encomendero*'s heir was recognized and was extended by stages to a third, fourth, and even a fifth life (Keen, personal communication). Eventually the *hacendado* class emerged, toward the end of the sixteenth century; the *hacendados* were landowners and were more independent of the crown (Gibson 1964:26, 58–97). For further information on the *encomienda*, see Gibson 1966 and Simpson 1950.

etzalli, Etzalcualiztli: *Etzalli*, maize and beans together. Etzalcualiztli, "The Eating of Maize with Beans," the prehispanic sixth month, equivalent to late May and early June. *Etzalli*, a ritual food, signified the agricultural abundance of the season, which was the only time that people were allowed to eat these two foods together. Impersonators of water deities were sacrificed and ceremonies were held in honor of these gods.

ezcahuitli, izcahuitli: edible blood-red worm from the lake. The name probably derives from *eztli*, "blood."

Glossary

Ezhuahuacatl: "Shedder of Blood," title given to one of four men (brothers or close relatives of the king) from whom a ruler was chosen when the king died. From *eztli*, "blood," and the verb *uauana*, "to cut or scratch."

hacendado: Owner of an *hacienda* or large landed estate.

Huauhquiltamalqualiztli: "Eating of Tamales [*huauhquiltamalli*] "Filled with Greens," another name for Izcalli, "Growth," eighteenth month of the year. Xiuhtecuhtli, fire god, was honored; a New Fire ceremony was held and a new image of the fire god was made of amaranth dough. Xiuhtecuhtli was the patron of rulers, so the sovereign played a prominent part in the ceremonies and there was a great dance of the lords. The special tamales were eaten. Every four years impersonators of Xiuhtecuhtli were sacrificed by fire.

Huehueteotl: "Old God," an aspect of Xiutecuhtli, fire god.

Huemac: Last ruler of Tula. In Durán's chronicle, the lord of Cicalco.

Huey Teocalli: "Great Temple."

Huey Tozoztli: "Great Vigil," fourth month of twenty days in the eighteen-month calendar, equivalent to the second half of April. Ceremonies were held in honor of the first fruits and of water and maize deities, also Quetzalcoatl. Important rites were conducted on the summit of Mount Tlaloc, east of Tenochtitlan, with rich offerings by the Aztec sovereign and rulers of other cities.

huipil: Feminine garment, a type of blouse or shift.

Huitzilopochtli: "On the Left of the Hummingbird," or "Left-Handed Hummingbird," possibly referring to the left of the sun, or the south. Huitzilopochtli was the Aztec patron deity, associated with war, the sun, sovereignty, and power. He was the son of Coatlicue, brother of the Huitznahua and of Coyolxauhqui, whom he defeated at Coatepec.

Huitzlampa: "Region of Thorns," refers to the south in general.

Huitznahua: "The Southerners," brothers and sisters of Huitzilopochtli and Coyolxauhqui.

Huitznahuatl Motelchiuh: Aztec official sent by Motecuhzoma II to receive Cortés in Cempoala.

Huitznahuatl Tecutli: "Lord of the South," a title. *Tecutli* or *tecuhtli* means "lord"; Huitznahuatl was the god of those destined to be sacrificed and the shrine dedicated to him was the Huitznahuac in the Great Temple precinct, where there was a *calmecac*. The title may refer to an association with the school or with the god.

icpalli: Low chair without legs, usually made of wood with a woven mat back, used by persons of high rank.

Ilhuicatl Xoxouhqui: "Blue Sky," appellation given to a statue of Huitzilopochtli in the Great Temple.

Itztapalapa: "Obsidian [Place] on the Water," from *itztli*, "obsidian," and *apan* "on the water."

ixcuahualli, itzcuahualli: Sacrificial knife.

Izquitecatl: Title, "Lord of the Place of Toasted Maize," from *izquitl*, "toasted maize," also a flower of pleasant odor.

Iztac Zolin Inemian: "Where White Quails Dwell" (see chap. I, note 5).
Iztapal Nacazcayan: Eighth level of the heavens, "Place Where There Are Corners of Obsidian Blades."
macehual (pl. *macehualtin*): Free commoners. They formed the majority of the population and included farmers, craftsmen, and traders. They paid tribute to the *tlatoani* or paid in labor to a nobleman. Some *macehualtin* were more affluent than others and had *mayeque* to work some of their land.
maguey: American agave, century plant.
Malinalxochitl: "Wild Grass Flower," Huitzilopochtli's sorceress sister, mother of Copil.
Malinche, Malintzin, Marina: Cortés's interpreter and mistress (see chap. LXIX, note 4).
maxtlatl: Breechcloth.
Mayahuel: Maguey goddess, personified century plant, which produces pulque, an intoxicating liquor. Although basically associated with this drink, which was used principally in ritual, the maguey plant had multiple uses, from material for roofing, and for making thread for weaving, to serving for autosacrifice with the sharp thorns at the ends of the leaves.
mayeque: Also called *tlalmaitl*. Tenants on the lands of *pipiltin* or noblemen, paying rent in kind on a share basis or by working the landlord's fields. They usually had their own plots, which could be transmitted by inheritance. Since they paid their landlords they were free from tribute to the ruler.
mestizo: Person of mixed ancestry, Indian and non-Indian.
Mexica-Aztec (or Aztec-Mexica): That branch of the Aztec people who settled in the Valley of Mexico and founded Tenochtitlan (see chap. II, note I).
Mexica, Mexitin (s. Mexicatl), Mexican: See Mexica-Aztec. Today the people of Mexico are called Mexican. Durán usually refers to the Mexica or Aztecs as Mexicans.
Mexico: When Durán says "Mexico" in his chronicle he is referring to Mexico-Tenochtitlan, capital of the Aztec empire (now Mexico City, capital of the country).
michhuauhtli: *Huauhtli*, seed amaranth (*Amaranthus hypochondriacus*), was the basic element of the ritual *tzoalli*. *Michhuauhtli* is a type of this plant whose seeds resemble fish roe (*michin* manes "fish" in Nahuatl).
Mictlampa: "Place of Death," associated with the north.
Mictlantecuhtli: "Lord of Mictlan," Land of the Dead; god of the last resting place of the deceased.
Mixcoatl: "Cloud Serpent," known in some areas as Camaxtli, god of the hunt. Mixcoatl has aspects similar to those of Huitzilopochtli—for example, war. He was patron of Tlaxcala and Huexotzinco.
Mocexiuhzauhque: Young man who served for a year in the temple as the surrogate of a god.
momoztli: Shrine placed at crossroads or in the marketplace. Momoztitlan means "Place of the *Momoztli*."
Moyotlan: "Place of Mosquitoes"; section of Tenochtitlan south of the Great Temple, a marshy area. One of the four original quarters of the city.

Glossary

Nahua, Nahuatl: Nahua: "he who speaks clearly," a person who spoke Nahuatl, a language "which sounds like a bell," according to Fray Alonso de Molina's sixteenth-century dictionary. A branch of the Uto-Aztecan linguistic group.

Nanahuatzin: "He Who [Is Covered] with Pustules," the humble god who threw himself into the fire in Teotihuacan and was transformed into the sun.

Neteotoquiliztli: "Impersonation of the God," ceremony when men wore the flayed skins of victims with insignia of different gods over them.

Ochpaniztli: "Sweeping of the Roads," eleventh month, equivalent to the first twenty days of September, in honor of the Mother Goddess. Houses, temples, and roads were swept clean; midwives and young warriors fought mock battles; impersonators of the Mother Goddess and maize deities were decapitated, then their flayed skins were worn by male dancers. An arrow sacrifice was held, its symbolism said to be fertilization of the earth by the victims' blood.

ocuiltamalli: "Tamale" made of edible worms.

Omecihuatl: "Lady Two," companion of Ometecuhtli in Omeyocan; female component of the creator pair. She was also known as Tonacacihuatl, "Lady of Our Sustenance," and Citlalicue, "Her Starry Skirt." Omecihuatl and Ometecuhtli were the primordial parents of the gods, the four aspects of Tezcatlipoca being their first children.

Ometecuhtli: "Lord Two," the male half of Ometeotl, "Divine Two," who dwelt in Omeyocan. Ometecuhtli was also known as Tonacatecuhtli, "Lord of Sustenance." For his many other names and attributes, see Nicholson 1971 (table 3).

Omeyocan: "Place of Duality," the thirteenth celestial level where the creator pair Ometeotl, the "Divine Two," dwelt.

Otomi: Order of high-ranking warriors among the Aztecs. Also an ethnic group.

Oxomoco: The first woman, companion of Cipactonal, conceived as an old sorceress, merging with maize-fertility goddesses. The gods had ordered her to learn how to spin and weave, women's chores. Some chronicles claim that Oxomoco was male.

palmo: Measure of length, approximately that of an outstretched hand, from thumb to little finger.

Panquetzaliztli: "Raising of the Banners," fifteenth month (late November and early December) in honor of Huitzilopochtli. Tezcatlipoca and Yacatecuhtli (the merchant god) were also propitiated. Paper banners decorated houses and fruit trees, the image of Huitzilopochtli was formed of amaranth dough and seeds, many victims were sacrificed to Huitzilopochtli, and merchants also sacrificed slaves. A highlight of the fiesta was a procession led by a priest carrying an image of Painal, Huitzilopochtli's deputy, from the Great Temple to different barrios in the city and back to the center of Tenochtitlan.

petlacalcatl: Principal steward, keeper of the ruler's treasure.

petlacontzitzquique: "Those who hold up the divine vessels and insignia," according to Durán (See chap. XXVIII).

pilli (pl. *pipiltin*): Noble, lord, person of high birth.

pulque: Intoxicating liquor obtained from the maguey, often referred to by Durán as *vino* (wine).
Quetzalcoatl: "Feathered Serpent" or "Precious Twin," god of knowledge and civilization, patron of the *calmecac* school, archetype of priests. The culture hero and high priest of Tula called Quetzalcoatl, when forced by Tezcatlipoca to leave his city, went to the Gulf Coast of Mexico, where he disappeared into the east, thus becoming the Morning Star. In this aspect he was called Tlahuizcalpantecuhtli, and Mixcoatl or Xolotl, his twin, was the Evening Star. As Ehecatl, Quetzalcoatl was the wind.
quetzaltlalpiloni: Feather adornment bound to a kind of "column" of hair on top of the head, worn by outstanding warriors.
Quiname: "Giants, men of great stature."
repartimiento: Allotment of Indians; see *encomienda*. After the New Laws of 1542–43 abolished forced labor, the *repartimiento* system obliged adult Indians to work in mines, in factories, on ranches, and in public works for a prescribed period. This compulsory labor was paid and was regulated by laws replacing forced personal services (Vigil 1987:300). *Repartimiento* and *encomienda* were synonymous in colonial Mexico, but *repartimiento* should not be confused with the late sixteenth century *repartimiento* or *cuatequil*, which was in fact an Indian labor draft.
talud-tablero: Architectural profile of a sloping wall (*talud*) combined with a rectangular upright panel (*tablero*), typical of many structures in Teotihuacan. When found elsewhere the *talud-tablero* usually indicates Teotihuacan influence.
Tamoanchan: A mythical paradise. Etymology uncertain but according to Sahagún it means "We Search for Our Abode."
techcatl: Sacrificial stone over which the victim was bent when the heart was extirpated.
tecpan: "Place of Lords," community and meeting house.
tecpatl: Flint knife used for cutting out the heart of the sacrificial victim. It was also a day sign in the calendar.
tecuhtli (pl. *tetecuhtin*): Man of high rank, one who held an important administrative position; outstanding warrior.
tecuitlatl: "Water excrement"; algae scraped from the lake's surface.
telpochcalli: "House of youth," where young men and women of the non-noble class were educated to become average citizens. They were taught by *telpochtlatoque*, "masters of young men," and by *ichpochtlatoque*, "mistresses of young girls," who were not religious but were lay instructors. The patron of the telpochcalli was Tezcatlipoca.
temalacatl: Round stone usually carved on the sides with scenes of feats in war. Used as a gladiatorial stone to which a victim was tied, where he fought with dummy weapons against well-armed warriors.
Templo Mayor: "Great Temple." In Mexico City, site of the Aztec religious center, the pyramid-temple that represented Coatepetl Hill.
Tenochca: Inhabitants of Tenochtitlan, Aztec capital in the Valley of Mexico. "Owners of the Prickly Pear Cactus [*tenochtli*]."

Tenochtitlan: "Place of the Prickly Pear Cactus," capital of the Aztec empire. In some sources Tenochtitlan is derived from Tenoch, one of the mythical founders of the city.

Teocolhuacan, Colhuacan, Huey Colhuacan: See chap. I, note 9.

teomama (pl. *teomamaque*): A *teomama*, "god-bearer," was one of the *teomamaque* who carried the image of the god Huitzilopochtli on the migration from Aztlan to the Valley of Mexico.

teooctli: "Divine wine," pulque drunk by prisoners who were to be sacrificed.

Teopan: "Place of the Temple [or God]," one of the four quarters in which Tenochtitlan originally was divided; to the east.

Teotihuacan: "Place Where the Gods [or Rulers] Are Made," great Classic metropolis (ca. A.D. 0–750) in the central Mexican highlands, whose influence extended in all directions.

Teotlachco: "Divine Ball Court."

teotlacualli: "Divine food," made of black pitch mixed with psychotropic plants and poisonous insects. The priests smeared their bodies with this as a magic protection.

Tepanec, Tecpanec: "People of the *Tecpan* [Palace]" or "People of the *Tepan* [Rocky Land]." Group settled in Azcapotzalco and Tlacopan (Tacuba).

Tepeyacac: "Nose of the Hill," that is, a ridge, in northern Mexico City. Today the shrine of Our Lady of Guadalupe, patroness of Mexico, stands in Tepeyac, called the Villa de Guadalupe. It is said that in ancient times Tonantzin, "Our Mother," may have been worshiped at this place.

Tepeyollotl: "Heart of the Hill," an aspect of Tezcatlipoca. God of caves, mountains, and darkness.

tepictoton: "Small molded ones," images of hills made of amaranth dough for festivities of the thirteenth month, Tepeilhuitl. The *tepictoton* were also considered to be *tlaloques*, Tlaloc's helpers.

tepixqui: One who oversees or directs the work of others, is in charge of people, a *calpulli* head.

teponaztli: Horizontal drum.

Tequihua (pl. Tequihuaque): Title given to distinguished warriors or a dignitary who was the head of a group of administrators.

tequitlato: One who is in charge of tribute. Official in a small community unit within a *calpulli*.

tequitque: Magicians, conjurers.

Tetamazolco: Place name, "On the Stone Toad."

Teteoinnan: "Mother of the Gods," an aspect of the Mother Goddess.

Teuctlamacazqui: Title of Tlillancalqui, who was sent by Motecuhzoma to the Gulf Coast to see if it was true that strangers (or gods) had arrived in houses on the sea.

teuctli or *tecuhtli* (pl. *tetecuhtin*): Indian of noble class.

Tezcatlipoca: "Mirror That Smokes," supreme god of prehispanic central Mexico, the god of fate, omnipotent, omnipresent, omniscient, associated with rulership. He had more appellation and aspects than any other deity: he was associated with the night as Tepeyollotl; he was the enemy, the warrior god, as Yaotl; he was eternally young as Telpochtli.

tezontle: A type of volcanic stone, porous and either gray or reddish in color.

Titles awarded to outstanding warriors and noblemen: see chap. XI.

Tizaapan: "In Chalky [or White] Water," a site between Colhuacan and Iztapalapa, next to the Huixachtepetl, "Hill of the Acacias," today called Cerro de la Estrella. Some scholars have mistaken a site called Tizapan in San Angel for the Aztec Tizaapan. Garibay (Durán 1967:II:578n. 1) calls attention to this misconception but, strangely, prefers the San Angel-Tizapan location.

Tlacatecatl: Inhabitant of Tlacatecco, residence of the Tlacateuctli, "People Lord" or Lord of the People.

Tlacatecpanecatl: "Lord of the Men's Palace." See chap. III.

Tlacaxipehualiztli: "Flaying of People" (*tlacatl* means "human being, person, people, men"). Tlacaxipehualiztli is usually translated as "Flaying of Men," since only men—war captives—were flayed during this ceremony. Women were flayed, however, during other rites (see Neteotoquiliztli). Beggars borrowed skins and went about asking for food. After twenty days of this they divided with the owners the maize, squash, beans, and other seeds given them. For a complete description of Tlacaxipehualiztli, see Durán 1977:172–85, chapter IX.

Tlacochcalcatl: "Prince of the House of Darts," from the Nahuatl *tlacochtli*, "propelled lance or dart," and *calli*, "house." The possessor of this title was one of four men (brothers or close relatives of the king) from whom a ruler was chosen when the *tlatoani* died.

tlacochcalli: "Armory," house of spears or darts. Name also given to an elaborate bower where an image of a recently deceased ruler, made of resinous wood, was placed. Offerings to the statue were made before it was removed from the bower and burned together with the dead ruler's body, before the statue of Huitzilopochtli.

Tlacopan: "In the Reeds," Tepanec city, now called Tacuba, part of Mexico City.

tlacotli (pl. *tlacotin*): Slave, servant.

Tlacuacuallo: "With [delicious] food." Huitzilopochtli's mantle, sometimes called this, was embroidered with a design of human bones.

Tlahuicole: Outstanding warrior from Tlaxcala, captured by the Tenochtitlan Aztecs.

Tlahuizcalpantecuhtli: "Lord of Dawn." See Quetzalcoatl.

Tlalhuica: Inhabitants of Cuauhnahuac (Cuernavaca) and surrounding area. Also spelled Tlahuica.

Tlaloc: God of rain and earth's fertility. Tlaloc was one of the most highly revered of all prehispanic deities. He was the god who fertilized the earth with his water and made the plants grow. The north side of the Great Temple was dedicated to him.

Tlaloc Tlamacazqui: Priest dedicated to Tlaloc.

tlaloque: Assistants to the rain god, seen as little Tlalocs. Four *tlaloques* were assigned to the four corners of the world, where they controlled the different types of rain. They also lived in caves and on mountain tops, where they worked with clouds and lightning. The *tepictoton*, mountain gods, were considered *tlaloque*.

tlamacazque: Priests.

Tlapallan: "Red Place," name of a mythical site; the east.

Tlatelolco: "On a Hillock of Sand." Originally Xaltilalli in Nahuatl: from *xalli*, "earth," *tlatel*, "mound or hillock," and *co*, "place of, on."

tlatoani (pl. *tlatoque* or *tlatoanime*): "He who speaks," "he who has the words," "the speaker"; that is, the ruler or, if the title is Huey Tlaoani (*huey*, "great"), the supreme ruler.

Tlauauanque: "Those who cut or gash skin." Four fully armed warriors who fought against a man who held only dummy weapons in the gladiatorial ceremony during the Tlacaxipehualiztli fiesta.

tlaxilacalli: Another name for a *calpulli*. A sector of the city.

Tlillan: "House of Darkness"; chamber where the statue of the goddess Cihuacoatl was kept.

Tlillan Calmecac: School where some of the *tlatoanime* and lords were taught as children.

Tlillancalqui: "Lord of the House of Darkness," from *tlilli*, "black or soot," and *calli*, "house." Title given to one of the four men from whom a ruler was chosen.

tochancalqui: "He who lives in our house." The man who set fire to Huitzilopochtli's magic weapon, the *xiuhcoatl*, with which Huitzilopochtli then struck off Coyolxauhqui's head.

Toci: "Our Grandmother," one of the names of the Mother Goddess. Toci was the patroness of midwives and healers.

Tonacatecuhtli: "Lord of Sustenance," one of the creator gods, also called Ometecuhtli. Tonacacihuatl was his companion.

Tonacatepetl: "Hill of Sustenance"; in mythology where grain was kept by ants but was discovered by Quetzalcoatl, who transformed himself into an ant in order to steal some grain, which eventually became the basic food for humans.

Tonantzin: "Our Revered Mother," an aspect of the Mother Goddess.

Tota: "Our Father," appellation given to the tree in a rite to Tlaloc during the month of Huey Tozoztli (second half of April), when a child was sacrificed in Lake Tezcoco and Tota, the tree, was sacrificed by being thrust into the water. Tota was also one of the names of the god Xipe Totec.

Toxcatl: "Dryness," fifth month (May 5–24), in honor of Tezcatlipoca. Household implements and agricultural and artists' instruments were "purified" by incense. Images of Huitzilopochtli and other deities were made of amaranth dough and rites to request rain were held. In Tlaxcala, Mixcoatl-Camaxtli was honored; here he took the place of Huitzilopochtli.

Tozoztontli: "Small Vigil," also called Xochimanaloya, "Offering of Flowers," third month (equivalent to March 26–April 14). Water and maize deities were honored; gardeners and those who worked with flowers made offerings to Coatlicue. Rites involved in planting were held in the fields and to the first flowers. Skins of flayed victims from the previous month, Tlacaxipehualiztli, were ritually buried in an artificial cave in the temple.

Tula: Ancient Toltec capital, now major city in the state of Hidalgo.

tzinitzcan: Bird of fine plumage, *Trogonorous mexicanus*.

tzitzimimitl (pl. *tzitzimime*): Malevolent women; mythical/supernatural women whose abode was celestial but who supposedly would descend to earth at the end of the Fifth Sun, to devour humanity.

tzoalli: Dough made of ground amaranth seeds (*Amaranthus hypochondriacus*), maize, *chian*, honey from the maguey plant, and at times blood. Amaranth was called *huauhtli* by the Aztecs. *Tzoalli* figures had ritual significance in the ancient festivals.

tzompantli: Skull rack, the 56th structure mentioned by Sahagún in the ceremonial precinct of Tenochtitlan. *Tzompantli* is also the name of a tree, *Erythrina americana*, whose leaves and bark have medicinal properties.

uitzoctli, uiztli, uictli axoquen: *Uictli* means hoe. *Uitzilin* or *huitzitzilin* means a small "song bird, hummingbird." *Axoquen* means "bird of white plumage"; also *uictliaxoquen* "bird image on the head of the hoe," the *uictli*.

vara: Spanish linear measure, about 0.84 meters. The metric system was introduced into Mexico by the Europeans, so of course Tlacaelel would not have been speaking of *varas* or meters.

Xipe Totec: "Our Lord, One Who Has a [Flayed] Skin," patron of metallurgists, also associated with vegetation. His feast was the Tlacaxipehualiztli.

xiuatlatl: "Turquoise blue spear-thrower," one of Huitzilopochtli's weapons.

xiuhcoatl: "Turquoise Serpent," also referred to as "Fire Serpent," one of Huitzilopochtli's insignia: his magic weapon with which he slew Coyolxauhqui and routed the Huitznahua.

Xiuhmolpilli: "Binding of the years," end of a 52-year cycle, comparable to a century.

Xiuhtecuhtli: "Turquoise Lord," "Lord of the Year," fire god also known as Ixcozauhqui, "Yellow Face," and Huehueteotl, "Old God." Xiuhtecuhtli was the patron of rulers, who were usually invested on the day 4 Acatl (Reed), the god's calendrical sign.

xiuhuitzolli: "Turquoise [or spiny] pointed diadem" worn by rulers.

xochiyaotl: Flower war, arranged to give practice in fighting to soldiers on either side, usually those of Tenochtitlan-Tlatelolco against men of the Puebla-Tlaxcala region.

Xoconochco: Province in southern Mexico. Now Soconusco, Tabasco.

Xocotl Huetzi: "Falling of the Fruits," tenth month of the prehispanic year. Harvest (falling fruit) was celebrated. This was also the main fiesta of Coyoacan. The festival was dedicated to the fire god and slaves were burned alive in his honor.

yolatl: "Heart water," a beverage given to soldiers "to alleviate the pains of war."

Yopican: Place of Yopico, a temple in the barrio of the same name, dedicated to Coatlicue.

Yopican Tecuhtli: "Lord of Yopican."

BIBLIOGRAPHY

ABBREVIATIONS

ADVG   Akademische Druck- u. Verlagsanstalt, Graz (Austria)
AHMNA   Archivo Histórico, Museo Nacional de Antropología (Mexico)
BNM   Biblioteca Nacional de Madrid
FCE   Fondo de Cultura Económica
HMAI   *Handbook of Middle American Indians*
IMEPLAM   Instituto Mexicano para el Estudio de las Plantas Medicinales
INAH   Instituto Nacional de Antropología e Historia
MNA   Museo Nacional de Antropología
SEP   Secretaría de Educación Pública, México
UCLA   University of California at Los Angeles
UNAM   Universidad Nacional Autónoma de México

Acosta, Joseph de
    1590   *De natura Novi Orbis*. Salamanca.
    1962   *Historia natural y moral de las Indias*. Ed. Edmundo O'Gorman. 2nd ed. México, D.F.: Fondo de Cultura Económica.

Aguilar, Fray Francisco de
    1977   *Relación breve de la conquista de la Nueva España*. 1560–1565. México, D.F.: Universidad Nacional Autónoma de México.

Alva Ixtlilxochitl, Fernando de
    1985   *Obras históricas*. 1625. Ed. Edmundo O'Gorman. 2 vols. Instituto de Investigaciones Históricas, Serie de Historiadores y Cronistas de Indias: 4. México, D.F.: Universidad Nacional Autónoma de México.

Alvarado Tezozomoc, Fernando
    1944   *Crónica mexicana*. 1598. México, D.F.: Leyenda.
    1949   *Crónica mexicáyotl*. 1609. Trans. Adrian León. México, D.F.: Universidad Nacional Autónoma de México.

Anales de Cuauhtitlan. See *Códice Chimalpopoca*

Anales de Tlatelolco
    1948   *Anales de Tlatelolco, unos anales históricos de la nación mexicana y Códice de Tlatelolco*. 1530. Trans. and ed. Heinrich Berlin. México, D.F.: Robredo y Editorial Porrúa.

Anawalt, Patricia Rieff
    1981   *Indian Clothing before Cortés*. Norman: University of Oklahoma Press.

Anderson, Arthur J. O.
    1982   Sahagún: Career and Character. In *Florentine Codex: General History of the Things of New Spain, Introductions and Indices*, no. 14, pt. 1, pp. 29–41. Santa Fe: School of American Research and University

of Utah.
Anonymous
1559–   *Actas de los capítulos provinciales de la provincia de Santiago de*
1587   *México, Orden de Predicadores.* Sixteenth-century manuscript in the AHMNA.

Badianus Manuscript
1940   *Badianus Manuscript (Codex Barberini, Latin 241).* 1552. Ed. Emily Walcott Emmart. Baltimore: John Hopkins University Press.

Barlow, Robert
1945   La crónica "X." *Revista Mexicana de Estudios Antropológicos*, vol. VII:65–87. México: Sociedad Mexicana de Antropología.

Barret, Ward
1977   *La hacienda azucarera de los marqueses del Valle (1535–1910).* Ed. Stella Mastrangelo. México, D.F.: Siglo Veintiuno.

Baudot, Georges
1974   The Last Years of Fray Bernardino de Sahagún (1585–90): The Rescue of the Confiscated Work and the Seraphic Conflicts, New Unpublished Documents. In *Sixteenth-Century Mexico*, ed. Munro S. Edmonson, pp. 165–88. Albuquerque: University of New Mexico Press.

1983   *Utopia e historia en México: Los primeros cronistas de la civilización mexicana (1520–1569).* Trans. Vicente González Loscertales. Madrid: Espasa-Calpe.

1988   Fray Rodrigo de Sequera: Devil's Advocate for Sahagún's Forbidden History. In *The Work of Bernardino de Sahagún: Pioneer Ethnographer of Sixteenth-Century Aztec Mexico*, ed. J. Jorge Klor de Alva, H. B. Nicholson, and Eloise Quiñones Keber, pp. 119–34. Studies on Culture and Society 2, Institute for Mesoamerican Studies. Albany/Austin: State University of New York/University of Texas Press.

Baudot, Georges, and Tzvetan Todorov
1983   *Relatos de la conquista.* Trans. Guillermina Cuevas. México, D.F.: Grijalbo/Consejo Nacional para la Cultura y las Artes.

Benson, Elizabeth P., ed.
1984   *Ritual Human Sacrifice in Mesoamerica.* Washington, D.C.: Dumbarton Oaks.

Berdan, Frances F.
1982   *The Aztecs of Central Mexico: An Imperial Society.* New York: Holt, Rinehart and Winston.

Beristáin y Souza, José Mariano
1883–   *Biblioteca hispano americana septentrional.* 1816–21. 3 vols. and
1889   supplement. Amecameca, Mexico: Colegio Católico.

Boone, Elizabeth Hill
1988   The Nature and Earlier Versions of Diego Durán's "Historia de las Yndias" in Madrid. In *Smoke and Mist: Mesoamerican Studies in Memory of Thelma D. Sullivan*, ed. J. Kathryn Josserand and Karen

Dakin, pt. I, pp. 41–58. BAR International Series 402. Oxford: BAR.

Broda de Casas, Johanna
1970   "Tlaxcaxipehualitzli: A Reconstruction of an Aztec Calendar Festival from the Sixteenth Century Sources." *Revista Española de Antropología Americana* 5:197–273. Madrid: Universidad de Madrid.

Broda, Johanna
1987   Templo Mayor as Ritual Space. In *The Great Temple of Tenochtitlan: Center and Periphery in the Aztec World*, ed. Johanna Broda, David Carrasco, and Eduardo Matos Moctezuma, pp. 61–123. Berkeley: University of California Press.

Brundage, Burr Cartwright
1972   *A Rain of Darts*. Austin: University of Texas Press.

Burkhart, Louise
1989   *The Slippery Earth: Nahua-Christian Moral Dialogue in Sixteenth Century Mexico*. Tucson: University of Arizona Press.

Bye, Robert, and Edelmira Linares
1983   The Role of Plants Found in the Mexican Markets and Their Importance in Ethnobotanical Studies. *Journal of Ethnobiology* 3(1): 1–13.

Calnek, Edward E.
1974   The Sahagún Texts as a Source of Sociological Information. In *Sixteenth Century Mexico: The Work of Sahagún*, ed. Munro S. Edmondson, pp. 189–204. Albuquerque: University of New Mexico Press.
1978   The City-State in the Basin of Mexico: Late Pre-Hispanic Period. In *Urbanization in the Americas from Its Beginnings to the Present*, ed. R. P. Schaedel, J. E. Hardoy, and N. S. Kinzer, pp. 363–70. The Hague: Mouton.

Carrasco, David
1982   *Quetzalcoatl and the Irony of Empire*. Chicago: University of Chicago Press.
1990   *Religions of Mesoamerica: Cosmovision and Ceremonial Centers*. San Francisco: Harper and Row.

Carrasco, Pedro
1971   Social Organization of Ancient Mexico. In *HMAI*, vol. X, pp. 349–75. 16 vols. Austin: University of Texas Press.

Carrasco, Pedro, and Johanna Broda, eds.
1976   *Estratificación social en la Mesoamérica prehispánica*. México, D.F.: INAH.

Caso, Alfonso
1958   *The Aztecs: People of the Sun*. Trans. Lowell Dunham. Norman: University of Oklahoma Press.

Castillo, Cristóbal del
1908   *Historia de los mexicanos desde su salida de Aztlan hasta la fundación de México*. Ed. Francisco del Paso y Troncoso. Florence:

Salvador Laudi.
Chadwick, Robert
    1971   Native Pre-Aztec History of Central Mexico. In *HMAI*, vol. XI, pp. 474–504. 16 vols. Austin: University of Texas Press.
Clavijero, Francisco Javier
    1780   *Storia antica del Messico*. Bologna.
    1945   *Historia antigua de México*. 4 vols. México, D.F.: Porrúa.
Clendinnen, Inga
    1991   *Aztecs*. Cambridge: Cambridge University Press.
Cline, S. L., ed.
    1989   *Conquest of New Spain, 1585 Revision by Bernardino de Sahagún*. Trans. Howard F. Cline. Salt Lake City: University of Utah Press.
Codex Borbonicus
    1974   *Codex Borbonicus*. Ed. Karl Anton Nowotny and Jacqueline de Durand-Forest. ADVG.
Codex Borgia
    1976   *Codex Borgia*. Biblioteca Apostolica Vaticana (Messicano Riserva 28). Ed. Karl Anton Nowotny. ADVG.
Codex Boturini. See *Códice Tira de la Peregrinación/Códice Boturini*
Codex Cospi
    1968   *Codex Cospi*. Ed. Karl Anton Nowotny, ADVG.
Codex Fejérváry-Mayer
    1971   *Codex Fejérváry-Mayer*. Ed. C. A. Burland, ADVG.
Codex Ixtlilxochitl
    1976   *Codex Ixtlilxochitl*. Ed. Jacqueline de Durand-Forest. ADVG.
Codex Laud
    1966   *Codex Laud*. Ed. C. A. Burland, ADVG.
Codex Magliabechiano
    1983   *Codex Magliabechiano and the Lost Prototype of the Magliabechiano Group*. Ed. Elizabeth Hill Boone. 2 vols. Berkeley: University of California Press.
Codex Mendoza
    1992   *Codex Mendoza*. Ed. Frances F. Berdan and Patricia Rieff Anawalt. 4 vols. Berkeley: University of California Press.
Codex Nuttall
    1975   *Codex Nuttall*. Ed. Zelia Nuttall and Arthur G. Miller. New York: Dover.
Codex Vaticanus B
    1972   *Codex Vaticanus B (Vaticanus 3773)*. Ed. Ferdinand Anders. ADVG.
Codex Vindobinensis Mexicanus 1
    1974   *Codex Vindobinensis Mexicanus 1*. Ed. O. Adelhofer. ADVG.
Códice Aubin
    1979   *Códice Aubin (Códice 1576)*. Ed. Antonio Peñafiel. México, D.F.: Innovación.
Códice Azcatitlan
    1949   Study of the Códice Azcatitlan by Robert H. Barlow. *Journal de la*

Societé des Americanistes, n. 5. 38: 103-35.
Códice Bodley
    1960   *Códice Bodley*. Ed. Alfonso Caso. México, D.F.: Sociedad Mexicana de Antropología.
Códice Chimalpopoca
    1945   *Códice Chimalpopoca*. 1558, 1570. Trans. Primo Feliciano Velázquez. México, D.F.: Imprenta Universitaria.
Códice Colombino
    1966   *Códice Colombino*. Ed. Alfonso Caso and Mary Elizabeth Smith. México, D.F.: Sociedad Mexicana de Antropología.
Códice Mendocino (Codex Mendoza)
    1979   *Códice Mendocino (Codex Mendoza)*. Ed. José Ignacio Echeagaray. México, D.F.: San Angel Ediciones.
Códices Becker I/II
    1961   *Códices Becker I/II*. Ed. Karl Anton Nowotny. ADVG.
Códice Tira de la Peregrinación/Códice Boturini
    1975   *Códice Tira de la Peregrinación/Códice Boturini*. Colección de Documentos Conmemorativos del DCL Aniversario de la Fundación de Tenochtitlan: Documento No. 1. SEP.
Códice Vaticano-Ríos
    1965   Códice Vaticano-Ríos (Vaticano Latino 3738). In *Antigüedades de México, basadas en la recopilación de Lord Kingborough*, ed. José Corona Nuñez, vol. III, pp. 7-313. 4 vols. México, D.F.: Secretaría de Hacienda y Crédito Público.
Colston, Stephen A.
    1973   Fray Diego Durán's "Historia de las Indias de Nueva España e Islas de la Tierra Firme": A Historiographical Analysis. Doctoral dissertation, UCLA.
    1977   A Comment on Dating the "Crónica X," *Tlalocan* 7: 371-77.
    1988   Fray Diego Durán and His Native Informants. In *Smoke and Mist: Mesoamerican Studies in Memory of Thelma D. Sullivan*, ed. J. Kathryn Josserand and Karen Dakin, pt. I: pp. 59-67. BAR International Series 402. Oxford: BAR.
Colston, Stephen, and Carlos Paredes
    1980   Un servicio de Fray Diego Durán a la Inquisición en 1586. *Antropología e Historia: Boletín del Instituto Nacional de Antropología e Historia* 3(29): 41-44.
Conquistador Anónimo
    1606   *Relatione di algune cose della Nueva Spagna*. Venice.
    1963   The Chronicle of the Anonymous Conquistador. In *The Conquistadors*, ed. and trans. Patricia de Fuentes, pp. 165-81. New York: Orion.
Cortés, Hernán
    1963   *Cartas y documentos*. 1522-43. México, D.F.: Editorial Porrúa.
    1971   *Letters from Mexico*. Trans. A. R. Pagden. New York: Grossman.
Couch, N. C. Christopher
    1987   Style and Ideology in the Durán Illustrations: An Interpretive

Study of Three Early Colonial Mexican Manuscripts. Doctoral dissertation, Columbia University, New York.

1989 Another Garden of Eden: Natural Imagery in the Durán Illustrations. In *I Coloquio de Documentos Pictográficos de Tradición Náhuatl*, pp. 123–35. Instituto de Investigaciones Históricas, Serie de Cultura Náhuatl, Monografía 23. México, D.F.: UNAM.

Dahlgren de Jordán, Barbro

1989 *La Mixteca: Su cultura e historia*. 2nd ed. México, D.F.: UNAM.

Davies, Nigel

1973 *The Aztecs: A History*. London: Macmillan.

1977 *The Toltecs until the Fall of Tula*. Norman: University of Oklahoma Press.

1980 *The Toltec Heritage: From the Fall of Tula to the Rise of Tenochtitlan*. Norman: University of Oklahoma Press.

1981 *Human Sacrifice in History and Today*. New York: William Morrow.

1986 *The Toltec Resurgence*. Norman: University of Oklahoma Press.

Dávila Padilla, Agustín

1955 *Historia de la fundación y discurso de la provincia de Santiago de Mexico, de la Orden de Predicadores*. Facsimile of first edition of 1625. Introduction by A. Millares Carlo. Mexico, D.F.: Academia Literaria.

Díaz, José Luis

1976 *Indice y sinonimia de las plantas medicinales de México*. México, D.F.: IMEPLAM.

Díaz del Castillo, Bernal

1939 *Historia verdadera de la conquista de la Nueva España*. 1632. 3 vols. México, D.F.: Pedro Robredo.

Dibble, Charles E.

1982 Sahagún's *Historia*. In *Florentine Codex: General History of the Things of New Spain, Introductions and Indices*, no. 14, pt. I, pp. 9–23, Santa Fe: School of American Research and University of Utah.

Durán, Diego

1581 Códice Durán. Manuscript in the Biblioteca Nacional de Madrid. Vitrina 26–11.

1854 *Historia de las Indias de Nueva España y Islas de Tierra Firme*. Manuscript, copy made in Madrid for José F. Ramírez, collection of the AHMNA, Mexico, no. 556 (15585).

1867– *Historia de las Indias de Nueva España y Islas de Tierra Firme*. 2
1880 vols. and atlas. Ed. José F. Ramírez. J. M. Mexico, D.F.: Andrade and F. Escalante (vol. I), I. Escalante (vol. II).

1951 *Historia de las Indias de Nueva España y Islas de Tierra Firme*. Ed. José Fernando Ramírez. 2 vols. México, D.F.: Editora Nacional.

1964 *The Aztecs: The History of the Indies of New Spain*. Trans. and ed. Doris Heyden and Fernando Horcasitas. New York: Orion.

1967 *Historia de las Indias de Nueva España e Islas de la Tierra Firme*. Ed. Angel María Garibay K. 2 vols. México, D.F.: Editorial Porrúa.

1971   Book of the Gods and Rites and the Ancient Calendar. 2nd ed., 1977. Trans. and ed. Fernando Horcasitas and Doris Heyden. Norman: University of Oklahoma Press.
1990a   Códice Durán. Ed. Electra and Tonatiuh Gutiérrez. México, D.F.: Arrendadora Internacional.
1990b   Historia de las Indias de Nueva España e Islas de la Tierra Firme. Ed. José Rubén Romero Galván and Rosa Camelo. México, D.F.: Banco Santander.

Duverger, Christian
1987   El origen de los aztecas. Trans. Carmen Arizmendi. México, D.F.: Grijalbo.

Edmondson, Munro S., ed.
1974   Sixteenth-Century Mexico: The Works of Sahagún. A School of American Research Book. Albuquerque: University of New Mexico Press.

Eguiara y Eguren, Johannes Josephus de
1944   Biblioteca Mexicana. 1755. 2nd ed., trans. Agustín Millares Carlo, ed. Federico Gómez de Orozco. México, D.F.: Fondo de Cultura Económica.

Enciclopedia de México
1977   Enciclopedia de México. 2nd ed. 14 vols. México, D.F.: Editorial Enciclopedia de México.

Fernández del Castillo, Francisco
1925   Fray Diego Durán, aclaraciones históricas. *Anales del Museo Nacional de Arqueología, Historia y Etnografía* 4, 3(3): 223–29.

Flannery, Kent V., and Joyce Marcus, eds.
1983   The Cloud People. Divergent Evolution of the Zapotec and Mixtec Civilizations. New York: Academic Press.

Florentine Codex. See Sahagún, Fray Bernardino de

Florescano, Enrique
1991a   La nueva imagen del México antiguo. *Vuelta* 15, no. 173: 32–38.
1991b   El nuevo pasado mexicano. México, D.F.: Cal y Arena.

Foshag, W. F.
1959   Mineralogical Attributions. In *Precolumbian Art: Robert Woods Bliss Collection*, pp. 51–60. 2nd ed. London: Phaidon Press.

Furst, Jill Leslie
1977   The Tree Birth Tradition in the Mixteca, Mexico. *Journal of Latin American Lore* 3(2): 183–226.

Furst, Peter T., ed.
1972   Flesh of the Gods: The Ritual Use of Hallucinogens. London: George Allen and Unwin.

García, Fray Gregorio
1981   Origen de los indios del Nuevo Mundo e Indias Occidentales. 1607. México, D.F.: FCE.

García Granados, Rafael
1952–   Diccionario biográfico de historia antigua de Méjico. 3 vols. Publica-
1953   ciones del Instituto de Historia, no. 23. México, D.F.: UNAM.

García Icazbalceta, Joaquín
   1941– *Nueva colección de documentos para la historia de México*. 5 vols.
   1944 México, D.F.: Chávez Hayhoe.

García Martínez, Bernardo
   1967 La Historia de Durán. *Historia Mexicana* vol. 18, no. 3:463–64. México, D.F.: El Colegio de México.

Garibay K., Angel María
   1953 *Historia de la literatura náhuatl*. 2 vols. México, D.F.: Editorial Porrúa.

Gerhard, Peter
   1972 *A Guide to the Historical Geography of New Spain*. Cambridge: Cambridge University Press.

Gibson, Charles
   1964 *The Aztecs under Spanish Rule*. Stanford: Stanford University Press.
   1966 *Spain in America*. New York: Harper and Row.
   1971 Structure of the Aztec Empire. In *HMAI*, vol. X, pp. 376–94, 16 vols. Austin: University of Texas Press.

Gillespie, Susan D.
   1989 *The Aztec Kings: The Construction of Rulership in Mexica History*. Tucson: University of Arizona Press.

Glass, John B.
   1975 A Survey of Native Middle American Pictorial Manuscripts. In HMAI, vol. XIV, pp. 3–80. Austin: University of Texas Press.

Glendinnen, Inga
   1991 *Aztecs, An Interpretation*. Cambridge: Cambridge University Press.

González Torres, Yólotl
   1988 *El sacrificio humano entre los mexicas*. 2nd ed. México, D.F.: FCE–INAH.
   1991 *Diccionario de mitología y religón de Mesoamérica*. México, D.F.: Larousse.

Hale, John R., et al.
   1975 *Age of Exploration Great Ages of Man*. 2nd ed. New York: Time Incorporated.

Handbook of Middle American Indians
   1964– *HMAI*. Ed. Robert Wauchope. 16 vols. Austin: University of
   1976 Texas Press.

Hassig, Ross
   1985 *Trade, Tribute, and Transportation: The Sixteenth Century Political Economy of the Valley of Mexico*. Norman: University of Oklahoma Press.

Hernández, Francisco
   1959– *Historia natural de Nueva España: Obras completas*. 1575. 7 vols.
   1984 México, D.F.: UNAM.

Heyden, Doris
   1974 La diosa madre: Itzpapálotl. *Boletín Instituto Nacional de An-*

tropología e Historia 2, no. 11: 3–14.
1975 An Interpretation of the Cave Underneath the Pyramid of the Sun in Teotihuacan, Mexico. *American Antiquity* 49(2): 131–47.
1976 El simbolismo de las plumas rojas en el ritual prehispánico. *Boletín Instituto Nacional de Antropología e Historia* 2, no. 18: 15–22.
1983a *Mitología y simbolismo de la flora en el México prehispánico*. México, D.F.: Instituto de Investigaciones Antropológicas, UNAM.
1983b "Reeds and Rushes: From Survival to Sovereigns." In *Flora and Fauna Imagery in Precolumbian Cultures: Iconography and Function*, ed. Jeanette F. Peterson, pp. 93–112. BAR International Series 171, Oxford, BAR.
1986a Metaphors, Nahual*tocaitl*, and Other "Disguised" Terms among the Aztecs. In *Symbol and Meaning beyond the Closed Community: Essays in Mesoamerican Ideas*, ed. Gary H. Gossen, pp. 35–43. Albany: Institute for Mesoamerican Studies, State University of New York.
1986b Xipe Totec: ¿dios nativo de Guerrero o hijo adoptivo? In *Arqueología y etnohistoria del Estado de Guerrero*, pp. 373–90. México, D.F.: INAH and Gobierno del Estado de Guerrero.
1989 *The Eagle, the Cactus, the Rock: The Roots of Mexico-Tenochtitlan's Foundation Myth and Symbol*. BAR International Series 484. Oxford: BAR.
In press *El Templo Mayor de Tenochtitlan en la obra de Diego Durán*, with contributions by Eduardo Matos Moctezuma and Miguel León-Portilla. México, D.F.: Instituto Nacional de Antropología e Historia-Proyecto Templo Mayor.

Historia de los mexicanos por sus pinturas
   1973 Historia de los mexicanos por sus pinturas. 1533–69. In *Teogonía e historia de los mexicanos: Tres opúsculos del siglo XVI*, ed. Angel Maria Garibay K., pp. 23–90. Sepan Cuántos 37. México, D.F.: Editorial Porrúa.

Historia de México (Histoire du Mechique)
   1973 Histoire du Mechique. In *Teogonía e historia de los mexicanos: Tres opúsculos del siglo XVI*. 1533–69. ed. Angel Maria Garibay K., pp. 91–116. 2nd ed. Sepan Cuántos 37. México, D.F.: Editorial Purrúa.

Historia Tolteca-Chichimeca. See Kirchhoff, Paul, et al.
Ixtlilxochitl. See Alva Ixtlilxochitl, Fernando de
Jiménez Moreno, Wigberto
   1938 Fray Bernardino de Sahagún y su obra. In *Historia general de las cosas de Nueva España, de Bernardino de Sahagún*, vol. I, pp. xiii–lxxiv. México, D.F.: Pedro Robredo.
   1956 Historia antigua de México. Mimeographed edition. Sociedad de Alumnos, Escuela Nacional de Antropología e Historia, México, D.F.

Keen, Benjamin
    1971   *The Aztec Image in Western Thought.* New Brunswick: Rutgers University Press.

Kellogg, Susan M.
    1986   Kinship and Social Organization in Early Colonial Tenochtitlan. In *HMAI, Supplement*, ed. V. R. Bricker, R. Spores, and P. A. Andrews, vol. IV, pp. 103–21. 16 vols. Austin: University of Texas Press.

Kingsborough, Lord (Sir Edward King)
    1964   *Antigüedades de México basadas en la recopilación de Lord Kingsborough.* Estudio de José Corona Nuñez, prologue Agustín Yañez. 4 vols. México, D.F.: Secretaria de Hacienda y Crédito.

Kirchhoff, Paul, Lina Odena Güemes, and Luis Reyes García, eds.
    1976   *Historia Tolteca-Chichimeca 1550–60.* México, D.F.: INAH/SEP.

Klein, Cecelia F.
    1988   Rethinking Cihuacóatl: Aztec Political Imagery of the Conquered Woman. In *Smoke and Mist: Mesoamerican Studies in Memory of Thelma D. Sullivan*, ed. J. Kathryn Josserand and Karen Dakin, pt. I, pp. 237–78. BAR International Series 402. Oxford: BAR.

Klor de Alva, J. Jorge, H. B. Nicholson, and Eloise Quiñones Keber, eds.
    1988   *The Work of Bernardino de Sahagún: Pioneer Ethnographer of Sixteenth-Century Aztec Mexico.* Studies on Culture and Society 2, Institute for Mesoamerican Studies. Albany/Austin: State University of New York at Albany/University of Texas Press.

Lafaye, Jacques
    1976   *Quetzalcoatl and Guadalupe: The Formation of Mexican National Consciousness, 1531–1815.* Trans. Benjamin Keen. Chicago: University of Chicago Press.

Laughlin, Robert M.
    1969   The Huastec. In *HMAI*, vol. VII, pp. 298–311. 16 vols. Austin: University of Texas Press.

León Pinelo, Antonio de
    1629   *Epitome de la biblioteca oriental i occidental naútica y geografica.* Madrid: Juan Gonzalez.

León-Portilla, Ascensión H. de
    1988   *Tepuztlahcuilolli: Impresos en náhuatl, historia y bibliografía.* 2 vols. Serie de Cultura Náhuatl, Monografías 22. Instituto de Investigaciones Históricas and Instituto de Investigaciones Filológicas. México, D.F.: UNAM.

León-Portilla, Miguel
    1963   *Aztec Thought and Culture: A Study of the Ancient Náhuatl Mind.* Norman: University of Oklahoma Press.
    1974   *Pre-Columbian Literatures of Mexico.* Norman: University of Oklahoma Press.

1978 *El Templo Mayor de Tenochtitlan, su espacio y tiempos sagrados.* México, D.F.: INAH.
Leyenda de los Soles. See *Códice Chimalpopoca*
Lienzo de Tlaxcala, El
  1983 *El Lienzo de Tlaxcala.* México, D.F.: Cartón y Papel de México.
Lockhart, James
  1991 Postconquest Nahua Society and Culture Seen through Nahuatl Sources. In *Nahuas and Spaniards: Postconquest Central Mexican History and Philology,* pp. 1–23. Palo Alto and Los Angeles: Stanford University Press and UCLA Latin American Center Publications.
Lombardo de Ruiz, Sonia
  1973 *Desarrollo urbano de México-Tenochtitlan, según las fuentes históricas.* México, D.F.: SEP/INAH.
Long-Solís, Janet
  1986 *Capsicum y cultura: La historia del chilli.* México, D.F.: FCE.
López Austin, Alfredo
  1973 *Hombre-Dios: Religión y política en el mundo nahuatl.* México, D.F.: UNAM.
  1988 *The Human Body and Ideology: Concepts of the Ancient Nahuas.* Trans. Thelma Ortiz de Montellano and Bernard Ortiz de Montellano. 2 vols. Salt Lake City: University of Utah Press.
Macazaga Ordoño, César, ed.
  1979 *Nombres geográficos de México.* México, D.F.: Cosmos.
Martínez, Maximino
  1987 *Catálogo de nombres vulgares y científicos de plantas mexicanas.* 2nd ed. México, D.F.: FCE.
Matos Moctezuma, Eduardo
  1988 *The Great Temple of the Aztecs: Treasures of Tenochtitlan.* Trans. Doris Heyden. London: Thames and Hudson.
Mendieta, Jerónimo de
  1945 *Historia eclesiástica indiana.* 1596. 2 vols. México, D.F.: Chávez Hayhoe.
Molina, Fray Alonso de
  1944 *Vocabulario en lengua castellana y mexicana.* 1571. Madrid: Ediciones Cultura Hispánica.
Motolinía, Fray Toribio de Benavente
  1971 *Memoriales o libro de las cosas de la Nueva España.* Ed. Edmundo O'Gorman. 1555. México, D.F.: Instituto de Investigaciones Históricas, UNAM.
Mullen, Robert James
  1975 *Dominican Architecture in Sixteenth-Century Oaxaca.* Phoenix: Center for Latin American Studies, Arizona State University.
Muñoz Camargo, Diego
  1966 *Historia de Tlaxcala.* 1598. Ed. Alfredo Chavero. Guadalajara: Edmundo Levy.

Nicholson, Henry B.
- 1957 Topiltzin Quetzalcoatl of Tollan: A Problem in Mesoamerican Ethnohistory. Doctoral dissertation, Harvard University.
- 1971 Religion in Prehispanic Central Mexico. In *HMAI*, vol. X, pp. 395–446. 16 vols. Austin: University of Texas Press.

Norman, Garth V.
- 1976 Izapa Sculpture. *New World Archaeological Foundation, Papers* 39(1–2). Provo: Brigham Young University.

Pasztory, Esther
- 1983 *Aztec Art*. New York: Harry N. Abrams.

Phelan, John Leddy
- 1970 *The Millennial Kingdom of the Franciscans in the New World*. 2nd ed. Berkeley: University of California Press.

Quiñones Keber, Eloise
- 1988 The Aztec Image of Topiltzin Quetzalcóatl. In *Smoke and Mist: Mesoamerican Studies in Memory of Thelma D. Sullivan*, ed. J. Kathryn Josserand and Karen Dakin, pt. I, pp. 329–44. BAR International Series 402. Oxford: BAR.

Radin, Paul
- 1920 *The Sources and Authenticity of the History of the Ancient Mexicans*. Publications in American Archaeology and Ethnology 17(1). Berkeley: University of California Press.

Ravicz, R., and A. Kimball Romney
- 1969 The Mixtec. In *HMAI*, vol. VII, pp. 367–99. 16 vols. Austin: University of Texas Press.

Relaciones geográficas del siglo XVI: México
- 1985–1989 *Relaciones geográficas del siglo XVI: México*. 1579–85. Ed. René Acuña. 10 vols. México, D.F.: Instituto de Investigaciones Antropológicas, UNAM.

Ricard, Robert
- 1966 *The Spiritual Conquest of Mexico: An Essay on the Apostolate and the Evangelizing Methods of the Mendicant Orders in New Spain, 1523–1572*. Trans. Lesley Byrd Simpson. Berkeley: University of California Press.

Robertson, Donald
- 1968 The Paste-Over Illustrations in the Durán Codex of Madrid. *Tlalocan* 5(4): 340–48.

Sahagún, Fray Bernardino de
- 1950–1982 *Florentine Codex: General History of the Things of New Spain*. 1561–82. Trans. and ed. Arthur J. O. Anderson and Charles E. Dibble. 12 books and introductory volume. Santa Fe: School of American Research and the University of Utah.
- 1969 *Historia de las cosas de Nueva España*. 2nd ed. 4 vols. México, D.F.: Editorial Porrúa.

Sandoval, Fernando B.
- 1945 La relación de la conquista de México en la "Historia" de Fray

Diego Durán. In *Estudios de Historiografía de la Nueva España*, pp. 49–90. México, D.F.: El Colegio de México.

Sandstrom, Alan R., and Pamela Effrein Sandstrom
  1986 *Traditional Papermaking and Paper Cult Figures of Mexico*. Norman: University of Oklahoma Press.

Simeón, Remí
  1965 *Dictionnaire de la langue náhuatl ou mexicaine*. ADVG.
  1988 *Diccionario de la lengua nahuatl o mexicana*. 6th ed. México, D.F.: Siglo Veintiuno.

Simpson, Lesley Byrd
  1950 *The Encomienda in New Spain*. Berkeley: University of California Press.

Smith, Michael E.
  1986 The Role of Social Stratification in the Aztec Empire: A View from the Provinces. *American Anthropologist* 88(1): 70–91.

Standley, Paul C.
  1961 *Trees and Shrubs of Mexico*. Contributions from the United States National Herbarium 23. 2nd ed. 3 vols. Washington, D.C.: Smithsonian Institution.

Sullivan, Thelma D.
  1971 The Finding and Founding of Mexico Tenochtitlan, Translation and Notes. *Tlalocan* 6(4): 312–36.
  1988 *Compendium of Nahuatl Grammar*. Trans. Thelma D. Sullivan and Neville Stiles, ed. Wick R. Miller and Karen Dakin. Salt Lake City: University of Utah Press.

Tezozomoc, Fernando Alvarado. See Alvarado Tezozomoc, Fernando

Todorov, Tzvetan
  1985 *The Conquest of America*. Trans. Richard Howard. New York: Harper and Rowe.

Torquemada, Fray Juan de
  1975– *Monarquía indiana*. 1615. 7 vols. México, D.F.: Instituto de
  1983 Investigaciones Históricas, UNAM.

Townsend, Richard F.
  1979 State and Cosmos in the Art of Tenochtitlan. *Dumbarton Oaks Studies in Pre-Columbian Art and Archaeology* no. 20. Washington, D.C.: Dumbarton Oaks.

Umberger, Emily
  1981 Aztec Sculptures, Hieroglyphs and History. Doctoral dissertation, Department of Art History and Archaeology, Columbia University, New York.
  1987 Antiques, Revivals, and References to the Past in Aztec art. *Res* 13: 63–106.
  1988 A Reconsideration of Some Hieroglyphs on the Mexica Calendar Stone. In *Smoke and Mist: Mesoamerican Studies in Memory of Thelma D. Sullivan*, ed. J. Kathryn Josserand and Karen Dakin, pt. I, pp. 345–88. BAR International Series 402. Oxford: BAR.

van Zantwijk, Rudolph
   1985 *The Aztec Arrangement: The Social History of Pre-Spanish Mexico.*
         Norman: University of Oklahoma Press.
Vargas, Ernesto, ed.
   1989 *Las máscaras de la cueva de Santa Ana Teloxtoc.* México, D.F.:
         Instituto de Investigaciones Antropológicas, UNAM.
Vigil, Ralph H.
   1987 *Alonso de Zorita: Royal Judge and Christian Humanist 1512–1585.*
         Norman: University of Oklahoma Press.
Vogt, Evon Z.
   1976 *Tortillas for the Gods.* Cambridge: Harvard University Press.
Warren, J. Benedict
   1973 An Introductory Survey of Secular Writings in the European
         Tradition on Colonial Middle America, 1503–1818. In *HMAI*, vol.
         XIII, pp. 42–136. 16 vols. Austin: University of Texas Press.
Wolinski, Arelene
   1987 Egyptian Masks: The Priest and His Role. *Archaeology* 40(1): 22–
         29.
Young, Serinity
   1987 Stars. In *The Encyclopedia of Religion*, vol. XIV, pp. 42–46. 15
         vols. New York: Macmillan.
Zavala, Silvio
   1935 *La encomienda indiana.* Madrid.
Zorita, Alonso de
   1971 *Life and Labor in Ancient Mexico.* 2nd ed. Trans. Benjamin Keen.
         New Brunswick: Rutgers University Press.

INDEX

Aatl, 53
Abad, 369
Acachinanco, 155, 369
Acacihtli, 51n
Acacitli, 216n
Acahualtzinco, 25
Acamapichtli, 48–50, 52–59, 71, 115, 243, 337; reign of, 579
Acamapichtzin. *See* Acamapichtli
Acamapilli. *See* Acamapichtli
Acapetlahuacan, 329
Acapichtlan, 15, 302, 336
Acaquilpan, 138
Acatl apechtli, 420–21
Acatzinco, 154, 155, 329
Acatzintitlan. *See* Mexicatzinco
Acazitli, 51–53
Achilhilacachocan, 330
Achitometl, 34–38. *See also* Toci
Acolhua, 225 & n.2
Acolhuacan, 126. *See also* Tezcoco
Acolman, 14, 17n
Acolnahuacatl (Tacuba king), 68
Acolneuhuac, 97n.2
Acosta, Joseph de, 3n, 571, 573
Actopan, 336
Acuecuexco (spring), 362–66, 369–72
Aculco, 141, 477–81
Aculhua. *See* Acolhua
Aculman, 330
Adultery, Aztec law vs., 210
Adultery flower, 52n.3
Agave. *See* Maguey
Aguilar, Francisco de, 519 & n
Ahuatl, 216n
Ahuauhtli, 45n.5, 349
Ahuexotl, 51 & n, 53, 216 & n
Ahuilizapan, 175–81, 197, 202
Ahuitzotl, 309–12, 394; and Chiapa campaign, 315–17; and Coyoacan dam project, 365–70; death of, 381, 382; enthronement of, 312–15, 318–23; as executioner, 338; funeral of, 382–86; and Huaxtec rebellion, 323–27; Nezahualpilli elegy for, 384; *persona* of, 341, 382; progeny of, 388; reign of, 579; religious pilgrimage of, 355–60; and Tecuantepec, 350–54, 374–79; and Teloloapan, 341–48; and Templo Mayor dedication, 328–41; and Tenochtitlan water needs, 362–70, 371–73; and Tzutzumatzin, 363–65, 372
Ahuitzotzin. *See* Ahuitzotl
Alauiztlan, 342, 344–48
Alcaraz (museum director), 566
Algae, edible, 11n, 46n.5, 205, 349
Alligators, men into, 433
Alphabet, Indian, 570
Altar of the Eagles, 428
Altars, Aztec, 170n.2
Alum, 204
Alvarado, Pedro de, 534, 551; ruse of, 535–37, 539, 542; at Tenochtitlan, 553, 554
Alvarado Tezozomoc, Fernando. *See* Tezozomoc, Fernando Alvarado
Amalech, 431 & n
Amalekites, 431n
Amaranth, 11n, 40n, 214, 362; as dough source, 40n (see also *Tzoalli*); flooded out, 370; Motecuhzoma II diet of, 487; as tribute, 55, 205, 206. See also *Ahuauhtli*
Amatla, 202
Amaxtlan, 349–50, 352–53
Amaxtli, 289n
Amber, 178–81, 203, 204, 274
Amequemecan, 14, 89, 141, 145 & n.4, 523–24
"Angry Lord." *See* Motecuhzoma II
"Angry Lord, He Who Shoots into the Sky." *See* Motecuhzoma I
Animals, 16; domesticated, 182; men into, 215 & n; as tribute, 203, 205, 207, 270, 302, 318. *See also* Fish; Fowl; Game; Hides, animal; Insects

609

Index

Anklets, 209, 280, 291, 297, 356
Annalists, pre-Conquest, 569
Annonas, 205
Antiquities of Mexico (Kingsborough), 4n.3
Ants, as tribute, 205
Apan, 330
Apanecatl, 51n
Apantecuhtli, 289 & n
Apazco, 385
Apples, 11n
Aqueducts, 67, 71n
Arachnids, as tribute, 205
Araras, 191
Armbands, 191; as booty, 356; for Cortés, 524; as funeral offerings, 291, 293, 466; of nobles, 356; royal, 209, 297, 305, 338, 356, 488; on sacrificial slaves, 295; as warrior bonus, 234
Armor, Aztec, 34n, 184, 205–206, 288
Arquebuses, 520, 521, 555
Arrows, 34n, 76, 77, 109, 119–20, 135, 153, 198; as coronation gifts, 323; flint-tipped, 206; as funeral offerings, 291, 293; as gift to gods, 158; human sacrifice by, 143 & n.2, 456–57, 459, 588; royal, 295; Spanish, 520; as tribute, 206, 412
Artillery, Spanish, 555, 561
Artists, Aztec, 503–504
Arzobispado Stone, 188n
Assyria, Jews to, 5
Astrologers, Aztec, 461, 463, 464
Atenco, 14
Atlacuihuayan, 33 & n.4
Atlapulco, 86–87, 95, 303
Atlas (Durán), 566, 567
Atlatlahuacan, 329
Atlatl, 34 & n, 38, 109n
Atlazol, 236, 237
Atlcahualo, 32n.2
Atlitlalaquian, 28
Atlixco, 329, 335, 436, 437, 470; as human food source, 233, 235; Tlacaelel focus on, 231
Atlixco (valley), 425–27, 436–39, 458
Atlixucan, 486

Atlpopoca (prov.), 380 & n
Atl tlachinolli, 41n
Atotonilco, 299, 300
Atotoztli, 49, 52, 115
Atzacualco (barrio), 58 & n
Atzitzihuacan, 329, 426, 436, 439
Auayucan, 453
Augustinians, in New Spain, 562
Auto de fe, 221
Autosacrifice: by Aztec kings, 282, 297, 298, 314, 356–58, 380, 390, 401, 424, 475, 525; by priests, 372, 475; in Tlachquiauhco, 472
Avocados, 11n, 205
Axayaca, 255
Axayacatl, 248–49, 253–56, 258, 309, 337, 388; death of, 290, 291; as executioner, 289–90; funeral of, 291–96; vs. Mechoacan, 277–82; memorialized in Chapultepec rocks, 290; progeny of, 388; reign of, 579; succession of, 248; and Sun Stone, 264, 277, 288–90; and Tarascan War dead, 283; as Tenantzinco ally, 263, 265–69; and Tlacaxipehualiztli, 272–74, 276; vs. Tlatelolco, 259–62; vs. Tliliuhquitepec, 286–87; vs. Toluca/Matlatzinco, 264–69; widows of, 294, 295; wounded in battle, 269
Axayacatzin. *See* Axayacatl
Axes, as medium of exchange, 86n
Axicoyo, 107, 202
Axicoyotzin, 81, 98
Axin, 424
Axolohua, 51 & n, 216
Axolotl, 51n
Ayauhcihuatl, 61–63
Ayotecas, 379
Ayotzinco, 14
Azazayakatl, 46n.5
Azcapotzalco, 29n, 45, 48, 49, 61, 506; as Aztec colony, 153; Aztec conquest of, 31n, 79–80 & n.5, 82–84, 97, 121, 129n.6; Aztec overtures to, 66, 73–74; Aztecs in thrall to, 52, 56–57, 243; Aztecs vs., 32, 80, 169, 202, 311 (*see also* Tepanecs, vs. Aztecs); and Coaixtlahuaca, 182, 183; Coyoacan vs., 100; decline of, 100; laborers

610

from, 130–31, 479; Moquihuixtli courting of, 255; as Tacuba ally, 437; Tepanecs of, 14, 29, 54, 590; Tlacaelel in, 75–77, 80, 258. *See also* Tepanecs
Azcatitlan Codex, 4n.2
Aztacoatl, 81, 98, 202
Aztahuacan, 135
Aztamecatl, 150
Aztatlan. *See* Teocolhuacan
Aztecs, 3n; Aztecs vs., 12n.1 (*see also* Moquihuixtli, vs. Tenochtitlan); character of, 18–19, 21, 81 & n.7, 83, 160; cruelty of, 6n, 166, 174, 178, 185, 229, 260, 352–53 (*see also* Human sacrifice); Cuauhtemoc charge to, 551; exodus of, 4n.2, 11–30, 590; fall of, 223 (*see also* Tenochtitlan, fall of); fear of, 202; Huitzilopochtli pledge to, 24–25; to Mexico (*see* Aztecs, exodus of); power of, 6n, 160–61, 192; riches of (*see* Tenochtitlan, treasure of); social divisions among, 192–93; subjects of, 302–303; subjugation of, 548; supreme, 233, 336; virtues of, 21. *See also* Aztlan; Chicomoztoc; Cihuacoatl; Colhuacan; Cuauhtemoc; Cuauhtlequetzqui; Huitzilihuitl (leader); Huitzilopochtli; Kings, Aztec; Meci; Nahuatl (lang.); Seven Caves; Tenochtitlan; Tlacaelel; Tlatelolco
Aztec slaves, 6n, 95, 100, 186, 201; as funeral offerings, 291–93, 383–85, 466; gift of, 373, 481, 502; Motecuhzoma II guarding of, 458; sacrifice of, 150, 245–46, 295–96, 307, 317, 383, 386, 428, 466, 481 (*see also* Prisoners of war, sacrifice of); as tribute, 206, 261, 262, 317, 329–31
Aztec statues, 227n, 427–28; of domestic gods, 350–51; of Huitzilopochtli (*see* Huitzilopochtli, statue of); priests and (*see* Tecuacuiltin); Spanish destruction of, 558; temple, 227, 231, 328, 356 (*see also* Huitzilopochtli, statue of); of warriors, 98. *See also* Chapultepec, carvings of; Huitzilopochtli, statue of
Aztlan, 21, 43n.2; Aztecs from (*see* Aztecs, exodus of); Aztecs in, 213–14 (*see also* Colhuacan). *See also* Chicomoztoc; Colhuacan; Teocolhuacan

Babel, Tower of, 9 & n.6
Bacon, Spanish, 500
Ball game, Aztec ritual, 83n
Banners, 82n.9, 150, 173
Banners, Feast of the, 407, 408n
Baptism, of Indians, 562, 576
Barbecue, 205
Bark: as funeral offering, 292; as tribute, 205; writing on, 82–83n.9 (see also *Amatl*)
Barley, 11n
Barlow, Robert, 571, 572
Barrios, 46, 82, 210; emigrants from, 345; leaders of (see *Calpixque*); systematic control of, 309; water for, 369. See also *Calpultin*
Barter system, Aztec use of, 86n
Bastards, rights of Aztec, 235
Battles, mock, 335. *See also* "Flower wars"
Beads, as Spanish trading trinket, 500–502, 517
Beans, 11n, 40n, 65, 153, 173, 177, 214; as booty, 317; gift of, 373, 502; for stonecutters, 481; storing of, 238; for Teloloapan emigrants, 348; as tribute, 55, 80, 205, 206, 317
Beef, Spanish, 500
Bees, 182, 206. *See also* Honey
Beggars, children of conquerors as, 533
Belcázar (conquistador), 10n.9
Bells, decorative, 275n.4, 293, 356
Beristáin (Spanish critic), 565
Beryl, 355–56, 377
Birds, 16, 26, 28; of Colhuacan, 213, 222; fallen warriors reincarnated as, 284n, 410n.1; as funeral offerings, 293; men into, 215 & n; mystic connotation of, 33n.3;

611

Index

sacrifice of, 38, 230 & n (*see also* Quail, sacrifice of); as tribute, 165, 203, 303, 327, 358, 400. See *also* Eagles; Eggs; Feathers; Fowl; Quail
Biscuit, Spanish, 497n, 500, 501
Bitumen, 435
Blacks, as Spanish shipmates, 510, 563
Bloodstone, 180, 203, 227
Blouses, 502, 524. See also *Huipiles*
Blowguns, 34n, 295
Bones: ceremonial, 389; as gifts to Aztecs, 274; jaguar, 297; musical, 151; as necklace elements, 210; as tribute, 204, 223, 224
Bonfires, victory, 343
Book of the Gods and Rites (Durán), 187
Books, pre-Conquest. See Codices
Booty, warrior right to, 317, 353, 379, 400, 421
Bowls, golden, 385
Bows (weapons), 139, 206, 291, 293, 295, 323. See also Arrows; Crossbows
Bracelets: as Aztec gifts, 276, 406; Aztec officers in, 178; bone, 158; as coronation gifts, 321, 322; gold, 226; Motecuhzoma II commission of, 497; of nobles, 356; royal, 314, 322, 352, 377, 385, 386, 406, 414; of Tarascan soldiers, 280; in Tizoc coronation ceremony, 304; as tribute, 303
Branding, of Indian slaves, 561
Brasil trees, 204
Brazier, "divine," 386, 389, 390
Bread(s), 166, 170; butterfly, 284; funeral, 293; maize, 157, 412, 509, 523; for Spaniards, 498, 509, 518, 523; as tribute, 177, 302
Breechcloths, 159, 167, 168; for Aztec emissaries, 334–35; ceremonial, 191, 274; of Colhuacan, 220, 221; as funeral offerings, 291–93; as gifts, 170, 173, 226, 274, 293, 304, 305, 321, 334, 340, 341, 373, 379, 405, 406; of priests, 368; royal, 190, 295, 297, 305, 314,

338, 385, 389, 390, 414; on statues, 428; as tribute, 185, 199, 261, 343, 358, 359; warrior, 209, 234, 379
Bridge(s): expeditionary, 420–21; false, 552–53; for Tlacaxipehualiztli stone, 480
Burning alive: of Aztec slaves, 593; as Cortés technique, 559
Butterflies, slain warriors reincarnated as, 284n, 410
Butterfly bread, 284
Butterfly mantle, 294
Buzzards, 203

Cabeceras, 329
Cacaloxochitl, 244 & n.3
Cacamatl Tecutli, 33
Cacao, 11n, 27, 159, 173, 176, 177, 182, 244 & n.3; of Colhuacan, 214; of Cuetlaxtla, 194; drinks from, 162, 214, 274, 509 (*see also* Chocolate); as funeral offering, 293; as gift, 373, 380, 481, 502; ground, 350; as money, 86n; for Motecuhzoma II enthronement festivities, 406; as privilege, 435; for Spaniards, 509; of Tecuantepec region, 349 & n; of Teloloapan, 344, 345, 348; as tribute, 165, 179, 181, 198–200, 203, 206, 274, 302, 318, 327, 336, 342, 347, 358, 375, 412.
Cacaoxochitl, 244 & n.3
Cactus. See Prickly pear cactus
Cakes: maize, 302, 320, 498, 500; as tribute, 302
Calendars, pre-Conquest, 4n.2, 569, 572
Calendar Stone, 264
Calimayan, 303, 315, 330
Calmecahuehuetque, 156 & n.7
Calmimilolco, 98n.2
Calpan, 16
Calpixque, 180, 471
Calpulalpan, 330
Calpules, 545n.1
Calpullali, 82
Calpulli, 167, 545n.1
Calpulteteo, 46
Calpultin, 46–47

612

Camaxtli, 138–39, 143, 459
Canals: Coyoacan-to-Tenochtitlan, 365–66, 368–69, 371; Tenochtitlan, 362, 552, 553, 558
Cannibalism, among Aztecs, 10, 192, 193, 233, 276, 407, 474; as privilege, 435; Spanish fear of, 542. *See also* Stews, of human flesh
Cannon, Spanish, 519–21. *See also* Artillery, Spanish
Canoes, 372
Capital punishment, 210, 447
Capuloac, 303, 330
Carnelian, 178, 180, 203, 227
Carpenters, 320, 341
Carpio, Bernardo del, 202
Carrots, 11n
Carthaginians, and Aztecs compared, 377
Carvings, Aztec, 121n, 192n.7; on *cuauhxicalli*, 188; of Templo Mayor, 227. See also *Chacmools*; Chapultepec, carvings of; *Temalacatl*
Cascalote, 204n
Caso, Alfonso, 572
Castilians, and Tezcocans compared, 14
Catholicism: Aztecs introduced to, 559–60; in Mexico, 560, 562–63, 575, 576; Motecuhzoma II and, 511, 530, 531; Tlaxcala and, 523. *See also* Baptism; Friars
Caualtzin, 98
Cauhtlecas, 225
Causeway, Xochimilco-to-Tenochtitlan, 110–12
Caves, as granaries, 485n
Ce Acatl. *See* Quetzalcoatl
Ce Atonal Tecuhtli, 175
Ce Cipactli, 318
Cempoala, 6n, 175, 273, 330, 512–15, 534–35
Censer-bearers, 277
Centipedes, 203
Century, Aztec, 445
Century plant. *See* Maguey
Centzon Huitznahua, 27n
Cereals, 11n
Cerro de la Estrella, 35n

Chachalayotl, 51 & n
Chachalmeca, 156 & n.7
Chacmool, 23n.2
Chalcas, exodus of, 13–14
Chalchiuhcueyecan, 508–10
Chalchiuhquiauh, 263
Chalchiuhtlicue, 308, 368–72
Chalchiuhtotolin, 387n
Chalco, 13n.4, 14, 32, 87n.3, 170; Ahuitzotl in, 358; and Ahuitzotl funeral, 383, 384; and Ahuitzotl successor, 387; artists of, 504; and Axayacatl funeral, 292; as Aztec ally, 118–19, 180, 196, 230, 266, 278, 281, 299, 324, 325, 342, 375, 378, 399, 422, 439; as Aztec colony, 153, 161, 236, 365; Aztec respect for, 147; Aztecs vs., 33–34, 121, 135–48, 184, 202, 288; vs. Chiapa, 315, 316; and Coaixtlahuaca, 182–84; and Coateocalli dedication, 434; Cortés in, 524; as Cortés ally, 525, 529, 548, 551, 555; Coyoacan appeal to, 87–90; Coyoacan-led conference at, 87–90, 93; and *cuauhxicalli* ceremony, 189; emigrants to Teloloapan region from, 345; Huaxtecs vs., 161; vs. Huexotzinco, 437, 438; and human sacrifice, 143n.2; maize of, 238; vs. Metztitlan, 300; Motecuhzoma II in, 414–15, 423; and Motecuhzoma II enthronement, 406; and Nezahualpilli funeral, 466; prisoners of, 335; shrines of, 355; vs. Spaniards, 547; Tecuantepec victory celebrated by, 353, 354; temple of, 358; and Templo Mayor, 225, 329, 338; Tizoc welcomed by, 297, 302; Totonac slave-shopping in, 240; traders from, 349; tribute from, 335. *See also* Chalcas
Chalco-Atenco, 89, 433
Chalk, ceremonial use of, 274, 289–90
"Chalk Leg." *See* Tizoc
Chalmeca, 23n.1
Chalmecatl, 22
Chaneques. See Dwarfs

613

Chanters, temple, 478
Chants, 570, 574
Chapanecas, 225
Chapultepec, 29–30, 72, 137; Aztecs at, 31–33, 42; carvings of, 21, 12in, 242–43, 290, 380, 481; Huemac to, 487–88; human sacrifice at, 186n; park at, 205n.5; waters of, 66–68, 363
Charcoal, 205, 207, 318, 509
Charles V, Holy Roman emperor, 560
Chastity: of Aztec schoolboys, 210; Motecuhzoma II enjoined to, 487
Chavero, Alfredo, 566, 568
Chia[n], 11n, 80, 173, 300 & n; as booty, 317; storing of, 238; for Teleloapan emigrants, 348; of Tenochtitlan, 362; as tribute, 80n.4, 205
Chiapa (prov.), 315–17, 330, 336, 346, 385
Chiapan, 202
Chiauhcoatl, 158
Chiauhtla, 14, 303
Chichicauhtla, 270
Chichimec. See Chichimecs
Chichimecateuctli, 22n
Chichimecs, 44n.3; as Aztec ancestors, 357, 440, 551; vs. Aztecs, 25–26; Coyoacan appeal to, 86–87; embroidery of, 203, nature of, 16–17; reform of, 18; weapons of, 34n. *See also* Aztecs; Chalco; Cholula; Huexotzinco; Tezcatlipoca; Tlaxcala; Tliliuhquitepec
Chichiquila, 179, 515–16
Chichiquilan, 197
Chichtli, 158
Chicomoztoc, 212nn.1, 2; Aztecs in, 213; Motecuhzoma I and, 212–23. *See also* Aztlan; Colhuacan; Seven Caves
Chiconauhtla, 330
Chicualoapa, 14
Chicuauhtlan, 301
Children: arming of Aztec, 139–40; Aztec, 160; as Aztec captives, 342; Aztec killing of, 80, 84, 85, 165, 179, 185, 229, 379, 494 (*see also* Children, sacrifice of); as Aztec slaves, 463; Chichimec, 16; of fallen warriors, 149, 284; Moquihuixtli of Tlatelolco, 260; as "precious jewels," 388n.3; registration of newborn, 309; sacrifice of, 6n, 10, 32n.2, 343, 366, 369, 371–72; sale of Aztec, 240; as Spanish captives, 557; as Spanish slaves, 561; as tribute, 206. *See also* Bastards; Orphans
Chile peppers, 11n, 22, 29, 40, 153, 177, 214, 350, 362; Ahuitzotl gift of, 373; of Colhuacan, 221; flooded out, 370; for Motecuhzoma II enthronement festivities, 406; for stonecutters, 481; storing of, 238; for Teloloapan emigrants, 348; as tribute, 55, 80, 155, 165, 185, 205, 207, 318, 327, 336, 412; as weapons, 195
Chimalhuacan, 13 & n.4, 330
Chimalhuacan del Río, 14
Chimalli, 34n
Chimalman, 51n
Chimalpopoca, 62, 63, 65–69, 243, 337; death of, 69 & n.6; reign of, 579
Chimaltecuhtli, 263, 269
Chimaltzin. *See* Chimaltecuhtli
Chinampaneca wars, 92n.6
Chinampa region, 91n.6, 225; and Ahuitzotl funeral, 383, 384; as Aztec ally, 266, 278, 281, 439; subjection of, 111n, 114, 375; Tizoc recognized by, 297, 302; tribute from, 335. *See also* Colhuacan; Cuitlahuac; Itztapalapa; Mexicatzinco; Mezquic; Xochimilco
Chinampas, 44–45n, 370
Chiquiuhtepec, 127
Chochos, 184 & n
Chocolate, 166, 179n, 186n, 408n; ceremonial use of, 294; drinks of, 170, 293, 322; gift of, 331, 334; perils of, 217, 219, 220, 222; slackers denied, 234; for Spaniards, 498, 500; as tribute, 177, 180, 181. See also Cacao

614

Chollolan. *See* Cholula
Cholula, 16, 17, 43nn.1,2, 410, 425; Ahuitzotl and, 320–23, 340; and Axayacatl funeral, 293; Aztecs and, 289, 319, 429, 433, 438–40, 452, 474; clay pipes of, 67n; and Coateocalli dedication, 433; "giant" founders of, 17n; Huexotzinco and, 449, 450; as human food source, 233, 235; and Motecuhzoma II enthronement, 402, 404; prisoners from, 329, 335; as Spanish ally, 549–51; Spanish atrocities in, 528–29; and Templo Mayor, 332–34; Tlacaelel focus on, 231, 262; traders from, 349
Christ, 445
Chronicles, pre-Conquest Mexican, 570–74. *See also* Codices; *Historia de las Indias de Nueva España e Islas de Tierra Firme* (Durán)
Chuchones. *See* Chochos
Cíbola, 10n.9, 23
Cicadas, 205
Cicalco, 485 & n, 486
Cicoac, 324
Cid, El, 202
Cihuacoatl (Aztec leader). *See* Tlilpotonqui
Cihuacoatl (goddess), 91n.6, 289 & n, 297, 424
Cihuahuaque, 141
Cihuatecpaneca, 23n.1
Cillan, 202, 315, 330, 346
Cilucan, 315
Cincalco, 485n
Cinnabrium, 150n.3
Cipactli, 307
Citlalcoatl, 81, 202
Citlalcoatzin, 98
Clavijero, Francisco Javier (Spanish Jesuit and chronicler), 565
Clay, drainage pipes of, 67 & n
Cloaks, 293, 295, 297, 356
Cloth, 159; as funeral offering, 292, 293; royal, 297; as tribute, 155, 165, 179, 185, 196, 198, 199, 203, 274, 302, 318, 328, 342. *See also* Cotton; Embroidery; Maguey

Clothing, 182; of Aztec executioners, 171; as booty, 95, 317; for Colhuacan, 214, 219; for Cortés, 524, 526; of Cuetlaxtla, 194; as funeral offering, 293; gift of, 124, 170, 173, 306, 307, 333, 340, 343, 379, 451, 481; for idols, 82–83n.9; inflammatory use of women's, 91–92; royal, 295, 297, 322, 369; for Teloloapan immigrants, 346, 348; in Tenochtitlan cache, 532; as tribute, 162, 165, 177, 200, 204, 237, 304, 327, 336, 342. *See also* Breechcloths; Cloth; Mantles
Clubs (weapons), 34n, 109
Coacuech, 159
Coaixtlahuaca, 182–85, 188, 202, 335, 470–72
Coanacoch[tzin], 467, 468, 550
Coas, 399
Coateocalli, 431, 433–36
Coatepec (hill), 25, 27n, 214–15, 221
Coatepec, 14, 303, 330, 483–85
Coatepetl. *See* Coatepec (hill)
Coatitlan, 166
Coatlalpan, 297, 302, 315
Coatlan, 98n.2
Coatlicamac, 13n.3
Coatlicue, 27n, 212 & n.2, 215, 217–23; statue of, 227
Coatlinchan, 14, 115, 121, 330
Coatlpopoca, 517–18
Coatzacualco, 223–24
Cochineal, 182 & n.2, 204
Cocotitlan, 140
Cocoyan, 182, 183
Cocuilan, 346
Codex Borbonicus, 4n.2
Codex Boturini/Tira de la Peregrinación, 4n.2
Códice Ramírez, 571, 572
Codices, 569–70; Aztec warriors celebrated in, 98 & n.6; Mixtec, 182n.1; pictorial, 328 & n.2
Colhuacan, 13, 29n, 32, 34–39, 43n.1, 45, 48n, 225n.2; and Ahuitzotl funeral, 383; as Aztec ally, 266, 315, 325; as Aztec colony, 153, 161; as Aztec enemy, 60, 93, 114, 202, 456; Aztec overtures to, 70; Aztecs in, 213–14; Aztecs

615

Index

to, 48–49; vs. Coaixtlahuaca, 183; and Coateocalli dedication, 434; Coyoacan appeal to, 87–90; and *cuauhxicalli* ceremony, 189; emigrants to Teloloapan region from, 345, 346; laborers from, 477, 478; magic of, 220 & n, 221; reputation of, 114; and Templo Mayor, 130–31, 329; and Tizoc enthronement, 297, 302; Tlacaelel allies from, 93–95, 99; traders with starving Aztecs from, 552. *See also* Achitometl; Aztlan; Chicomoztoc; *Chinampa* region

Colhuas, exodus of, 13

Collars, slave, 329 & n

Colomaxcatl, 288

Colombia, Belcázar in, 10n.9

Colors, symbolism of, 43–44n.2, 440–41 & n, 559n

Coltzin, 270

Columbus, Christopher, 3n

Comet(s): "meaning" of, 145n.3, 223; over Tenochtitlan, 460–62, 464, 481, 483, 486

Conch shells, as tribute, 175, 177, 181. *See also* Shells, musical

Concubines, 52n.3, 204, 206, 356, 411

Conjurers. *See* Magicians

Conversion, religious: as Cortés goal, 533; as friar goal, 575; as Spanish goal, 6

Cookware, 153

Coots, 26

Copal, 83n, 368, 369. *See also* Incense, ceremonial *copal*

Copil, 31–33, 41, 42

Copper, 86n, 275n.4

Cormorants, 213

Corn. *See* Maize

Coronado, Francisco de, 10n.9

Cortés, Hernán, 6, 219n, 568, 569; arrival of, 6n, 468, 495n.2, 499n, 502, 510; assassination attempt on, 528; and Aztec treasure, 559; cruelty of, 528–29, 536, 548, 559; divine assistance for, 543; and human sacrifice, 512; land holdings of, 15 & n; as marquis, 15n; Motecuhzoma II and, 515–18, 524, 526, 528–33, 536, 540; and Narváez, 534–35, 536n.2; non-Aztecs courted by, 548; at Otumba, 546–47; piety of, 533, 540, 559–60, 563; post-Tenochtitlan conquests of, 560–62; as Quetzalcoatl "emissary," 7n, 497n; and Tecoac battle, 518–21; in Tenochtitlan, 246, 515–28, 530–44, 548, 555–60; to Tenochtitlan, 529–30; at Tlatelolco, 26n.4

Cotton, 15, 203n.2, 342; armor of, 205–206; Aztec trade in, 106; for Colhuacan, 214; destruction of, 436; Motecuhzoma II gift of, 502; privilege of wearing, 234, 435, 454; of Teloloapan region, 344, 345, 348; as tribute, 185, 200, 203, 206

Couixco, 170, 303, 336

Coward(s): punishment of, 444; Tizoc as, 307; Tlacaelel focus on, 234–35

Coyoacan, 14, 29, 32, 45; Axayacatl feted by, 270; Aztec absorption of, 96, 100–102, 104, 153, 161; Aztec emissaries to, 362–65; Aztecs vs., 68, 72, 83–95, 202; Cortés in, 15n, 525–26; as Spanish ally, 525–26, 529; temple workers from, 130–31. *See also* Maxtlaton; Tepanecs; Tzutzumatzin

Coyoacanos, 112

Coyolcue, 152–53, 155, 157–58

Coyolxauh[qui], 26, 27 & n, 191n.4, 212n.2, 328 & n.3

Coyopetlayo (hill), 153

Coyuchi, 203n.2

Cozcatlohtli, 289

Cranes (birds), 213

Crayfish, 46n.5, 179

Crocodiles, in Mesoamerican myth, 33n.3. *See also* Alligators

Crónica Mexicana (Tezozomoc), 571

Crónica X, 147n, 572, 573

Crops, of ancient Mesoamerica, 10–11n.10

Crossbows, Spanish, 520, 555

Cross-dressing, by Aztec leaders, 91n.6

Crown, royal feathered, 352

Cuachics, 164, 279–81
Cuachtli, 150
Cuacuauhtin, 191
Cuacuauhtzin, 260–61
Cuahpanohuayan, 266
Cuatecpan, 23n.1
Cuatecpan Tecutli, 22
Cuateotl, 84–90, 118, 132–33, 145 & n.4
Cuatlecoatl, 53, 54n.5, 98, 202
Cuauhacan, 315
Cuauhapazco, 303
Cuauhcalli, 192
Cuauhchinanco, 324–25
Cuauhcipalli, 297
Cuauhcoatl, 213–14, 217. *See also* Cuauhtlequetzqui
Cuauh Huehuetque, 279, 283, 301
Cuauhmatlatl, 421
Cuauhnahuac, 15, 63, 244, 302, 336, 384, 548; Aztec conquest of, 121; today (*see* Cuernavaca)
Cuauhnochtli, 183, 199–200
Cuauhquechol, 105
Cuauhquechollan, 329, 436, 439
Cuauhquiahuac, 99n.7
Cuauhtemallan (prov.), 380 & n
Cuauhtemoc[tzin], 47n, 262n.4; capture of, 556; death of, 562 & n.3; named king, 538, 545, 547; reign of, 579; vs. Spaniards, 539–41, 546–49, 551–56
Cuauhtexcac (cliff), 146
Cuauhtinchan, 154, 155, 329
Cuauhtitlan, 255, 385, 539, 547, 548
Cuauhtlalpan, 230, 302, 335, 345, 346, 375; and Ahuitzotl funeral, 383, 384; as Aztec ally, 236, 299, 375, 539, 548; vs. Spaniards, 547. *See also* Otomi
Cuauhtlecoatl, 81
Cuauhtlequetzqui, 32, 41–44, 51 & n, 53, 216
Cuauhtli (eagle), 186
Cuauhtochco, 237
Cuauhtzitzimitl, 81, 98, 202
Cuauhuacan, 202, 330, 346
Cuauhuanecas, 225
Cuauhuehuetque, 156 & n.7
Cuauhxicalli, 172, 186–93, 297, 386, 390

Cuauhximalpan, 270
Cuauhxochitl, 193
Cuauitl (tree, wood), 186
Cuautla, 15n
Cuaxomotitlan, 135
Cuaxopas, 14
Cuba, 399, 495n.2, 534
Cucurbits, 40n
Cuecuech, 84, 90, 92–93
Cuepan (barrio), 58 & n
Cuernavaca, 15n, 63
Cuetlaxtecatl, 274
Cuetlaxtla (prov.), 175, 179–81, 188, 194–201, 244–45, 293, 302, 496
Cuetlaxtlan, 508–10
Cuextlan, 202
Cueyatzin, 256, 258
Cuitlahuac (king), 538n.7, 579
Cuitlahuac, 13, 87 & n.3, 116n; artists of, 504; as Aztec colony, 153, 161; Aztecs vs., 116–21, 202; Coyoacan appeal to, 88–90; and *cuauhxicalli* ceremony, 189; divers from, 480; emigrants to Teloloapan region from, 345, 346; laborers from, 130–31, 477, 478; and Templo Mayor, 130–31, 329; Tizoc welcomed by, 297; today (*see* Tlahuac); traders with starving Aztecs from, 552. *See also* *Chinampa* region
Cuitlalpitoc, 495, 496, 498–502
Cuitlatenanco, 303
Cuixtlahuac. *See* Coaixtlahuaca
Culhuacan. *See* Colhuacan
Culhuas, 36n
Cypress, 26

Dam, Coyoacan, 365–66, 370–72
Dancing, ceremonial, 275, 435, 479, 536–37; coronation-related, 305–307, 321, 322, 406; for Cortés, 512, 523, 531; during flaying ceremony, 172; funerary, 150–51, 284, 296; to honor gods, 524n; during Huauhquiltamalqualiztli, 586; by prisoners of war, 166, 170, 186n, 473; as sacrifice element, 157; victory-related, 343, 433, 455
Darts: Aztec, 109 & n, 119–20, 150,

Index

165, 198, 206; Chichimec, 519; Huaxtec, 165
Davies, Nigel, 18n
Dávila Padilla, Agustín, 565, 571
Dead, Land of the, 285n.4, 583. *See also* Underworlds, Aztec
Death: Aztec tradition and warrior, 556; hunger-induced, 92. *See also* Funeral(s)
Deer, 16, 166, 177, 205, 270, 302, 318, 406
Deerskins, 82n.9, 155
"Descending Eagle." *See* Cuauhtemoc
Devil, 215, 221, 245, 308, 475, 487
Diadems, 305; as funeral offerings, 291, 293, 466; as gifts, 226, 321, 323, 336, 340, 406; heron-feather, 367; royal, 297, 304, 313, 314, 321, 338, 356, 369, 372, 377, 385, 406, 407, 435 (see also *Xiuhuitzolli*)
Díaz del Castillo, Bernal, 6n, 399n
Dictionaries, of Indian words, 575
Dikes, Tenochtitlan, 370, 552
Dinnerware, royal, 385, 532
Divers, professional, 480
Divine Wine/Liquor, 157, 172, 186 & n
Dogs, 182; Aztec killing of, 178, 229; Indians run down by, 559, 562
Dominicans: as chroniclers, 569; Durán, 567; in Mexico, 560, 567. *See also* Durán, Diego
Dragonflies, 46n.5
Dreams: interpretation of, 145n.3; Motecuhzoma II interest in, 490–93
Drought, 238–41
Drums, 301, 304, 305, 356, 435, 519, 537; funeral, 149–51, 386; royal, 352–53; sacrifice-related, 171, 274–75, 296; types of, 275n.4; victory, 317, 327, 343, 433, 455, 473
Ducks, 26, 182, 213, 220, 334, 349
Duennas, 411, 533
Durán, Diego: editorializing of, 439n; and Inquisition, 221n; life of, 567–68; praise for, 565, 567, 571, 574–76; purpose of, 575–77; as reporter, 339n.1; sources of, 569; syntactical problems of, 566; works by, 568. *See also Historia de las Indias de Nueva España e Islas de Tierra Firme*
Dwarfs, royal, 295, 296, 307, 356, 357, 466, 483, 485n, 486, 488
Dyes, 182 & n.2, 185, 204 & n

Eagle garments, 424
Eagle Knights, 187, 435
Eagles: Aztecs dressed as, 339n.1, 474, 531; as Mexican symbol, 41n; as Motecuhzoma aide, 483, 484, 485; mystic character of, 41, 42, 44, 357; as tribute, 203, 207; Tzutzumatzin use of, 364
Eagle Shrine, 389
Eagle vessel. *See Cuauhxicalli*
Eagle Warriors, 99n.7, 449n
Ear pendants: as funeral offerings, 291, 293, 466; as gifts, 226, 276, 304–306, 406, 497; of nobles, 355; royal, 295, 297, 304, 314, 356, 377, 385, 390, 406, 414, 424; on statues, 428; of Tarascan soldiers, 280; as warrior bonus, 234. *See also* Earrings
Ear plugs, 262, 274, 284, 321, 322, 338, 340; hierarchy of, 209
Earrings, 164, 170, 173, 295. *See also* Ear pendants
Ears: adornment of, 178 (*see also* Ear pendants; Ear plugs; Earrings); ritual amputation of, 114 & n.3
Earth, eating of. *See* Geophagy
Ecatepec, 29, 281, 385, 506
Ecatzinco, 13
Eggs: edible insect, 46n.5, 349; for Spaniards, 509, 518
Eguiara (Spanish historian), 565
Egypt: Hebrew exodus from, 431n; priests of, 171n.6
Elephants, of prehistoric Mexico, 17n
El Salvador, 380n
Embroidery, 203, 204
Emeralds, 227, 297
Emery, 417
Encomiendas, 561

618

Enríquez, Martín, 362
Epazoyocan, 330
Epcoahuatl, 202
Epcoatl, 53, 54n.5, 81
Epcohuatzin, 98
Eunuchs, royal, 356
Executioners, Aztec, 169–72, 190. *See also* Chachalmeca; Human sacrifice
Ezcahuitli, 45–46n.5, 56 & n, 92
Ezekias, king of Jerusalem, 4
Ezhuahuacatl, 137–38, 142–43
Ezra (bibl.), 5

Face painting, by Aztec warriors, 164
Famine, 238–41. *See also* Starvation, in Tenochtitlan
Fans, decorative, 158, 293, 347
Fasts, 151, 192, 296, 466
Feathers, 159, 176, 182, 191, 209–10, 218, 537; as booty, 95, 317, 356; for Chalchiuhtlicue, 372; of Chichimecs, 519; for Colhuacan, 220; commoners barred from wearing, 234; of Cuetlaxtla, 194; as diadem element, 226 & n.3; eagle, 297; embroidery using, 204; for food, 552; as funeral offering, 291–94, 383–85, 466; as garland element, 276; as gifts, 123, 124, 170, 173, 290, 322, 348, 380, 406, 417, 468; as gift to gods, 158, 357, 475; as headband decoration, 321; Huaxtec battle, 164; Motecuhzoma II and, 414, 468, 474; of nobles, 356; in pierced noses, 147, 355–56; of priests, 171; ritual use of, 43 & n.1, 76, 190, 191, 274, 275, 290; royal, 305, 314; on sacrificial slaves, 295; shields inlaid with, 206; for Spaniards, 499, 512, 524, 525, 529, 550; on statues, 428; and status, 167; Tarascan soldiers adorned with, 280; of Teloloapan, 348; as temple adornment, 227; Tenochtitlan cache of, 532; Tlatelolco nobles stripped of, 262; trade in, 349 & n; as tribute, 165, 179–81, 198–201, 203, 206, 237, 261, 274, 302, 303, 318, 327, 336, 358, 359, 375, 376, 473; as virgin adornment, 524n; war announced by, 152 & n; warriors and, 178, 184, 234, 235, 355, 380, 441 & n
Feather workers, 319, 336, 341, 497
Festivals, 40, 91 & n.5, 170–74, 191n.4
Fire, human sacrifice by, 139–42, 456, 457, 459. *See also* Burning alive
Fire priests. *See* Tlenamacaque
Fire serpent, 290. See also *Xiuhcoatl*
Fisga. *See* Atlatl
Fish, 15, 26, 28, 92; Aztec trade in, 45, 46 & n.5, 105; barbecued, 165; of Colhuacan, 214, 220, 222; in Coyoacan dam canals, 368; of Cuetlaxtla, 194; as gift, 334; golden, 370; men into, 433; for Motecuhzoma II enthronement festivities, 406; for Spaniards, 509; as tribute, 55, 63, 180, 181, 198, 200, 302, 318, 400, 415
Fishermen, 341
Five Suns, 445
Flaying: at Motecuhzoma II pleasure, 485; ritual (*see* Tlacaxipehualiztli)
Fleas, 359
Flies, edible, 46n.5, 349
Flint, 34n, 165, 206
Floating gardens. See *Chinampas*
Flooding, of Tenochtitlan, 370–73
Florida, de León in, 10n.9. *See also* La Florida
Florists, 319
Flour, 207, 285, 350, 368, 412
Flower(s), 15, 26, 306–307, 537; for Aztec emissaries, 334; certain persons denied, 234; of Cicalco, 485; of Colhuacan, 214, 220, 221; coronation, 304, 321, 322; for Cortés, 515, 523, 529, 530; death in war as, 410n.2; flood-ravaged, 370; funeral, 285, 293, 294; as gifts, 276, 306, 331, 333, 334, 369; as privilege, 435; for returning warriors, 433, 437; as sacrifice

element, 157, 230, 288, 301, 401, 473; for Teloloapan emigrants, 348; of Tenochtitlan, 362; on Tlacaxipehualiztli stone, 480; as tribute, 55, 205, 302, 327. See also *Tetlaxincaxochitl*
"Flower wars," 286n, 402, 437n
Flutes, 275n.4, 301, 317, 343, 356, 368, 372, 433, 435, 455, 473
Flyers Dance. See *Volador*
Food: royal, 435; treasure exchanged for, 552; as tribute, 165
Forestation, of Tenochtitlan, 373
Fowl, 162, 170; Aztec killing of, 229; as funeral fare, 293; for Motecuhzoma II enthronement festivities, 406; for Spaniards, 498, 509, 523; as tribute, 207, 318, 336. See also Eggs; Waterfowl
Fowlers, 341
France, Twelve Peers of, 202
Franciscans, in Mexico, 47n, 560, 569. See also Olmos, Andrés de; Sahagún, Bernardino de
Franco, Alonso, 565
Friars, of New Spain, 521, 561, 563, 568, 571; vs. mixed bathing, 39n.8. See also Augustinians; Dominicans; Franciscans
Frogs, 28, 92; Aztec trade in, 45, 46n.5, 334; in Coyoacan dam canals, 368; golden, 370; as tribute, 55, 63, 415
Fruit, 11n, 15, 165, 166; for Aztec emissaries, 334; for Motecuhzoma II enthronement festivities, 406; for Spaniards, 498, 509, 518, 523; of Teloloapan, 344, 345, 348; as tribute, 205, 302, 318, 336, 342
Funeral(s), 122, 123, 149; of Ahuitzotl, 382–86; of Axayacatl, 291–96; of fallen warriors, 149–52, 283–90, 428, 437, 441, 455; of Itzcoatl, 122; of Motecuhzoma I, 245–46; of Motecuhzoma II, 545; of Nezahualpilli, 466; of Tizoc, 307–308

Game (meat), 336, 509
García, Gregorio, 3n

Gardens: of Nezahualcoyotl, 71n; of Tenochtitlan, 205n.5, 362, 373. See also *Chinampas*
Garibay K., Angel María, 573, 574, 576
Garlands, 234, 276
Geese, 26, 203, 220, 334
Gem cutters, 319. See also Jewelers; Lapidaries
Gems, 43 & n.1, 159, 176, 209, 218, 319, 367; Aztec traders and, 349 & n; as booty, 95, 317; ceremonial use of, 190; for Chalchiuhtlicue, 371, 372; as crystal, 203; as funeral offerings, 291–93, 383–85, 466; as gifts, 123, 124, 290, 306, 307, 321, 322, 341, 405, 406, 417; as gift to gods, 357, 475; for maize, 552; Motecuhzoma II and, 414, 449, 459, 468, 474; of nobles, 355, 356; of Quetzalcoatl, 497n; royal, 305, 307, 314, 321, 356; as sacrifice element, 295; for Spaniards, 499, 512, 524, 525, 550; Spaniards doomed by Aztec, 543–44; of Tenochtitlan cache, 532; into Tenochtitlan lake, 370; as tribute, 165, 180, 181, 197, 201, 206, 224, 227, 261, 270, 278, 302, 303, 318, 336, 358, 359, 375, 376, 473; as warrior adornment, 178, 184, 235, 280, 380, 441 & n; worship of, 203. See also Jewelry; Pearls
Genealogies, Native American, 4n.2, 569
Geophagy, 158 & n, 180, 186, 230–31, 288, 301, 327, 343, 401, 415, 440, 455, 473; by Ahuitzotl, 357, 369; by Aztec nobles, 369
Ghosts, Native Americans and, 276
Giants, 17–18. See also Quiname
Girdles, 293
Glass, volcanic, 34n. See also Obsidian
Glyphs, 39n.9, 47n
Gods, Aztec, 64, 431, 569; Aztecs dressed as, 170–72, 274, 289, 290, 308, 338–39 & n.1, 366–68; Motecuhzoma II reproach of, 525; statues of domestic, 350–51. See

also *Calpulteotl; Calpulteteo;* Chalchiuhtlicue; Huitzilopochtli; Mother Goddess; Quetzalcoatl; Tezcatlipoca; Tlaloc; Toci

Gold, 27, 43 & n.1, 159, 176, 182, 209, 218, 385; Aztec traders and, 349 & n; as booty, 95, 356; ceremonial use of, 190; for Cortés, 524; of Cuetlaxtla, 194; for food, 552; funeral offerings of, 291–93, 383; as gift, 124; as medium of exchange, 86n; Mixtec working of, 182n.1; for Motecuhzoma II, 414; of Quetzalcoatl, 497n; shields adorned with, 206; Spaniards doomed by Aztec, 543–44; Spanish lust for, 559; Tenochtitlan cache of, 532; as tribute, 165, 180, 181, 198–203, 206, 223, 224, 303, 336, 358, 375, 376; as warrior gift, 178, 184, 235, 280, 380

Goldsmiths, 497

González, Fernán, 202

Gophers, 205

Gourds, 11n, 182, 285; bowls from, 186; ritual use of, 150 & n.2, 156, 204, 355; as tribute, 204

Grain, 238, 239. See also Maize

Grammars, Mexican Indian, 575

Great Temple. See Templo Mayor

Greeks, paganism of ancient, 577

Greenstones, 178, 180, 203, 227. See also Jade

Grijalva, Juan de, 495n.2

Gruel, 166, 239, 300. See also *Atole*

Guatemala, 4n.2, 158, 380n, 561

Guavas, 205

Guaxaca, 202, 223–24, 227–30, 236–37, 376

Guzmán (Spanish officer), 556

Hair, symbology of Aztec, 226n.3, 275, 283 & n, 287, 294, 427, 440, 454, 467, 524 & n; king and, 390; priests and, 355

"Handful of Reeds." See Acamapichtli

Hares, 16, 270, 318, 406

Hawks, 203

Headbands, 164, 274, 280, 301, 304, 321, 322, 355, 356, 414

Headdresses, 191, 434–35, 488

Heavens, Aztec, 339n.1, 391 & n, 583

Helmets, honorary warrior, 90

Herbs, 16, 164

Hernández, Francisco, 17n

Hernández de Córdoba, Francisco, 495n.2

Herons, 26, 203, 213, 220, 334, 367

Herrera, Antonio de, 575

Hides, animal, 159, 276; as booty, 356; as funeral offerings, 293; as gifts, 340; as gift to gods, 158, 357; as tribute, 180, 181, 197, 199, 200, 270, 303, 316. See also Deerskins

Hippolytus, Saint, 484n

Historia de las Indias de Nueva España e Islas de Tierra Firme (Durán): history of, 565–67; and other chronicles, 571–74. See also Durán, Diego

Historia de la venida de los indios (Tovar), 571

Historia natural y moral de las Indias (Acosta), 571

History: as Aztec school subject, 581; Durán view of, 576, 577

Hoes, martial use of, 109

Honduras, 4n.2, 568

Honey, 165, 206, 343, 408n

Honeycombs, 206

Honor, importance to Aztecs of, 455

Horns (musical instruments), 519, 531. See also Trumpets

Horses, Spanish, 510, 511, 513, 518

Hoshea, king of Israel, 4

Hot Country/Lands, 170, 225, 244; Ahuitzotl and, 383, 384, 387; artists of, 504; Aztec dominance of, 236, 278, 282, 299, 365; Aztec support in, 375, 378, 439, 548; and *cuauhxicalli* ceremony, 189; emigrants to Teloloapan region from, 345; Motecuhzoma II and, 406, 492; and Nezahualpilli funeral, 466; Spanish subjugation of, 560–61; Tecuantepec victory celebrated in, 353, 354; Tezcoco vs., 465; and Tizoc enthrone-

621

ment, 302; tribute from, 336. *See also* Acapichtlan; Actopan; Cuauhnahuac; Huaxtepec; Matlatzinco; Xilotepec; Xocotlan; Yauhtepec
Houses, of Tenochtitlan, 209, 435
Huacalxochitl, 244 & n.3
Huacaman, Mex., 98n.2
Huauhtli. *See* Amaranth
Huaxteca, the, 244n.2, 324, 335
Huaxtecs, 43n.1; Aztecs and, 160–65, 188, 273n, 323–27, 404, 409, 430, 440; and human sacrifice, 143n.2; as Metztitlan ally, 300; sacrifice of, 339n.1; Tlacaelel disdain for, 231
Huaxtepec (park), 205n.5
Huaxtepec (prov.), 15, 244 & n.2, 245, 292, 302, 336, 513, 548, 561
Huehue Motecuhzoma. *See* Motecuhzoma I
Huehueteotl-Xiuhtecuhtli, 59n.2
Huehuetl, 275n.4
Huehuetlatolli, 298n, 569
Huehue Zaca, 81, 202
Huehuezcan, 98
Huemac (Cicalco ruler), 485–88
Huexotla, 290
Huexotzinco, 16, 17, 146–47, 320, 340; and Axayacatl funeral, 293; Aztecs and, 121, 288, 319, 410, 425–27, 429, 433, 436–38, 440, 449, 452, 457, 474; character of, 470; and Coateocalli dedication, 433; as human food source, 233, 235; and Mixcoatl, 587; Moquihuixtli and, 249–50; and Motecuhzoma II enthronement, 402, 404; prisoners from, 335; as Spanish ally, 549, 551; and Templo Mayor, 334; Tezcoco vs., 376; Tlacaelel focus on, 231; Tlatelolcas vs., 262; Tlaxcalans vs., 446, 449
Huexotzinco (prov.), 329
Huexutla, 14
Hueyapan, 13 & n.4, 329, 561
Hueynacaztli, 179 & n
Huey Tecuilhuitl, 186n, 408n
Huicton, 216 & n
Huipiles, 91n.6, 204, 293
Huitzilan, 369

Huitzilihuitl (king), 53, 54n.5, 59–66, 81, 243, 337; reign of, 579
Huitzilihuitl (leader), 29, 33, 34, 42, 142
Huitzilopochco, 477, 478; Ahuitzotl and, 358, 383; as Aztec ally, 266, 315, 325; vs. Coaixtlahuaca, 183; and Coateocalli dedication, 434; shrines of, 355; and Templo Mayor, 329; today (*see* Churubusco)
Huitzilopochtli, 8n, 12n.1, 19n.1, 23, 24, 27–28, 31–34, 39–46, 49–51 & n, 53n, 55, 56 & n, 58–60 & n, 71, 73, 74, 88, 96, 105, 116, 117, 121, 125, 127, 130–32, 139, 140, 155, 157, 158, 166, 170, 177, 180, 186, 191n.4, 199, 200, 212 & n.2, 213, 215, 217, 218, 225n.1, 226, 230, 231, 233, 273n, 288, 289n, 294, 298, 301, 302, 313, 340, 357, 370, 384, 398n, 408n, 491, 502, 536; Axayacatl corpse as, 294; birth of, 27n, 212n.2, 213; Chalco reverence for, 358; vs. Copil, 32; Cortés treated like, 530; and Coyolxauhqui, 27–28n; dances honoring, 524n; and eagle, 339n.1; gifts for, 357 (*see also* Human sacrifice); "hunger" of, 287 & n; impersonation of, 289; Spaniards vs., 219n, 538; statue of, 270, 296, 297, 302, 308, 314, 338, 343, 357, 386, 428, 536, 538; Tenochtitlan "home" of, 46 (*see also* Templo Mayor); and Tizoc enthronement, 302; as Tlatelolco god, 260; and Toci, 36–38. *See also* Coatlicue; Huitznahua (Huitzilopochtli brothers)
Huitzitzilapan, 270
Huitznahua (Aztec emigrant), 26
Huitznahua (barrio), 98n.2
Huitznahua (Huitzilopochtli brothers), 191n.4
Huitznahuac (barrio), 23n.1
Huitznahuatl [Tecutli], 22, 283
Huixachtecatl, 107n, 445–46
Huixachtepetl, 35n
Huixachtlan, 445
Human sacrifice, 140–43 & n.2, 152n, 156–57, 191–92, 339n.1; ac-

celeration of, 233–34; of children, 6n, 10, 32n.2, 343, 366, 369, 371–72; Cortés and, 512; by falling, 457n; by fire, 456, 457, 459; funerary, 57; for food only, 474; Motecuhzoma II and, 525; during New Fire ceremony, 446; priests of (see Chachalmeca); of prisoners of war, 10, 140–42, 149, 155, 165, 166, 180, 186–87, 189–90, 229–31, 288–90, 292, 307, 322–23, 329, 330, 335, 338–40, 352, 407, 429, 435–36, 448–49, 455–57, 459; of slaves, 150, 245–46, 295–96, 307, 317, 383, 386, 428, 466, 481 (see also Human sacrifice, of prisoners of war); of Spanish soldiers, 553–54; on Sun Stone, 264 & n; temple dedication–related, 329, 330, 335, 338–40; Tlacaelel penchant for, 233, 311; of Tlahuicole, 449n; of women, 186n, 466. See also Fire sacrifice; Tlacaxipehualiztli; Toci

"Hummingbird Feather." See Huitzilihuitl (king)

Hunchbacks, royal, 295, 296, 307, 356, 357, 466, 483, 485, 486, 488, 501

Hunters, professional, 341

Hymns, Aztec, 230, 275, 282, 283, 285, 294, 501

Ichcaxochitl, 294
Icnopilli, 289 & n
Icpatepec (prov.), 399, 409
Iglesia, Ramón, 575
Ihuitltemoc, 53, 54n.5
Ilancueitl, 49, 50, 52–54, 115
Ilhuicatzitzquique, 227
Image(s), wood, 40n; of dead Axayacatl, 294–96; of fallen warriors, 284–85, 288
Incas, 344–45n
Incense, ceremonial *copal*, 82, 83n, 277, 356, 368, 478, 480, 502; for Chalchiuhtlicue, 371, 372; dispensers of (see Tlenamacaque); elders' use of, 186, 301, 347; and human sacrifice (see Incense, and prisoners of war); kings and, 297–98, 305, 356, 369, 380, 389, 390, 435 (see also Incense, and royal funerals); and prisoners of war, 180, 186, 230, 290, 446; and royal funerals, 295, 386; Spaniards greeted with, 531; today, 83n; during Toxcatl, 592; victory celebrated with, 433, 455, 473; warrior widows and, 286; warrior wives and, 162

Indian corn. See Maize
Inheritance, kingship by, 468–69
Ink, mineral, 204
Inquisition, Spanish, 221, 576
Insects: as dye source, 182n.2; as human food, 16, 205; as pitch ingredients, 60n; as *teotlacualli* ingredient, 189n; as tribute, 203, 205

Inspectors, tribute, 320
Intoxication, Mixtecs and prophecy-induced, 472, 473
Ipalnemoani. See Tezcatlipoca
Israel, ten tribes of, 3n, 4–10
Itzacalco, 40
Itzcoatl, 52n.3, 53, 71–81 & nn.6,7, 88, 91 & n.6, 94, 100–101, 105–108, 243, 271, 337; accomplishments of, 121; as Azcapotzalco king, 83; and Chalco, 118; and Cuitlahuac, 116–19, 121; death of, 121–22; kin of, 81 & n.6, 97–98; reign of, 579; and Tezcoco, 129; titles awarded by, 96–99; and Xochimilco, 112, 113

Itzmiquilpan, 299, 300
Itzpapalotl, 171 & n.3, 289 & n
Itztapalapa (park), 205n.5
Itztapalapa, 39, 135; Ahuitzotl and, 358, 383; as Aztec ally, 266, 315, 325; vs. Coaixtlahuaca, 183; and Coateocalli dedication, 434; Motecuhzoma II in, 423; shrines of, 355; and Templo Mayor, 329, 477, 478; Tizoc welcomed by, 297, 302, 303. See also *Chinampa* region

Itztapalucan, 330
Itztonpatepec, 141, 143
Itzucan, 354
Ixcuahualli, 171. See also Knives, sacrificial

623

Index

Ixcuetlatoc, 98
Ixnahuatiloc, 98n.3
Ixtlilcuechahuac, 436, 437
Ixtlilxochitl, 71, 467, 468, 550, 555, 569–70
Izapa, 33n.3
Izcahuitli, 45n.5
Izhuatlan (prov.), 202, 349–50, 351
Izquitecatl, 22, 289 & n
Izquixochitl, 244 & n.3
Iztaccihuatl, 40n
Iztac Tollin Ymaucan. *See* Cholula
Iztac Uexotl Yhicacan. *See* Cholula
Iztac Zolin Inemian, 8 & n
Iztapaltetitlan, 266
Izucan, 423

Jackals, men into, 215
Jade, 24–25n, 43n.1, 190, 209, 285n.4, 297
Jadeite, 25n.3
Jaguar(s), 159, 207n, 214; in Aztec necrology, 285n.4; Aztecs dressed as, 339n.1, 474, 531; men into, 215; pelts of, 180, 197, 297, 303, 321, 340, 356, 357, 377; as tribute, 203, 207; Tzutzumatzin changed into, 364
Jails, Aztec, 457, 461, 493
James, Saint, 558
Jericho, Jews to, 74
Jerusalem, Solomon at, 130
Jesters, Aztec, 478, 480
Jewelers, 319. *See also* Gem cutters; Lapidaries
Jewelry, 159, 176, 284; as booty, 356; as funeral offering, 291, 383, 385, 466; as gift, 226, 274, 451; as gift to gods, 158; in pierced noses, 147 (*see also* Nose plugs); royal, 356, 385; for Spaniards, 499, 524; Tenochtitlan cache of, 532; as tribute, 203, 237; as warrior adornment, 178, 184. *See also* Gems
Jews: and Aztecs compared, 24, 25, 73–74, 100, 130, 444; out of Egypt, 431n; Native Americans as, 3 & n, 4–10; as Spanish enemies, 440
Jícama, 11n

Joseph (bibl.), 100
Judges, Aztec, 210, 454, 463. *See also* Justice, Aztec
Justice, Aztec, 193, 210 & n

Kings, Aztec, 103, 123; certification of, 128n.4; chronology of, 579; deity of, 157; dress of, 208–209; election of, 60, 468–69; as gods, 282; laws affecting, 208–209. *See also* Acamapichtli; Ahuitzotl; Axayacatl; Chimalpopoca; Cuauhtemoc; Cuitlahuac; Huitzilihuitl; Itzcoatl; Motecuhzoma I; Motecuhzoma II; Tizoc
Kingsborough, Lord, 4n.3
Knights of the Sun, 191–93. *See also* Cuachics
Knives, sacrificial, 171n.3, 190, 289–90, 386

Labrets, 124, 284; as funeral offerings, 291, 293; as gifts, 170, 173, 226, 274, 276, 304–306, 321, 322, 340, 497; hierarchy of, 209; of nobles, 355; royal, 295, 304, 305, 314, 338, 356, 377, 386, 390, 406, 414, 424; on statues, 428; of Tarascan soldiers, 280; of Tlatelolco nobles denied, 262; as tribute, 303; warrior, 164, 178, 234
La Florida, 10 & n.9
Lake(s), Mexican: of Mexican basin, 400n; of Tenochtitlan, 45 & n.5, 48, 51, 64, 66, 92n.7
Lances: Aztec, 34n, 119, 135; Spanish, 519, 553
Lapidaries, 336, 341, 417, 497. *See also* Gem cutters
Las Higueras, 562
Laurel (tree), 151, 295, 296
Laws: of Motecuhzoma I, 208–11; pre-Conquest records of, 569. *See also* Justice, Aztec
Leaches, 368
Leather, 301
Leggings, 305, 466
Leg ornaments, 314, 321, 322, 323, 338, 340, 352, 356, 377, 385, 386, 414, 488, 497

León, Ponce de, 10n.9
Lettuce, 11n
Libraries, of Tezcoco, 71n. *See also* Books
Lice, 359
Lienzos, 4n.2
Lime (calcareous material), 80, 130, 205, 207, 225, 226, 365
Lions, Durán and, 207n
Lip plugs. *See* Labrets
Lizards, 16
Llorona, La, 490 & n
Locusts (insects), 16, 205
López, Martín, 550
Lords, Feast of the, 407
Lumber, 205, 317

Macana, 323
Macaws, 165, 191, 327
Macuahuitl, 34n
Macuilxochtitla, 179
Macuilxochtitlan, 197
Magicians. *See* Sorcerers
Magpies, 26
Maguey, 11n, 82n.9; clothing of, 203, 204; as commoner fiber, 209, 454; drought vs., 238; honey, 238; paper of, 82n.9; as pulque source, 285n.3; slings made of, 34n, 206; Tlatelolco nobles in, 262; worms, 45n.5. *See also* Pulque
Maize, 10n.9, 22, 29, 40n, 65, 153, 173, 177, 178, 214, 222n, 350; Aztecs vs. Xochimilco, 107; blue, 368; as booty, 317; cakes of, 302, 320, 398, 400; of Colhuacan, 221, 222; destruction of, 436; divination by, 493; drought vs., 238; flood-ravaged, 370; in funeral rites, 151; as gift, 502; gruel of, 166; mystic connotations of, 33n.3; riches exchanged for, 552; ritual use of, 157; for slaves, 240; for Spaniards, 518; for stonecutters, 481; storing of, 238; for Teloloapan emigrants, 348; of Tenochtitlan, 362; as tribute, 55, 56, 80, 205, 206, 238, 317, 412. *See also* Tortillas
Malacaquetzalli, 294

Malinalco, 23, 25, 31, 47, 303, 315, 330, 504, 513
Malinaltzinco, 303
Malinalxochitl, 24–25, 31 & n
Malinche, Malintzin. *See* Marina
Mamey, 205
Mammoths, 17n
Manioc, 11n
Mantas (blankets), 86n
Mantles, 167, 168, 176, 177, 209; for Aztec emissaries, 334–35; as booty, 356; butterfly, 294; ceremonial, 191; of Colhuacan, 214, 219–21; for Cortés, 525, 526, 550; as funeral offerings, 150–52, 291–93, 383, 384, 466; as gifts, 170, 173, 226, 274, 276, 290, 293–94, 304–307, 321–23, 334, 340, 341, 343, 373, 405, 406, 417, 459, 468, 474, 502; as gift to gods, 475; royal, 190, 208–209, 304, 305, 314, 338, 348, 352, 356, 377, 385, 390, 414, 440, 487; Spaniards doomed by Aztec, 544; for statues, 328, 428; for stonecutters, 481; in Tenochtitlan cache, 532; Tlatelolco nobles stripped of, 262; as tribute, 162, 180, 181, 185, 199, 203, 206, 261, 270, 303, 343, 358, 359, 376, 412; warrior, 209, 234
Mapa de Sigüenza, 4n.2
Marina (Malinche) (Cortés translator), 499–500, 510, 515, 516, 520, 523, 530, 555, 556
Markets, 86
Marquesado, the. *See* Hot Country
Marquesado del Valle de Oaxaca, 15 & n
Marriage, 52n.3, 61–62, 81n.6. *See also* Polygyny; Widows; Wives
Mary (bibl.), 543, 558, 563
Masons, 320, 341, 365. *See also* Stonecutters
Matlatzincas, mass sacrifice of. *See* Tlacaxipehualiztli, for Matlatzincas
Matlatzinco, 170; and Ahuitzotl funeral, 384; Aztecs and, 202, 265–69, 280–81, 299, 315, 539; vs. Coaixtlahuaca, 183; emigrants to

Index

Teloloapan from, 346; vs. Huexotzinco, 438; and Templo Mayor, 330; Tizoc welcomed by, 297, 302; tribute from, 336
Mat makers, 341
Mats, as tribute, 204, 207, 318
Maximilian, emperor of Mexico, 566
Maxtla[ton], 68 & n, 84–88, 90–92, 100–102
Maxtlalxochitl, 54n.5
Maya, 33n.3
Mazahuacan, 202, 236, 315, 330, 335, 345, 346
Mazahuas, 170, 225, 297, 300, 384
Mazatlan, 34, 374–79
Meal, bean, 412
Meat, 170, 180, 181. *See also* Barbecue; Game
Mecantzin, 98
Mechoacan, 23, 319; Ahuitzotl and, 320–21, 331, 340; Aztecs of, 25, 47; Aztecs vs., 166, 277–82, 288, 347, 392, 409, 430, 433, 449n, 474 (*see also* Tarascans); and Coateocalli dedication, 433; and Motecuhzoma II enthronement, 402, 404; natives of, 470; and Templo Mayor, 334; Tlacaelel disdain for, 231
Meci, 21, 48, 51 & n
Mecitin. *See* Aztecs
Mendieta, Jerónimo de, 573
Mendoza, Antonio de, 561, 563
Mercenaries, Aztecs as Colhuacan, 72n.8
Mesoamerica, prehispanic, 4n.2. *See also* El Salvador; Guatemala; Honduras; Mexico; Nicaragua
Mestizo(s): 262n.4
Metal workers, 319. *See also* Goldsmiths; Silversmiths
Metates, 153
Metepec, 330
Metztitlan, 319; Ahuitzotl and, 320, 331, 340; Aztecs and, 288, 289, 299–301, 307, 392, 430, 433, 474; and Coateocalli dedication, 433; Huaxtec support for, 324; and Motecuhzoma II enthronement, 402, 404; natives of, 470; and Templo Mayor, 334

Mexica-Aztecs. *See* Aztecs
Mexicalcingo, 39n.9
Mexicano. *See* Nahuatl
Mexicans. *See* Aztecs
Mexicas. *See* Aztecs; Mexicans
Mexicatzinco, 39 & n.9; Ahuitzotl and, 358, 383; as Aztec ally, 266, 315, 325; vs. Coaixtlahuaca, 183; and Coateocalli dedication, 434; laborers from, 477, 478; shrines of, 355; and temple dedication, 329; Tizoc welcomed by, 297, 302. *See also Chinampa* region
Mexico, 4n.2; Aztecs to (*see* Aztecs, exodus of); chronicles of, 569; Cortés holdings in, 6n, 15n. *See also* Aztecs; Tenochtitlan; Valley of Mexico
Mexico, Gulf of, 495n.2
Mexico, Valley of. *See* Valley of Mexico
Mexico City, 13n.4, 15n, 32n.2, 33n.4, 45n.4, 48n, 170n.2, 53In; barrios of, 46; creation of, 558, 559; 1985 earthquake in, 47n; Tlatelolco and, 47n. *See also* Coyoacan; Templo Mayor; Tenochtitlan
Mexico-Tenochtitlan. *See* Tenochtitlan
Mexico-Tlatelolco. *See* Tlatelolco
Mexitin. *See* Aztecs; Mexicans
Mexitzin, 51n
Mezcatitlan Lagoon, 10n.9
Mezquic, 13, 87 & n.3, 88, 552; artists of, 504; as Aztec colony, 161; and Coateocalli dedication, 434; divers from, 480; emigrants to Teloloapan from, 346; laborers from, 478; and temple, 130–31, 329; Tizoc welcomed by, 297. *See also Chinampa* region
Miauatlan (prov.), 349–50, 351–52
Mice, 16
Michoacan, 6n
Mictecacihuatl, 285n.4
Mictlan, 223–24
Mictlancuauhtla, 495 & n.1
Mictlantecuhtli, 59n.2, 285n.4, 485n
Midwives, 186n

626

Milpa, 104
Milpas, 483
Mines, Indians as laborers in, 561
Miscarriage, cooking aroma–induced, 92
Mixcoatl, 289 & n
Mixiuhcan. *See* San Pablo, Mex.
Mixquic, 87n.3
Mixtecs, 3n, 182n.1, 184n; Aztecs and, 202, 229, 428, 429, 440; manuscripts of, 4n.2; tribute from, 335. *See also* Coaixtlahuaca; Tlachquiauhco; Yancuitlan; Zozola
Mizquetecas, 315
Mocexiuhzauhque, 460
Moctezuma. *See* Motecuhzoma I
Moles, 16
Momoztitlan, 93 & n
Momoztli, 93n
Montezuma. *See* Motecuhzoma I
Montúfar, Alonso de, 264
Moors, Spain and, 440
Moquihuix[tli], 249–60
Moses, and Quetzalcoatl compared, 7
Mosquitoes, 205
Motecuhzoma I, 113–14 & n.2, 81, 98, 160, 202, 337, 408, 531; and Ahuilizapan, 175–77, 180–81; and Chalco, 130, 132–49; and Chicomoztoc, 212–13; and Coaixtlahuaca, 183, 186, 193; and Coatzacualco, 223; and *cuauhxicalli* ceremony, 186–91, 193; and Cuetlaxtla, 194–201; death of, 245, 247; dynastic plans of, 309–10; as executioner, 190; and great famine, 238–40; and Guaxaca, 227–30, 236–37; and Huaxtecs, 161, 166, 167 (*see also* Tlacaxipehualiztli); and Huaxtepec, 244–45; laws of, 208–11; progeny of, 388; reign of, 579; renown of, 210, 298; statue of, 242–43, 290; and temple, 130–32, 169, 224–27, 231; and Tepeaca, 152–55, 157–59; and Tezcoco, 123–26, 128, 129; war policy of, 233–34, 236
Motecuhzoma II, 223; and Atlixco campaigns, 427–28, 437; baptism of, 531; and Coateocalli, 431, 433–36; and Cholula, 438–41; and comet, 460–63, 481, 483, 486; and Cortés, 515–18, 524, 526, 528–33, 536, 540; Cortés on, 399n; cruelty of, 398, 411, 476, 485, 491, 493, 494, 545; death of, 529, 545; on defeat in battle, 440–41; dictates of, 394–98; election of, 389–93; enthronement of, 402–408; flight of, 488; fondness for human flesh of, 474; frustrated rage of, 453–54, 457; and Huexotzinco, 446–51; vs. Icpatepec, 409; imprisonment of, 530–31, 534–45; in mountain cave, 483–84; Nezahualpilli charge to, 391; and Nezahualpilli successor, 467; as orator, 405; people vs., 540–41, 545; *persona* of, 474, 477; progeny of, 511, 538–39, 545; reign of, 579; renown of, 393; and Spaniards, 7n, 495–518 (*see also* Motecuhzoma II, and Cortés); as Spanish spokesman, 540; and Tlacaxipehualiztli stone, 476–81; vs. Tlachquiauhco, 471–73; and Tlahuicole, 447–48, 449n; and Toci festival, 456–57; vs. Totonacs, 6n; vs. Totopec/Quetzaltepec, 419–23; Totoquihuaztli charge to, 391–92; and tribute, 359; tyranny of, 6n, 506; and Tzocoztli, 460, 461
Motecuhzoma Ilhuicamina. *See* Motecuhzoma I
Motecuhzoma Xocoyotzin. *See* Motecuhzoma II
Motecuzoma. *See* Motecuhzoma I
Motelchiuh, 515–17
Moteuczoma. *See* Motecuhzoma I
Mother Goddess, 524n
Mountain lions. *See* Pumas
Mourners, professional, 382
Moyotla[n], 58 & n
Mozauhque, 156 & n.7
Munoz Camargo, Diego, 449n
Murals, 43n.2, 150n.2
Mushrooms, hallucinogenic, 307, 322 & n.1, 407, 408n, 475
Music, ceremonial, 287, 435, 480;

battle-related, 259, 519; coronation, 321; at Coyoacan dam opening, 368; funerary, 283–85, 301, 386; victory-related, 317, 327, 343, 433, 455, 473
Musical instruments, Aztec, 275n.4

Nacazcolotl, 204 & n
Nagual, 215n
Nahual, 215n
Nahualism, 215n
Nahuatl (lang.), 14n; counting in, 391n; as Durán tongue, 155n, 568, 575; glories of, 70; Huitzilopochtli affinity for, 273n
Narcotics, 186n. See also Mushrooms, hallucinogenic
Narváez, Pánfilo de, 534–36 & n.2, 542
National Museum of Anthropology (Mexico City), 188n, 227n, 322n.2; Duraniana in, 566
National Palace, 531n
National Pawn Shop, 531n
Native Americans: and corn, 222n; nature of Mesoamerican, 409; origin of Mesoamerican, 3–11; as Spanish allies, 6n. See also Aztecs
Nauholin, 191
Nauhtlan, 517
Nauhyotl, 48–49 & n
Near East, Native Americans as immigrants from, 3n
Necklaces, 210, 291, 356, 405, 488, 510, 529, 530
New Fire ceremony, 107n, 445–46
New Spain, 20, 345n. See also Mexico; Tenochtitlan
Nexticpac (plain), 140
Nezahualcoyotl, 57 & n, 71 & n, 88, 121, 123–29, 225, 235–36, 278, 291; death of, 290; gardens of, 205n.5; Tlacaelel and, 248
Nezahualcoyotzin. See Nezahualcoyotl
Nezahualpilli. See Nezahualpiltzintli
Nezahualpiltzintli, 290, 335, 371–72, 458–59, 485, 550; at Ahuitzotl funeral, 382–86; and Ahuitzotl successor, 387–88, 390–91; and Axayacatl funeral, 291–92; death of, 465–66; as executioner, 338; and Huaxtec rebellion, 324; magic powers of, 452, 459, 461–62, 481; and Motecuhzoma II, 452–53, 459, 461–62, 465–66, 475, 481; *persona* of, 376; progeny of, 467, 468; respect for, 344; and Teloloapan resettlement, 344–45; and temple dedication, 330, 331, 337–38; at Tizoc coronation, 304; and Tizoc successor, 310–11; and Xoconochco campaign, 376
Nicaragua, 4n.2, 380n
Noah, 3n
Nobles, Aztec, 78–82, 96, 101, 103, 192–93, 387; dress of, 208, 209; laws affecting, 208–10. See also *Pipiltin*; Titles, Itzcoatl assignment of
Nochtepec, 303, 336
Nomads, Aztecs as, 12n.2. See also Aztecs, exodus of
Nonoalco-Tlatelolco Housing Development, 47n
Nonohualcas, 273
Nopal. See Prickly pear cactus
Nopallan (prov.), 399
Nose pendants, 170, 173, 291
Nose plugs, 191, 284, 295; as funeral offerings, 466; as gifts, 276, 304–306, 321, 322, 340; as gift to gods, 158; hierarchy of, 209; Huaxtec, 164–65; of nobles, 355–56; royal, 297, 304, 305, 313, 356, 377, 385, 390, 406, 414, 424; on statues, 428
Noses, pierced, 147, 190. See also Nose plugs
Nuño de Guzmán, 10n.9
Nurseries, plant, 205n.5

Oaxaca (state/prov., Valley of), 15n, 182n.1, 351, 567
Oaxtepec. See Huaxtepec
Obsidian, 30, 34n, 66 & n.2, 171n.3, 206, 289n, 323
"Obsidian Serpent." See Itzcoatl
Oceloapan, 179
Oceloicpalli, 297

Ocelopan, 51 & n, 53, 216n, 236
Ocelots, 159, 207n; men into, 215; pelts of, 180, 197, 356, 357; as tribute, 203, 207
Oceoloapan, 197
Ochre, 82, 190, 191, 204
Ococal, 51 & n
Ococaltzin, 55, 56
Ocopetlayuca. *See* Tuchimilco
Ocopetlayucan, 111
Ocopilla, 25
Ocoteteuctin, 150
Ocotl, 150
Octli. *See* Pulque
Ocuila, 95, 290, 303, 315
Ocuilan, 330
Ocuiltamalli, 46n.5
Ocuituco, 13 & n.4, 561
Officials, Aztec, 210 & n, 309, 319; tribute-focused (see *Tequitlato*). *See also* Acolnahuacatl; *Calpixque*; *Petlacalcatl*
Ol[l]in. *See* Rubber
Olinalan, 303
Olmos, Andrés de (Franciscan missionary), 570, 573, 574
Ololiuhgui, 60n, 189n
Omacatl, 506
Omecihuatl, 59n.2
Ometecuhtli, 59n.2
Opochtli, 289 & n
Opochtzin, 48, 49, 52, 170
Oquiz, 506
Oracles. *See* Soothsayers
Oranges, 11n
Orators, Aztec, 70–72
Orchards, 15, 362
Orizaba. *See* Ahuilizapan
Orphans, royal largesse to, 306, 400, 408, 415
Otlatlan, 351
Otomi (Aztec warriors), 26n, 164, 281, 306
Otomi(s) (Mexican people), 14, 26 & n, 346, 383; at Ahuitzotl funeral, 384; as Aztec allies, 539; Aztec contempt for, 273n; as laborers, 225, 365, 478–79; vs. Spaniards, 546, 547; of Xilotepex, 316
Otompan, 14, 330

Otumba (plain), 546–47
Our Lady of Remedies, 544, 546
Owls, as ill omen, 144–45 & n.3
Oztoman, 342, 344–48
Oztoticpac, 329
Oztoyocan, 330

Pachimalcatl Tecuhtli, 104
Pachuca, 33n.3
Paganism: Durán vs., 431n; Spain vs., 440; virtues of, 577
Pahuacan, 369
Painters (artisans), 320, 341. *See also* Artists
Painting(s): Aztec, 121; Native American, 3, 4 & n.2, 7–8, 16; of newly arrived Spaniards, 503–505. *See also* Face painting; *Lienzos*; Murals; *Pinturas*; Rolls, pictorial
Paints, 82, 204
Palace, Aztec: laws of, 208, 210
Palenque, 33n.3
Panquetzaliztli, 191n.4, 408n
Pantitlan, 98n.2
Papagayo River, 420n
Papalotilmatli, 294
Papalotlan, 330
Papalotlaxcalli, 284
Papayecan, 426
Paper, 82 & n.9, 292, 478. *See also Amatl*
Pardon, royal, 210
Paredes, Diego de, 202
Parks, 205n.5
Parrots, 165, 203, 327
Partidor, Martín, 561
Paschal candle, 445–46
Patzcuaro, Lake, 34n
Patzcuaro, 23 & n.2
Pawnee Indians, 143n.2
Pearls, 204
Pears, 11n
Peas, 11n
Pelicans, 334
Pellet bows, 295
Penitent(s): Motecuhzoma II as, 487; priestly (see Mozauhque)
Peñol (knoll), 370
Perfume, as Aztec gift, 276
Peru, 535

629

Petaca, 359n
Petlacalcalli, 359n
Petlacalcatl, 303, 359n
Petlacontzitzquique, 227
Pharaoh, 171n.6
Philosophers, pre-Conquest Mexican, 570
Piaztlan, 303, 336
Pictographs, pre-Conquest, 570
Pilhoacazintli. *See* Tezcatlipoca
Pilli. See Nobles, Aztec
Pineapples, 165, 205
Pinelo, León, 565
Pinotl, 180–81, 244, 496
Pinturas, 121
Pintura peregrina, 245n
Pipiltin, 52n.3. *See also* Nobles, Aztec
Pita, 297
Pitch: ritual use of, 60 & n, 76 & n, 77n, 189 & n, 220, 299, 386, 406, 531; yellow, 424
Pizarro, Gonzalo, 535
Plague, 5
Plants: of ancient Mesoamericans, 10–11n.9; of Colhuacan, 220, 221; as tribute, 55, 56. *See also* Fruit; Seeds; Trees; Vegetables
Plasterers, 320
Plates, gold, 385
Platters, gold, 532
Plumes. *See* Feathers
Poctla (prov.), 202
Poems, pre-Conquest, 570, 574
Polygyny, 52n.3, 435
Poor, royal generosity to, 306, 341, 400, 408
Poplars, 26
Popocatepetl (volcano), 13n.4, 40n, 380n
Popolocas, 184n
Potters, 319, 341
Pottery, 207
Prickly pear cactus, 11n, 21, 32, 33n.3, 41 & n, 42, 44, 182, 238, 347
Priests, Aztec, 83n, 301, 355, 356; and Ahuitzotl investiture, 314; after Aztec defeat, 427, 440; blackened, 486n; at Coateocalli dedication, 435; Cortés welcomed by, 531; and Coyoacan dam ceremonies, 368; as executioners, 339; and flaying ceremony, 171–72, 478, 480; funerary rites of, 150n.2, 151, 295, 386; hierarchy of, 155–56; killing of, 538; Motecuhzoma II and, 457, 461, 462, 475, 491–92; and New Fire ceremony, 446; perquisites of, 210; records of, 569; and returning warriors, 473; and sacrifice rites, 230, 270, 287, 338–39 & n.1. *See also* Fire priests
Prisoners of war, 166–67, 271, 301, 327, 400, 433, 455, 458, 473; flaying of (*see* Tlacaxipehualiztli); killing of, 72n.8 (*see also* Prisoners of war, sacrifice of); pre-sacrifice respect for, 443–44; sacrifice of, 10, 140–42, 149, 155, 165, 166, 180, 186–87, 189–90, 229–31, 288–90, 292, 307, 322–23, 329, 330, 335, 338–40, 352, 407, 429, 435–36, 448–49, 455–57, 459; as tribute, 329, 330
Prophets, Aztec, 464, 493. *See also* Soothsayers
Prostitutes, 283n, 524n
Puebla, 16, 182n.1
Puebla-Tlaxcala region, Aztecs in. *See* "Flower wars"
Pulque, 152, 170, 186n, 285n.3, 295. See also *Teooctli*
Puma(s), 159, 207n; pelts of, 340; priest dressed as, 339n.1
Pumpkin seeds, 153, 155, 165, 177, 205–207, 327, 336, 412
Pyramids, 17n, 191–92 & n.6

Quail: sacrifice of, 245, 270, 282, 297, 298, 305, 356, 358, 369, 372, 380, 390, 406, 475, 478, 480; as tribute, 177, 205, 270, 302, 318
Quauhuitlicac. *See* Cuicatlicac
Quauitlehua, 32n.2
Quecholac, 329
Quechua (lang.), 344–45n
Quetzalacxoyatl, 467–68
Quetzalacxoyatzin. *See* Quetzalacxoyatl
Quetzalatl (river), 300, 420

630

Quetzalayotl, 273–74
Quetzalcoatl, 43n.1, 48n, 59n.2, 170, 243 & n, 289n, 298n, 501, 504, 530; Cholula obeisance to, 408n; dead Axayacatl as, 294; impersonation of, 289; miracles of, 7 & n; Spanish commander as, 497–98
Quetzalcuauh, 141
Quetzaltepec, 417–23, 425
Quetzaltlalpiloni, 226 & n.3
Quiahuiztlan (prov.), 6n, 273–74
Quiauhtzin Tecuhtli, 288
Quilaztli, 505–506
Quimichtla, 179
Quimichtlan, 197
Quiname, 16, 17 & n
Quiztohozin, 88

Rabbits, 16, 166, 406; as tribute, 177, 205, 270, 302, 318. *See also* Hares
Rafts: horticultural (see *Chinampas*); Teuctepec invaded on, 432; as tribute, 372. *See also Acatl apechtli*
Rain, 196n
Ramírez, José Fernando, 566–68
Ramírez de Fuenleal, Sebastián, 573
Rape: of Aztec women, 86; of Tlatelolco ladies, 249
Rasping bones/stones, 275n.4
Rattles, 164, 209, 275n.4, 295, 368
Ravens, 203
Real estate, records of pre-Conquest, 569
Red (color), significance of, 150n.3
Religion: Aztec, 19, 21, 26 (*see also* Gods, Aztec; Priests, Aztec; Seven Caves, gods of; Temples, Aztec); Christian (*see* Catholicism); mushrooms and modern Mexican, 322n.2; pictorial representations of Native American, 4n.2. *See also* Rites, religious
Repartimientos, 561
Resin, 206
Revisionism, Aztecs and historical, 81–82n.7
Rice, 11n

Rites, religious: pre-Conquest chronicles of, 569
Rock crystal, 178, 203, 227
Rodents, 205
Rolls, pictorial, 4n.2
Rome, ancient: paganism of, 577; sacking of, 317
Roots, as food, 16
Roses, Durán and, 207n
Rouge, Indian women use of, 524 & n
Rubber: ceremonial use of, 40n, 82, 83n, 274, 368, 478; for Chalchiuhtlicue, 371, 372; as rouge, 367
Rubies, 227

Sacrifice(s): human (*see* Human sacrifice); by Jews, 444; by "war widows," 350–51
Sage, 80n.4. *See also Chia[n]*
Sahagún, Bernardino de, 47n, 568, 569, 573, 574
Salamanders, 46n.5
Salt, 153; punitive sowing of, 412; as tribute, 155, 185
Saltillo, 345n
Salvador, 4n.2. *See also* El Salvador
San Antonio, 40, 369
Sand, 225, 226, 365, 417
Sandals, 159, 167, 168, 177; as funeral offerings, 291; as gifts, 170, 173, 274, 304, 322, 340, 405; jaguar-skin, 297, 305; privilege of wearing, 192, 435, 454; royal, 208, 297, 305, 314, 338, 385, 386, 389, 390; rubber-soled, 83n; Tlatelolco nobles stripped of, 262; as tribute, 155, 162, 177, 207, 303, 412
Sandoval, Fernando B., 571
San Francisco Colhuacan, 48n
San Hipólito, church of, 484n
San Juan (barrio), 46
San Juan de Ulúa, 495n.2
San Martín (barrio), 14, 556
San Pablo (barrio), 40, 46, 369
San Pedro Tlahuac, 116n
San Sebastián (barrio), 46
Santa María la Redonda (barrio), 46

Index

Santiago (barrio), 47
Santiago Tlatelolco, 568
Santo Domingo, 560
Sapodilla tree, 171 & n.4
Sapotas, 205
Sashes, 170, 173, 305
Savants, Aztec. *See* Calmecahuehuetque
Scallops, 175
Schools: Aztec, 210, 312, 314, 337, 392, 395, 396 (see also *Calmecac*; *Telpochcalli*); Spanish-run Indian, 568
Scorpions, 203
Sculptors, 341, 477. *See also* Stoneworkers
Sculpture. *See* Carvings
Seashells, decorative use of, 43n.1
Seat makers, 341
Seats (furniture), 204, 207, 318
Seeds, edible, 214; of Colhuacan, 221; for Teloloapan emigrants, 348; as tribute, 80, 317, 327, 412. See also *Chia[n]*; Pumpkin seeds
Selim I, sultan, 399
Serpents. *See* Snakes
Servants, conquered Indians as Spanish, 561
"Setting Sun." *See* Tizoc
Seven Caves, 3n, 10 & n.9, 11, 21; Aztec exodus from (see Aztecs, exodus of); gods of, 22. See also Chicomoztoc
Seven Cities of Silver. *See* Cíbola
Shalmaneser, king of Assyria, 4
Shells: of Cuetlaxtla, 194; as gifts, 274; musical, 275n.4, 301, 317, 343, 356, 368, 372, 433, 435, 455, 473, 480, 502, 519, 531; as necklace element, 210; as tribute, 204, 223, 224, 274. See also Conch shells; Seashells
Shields: Aztec, 34n, 66 & n.2, 76, 77, 119, 120, 135, 139, 150, 153, 178, 198, 206, 234, 553; Chichimeca, 519; of dead warriors, 150; executioner, 171; as gifts, 124, 294, 323, 340, 348, 417, 451, 459, 474; Huaxtec, 165; royal, 375, 437; as sacrifice element, 157; for statues, 428; Tarascan, 279; in Tenochtitlan cache, 532; Tepanec, 79 & n.2; as tribute, 206, 303, 318, 358, 359, 376, 412, 473; as warrior bonus, 234; Xochimilca, 109
Ships, Spanish, 499, 503, 507–10; scuttling of, 528; and Tenochtitlan invasion, 549, 551, 556; Tezcoco-built, 550
Shrieks, battle, 79 & n.3, 94, 108, 109, 136, 139, 165, 185, 259, 267, 326, 353, 378, 399, 426, 544
Shrimp, 45, 165, 179
Shrines, Aztec, 46, 337, 355, 361; domestic, 40n; of Huitznahuatl (*see* Huitznahuac); idols of, 162; marketplace, 157; of Toci, 457n. *See also* Coateocalli; *Momoztli*
Sickness, hunger-induced, 92
Sierra Nevada, 15, 146
Signs, interpretation of hortatory, 145n.3
Silver, 27, 43 & n.1, 159, 200, 206, 218, 235, 385; of Quetzalcoatl, 497n
Silversmiths, 336, 341
Skirts, 204, 293, 502, 524
Skull rack, 190, 274, 276, 288, 290, 341
Slaves: Aztec (*see* Aztec slaves); Aztecs as, 240; Indians as Spanish, 561. *See also* Prisoners of war
Slings (weapons), 34n, 57, 135, 198, 206, 412
Smallpox, 538n.7, 563
"Smoking Shield." *See* Chimalpopoca
Smoking tubes, 319, 341
Snails, 194, 204, 210, 223
Snakes, 16, 214; bones of, 210; in Coyoacan dam canals, 368; as Mexican symbol, 41n; mystic significance of, 41n; ritual paper, 190–91 & n.4; sacrifice of, 200; of Tizaapan, 35–36; as tribute, 197, 200, 203; Tzutzumatzin transformed into, 364
Snow, 160
Solomon, temple of, 130
Songs, ritual, 277, 304–305, 478, 479; of condemned prisoners,

632

301, 327, 473; coronation, 321; flaying, 171; funerary, 149–51, 283–85, 294–96, 385, 428; of Spanish murderers, 538; victory, 343, 433, 455. *See also* Chants; Hymns

Soot, 206, 352

Soothsayers, Aztec, 461, 463, 464, 475, 495, 512

Sorcerers, Aztec, 464, 485, 493–95; to Colhuacan, 214–22; Cuauhtemoc and, 540; Motecuhzoma II and, 461, 463, 475, 485, 493–95; vs. Spaniards, 512–15

Spain: enemies of, 440; honorary titles in, 102, 103; Turkey and, 434, 440. *See also* Spaniards; Spanish conquest

Spaniards, in New World, 495n.2; arrival of, 6 & n, 468, 495n.2, 496 (*see also* Cortés, Hernán — arrival of); avarice of, 531–33, 543–44; cruelty of, 166, 178, 410, 528, 537, 560 (*see also* Cortés, Hernán — cruelty of); devastation by, 317; flowers for, 529; mutiny among, 562; *persona* of, 528. *See also* Cortés, Hernán

Spanish conquest, 5, 129n.6, 223, 521n, 560–62. *See also* Cortés, Hernán; Spaniards, in New World; Tenochtitlan, fall of

Sparrow hawks, 203

Spears, Aztec, 109n, 553

Spiders, 203

Spirulina, 11n

Squash, 11n, 55, 362

Staff (stick), royal, 435

Star Hill, 107n

Stars, 582. *See also* Citlalco

Starvation, in Tenochtitlan, 552, 555, 557. *See also* Famine; Sickness, hunger-induced

Statues: Aztec (*see* Aztec statues); of Chalco temple, 358; on Tenochtitlan-Tlatelolco border, 258n.2; for Tlatelolco target practice, 251–52

Steam bath. See *Temazcalli*

Stewards, Aztec territorial, 129

Stews, 162, 498, 500; of human flesh, 284

Stilts, as festival resource, 9n.7

Stone(s): aquatic, 204; for Coyoacan dam, 365; as necklace element, 210; precious (*see* Gems); rasping, 275n.4; sacrificial, 322–23n.3, 328 & n.3, 474, 476, 477 (*see also* Sun Stone; *Temalacatl*); for temple, 130–33, 225, 226; as tribute, 80, 105, 204–207; volcanic (see *Tezontle*); as weapons, 120, 135, 198; working of, 188. *See also* Cuauhxicalli; Sun Stone; Sun stones; *Temalacatl*

Stoneworkers, 328, 341, 477–78, 481

Sugar, 15n

Suicide, by defeated Aztecs, 557

Sun: Aztec concept of (*see* Huitzilopochtli); Chichimec worship of, 18

Sun Stone, 17n.3, 191, 286, 288–90, 297, 302 & n.2, 307, 322, 338, 386; Axayacatl and, 264; inauguration of, 278, 339n.1; Tlacaelel and, 276–77

Sun stones, 188n

Sweeping, ritual, 161, 162

Swords: Aztec, 34n, 66, 76, 109, 135, 139, 150, 153, 198, 294, 553; Chichimeca, 519; executioners', 171; gifts of, 294, 451; obsidian-bladed, 323, 378; royal, 375, 437, 440; Spanish, 553; for statues, 428; stone-bladed, 279; as tribute, 412; Xochimilca, 109

Tacuba (prov.), 14, 29, 32, 45, 170, 465; and Ahuitzotl coronation, 312–14; and Ahuitzotl successor, 387, 390; Axayacatl feted by, 270; and Axayacatl funeral, 292; as Aztec ally, 176, 196, 265, 270, 278, 286, 299, 342, 344, 375, 411, 420, 429, 431, 432, 435, 438–39, 446, 447, 453, 455, 472, 531; as Aztec colony, 161, 365; vs. Aztecs, 68, 72 (*see also* Tacuba, as Spanish ally); vs. Chiapa, 317; and Coaixtlahuaca, 182, 183; and Coateocalli dedication, 434; and *cuauhxicalli* ceremony, 189, 191; Huaxtecs vs., 161; vs. Huexotzin-

Index

co, 436–38; and Nezahualpilli funeral, 466; prisoners of, 335; and Spaniards, 524–25; as Spanish ally, 529, 548, 551, 555; and Tecuantepec victory, 353, 354; and Templo Mayor, 131, 224–25, 331, 335; and Tizoc enthronement, 297, 298, 302, 304, 307n; vs. Tlachquiauhco, 471; Totonac slave-shopping in, 240; Tzutzumatzin mourned in, 367. *See also* Tepanecs; Totoquihuaztli; Triple Alliance
Tacubaya, 14, 33n.4
Toltecs, 88n
Tamales, 239 & n, 350, 509
Tamapachco, 324
Tamemes, 511
Tarascans, 23 & n.2; Aztecs vs., 23n.2, 273n, 278–82, 347; today, 34n
Tassels, commemorative, 355
Taxes, 46n.6, 262 & n.3, 435; collection of (see *Calpixque*)
Teachers, Aztec, 210. See also *Ichpochtlatoque*; *Telpochtlatoque*; Tutors
Tecalli, 154, 155, 329, 331
Tecamachalco, 329
Tecayehuatl, 446–47, 449–51
Tecayehuatzin. See Tecayehuatl
Tecciztlan, 14, 330
Techichco, 134, 135–36, 479
Tecoac, 231, 233, 329, 330, 332, 334, 335, 340, 518–22
Teconal, 250, 251, 254, 255, 258, 259; death of, 260, 261
Tecpan (barrio), 98n.2
Tecpan, 47n, 87n.2, 98n.2
Tecpanecs. See Tepanecs
Tecuacuiltin, 156–57, 171
Tecuantepec (prov.), 349–53, 356, 360, 374–79, 413–14
Tecuantepeque, 202
Tecuilhuitontli, 408n
Tecuitlatenco, 119
Tecuitlatl, 46n.5
Tecutli. See *Tetecuhtin*
Tehuantepec, Isthmus of, 15n
Teimatini. See Tezcatlipoca
Teixpan miquiz teuicaltin, 292

Teloloapan, 341–42, 344–48
Telpochcalli, 53n
Telpochtli. See Tezcatlipoca
Temalacatl, 169, 174, 186n, 449n, 477
Temazcalli, 39 & n.8, 41
Temazcaltitlan, 41
Temoac, 13
Temples: Ahuitzotl tour of, 355–58; Aztec (*see* Tenochtitlan, temples of); burning of, 94, 127, 128, 185, 229, 269, 316, 326, 412, 421, 423, 472; dignitaries of, 156; human residents of Aztec (*see* Mocexiuhzauhque); Spanish demolition of Tenochtitlan, 558; of Tacuba, 458; of Tenochtitlan, 22, 26, 46, 64, 156, 224–27, 307, 337, 355–57, 558 (*see also* Templo Mayor); of Tezcoco, 458; of Tlatelolco, 261, 262. See also Coateocalli; Great Pyramid Temple; Shrines
Templo Mayor, 188n, 192n.7, 226n.4, 262n.4; Ahuitzotl in, 356–57; carvings of, 28n.6; as Cortés objective, 555; dedication of, 328–41; massacre in, 536n.2, 537–39, 542, 544; Motecuhzoma II shrine in, 431; Spanish occupation of, 555. See also Coatepec; Huitzilopochtli, statue of
Tenamazcuicuil, 134–35
Tenamaztli, 98
Tenango, 14
Tenantzinco, 263–69, 330
Tenayuca, 14, 255, 385, 506, 539, 547
Tenoch, 51 & n, 53, 216 & n, 258n.2
Tenochtitlan, 19n, 20, 28n, 41 & n; after Azcapotzalco victory, 82–84; and Coaixtlahuaca, 182; Cortés and, 484n, 518, 550–56; Cuauhtemoc restoration of, 547; fall of, 246, 484n, 548, 549, 556–57; founding of, 12n.1, 43–47; glories of, 319; growth of, 64, 66; Huexotzinca refugees in, 446–47, 449, 450; lake at, 45 & n.5, 48, 51, 64, 66, 92n.7; layout of, 539, 542, 549; population of, 6 & n; postflood rebuilding of, 373; and

634

prickly pear cactus, 33 & n.3; razing of, 558, 559; recollections of, 569; Sevillian martyr of, 554; structural problems of, 226n.4; as supreme, 218; temples of (*see* Temples, of Tenochtitlan; Templo Mayor); Tezcoco rape of, 128n.3; treasure of, 531–32, 534, 558–59, 562n.3; water problems of, 362 (*see also* Flooding, of Tenochtitlan). *See also* Cuepopan; Kings, Aztec; Mexico City, Mex.; Moyotlan; Palace; Teopan; Triple Alliance
Tenochtli. *See* Prickly pear cactus
Tents, 153, 154, 278–79
Teocalli de la Guerra Sagrada, 33n.3, 41n
Teocolhuacan, 10, 36n
Teoixhuacan, 179, 197
Teomamaque, 19n, 51n
Teonacaztli, 214
Teonanacatl. *See* Mushrooms, hallucinogenic
Teooctli. *See* Divine Wine
Teopan[tlaca] (barrio), 58, 59n.1
Teoquizqui, 145
Teotecomatl, 285
Teotenanco, 303, 330
Teotihuacan (archaeological site), 17n, 29n, 150n.2, 173n, 546, 559n
Teotitlan, 237, 336
Teotlachco, 27
Teotlacualli, 60n, 189n
Teotlala, 303
Teotliztac, 303
Tepanecapan, 324, 325
Tepanecs, 29, 45, 54; and Atlixco campaign, 426; as Aztec allies, 154, 180, 230, 266, 281, 378, 399, 413, 422, 423, 426; vs. Aztecs, 68–80, 97; Aztec tribute to, 60–63; as Aztec vassals, 69n.5, 277, 365; vs. Chiapa, 315, 316; Coaixtlahuaca vs., 183, 184; Cortés embraced by, 525; empire of, 69n.5; exodus of, 13, 14; as merchant traders, 349; vs. Metztitlan, 300; Nezahualcoyotl vs., 129; political system of, 80–81n.5; vs. Spaniards, 547; subjugation of, 129n.6; to Teloloapan region, 345; and Templo Mayor, 338; today, 13n.4. *See also* Azcapotzalco; Coyoacan; Tacuba; Tezozomoc[tli]
Tepanquizqui, 105
Tepan tlacaltin, 292
Tepeaca, 149, 152–55, 159, 188, 202, 293, 329, 335
Tepechpan, 14, 330
Tepecuacuilco, 303, 336
Tepeilhuitl, 40n
Tepemaxalco, 303, 315, 330
Tepepulco (hill and town), 330, 400, 415
Tepetecuhtli, 175, 195
Tepetlan, 303
Tepetlaoztoc, 14, 330
Tepetlixpan, 13
Tepetzinco, 32 & n.2
Tepexi, 385
Tepexpan. *See* Tepechpan
Tepixqui, 469
Teponaztli, 274–75 & n.4, 296, 305
Tepoztecatl, 289 & n, 339n.1
Tepoztlan, 13, 292, 513, 548, 561
Tepoztopilli, 34n
Teptzotecas, 385
Tequiciztlan, 127
Tequihuaque, 306
Tequitlatos, 469, 491
Tequitque, 485
Tequixquiac, 28
Terra cotta, 192n.7
Tetecuhtin. See *Tecuhtli*
Tetecuhtin, 22–23n
Tetela, 13 & n.4, 561
Tetelan, 329
Teticpac, 342
Tetlaxincaxochitl, 52n.3
Teucnene, 175
Teuctepec, 431–33, 442–43, 445, 446
Teuctlamacazqui. *See* Tlillancalqui
Teuctlehuac, 69 & n.6
Teuctli. *See* *Tetecuhtin*
Texiptla, 488–89, 494
Texocotl, 11n
Textiles, Otomi, 26n
Teyacac, 108
Tezacatetl, 51 & n, 53, 216 & n
Tezcacoac, 97n.2

Tezcacoacatl, 51n
Tezcatlipoca, 44n.3, 53n, 66n.2, 387n, 398n, 536; Chalco reverence for, 358; dances honoring, 524n
Tezcocans, exodus of, 14–15
Tezcoco, 14, 29n, 45, 48, 49, 170, 225 & n.2; and Ahuitzotl coronation, 312, 313; and Atlixco campaign, 426, 427; as Aztec ally, 176, 180, 196, 230, 265, 266, 270, 278, 281, 286, 299, 300, 324, 325, 331, 342, 344, 375, 378, 399, 413, 420, 422, 423, 426, 427, 438–39, 446, 447, 453, 455, 472, 531, 539; as Aztec colony, 124, 125, 153, 161, 277, 365; as Aztec conqueror, 60, 128n.3; Aztec overtures to, 64, 70, 71; Aztecs vs., 202; Aztecs "vs.," 126–27, 128n.3; vs. Chiapa, 315–17; and Coaixtlahuaca, 182–84; and Coateocalli dedication, 434; Cortés in, 549, 550; Coyoacan appeal to, 87, 88; and *cuauhxicalli* ceremony, 189, 191; Durán in, 567, 568, 574–75; Durán praise for, 15; emigrants to Teloloapan from, 345; holdings of, 330; Huaxtecs vs., 161; Huexotla vs., 290; Huexotzinco vs., 438; laborers from, 478; memoirists of, 569; merchants of, 349, 428–29; vs. Metztitlan, 300; prisoners of, 335; as royal farm, 238; and Spaniards, 524–25, 547; as Spanish ally, 548, 550, 551, 555; splendor of, 550; Tecuantepec victory celebrated in, 353, 354; and Templo Mayor, 130–31, 224–25, 338; Tenochtitlan and, 330–31; and Tizoc enthronement, 297, 298, 302, 307n; vs. Tlachquiauhco, 471; today, 13n.4, 71n; Totonac slave-shopping in, 240; as Tula ally, 436–37; Tzutzumatzin mourned in, 367; and Xocomochco campaign, 376. *See also* Nezahualcoyotl; Nezahualpiltzintli; Triple Alliance
Tezcotzinco, 71n
Tezmeluca, 550

Tezontepec, 300, 330
Tezontle, 365
Tezoyocan, 330
Tezozomoc, Fernando Alvarado, 69n.5, 571–73
Tezozomoc[tli] (Tepanec king), 54–56, 61–63, 65–69 & n.5, 263, 265–69
Theft, punishment for, 210
Thieves: Aztec soldiers as, 178 (*see also* Booty, warrior right to); New Spain Spaniards as, 410
Thirteen, as mystic number, 289n
Thread, 182, 587
Thrushes, 26
Tigers, Durán and, 207n
Time, Aztec concept of, 445
Tira de la Peregrinación. See *Codex Boturini/Tira de la Peregrinación*
Titles, Itzcoatl assignment of, 97–99, 102–103
Tizaapan (Aztec grant), 35–38, 52
Tizaapan (barrio), 52, 107 & n
Tizapan, 35n
Tizoc, 309, 337, 388; death of, 307; enthronement of, 291, 296–99, 302–307; and Metztitlan campaign, 300–301; progeny of, 388; reign of, 579
Tizocic. *See* Tizoc
Tizocicatzin. *See* Tizoc
Tizocic Tlalchiuhtonatiuh. *See* Tizoc
Tizoc Stone, 188n
Tizoc Yahuacatl, 183
Tlacacaliztli, 143n.2
Tlacacochtoc, 53, 54n.5, 98 & n.5
Tlacacuitlaua, 68
Tlacaelel, 72 & n.9, 74–82, 91, 93–97, 99–101, 202, 208, 271, 287, 288, 560; as acting king, 299, 302; and Ahuilizapan, 175, 176, 180; and Ahuitzotl, 309–15, 320, 322; ambitions of, 231–32; and Axayacatl funeral, 290, 291, 293; and Chalco, 133–48; and Chiapa campaign, 315, 317; and Chicomoztoc, 212–16, 218, 221–23; and Coaixtlahuaca, 183; and *cuauhxicalli* ceremony, 186–87, 189–91, 193; and Cuetlaxtla, 194–

97, 199–201; and Cuitlahuac, 117, 119–21; dark side of, 169, 173n, 233, 272; death of, 361; as executioner, 190, 289–90, 338; and great famine, 238–39; and Huaxtecs, 161, 162, 164, 166, 323–24, 327; and Huaxtepec gardens, 244, 245; kingship rejected by, 247–48; vs. Mechoacan, 277–78; and Metztitlan debacle, 301; as military preceptor, 234–36; after Motecuhzoma death, 247–48; as old man, 233, 253, 265; power of, 311; and prisoners of war, 301; renown of, 361; statue of, 242–43; and Sun Stone ceremony, 286, 288–90; and Tarascan disaster, 282; and Teloloapan resettlement, 344, 345; and Templo Mayor, 130–31, 224, 226, 307, 328, 331, 333, 337, 338; and Tepeaca, 152–55, 158–59; and Tezcoco, 126–28; titled, 97 & n.2; and Tizoc enthronement, 303, 304, 306, 307n; and Tizoc funeral, 308; and Tlacaxipehualiztli, 272, 273, 276; and Tlatelolco rebellion, 253–56, 258–59, 262; vs. Toluca/Matlatzinco, 264, 265, 269–70; and Xochimilco, 107–108, 112, 113
Tlacahuepan, 53, 54n.5, 81, 98, 141, 202, 425–27
Tlacatecatl, 147
Tlacatecpaneca, 23n.1
Tlacatecpanecatl, 22
Tlacatlacualli, 284
Tlacatlan, 102
Tlacaxipehualiztli (flaying ritual), 169–74, 186n, 339n.1, 343, 429, 473–75, 591, 592; for Matlatzincas, 272–76; stone for, 477–81
Tlacaxipehualiztli (month), 170
Tlachco, 303
Tlachitonatiuh. *See* Tizoc
Tlachmalac, 303
Tlachquiauhco, 470–73
Tlachtonco, 487–88
Tlacitla, 179
Tlacochalca, 23n.1
Tlacochcalcatl Tecutli, 22

Tlacochcalco, 284
Tlacochcalli (armory), 150
Tlacochcalli (bower), 294, 385
Tlacochtoc, 98n.5
Tlacocomolco, 32
Tlacopan. *See* Tacuba
Tlacotepec, 13, 303, 315, 330
Tlacozauhtitlan, 336
Tlacuilocan, 141
Tlahuac, 87n.3
Tla[l]huica, 548
Tlahuicas, 300, 315, 349, 422
Tlahuicole, 447–49 & n
Tlalanapan, 330
Tlalcozauhtitlan, 303
Tlalmanalco, 14, 400
Tlalnepantla, 14, 547
Tlaloc, 225n.1, 289 & n, 294, 339n.1, 368, 485n
Tlalocan, 485n
Tlalpiloni, 226n.3
Tlaltecatzin, 402
Tlaltecuhtli, 308n
Tlaluacpan, 121
Tlaluicas, 13, 15, 230
Tlamacazque, 156 & n.7
Tlamimilolpan, 13 & n.4
Tlamimilulpan, 329
Tlapallan, 98n.2
Tlapanecs, 335, 336
Tlapechhuacan, 140, 141, 478
Tlapitzahuayan, 138–40, 358, 400, 479
Tlaquilpan, 330
Tlaquiltenango, 15
Tlatectla, 197
Tlatelolco, 47–48, 50, 72; as Aztec ally, 262, 442, 443, 453, 458, 459, 555–56, 558; Aztec sack of, 261; and Aztec treasure, 559 & n, 562n.3; Cortés seizure of, 262n.4; Cuauhtemoc as king of, 546; humiliation of, 261–62; independence of, 249; Motecuhzoma II and, 406, 411–12, 441–44; rebellion of, 249–60; temple of, 412; today, 47n; warriors punished in, 454. *See also* Cuauhtemoc; Moquihuixtli
Tlatlatepec (prov.), 380 & n
Tlatlauhquitepec, 245, 335

637

Index

Tlatlauhqui Tezcatl. *See* Tlacaxipehualiztli
Tlatoani, 22–23n
Tlatoanime. See Tlatoani; Tlatoque
Tlatocaithualli, 305
Tlatolzaca, 53, 54n.5, 81, 202
Tlatoque. See Kings, Aztec; *Tlatoani*
Tlatzcayucan, 330
Tlauauanque, 272
Tlaueloc, 98
Tlauitol[tzin], 467, 468
Tlaxcala, 15, 17, 175, 176, 182n.1, 425, 429; as Ahuilipan ally, 178; Ahuitzotl and, 320, 331, 340; and Axayacatl funeral, 293; as Aztec ally, 410; and Aztecs, 194, 197, 199; Aztecs vs., 6n, 53, 319, 392, 433, 438, 440, 447–48, 452–55, 474, 526; character of, 470; and Coateocalli dedication, 433; Cortés refuge in, 246; Cuauhtemoc appeal to, 547–48; as Cuetlaxtla ally, 197; gods of, 592; as Huexotzinco ally, 457–58; as human food source, 233, 235; Moquihuixtli and, 250; and Motecuhzoma II, 402–404, 408, 409; prisoners from, 329, 335; Spaniards in, 547–48; as Spanish ally, 16, 522–24 & n, 529, 541, 543, 547, 549, 551, 553, 555; and Sun Stone ceremony, 289; and Templo Mayor, 332–34; and Tenochtitlan treasure, 559n; Tlacaelel focus on, 231; Tlatelolco vs., 262; traders from, 349. *See also* Puebla-Tlaxcala region
Tlaxcalans, exodus of, 13, 15–16, 562n.3
Tlaxcaltecas. *See* Tlaxcalans
Tlaxtlan, 336
Tlayacapa, 13
Tlayacapan, 315, 329, 548, 560
Tlazolteotl, 98
Tlehuitzilin, 273
Tlenamacaque, 156 & n.7, 277, 290
Tlilatl (spring), 362–66, 370–72
Tlilcuatzpal, 269
Tliliuhquitepec, 171n.3, 286n, 425; Ahuitzotl and, 320, 340; Aztecs and, 286–87, 289, 290, 362, 429–30, 433, 438; and Coateocalli dedication, 433; as human food source, 233, 235; Moquihuixtli and, 250; and Motecuhzoma II enthronement, 404; prisoners from, 335, 339n.1; and Templo Mayor, 332, 334; Tlacaelel focus on, 231; Tlatelolcas vs., 262
Tlillan, 297
Tlillan Calmecac, 313
Tlillancalqui, 199–200, 495–503, 505, 509–13. *See also* Teuctlamacazqui
Tlilpotonqui, 361, 388n.2, 394, 396, 415, 423, 434, 440, 453, 455; and Ahuitzotl successor, 388–90; as Cihuacoatl, 424; and Coateocalli dedication, 435–36; and Icpatepec campaign, 411; and Motecuhzoma II enthronement, 400, 405; at Nezahualpilli funeral, 466; vs. Yancuitlan/Zozola, 429
Tloque Nahuaque. *See* Tezcatlipoca
Tobacco, 157, 306–307, 319; for Aztec emissaries, 334; ceremonial use of, 150n.2, 156, 157, 285, 294; as funeral element, 293; as gift, 304, 306, 321, 322, 331, 333, 334, 369; Motecuhzoma II burned by, 484, 485; as privilege, 435; for sacrifice victims, 230, 288, 301, 401, 473; certain persons denied, 234; for Teloloapan emigrants, 348; in *teotlacualli*, 189n; as tribute, 177, 327
Tochimilco, 111
Tochpan, 188, 202, 237, 335
Tochtepec, 335
Tochtla, 302
Toci, 37–38, 170, 289 & n, 456–57 & n, 459, 462, 529
Tocititlan (shrine), 457–59, 462, 480, 529–30
Tocoltecatl, 107
Tocpacxiuh, 522
Tocpaxochiuh, 467, 518
Tocuillan, 97n.2
Tolpetlac, 29

638

Toltecs, 23n.2, 36n, 43n.1, 48n, 88 & n, 504; as Aztec ancestors, 485n; decline of, 25n.4. *See also* Colhuacan; Culhuas; Tula
Toluca, 202, 263, 265–69, 302, 303, 330
Tomatoes, 11n, 55, 214, 221, 362, 370
Topiltzin. *See* Quetzalcoatl; Xipe Topec Tlatlauhqui Tezcatl
Torch pine, 206
Torquemada, Juan de, 477n
Tortillas, 153, 162, 177, 178, 183, 239n, 350; funerary, 284; as gift to gods, 350; for Spaniards, 509, 510
Tota. *See* Xipe Totec Tlatlauhqui Tezcatl
Totec, 171, 172, 425, 486
Toteoci Tecuhtli, 132–33, 145n.4
Toteociteuctli, 89, 118
Totolapan, 13, 315, 329, 548, 561
Totoltecas, 303
Totolzinco, 127, 330
Totonaca, 179
Totonacs, 6n, 240–41
Totopec, 419–21, 425
Totoquihuaztli, 236, 324; Ahuitzotl and, 344, 345, 371; at Ahuitzotl funeral, 383, 384; and Ahuitzotl successor, 387, 390–92; Axayacatl and, 248, 278; death of, 402; and Templo Mayor, 225
Tototectin, 173–74
Tototepec, 417–18
Tovar, Juan de, 565, 568, 570–74
Town hall. *See Casa real*
Toxcatl, 536–37
Toxiuhmolpilli, 445
Tozapan, 202, 302
Trade, nature of Aztec, 86n
Treasury, royal, 359–60
Trecena, 289n
Trees, 26, 581; of Colhuacan, 214; drought vs., 238; as tribute, 55, 205, 206. *See also* Lumber; Wood
Tribunals, Aztec, 210
Tribute, 43n.1, 103, 202–207, 270, 328, 343, 358, 415; for advancing troops, 177; Ahuilizapan refusal to pay, 175; Ahuitzotl distribution of, 359; Aztec payment of, 54–57; from Chiapa, 317; from Coaixtlahuaca, 185, 193; from Coatzacualco, 223; collectors of (see *Calpixque*); coronation-related, 302–304, 318; from Cuetlaxtla, 179–81, 194, 196–201; exemption from, 435, 465; from Huaxtecs, 165; mechanics of, 323, 336 (see also *Calpixque*); from Miauatlan, 352; from Mixtecs, 473; at risk, 375; Spanish, 585; from Tecuantepec, 353; from Teloloapan, 342; temple dedication-related, 335–36; from Tenochtitlan commoners, 309, 335; from Tepeaca, 155; Tezcoco and, 330–31; Tizoc enthronement financed by, 302–304; from Tlatelolco, 261, 262, 412; war over, 105n; waylaying of, 470–71
Triple Alliance, 129n.6. *See also* Tacuba; Tenochtitlan; Tezcoco
Trumpets, Aztec, 275n.4
Tuchimilco, 13
Tula, 33n.3, 43n.1; as Aztec ally, 539; Aztecs to, 25 & n.4, 28; vs. Coaixtlahuaca, 183; vs. Huexotzinco, 436–38; memoirists of, 569; vs. Spaniards, 547; Spanish biscuit to, 497n. *See also* Toltecs
Tulan, 183
Tulantzinco, 162, 330, 539
Tulla, 385
Tultitlan, 385
Tuna (nopal fruit), 11n
Turkey (country), Spain and, 434, 440
Turkey(s) (fowl), 165, 166, 178, 182; as booty, 317; as burial offerings, 387n; as respected bird, 387n; as royal dish, 406; for Spaniards, 500, 509, 510, 518; as tribute, 207, 302, 318
Turquoise, 43n.1
Turtles, 175, 177, 181, 194, 204
Tutors, execution of, 411
Tuzapan, 324
Tuzapanecs, 335
Tzacualcatl, 68

Index

Tzacuallan, 330
Tzacualpan, 303, 336
Tzapotl, 171 & n.4
Tzapotl Calli, 171
Tzatzcantitlan, 151
Tzauctla, 179
Tzaueyucan, 270
Tziccoatl, 302
Tzinacantepec, 303, 315
Tzinccoac, 335, 336
Tzitzimime, 328
Tziuac calli, 150
Tziuhcoac, 202, 334
Tzoalli, 40n. *See also* Amaranth, as dough source
Tzocoztli, 460, 461
Tzocuicatl, 285
Tzompanco, 27, 29
Tzompanteuctli, 376, 481, 485
Tzompantitlan, 170
Tzompantli (skull rack), 81, 170n.2, 202. *See also* Skull rack
Tzompantzin, 98
Tzontemoc, 98
Tzutzumatzin, 362–65, 367, 371

Uanitl, 506
Ueitihuacan, 330
Uexotla, 330
Uitzilan, 330
Uitzoco, 303, 336
Underworlds, Aztec, 339n.1

Valencia, Martín de, 573
Valle, Marqués del, 468
Valley of Mexico, 12n.1, 29n
Vanilla, 11n, 214
Varas, 112
Vegetables, 11n, 80, 205, 206, 214, 317
Veracruz, 15n, 495n.2, 534, 536n.2, 547, 550
Vespucci, Amerigo, 3n
Vessels (drinking utensils), gold, 532
Veterans, Aztec war. *See* Cuauhuehuetque
Virgins, Indian, 524n
Volador, 143 & n.1
Volcano, 349
Vote, as Aztec privilege, 435

Waistbands, warriors', 209, 321–23, 379
War: ritualistic preparations for, 76 & n, 77
Warriors, Aztec: funeral rites for fallen, 149–52, 283–90, 428, 437, 441, 455; honoring of, 167–68; Motecuhzoma II punishment of, 454; victory-related generosity of, 416. *See also* Cuachics; Cuauh Huehuetque
Warriors of the Sun, Order of, 306, 435
Water amaranth. *See Ahuauhtli*
"Water Face." *See* Axayacatl
Waterfowl, 92; Aztec trade in, 45, 46, 105; of Colhuacan, 220, 222; as gift, 334; Tlatelolco youth vs., 252; as tribute, 56, 63, 400, 415; vanquished Tlatelolcas as, 261. *See also* Ducks; Geese
"Water Monster." *See* Ahuitzotl
Weapons, 30, 34 & n; as gifts, 123, 124, 294, 323, 340, 348, 459, 474; royal, 352, 375; for statues, 428; surrender of, 454; Tarascan, 279; in Tenochtitlan cache, 532; as tribute, 206, 261, 303, 318, 358, 359, 376–77, 412, 473; as warrior bonus, 234
Weasels, 16, 205
Wheat, 11n
Whistles (musical instruments), 275n.4, 343, 433, 435, 473, 480
Whistling jars, 275n.4
Widows, Aztec war, 149, 151, 283–86, 302, 400, 408, 415, 440, 463
Wigs, Aztec ceremonial, 275
Wildcats, 16, 203, 207 & n, 214, 215, 303
Wild fig, 82n.9
Willows, 26
Winding cloths, 150
Wine, 322, 350, 435, 500, 501; Aztec (*see* Pulque). *See also* Divine Wine
Wives: of absent warriors, 350–51; of Motecuhzoma II, 487, 538–39, 545; rites of warriors', 161–62; royal, 356. *See also* Polygyny; Widows
Wizards. *See* Sorcerers

640

Women: arming of Aztec, 555; Aztec killing of, 80, 84, 165, 179, 185, 229, 342, 379, 471 (*see also* Women, sacrifice of); for Cortés, 523, 524; flaying of, 170n.1, 591 (*see also* Women, sacrifice of); Moorish, 434n; Moquihuixtli use of Tlatelolco, 260; Motecuhzoma II murder of, 494; rape of Aztec, 86; sacrifice of, 186n, 466; for Spaniards, 511, 523, 534 (*see also* Women, for Cortés); as Spanish captives, 556, 561; as symbols of cowardice, 91–92; as tribute, 327; as war widows, 149, 151, 283–86, 302, 400, 408, 415, 440, 463. *See also* Concubines; Duennas; Midwives; Prostitutes; *Tzitzimimitl*; Virgins; Widows; Wives
Wood: as funeral offering, 292; for Spaniards, 509; for temple, 130, 131, 225, 226; as tribute, 80, 105, 205, 207, 318. *See also* Bark; Charcoal; Lumber
Woodcutters, 320
Workmen, as tribute, 317
Worms, edible, 16, 45–46n, 205, 349
Writers, pre-Conquest, 569

Xalatlauhco, 86–87, 95, 303, 348
Xaltelulli. *See* Tlatelolco
Xaltepec (prov.), 409
Xaltianquizco, 420 & n
Xaltilalli. *See* Tlatelolco
Xaltocan, 29
Xayacamachan, 332
Xicalli (vessel), 114n, 186
Xiconoc, 81, 98, 134–35, 202
Xicotencatl, 194, 523
Xilomatzin, 87
Xilotepec, 315–17, 330, 336, 346, 383, 385, 539
Xipe Totec, 173, 289n, 339n.1
Xipe Totec Tlatlauhqui Tezcatl, 275n.5
Xiquipilco, 202, 225, 290, 315, 330, 346, 385
Xiuhcoatl, 27n, 191n.4, 290
Xiuhtecuhtli, 91n.5, 398n
Xiuhtecuhtli-Ixcozauhqui, 142
Xochhuehuetlan, 303

Xochiacan, 330
Xochimilcas, exodus of, 13
Xochimilco, 13 & n.4, 32, 170, 506; and Ahuitzotl funeral, 383; and Ahuitzotl successor, 387; and Axayacatl funeral, 293; as Aztec ally, 153, 180, 196, 230, 266, 281, 299, 324, 325, 342, 375, 399, 439, 531; as Aztec colony, 161, 236, 365; Aztecs vs., 72n.8, 102, 104–11, 112, 115, 202; breaking up of, 112–13; vs. Chiapa, 315, 316; and Coaixtlahuaca, 182–84; and Coateocalli dedication, 434; Colhuacan vs., 114; Cortés support in, 529; Coyoacan appeal to, 87–90; and *cuauhxicalli* ceremony, 189; divers from, 480; emigrants to Teloloapan region from, 345; floating gardens of, 45n.4; Huaxtecs vs., 161; laborers from, 477, 478; vs. Metztitlan, 300; and Motecuhzoma II enthronement, 406; and Nezahualpilli funeral, 466; prisoners of, 335; as royal farm, 238; vs. Spaniards, 547; as Spanish ally, 548, 551; and Templo Mayor, 130–31, 329, 338; and Tizoc enthronement, 297, 302; Totonac slave-shopping in, 240; traders of, 428–29, 552; tribute of, 335. *See also* Chinampa region
Xochinacaztli, 244 & n.3
Xochiquetzal, 524n
Xochitepec, 109
Xochitl Olinqui, 116–18, 120
Xochitl Tecuhtli, 325
Xochiyaoyotl, 410
Xochtla, 202
Xoconochco (prov.), 158, 202, 374–79. *See also* Soconusco
Xoconochnopaltitlan, 79
Xocotitlan, 202, 315, 330, 346, 384
Xocotl, 142
Xocotlan, 336
Xocotlecas, 225
Xocotl Huetzi, 91 & n.5, 142
Xolotla (prov.), 349–50, 352–53, 374–79
Xomimitl, 216n

641

Index

Xuchimiquiztli, 410
Xumiltepec, 13

Yacamapich, 506
Yacapichtlan, 292, 548, 560
Yacaxapo Tecuhtli, 104, 106
Yahualiuhcan, 119, 286
Yams, 205
Yancuitlan, 428–29
Yaoteuacan, 329
Yaotl. *See* Tezcatlipoca
Yauhtepec, 15, 244, 292, 302, 336, 513, 548
Yetocomatl, 156
Yohualahuan, 172, 289 & n, 294, 339n.1
Yolatl, 280
Yollometl. *See* Xipe Totec Tlatlauhqui Tezcatl
Yolloxochitl, 244 & n.3
Yolotlicue, 227n
Yopi, 170, 275 & n.5, 298
Yopica, 23n.1
Yopican Tecuhtli, 22

Yopico (barrio), 99n.8
Yopico (temple), 171n.5, 298
Yopico Calmecac, 171n.5
Yopi-Tlapanec region, 99n.8
Yopitzinco, 231, 275n.5, 320–23, 340, 430, 433
Yopitzontli, 275
Youallan, 303, 336
Yucatan, 43n.1, 495n.2
Yxnauatliloc, 98 & n.3
Yzquiteca, 23n.1

Zacancatl, 84–85
Zacatecas, 348n
Zacatlan, 262, 332, 334, 335, 340
Zacatlaxcalli, 204 & n
Zacatzontitlan, 330
Zacualpa, 13
Zapotecs, 229, 335, 379, 440
Zapotitlan, 429
Zocalo, 53In
Zopachtzinco, 522
Zoquitzinco, 330
Zozola, 428, 429

www.ingramcontent.com/pod-product-compliance
Lightning Source LLC
Chambersburg PA
CBHW030101010526
44116CB00005B/53